Principles of Employment Law

Michael Jefferson, MA (Oxon), BCL

Lecturer in Law

The University of Sheffield

Cavendish
Publishing
Limited

London • Sydney • Portland, Oregon

Fourth edition first published in Great Britain 2002 by
Cavendish Publishing Limited, The Glass House,
Wharton Street, London WC1X 9PX, United Kingdom
Telephone: + 44 (0)20 7278 8000   Facsimile: + 44 (0)20 7278 8080
Email: info@cavendishpublishing.com
Website: www.cavendishpublishing.com

Published in the United States by Cavendish Publishing
c/o International Specialized Book Services,
5804 NE Hassalo Street, Portland,
Oregon 97213-3644, USA

Published in Australia by Cavendish Publishing (Australia) Pty Ltd
3/303 Barrenjoey Road, Newport, NSW 2106, Australia

© Jefferson, M	2000
First edition	1994
Second edition	1995
Third edition	1997
Fourth edition	2000
Reprinted	2002

British Library Cataloguing in Publication Data
Data available

Library of Congress Cataloguing in Publication Data
Data available

ISBN 1-85941-468-0

1 3 5 7 9 10 8 6 4 2

Printed and bound in Great Britain

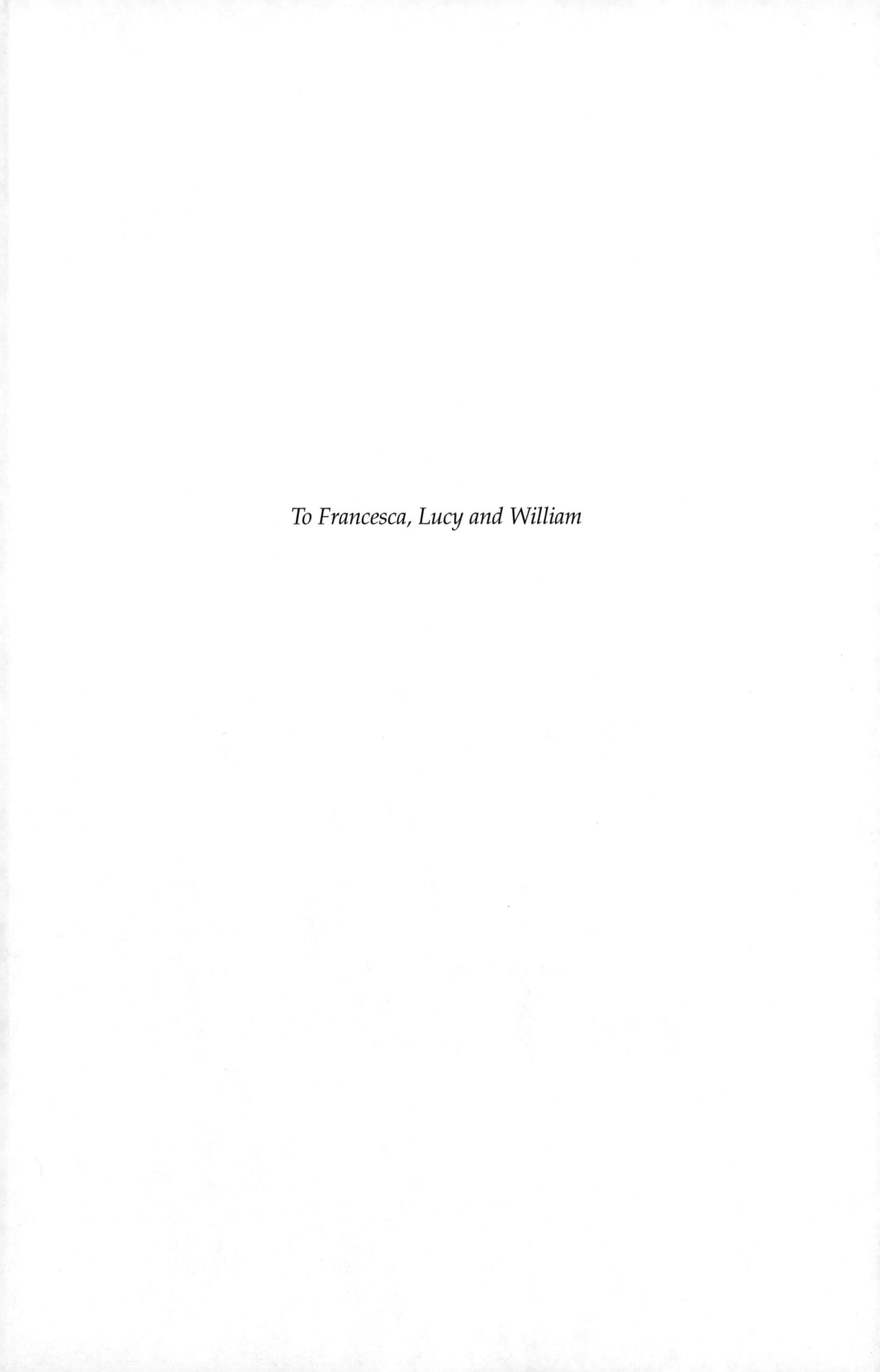

To Francesca, Lucy and William

PREFACE

The fourth edition of this book continues the pattern established in the earlier editions. The opening chapters consider the framework of employment law in the 1990s; Chapters 3–12 deal with individual employment law; and Chapters 13–16 deal with collective labour law. A list of recommended reading is given at the end. The topics covered are those normally found on a UK employment law course.

The fourth edition is published at a time of great change. Since the third edition, the Employment Relations Act 1999 has been passed; there is, for the first time, a national minimum wage in the UK; for many workers, the maximum number of working hours is now controlled; and protection has been afforded whistleblowers by the Public Interest Disclosure Act 1998. Judicial interpretation of statutory provisions continues apace: while many of the reforms of the Conservative years have been accepted (such as pre-strike ballots), a process of reversing some of the restrictions on unions has been set in train. The mood was summed up by Lord McCarthy in the House of Lords: 'I say to you, rejoice, rejoice, rejoice. We are beginning to reverse the nine weary Bills we had between 1980 and 1993.' (*Hansard*, 10 May 1999, Col 1019). Employment law students live in exciting times!

I have tried to state the law as at 1 November 1999, but have been able to include updates at proof stage, bringing the book into the 21st century.

Michael Jefferson
20 January 2000

CONTENTS

Contents

Contents

8   COMMON ISSUES IN REDUNDANCY PAYMENTS AND UNFAIR DISMISSAL

Contents

TABLE OF CASES

TABLE OF STATUTES

TABLE OF STATUTORY INSTRUMENTS

TABLE OF EUROPEAN COMMUNITY LEGISLATION

TABLE OF ABBREVIATIONS

ACAS	Advisory Conciliation and Arbitration Service
CAC	Central Arbitration Committee
CRE	Commission for Racial Equality
DRC	Disability Rights Commission
EPA	Equal Pay Act 1970
ERA	Employment Rights Act 1996
EOC	Equal Opportunities Commission
IRA	Industrial Relations Act 1971
RRA	Race Relations Act 1996
SDA	Sex Discrimination Act 1975
SEA	Single European Act 1986
TGWU	Transport and General Workers' Union
TULR(C)A	Trade Union and Labour Relations (Consolidation) Act 1992
TUPE	Transfer of Undertakings (Protection of Employment) Regulations 1981
TURERA	Trade Union Reform and Employment Rights Act 1993

CHAPTER 1

MODERN EMPLOYMENT LAW

1.1   Ideological conflict

Employment law has been one of the most important areas of conflicting ideologies in the UK over the last 35 years. It has been affected by economic, political and social theories. Party politics have played a large part. Free market economists have sought to destroy the power of trade unions, which are seen as impeding business by acting as a restraint on management (at the stages of both hiring and firing) and as pushing up prices by gaining larger pay increases for their members than those given to non-members. Global competition has hit the UK hard. The control of inflation is the goal and full employment and welfare benefits are not even on the agenda. A role is reserved for unions: that of acting as a society negotiating benefits such as reduced health insurance premiums for members. Linked with this view of unions are the continuing privatisation of former State-run utilities; the emphasis on personal bargaining, flexible contracts and self-employment; the rise of multi-national companies; worldwide competition; and compulsory competitive tendering for various functions such as the collection of dustbins. Employment law can be used to promote such policies, just as it can be used to promote social policies.

Advocates of the market economy have been aided by changes to the UK workforce. There has been a shift from manufacturing and heavy industries such as shipbuilding and mining to the service sectors, for example, tourism and the activities of the City; there has been a move away from full time to part time work and from permanent jobs to temporary ones; and there has been an increase in the number of women as a proportion of workers. Unions have traditionally found difficulty recruiting in service industries and among part-timers and women. The rise of part-timers to around 28% of the workforce and the proportion (85%) of those jobs performed by women have hit the unions hard and have, to some degree, obliged them to re-order their priorities.

The policy of the Conservative Government was to undermine the ability of unions to regulate industrial relations with management through collective bargaining. It encouraged the non-recognition of unions and the introduction of personal contracts, that is, contracts which are imposed on employees rather than negotiated between unions and management. Industry-wide collective agreements covered 60% of the workforce in the private sector in 1950, but at present they cover under 10%. Union immunities were seen as 'privileges' causing unemployment and a weak economy. How much of the undermining of unions since the Conservatives' election victory in 1979 was due to that Government's substantial changes in the law and how much was due to other factors such as demography is impossible to say. The industrial scene has altered radically over the last 30 years. Since the 1960s, many manual jobs have disappeared; women are entering the labour market in greater numbers than before; and the methods in which jobs are performed and the content of employment contracts have changed enormously. It is expected that, by 2001, women will form more than half of the workforce. It must, however, be remembered that the most efficient system is not necessarily a free market system (as the deregulation of buses outside London demonstrates), and economic efficiency does not take into account other possible bases for unions, such as providing training in democracy. Certainly, a firm with 6,000 workers cannot effectively bargain with each worker individually. Collective regulation reduces the cost of contracting. The Conservative Government considered, nevertheless, that the move to individual contracts was 'healthy' (see *People, Jobs and Opportunity*, Cm 1810, 1992). The reality is that employers have been imposing standard form contracts on workers and dismissing those who do not agree. Contract law can be exploited by those who hold power in a relationship. Moreover, because the employment contract is intended to be of indefinite duration in many instances and, as a result, it cannot from the start cover all eventualities, there is room for the development and imposition of novel work practices.

1.1.1 Pro-unions

Supporters of unions may turn free market ideas on their head. Management prerogatives should be restrained: why should the law permit a long serving employee to be sacked at any moment? Employees like citizens have human rights. Membership of a union carries with it various advantages, one of which is that overall members are paid more than non-members. Unions exist to protect their members and advance their interests. From 1906 to 1979, a characteristic, perhaps the main one, of the UK labour market was the growth of management-union negotiations, otherwise known as collective bargaining. The number of union members reached its peak in 1979 (13.3 million). In 1992, there were some 9.5 million union members, a decline of 3.7 million since 1979. The figure in 1994 was 7.2 million. In 1979, over half of the workforce were members of a union; in the late 1990s, only a third were. Furthermore, employees who were not union members were often covered by collective bargaining. This coverage has also fallen drastically, from 77% of all employees in the late 1970s to 47% in 1990, and this percentage continued to drop throughout the 1990s. At present, it is at about 35%. The decline has been particularly marked in the private sector and among full time manual workers. By far the largest union is UNISON. Despite their decline, unions remain the largest voluntary bodies in the UK.

1.2 An industrial relations theory

The next part of this chapter briefly considers one of the classic theories of industrial relations. With reference to the model which this analysis provides, modern employment law can be discussed. The theory postulates three 'frames of reference': unitary; pluralist; and conflictual. By understanding a little about industrial relations, the reader may see how the changes in the law over the last 20 years fit together without becoming overwhelmed by the details.

1.2.1 The unitary frame of reference

The unitary frame of reference is such that business entrepreneurship is seen as the touchstone by which all activities within the firm are judged. Any development which does not promote the business is to be neutered. The outcome for workers is that, at the end of the day, they will somehow share the profits of their successful enterprise. On this approach, unions have no relevance except as bodies involved in the provision of welfare benefits and financial services. Because they are not necessarily in tune with the advancement of the firm, they have no collective bargaining function. Negotiation and compromise, as well as employee participation in decision making, are simply not on the agenda for they potentially hinder the company's objectives. Challenges to managerial prerogatives are viewed as illegitimate. The State can be brought in to control challenges to management. For example, strikes may be made illegal on the ground that they disrupt commerce. Economic efficiency is the grail. Subordination of workers to management is a staging post on that trail.

1.2.2 The pluralist frame of reference

The pluralist doctrine notes that the various participants in business undertakings may have different perceptions. What one group wants from the enterprise may conflict with what another section desires. These aspirations are legitimate. Reconciliation of these divided interests is part of the nature of industrial relations. Law may be one of the forces through which interests may be compromised. Unions can be seen as an aid to achieving a balance between the wishes of employers and employees. An individual employee normally cannot bargain on even terms with employers. The relationship is one of subordination of employees to employers (see the control test in Chapter 3). This subordination has been increased in recent years through the introduction of profit related pay, performance related pay and appraisal systems. Employees, by joining together to form unions, can negotiate more equally with employers than can one person. The collective interests of employees represented by trade unions, therefore, constitute a good thing. Collective bargaining, being an expression of such an ideology, is to be cherished. Where it does not exist, it is to be encouraged to begin, perhaps by the intervention of the State (for example, in England, through wages councils). Similarly, because collective bargaining is a continuing matter and the parties have to function together when they are not in dispute, reconciliation between their desires can, if necessary, be provided by the State. Pluralism was abandoned by the Conservatives in the period from 1979–97 but has since been making a comeback.

1.2.3 The conflictual frame of reference

To the pluralist, the advent of trade unions is seen as an attempt at equalising the power relationship between employers and employees. For adherents of Marxism in its various forms, pluralism is defective. There is no level playing field between employees, even when backed by unions, and employers. The whip-hand, to change the metaphor, is held by employers. Lasting compromise is not possible. The interests either of one side, capital, or of the other, labour, must prevail. At present, capital exploits labour; in a Western style economy, unions may reduce that exploitation but they cannot defeat it. In the long run the means of production will move from the capital holding group to the labouring classes but, for the moment, capitalists control workers' terms of employment. Collective bargaining can ameliorate but not destroy the fundamental inequality between the classes.

1.3 The law and industrial relations

Governments have used the law in several different ways since the Second World War. From the early 1960s, shifts in policies have led to substantial amendments in the law. Changes to the law have come thick and fast. Nevertheless, remnants of pre-1960 law are still in existence.

1.3.1 Role of law

The role of the law in industrial relations may be seen as reflecting the first two of the frames of reference stated in the previous section. There has, over the last 40 years, been an increasing involvement of law in the relationship between employers and workers, but its function has been subject to several significant changes. The law relating to trade unions between 1799 and the 1950s is an oft told story. The principal statute was the Trade Disputes Act 1906, which withdrew common law liability from unions if they were acting in contemplation or furtherance of a trade dispute. This phrase has come to be known as the 'golden formula', a term coined by Lord Wedderburn, the doyen of UK labour lawyers. Despite the increase in law affecting employees over the last 35 years, it is thought that the employment relationship in England and Wales is the least regulated in the EC. This section concentrates on the years after the Second World War. It is through this framework that the employment law of the 1980s and 1990s can be seen. The rest of this section attempts, in a short span, to provide that conceptual structure.

1.3.2 The start of the modern era

In the 1950s, State intervention was slight. Unions did not want the State to intervene. They had won their rights by industrial muscle and negotiation. In the famous words of Otto Kahn-Freund, 'What the State has not given, the State cannot take away' (in Ginsberg, M (ed), *Law and Opinion in England in the 20th Century*, 1959). The Government, it may be said, broadly supported pluralism. The State, which was itself an employer of many workers, acted as a model employer; that is, since the First World War, it strove to encourage its employees to join unions and thereby develop collective bargaining. Since the 19th century, it had, in its other role as legislator, enacted laws in favour of health and safety, such as those preventing children working as chimney sweeps and women working underground (this type of law is often known as 'protective legislation'). It helped to arrange settlements in industrial disputes through institutions such as the Industrial Court, which was established in 1919. In some industries where workers had suffered grave exploitation, there had existed wages councils since 1909. Such bodies were seen as temporary expedients, designed to be abolished when collective bargaining grew strong enough. They were 'props' to collective bargaining, intended to encourage the flourishing of such bargaining and to be abolished once employers and unions were negotiating continuously and successfully. Wages councils constituted a strong illustration of direct State intervention in the employer-employee relationship. The minimum level of pay was regulated by inspectors appointed by the State and there was a criminal sanction for failure to pay that amount. By the late 1950s, State intrusions, such as contracting in to unions' political funds and wartime compulsory arbitration, had been abrogated. Even the courts, not regarded as workers' friends, had, since the early years of the last century, adopted a policy of non-intervention in some aspects of trade unionism. For example, the pursuit of a closed shop had been held to be legitimate. Unions were free to conduct industrial campaigns. Industrial conflict and its evolution were concomitant parts of Hugh Clegg's *The System of Industrial Relations in Great Britain*, an influential book published in 1954.

1.3.3 Collective *laissez-faire*

In the book mentioned above, Otto Kahn-Freund, the leading commentator on industrial relations at that time, saw the situation in terms of the law's non-intervention in the collective bargaining process. He did not doubt that the law could and did act as an auxiliary support to the practice of collective bargaining, but he described the scene in terms of 'collective *laissez-faire*', also called voluntarism and abstentionism. By this phrase he meant that, by and large, the State did not play a part in the procedure and merits of industrial conflict. The parties dealt with problems by themselves. Law was used only when the collective powers were too disparate. The joint regulation of industrial matters was seen throughout the world as the UK's greatest contribution to industrial relations. Unions were seen as the embodiment of the democratic will. By comparison with the position of the unions in Nazi Germany and the Soviet Union, British unions were not an arm of the State, and this separation was undoubtedly a good thing. Besides providing a description of the scene, Kahn-Freund gave an analysis which to some degree (such as the separation of unions and the State) was a prescription for good industrial relations. Both sides of industry *ought* to be left alone. After all, they were directly involved. Compromises could be reached without State intervention. There was no need for the State to penalise one of the parties to a dispute. Indeed, the governments of the day seem to have decided on a policy of non-intervention. Law merely exacerbated inter-group disputes. It was too blunt an instrument to resolve disputes satisfactorily, for the parties had to live with each other after the law had moved on. The law was inflexible; collective bargaining was pliable and was, therefore, suitable to a mature industrial relations system. Neither side wanted agreements to commit all parties to exact obligations. This attitude was reflected in the views of union leaders. It seems almost ludicrous to recall that, when wages councils were instituted in 1909, they were castigated by some union leaders as interfering with the employment relationship.

1.3.4 Auxiliary legislation

It should, however, be noted that not even in the 1950s did the law play no part in industrial relations. Collective bargaining did not exist where it was most needed. Kahn-Freund thought that the laws then existing were a gloss on collective bargaining. Yet the laws were important. Wages councils, the Fair Wages Resolution (by which the Government enforced the level of pay generally existing in the industry among its contractors, an early form of what is now called contract compliance), factories legislation, and the Truck Acts (under which, for instance, workers could not be paid in tokens redeemable only in company owned 'tommy shops') existed. There was also legal intervention in specific industries such as dock working. Such supporting or auxiliary mechanisms, which aimed to extend collective bargaining into areas where it was weak or non-existent, were quickly seen by the Conservative Government in the post-1979 era as restrictive of market forces and as preventive of the creation of jobs.

1.3.5 Beginning of 'floor of rights'

In 1963 came the harbinger of statutes giving rights to employees. The Contracts of Employment Act 1963 provided for minimum lengths of notice periods to be given to employees, that length depending on the number of years the relevant employee had worked for the employers, and for a written statement of the terms of employment. The Redundancy Payments Act 1965 continued the process of legal intervention in areas that were previously the sole domain of collective bargaining. These two statutes, now consolidated in the Employment Rights Act (ERA) 1996, remain in their essentials unchanged. These statutes constitute the beginning of the 'floor of rights', the minimum rights of employees. The Government was also concerned to restrain judicial activism in industrial conflict. It reversed *Rookes v Barnard* (1964) in the Trade Disputes Act 1965.

1.3.6 Unions and economic decline

In the 1960s, commentators viewed the economic decline of the UK with alarm. One failure singled out for criticism was the increase in 'wild cat' industrial action, that is, action that was not union-backed. Industry-wide agreements seemed to be in decline, being replaced by plant bargaining. There was apparently less control by union officials over shop stewards than previously. There was some talk of union corruption, especially Communist infiltration into the electricians' union in the 1950s, and of agitators, such as the seamen's dispute of 1966. Some employers said that there were too many unions in the workplace and that multi-unionism led to demarcation disputes. The courts seem to have reacted to these concerns by creating new torts. Being new, they were not subject to the normal statutory immunity for industrial action. Another area where the judges intervened was in disputes between the unions and their members. In the 1950s, the courts introduced the concept of natural justice into that relationship and, in the 1960s, they began to develop the idea that workers had a right to work, enforceable against the unions (but not against employers).

1.3.7 Donovan

The Donovan Commission (*Report of the Royal Commission on Trade Unions and Employers' Associations*, Cmnd 3623, 1968) was established to comment on the defects of the UK's industrial relations, including wage drift (local pay rates rose above the level agreed nationally), and to suggest reforms. The Commission considered that more formal procedures than those previously adopted should be followed. Rather than industry-wide bargaining, agreement was to be reached at plant or company level. The aims were to improve productivity, resolve grievances quickly and establish stable pay bargaining. The law was to play only a minor role in industrial relations, for 'properly

7

conducted, collective bargaining is the most effective means of giving workers the right to representation in decisions reflecting their working lives, a right which is or should be the prerogative of every worker in a democratic society' (para 212). Collective bargaining was seen as the best way of making industrial relations orderly.

1.3.8   *In Place of Strife*

The Government's proposed solutions, which included penal sanctions for unofficial strikes, were found in a White Paper entitled *In Place of Strife*, 1969. Its recommendations were followed by industrial unrest and were lost with the election defeat in 1970.

1.3.9   Industrial Relations Act 1971

The Industrial Relations Act (IRA) 1971 was largely based on United States' experience. This 'legal transplant' used American terms and concepts such as bargaining agents and bargaining units, these being an attempt to abolish multi-union workplaces. It was a comprehensive and radical Act. Labour law was divorced from prior laws. New torts, called unfair industrial practices, and a new court, the National Industrial Relations Court (NIRC), were created. Unions were given a right to be recognised by employers and employees obtained for the first time a right to a remedy for unfair dismissal. Collective agreements were legally enforceable, unless a term stating 'This is not a legally enforceable agreement' was included. Such a term was known as a TINA LEA clause. It seems that only one collective agreement did not have such a clause in it. Attempts were made, with little success, to improve union rule-books. Also unsuccessful was the enactment of a power to order a ballot before a strike. This power was used only once. The union won by a six to one majority, and the employers granted a substantial pay increase. Exemption from liability for strikes was predicated on unions registering under the IRA 1971.

1.3.10 Its failure

Most unions, led by the Trades Union Congress, got round the IRA 1971 by refusing to register. In this way, the IRA 1971 quickly became a dead letter. Managements did not seek to destroy collective bargaining. The 1970–74 Government was defeated in a general election after the three day week.

1.3.11 Labour Government 1974–79

Two matters deserve comment: first, the increasing use of the law in areas where traditionally there had been collective *laissez-faire*; and, secondly, the use of the law in non-traditional areas.

1.3.12 Pro-employees

The Government, having abolished the IRA 1971, returned to the pre-1971 structure but re-enacted the unfair dismissal provisions of that statute. Amendments were made to extend employees' and unions' rights against employers. For example, the qualifying period for unfair dismissal was reduced and the legality of the closed shop was widened so that only persons who objected on grounds of conscience to membership of a union had a remedy for being excluded from a job (though, in practice, the closed shop agreement often had a 'conscience clause' permitting the retention of such workers). Unfair dismissal, which is now seen as the core of employment law, is also central to negotiation outside law. The law was sweeping into areas previously occupied by collective bargaining. Moreover, law was not always as successful as settlements without legal intervention. Outside law, re-employment was the principal remedy, whereas under law the remedy most frequently granted was compensation and that often at low levels. Nevertheless, the law was now taking a leading part in industrial relations. The Government also intervened between employers and employees and unions and their members in the Sex Discrimination Act 1975 and the Race Relations Act 1976. These statutes can be seen as the start of a movement in employment law towards treating non-discrimination as a fundamental principle. Fair treatment can also have an economic basis; workers are demotivated by unlawful discrimination and employers lose out on talent if they do not select employees from a broad pool of potential applicants. ACAS was created in 1975. Its functions are discussed in the next chapter.

1.3.13 Pay and training

The Government shied away from using the law to restrain pay deals but did introduce wage restraint. Various training schemes were established. Both work relationships and wages were being regulated by law. The first training legislation was the Industrial Training Act 1964 and the first Prices and Incomes Act dates from 1966. Both aspects continued in the 1970s.

1.3.14 Social contract

The two sides of government policy, industrial training and prices and incomes, were summed up in the term 'social contract'. The unions moderated their pay claims in return for economic and social rights granted by law. These rights included one whereby unions could oblige an employer in a certain industry to increase wages to the general level found there (Sched 11 of the Employment Protection Act 1975). Other rights included time off for trade union purposes, maternity rights, and the compulsory notification to unions of redundancies. This period is sometimes, in political terms, seen as an era of corporatism. Unions were joining the Government in tackling the problems of the UK's economic decline in return for the grant of various rights. As some unionists would maintain, rights granted by law can be taken away by law.

1.3.15 European Community law

In this era, the influence of EC law was slight. English law contained or seemed to contain guarantees at least equal to those provided by EC legislation. The Equal Pay Act 1970 was thought to embody the concepts of Art 119 of the Treaty of Rome (now Art 141 of the EC Treaty). The procedure for handling redundancies found in ss 99–107 of the Employment Protection Act 1975 seemed to constitute the UK's equivalent of the Collective Redundancies Directive of 1975 (75/129). To modern students, the minimal effect of EC law stands out. Even today, except in respect of equal pay, EC law hardly affects the terms and conditions of many workers and, except in relation to the social dialogue (see Chapter 2), there is still little effect on unions, which are being given information and consultation rights, not rights to bargain collectively.

1.3.16 Winter of discontent

The 1978–79 'winter of discontent' led to the downfall of the Labour Government. It was replaced by a government of a different hue, which extensively used law in the pursuance of its policies.

1.3.17 Conservatives' approach

It has been a matter of debate whether the anti-union stance of the previous Government can be seen as a trend underlying all amendments in labour law since 1979 (a thread, the source of which was Mrs Thatcher's espousal of Friedrich von Hayek's theories contained in books such as *The Road to Serfdom*, 1944, and *Law, Legislation and Liberty*, a triple-decker work, the third volume of which appeared conveniently in 1979), or whether the Government reacted to circumstances, or whether there was a mixture of the two. Certainly, there was no immediate radical overhaul of the law the Heath Government had performed in 1971. Changes were made piecemeal. An analysis of each provision in each successive statute suggests the last. The keynote was opportunism within a broad range of continuing policies. For example, when Parliament enacted a law stipulating that voting members of unions' national executive committees had to be elected at least once every five years, the Government seemed to have overlooked the fact that at least one influential non-voting member, Mr Scargill, leader of the National Union of Mineworkers, did not have a vote. The Government changed the law by means of the so called 'Scargill clause' to meet its demand that non-voting members should now be elected. The policy of undermining union leaders, who were seen as overmighty subjects, was followed by a measure which was virtually *ad hominem*, directed at one particular union leader. Some changes in the law have misfired. If pre-strike ballots were introduced to divide union members from the leadership, that aim has spectacularly miscarried. Over 90% of such votes result in the support for the union's stand and unions had been given a further weapon in collective bargaining. While the Conservative approach to anti-union legislation has often been described as 'step by step', it was not that one step has been followed by another according to a pre-existing plan. Rather, there was an Act, followed a short while later by another statute on the same topic, dealing with the shortcomings of the previous Act. Policy objectives have also changed since 1979. Therefore, it cannot be said that there was a continuous implementation of one blueprint for changing industrial relations. Certainly, nobody in 1979 would have been able to write the present laws relating to lawful industrial action: they are far too complex for that! Since employment legislation is seen as an arm of economic policy, there appeared to be no end in sight. Among recent suggestions were the removal of employment protection for employees working in small firms and the reduction in health and safety rules. Further measures could have been expected had the Conservatives won in 1997.

The general policy of restriction (see below) underlies much of the legislation but there have been other factors at work. One of these factors has been the influence of EC law, which is seen by some Conservatives as permitting socialism to enter by the backdoor, having been thrown out of the front. Unions have reversed their anti-EC stance, seeing the Community as their one hope in a world of anti-unionism. EC-wide norms on matters such as working hours would have undermined government policies. Some EC law was welcomed by the Government. An example is the removal of restrictions on women's working nights, on heavy work and underground work (s 9 of the Employment Act 1989). This protective legislation was seen by the Government as being a barrier to competition. Instead of extending the legislation to men (which would also not have been sexually discriminatory), the Government removed it totally. Some EC-based laws were not welcomed. These include the implementation of equal pay for work of equal value in the Equal Pay (Amendment) Regulations (SI 1983/1794) and the partial enactment of the Acquired Rights Directive (77/187) by the Transfer of Undertakings (Protection of Employment) Regulations (SI 1981/1794). Those latter amendments were not in line with government policy. The issue of the European Commission's Social Policy is discussed in Chapter 2. Here it can be stated that the Government cannot override existing EC legislation, which is, moreover, subject to wide interpretation by the European Court of Justice.

1.3.18 Claimed success

The Conservatives claimed success for their approach (which is called 'deregulation' by their supporters and 'restriction' by their detractors): there was increased productivity, decreased industrial action and improved communication between management and workers. Recently, there has been a limit placed on public sector wage claims, a limit which is inconsistent with the professed policy of leaving industrial relations to employers and employees. Increased automation, worldwide competition, long lasting recessions and unemployment have aided these developments, but the increased use of the law has bolstered some of the claimed successes. Nevertheless, the UK's productivity remains stubbornly below that of many competitors, and some pundits argue that the country suffers from a shortage of skills.

1.3.19 Major legal changes

The following is a brief description of some of the major changes in industrial relations law made by the Conservative Government in the 1980s and early 1990s, together with the relevant statute or statutory instrument. The Government saw itself as restraining unions' bargaining power.

1.3.20 Reduction of employees' rights

The restrictions on rights of employees against employers are listed below, together with the original statute:

- The right to return after pregnancy was limited and made subject to complex law concerning written notices: ss 11–12 of the Employment Act 1980.

- After various increases in the qualifying period, the rule from 1985 to 1999 was that only employees with two years' service have a claim for unfair dismissal: Unfair Dismissal (Variation of Qualifying Period) Order 1985 (SI 1985/782). There is, however, still an exception for dismissal on trade union grounds. Protection against unfair dismissal extends from the moment of employment. The burden of proving reasonableness in unfair dismissal no longer lies on the employers, and employment tribunals must take into consideration the size and administrative resources of the firm: s 6 of the Employment Act 1980, amending what is now s 98(4) of the ERA 1996. These changes may simply reflect what tribunals were already doing. It is no longer unfair for employers to re-employ former strikers selectively where the workers were engaged in official action: s 3 of the Employment Act 1990. Official industrial action occurs when a union authorises or endorses it and fails to repudiate it.

- There have been various changes to procedure in industrial tribunals, which, since 1998, have been renamed employment tribunals. Deposits of up to £150 may be required from applicants (that is, from employees): s 20(1) of the Employment Act 1989; and there are now pre-hearing reviews by tribunal chairs: s 20(2) of the Employment Act 1989. Both came into force in 1993.

- The right to reasons for dismissal found in s 92 of the ERA 1996 is now available only to persons employed for at least two years: s 15 of the Employment Act 1989. The previous qualifying period was six months.

- There is no right to particulars of disciplinary procedures in firms which have fewer than 20 employees: s 13 of the Employment Act 1989.

- The protection given to young people by wages councils has been abolished: s 12(3) of the Wages Act 1986. Wages councils could no longer give more than one rate for minimum wages: s 14 of the Wages Act 1986. The Trade Union Reform and Employment Rights Act 1993 abolished wages councils except for the Agricultural Wages Board. Criminal liability for unauthorised deductions from wages has been abrogated: see Sched 1 of the 1986 statute, which repealed various statutes including the Truck Acts 1831–1940 and the marvellously named Payment of Wages in Public Houses Prohibition Act 1883. By s 19 and Sched 2 of the Employment Act 1980, the Road Haulage Wages Act 1938, which provided for the equivalent of a wages council in that industry, was repealed.

- Various legislation in favour of groups of workers has been repealed. The one which caught most media attention was the removal of the law that women could not work underground: s 9 of the Employment Act 1989. That statute also removed restrictions on women being engaged in heavy and night work, though the latter restraint already had many exemptions. Limits on young persons' hours of work have been removed: s 10 of the Employment Act 1989.

- Attempts by Labour councils to impose contract compliance have been made illegal: ss 17–20 of the Local Government Act 1988. No longer is it possible for councils to impose conditions on employers before granting contracts, except in respect of race relations (s 18). This change in the law has prevented councils acting as model employers.

- Time off for trade union duties has been restricted to situations where the union is recognised by the employers on the topic under discussion: s 14 of the Employment Act 1989.

The then Government did not rely on empirical evidence which demonstrated that employment protection laws did not affect management decisions; deregulation was based on untested assumptions.

Despite these many and varied reductions in the rights of employees, there were occasions when the Government introduced extensions to their rights. Most of these were the result of EC legislation (see Chapter 2) but there were other isolated changes, including the new rights laid down by the Disability Discrimination Act 1995.

1.3.21 Policy of restriction

Restrictions imposed on trade unions are listed below:

- Unions have been made liable in tort: s 15 of the Employment Act 1982. Simon Auerbach, *Legislating for Conflict*, 1990, called this amendment 'the pivotal provision ... of the whole *corpus* of legislation' (p 232). Unlawful acts not repudiated by trade union officials including shop stewards gave rise to vicarious liability to a maximum of £250,000 per action per employer: s 15 of the Employment Act 1982 and s 6 of the Employment Act 1990.

- Immunity for trade unions for inducing breach of or interfering with contracts has been limited to secret ballots of all those workers who may be called upon to act: ss 10–11 of the Trade Union Act 1984 and s 16 of the Employment Act 1988. Further restrictions on the conduct of ballots before industrial action were added in 1993. One development, major in terms of theory if insignificant as yet in practice, is the citizen's right of action discussed in Chapter 16.

- The golden formula immunity for acts done in contemplation or furtherance of a trade dispute has been limited to disputes between workers and their employers: s 18 of the Employment Act 1980.

- Picketing is lawful only at the place of work by those engaged in industrial action: s 16 of the Employment Act 1980.

- Secondary action is now confined to attendance at lawful picket sites: s 4 of the Employment Act 1990. This limitation began as s 17 of the 1980 Employment Act, which produced extremely complicated laws. The Government reacted to criticism by the International Labour Organisation's Committee of Experts' Report of 1989 that the law was in breach of Convention 87 on Freedom of Association and the Right to Organise for not affording sufficient protection to employees by abolishing the immunities for secondary action which remained after the 1980 statute. That was assuredly not the intention of ILO. The exception for secondary picketing is more apparent than real: see Chapter 16.

- Industrial action to enforce a closed shop is illegal: ss 10–14 of the Employment Act 1982 and s 10 of the Employment Act 1988.

These amendments to the law were designed to give employers the power to resist trade unions' claims.

1.3.22 Union autonomy reduced

The internal regulation of trade unions has been amended as follows:

- various rights have been granted to members against their unions, for example: the right to a ballot before industrial action (s 10 of the Trade Union Act 1984 and s 1 of the Employment Act 1988); the right not to be unreasonably excluded from membership (s 4 of the Employment Act 1980); and the right not to be disciplined for refusing to participate in industrial action (s 3 of the Employment Act 1988). These rights were extended in 1993;

- the Government has enacted provisions in relation to elections for members of unions' national executive. For example, independent scrutineers must be appointed and voting must be on the basis of one person, one vote: Pt 1 of the Trade Union Act 1986, as amended;

- unions must not indemnify members who execute unlawful instructions: s 8 of the Employment Act 1988;

- the Commissioners for the Rights of Trade Union Members and for Protection against Unlawful Industrial Action were appointed. (Refer to Chapter 2.) Both offices were abolished by the Employment Relations Act 1999.

Unions are now very much more highly regulated than they were before the 1970s. Their power to protect members has been reduced. The effect has been to rely more on market forces to regulate industrial relations. Insofar as the Conservative Government had freedom of action (it is sometimes forbidden to act by European Community law), individual employment protection 'rights' have been reduced in order to reduce burdens on businesses. It is perhaps because there is so much legislation that the intervention of the courts in strikes and in disputes between unions and members that the previously expressed concerns about judicial interference have died down. Scope for judicial intervention has been reduced.

1.3.23 Consolidation of law

Provisions dealing with unions are now found in the Trade Union and Labour Relations (Consolidation) Act 1992. Much of statutory employment law outside the area of discrimination was consolidated in 1996.

1.3.24 Model employer role abrogated

The Government withdrew from its role as a model employer. No longer did it promote trade unionism. It abrogated the Fair Wages Resolution 1946, and abolished the right to belong to a trade union for Government Communications Headquarters workers ostensibly on the grounds of national security. It repealed the right of employees to obtain wages at the general level in the relevant industry (Sched 11 to the Employment Protection Act 1975) and the right of unions to recognition (s 11 of the same Act). It abolished several tripartite bodies (that is, bodies with representation from unions, employers and independents), such as the Manpower Services Commission.

1.3.25 Employers' view

The then Government was supported by the success of some employers in crippling and defeating unions. The failure of the miners' strike 1984–85 stands out, but there have been other major victories for employers, such as the transfer of part of the London newspaper industry to Wapping and the reorganisation of ferries which led to the P & O dispute. Many other trials of strength have occurred, such as the dismissal of 89 women workers at Middlebrook Mushrooms near Selby, North Yorkshire, for going on strike in response to a proposed wage cut. Some employers have demonstrated that they are willing to use the courts to restrain industrial conflict.

1.3.26 Decline of unions

There is no doubt that the industrial scene has changed much since 1979. Union membership and density are down. Financially, some unions have been hard hit. Mass picketing away from the workplace has virtually disappeared. The closed shop has been undermined both by legal sanctions and employers' withdrawing from schemes, an example being British Rail. Recognition has sometimes been withdrawn. The decline of recognition was also affected by the decline of the number of employees in unions. The introduction of a right to recognition in 1999 does not necessarily mean that collective bargaining will resume its former importance. How much of the change is due to legislation is at least for the moment impossible to tell, but Conservative laws have affected the power relationship in the workplace. That effect, and the volume of legislation, continued right to the end of John Major's administration.

1.4   The Major era

Conservative appetite for change did not decrease. Several suggestions for amendment to the law were made but not enacted. One idea was the prohibition of strikes in essential industries. Another was that persons paying the political levy to trade unions should have to opt-in to doing so. A third possible change was to make collective agreements legally binding. This long standing proposal seems to have been rejected because it reflects corporatist notions. Moreover, derecognition would be impeded if recognition agreements were contractual. The Green Paper, *Industrial Relations in the 1990s* (Cm 1602, 1991), considered other proposals, many of which formed part of the Trade

Union Reform and Employment Rights Act 1993. One suggestion was a right to restrain unlawful action which affects the provision of public services, an idea which resurfaced at the Conservatives' 1996 conference. The Green Paper, *Industrial Action and Trade Unions* (Cm 3470, 1996), proposed making illegal industrial action which had a disproportionate or excessive effect. Workplace ballots could be made illegal. The 1996 Green Paper also proposed an increase in the length of notice to employers from seven days to 14, the imposition of a requirement that industrial action should be supported by a majority of those entitled to vote (and not just of those who do vote), and the re-balloting of union members at intervals during industrial action. Among other proposals were the abolition of the right to certain information for collective bargaining purposes and the right to time off with pay for union duties and to time off without pay for union activities. These rights are discussed in Chapter 14.

The Conservative Government continued to support flexible working practices, individual contracts, and the use of the law in industrial disputes. It boasted in *Britain – the Preferred Location* (1993) that 'labour costs in the UK continue to be low … the UK has the least onerous labour regulations in Europe, with fewer restrictions on working hours, overtime and holidays … [T]here is no legal requirement to recognise a trade union …'. It promised in the White Paper, *Competitiveness: Helping Business To Win* (1994), to keep industrial relations law under review. On the other side of industry, there has been debate as to whether unions' immunities against common law liability should be recast as positive rights and whether those rights (or even a modified system of immunity) should be enforced in labour courts separate from the ordinary court structure. Both recommendations reflect trade unionists' concern that ordinary courts, with their emphasis on individualism, are unlikely to adopt a neutral stance in disputes between employers and employees and have in the past restricted immunities which Parliament has granted to unions. Comments on the effect of the immunities by the judges encouraged the Government to narrow the protection afforded to unions. If judges cannot be trusted to enforce the law, some other mechanism is needed. There is also some debate as to whether a full blown system of basic human rights for workers should be introduced.

The issue of immunity is dealt with in Chapter 16, below. In conclusion, collectivism has been undermined but not eradicated and there still are no fundamental employment law rights in English law, while on the individual employment law side deregulation continued in the 1990s. A government amendment to the Trade Union Reform and Employment Rights Bill in May 1993, which was enacted, is the epitome of these policies. No longer is it unlawful (as the Court of Appeal has twice said it is, though in 1995 the House of Lords overturned that decision) to offer financial inducements to employees to renounce union membership.

1.5   The Labour Government

The White Paper, *Fairness at Work*, emphasised that Labour would not be abolishing all the Conservative anti-union laws. 'There will be no going back. The days of strikes without ballots, mass picketing, closed shops and secondary action are over ...' (Tony Blair's foreword). There have, however, been major changes to the law: working time; parental leave; time off for domestic emergencies; amendments to the Transfer of Undertakings (Protection of Employment) Regulations 1981 and to the Sex Discrimination Act 1975 to accommodate those undergoing gender re-assignment; as well as the prohibition of blacklists of union members. The enactment of a right to be accompanied at a disciplinary hearing and the introduction of a statutory recognition procedure are also of importance.

MODERN EMPLOYMENT LAW

Ideological conflict over the role of trade unions has been a feature of UK politics for many years. At present, free market economic theory prevails. The labour market has been deregulated and unions have been re-regulated.

Frames of reference

Industrial relations experts sometimes model their subject through the use of three 'frames of reference': unitary, pluralist and conflictual. In a unitary firm, the workers are seen as part of a team. Their interests are subordinated to the firm. Unions are not legitimate, for they interfere with the company's smooth running by introducing different interests. Pluralism is the thesis by which the power of workers is increased by their banding together to form unions. Only by their so doing is their power made equivalent to that of employers. A conflictual frame of reference is that postulated by Marxists. In the contest between capital and labour, there can be no long lasting equilibrium. Only when workers control the means of production, exchange and distribution will there be industrial peace.

Law and industrial relations

Legislation has increasingly intervened in the relationships among employers, employees, and unions. Conservative Government policies were concerned with reducing employees' rights (with the effect that managerial prerogative was increased) and restricting union freedom of manoeuvre. These policies were subject to the laws of the European Community. During the last years of the Conservative Government, the Trades Union Congress viewed the EC as the sole possible source of salvation for workers. The Conservative opposition to the European Union stymied the introduction into the UK of employment rights under the Maastricht Treaty and several draft directives were held up.

The future

The policy of deregulation (or re-regulation) would have been set to continue, had the Conservatives won in 1997. Ideas exist to modernise the structure of labour law as it existed from 1906 to the end of the 1970s. For over a decade, there has been a debate whether a system of positive rights (for example, the right to strike) and a structure of labour tribunals outside the present judicial hierarchy would uphold workers' rights in a manner more advantageous to employees than the present system. The advantage of autonomy is that it prevents common law such as contract impeding legal developments.

The Employment Relations Act 1999 introduced several new rights for workers, including parental leave. Unions obtained a (highly complex) statutory right to be recognised.

CHAPTER 2

INSTITUTIONAL MATTERS

2.1 Institutions

This section deals with bodies created by law to tackle industrial relations issues. The first difficulty is to determine which body deals with the claim at first instance.

2.1.1 County court or employment tribunal?

The court or tribunal in which an employment case is heard depends on the origin and nature of the claim. In respect of contractual actions such as wrongful dismissal, the trial may take place in the county court or High Court in the normal way, although neither court has a great deal of experience of employment law. Legal aid is available and the limitation period is six years. Appeals lie to the Court of Appeal and then the House of Lords. Statutory claims are heard in employment tribunals, which are creatures of statute; that is, their jurisdiction is circumscribed by the power entrusted to them by Parliament. Exceptionally, employment tribunals have been ready to hear cases based on European Community (EC) law even though domestic law does not empower them to do so. There has been some discussion whether employment tribunals can lawfully act in this way, but no successful challenge to jurisdiction has been mounted. Some contractual actions on termination of the contract of employment in employment law have been transferred to the employment tribunals, subject to an upper monetary limit. See 2.2.1, below. There is nowadays no limit on claims in respect of racial or sexual discrimination and there never has been a restriction on the amount which an employee can claim has been unlawfully deducted from wages. The limit on contractual claims could be seen as anomalous. Personal injury claims are excluded from transfer. Appeals from employment tribunals go to the Employment Appeal Tribunal (EAT) and thence to the Court of Appeal in the usual way. Diagrammatically the appeal system can be represented thus:

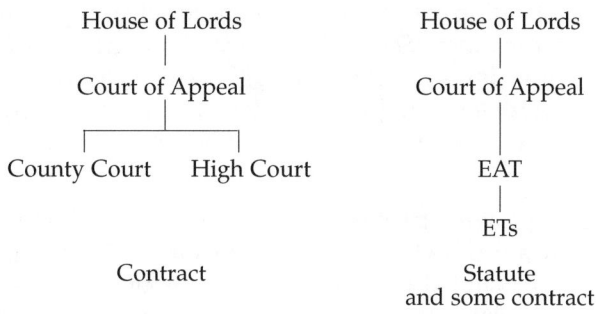

House of Lords	House of Lords
Court of Appeal	Court of Appeal
County Court High Court	EAT
	ETs
Contract	Statute and some contract

Reference to the European Court of Justice (ECJ) may be made by any of these bodies including employment tribunals under Art 234 (formerly Art 177) of the Treaty Establishing the European Community. The reference is made in the usual way. The power to refer has been utilised by the various employment law courts and tribunals. For example, the ECJ answered a reference from the House of Lords in the pregnancy discrimination case of *Webb v EMO Air Cargo (UK) Ltd* (1993).

2.2 Tribunals

This section deals with the tribunals particular to labour law. Employment tribunals were expected to be cheap, speedy and accessible bodies, but there has been an increasing juridification of their functioning. Appeals lie to the Employment Appeal Tribunal.

2.2.1 Employment tribunals

Employment tribunals are the judicial bodies in which most statutory employment claims are heard and determined. Over the last 15 years, their caseload (but not their resources) has increased sixfold. For example, there were over 70,000 applications in 1995–96 and almost 92,000 in 1998–99. In 1993–94, 71,661 claims were registered and 25,659 cases heard, an increase of some 250% over 1989–90. The numbers have continued to increase from 1994:

- Industrial tribunals, which since the Employment Rights (Dispute Resolution) Act 1998 have been called 'employment tribunals', were established by Parliament in 1964. They are composed of a lawyer chair, who must be a solicitor or barrister of seven years' standing, and two lay members, 'wingmen', one from the employers' side of industry and commerce and one from the employees' side. In 1996–97, there were 79 full time and 195 part time chairs. The Conservative Government tried to extend the categories of persons who are appointed wingmen beyond those nominated by organisations such as the CBI and Trade Union Congress. The lay members can outvote the lawyer chair, surprisingly, even on questions of law. The laypersons' function is to use their knowledge and understanding of industrial relations to solve employment disputes in a practical manner (*Sogbetun v London Borough of Hackney* (1998)). The use of non-lawyers explains the oft-used phrase that employment tribunals are 'industrial juries'. There are approximately 75 full time and some 200 part time chairs. The number of lay members is about 2,200.

- The jurisdiction of employment tribunals is extensive. The first main power was over the award of redundancy payments in 1965. Since then, jurisdiction has vastly expanded to cover, for instance, unfair dismissal and sexual and racial discrimination in the employment sphere. There are now over 50 jurisdictions. A substantial proportion of cases involved unlawful deductions from wages. Recent statutes which have given the tribunals more jurisdiction include the Deregulation and Contracting Out Act 1994, the Sunday Trading Act 1994 (now part of the Employment Rights Act (ERA) 1996) and the Disability Discrimination Act 1995. There is, however, no jurisdiction to hear a claim under the law established in *Francovich v Italian Republic* (1990) (see 2.4.5, below) (*Secretary of State for Employment v Mann* (1996)). The claim must be made in the High Court. The Court of Appeal refused the appeal (*sub nom Potter v SSE* (1997)). This is not an employment law claim but an action against the State akin to the tort of breach of statutory duty. There is also no jurisdiction to hear a free-standing EC claim (*Barry v Midland Bank plc* (1997)).

- Employment tribunals are empowered to disregard the rules of evidence. While not informal (for instance, oaths are sworn), they can be substantially less intimidating to applicants than the county court, though procedure, which is largely governed by the Employment Tribunals (Constitution and Rules of Procedure) Regulations 1993, SI 1993/2687, varies from tribunal to tribunal. The chair plays the key role in controlling procedure.

- Research has demonstrated that applicants with representation by lawyers are twice as likely to win than those without. Some of the difference may be accounted for by the fact that lawyers may be used only in circumstances where there is some likelihood of success. Experienced lawyers know the ropes and may be familiar faces to the chairpersons. Since legal aid is not available for representation before employment tribunals and employers normally have more money than employees they have dismissed, there is an imbalance. Part of this imbalance is sometimes rectified by the use of lawyers paid for by unions. Chairs may (but need not) help unrepresented claimants. There have been calls over many years for legal aid to be extended to some tribunals, including employment tribunals.

- Employment tribunals can act swiftly. Often, cases are disposed of within a few weeks of the application being made.

- If the defendant or the employment tribunal considers that an argument is unlikely to succeed, the employment tribunal may order a pre-hearing review. At the review, the employment tribunal may order a deposit of up to £150 from the party whose contention may well be rejected and he is warned that the deposit will be forfeited and costs awarded against that party if he continues in his contention. If he then loses and costs are awarded against him, the deposit is first used to defray part of the costs. There were 795 pre-hearing reviews and deposits were required in 402 cases in 1995–96. Pre-hearing reviews may be conducted by the chair sitting alone.

- The increasing use of lawyers has led to charges of excessive legalism and of increased length of hearings caused by lawyers' prolixity. The European Court of Human Rights held in *Darnell v UK* (1993) that the delays in unfair dismissal cases breached Art 6(1) of the European Convention on Human Rights, which states that 'everyone is entitled to a ... hearing within a reasonable time ...'. A public apology was held not to be a sufficient remedy and the court ordered the UK to pay damages of £5,000. It must, however, be remembered that some aspects of employment law are in themselves complex and that the loss of a job is an extremely important matter. Income, career, and often personal satisfaction depend on jobs. Loss of a job can be traumatic. The 'day in tribunal' may help to reduce such stress. Legalism is reduced by the presence of lay tribunal members and by the fact that one tribunal is not bound by the decisions of other employment tribunals.

- Normally, there is a lawyer in the chair plus two 'wingmen'. If the parties consent, the powers of an employment tribunal can be exercised by the chair and just one lay member (s 4 of the Employment Tribunals Act 1996). The aim is to save money. The Act permits the chair to sit alone in various classes of cases, for example, where the respondents do not contest the case, the claim is one for interim relief, and the complaint is of an unlawful deduction from wages contrary to the ERA 1996. The Employment Rights (Dispute Resolution) Act 1998 extended this list to include matters where the chair is to hear the case alone unless he decides otherwise. Among those jurisdictions are redundancy payments, deductions from wages, written statements, failure to pay protective awards and failure to pay compensation for breach of the information provisions in respect of transfer of undertakings.

- Where the same issue is being litigated in both the High Court and an employment tribunal, the chair has a discretion to stay the tribunal proceedings pending the outcome of the civil proceedings. This situation used to occur especially when wrongful dismissal actions had to be heard in the civil courts, but, as most termination claims fall within the concurrent jurisdiction of employment tribunals (see below), this issue should lose its importance. Some breach of contract claims (whether express, implied or imposed by law) arising on termination, such as claims for payment in lieu of notice and holiday pay as well as actions for wrongful dismissal (but there is no power to issue declarations or injunctions or for employers to bring actions, though they may counterclaim), form part of the concurrent jurisdiction of tribunals and courts. The Employment Tribunals Extension of Jurisdiction (England and Wales) Order 1994 (SI 1994/1623) excludes covenants on restraint of trade, obligations of confidentiality, copyright and other intellectual property rights (all of which may involve difficult areas of law) and the provision of living accommodation, and all claims above

£25,000. They are heard by the lawyer chair sitting alone unless he decides differently. Various matters must be taken into account by the chair before deciding to sit alone, including whether a case discloses an issue of law which it is desirable for a lawyer to resolve and whether other issues between the parties are being dealt with by the full tribunal or just by the chair. The chair may decide to move from sitting alone to sitting with the other members. It should be noted that, where jurisdiction has been transferred, the ordinary courts may still hear the case: jurisdiction is concurrent, not exclusive. One problem is that employment tribunals cannot hear contractual actions except those concerned with the termination of the contract. For example, a deduction of pay for taking part in industrial action may give rise to a dispute and, if so, the claim is heard in the civil courts because it does not involve the termination of the contract.

- Costs are rarely awarded against former employees (though see above regarding the pre-hearing review). After all, applicants may still be out of work. When costs are awarded, the applicant has been frivolous, vexatious or unreasonable or has acted abusively or disruptively.

- The Employment Rights (Dispute Resolution) Act 1998 permits the use of legal officers to aid chairs. They will deal with interlocutory matters such as requests for further and better particulars and for the discovery of documents, as well as dealing with settled and withdrawn cases. It is hoped that legal officers will speed up the tribunal process. They will not be able to conduct pre-hearing reviews or hear and determine proceedings (unless the applicant has withdrawn her claim or the parties have reached a settlement).

- The 1998 Act also empowered ACAS to set up a mechanism for resolving unfair dismissal disputes by arbitration. It is expected that this scheme will come into force in spring 2000. Entry into the scheme is voluntary. It is uncertain what effect this scheme will have on the tribunal system.

The Conservative Government published a Green Paper, *Resolving Employment Rights Disputes: Options for Reform* (Cm 2707, 1994). The main proposals were to encourage voluntary arbitration as an alternative to the tribunal system, to encourage applicants to use internal procedures (compensation may be reduced if they are not used), to improve information to employers and to extend the powers of chairs to sit alone. For a devastating critique, see Tsamados (1995) *Legal Action* (March) 6, pp 6–7. Many of these proposals were enacted by the Labour Government in the Employment Rights (Dispute Resolution) Act 1998. It did not propose the replacement of the accusatorial system with one based on the inquisitorial approach, which may be more suitable.

John K MacMillan has recently written:

> The Department of Trade and Industry predicts that the reduction to one year in the qualifying period for bringing unfair dismissal claims, the lowering of the small employer threshold from 20 to 15 in disability discrimination cases and the various new jurisdictions which employment tribunals seem to be perpetually acquiring, the most important of which are the Working Time Regulations 1998, the National Minimum Wage Act 1998 and the Public Interest (Disclosure) Act 1998, will increase [the annual workload] to around 110,000. There is no indication of any, let alone any comparable, increase in resources [(1999) 28 ILJ 33, pp 45–46].

Several commentators have proposed the creation of specialised tribunals to deal with discrimination claims, arguing that tribunals do not have sufficient experience to deal with the difficult legal issues which arise in such claims. It is suggested that, while there is a great deal of force in such a proposal, it fails at the point of distinguishing discrimination and 'normal' employment claims: what is to happen if an employee claims that the same act constitutes an unfair dismissal and sexual discrimination?

2.2.2 Employment Appeal Tribunal

Most of the work undertaken by the EAT consists of the hearing of appeals from employment tribunals, including (since 1998) appeals in contract cases. Usually, only questions of law can be appealed. One exception is that appeals from determinations of the Certification Officer may be made on issues of fact (s 256 of the Trade Union and Labour Relations (Consolidation) Act (TULR(C)A) 1992). Similarly, appeals against a refusal by the Certification Officer to list a union (s 9(4)) may involve questions of fact. Appeals on questions of fact may also be made in cases of exclusion or expulsion from a union. There were 941 appeals in 1994 and 998 full appeals in 1995–96. Between 1998 and 1999, the EAT disposed of 1,323 cases. Like employment tribunals, the EAT is composed of a lawyer chair (often a High Court judge) and two or sometimes four lay members, and again the laypersons can outvote the lawyer even on questions of law. The number of employee and employer representatives must be equal, unless the parties agree differently. If an employment tribunal chair is empowered to sit alone, on appeal so may an EAT judge. With consent, the case may be heard with one or three lay persons. One judge is nominated President of the EAT. In terms of precedent, the EAT binds employment tribunals and is bound by the Court of Appeal and the House of Lords. The EAT has original jurisdiction over exclusion and expulsion claims against unions unless the employee has been admitted to membership (s 67(2) and s 176(2)). Other points of interest are listed below:

- the EAT could have been called a court. It is indeed a superior court of record. However, the Government which established it did not wish the EAT to be considered in the same way as its precursor, the National Industrial Relations Court, which was instituted by the previous

Government in the Industrial Relations Act 1971. That court was inextricably linked to that piece of legislation and, on the repeal of the Act, the court was abolished. Many trade union members have, moreover, had a dislike for law, seeing it and its courts as being run by a judiciary opposed to the interests of unions. The name 'Employment Appeal Tribunal' was, therefore, chosen to ensure that the body was not tainted by the nature of its predecessors;

• problems for the EAT have included its workload and its position in the hierarchy. To cut down on the number of appeals, it can call disputes 'questions of fact', which are not appealable. However, to do so can lead to one employment tribunal directly contradicting another tribunal on exactly the same facts. For example, the issue of whether a worker is an employee is a question of fact. If a company dismisses part of its workforce, some workers being in Southampton, some in Sheffield, one tribunal might hold that the workers are employees, and another that they are not. The first set of workers can claim a remedy for being unfairly dismissed, whereas the second cannot. This inconsistency is discreditable to a system of law. One potential escape route was for the EAT to lay down guidelines for employment tribunals. The EAT used guidelines on several occasions, thereby alerting employment tribunals to considerations which they should take into account. The Court of Appeal has, however, rejected the use of guidelines on several occasions. Employment tribunals are instructed primarily to consider the words of the statute and to apply them to the facts. There is now little guidance outside of statute and precedent. The result is a wilderness of decisions, and the outcome of employment tribunals' determinations are not always predictable.

2.3   Other institutions of English employment law

Since the mid-1970s, governments have created various bodies for the purpose of resolving industrial conflicts and assisting employees both against their employers and their unions.

2.3.1   Advisory Conciliation and Arbitration Service (ACAS)

The name of the Advisory Conciliation and Arbitration Service (ACAS) reflects, to a large extent, what it does. Its principal role when it was created at the start of the 1974–79 Labour administration was to assist in the improvement of industrial relations, especially through the widening and deepening of collective bargaining. That principle survived until 1993 and was enshrined in s 209 of TULR(C)A 1992. However, it was undermined by the Conservative Government's commitment to individual bargaining and to the diminution in power of trade unions and their consequent sidelining. Since 30 August 1993, ACAS no longer has a duty to encourage collective bargaining. It is not, however, prevented from giving support to collective bargaining. The Conservative Government amended the law in 1993 to emphasise ACAS's functions in aiding settlement of industrial disputes as part of its principal duty of improving industrial relations. The Labour Government in 1999 placed a duty on ACAS to 'promote industrial relations' but it did not restore ACAS's duty to encourage the extension of collective bargaining. It reasoned that it did not wish to be seen as being in favour of collective bargaining. There is no duty on the parties to resort to ACAS. Submission is voluntary. ACAS adopts a neutral stance between employers and employees.

Composition (ss 247–49)

Like employment tribunals and the EAT, ACAS has a tripartite structure. It is governed by a council of nine. Three members are independent, three represent employers and three represent unions. It is seen as an impartial body. The Chair is appointed by the Secretary of State. Funding is provided by the Government. Despite such possible sources of interference, the Service has retained its independence, the separation being confirmed by s 247(3) of TULR(C)A 1992. No government minister may direct ACAS as to how to exercise its functions. The original intention was to keep the Service separate from government policies on pay.

The main functions of ACAS are listed below, but it has others, for example, the maintenance of the list of independent experts who are involved in claims for equal pay for work of equal value.

Advice (s 213)

ACAS provides a large amount of written and oral advice each year on industrial relations matters. Much advice is given over the phone. There were over half a million enquiries each year in the late 1990s. Before 1993, ACAS had a wider duty, in that it could give advice on employment and not just on industrial relations matters. The reference to advice on collective issues was dropped in the revised wording, but there is nothing to stop ACAS giving advice on collective negotiation, and it frequently does so. ACAS also publishes various booklets, the most important of which is 'Discipline at Work' (1987). Section 213 gives a lengthy though non-exclusive list of the matters on which ACAS may advise. They include union recognition, joint consultation, discipline, pay systems and staff turnover. Since 1 April 1994, ACAS has been obliged to charge for its handbooks and advisory booklets.

Conciliation (s 210)

What may be called 'collective conciliation' is the process by which the Service seeks to bring parties in dispute together in an attempt to resolve industrial strife. One party must request the intervention. The aim is not to use an umpire to settle the dispute (or apprehended dispute) but to provide an opportunity for the sides to find a solution away from the heat of battle. ACAS can provide an independent conciliator whose function it is to encourage the parties to reach a settlement. Collective conciliation is important because, if it fails, industrial conflict may take place. It is thought that rolling strikes (for example, one strike a week for several months) are harder to conciliate than all-out strikes. The Service received 1,207 cases for collective conciliation in 1992; 1,211 in 1993; 1,313 in 1994; 1,321 in 1995; and 1,306 in 1996. About half the requests involved disputes concerning pay or terms and conditions of employment. ACAS Reports made during the 1990s stated that in 90% of referrals it had obtained a settlement or had encouraged the parties to make substantial progress towards a settlement. The 1995 Report noted that both sides of industry were resorting more and more to the law. Food, drink and tobacco comprise the sectors of industry most often in need of collective conciliation.

Individual conciliation (s 18 of the Employment Tribunals Act 1996) occurs when an ACAS officer acts to seek a settlement between employees and the party claimed against. Often, it is only by talking to the officer that the applicant realises the strength or weakness of his claim. When an employee applies to an employment tribunal, either against the union (for example, for being unjustifiably disciplined contrary to s 290(a) of TULR(C)A 1992) or against his employers (for example, for a remedy for breach of the right not to be unfairly dismissed), the matter is referred to one of these officers, who attempts to find grounds for a settlement before the case reaches the tribunal. Neither party is obliged to assist the conciliation officer. The scheme is free to both parties.

Thousands of claims are referred each year, the majority of which involve unfair dismissal. The number is rising year by year: in 1998, there were over 113,000. ACAS started conciliating in claims for breach of the contract of employment in 1994 and received over 3,000 requests in that year. What is surprising to a long term student of ACAS is that in 1998 there were more claims involving breach of contract and deductions from wages (over 48,000) than unfair dismissal (almost 43,000). From its inception, the largest number, often by a large percentage, of individual conciliation cases had involved unfair dismissal and the fact that it has been superseded by contractual actions is astonishing. ACAS does not have the power to conciliate in claims involving written statements and applications for interim relief. If a settlement is reached, it must be recorded on form COT 3 to be binding between the parties. Such a settlement is not void as being an attempt to evade the prohibition on contracting out of the provisions of the ERA 1996. There is concern that settlements often result in payments substantially below those which the applicant would have obtained had the claim gone to tribunal.

The Trade Union Reform and Employment Rights Act 1993 and the Employment Rights (Dispute Resolution) Act 1998 widened the law on compromise agreements with which ACAS is not involved. Where individual conciliation fails, the employee can go to the employment tribunals if the matter falls within the jurisdiction of those institutions. About one-third of unfair dismissal conciliation cases result in re-employment. The figure for employment tribunals is under 3%. Perhaps half of ACAS's time is spent on unfair dismissal conciliation. ACAS conciliation work in individual cases is outstandingly successful. In terms of costs, it was estimated that a settlement conciliated by ACAS costs £267 (1994 figures), whereas the cost per completed case at an employment tribunal was £966, which in itself was only two-thirds of the 1988–89 figure. The Chair of ACAS is proud of the savings to the public purse.

Arbitration (s 212)

If both parties agree, a dispute may be referred to ACAS for arbitration. The possibility of settlement by conciliation must first be considered. The arbitrator (there is normally only one, but a panel may be appointed) will decide between the competing claims and can reach a compromise (unless the parties agree on 'pendulum arbitration', in which case the arbitrator must accept in full one side's claim). The arbitrator is chosen from a list kept by ACAS or the Central Arbitration Committee. ACAS officers do not themselves undertake arbitration. The arbitrator's decision is not legally binding. With the consent of the parties it may be published. The number of arbitrations has been declining since the 1970s. ACAS never dealt with more than 260 arbitrations in the 1980s. In 1994, there were 156; in 1995 there were 136; and, in 1996, ACAS reported 117 requests. The award is not enforceable in a court. Sometimes the parties use an ACAS arbitrator without the dispute being formally referred. For further details, see Mumford (1996) 34 BJIR 287.

Inquiry (s 214)

ACAS may conduct inquiries into any industry (for example, newspapers) or undertaking. Only four inquiries have been held so far. There is also provision (s 215) for the Secretary of State for Trade and Industry to refer industrial disputes to courts of inquiry. An example was the Grunwick dispute (1977).

Codes of Practice

ACAS may issue, revise and revoke Codes of Practice for the purpose of improving industrial relations (s 199). The Secretary of State must give his approval, as must Parliament. The Codes seek to disseminate information about good practice. Breach of a Code does not in itself found liability, but may be taken into account by the Central Arbitration Committee or an employment tribunal when judging an issue (s 207). The ACAS Codes are:

- No 1: Disciplinary Practice and Procedures in Employment 1977, revised in 1997 and in force from 5 February 1998;

- No 2: Disclosure of Information to Trade Unions for Collective Bargaining Purposes 1977, revised in 1997; and

- No 3: Time Off for Trade Union Duties and Activities, which was revised in 1991 and 1997.

The Secretary of State for Trade and Industry (formerly the Secretary of State for Education and Employment) also has the power to issue, revise and revoke Codes of Practice (ss 203–06). ACAS must be consulted, and Parliament must assent to them. These Codes have the same legal effect as ACAS Codes, except that courts may also take them into account. (When the National Disability Council issues a Code, both courts and tribunals will be entitled to take it into account.) The power has been exercised in relation to the closed shop, picketing and industrial action and notice to employers, the last being revised in 1995 to take account of the legislation of the early 1990s. ACAS did not wish to draw up these Codes because it was thought that its reputation for unbiased advice would be blemished. The Secretary of State's Codes have been criticised as extending anti-trade union measures beyond those approved by Parliament. In *Thomas v National Union of Mineworkers (South Wales Area)* (1985), Scott J controversially suggested that the Code of Practice on picketing's recommendation that the maximum number of pickets should be six at each entrance was law: more than six would constitute intimidation. His statement was controversial because the maximum number had not been so stated in a statute or in a judicial decision. This 'back door' legislation has been attacked as being unconstitutional – law should be laid down by Parliament and the courts, not in non-binding Codes of Practice.

By s 251A, as inserted by s 44 of the Trade Union Reform and Employment Rights Act 1993, ACAS may charge for its services. Except for conferences and some publications, it does not do so.

The Conservative Government intended to create an arbitration scheme under ACAS auspices to deal with unfair dismissal claims. Arbitration would be voluntary. Any employment law disputes would be allowed to go to binding arbitration. The Labour Government legislated for this in the Employment Rights (Dispute Resolution) Act 1998 and it is expected that the scheme will apply from spring 2000.

2.3.2 Central Arbitration Committee (CAC)

The CAC was established in 1975 (though its predecessors date back to 1919) to deal with arbitrations in industrial disputes. Since its inception, its chair has been Sir John Wood, but he retired in 1998 before the powers of the CAC were extended to cover the statutory recognition procedure. There is currently no chair, though the two deputies act up. Arbitration committees are established, composed of an independent neutral chair together with an equal number of representatives of employers and employees. The expectation is that they will reach unanimous decisions, but the chair's vote can outweigh all other votes. The CAC encourages the parties to reach a settlement by suggesting compromises and ways forward. It is more proactive and interventionist than the other bodies discussed here. It has no power to compel the attendance of witnesses.

The two remaining functions of the CAC are: first, arbitration over matters referred to it by ACAS; and, secondly, arbitration concerned with the disclosure of information for collective bargaining purposes. The first is voluntary, the second is compulsory. The highest number of voluntary arbitrations was 11 in 1976. There were none in the 1990s. There is no appeal from a determination of the CAC, but there is the possibility of judicial review. The Committee need not give reasons in its first jurisdiction but it has decided to state its 'general considerations' for reaching its conclusions. In the second jurisdiction, it must give reasons (ss 183–84 of TULR(C)A 1992). In 1995, the CAC received 30 references, all under the second head, discussed in Chapter 14. For the most part, the information concerns finance, restructuring plans, workforce composition, grading and managing change (for example, relocation and privatisation). Formal awards are rare, perhaps one per year (under 20% of cases go to a full hearing), but the CAC has twice formally stated that employers have not complied with an award. Unlike the Equal Opportunities Commission and the Commission for Racial Equality, the courts have not intervened very much to correct any excesses of jurisdiction by the CAC. At the time of writing, the CAC is about to undergo a revamp to enable it to deal with the statutory recognition procedure laid down in the Employment Relations Act 1999.

2.3.3 The Equal Opportunities Commission (EOC) and the Commission for Racial Equality (CRE)

These institutions were established under the Sex Discrimination Act (SDA) 1975 and the Race Relations Act (RRA) 1976 respectively. Their composition comprises between eight and 15 commissioners, who may be part-timers, together with a chairperson. Their functions are similar:

- the promotion of equal opportunities;

- the elimination of discrimination;

- the review of legislation (various documents have been issued but the Government has not endorsed them);

- the striking down of discriminatory job advertisements (see Chapter 6); and

- the conduct of inquiries ('formal investigations') into discrimination.

The Commissions deal with enquiries both in writing and over the telephone. Major areas of concern include victimisation, equal opportunities, maternity and the 'like work' method of acquiring equal pay. The Commissions are empowered to deal with individual claimants where the application is a test case which raises a matter of principle, and it is unreasonable to expect the person to deal with the application unaided, or 'if there is any special consideration' (s 75 of the SDA 1975; s 66 of the RRA 1976). The EOC has adopted a test case strategy. It has attempted to use cases to move English domestic law into line with EC law when the latter is more favourable to applicants than the former. Without such financial assistance, applicants would not have been able to pursue their claims and the law would not have changed so rapidly. The EOC granted legal assistance in 47 cases and legal advice in 18 cases in the year ending 31 March 1999. The CRE received 1,657 requests for assistance in 1998. The CRE granted finance for representation in 112 cases in 1992 and 206 in 1995. The House of Lords held in *R v Secretary of State for Employment ex p EOC* (1994) that the EOC has the power to bring judicial review proceedings to clarify the relationship between UK and EC law as to sex discrimination. The effect was to strike down a long standing rule as to qualifications for employment protection found in statutes. This case was a real success for the EOC after a number of defeats during the Thatcherite era.

The Commissions are empowered to apply to the appropriate county court for an injunction to restrain instructions to discriminate, attempts to procure discrimination, and pressure to discriminate (ss 39–40 of the SDA 1975; ss 30–31 of the RRA 1976). The organisations may also seek injunctions to abrogate discriminatory practices (s 37 of the SDA 1975; s 28 of the RRA 1976).

Formal investigations (s 57 of the SDA 1975; s 48 of the RRA 1976) might be seen as the cutting edge of the enforcement of non-discriminatory policies. Individual cases improve the lot only of those employees who made the claim. Formal investigations can, however, be targeted at companies with a view to securing their compliance with the legislation. Individual claims in legal theory benefit only individuals; formal investigations have the potential to benefit members of groups. However, such hope has been dashed. Judicial interpretation has restricted the Commissions' potential powers (see especially *Re Prestige Group Ltd* (1984), where the House of Lords held that the Commissions could not inspect a firm on their own initiative: there had to be a least some grounds for suspecting that the firm was discriminating unlawfully), but there is still scope for a more active use of this tool than has occurred over the past decade. The CRE did not commence any formal investigations in 1995, but there was a resurgence of interest in such investigations in the late 1990s.

The Commissions have the power (ss 60 and 67 of the SDA 1975; ss 51 and 58 of the RRA 1976) to issue non-discrimination notices ordering the employers not to discriminate where there is unlawful discrimination, a discriminatory job advertisement or practice, pressure to discriminate, or an act in breach of an equality clause inserted in an employment contract by virtue of the Equal Pay Act 1970. The notices order the employers to comply with the requirements stated in them. For example, an employment agency in West Yorkshire was told to desist its discriminatory practices and to permit the EOC to monitor the situation for five years. Employers have the opportunity to make representations but not to cross-examine members of either Commission. Employers must inform the Commission as to the manner in which they have complied with the notice. There is a right of appeal against a notice to an employment tribunal. The appeal can be on the grounds that a fact relied on by one of the Commissions is open to challenge. The notice is enforceable by a county court injunction if the employers are likely to discriminate again within five years of the notice. However, if the employers did not challenge the legality of the notice when first issued, an employment tribunal must first consider that issue.

If the Commission has acted *ultra vires*, judicial review is available. The Commissions have at times been found to have exceeded their powers, principally on the grounds that formal investigations cannot be used unless there is at least suspicion that the employers have been acting discriminatorily. Much has been written on the failure of formal investigations to extirpate unlawful discrimination. The writing is often to the effect that sexual and racial discrimination are based on discrimination against groups, such as women in general, not against individuals within a group, such as a particular woman. Using the law to prevent discrimination against a specific woman does not attack the root of the problem – discrimination against women in general. Formal investigations can, however, deal with discrimination against groups. The current failure of the formal investigation mode and the lack of fit between the problem of discrimination against groups and the emphasis on individual enforcement has led to the suggestion that there should be instituted 'class actions' such as exist in the USA, that is, claims on behalf of a group. English law is perhaps moving towards such a concept. Equal pay claims have been made by representatives of groups such as speech therapists ('representative actions'), but there is no possibility in the near future of the Government creating the class action mode of enforcement. It is a matter for debate whether a more strategic use could be made of representative actions than heretofore.

The Commissions may issue Codes of Practice in their respective areas. These Codes have the same legal authority as those issued by ACAS. The CRE issued one in 1984 on 'The Elimination of Racial Discrimination and the Promotion of Equality of Opportunity in Employment' (one employment tribunal, in a case involving discrimination against a person of Anglo-Dutch origin by a Japanese firm, said that it was 'reprehensible' not to refer to the Code) and the EOC issued one in 1985 on 'The Elimination of Discrimination on the Grounds of Sex and Marriage and the Promotion of Equality of Opportunity in Employment'. The EOC issued a Code of Practice on equal pay (which came into force in 1997). TURERA 1993 gave the EOC the power to issue that Code of Practice. This was the first Code on equal pay in any Member State of the EC. The EOC, in its proposals for reform, *Equality in the 21st Century: A New Approach* (1998), suggested that employers should be made to review their pay systems in accordance with this Code of Practice. If the employers refused to do so, or did so inadequately, the EOC would be empowered to devise a programme for them. If they still failed to comply, the EOC would be able to bring proceedings in the employment tribunals.

2.3.4 Certification Officer

By s 254 of TULR(C)A 1992, a provision which dates back to 1975, there exists the position of Certification Officer. He fulfils the following principal duties:

- maintaining the list of trade unions;

- issuing certificates of independence to unions;

- keeping records of annual membership and financial returns from unions;

- keeping various other union records including copies of union rules;

- enforcing the law on elections of union officers;

- enforcing the law on ballots to establish political funds and on political expenditure; and

- investigating union finances and appointing an inspector when fraud is suspected.

The first two duties were given to the Certification Officer when the office was first created. The other ones were given by the Conservative Government as part of their policy of intervention in unions' internal affairs. The Employment Relations Act 1999 transferred many of the functions of the Commissioner for the Rights of Trade Union Members to the Certification Officer. In 1992, six certificates of independence were issued but there were none granted in 1995. In the late 1990s, certificates tended to be granted mostly to unions formed by the amalgamation of two or more unions. Appeal lies to the EAT.

The Employment Relations Act 1999 abolished the offices of the Commissioner for the Rights of Trade Union Members and the Commissioner for Protection against Unlawful Industrial Action. Most of the functions of the former were transferred to the Certification Officer.

2.4 Membership of the European Community

This topic is vast and expanding. Membership of the EC has affected UK law in many different ways. There is a move towards harmonisation or convergence of the labour laws of the Member States but the process has a very long way to go. UK politics have also had a major impact on EC law. UK opposition stifled most attempts to enact EC legislation in the period after 1979. In the last few years, the European Court of Justice (ECJ) has become more pragmatic in its approach to issues such as equal pay than previously. It has become less doctrinaire and more conservative. Perhaps its judges are afraid of losing some of their powers. The Chair of the London North employment tribunal issued a heartfelt plea in *Downer v Onyx UK Ltd* (1995):

The tribunals are at present subject to Euroclaim-hysteria to an extent which is likely to bring the tribunals to a standstill with the volume and complexity of the claims ...

2.4.1   Effect on UK law

By s 2(1) of the European Communities Act 1972, the UK accepted that EC law, created under the Treaty of Rome, now called the Treaty Establishing the European Community (EC Treaty), would be enforced in the UK. Some parts of EC law were indeed 'directly applicable', that is, such provisions apply without enactment by the national Parliament:

- EC law constitutes a new legal order which is superior to national law: *Costa v ENEL* (1964), a decision of the ECJ. Inconsistent domestic law which falls short of EC law is displaced. The national courts are, therefore, under a duty to disapply national law which conflicts with EC law. They must do so without waiting for the domestic legislature to abrogate domestic law. UK courts accepted this principle, which applies even though the domestic legislation was enacted after the relevant EC provision: *Factortame v Secretary of State for Transport* (1989), a decision of the House of Lords. The same court ruled in *R v Secretary of State for Employment ex p EOC* (1994) that Acts of Parliament can be disapplied (in effect, struck down) by the judge in judicial review proceedings even though no directly effective right had been given to the body bringing the action.

- EC law applies not only to contracting States but also to individuals (*Van Gend en Loos v Nederlandse Administratie der Belastingen* (1963)). However, for individuals to gain rights under EC legislation, the relevant provisions must be unconditional and sufficiently precise. For example, Art 141 (formerly Art 119) of the EC Treaty, which deals with equal pay, fulfils those criteria in respect of direct discrimination. Accordingly, individuals can rely on that Article. The beneficiaries of the right must be identified, as must the nature and content of that right. This method of ensuring that individuals gain rights in EC law is called 'direct effect'. A provision can have direct effect even though, like Art 141, it is addressed to Member States.

Directives can also have direct effect. The UK was required to implement the Working Time Directive (93/104) by 23 November 1996. It did not do so. In *Gibson v East Riding of Yorkshire Council* (1999), the applicant, a swimming instructor employed by a local authority, claimed that, under the Directive, she was entitled to annual holidays, even though the Directive had not yet been implemented. The EAT held that the relevant Article of the Directive was clear, precise and unconditional. Essentially, it was directly effective against an emanation of the State such as a local authority. Her contract, which previously did not contain a term as to annual holidays, was varied to provide such a term. It was immaterial that her hourly rate of pay took into account the fact that she was not paid during school holidays. However, Art 118 (now Art 137) of the Treaty, which states that one of the objectives of the Community is the harmonisation of '… labour law and working conditions …, law of trade unions, and collective bargaining between workers and employers', is not directly effective. Similarly, Blackburne J held in *Griffin v South West Water Services Ltd* (1995) that the Collective Redundancies Directive (75/129) was not sufficiently clear, precise and unconditional to have direct effect because he could not state exactly which people were workers' representatives by looking solely at the Directive. It is, however, suggested that on the facts the High Court was incorrect. The relevant trade union within the Directive was the workers' representative. The fact that the employers did not recognise the union was irrelevant in EC law – recognition mattered only in English law. In practice, the union represented the workers. Accordingly, the union was the beneficiary of the duty imposed on the employers to consult with workers' representatives. Therefore, on the facts, the obligation was sufficiently clear, precise and unconditional.

2.4.2 Several forms of EC law

There are several forms of EC law. The type of direct effect which EC law has depends on the form of the legislation. The Articles in the EC Treaty and in regulations (which should not be confused with statutory instruments called regulations adopted under UK statutes) apply both against the Member States and individuals, the latter term encompassing companies (see *Defrenne v SABENA (No 2)* (1976), where Art 141 was for the first time invoked against a private company). Accordingly, an employee has a right of action under these forms of legislation against the State and non-State bodies and individuals such as employers. This direct effect is both 'vertical' and 'horizontal'. A claim may be made vertically against the State or horizontally against individual defendants. Therefore, an employee can sue a State organisation which acts as an employer or a private company for equal pay in reliance on Art 141. However, another form of Community legislation, directives, are only vertically directly effective. That is, the rights embodied in directives can be enforced only against State organisations, not against non-State employers (*Marshall v Southampton and South West Hants AHA* (1986)). The right against the State is based partly on the wording of Art 249 (formerly Art 189) of the EC Treaty, which defines the nature of the various forms of Community legislation, and partly on the theory that a law is presumed to have been enacted to promote some purposes and, therefore, the law should be used to fulfil that purpose (*effet utile*). In the *Marshall* case, a female dietician at a hospital had to retire at 60 whereas males could work until the age of 65. UK law permitted this difference. The ECJ held that the relevant directive, the Equal Treatment Directive 1976 (76/207), was directly effective but only vertically so. The State was in breach of its duty under the Directive to equalise retirement ages but only in relation to employees working in the State sector. It should be remembered that directives are not even vertically directive effective unless they are unconditional and sufficiently precise. For example, it has not yet been determined by the ECJ whether the Directive on Acquired Rights (77/187) is sufficiently clear, precise and unconditional to be enforceable against the State or an emanation of the State. Lord Hoffmann, in *Mann v Secretary of State for Employment* (1999), put the argument about directives thus:

> The principle that directives do not have horizontal effect between private parties is based upon the notion that ordinary citizens are entitled to rely upon clear provisions of domestic law until they have been changed in accordance with a directive.

Recommendations are a developing source of EC law. The EC Treaty states that they do not have binding effect but they have come to be seen as 'soft law'; that is, something which the national court should take into account. There are recommendations in the sphere of labour law on sexual harassment, vocational training for women, hours of work and holidays, and flexible retirement.

2.4.3 The problem of vertical direct effect

The problem of vertical without horizontal direct effect is particularly acute in EC employment law because most of this is in the form of directives. Examples include the Equal Treatment Directive (76/207) and the Directive on Acquired Rights (77/187). More recently, the Directive on an Employer's Obligation to Inform Employees of the Conditions Applicable to the Contract of Employment Relationship (91/533) obliges the Government to alter English law on written particulars: see Chapter 4. The aim of directives is to permit Member States some degree of control as to how they are to be fitted into existing national law. Absolute uniformity across the EC is not required. The accent is on the harmonisation of national laws, a useful concept when the labour law and traditions of the national States are as varied as they are. The outcome of *Marshall* is that individuals can use directives against institutions of the State, that State not having implemented them or having implemented them incorrectly.

The theory which the ECJ has accepted which underlies the vertical but not horizontal effect of directives is that States should not be able to rely on their own wrong, that is, their failure to enact directives either at all or sufficiently. Article 10 (formerly Art 5) of the EC Treaty instructs Member States to take all appropriate measures to ensure the fulfilment of any obligation arising under the Treaty or resulting from the action of Community institutions. The theory is applicable only against States, not otherwise. After all, it is not private employers who are at fault in failing to implement directives properly. As can be predicted, there is a growing body of law as to what constitutes a State authority (which is called an emanation of the State) and what does not. In *Foster v British Gas plc* (1991), the ECJ held that a State employer is:

> ... a body, whatever its legal form, which has been made responsible, pursuant to a measure adopted by the State, for producing a public service under the control of the State and has for that purpose special powers beyond those which result from the normal rules applicable in relations between individuals.

Applying this definition, the House of Lords held that, before privatisation, British Gas was an emanation of the State. British Gas paid £800,000 in an out of court settlement to 16 women who had to retire at 60 where men could work until 65. In *Marshall*, an English Health Authority was held to be a State body, but private employers are not emanations of the State (*Duke v GEC Reliance* (1988)). The approach of English courts has been to require all three elements of the *Foster* definition: a service to the public; a service which is under State control; and a body which has special powers. The following case is illustrative. A privatised water company was held to be an emanation of the State in *Griffin v South West Water Services Ltd* (1995) largely because of the amount of control the Government exercised over the service provided by the company. It did not matter that the State did not have control over the company itself. It was conceded that the company had special powers and performed a public service. It was immaterial that the service provider was a commercial operator and that its legal personality was that of a company. Presumably, British Telecom is an emanation of the State despite its corporate status and profits.

The court in *Doughty v Rolls Royce plc* (1992), applying the *Foster* criteria, held that a company which is 100% owned by the State is not an emanation of the State if it is a commercial undertaking. This decision is slightly controversial, for it seems that the criteria in *Foster* are to be as separate, not cumulative, ones. The Court of Appeal held that a voluntary aided school was an emanation of the State because, although education was not a service under the control of the State and the governing body had no special powers, it was part of the State system (*National Union of Teachers v Governing Body of St Mary's Church of England (Aided) Junior School* (1995)). The court stressed that the criteria in *Foster* were not to be applied strictly. Blackburne J in *Griffin* said that the issue was whether the service was under State control, not whether the body was.

There is criticism that EC law ought not to be predicated on whether or not a State organisation is the employer. The same rules ought to apply irrespective of the nature of the employers. Those employed by private employers ought not to have fewer rights than those employed by State organisations. The answer to this criticism given in *Foster* is that the distinction would not exist if the State had fully implemented the Directive. Nevertheless, as Paul Skidmore wrote in (1995) 58 MLR 744, p 750, '... the wide ambit of emanation of the State, to include private sector enterprises which are providing public services, does not sit easily with the original rationale of direct effect, which was to prevent the State from relying on its own failure to implement'. The UK Government has in fact on one occasion equalised rights of employees of State and non-State bodies. The SDA 1986 changed national law so that retirement ages for men and women were made the same whether they were employed by State or non-State employers.

2.4.4 Indirect effect

One might have thought that the ECJ's ruling that directives had only vertical direct effect was the end of the story. Recently, however, the ECJ has introduced two doctrines which, to some degree, get round the distinction between vertical and horizontal direct effects. The first doctrine, sometimes known as 'indirect effect', is that national courts must construe national laws so as to give effect to EC directives as far as it is possible to do so. It is irrelevant whether the directive is or is not directly effective. In *von Colson v Land Nordrhein-Westfalen* (1984), the first case in which the ECJ ruled on this point, it was said that:

> ... in applying national law and, in particular, those provisions of national law specially introduced to give effect to a directive, the national court is bound to interpret its national law in the light of the text and of the aim of the directive ...

In that case, Mrs von Colson sought compensation in the German courts for being discriminated against when she sought a job with non-State employers. German law provided for only a low level of compensation in such circumstances. Though the relevant source of EC law, the Equal Treatment Directive, was not horizontally directly effective, the ECJ held that, in the light of Art 10 (formerly Art 5), national courts are under an obligation to construe national law so as to effectuate a directive's purpose, at least when national legislation was specifically introduced to implement the relevant directive. Sanctions for breach of EC law are left for the normal authorities but they must not be ineffective, as the German one was. For example, compensation must be adequate. UK courts have accepted that they are under this duty: *Pickstone v Freemans plc* (1989) and *Litster v Forth Dry Dock & Engineering Co Ltd* (1990), both decisions of the House of Lords.

The House of Lords also accept that the duty to construe national legislation in conformity with EC norms applies even though the relevant directive is not directly effective between the parties because the employers are not an emanation of the State, as in *Webb v EMO Air Cargo (UK) Ltd (No 2)* (1995). There is no need for the domestic statute to be passed after and in consequence of a directive. It is usually considered that cases such as *Duke v GEC Reliance*, in which the House of Lords held that the SDA 1975, being enacted before the Equal Treatment Directive, could not be construed in such a manner as to give effect to it, are incorrect.

That *Duke* is wrong seems to have been confirmed by *Marleasing SA v La Comercial Internacional de Alimentacion SA* (1992), in which the ECJ held that national courts must construe national law, so far as possible, to implement the objectives of directives whether that law pre- or post-dates the relevant directive. The House of Lords held in *Webb v EMO Air Cargo (UK) Ltd* (1993) that national courts can construe in conformity with EC obligations only if on the words of the national legislation such an interpretation is possible. The House stated that an English court 'must construe domestic legislation in any field covered by a Community directive so as to accord with the interpretation of the directive as laid down by the European Court ... whether the domestic legislation came after or, as in this case, preceded the directive'. On this point, *Duke* is a dead duck. The House did, however, cite *Marleasing* for the proposition that domestic legislation must be capable of being construed in accordance with Community law, and it applied *Duke* for the proposition that a Community interpretation could not be used where it would distort the meaning of English law. For an application of this rule in the area of indirect sex discrimination, see *Bhudi v IMI Refiners Ltd* (1994) in Chapter 6.

The ECJ in *Coloroll Pension Trustees Ltd v Russell* (1995) went further than it did in *Marleasing* and held that:

> ... national courts ... are ... bound ... to the full extent of their discretion under national law, to interpret and apply the relevant domestic provisions in conformity with the requirements of EC law and, where this is not possible, to disapply any incompatible domestic conditions.

The effect of the obligation laid down in *von Colson* to construe national law so as to effectuate EC law is one method of reducing the State/private distinction which is seen as undermining the effectiveness of directives. It should, however, be noted that, until there is national legislation on the topic at issue, there is nothing for the courts to interpret.

English courts have accepted that the duty in *von Colson* is paramount over English 'rules' and canons of statutory interpretation such as the literal rule and the presumption that words and phrases are not to be added to statutes. However, the Lords in *Webb* held that it may be that national courts cannot interpret directives until their true import has been determined, sometimes by a reference to the ECJ. The House of Lords also decided that the national legislation had to be open to construction in accord with Community law, but see *Marleasing*, above. Can the process be called 'construction' if national legislation is disregarded when its terms are directly contradictory to EC directives?

2.4.5   Cause of action against the State

In *Francovich v Italian Republic* (1992), the ECJ held that individuals (including, of course, employees) have a cause of action against the State for damages in national courts for losses suffered as a result of its failure to implement at all or to implement completely a directive. The facts of *Francovich* were as follows. Directive 80/987 relates to the harmonisation of national laws on protecting employees on the insolvency of their employers. Article 11 requires Member States to establish institutions which would guarantee wages owing but not paid at the time of insolvency. Italy did not implement the Directive. The Commission brought an action against Italy under Art 226 (formerly Art 169) of the EC Treaty (see 2.4.6, below). This action was successful. Workers were left with unpaid salaries on insolvency. The ECJ held that Art 11 of the Directive was not sufficiently precise and unconditional because it did not specify which institution was to guarantee pay on insolvency. The State was not the institution. Therefore, the State was not liable for not implementing the guarantee of the payment of wages; rather it had failed to designate the responsible non-State body. Accordingly, Art 11 was not directly effective. However, the ECJ held that the Italian State was liable to pay compensation for its failure to implement the Directive. Member States had to implement directives to protect individuals' rights which derive from EC law. That protection would be diminished if there was no sanction for non-implementation and, in the light of Art 10 of the Treaty, national authorities were under a duty to take appropriate measures to secure the fulfilment of EC law. It did not, therefore, matter that the right was not directly effective. The Court stated that damages were available for non-implementation of a directive where:

- that directive was intended to confer rights on individuals (certainly, if the Community provision is directly effective, it was intended to confer rights on individuals);

- the width of that right could be identified from the text of the directive; and

- there was a causal nexus between the State's breach and the loss suffered by the intended beneficiary. Whether there was a causal nexus is for the national courts to decide.

This right to damages was subject to national law provisions governing analogous rights in that legal system – in England presumably the provisions under tort of breach of statutory duty – and was enforceable in national courts. The conditions for enforcement of the right should not be such that enforcement was impossible in practice to achieve or excessively difficult to obtain. There was no need to wait for the outcome of Art 226 (formerly Art 169) enforcement proceedings. A State is liable whether or not it intended to break EC law and whether or not it knew of the breach.

In *Brasserie du Pêcheur SA v Germany* (1996) and subsequent cases, the ECJ held that rights arising indirectly under the principle in *Francovich* were to be treated as those arising from the Treaty, such as the right to equal pay and those arising out of the doctrine of vertical direct effect of directives. It is irrelevant whether the Community law is directly effective or not. Where there was a breach of any of the rights, it was immaterial whether the breach was by the legislature, the executive or the courts. Provided that the law was intended to confer rights on individuals, the issue of failure to implement those rights depended on whether the failure was 'sufficiently serious'. The question of whether the breach was sufficiently serious depends on the gravity of the State's failure. The national courts are to determine this issue, taking into account the precision and clarity of the law, the amount of discretion afforded to the national authorities, the voluntariness or otherwise of the breach, the excusability of any error of the law, the fact whether the failure was caused or contributed to by an EC institution, and the Member State's adoption or retention of measures in general which are contrary to EC law. No guidance was given as to the weight to be attached to each element. The principle of legal certainty has surely been broken.

Failure is deemed to be sufficiently serious if the ECJ has ruled that the Member State is in breach, if a Member State has manifestly and gravely exceeded its powers or if no action has been taken by the State. If the failure was sufficiently serious, damages are assessed in such a way that the victim is compensated for any loss (including loss of profits) and, as the ECJ held in *von Colson*, national rules must not be such that they make it impossible or very difficult for compensation to be obtained. Normal rules, such as mitigation and contributory negligence, apply. *Francovich* claims are subject to national limitation periods if they are worded to apply to them. The *Brasserie du Pêcheur* principles also apply when a State had incorrectly transposed a directive. An example of this failure to implement a directive is the UK Government's failure in respect of the Working Time Directive (93/104), which should have been implemented by 23 November 1996. The failure to transpose the Directive was sufficiently serious (*R v Attorney General for Northern Ireland ex p Burns* (1999)).

2.4.6 Infringement proceedings

By virtue of Art 226 of the EC Treaty, the European Commission may bring 'infringement proceedings' in the ECJ against Member States for their failure to give effect to EC law, as when, for example, directives are not enacted. The Commission instituted such proceedings against the UK for failure to enact provisions giving the right to equal pay for work of equal value (*EC Commission v UK* (1982)). Proceedings were also brought by the Commission against the UK for non-implementation of the Acquired Rights Directive (77/187) and the Collective Redundancies Directive (75/129) where there were no employee representatives to consult. There is also the possibility under Art 227 (formerly Art 170) of the Treaty of a Member State's bringing an action in the ECJ against another Member State for breach of Community obligations, though politics generally rule out such proceedings. The Treaty of Maastricht inserted a provision into the EC Treaty by which the ECJ may fine a State for failure to abide by EC law. The Treaty, as amended, is silent as to the sanction for failure to pay the fine. The Commission has often reported that Member States have not complied with EC law. The UK Government claims that, of all the members, it is the one which complies best with EC laws.

2.4.7 Present EC and UK social policy

The history of EC social (or employment) policy is normally divided into three stages. The first stage was from the inception of the EC by the Treaty of Rome (in 1957) to the early 1970s. During this period there was little development. Employment law was not a concern of the founding fathers of the EC. They seem to have believed that living conditions would automatically rise through the functioning of the common market and that, for that reason, there was no need for special provision in the Treaty to give workers rights against their employers. In the Treaty there was Art 119 (now Art 141) on equal pay for women and men, a provision inserted at the insistence of the French so that their products would not be undercut in price by other countries which did not have equal pay laws. Little was done to implement that Article. Article 136 (formerly Art 117) speaks of the progressive raising of living standards of workers, but that Article is not legally enforceable. The Preamble to the EC Treaty embodies the same concept. Article 137 (formerly Art 118), also not legally enforceable, provides for co-operation among Member States on social matters, including employment law.

The second stage was the mid and late 1970s, when the EC, through its Social Action Programme 1974–76, enacted several directives such as the ones mentioned above on equal treatment and acquired rights. This period marked a shift from the EC being seen as a purely economic common market to being seen as a 'Community with a human face'. The third period, from the late 1970s to the present, has been one of stagnation to a large degree, except in relation to health and safety. For example, the Commission's Social Action Programme of 1995 was a measure aimed largely at consolidating existing law. The EC is less interventionist nowadays than it was in the 1970s. Advances in workers' rights have been made by the ECJ. Even this institution at present seems to be in retreat from its wide ranging approach in the 1980s. The work of the European Commission and Council, the central organs of the EC, has been stultified by the intransigent UK Government of 1979–97, sometimes supported by other States. For this reason, the Commission has resorted to 'soft law' in labour affairs, such as the Opinion on the equitable wage, the Memorandum on equal pay for work of equal value, and the Recommendation and Code of Practice on sexual harassment. Because of the UK's tactics, the EC also tried to legislate by means of agreements between the social partners, the two sides of industry. The union side is represented by the European Trades Union Council (ETUC), the employers, by CEEP and UNICE, bodies which respectively represent small to medium and large employers. UK intransigence paradoxically led to power being given to unions at the European level. The social partners negotiate an agreement which is then extended to all workers by means of a directive. The European Parliament plays no part in this process and the Council cannot amend it. It was by this method of legislation that the Directives on Parental Leave (96/34) and Part Time Work (97/81) were enacted.

UK unions are now in favour of the EC, a U-turn of their previous attitude. Collective bargaining, undermined in the UK by government policy, has been encouraged in the EC and may develop further. An alternative view to that just stated is that the UK Government of 1979–97 blocked EC measures which would impose financial and administrative burdens on businesses that would have undermined British competitiveness in world markets and would have reduced job opportunities. Conservative policy prevented, among other matters, laws on employee participation (industrial democracy) under the draft European Company Statute, led to the refusal to join the Charter of Fundamental Social Rights 1989, which the other 11 (at that time; later there were 14) Member States had signed, including draft measures under this Social Charter (except health and safety ones), and resulted in the non-acceptance of the Social Chapter (contained in a Protocol) of the Maastricht Treaty. When Austria, Finland and Sweden joined the EC they committed themselves to the Protocol. The Labour Government accepted the Social Chapter, which is now part of the Treaty of Amsterdam.

Government policy during 1979–97 was to hold down wage costs so that employers would be able to compete in the world market. One aim behind non-acceptance of the Social Charter and Chapter was to undercut the developed States' prices for products, thereby gaining a competitive advantage over them; and, with reduced labour costs and expanding markets, employment opportunities would be created. The negative effect of the opt-out was that the UK had no direct input into directives which affect UK citizens and companies. Member States have agreed on qualified majority voting for various matters such as equality, working conditions and informing and consulting workers (the European Works Councils Directive (95/45), which was the first directive to be passed under the Protocol (it should have been implemented by 22 September 1996)), but unanimity is still needed in respect of others, for example, the rights of dismissed workers. It should be noted that Directives such as the European Works Councils Directive, which did not apply to the UK because they were adopted under the Maastricht Protocol, *did* bind UK companies which have employees in other EC Member States. The exceptions remain in force after the Treaty of Amsterdam. There have been developments in the attempts to convert the rather vague policy aspirations of the 1989 Charter into hard law. For example, in 1993 the Commission issued an Opinion (which is non-binding) on equitable wages.

The Social Policy Agreement attached to the Treaty of Maastricht 1993 was originally not adhered to by the UK. It was the Labour Government which, in 1997, agreed to be bound by the Agreement. The agreement has now become part of the Treaty of Amsterdam 1997, which came into force in 1999. Labour law matters can be divided into three categories:

(1) the EC has competence over the working environment, health and safety, conditions of work, equal treatment and those excluded from the labour market. Votes on these matters may be by qualified majority voting;

(2) matters concerning the social protection of workers, rights on termination, rights of representatives and collective defence fall within the remit of the EC but voting must be unanimous;

(3) the EC has no competence over pay, the right to associate, the right to strike and lockouts.

The Commission has, since 1990, sought to relaunch European social policy through stimulating discussion, using the Social Chapter, modifying draft directives to attune them to the requirements of business and using 'soft' law such as Codes of Practice and Recommendations. Its priority, however, was stated in the Green Paper, *European Social Policy: Options for the Union* COM (93) 551, 1993: 'The next phase in the development of European social policy cannot be based on the idea that social progress must go into retreat in order for economic competitiveness to recover.' There is now, however, greater emphasis on job creation, which may be at the expense of employment rights.

2.4.8 The importance of accepting the Single European Act 1986

While the Conservative Government generally opposed EC developments in employment law (it opposed all changes except in relation to health and safety and sexual discrimination), it did ratify the Single European Act (SEA) 1986. The importance of accepting the SEA can be demonstrated thus. When the EC Council of Ministers proposes to enact labour legislation (or any law in any field), it has to find a legal basis for doing so in the EC Treaty. In the Treaty as originally drafted, besides Art 141 (formerly Art 119) (equal pay), there were two possible legal bases for labour law. By Art 94 (formerly Art 100), the Council may issue directives, when the Commission so proposes, which will lead to the harmonisation (approximation) of the laws of Member States in order to secure the successful implementation of the common market. (If the Council thought that the UK would not use its opt-out, it could propose a measure affecting social rights under Art 94 (previously Art 100)). By Art 308 (formerly Art 235), directives may be issued to attain a Treaty objective when the Treaty itself does not provide specifically in any other Article for such a power. Under both Arts 94 and 308, votes have to be unanimous. Accordingly, one State could block draft directives. The SEA 1986 added a new Article, Art 100A (now Art 95), to the Treaty. It provides that 'measures necessary for the establishment and functioning of the internal market' can be adopted by the Council on a 'qualified majority' vote. That last term signifies that the votes of Member States are not equally weighted but are weighted according, approximately, to the State's size. By this method the objection of one State, even a large one such as the UK, could be overridden.

In the Europe of 15 Member States, 62 votes are needed out of 87. However, the later part of Art 95 takes away a large part of what the earlier part has given in the employment sphere by stating that unanimity remains necessary where 'the rights and interests of employed persons' are affected. This stipulation would seem on its face to prevent the adoption of EC employment laws by the qualified majority voting system. There has been much debate about the width of the later part of Art 95, especially in the light of Art 137 (formerly Art 118A), which also derives from the SEA 1986. Article 137 provides that Member States should encourage the health and safety of workers, especially in the working environment, and empowers the Council to enact directives on this matter by qualified majority voting. 'Health and safety' is read widely to include all factors, physical or otherwise, capable of affecting the health and safety of the worker in the working environment. That power is subject to the stipulation that health and safety measures should not impose administrative, financial or legal constraints which affect the creation of small and medium business enterprises. This proviso is very vague. Certainly, small businesses can be the subject of health and safety law at EC level. One aspect of that debate is whether maternity rights form a part of the law of 'the rights and interests of employed persons' within Art 95, in which case unanimous voting is required, or whether they constitute part of the law of health and safety in the workplace, in which eventuality Art 137 applies and qualified majority voting is possible. The same may be said of sexual harassment at work.

The Action Programme laid down by the Commission in 1989 based on the Social Charter has been successful only in relation to health and safety matters, that is, those measures based on Art 137. Draft directives on other matters have not been implemented because of opposition largely from the last UK Government. The Secretary of State for Employment opposed the proposed Directive on posted workers because of the possible effect on jobs of British workers in Germany. To give them the same rights as German workers would result in their being sacked.

The Social Action Programme for 1995 onwards contains 21 measures, most of which consolidate existing law. The Conservative Government blocked draft directives on paternity leave and part time workers. There have already been Council Recommendations on social protection and profit sharing and an Opinion on the equitable wage. As part of an attempt to 'humanise' work – the UK has the largest proportion of workers in the EC who work more than 48 hours per week – the Working Time Directive may be seen as one aspect of the EC policy of attempting to reconcile family and professional life. It came into force on 23 November 1996 in the rest of the EC. Those affected by non-implementation can sue the State. The principal provisions are these:

(a) workers must not be subjected to any detriment if they refuse to work for more than 48 hours (including overtime) in any seven day period: there is nothing to stop employees agreeing to work for more than that time;

(b) they must have a minimum of 11 consecutive hours rest per day, a rest break when the working day exceeds six hours, and a minimum of 35 hours uninterrupted rest per week (or 24 hours if objective technical or organisational conditions so dictate);

(c) night workers must not work more than eight hours in a 24 hour period and, if night work causes health problems, the worker is to be transferred onto day work;

(d) workers are to have three weeks' paid holiday per year, rising to four weeks in 1999.

The exceptions to the Directive are huge and include airport employees (including ground staff), agricultural workers, health workers, security guards, dock workers and telecommunications staff. Work carried out on a voluntary basis is excluded from the Directive. This exclusion will be reviewed in 2003.

The UK Government's challenge to Art 137, formerly Art 118A, as the legal basis failed in *United Kingdom v Council of the European Union* (1997) except in so far as the court accepted the UK Government's contention that Sunday should not be included in the weekly rest period laid down by the Directive. The Young Persons Directive (94/33) was adopted as a health and safety measure. The UK Government negotiated a deferment of the application of some of the Directive to the year 2001, whereas it applies to the rest of the EC from 1996. It should be noted that the UK is bound by directives founded on Arts 95 and 137 despite the refusal to accept the Social Charter and the Social Chapter. For legal scholars, this is all very interesting, but there remains no solid legislative underpinning of EC social policy. After all, much of EC social policy is predicated on implementing the internal market, not on protection for workers pure and simple. One effect of the 'treaty-base game' (that is , the need to find a legal basis for directives in the Treaty) and the UK opposition of 1979–97 was that EC law is not extensive in its coverage. Much of it relates to discrimination and health and safety.

One final matter to be noted is that the EC Commission is placed under a duty to encourage the so called 'social dialogue' between employers' groups and unions as a result of the SEA 1986. This duty was followed up by the Treaty on European Union (the Maastricht Treaty), one Protocol of which provides for Member States to delegate the implementation of directives to the social partners and for Member States to put into law agreements reached by them. Such amendments are called 'framework agreements'. This power is now found in Arts 138–39 of the EC Treaty. The first formal agreement made by the social partners under the Protocol on social policy annexed to the Maastricht Treaty was that on parental leave. This agreement did not apply in the UK, which until 1999 had no law on leave for parents. Other agreements concern part time and fixed term work. UNICE, the employers' organisation, has refused to enter into negotiations with its social partners about informing and consulting workers in the EC. The baton has passed to the Commission, which in late 1998 published a draft directive which was adopted in June 1999. It will come into force on 28 June 2001.

The European Works Council Directive was adopted under the Agreement on Social Policy in the Treaty of Maastricht. Since the Conservative Government had opted out of the Treaty, the Directive did not apply to the UK. However, the Labour Government accepted the Directive in 1997 and the implementation date was December 1999. The Directive provides for the establishment of an EWC or a procedure for informing and consulting employees in every undertaking which has 1,000 or more employees in the EC and Norway, Iceland and Liechtenstein and at least 150 employees in at least two Member States. Central management, if located in the EC, or its agent, if located elsewhere (or if there is no agent, the management of the establishment in the EC with the most employees), is required to set up a 'special negotiating body'. This body, which has three to 17 members elected in accordance with national rules, decides whether there is to be an EWC or a procedure for informing and consulting. If an EWC is to be established, its composition, functions and term of office are determined by the SNB. If the SNB cannot decide on these matters, there are default provisions. The EWC has the right to meet with central management once a year for information and consultation. The matters to be covered include 'the economic and financial situation, the probable development of the business ..., substantial changes concerning organisation, introduction of new working methods, ... mergers, cutbacks or closures of undertakings, and collective redundancies'. The remedy is a complaint to the CAC. This obligation is, however, restricted: information which would seriously harm the business is not to be transmitted and neither is confidential information. These rights are in addition to those introduced by the Collective Redundancies and Acquired Rights Directives.

There is protection against unfair dismissal and detriment. Employees and employee representatives who are members of a SNB or an EWC are entitled to time off to undertake their duties.

2.4.9   The Labour Government and the EC

The post-1997 Labour Government ratified the Treaty of Amsterdam which came into force in 1999. Among other matters, the Treaty consolidates the previous Treaties relating to the EC (renumbering the Articles) and it gives a legislative basis for EC law on racial discrimination. The Government abrogated the opt-out from the Maastricht Treaty 1993, the Social Policy Agreement of which was incorporated into the Treaty, and it adopted the European Works Council Directive and the Parental Leave Directive in December 1997 and the Part Time Work Directive in April 1998. These Directives remained unchanged in their wording and therefore the UK had two years from December 1997 and April 1998 respectively to comply with them.

2.4.10 Conclusion

With regard to both domestic and EC institutions, the position has altered substantially over the last quarter of a century. In the late 1960s, the UK was not even a member of the EC. The industrial scene was based on informal means of dispute resolution. Even unjustifiable dismissals and industrial conflicts were largely a matter for negotiation between the employers and employees, the latter sometimes supported by trade unions. Many employment law rights, such as those in the area of sexual discrimination, bypass collective bargaining and use employment tribunals. Custom and practice has partly been replaced by law, but still exists. Despite changes to EC law over the past 25 years, EC employment law remains of limited relevance to most employees. The principal areas where it has had an impact are sex discrimination and health and safety. Equal pay has long been viewed as one of the foundations of the Community. Substantial areas of law remain unaffected. There is no EC law as yet on unfair dismissal or race discrimination. Weiss puts it this way: 'Social policy still remains accidental and fragmentary.' (in Blanplain, R (ed), *Labour Law and Industrial Relations in the European Union*, 1998, p 199.) Moreover, even where there exists EC law, enforcement of that law is largely dependent on national authorities. It was not until 1993 that there was an English statute in the sphere of employment law where a substantial number of sections derived from EC law.

EC labour law in the 1990s was in something of a backwater. Not only did the Conservative Government in the UK oppose extensions of workers' rights but other States did too; and the ECJ acted more conservatively than before, perhaps being influenced by the number of right wing administrations in the Member States. The Social Dialogue was a way of avoiding these limitations but it has not produced much in the way of social policy advances. Nevertheless, there are indications that in this new millennium there may be extensions to laws, particularly those relating to discrimination, as a result of the Treaty of Amsterdam.

INSTITUTIONAL MATTERS

Institutions; tribunals

English employment law is bedevilled by the jurisdictional problem of knowing in which court or tribunal a claim should be brought. Employment tribunals have concurrent jurisdiction with the ordinary civil courts in most claims involving termination of contracts for sums under £25,000. Applications involving, for example, redundancy payments and unfair dismissal are determined by employment tribunals with appeal to the Employment Appeal Tribunal. Other English institutions include the well known ACAS, the Central Arbitration Committee, the three organisations dealing with discrimination (namely, the Commission for Racial Equality, the Disability Rights Commission and the Equal Opportunities Commission) and the Certification Officer. The text considers their powers and offers some criticism. If a claim is heard in the county courts or the High Court, legal aid is available. The limitation period in a contract action is six years. If the applicant seeks a remedy before an employment tribunal there is no legal aid. The limitation period is dependent on the nature of the claim. For example, in an unfair dismissal case the time limit is, generally speaking, three months from the effective date of termination.

Membership of the European Community

The accession of the UK to the European Community has led to several amendments being made to English labour law. One of the main institutional issues at present is the vertically but not horizontally direct effect of directives. The ECJ has ruled that national laws must be construed to give effect to directives and that individuals have a right of action for damages against the state for non-enactment of directives. Despite such developments by the ECJ, the Conservative Government opposed recent proposals in the sphere of employment law (social policy) such as the Social Charter of 1989 and the Social Chapter of the Maastricht Treaty. However, acceptance of the SEA 1986 has led to attempts to find legal bases in the Treaty of Rome in order to get round the objections of various EC governments, including that of the UK, to giving workers more rights than they have at present. Examples of draft directives to which the Government were opposed are those on parental leave (especially for fathers), worker participation and proportional rights for part time employees. There was no relenting on opposition to various parts of the Social Charter such as fair wages. The Labour Government implemented the Social Chapter. New areas of law, such as the limitation of the working week, have come into force.

CHAPTER 3

FORMATION OF THE CONTRACT OF EMPLOYMENT

3.1 Employment contracts are contracts

A contract of employment, often called a service agreement or a contract of service, is a contract. Therefore, general contractual principles covered in contract or common law courses are applicable in the law of employment. For example, material relating to offer and acceptance, consideration and illegality underlies employment law, and the cases in contract and employment law are to some degree interchangeable. The equivalent to offer and acceptance in contract law is the hiring of the employee; and, as we shall see, the extensive law on dismissal is based on breach of contract. Normally, there will be no problem with the intent to create legal relations. The parties intend, generally speaking, that the employee will work for money. Therefore, there is consideration and the parties intend legally to be bound. A possible exception to this principle concerns ministers of religion, who may sometimes not work under a contract. The relationship may be spiritual, not contractual. The same problem may arise in both non-employment contract law and employment law: did illness frustrate this contract? Is a minor bound by a contract? Lord Evershed MR in *Laws v London Chronicle (Indicator Newspapers) Ltd* (1959) aptly summarised this idea: 'A contract of service is but an example of contracts in general, so that the general law of contract is applicable.' In legal terms, a contract of employment is a binding agreement made voluntarily and the duties are agreed by the parties either personally or through employers' associations and trade unions. This relationship between workers and their employers is essentially a late 19th century construct. Before then, employees could be prosecuted for leaving their jobs.

3.1.1 Specialised nature

The contract of employment is, however, a specialised form of contract. Just as with other special types of contract such as the sale of goods and agency, different rules have been superimposed on those contractual arrangements classified as employment ones. Indeed, in some respects, employees can be seen as having a status. Parliament has intervened, largely in favour of the individual employee, to rectify what were perceived as abuses. For instance, rights have been given to workers to claim in respect of discrimination on racial and sexual grounds where no such rights existed at common law, and employers cannot derogate from these rights by contract. In addition, the right to a remedy for unfair dismissal can be seen as an attempt to obtain a 'level playing field' at the point of termination of employment.

Moreover, many employees have their terms and conditions negotiated by trade unions: it is rare for an individual employee to bargain with his employers. The intervention of unions can also be seen as an attempt to create a level playing field. Nevertheless, the contract of employment remains the 'cornerstone', as labour lawyers put it, of employment law. It is the foundation for a series of statutory entitlements such as those relating to redundancy payments and unfair dismissal. Moreover, if for some reason an employee is not entitled to a statutory claim, the common law contract remains as a source of rights; on occasions, indeed, contractual and statutory rights can be claimed at the same time, and the contractual remedy may be worth more in financial terms than the statutory one.

The mechanism for imposing equal pay is an equality clause, a contractual term. In general, the parties cannot agree that an employee's statutory entitlements should be diminished, but they may agree to extend them. The statutory notice period to be given to an employee on termination of the contract of employment cannot be reduced by contract between the employers and the employee but a greater length of notice period can contractually be agreed by the parties. In the jargon, employment law provides a 'floor of rights' which cannot be undercut by agreement, but the parties can agree to build on that floor of rights to provide an employee with greater benefits than those stipulated by Parliament. Accordingly, it may be said that the contract of employment is a contract but it is not just a contract; it is also the vehicle through which Parliament has given the employee various rights.

3.2 Who is an employee?

Many, but not all, labour law rights are dependent on the applicant's being an employee. In most circumstances, there is no problem. Where there is difficulty, the courts and tribunals refer to various common law tests. Unfortunately, there is no statutory definition and no one test has been universally approved. The Employment Relations Act 1999 gives the Secretary of State for Trade and Industry the power to extend statutory employment law to workers who are not employees. The aim is to prevent technical evasions of the law such as that achieved in *Express & Echo Publications Ltd v Tanton* (1999) (discussed below, 3.3.18) while not affecting those who are genuinely self-employed.

3.2.1 Contract of service or for services?

Once one has determined that there is a contract at all, the problem is to consider whether or not that contract is one of employment. Lawyers distinguish between employees and those people who work for a living but are not employees. Most of those in the latter group are usually called independent contractors or self-employed. Such persons, who constitute some 13% of the workforce, are said to work under a contract *for* services. It should be recalled that an employee works under a contract *of* service. In old-fashioned terminology a contract *of* service constitutes the relationship between masters and servants. The distinction between employees and independent contractors is of fundamental importance to employment law but is not always clear-cut, as we shall see. EC law, generally speaking, applies to 'workers', a wider term than 'employees'. Workers include those independent contractors who personally do the work, but excludes professionals who contract with clients. Besides employees and the self-employed, there are other sorts of workers, such as apprentices and office holders. Different rules attach to such workers.

3.2.2   Importance of distinction

Smith and Wood, *Industrial Law*, 6th edn, 1996, p 9, wrote: '... the independent contractor may be in a better monetary position while working, but at a grave disadvantage if he falls off a ladder or is sacked.' In *Lane v Shire Roofing Co (Oxford) Ltd* (1995), the Court of Appeal stressed that where the claim involved an issue of safety at work the court or tribunal should lean towards finding that the worker was an employee. Cases where the courts and tribunals have stated that there was no mutuality of obligations (see below) may have been decided differently if they had raised issues of health and safety. Accordingly, decisions may have an element of policy in them, though rules and principles are to the fore. It is not beyond the bounds of possibility that a worker may be an employee for one purpose (such as unfair dismissal law) but self-employed for another (for example, tax). See, however, 3.8, below.

3.2.3   Differences

The significance of the distinction between employees and independent contractors is outlined in the differences listed below:

- Employees owe employers certain obligations which independent contractors do not owe. For example, in every contract of employment, there is an implied duty that an employee will serve his employers faithfully, an obligation sometimes known as the duty of fidelity. The nature and extent of such common law implied terms are discussed in the next chapter.

- Similarly, employers may owe employees obligations which they do not owe to independent contractors. Under the Health and Safety at Work Act 1974, employers must adopt a higher standard of care towards their employees than towards independent contractors who work for them. Protection on the transfer of an undertaking applies only to employees and apprentices.

- By virtue of the doctrine of vicarious liability, employers are liable for the torts of their employees committed in the course of employment, but rarely are employers liable for the torts of independent contractors. For example, in *Hillyer v Governors of St Bartholomew's Hospital* (1909), the Court of Appeal held that on the facts a consultant at a hospital was self-employed. Therefore, the hospital was not liable to compensate a patient harmed by the consultant's negligent operating technique. Nurses were similarly not employees of the hospital because they took their orders from the surgeon, a fascinating ruling but one logically acceptable under the control test discussed below.

- Sometimes, Parliament has enacted laws for the benefit of employees. If employers break such laws, employees can sometimes sue their employers for breach of statutory duty, a tort. If employers owe such duties only to employees, they do not owe them to independent contractors, and the self-employed cannot sue for breach. For more detail on vicarious liability and breach of statutory duty, refer to a standard tort textbook.

- Parliament may give rights to employees only. The principal rights against employers are now found in the Employment Rights Act (ERA) 1996. Two illustrations suffice: s 94 provides employees with a right to a remedy for unfair dismissal; s 135 provides for payments on redundancy. These rights form the core of employment law. They are not available to the self-employed. The more persons who are classified as self-employed, the smaller is the number of those entitled to claim statutory employment rights.

- Certain State benefits such as sickness pay and statutory maternity pay apply only to employees (and some office holders).

- The self-employed may be financially better off than employees because of the tax system. They pay tax under Sched D, whereas employees pay under the PAYE (pay as you earn) scheme under Sched E. For the advantage see a revenue law text. Independent contractors may be able to recover more of their expenses than can employees. For these reasons some workers prefer to be self-employed. An illustrative case is the decision of an employment tribunal in *Jennings v Westwood Engineering Ltd* (1975). A worker chose to receive his pay without deduction of tax. On being sacked, he claimed a remedy for unfair dismissal. The tribunal determined that he was an employee. (However, he could not obtain redress because his contract was illegal in that it was one designed to defraud the Revenue.)

- Independent contractors may have to register for VAT (value added tax); employees do not.

- Employers may benefit from having independent contractors as workers. They do not have to pay sick pay or pensions, and often fringe benefits are restricted to employees. They can reduce expenditure on administration because they do not have to establish a system of deducting income tax or national insurance from the self-employed workers' pay. There is no levy for industrial training. And, since unions find grave difficulty in recruiting the self-employed, employers may not have to deal with trade union officials and shop stewards.

- Employees but not independent contractors are preferential creditors on the bankruptcy of their employers.

According to the *Labour Market Trends* of January 1996, there are over three million independent contractors, an increase of one million since 1979. The Labour Force Survey from mid-1994 found that some 75% of the self-employed were male and that the greatest concentration of independent contractors occurred in catering, construction and distribution. The move towards self-employment was in line with the thinking of the Conservative Government. The burden of employees' rights was lifted from employers, and the employers did not have to pay wages during a downturn in business: the workers suffered instead because they were dismissed without compensation.

3.3 The tests

Courts and tribunals have adopted several different tests of employment status. The modern approach is to consider all the factors, give weight to each of them and put them into a pan. If the balance of the pan tips towards employment, the worker is an employee; if not, the worker is an independent contractor.

3.3.1 No statutory definition of employment

For the reasons stated above, it is important to distinguish between employees and independent contractors. Often the distinction is easily drawn. The writer of this book is an employee of the University of Sheffield. He is hired (and perhaps fired) by that institution; pay, sick pay and holiday pay come from it; the University deducts income tax under the PAYE scheme. He may be working side by side with an independent contractor who is doing very much the same kind of work. A part time tutor is likely to be self-employed. He may work part time as an assistant solicitor, that is, be employed by the partners of his firm of solicitors, but work for three hours a week as a tutor at a university or college. An actor who taught drama part time at a school was held to be self-employed in *Argent v Minister of Social Security* (1968). The distinction between the two types of workers cannot therefore reside in the nature of the job which they are doing. If a full time lecturer and a part time lecturer tutor labour law, they are engaged in the same task. Similarly, the same drains may be unblocked by a plumber employed by the council and one who is self-employed. There is no definition of employment or self-employment provided by Parliament. Section 230 of the ERA 1996, the definition section, states merely that an employee is a person who works under a contract of employment. For the purposes of the statute, a contract of employment covers both a contract of service and a contract of apprenticeship. Judge made law does, however, provide a number of tests by which workers may be divided into employees and independent contractors. These tests are best viewed historically in order to understand the current law.

3.3.2   Variable statutory coverage

It should be noted that the rights given to workers by Parliament are not always restricted to employees and apprentices. Each statute must be considered to determine coverage. For example, the Sex Discrimination Act 1975 applies by virtue of s 82(1) to employees, apprentices and those who 'contract personally to execute any work or labour'. This phrase covers a substantial number of the self-employed such as jobbing gardeners.

3.3.3   Control test

The control test was developed by the judiciary in the late 19th century. It is no longer applied by itself but is a part of the modern tests.

3.3.4   Definition and criticism

The classic statement of the control test is that of Bramwell LJ in *Yewens v Noakes* (1881): an employee is 'subject to the command of his master as to the manner in which he shall do his work'. If the alleged employers have control over what the worker does and how he does it, he is an employee. A self-employed person is told what to do, but not how to do it. This test is simple to use in relation to some workers such as domestic servants, farm workers, and factory hands. It is, however, impossible to use with regard to many modern jobs. One would not wish the Chair of British Airways to order a pilot how to land at an airport during a sandstorm; yet the pilot may well be an employee. One would not want the chief executive of an NHS trust to tell a consultant how to perform microsurgery. If the control test were applied, the pilot and the surgeon would be self-employed. The test breaks down when dealing with complicated jobs. Persons performing such jobs are employees but they would be categorised as self-employed by this test. The test has for this reason fallen into desuetude.

The defective nature of the control test can clearly be seen from *Collins v Hertfordshire County Council* (1947). Employers are, generally speaking, liable for the torts of their employees committed in the course of employment but not the torts of independent contractors. In this case, a patient was injured through the negligence of both the resident junior house surgeon and the operating surgeon. With regard to the house surgeon there was no problem. She was an employee and the hospital was liable for her negligence. The visiting operating surgeon worked part time and on a temporary basis at the hospital, although he did have a basic salary and set hours. The court held him not to be an employee. Therefore, the hospital was not responsible for his negligence. The outcome was unfortunate. Whether a plaintiff could successfully sue the alleged employers vicariously depended on whether the person who performed the wrongful act was an employee. If the tortfeasor was an independent contractor, the sole right to sue lay against him and he might be a 'man of straw' – unable to pay damages for his wrongdoing.

3.3.5 Continued criticism

Moreover, the fact that there is control is not by itself sufficient to show that there is a contract of employment. In *Gould v Minister of National Insurance* (1951), Mr Gould was a music hall artiste. The owners of music halls who engaged him could control what he did to a large degree. They could, for example, tell him at what time he was to appear on stage and order him not to use offensive words and gestures. Nevertheless, he was not an employee. He provided his skill, his personality and his performance. The control which management exercised related solely to the desire not to offend the audience and to keeping the theatre running smoothly. On the other hand, musicians in an orchestra have been held to be self-employed despite the amount of control which the conductor had over their playing: *Addison v London Philharmonic Orchestra* (1981). Control, therefore, is no longer decisive but it remains one of the elements to be taken into account.

3.3.6 Present use

While the control test is no longer decisive, it remains a factor in some of the other tests. In the 'multiple' test, which derives from *Ready Mixed Concrete (South East) Ltd v Minister of Pensions and National Insurance* (1968), control was one element in determining whether a driver was an employee or self-employed. There was a large amount of control, but such control was not determinative, for the driver was held to be an independent contractor. The full facts of *Ready Mix* are stated below.

3.3.7 Right to control

For these reasons, the courts attempted to update the control test. The right of control was seen in *Short v Henderson Ltd* (1946) as being one of the factors of the *'indicia'* test discussed below. Indeed, in one case, *Mersey Docks and Harbour Board v Coggins & Griffith (Liverpool) Ltd* (1947), the House of Lords treated the right to control as a separate, substantive test. The Court of Appeal had earlier done the same in *Walker v Crystal Palace FC* (1910). A football club had the right to control a player, even though they did not control what he did during the match. One criticism of the 'right to control' test is that it is circular: when is a worker an employee? When the employers have a right of control. When do employers have a right of control? When the worker is an employee. Another way forward was used by Denning LJ, as he then was, in *Cassidy v Minister of Health* (1951). He noted that the control test did not adequately deal with skilled workers such as surgeons. He considered that hospitals should be liable for the torts of their surgeons, no matter whether the surgeon was an employee or self-employed. The hospitals after all engaged staff, or they chose them for their ability in performing their job functions; and they could dismiss them. Therefore, they should be vicariously liable for the torts of their surgeons. In *Cassidy*, the plaintiff lost some fingers because of the carelessness of the surgeon. He sued the hospital. The Court of Appeal decided that he was entitled to damages from the hospital because he had entrusted himself to that body. The organisation of the hospital had led to the negligence; therefore, the hospital was responsible.

3.3.8 Organisation test

To remedy the defects of the control test Denning LJ instituted a new test, the organisation test, in *Stevenson Jordan and Harrison v MacDonald and Evans* (1952). He said that whether a person was an employee or not no longer depended on whether he submitted to orders but:

> ... it depends on whether the person is part and parcel of the organisation. A person under a contract of service does his work as an integral part of the business whereas a person under a contract for services – although he might do his work for the business – is not integrated into it but is only an accessory to it.

This test would have led to both surgeons being employees in *Collins v Hertfordshire CC* (1946), above.

3.3.9 Criticism

The organisation test may be criticised. First, it sometimes gives the incorrect answer. Homeworkers, such as knitters, may be an integral part of the organisation but many are self-employed. There are well over half a million homeworkers and this issue is of importance to them. The fact that they work when they want, may provide their own equipment and can have others helping them point towards self-employment. Similarly, a cleaner in a government office is still an employee even though his job has been privatised. The job remains an integral part of the enterprise of running a government office. It is merely the employers who have changed. A cleaner may, however, be self-employed yet still be an integral part of the organisation. If, for example, local government contracts out the cleaning of a building, a former employee tenders for the job, obtains it and does exactly the same job on the cleaning as he did before the contracting out, he is now self-employed. The same applies to subcontractors in the private sector. Secondly, the test may be difficult to apply. Is the window cleaner who cleans windows at a brickworks part and parcel of the organisation (as Denning LJ put it in *Bank voor Handel en Scheepvaart NV v Slatford* (1953))? Some window cleaners may be employees, some self-employed, but the test does not enable a judge to differentiate. Thirdly, the organisational test may add nothing to the control test. Determining who was part and parcel of the organisation could only be done by determining whether such workers were under the control of their employers. MacKenna J in *Ready Mix* (1968) was strongly of this opinion. All in all, it is uncertain as to when a worker is or is not part of an organisation.

3.3.10 Current use

Despite such criticism, the organisation test is sometimes utilised as an additional test to support a conclusion. In *Davis v New England College of Arundel* (1977), the judge stated:

> ... whether one applies the test of control, or whether the applicant was part of the organisation of the college, the answer is plainly the same.

Similarly, in *Whittaker v Minister of Pensions* (1966) the judge held that a trapeze artiste was an employee because:

> ... she had no real independence and had to carry out her contractual duties as an integral part of the business of the company.

3.3.11 Ordinary person test

The courts realised that the tests already mentioned did not easily fit the fact situations. Novel tests were adopted. One of these tests may be called the 'ordinary person' test. In the words of the judge in *Collins v Hertfordshire* CC:

> ... was his contract a contract of service within the meaning which an ordinary person would give to the words?

This test was approved by the Court of Appeal in *Cassidy v Minister of Health* and used in *Whittaker v Minister of Pensions*.

3.3.12 Criticism

There are, however, drawbacks. First, who is the ordinary person? If it is the judge, this test does not help her. If it is someone else, how does the judge know what the ordinary person thinks? Secondly, surely an ordinary person will never have heard of a contract of service. Thirdly, it may be difficult for legal advisers to say, before a case is heard, whether an individual is an employee or not. Despite such criticisms, this test has been used in recent times (*Withers v Flackwell Heath Football Supporters Club* (1981)). If policy issues, however, govern whether a person is to be deemed to be an employee, the 'ordinary person' test does not straightforwardly promote those policies.

3.3.13 *Indicia* test

A second test from the late 1940s comes from the speech of Lord Thankerton in *Short v Henderson Ltd* (1946). He said that there were four indicators – *indicia* – of a contract of employment:

(a) the employers' power to select an employee;

(b) their payment of wages;

(c) their right to control the manner in which work was done; and

(d) their right of suspension or dismissal.

3.3.14 Criticism

This approach was criticised in *Ready Mix* on the grounds that factors (a), (b) and (d) helped simply to establish whether there was any contract at all, not whether the contract was one of employment. The remaining element, right of control, was the old control test updated to the mid-20th century.

3.3.15 Multiple test

Lord Wright in *Montreal Locomotive Works Ltd v Montreal* (1947), a Privy Council authority, postulated a second four part test. The court should consider:

(a) control;

(b) ownership of the tools;

(c) the chance of profit; and

(d) the risk of loss.

He did not think that these four factors were conclusive. Other elements might have to be added. Such an attitude gave rise to the modern approach to distinguishing employees from independent contractors.

3.3.16 *Ready Mix* case

One of the well known staging points on the way towards the current thinking is *Ready Mixed Concrete (South East) Ltd v Minister of Pensions and National Insurance* (1968). The company sacked its drivers, sold its lorries to them, and re-engaged them under some kind of contract. The written contract stated that the drivers had to wear the company's uniform, use the lorries only on company business, place them at the company's disposal for a set number of hours and obey the foreman's orders. These factors pointed to the existence of a contract of employment. However, other elements pointed towards the drivers' being self-employed. They had to maintain the lorries and pay running costs. They could own more than one lorry and hire substitute drivers. They had no set hours or meal breaks. They decided on routes and how to drive the lorries. They paid their own tax and national insurance. The judge said that there were three conditions which had to be satisfied before there existed a contract of employment:

- the employee had to agree to provide his own skill in the performance of a service for his employers in return for payment;

- the employers had to have some degree of control; and

- the other terms of the contract must not be inconsistent with the existence of a contract of employment.

3.3.17 Decision in *Ready Mix*

On the facts the drivers were self-employed. Though there was some element of control, a term which included 'the power of deciding the thing to be done, the means to be employed in doing it, the time when and the place where it shall be done', they did not have to work personally for the firm. They could provide substitutes, a strong but not decisive indication of self-employment. Furthermore, some terms of the contract were not consistent with there being a contract of employment. Yet, as can be seen from the facts, many were, and some factors were indecisive. The drivers were paid according to the work they did. One might think that this element pointed towards their being self-employed, but some employees are paid by results, for example, piece workers and those on commission.

3.3.18 Modern approach

The multiple test in *Ready Mix* has developed into what is sometimes called the pragmatic test. The judge or tribunal members weigh up all the factors pointing towards the existence of a contract of employment and all the factors pointing towards a contract for services. No one factor is determinative, except that, if the worker need not perform the services personally, he is not an employee. For instance, the fact that a company pays a person's tax and national insurance does not automatically mean that he is an employee (*O'Kelly v Trusthouse Forte plc* (1984), among other cases). Similarly, the fact that a firm does not pay a worker's tax and national insurance does not mean that he is automatically self-employed (*Davis v New England College of Arundel* (1977)). A casual vision mixer was held to be self-employed even though he did not provide the tools of his job (*Hall v Lorimer* (1994)). The requirement of personal service for a contract of employment was laid down by the Court of Appeal in *Express & Echo Publications Ltd v Tanton* (1999). A contract of service is a contract of personal service. If the worker can provide a substitute, there is no contract of personal service and therefore no contract of service. The first step in the *Ready Mix* test, that the worker, to be an employee, must provide his own skill, supports the *ratio* of *Tanton*. However, this would mean that employers could easily evade the law of employment by inserting a clause that the worker need not perform services personally. Surely that cannot be right?

It must be questioned whether the first criterion adds anything to the other two. Both the self-employed and employees agree to work in consideration of payment (*Airfix Footwear Ltd v Cope* (1978) and *Thames Television Ltd v Wallis* (1979)). In *Market Investigations Ltd v Minister of Social Security* (1969), Cooke J gave some indication of the sort of factors which may be relevant when determining whether there was a contract of employment present. Control was always relevant but other factors might include:

- whether the worker provided his own equipment;
- whether he could hire helpers;
- whether he had some financial risk;
- whether he could profit from the job through what the judge called 'sound management'; and
- whether he had responsibility for investment and management.

There is, however, no checklist of relevant factors. All factors must be weighed in the balance. The Court of Appeal in *Hall v Lorimer*, above, said that the list of factors in *Market Investigations* should not be gone through like a checklist. In some cases they may be of little use. For example, in *Hall v Lorimer*, working for several firms and the shortness of each job were significant elements. The court or tribunal should not apply the factors mechanically. In that case, the worker was not responsible for investment decisions and management of his business but he was self-employed.

3.3.19 Examples

An example of such balancing can be seen in *Hitchcock v Post Office* (1980). A sub-postmaster had to carry out the instructions of the Post Office and he had to tell the head postmaster if he was going to be absent for three days or more. However, he could delegate the performance of his duties and took the risk of profit and loss. The latter factors outweighed the former. Accordingly, the sub-postmaster was self-employed. The case demonstrates that a court or tribunal must weigh the factors, not simply count them. One 'heavyweight' factor can outweigh four 'lightweight' factors. Other factors which may be important include: whether the person works at home or at a workplace; whether he can work for another firm, and whether the work is casual. The effect is that it is difficult in hard cases to look to authorities for guidance.

A second illustration is *McManus v Griffiths* (1997). A document called a 'contract of employment' stipulated that the worker was to run a catering business on the premises of a golf club. The contract was one of personal service and the club provided the equipment. There were clauses concerning her salary, duties and holidays. Nevertheless, the court held her to be self-employed. The club had no right to any of the profit and this factor was the overwhelming indication that she was in business on her own account.

3.3.20 Mutuality of obligations

One factor which has recently come into prominence is whether there exists 'mutuality of obligations' between the parties. A major case is *Nethermere (St Neots) Ltd v Gardiner* (1984). The plaintiffs were outworkers: they made clothes at home. They were paid by the piece. There was no obligation to work at set times to do a certain amount of work. The Court of Appeal held that they were employees, largely because there was a regular arrangement over a period of time whereby the homeworkers would do the work. They had the expectation of being given work. This expectation was transmuted into contracts of employment through the providing and accepting of work over a lengthy period. Kerr LJ said:

> ... the inescapable requirement concerning the alleged employees ... is that they must be subject to an obligation to accept and perform some minimum or at least reasonable amount of work for the alleged employer.

It must be said, however, that all contracts, even ones of self-employment, have an irreducible minimum.

An example of a case where there was no mutuality of obligations is *Clark v Oxfordshire HA* (1998). The applicant worked for a 'bank' or 'pool' of nurses. She was offered work when it was available. The court held that there was no global contract of employment because the the defendants were under no duty to offer work and the nurse was under no obligation to accept it. A similar decision was reached by the Privy Council in *Cheng v Royal Hong Kong Golf Club* (1998). A golf club was not obliged to provide a caddie with work and he had no obligation to work. He had no sickness, pension or other benefits which the employees of the defendants had and he was paid per round. It was held that there was no contract of employment between the parties. Lord Hoffmann, dissenting, advised that he was a casual employee of the club, just like a jobbing gardener:

> ... the club had selected the claimant as a caddie, trained him, equipped him with a uniform and a locker ... determined his rate of payment, established the system on which he would be allocated to individual members to carry their clubs, exercised disciplinary powers over him, paid him and had the right to dispense with his services.

Mutuality of obligations was, in his view, irrelevant to one-off (non-continuing) contracts of employment.

3.3.21 Criticism of mutuality

One difficulty with the mutuality of obligations doctrine is that it may lead to results which are not in accord with the policy of widening the concept of 'employee' so that workers may claim on being dismissed unfairly. Those who work in temporary jobs or part time or as casual labourers may not be included within the scope of the legislation. Since perhaps one-third of the UK workforce is engaged in such jobs, and since more and more workers for the foreseeable future will work in them (the number of full time jobs occupied by males is decreasing, while the number of part time jobs held by women is increasing), the effect of this doctrine is not in tune with the legislative objective. Such workers are called 'atypical' workers but they are in fact becoming typical. This problem has arisen in an important case: *O'Kelly v Trusthouse Forte* (1984). Here, the plaintiffs were 'regular casuals'. They came in to help at banquets and similar functions. They often came in at set hours on set days. In industrial relations terms, they formed a secondary labour force. The core workers did their jobs full time and did work daily and regularly. It could be said that there was a tertiary labour force who came in when asked. The 'regular casuals' fitted in between. It might have been thought that these were the very sort of persons whom employment law should protect. The Court of Appeal could have held that the regular casuals were employees. They worked frequently for the defendants; they had no other jobs; they apparently could not provide substitutes; the hotel where they worked gave them uniforms; they did not lay out capital or share in the financial risks.

The court decided that the workers were self-employed despite such factors. The court seems to have been impressed by the custom and practice of the business and by the intention of the parties that the waiters were not employees. There was no mutuality of obligations. The employers were under no duty to provide work and the workers were under no obligation to do work, though in practice they would not refuse it for, if they did, they would not be offered more work. It should be noted, however, that, generally speaking, employers have no duty to provide work and the effect of this decision is that a large and growing class of workers is not protected by the employment legislation. Moreover, not even the Court of Appeal has applied the mutuality of obligations principle (*McLeod v Hellyer Bros* (1987)), though compare the decision in *Scarah v Fish Container Services Ltd* (1995) where the Court of Appeal held that there was no mutuality of obligation between those who unloaded crates of fish and the defendant company so that there was no global contract covering the period of work because they were not obliged to turn up to work.

Once the 'regular casual' workers have begun to work, there is, contrary to *O'Kelly*, mutuality of obligation. The fact that they need not accept work is irrelevant if they have done so. *O'Kelly* has been criticised on other grounds. If one enquires in the terms of the next test whether the waiters were in business on their own account, it is impossible to say that they ran the risk of profit or loss. They were not entrepreneurs but were under the control of the hotel managers. Furthermore, employers should not be able to deprive workers of the protection of employment legislation. The outcome of the case permitted the employers to get rid of pro-union workers with no financial loss to themselves.

O'Kelly should now be read subject to *Carmichael v National Power plc* (1998). The Court of Appeal ruled that guides to a power station working on a 'casual as required' basis were employees because the employers were subject to an implied term that they would provide a reasonable proportion of the work to each worker and the workers were subject to an implied term that they would accept it. Accordingly, there was mutuality of obligations. This ruling is a break from earlier law. More casual workers will be held to be employees than had previously been the case. In January 2000, the House of Lords reversed *Carmichael*, holding that the issue of whether a worker was an employee was one of fact, which the court could not interfere with. The reasoning of the Court of Appeal was not in issue.

3.3.22 Independence test

A test formulated by Cooke J in *Market Investigations Ltd v Minister of Social Security* (1969) was:

> ... is the person who has engaged himself to perform those services performing them in business on his own account?

If a person invests money in his job, he is likely to be self-employed. If a plumber works when he wishes, buys the tools and can send someone else in his place, the plumber is likely to be self-employed. If, however, the worker is provided with tools and materials, he is likely to be an employee (*Airfix Footwear Ltd v Cope* (1978)). This test has been used several times. For example, *Young & Woods Ltd v West* (1980), a decision which is described below (3.4.6), and the Privy Council in *Lee v Chung* (1990), where a casual construction worker in Hong Kong was held to be an employee because he ran no risk of profit or loss while working, approved Cooke J's approach. The Court of Appeal in *Lane v Shire Roofing Co (Oxford) Ltd* asked: '... was the workman carrying on his own business, or was he carrying on that of his employers?' This definition of an independent contractor has been criticised as in reality being the outcome of the other tests and not a test in its own right, but it has certainly been used by the courts and tribunals independently of the other tests. Moreover, casual workers may not be in business on their own account, but they are not necessarily employees: *Wickens v Champion Employment* (1984), in which temporary workers were held not to be employees of an employment agency. The EAT held that the agency had no duty to secure work for them and they had no obligation to accept any work secured for them by the agency.

3.3.23 Difficulty of deciding

The answer to the question whether a worker is an employee or self-employed is sometimes controversial. For example, in *Barnett v Brabyn* (1996), the High Court held that an engineer was self-employed for tax purposes despite his being under control of the firm, working solely for it, being paid holiday pay and he would have received sick pay had he been ill. He ran no risk of profit or loss. In the light of other cases such as *Market Investigations*, it might have been expected that the engineer was an employee.

3.4   Labels

This section discusses the situation where there is an express term in the contract that the worker is an independent contractor. This issue is sometimes known as 'labels'. Despite the doctrine of freedom of contract, the courts and tribunals have cut through the label to reveal the true situation.

3.4.1   The problem

A problem which sometimes arises is when all or most of the elements point in one direction but there is a clause in the contract between the worker and the company which states that he is self-employed. Is he an employee or an independent contractor? Take, for example, a building worker who works on what is called 'the lump'. The labourer takes a job on the basis that he is to be treated as a 'self-employed labour only sub-contractor'. Most other factors, for example, wages, times of work and personal service, point towards his being an employee. While in work the labourer enjoys the advantages associated with being self-employed (though there are special revenue rules which apply to working on the lump), but what happens if he is injured or wishes to claim statutory rights? He can do so only if he is an employee.

An illustration of a tribunal's searching for the true nature of the contract is *Catamaran Cruisers v Williams* (1994) (EAT). The worker, in order to avoid PAYE, established a company and sold his services to a firm which provided a riverbus facility on the Thames. He paid tax on the money he received from the company (which was given to it by the riverbus firm) and the company paid corporation tax. It was held that he was an employee for the purposes of his claiming employment law rights. The fact that there was a company between him and his employers did not affect the substance of the transaction.

Another case illustrative of the problem dealt with in this section is *City and East London Family Health Services Authority v Durcan* (1996). A dentist working in private practice worked for five hours a week at a hospital providing emergency services. The contract stated that he was an independent contractor. The EAT held that he was not in business on his own account but was an employee for those five hours despite the label.

3.4.2 *Ferguson's* case

One of the main authorities is *Ferguson v John Dawson & Partners (Contractors) Ltd* (1976). Mr Ferguson was a worker on the lump. He fell through the roof of a building and was injured. He contended that the company was liable for the tort of breach of statutory duty for failing to provide a guard rail. By a majority, the Court of Appeal held that he was an employee. Therefore, he was awarded damages. The majority held that the label of self-employment was simply a smokescreen which hid the true relationship. That smokescreen could be pierced by the courts and the true relationship discovered. Later cases have followed the majority in *Ferguson*: *Davis v New England College of Arundel* (1977); *Tyne & Clyde Warehouses Ltd v Hamerton* (1978); and *Thames Television Ltd v Wallis* (1979).

3.4.3 The dissent

The dissenting judge, Lawton LJ, would have given the worker no compensation. He stated that there was no reason why a person could not be self-employed if he chose, and it was against public policy for a person to be an employee for the purpose of tort law but self-employed in relation to tax. 'The prime object of the bargain', he said, was that the plaintiff had the status of self-employment.

3.4.4 *Massey's* case

The case with which to compare *Ferguson* is *Massey v Crown Life Insurance Co* (1978). The applicant was a branch manager for the defendants. There was no doubt that he was at that stage an employee. Later, the parties agreed that he should become self-employed. After taking independent professional advice, he accepted his new status. He was taxed as self-employed and he paid national insurance as a self-employed person. He was dismissed. He claimed compensation for unfair dismissal. He could succeed only if he was an employee. The Court of Appeal held that he was self-employed. The court stated that the parties could not alter the true relationship by putting a label on it falsifying the real situation. However, if the relationship was not clear, the label was strong evidence of what the relationship was. In *Massey*, there was no attempt to defraud the Revenue, unlike in *Ferguson*: it was an agreement to treat the former employee as self-employed. By choice the worker had, during the running of his contract, agreed to change his relationship.

3.4.5 Decision in *Massey*

The judgment in *Massey* was unanimous. The court was influenced by the fact that the manager had altered his status for tax purposes. The judges did not want him to be self-employed for the purposes of taxation but an employee for unfair dismissal purposes. Lawton LJ, the dissentient in *Ferguson*, said in *Massey* that:

> *Ferguson* clearly established that the parties cannot change a status merely by putting a new label on it. But, if in all the circumstances of the case, including the terms of the agreement, it is manifest that there was an intention to change status ... there is no reason why the parties should not be allowed to make that change.

3.4.6 *Young & Woods v West*

The principal authority is now *Young & Woods Ltd v West* (1980). The applicant was a sheet metal worker. He was engaged as a self-employed person and the Inland Revenue treated him as such. He was dismissed and claimed compensation for unfair dismissal. The Court of Appeal did not accept the words of Lawton LJ quoted above. The court held that the label was one factor which a court or tribunal had to take into account. It was decisive only when, all other factors having been weighed, there was still doubt as to the nature of the contract. The court thought that more weight should be attached to a label if there had been a deliberate change in the relationship than otherwise, the situation which had occurred in *Massey*, or if the type of job was unusual. In *Massey* the post was unusual. In the present case, there was nothing unusual about the job. The court did not consider, however, that an intent to change the status should automatically take effect; rather, the label was a factor in the equation. On the facts of the case, the label was not decisive because the other elements pointed towards employment: they were not evenly balanced. The applicant worked alongside employees doing the same work as he did. There was no doubt as to the relationship, disregarding the label. Therefore, the label was not decisive. Accordingly, the applicant was an employee.

3.4.7 Tax consequence

The court did, however, say that courts or tribunals which characterised a relationship as one of employment which had been thought to be one of self-employment should inform the Revenue to recoup back tax on an employment basis (PAYE). The result might be that the employee would lose more on tax than gain on compensation for unfair dismissal.

3.4.8 Avoidance provision

It should be noted that s 203 of the ERA 1996 prevents the parties from contracting out of the rights provided in that statute. To permit 'labels' would defeat this non-contracting-out rule. This policy has been effected to some extent by the courts in their decisions on labelling. No court or tribunal has yet held that a label is an attempt to evade the application of the Act.

3.4.9 Critique

One criticism of the 'label' cases is that they are not easily squared with the doctrine of freedom of contract. By that principle, contractual parties should be free, subject to some limitations based on public policy, to determine their relationship. If they have chosen to state whether orally or in writing that a worker is an independent contractor, why should the courts intervene to change the nature of the relationship? The fact that the worker does not realise all the consequences of being self-employed is not to the point. After all, the parties are bound by the contract in general whether or not they understood the terms. Moreover, the worker has taken the financial benefits of being self-employed. Should he now not take the disadvantages? The opposing view is that employment legislation is to protect workers and therefore coverage should be broad.

3.5 Special types of workers

The law has found difficulty in dealing with several classes of workers. Separate treatment is made of these categories. The principle is that tribunals and courts apply the above-stated tests to determine status. It should be noted that a probationary employee is an employee despite being on probation.

3.5.1 Office holders

Where a person holds an office (defined as a permanent post which exists independently of the person who holds it), he is neither employed nor self-employed (though there is also authority which holds that an office holder may also be an employee). He falls into a separate category called 'office holders'. Police constables comprise the principal illustration of this class. They do have some of the rights held by employees, such as written terms, minimum notice period and redundancy payments, but they are subject to specialised terms and conditions in the performance of their duties. There are other office holders, such as registrars of births, marriages and deaths, prison officers (who are deemed to be employees for the purposes of the ERA 1996), Justices of the Peace, judges, trade union officials, trustees and Salvation Army officers. For the purpose of discrimination legislation, a chief constable is deemed to employ the police officers who work under him.

3.5.2   Clergy

The courts have said that some clergy are neither office holders nor employees because there is no intent to enter into legal binding relations, for example, *Davies v Presbyterian Church of Wales* (1986). However, it has been held that priests of various religions including Islam and Judaism are employees. Similarly, in *Coker v Diocese of Southwark* (1995) (which on appeal was called *Diocese of Southwark v Coker*) Professor Rideout, Chair of the London South employment tribunal, said that an Anglican assistant curate was an employee. He criticised an earlier case which had held that the relations between the Methodist Church and a minister were purely spiritual: the spiritual nature of the work did not preclude a contract. The Church of England exercised a high degree of control. In sum, the curate was under a contractual duty to adhere to Church rules. Because he was an employee, he could bring a claim for unfair dismissal. On appeal (1996), the EAT held that Professor Rideout was incorrect. The assistant curate was an office holder. Working in that capacity was inconsistent with being an employee. There are conflicting decisions on Muslim religious leaders, and a Sikh priest has been held not to be an employee.

3.5.3   Trainees

Persons in training who do not have contracts of apprenticeship may also fall into a special class called 'appointees for training' by Lord Denning MR in *Wiltshire Police Authority v Wynn* (1980). The Court of Appeal determined that despite wages and hours of work, a police cadet was neither an employee nor an independent contractor. A university research student seems to be in a similar position (*Hugh-Jones v St John's College* (1979)). *A fortiori*, undergraduates are not employees. However, an articled clerk is an employee (*Oliver v JP Malnick & Co* (1983)). Accordingly, the fact that a worker is undergoing training is not decisive of the issue of whether he is an employee or not.

3.5.4   Difficult jobs

The above two classes of workers form exceptions to the usual division into employees and independent contractors. The next two categories constitute types of workers where rules have been developed to deal with the nature of the worker.

3.5.5   Workers' co-operatives

A worker in a co-operative venture registered as a limited company was held to be an employee in *Drym Fabricators Ltd v Johnson* (1981). Facts may, however, lead to another conclusion, as in *Addison, above*.

3.5.6 Directors

Perhaps surprisingly, a director may be an employee and may be so despite the fact that he runs the company. Cohen J made the point in *Trussed Steel Concrete Co Ltd v Green* (1946):

> When I find a man who is bound to devote his whole time to the affairs of the company, to do all in his power to develop and extend the business of the company, not to engage in any other business and who is engaged on the terms that his employment may be determined by notice in writing, I find it impossible to say that he is not employed by the company.

A company has a legal personality separate from the natural persons who own and manage it. For example, like a natural person, a company can employ people, whether as factory floor workers or as directors. A general meeting must approve contracts of employment given to directors for over five years.

The fact that the director works full time for the company is presumptive of employee status. It was once thought that the person who is a director and the controlling shareholder cannot be an employee. However, it is now clear that such a person can be an employee (*Secretary of State for Trade and Industry v Bottrill* (1999)).

3.5.7 *Lee's* case

The main authority is *Lee v Lee's Air Farming Ltd* (1961), a decision of the Privy Council on appeal from New Zealand. The deceased owned all the shares except one in a company. He was killed in a flying accident. His widow claimed compensation. By the law of New Zealand as it then was, she could succeed only if the deceased was an employee of the company. The Judicial Committee held that he was an employee even though the company was a 'one-man company', he being the one man.

3.5.8 *Parsons's* case

A director is not, however, always an employee. A contrasting case is *Parsons & Sons Ltd v Parsons* (1979). The applicant sought compensation for unfair dismissal when he was removed by his brothers from his directorship. The Court of Appeal noted that he was regarded as self-employed for the purposes of national insurance; he did not receive a salary but directors' fees; and the firm's accountant regarded him as self-employed. He was held to be an independent contractor. One indication that he was not an employee was that he had no written contract of employment (or written memorandum) as required by what is now s 318 of the Companies Act 1985. Similarly, the mere fact that the director does some work for the company does not make him an employee. If he owns most of the shares, it is likely that he is not an employee.

3.5.9 Partners

A partner is self-employed. The partner is the employer. A junior partner who shares in the equity is a partner. An equity partner is not an employee. Care must be taken to distinguish true partners from salaried partners, the latter being employees, whereas the former share the profits, often in proportion to the amount of capital each has invested.

3.5.10 Agency workers

Agency workers are those workers who are sent by employment agencies to work in firms. Whether such workers are employees or self-employed depends on the general law and often they will be independent contractors (as when temporary secretaries, 'temps', go from job to job to cover holiday absences). Indeed, where a worker agrees with one firm to work exclusively for another, it is thought that there is neither a contract of service nor one for services but a contract *sui generis (Construction Industry Training Board v Labour Force Ltd* (1970)). If, however, the terms of the contract such as those indicating that the worker was subject to a large degree of control by the agency (but omitting reference to the label of employment or self-employment) indicate that the worker is an employee, he is so. In *McMeechan v Secretary of State for Employment* (1997) – where there was a grievance procedure, the worker was paid weekly and was under a duty of faithful service – a clause in his contract providing that he was self-employed was held not to be determinative of the true relationship. A locum doctor was held not to be an employee of the agency which sent him to jobs because he could choose whether to work or not and the sole control the agency exercised over him was a monitoring one (*Sreekanta v Medical Relief Agency (Stoke-on-Trent) Ltd* (1995)). A fitter/machinist was held to be an independent contractor in *Pertemps Group plc v Nixon* (1994) because all the terms of the contract so indicated. Accordingly, if the alleged employers do not have a sufficient degree of control and the workers are not obliged to take a job, the likelihood is that they are not employees of the agency. Three situations may be distinguished:

(a) if employers take on a person and he is under an obligation to do the work personally, he is likely to be an employee;

(b) if the firm contacts the agency for a worker but there is no duty on the agency to provide a specific person, the worker may well not be an employee of the firm;

(c) if the company pays the agency for the worker and the agency pays the worker, there is no contract between the company and the worker. The agency may be the worker's employer. This determination will be supported by the agency acting as if it were the employer, for example, by deducting tax and national insurance. An agency, however, may have no duty to find work for the persons on its books.

3.5.11 Crown employees

Crown employees may work under a contract, for example, *Reilly v R* (1934). In *R v Lord Chancellor's Department ex p Nangle* (1991), the Divisional Court held, contrary to previous authority, that the Crown may intend to create legal relations. However, the Crown is not bound by an Act of Parliament unless the statute says so. For some purposes, such as unfair dismissal (see s 191 of the ERA 1996), civil servants are treated as employees, but for some other employment law purposes they are not. Central government employees cannot claim statutory redundancy payments (s 191(2)). There are other exemptions and exceptions which are well discussed by Fredman and Morris in *The State as Employer*, 1989. It should be noted that, since 1990, NHS employees have been entitled to redundancy payments and, since 1993, members of the armed services have been entitled to claim many employment rights. There seems to be something of a paradox here. Some public employees are for some purposes being assimilated into the category of ordinary employees, whereas other public employees are becoming more separated from ordinary employees because of the availability of judicial review.

3.6   Law or fact?

In the light of the difficulties which courts and tribunals have come across when determining whether a contract is one of employment or for services, it has been said that the issue is one of fact for the fact finding tribunal. The strongest authorities to that effect are the House of Lords decision in *Carmichael v National Power plc* (2000) and the Privy Council decision in *Lee v Chung* (1990). Only where the difficulty relates solely to the construction of a written document is the question one of law (see *Davies v Presbyterian Church of Wales* (1986)). The House of Lords held that the status of a Methodist minister was to be determined by construing the applicant's written contract with the outcome that the decision of the employment tribunal was appealable). The legal effect is that, in general, questions of fact cannot be appealed to the EAT and thence to the Court of Appeal and House of Lords. The practical effect is that the EAT cannot intervene (except where the employment tribunal has misdirected itself as to law or where the result is 'perverse') in order to correct inconsistent decisions by employment tribunals: on the same facts, one worker may be an employee (and therefore able to make a claim for unfair dismissal, for example) and another worker an independent contractor. Such an approach does not reflect creditably on a legal system. The determination that the issue is a question of fact is often said to be the result of the higher tribunals' striving to reduce their workload. See, for example, Lord Griffiths in *Lee v Chung*. It is an unfortunate side effect of their doing so that some workers may be deprived of rights to which they would otherwise be entitled. Should administrative convenience be permitted to defeat rights?

3.7   Who are the employers?

It may be certain that a worker is an employee but not who employs him. A person may have two employers, for example, a person may work for one employer in the morning and another in the afternoon. The problem really comes when one firm sends an employee to another firm for a certain time or to complete a set task. The basic rule is that the first firm remains the employer unless the employee has consented to the move. In *Mersey Docks and Harbour Board v Coggins & Griffith (Liverpool) Ltd* (1947), the Board had loaned a crane and its driver to a firm. He was careless and an accident happened. The Board was held by the House of Lords to be still the worker's employer and so liable vicariously for the employee's negligence.

3.7.1   Exception

At times, however, the second firm is the employee's employer. In *Garrard v AE Southey & Co* (1952) the plaintiff was loaned by the first defendant to the second defendant. The latter's foreman controlled what the worker did and how he did it. The worker was injured. He sued both defendants for negligence. The court held that the second defendant was his employer and was liable. The court said that, if the employee's labour alone was loaned, it would often be that the hirers are his employers, but, if he is loaned with a complex piece of machinery, it may well be that the first firm remains the employer.

3.8   General criticism

In law, there is a doctrine that 'one cannot blow hot and cold'. Differently put, one cannot, for example, be two inconsistent things at the same time. In the present context, one cannot in English law, it would seem, be an employee for one purpose but self-employed for another. If one is an employee for the purposes of the employment legislation, one is also an employee for tax purposes (*Calder v H Kitson Vickers Ltd* (1988)). That is why the employment tribunal, having re-characterised a worker as an employee from being an independent contractor, informs the revenue authorities of the change. Nevertheless, first, there is no clear dividing line between employees and independent contractors; secondly, the answer to the question whether a worker was an employee or self-employed may be 'result-pulled', that is, a court or tribunal may hold a worker to be an employee if such is in tune with some policy. This attitude may be seen especially in cases involving vicarious liability.

To gain damages from someone, the plaintiff has to prove that the person who injured him was an employee. The court in order to be able to award damages to a person who has been injured must hold that the worker was an employee and accordingly does so. For this reason, cases on vicarious liability should be treated carefully when applying them into the area of employment protection. Similarly, in order to have jurisdiction to hear a case on unfair dismissal the employment tribunal must hold a worker to be an employee. Therefore, it does so determine. In tax matters, the courts may be striving to prevent evasion. Searching for the dividing line between employees and independent contractors is a sterile task, but a virtue could be made of the difficulty in drawing the line. Decisions could be expected to be context-specific. A ruling that a worker was an employee for the purposes of vicarious liability would not automatically mean that he was one for unfair dismissal purposes, for the policies behind these doctrines are different. Vicarious liability protects injured third parties, whereas unfair dismissal does not.

Certainly, there is no one factor which marks out a contract of employment. A factor which is important in one case may be insignificant or not present in the next. The judge or tribunal has to weigh up the factors in the context of each particular case. Since the policy behind the various rulings about employment status vary so markedly, it is not surprising that the judiciary have failed to come up with a simply stated and easily applied test. While the multiple test is the one which is most often used, there is nothing in the cases to prevent the courts or tribunals from running together the tests, giving priority to one test rather than the multiple test or inventing new tests. The sole test which stands rejected is the first, the control test.

Government policy in the period 1979–97 was in favour of the switch from employees to independent contractors. The effect, it was hoped, was to unleash the hidden hand of the market with consequential reductions in permanency of employment and the level of pay. One result in employment law is that proportionately fewer workers are able to claim their statutory protection rights than in 1979.

FORMATION OF THE CONTRACT OF EMPLOYMENT

Employment contracts are contracts

A contract of employment or of service is an example of contracts in general, but it has specialised features due to statutory intervention in favour of individual employees. Despite parliamentary inroads, contract remains the cornerstone of employment law (*Laws v London Chronicle* (1959)).

Who is an employee?

Many rights are granted to employees but not to other workers, in particular, the self-employed. The distinction is therefore important (*Hillyer v St Bartholomew's* (1909)).

The tests

Parliament has not defined an 'employee'. Employees must perform the work personally: *Express & Echo Publications Ltd v Tanton* (1999). The courts and tribunals have used a variety of tests to distinguish employees from the self-employed: control, right to control, organisation, ordinary person, *'indicia'*, multiple, the modern or pragmatic approach and independence:

- control: *Yewens v Noakes* (1881);

- organisation: *Macdonald and Evans v Stevenson Jordan and Harrison* (1952);

- ordinary person: *Collins v Herts CC* (1947);

- *indicia*: *Short v Henderson* (1946);

- multiple: *Ready Mix* (1968);

- modern approach: *Market Investigations* (1969); mutuality of obligations: *Nethermere v Gardiner* (1984); *Carmichael v National Power plc* (1998);

- independence: *Market Investigations* (1969).

Labels

If the parties agree on the status of the worker, effect will be given to such oral or written statement, provided that the 'label' does not hide the true relationship:

- *Ferguson v John Dawson* (1976);
- *Massey v Crown Life* (1978);
- *Young & Woods v West* (1980).

Special types of worker

Some persons form specific classes of workers. An example is office holders. Other types of workers require particular treatment, Crown employees being an illustration (*Wiltshire PA v Wynn* (1980); *Lee v Lee's Air Farming* (1961)).

Law or fact?

Surprisingly, the determination of whether a worker is an employee or an independent contractor is a question of fact, except where the matter is one of the construction of a written document (*Lee v Chung* (1990)).

Who are the employers?

The question whether an employee is employed by the employer who loaned him out or by the employer who hired him is resolved by considering the factual matrix of the case (*MD and HB v Coggins and Griffith* (1947)).

General criticism

The outcome in the cases may be 'result-pulled' because of policy. There is no list to be ticked off in deciding whether a contract is one of employment. Factors have to be weighed. The courts and tribunals are at liberty to apply more or less any of the tests used since the Second World War.

CHAPTER 4

THE COMMON LAW OF CONTRACT

4.1　Common law contract

In the last chapter, it was noted that the contract of employment is a contract. Therefore, general contractual principles, such as the doctrines of consideration and privity, apply to service agreements. Just as in general contract law, a term is void if it is meaningless or too vague, so a term in an employment contract will fail for the same reason. Therefore, a clause that the employee would receive terms to be mutually agreed would be too vague to be enforced. This chapter begins by examining three matters of contract law as they apply to employment contracts: minority, illegality and form. Linked with form is the statutory provision of written terms of employment. Also considered are express and implied terms, the latter supplementing the former. While contracts of employment are becoming more formal than previously, offer and acceptance can be simple: 'Will you start on Monday at 8 am?' 'Yes.' The terms of a contract may derive from various documents such as the company handbook. In the event of a dispute, it may be very difficult to discover what the parties are to be taken to have agreed. Some matters in contract have been affected by statute. This chapter looks at deductions from wages and the length of the working day, as well as the national minimum wage.

4.1.1　Continuing importance

Although statutory rights have, to a large extent, replaced contractual rights, contract nevertheless remains important. For example, the law of covenants in restraint of trade and the law governing wrongful dismissal are contractual in nature. Whether there has been a dismissal for statutory purposes, for example, in the context of unfair dismissal, is very largely determined by contract. On the collective side of employment law, determining whether there are unlawful means in the action for inducing breach of contract depends on the contract of employment, and, while there are several statutory glosses, the relationship between a union and its members is based on contract.

4.2　Offer and acceptance

As with other contracts, offer, acceptance, consideration and intention to create legal relations (the last requirement being presumed unless the contrary is demonstrated) must be present. An offer need not be in any set format. It could be a notice pinned on a board, though the notice is likely to be an invitation to treat. An advertisement may or may not be an offer, as every first year law student knows from *Carlill v Carbolic Smoke Ball Co* (1893). If the job advertisement is part of the contract, it overrides the employers' attempt to substitute different terms unilaterally. In *Financial Techniques Ltd v Hughes* (1981), an advert stated that the job had a profit sharing scheme. The employers argued that the scheme was discretionary. The Court of Appeal held that the phrasing of the advert was inconsistent with that argument. A contrasting authority is *Puntis v The Governing Body of Isambard Brunel Junior School* (1996). A deputy head's oral assurances that a temporary promotion would be made permanent were not contractual because there was no offer and acceptance, no consideration and no intent to create legal relations.

The Asylum and Immigration Act 1996 came into force on 27 January 1997. Employers are guilty of a summary offence if they employ a person aged 16 or over who is subject to immigration control and who does not have permission to work in the UK. The maximum fine is £5,000. The employers have a defence if the employee produced a document relating to himself which was one specified in the relevant statutory instrument, such as a UK birth certificate or a document from the previous employers stating his national insurance number, and they have kept it or a copy.

Offers may be made subject to conditions such as a medical examination. It is thought that an offer of employment subject to satisfactory references is to be tested subjectively: did these employers consider the reference to be satisfactory? (*Wishart v NACAB* (1990)). Acceptance may be a simple nod or handshake. Terms tend to be dictated by employers, though there may be 'chaffering' (negotiation) over some terms, especially pay, and sometimes, terms may be laid down in a collective agreement. Just as in general contract law, there may be a collateral contract. In *Gill v Cape Contracts Ltd* (1995), the plaintiff was told by the defendants that the job he was to do would last for at least six months. However, before he could take up the job, they repudiated the contract. Since he had acted to his detriment (by giving up his current job) in reliance on their representation, he was entitled to damages for breach of contract.

If there is no contract, obviously there cannot be a contract of employment. A prisoner does not have a contract of employment with the Prison Service. There is a duty to work but only a discretion to pay for the work.

4.3 Infancy

The law relating to minors' contracts applies to employment contracts (and, indeed, contracts for services). An infant (that is, a person under 18) is bound by an employment contract if overall it is for his benefit. For example, a boy of 16 can agree to serve at low wages as a trainee chef in the expectation that he will be able to use his training and experience in later life. In *Chaplin v Leslie Frewin (Publishers) Ltd* (1966), a contract with Charlie Chaplin's son, Michael, to write a book, was binding because he received an adequate amount of money in return for his work. In comparison, an agreement was void in *De Francesco v Barnum* (1890). There were onerous obligations on a 14 year old but little obligation on her employers. It is possible for a term which is not for the infant's benefit, such as a covenant in restraint of trade, to be severed.

4.4　Illegality

The law of illegal contracts applies to contracts of employment. Contracts tainted with illegality or immorality cannot be enforced by courts or tribunals. Such agreements may be contrary to public policy at common law or expressly or impliedly prohibited by Parliament. A contract which is illegal *ab initio* is not enforceable by either party. The fact that the plaintiff or applicant does not know of the illegality is irrelevant. This law is laid down in the well known contract case of *St John Shipping Corp v Joseph Rank Ltd* (1957). An illustrative employment case is *Corby v Morrison* (1980). An agreement to pay £5 without deducting tax made the agreement illegal at and from its commencement.

If the contract is illegal, an employee cannot rely on any contractual or statutory rights to which he would otherwise be entitled, such as the rights to be awarded damages at law for wrongful dismissal and to be granted a remedy for unfair dismissal under statute. In *Cole v Stacey* (1974), an employee received additional tax free pay. The contract was void for illegality and the right to a redundancy payment was lost. If there is a period of illegality, continuity of employment for (for example) the purpose of determining the qualifying period for unfair dismissal is broken (*Hyland v JH Barker (Northwest) Ltd* (1985)).

If the illegality occurs during a contract and is then stopped, one cannot add together the two lawful periods to create one period of at least one or two years' duration for the purpose of claiming statutory employment rights involving, for example, redundancy payments, unfair dismissal and written reasons for dismissal: *Attridge v Jaydees Newsagents Ltd* (1980), an unreported decision of the EAT. This case and the previous one illustrate the proposition that a contract, once illegal, can become lawful again. In the opinion of the writer, it is the height of absurdity that the doctrine of illegality applies even in the areas of sexual and racial discrimination. An employee who is dismissed on racial grounds, therefore, has no claim when he received pay without deduction of tax or national insurance, because the concept of dismissal is based on contract law. If an employee is sacked on racial grounds, he has no claim if he has been employed under an illegal contract.

In *Leighton v Michael* (1996), the EAT avoided this conclusion by holding that the claim was one which was not based on an illegal contract. A claim in respect of discrimination (provided it was not one founded on dismissal which is grounded on contract) was not one which failed on that ground. Mummery J referred to the Equal Treatment Directive (76/207), under which 'men and women shall be guaranteed the same [working] conditions without discrimination on grounds of sex'. He deduced from this proposition that 'the emphasis is on the objective conditions of working rather than the legally enforceable nature of the contract under which work is done'. There is no similar law on race discrimination.

A major criticism of *Leighton v Michael* is that a sex discrimination claim, just as much as one for unfair dismissal, requires a contract. Admittedly, the type of working arrangement is wider in discrimination law than in unfair dismissal law; nevertheless, a contract is necessary. The EAT in *Hall v Woolston Hall Leisure Ltd* (1998) stated that it found difficulty with *Leighton v Michael*, but applied it 'in the interest of comity'. In a later case, *Chilton v HM Prison Service* (1999), the EAT held that *Leighton* was a well established authority which should be followed in the interests of consistency, despite the fact that it created a distinction between sex discrimination and unfair dismissal claims. An employee will be deprived of employment rights even though, for example, the amount of untaxed pay was small in comparison with the gross wages and even if the scheme to defraud the Revenue was instituted by the employers (*Newland v Simons & Willer (Hairdressers) Ltd* (1981)). The EAT held that the Parliamentary policy of widening the rights of employees did not prevail against the common law policy of safeguarding the Revenue. See, however, 4.4.5, below.

4.4.1 Statutory rights negated

Accordingly, even though it is the contract which is void, statutory rights are not enforceable. If only employees may claim various rights, 'employee' is defined in terms of working under a contract of employment or apprenticeship. If there is no contract, there is no contract of employment. Statutory rights are dependent on there being such a contract. (This argument reinforces the view that contract remains the 'cornerstone' of employment law.)

4.4.2 In performance

There are exceptions to the rule about illegality.

Mode of performance

If the unlawfulness was not present at the inception of the contract but came about as a result of the method in which it was performed, the agreement is not automatically unenforceable. In *Coral Leisure Group Ltd v Barnett* (1981), the hiring of prostitutes for clients was held not to be part of an employee's terms of employment but merely a way in which his job was performed. The contract was lawful at the start, but was performed unlawfully. It is not always certain whether a contract is illegal from its inception or becomes so only during performance. *Corby v Morrison*, above, could have been treated as one in which only the performance was unlawful: the illegal payment occurred during the running of the contract. It seems that contracts in which there is a payment of wages without deduction of tax or national insurance will be void automatically.

4.4.3 Knowledge

The last sentence is, however, contradicted by a number of other cases. In relation to contracts illegal in performance, an employee will lose his rights only if he knew of the illegality. This principle has been used in tax evasion cases (*Tomlinson v Dick Evans 'U' Drive Ltd* (1978) (*obiter*), *Davidson v Pillay* (1979) and *McConnell v Bolik* (1979)). In the latter two cases, the employee did not know of or participate in the illegal transaction. In the first case, the employee *did* know of the illegality. He was paid a £15 per week bonus out of petty cash and did not pay tax on it. The EAT held that both parties 'were in it up to the neck'. In *Salvesen v Simons* (1994), the employee, an estate manager, was paid largely free of tax. The Scottish EAT held that it was immaterial that he did not know that what he was doing was unlawful. What he knew was the fact of the arrangement, and that knowledge was sufficient. Therefore, he could not claim a remedy for unfair dismissal.

Attempts to avoid tax are as lawful in employment law as in the general law. Payment to the applicant's spouse so as to reduce income tax and national insurance liabilities is lawful (*Lightfoot v D & J Sporting Ltd* (1996) EAT). If, however, the payment is a bonus, given, for example, when a greyhound wins a race, the trainer's contract is not unenforceable even though he knew that the payment was free of tax (*Annandale Engineering v Samson* (1994)). The test for knowledge is a subjective one: did the employee know of the illicit activity? It is not material that the employee ought to have known of the illegality (*Newland v Simons & Willer (Hairdressers) Ltd*, above). Therefore, as the EAT said, 'stupidity or misunderstanding or inexperience' can provide the employee with a defence. When the employee *does* come to know of the illegality, he must do all he reasonably can to stop it (*Davidson v Pillay*). Compare this with *Begacem v Turkish Delight Kebab House* (1988), an unreported EAT decision. The employee was paid in cash. No national insurance contributions or tax was deducted. He asked his employers why this was so, but he was always assured that all was fine. The tribunal held that the employee could not have a remedy for being unfairly dismissed. He should have told the Revenue of the illegality so that his true situation could be investigated.

4.4.4 Gravity: the role of public policy

Not every illegality is sufficiently heinous to avoid the contract. Illegality will take effect, at least if it is a statutorily based one, if Parliament must have intended to make the agreement void. (Similar thinking pervades the previous point. The fact that, while performing the contract, an employee has done something illegal does not make a service agreement void. For example, a lorry driver's contract will remain in existence even if he has broken the speed limit.) Because of this principle, it is uncertain whether cases such as *Tomlinson v Dick Evans 'U' Drive*, above, survive in their entirety. In that case, the EAT noted that the employee may be less blameworthy than the employers but decided that 'even in such cases the evil lies in the dishonesty in which the employee knowingly participated'. There were, therefore, no degrees of blame.

However, the courts have recently established that public policy is not dictated by the sort of considerations which applied in *Tomlinson*. In *Hewcastle Catering Ltd v Ahmed* (1991), the Court of Appeal held that two employees could complain of unfair dismissal when their employers had instructed them to participate in a scheme to evade VAT. Kerr LJ said that the relative moral culpability of the parties may be relevant in ascertaining whether employment law rights would be unenforceable because the underlying contract was tainted by fraud. On the facts, the Court of Appeal held that public policy did not operate to render illegal the employees' contracts. There was nothing in the contracts of employment which stated that the workers had to participate in the fraud. They did not benefit from it. It was the employers' duty to make VAT returns. The fraud would presumably have continued without the employees' participation. And, if the employees lose their right to claim, others would be deterred from disclosing illegality, a significant point which is applicable to cases dealing with fraud on the Revenue instigated by employers.

Therefore, in this situation, employees may claim, even though they know of and participate in the scheme. It may be suggested that, in order to save employees being deprived of their employment protection rights, Parliament should change the law to make the doctrine of illegality inapplicable to such claims.

4.4.5 Severance

The doctrine of severance of illegality can apply to employment contracts (*Kearney v Whitehaven Colliery Co* (1893)). It is thought that severance of frauds on the Revenue is not permissible.

4.4.6 Servile incidents

One last point on illegality is that a contract is unlawful if there are 'servile incidents' attached to it. Perhaps an example might be a contract of employment under which an employee agreed not to move house at all without the employers' permission.

4.5 Form: in writing

Because the contract of employment is a contract, there must be consideration (or a deed). There is no set form and, in general, writing is not required. There are, however, some exceptions:

- there are various complex rules on the right to return to work after maternity. An employee must inform her employers in writing at least 21 days before her absence because of pregnancy that she intends to return (s 82(1) of the Employment Rights Act (ERA) 1996). If requested by her employers, she must give written confirmation seven weeks after birth that she intends to return. If the employers do so request, they must include in writing a statement that she will lose her right to return unless she replies within two weeks of receipt or as soon as possible thereafter (s 80(2) and (3) of the ERA 1996);

- an employee working under a fixed term contract of two years or more can waive his rights to a redundancy payment in writing (s 197 of the ERA 1996);

- contracts of apprenticeship must be in writing and signed, as required by common law;

- a merchant seaman's contract must be in writing signed by him and on behalf of the employers (s 25 of the Merchant Shipping Act 1995). This provision applies only to seamen on UK registered ships;

- some deductions from pay must be in writing or evidenced in writing (s 27 of the ERA 1996). This stipulation does not apply to deductions for industrial action. It will not surprise the reader that deductions from wages for income tax do not need to be in writing.

4.6 Written statement

Once an offer of employment has been accepted, there is a contract of employment in existence. Since the contract may be made orally or partly orally and partly in writing, there may be disputes over terms. The topic of implied terms is treated later. This section considers one way in which disputes over contractual issues may be avoided.

4.6.1 Basic consideration

Employers must provide to persons to whom the Act applies (basically, employees who have worked for at least a month) a written statement of the main terms and conditions of employment within two months of the employee's starting work: s 1 of the ERA 1996, part of which derives from the Trade Union Reform and Employment Rights Act 1993. The relevant part of the 1993 Act enacts the Written Particulars Directive (91/533). (This Directive has other names, for example, 'terms and conditions'.) The Directive is one of the few areas of EC law which derives from UK law. That UK law was enacted by the Conservatives but they abstained in the vote on the Directive. Part of the preamble to the Directive states that the aims of the new provisions are 'to provide employees with improved protection against possible infringements of their rights and to create greater transparency in the labour market'. The implementation of the Directive has led to an increase in the amount of paper an employee receives, which may or may not be a good thing. 'Transparency' is not enhanced by a highly detailed written document.

UK law, which dates from 1963, is also based on transparency. Employees should know their rights and duties. Employees already in work on 30 November 1993 are not entitled to the new style statement unless they request one. The employers have two months in which to reply. This document is also called the 's 1 statement' and 'written particulars'. One can see that the statement is not the contract of employment. The contract is made at the start of employment, but the statement need not be given until two months have elapsed. Therefore, by the time the statement is given, the worker is already doing his job under a contract of employment. The Directive applies to 'every paid employee having a contract of employment relationship'. The ERA 1996 applies, however, only to employees, that is, to those who work under a contract of employment. Whatever 'employment relationship' means, it is wider than the UK understanding of what employees are. Therefore, UK law falls short of EC law.

There are various categories of workers to whom this statement need not be given. These include merchant seamen working under a crew agreement (this provision is inconsistent with the Directive, which has no such exception), those working wholly or mainly outside Great Britain, and share fishermen (that is, those paid by a share of the catch). The previous exception of part time employees was abolished by the Employment Protection (Part-Time Employees) Regulations 1995 (SI 1995/31), which came into force in 1995. Even if the exception had not been abolished by UK law, it would have fallen foul of the Part Time Workers Directive (97/81), which has to be implemented in the UK by 7 April 2000. The statement must be given to the employee even though he left the employment within two months of the date of commencement.

4.6.2 Contents

The matters which must be included in the written statement are:

Principal statement

- the identity of the parties;
- the date of commencement;
- job title or a brief description of the work (there is no requirement that a job description is included);
- whether employment with a previous employer is to be counted towards continuity of employment (this is important because only continuous service counts towards the one or two year qualification period for employees and because the amount of compensation depends on the length of continuous employment);
- the amount of pay (presumably, a reference to the national minimum wage will be sufficient);
- when remuneration is paid;
- any bonus or commission;
- the hours of work;
- holidays and holiday pay;
- public holidays;
- title of the job (employers should include wide ones, for example, 'secretary', not 'typist', in order to obtain flexibility from their workforce);
- the place of work, an important matter in relation to redundancy and picketing. Where the employee works at various places, the statement should so state and should give the employers' addressess.

The principal statement must be one document, but particulars may be given in instalments, provided that the two month deadline is not exceeded and the principal statement remains as one document.

Particulars

- any terms as to sickness or injury including sick pay;
- length of notice (reference may be to the statutory minimum periods of notice (considered in Chapter 7) or to a collective agreement);
- pensions, including whether there is a contracting out certificate;
- if the work is temporary, its duration;

- any collective agreements which affect the employee's terms and conditions; if the employers were not a party to the agreement, the identity of the person who made it is to be stated;

- where the employee is to work outside the UK, the period of work abroad, currency of pay, any additional benefits, and any term relating to return to the UK;

- disciplinary and grievances procedures (see below). Section 13 of the Employment Rights (Dispute Resolution) Act 1998 inserted s 127A into the ERA 1996, whereby compensation for unfair dismissal is reduced if the employee fails to use an internal appeals procedure.

These matters need not be in the same document as the principal statement. If they are not, they must be in a document (or collective agreement) which the employee has a reasonable opportunity to read in the course of employment or which is otherwise reasonably accessible. A company handbook is the sort of document which may contain these particulars. The provision as to collective agreements is novel for, until now, most union-management agreements have largely been incorporated into contracts by implied reference. If no particulars on pensions, sick pay, holidays and working outside the UK apply, that fact must be stated (for example, there may be no pension).

References to collective agreements seem out of date in this era of union decline and personal contracts. It should be noted that collective agreements, where they exist, are generally speaking not binding. The fact that the written statement refers to a collective agreement does not mean in itself that that agreement is incorporated into individual employees' terms.

The list of matters which must be included in the written statement comprises the main terms and conditions one might expect to see in a contract of employment.

4.6.3 Disciplinary procedures

There need be no statement about grievance and discipline in relation to health and safety. Disciplinary rules need not be given in firms employing fewer than 20 employees (s 3(3) of the ERA 1996) (this figure includes associated employers). Section 3(3), which was inserted by s 13 of the Employment Act 1989, is interesting. It was apparently introduced as a result of the Government's efforts to reduce administrative burdens on small employers. One might, nevertheless, justifiably say that parties to a dispute should know where they stand; small employers are not exceptional. Looking at the matter from the viewpoint of the employee, there is no justification for this inequality. Moreover, while disciplinary and grievance procedures need not be as formal in small workplaces as in large unionised workplaces, one would expect the State to encourage the settlement of disputes without recourse to courts and tribunals. It should be noted that the ACAS Code of Practice, 'Disciplinary

Practice and Procedures in Employment' (1977) applies to all workplaces, irrespective of size. Even if the employers have fewer than 20 employees, they must give details of the person to whom an individual can take grievances. It should be noted that the Directive does not insist that disciplinary procedures are included in the statement. In this respect, UK law is more favourable to employees than EC law.

4.6.4 Changes

Any changes to the statement must be notified to the employee *individually* at the earliest opportunity and not later than a month after the change (s 4). Changes in respect of matters other than those found in the principal statement need not be given to each employee. It is sufficient that he has reasonable access to them, for example, in a company journal. It should be remembered that the contract of employment, being a contract, cannot be changed without agreement. New particulars need not be given if the employee is re-employed within six months of leaving employment and the terms of the job are unchanged. If there has only been a change of employer, the new one need just inform the employees of the change, but notice of the change must include the date of the start of continuous employment. Individual notification of changes may not be required by EC law. Conspiracy theorists may see this law, which was introduced in 1993, as part of the decollectivisation of industrial relations.

4.6.5 Enforcement

If the employers do not provide a statement (and it is often said that employers do not comply with this obligation) or there are omissions in it and there is a dispute over the statement, they or the employee may refer the matter to an employment tribunal under s 11 of the ERA 1996. There is no power to award compensation, even where the applicant has suffered loss through the employers' failure to include one of the written particulars in the statement. It is suggested that this lack of a power to award compensation is inconsistent with EC law, which demands effective (that is, deterrent) remedies so that directives are enforced. The tribunal may only confirm, amend or substitute particulars. It does not have the power to fine employers. It had this power in 1963 when the jurisdiction was first established, but it was quickly lost. Since the tribunal has the power to write in terms, it is better for employers to state a term at the start of the employment relationship. Where the employers must include a matter (for example, the name of the parties), the tribunal, it has been stated *obiter*, must insert a term.

If the dispute relates to an item which is not mandatory, such as sick pay, the tribunal will insert a term if the parties expressly or impliedly had agreed to it (*Eagland v British Telecommunications plc* (1993)). If there is no agreement, the tribunal should so state. In *Mears v Safecar Security Ltd* (1983), the Court of

Appeal decided that a tribunal had jurisdiction to amend inaccurate particulars, a point which had been unclear. There is no power deriving from the written statement to invent contractual terms. For example, if, as in *Eagland*, there is no reference to sick pay, the tribunal cannot create such a term. There is a time limit of three months from the termination of employment or within a reasonable time thereof if it was not reasonably practicable for the employee to claim within three months. It has happened that employees who made a claim under s 11 have been dismissed for doing so. Section 104 of the ERA 1996, which comes from the Trade Union Reform and Employment Rights Act 1993, deems a dismissal for bringing such a claim an automatically unfair reason for the purposes of unfair dismissal (see Chapter 11).

4.6.6 Jurisdiction

An employment tribunal can declare what the parties meant to include. It cannot go further and interpret the terms. For instance, in *Cuthbertson v AML Distributors* (1975), a tribunal was able to state that an employee should not be dismissed without reasonable notice, but it could not say how long that notice was. It was for the civil courts to determine that issue. The EAT took a similar view in *Construction Industry Training Board v Leighton* (1978). A tribunal could declare that an employee was owed so much a year, but it could not rule whether or not that amount included a bonus. The Court of Appeal approved this stance in *Mears*.

4.6.7 Criticism

The remedy is weak and there is a possibility that, if the employee did apply to a tribunal for amended particulars, he might be dismissed. It is suggested that English law falls short of the EC Directive in failing to provide an effective remedy. From the viewpoint of employers, the 1993 amendments are onerous. The response is that the statement contains the fundamental rights of the parties and may lead to the prevention of disputes.

4.6.8 Legal status

The written statement is not the contract of employment; it is only evidence of the contractual terms. It is a document provided unilaterally by employers and, unlike a contract, it is not (potentially) subject to negotiation. Therefore, it is only declaratory of the employment contract. If the statement is the sole evidence of the terms, it is treated as strong evidence (*System Floors (UK) Ltd v Daniel* (1982)) but is not conclusive (*Turiff Construction Ltd v Bryant* (1967)). It may be the law there is a heavy burden of proof on employers to show that the written statement does not accord with the contract, whereas employees have only a burden of persuasion to show the same (*System Floors (UK) Ltd v Daniel* (1982)). The different standards of proof reflect the law that it is the employers' obligation to provide the written statement. Under Directive 91/533, the employer bears the burden of showing that the statement is wrong in any particular. The Directive did not alter the legal status of the document.

An example of a decision that a statement is not the contract of employment is *Hawker Siddeley Power Engineering Ltd v Rump* (1979). In the statement was a mobility clause. However, the employee had been orally assured that the clause would not be enforced. This oral assurance, a contractual term, overrode the statement, which was in writing. It may not always be obvious whether a document is the contract of employment or the written statement, and care is needed, in that a document entitled 'contract of employment' may be the written particulars and one headed 'written statement' may be the contract of employment.

4.6.9 Transmutation

There is one situation where the statement is treated (miraculously) as being the contract of employment, and that is where the employee signs it as being the contract. It is insufficient to sign it simply in acknowledgment that it has been received. This was held in the Court of Appeal case of *Gascol Conversions Ltd v Mercer* (1974). There was a dispute over the number of hours the employee had to work. The court held that the statement which was entitled 'Non-staff employees' contract of employment' was conclusive because the employee agreed it as being the new contract. This effect was said to derive from the parol evidence rule. This case shows the importance of getting the correct term into the written statement. And, since one has to get the right term into the statement, one ought to get the right term into the contract, even when the statement is merely evidence of the contract.

Gascol has been criticised for blurring the distinction between the contract of employment and the written statement. In the case's favour is the successful argument that the employee had considered the content of the statement and had decided not to protest. There was no other evidence of the terms. Therefore, it could be said that the parties had reached a written agreement, a contract of employment, which took the form of a written statement.

4.6.10 Not contract

The law is that the written statement is not a contract, subject to *Gascol*. The contrast may be seen from another Court of Appeal decision, *Robertson v British Gas Corp* (1983) which, like *System Floors Ltd v Daniel*, approved *Gascol*. The employee was due a bonus under his contract. The employers withdrew the bonus and said so in the written statement. The court held that the employee was still legally entitled to the bonus under the contract. Since the statement was not the contract, it did not apply. (Indeed, the statement was not given until the employee had worked for seven years.) For the employers to win, they would have to negotiate the contract to get rid of the bonus, or use the *Gascol* approach. The fact remains that the change of such a term in the contract cannot be foisted on the employee. If there is no other evidence of the contract, saying that the written contract is not the contract of employment wears a little thin.

4.7 Express terms

Subject to general principles of law such as illegality and restraint of trade, the parties can agree on anything; for example, I can agree to serve you as a shoe-shine boy for 1p a year. Fortunately for me, the courts have set their face against the specific performance of contracts of personal service. The principal remedy for breach of an express or implied term is damages. Such claims are heard in the ordinary civil courts, the county court and the High Court (normally the Queen's Bench Division). Employment tribunals have concurrent jurisdiction over most contractual claims on termination, provided the amount claimed is under £25,000. Some contracts, especially of managers and specialists, are formal; many are not. Express terms override particulars in the written statement. In *Hawker Siddeley Power Engineering Ltd v Rump* (1979), an oral promise that he would not be asked to work outside the south of England, made when he was engaged, overrode references in the statement to a collective agreement which provided for employees to be moved anywhere across the country.

4.7.1 Definition

Express terms are those which the employer and employee have agreed, whether orally or in writing. For example, if the employer says 'I offer you the post of Sales Manager at £20,000 per annum, plus a car commensurate with your status', and the employee says 'I accept', there is a contract of employment with several express terms:

- the job of Sales Manager;
- the pay; and
- the car.

To find out, for example, what the post of Sales Manager entails or what type of car he will get, we have to look elsewhere, perhaps to the company handbook. Conditions set out in the handbook may be incorporated by reference into the contract of employment. Those conditions, ones which are not expressly stated by the parties, are called implied terms (see below).

It should be noted from the above that not all terms in a contract need to be express ones – indeed, it is still rare to find a contract where all the terms are expressed – but implied terms are just as binding as express ones. So, if the job description of the Sales Manager does not expressly state that part of the work involves telephone sales, but the job implicitly does, then that implied term applies just as if it were an express one. A second point to remember is that, if there is a conflict between an express term and an implied one, the express term prevails. For example, if a person is employed as a Sales Manager, he is not subject to an implied term that he must help out in the production process as and when required. An express term would be needed in that case. See, also, 4.9.3, below.

Sometimes, an express term will need interpretation. In *Glitz v Watford Electric Co Ltd* (1979), an employee was taken on as 'copy typist/general clerical duties clerk'. The EAT held that her duties in respect to the second part of her job title included operating a duplicator. The tribunal added that, in a small firm, it was to be expected that job descriptions would be written broadly, with the result that workers should expect to be flexible. An express written term may be qualified by an express oral term. For example, an express mobility clause may be subject to an oral term that it will not be enforced when to do so would take the employee out of daily commuting distance.

4.7.2 Advantages

Advantages of express terms over implied ones are as follows:

- There is little or no room for dispute. Take, for example, a clause which provides, 'You are employed at any of the company's factories'. A worker has made widgets all her life at the firm's Leeds works. Because of a lack of orders, the company decides to close down the Leeds works and concentrate production in Halifax. Since the employee is employed at any of the factories, there can be no dispute that the company is entitled to close down the Leeds branch and transfer the employee to the same job at Halifax. Obviously, there will be a saving in time and money if disputes over the meaning of employment terms can be avoided. Grievance procedures and litigation are thereby avoided.

- This advantage is also perceived in legal terms. If a claim is made by the employee on the facts above, it will fail. The closure of the Leeds factory will not amount to a dismissal; therefore, there is no liability for wrongful dismissal, unfair dismissal or redundancy payments, because each of these claims is based on the requirement of a dismissal. Even if there is a dismissal, there is no redundancy if, as on the above facts, not all of the firm's works have closed. (A term which permits transfer between offices and branches, etc is generally known as a 'mobility clause'.) Another example similar to the one involving a transfer from one place to another is a term which states the employee's task in wide terms. (This type of term is sometimes called a 'flexibility clause'.) If an employee works as a press operator at a hot water bottle factory, and there is a clause stating that he is employed not just on presses but also on sweeping and cleaning duties, he is legally obliged to do those duties as well as being a press operator.

- Some express terms, such as covenants in restraint of trade, apply post-employment; some implied terms, particularly confidentiality, can also survive termination of the contract of employment. The employee will know the express term but will not realise that he is bound by an implied term. The effect is that the employee may well have breached the implied term even before he realised that it existed. Therefore, the implied term often does not take effect at all, so as to prevent the employee's breaking it.

4.7.3 Disadvantage

The drawback with an express term is the converse of the advantage. If it is stipulated that an employee works in 'Leeds or Halifax', what happens if both of those works are closed down in order to create a super-factory in Bradford? Legally, the employee is not obliged to accept the transfer, and this is so despite the fact that Bradford is near Leeds and within commuting distance. If, however, there had been no express clause, a term might have been implied that, although the employee normally worked in Leeds, he could be transferred to any place within reasonable commuting distance, and the courts have been prepared to imply such a term (see below for how this is done). The secret is to draft express terms widely. Rather than say that the worker is employed in 'Leeds or Halifax', it is better to say 'anywhere in the UK' or 'any of the company's workplaces'.

4.7.4 *Nelson v BBC*

However, an example which worked against the employers is *Nelson v BBC* (1977). One might expect that employers would wish to argue against redundancy because, if they lose, they will have to make the statutory redundancy payment. However, if there is a redundancy, they will have to make only a payment for that, and they may be able to avoid compensation for unfair dismissal. Since the amount for unfair dismissal usually substantially exceeds the amount for redundancy, employers may for this reason argue redundancy. In *Nelson*, there was an express term that the employee would work when and where the BBC demanded. The BBC closed down its Caribbean service where he worked. The court held that, since only one of the services had been cut back, he was not redundant.

4.7.5 Advice to employers

Since certain terms have to be in the written statement and since the statement can refer to other documents such as a written contract of employment, it is administratively convenient for employers to provide employees with one document. This document should be provided at the start of employment so that any disputes are nipped in the bud.

4.8 Restraint of trade

Restraint of trade clauses are express terms which directly or indirectly seek to restrain an employee (working either alone or for another firm) from competing with the employer during or after employment. The courts look to the substance of the clause, not to its form. For example, a rule that football clubs would not engage a footballer whose contract had been terminated by one club without the consent of that club was a covenant in restraint of trade. A clause may read, 'the employee agrees that he will not solicit persons who have been clients of the company within two years preceding termination for six months after such termination'; or 'the employee covenants that she will not disclose or use any confidential information belonging to the company'; or 'the employee stipulates that he will not work in any business competing with that of the employer within a radius of five miles from Sheffield Town Hall for two years from the termination of employment'. A restraint of trade clause may be added to the end of a garden leave clause (see 4.9.15, below), thereby providing employers with increased protection for their interests (*Crédit Suisse Asset Management Ltd v Armstrong* (1996)).

4.8.1 General

While the rules are easy to state, they are hard to apply, and this aspect of the contract of employment is predominantly one for the lawyers, in respect to both drafting and enforcement. The basic principle is that the courts do not like covenants in restraint of trade. They see a conflict between the employers' freedom to protect their business and an employee's freedom to move to another job or to set up another firm.

4.8.2 Basic rules

The rules were laid down at the turn of the century in a series of cases culminating in *Herbert Morris Ltd v Saxelby* (1916):

- Employers may protect only legitimate proprietary interests. While the list of those interests is not closed, in employment law there are two such interests: trade secrets and customer connection (a no-poaching agreement seems also to fall within the doctrine as protecting the employers' interest in a stable workforce: *Alliance Paper Group plc v Prestwich* (1996), not following contrary authority, but applying an unreported Court of Appeal decision). An employer cannot gain protection from competition *per se*. The Court of Appeal case which is contrary to *Prestwich* is *Hanover Insurance Brokers Ltd v Schapiro* (1994). The court held that a no-poaching clause did not protect a legitimate proprietary interest and therefore was unreasonable as seeking to prevent competition *per se*.

- A restraint is valid only if it is reasonable both between the parties and in the interests of the public. (As stated above, there is debate whether express terms are subject to an implied duty on employers not to exercise them unreasonably, but in respect of restraint clauses there is an inbuilt requirement of reasonableness.)

The burden of proof is on the employers, except in relation to the public interest, where it is on the party asserting that the covenant is unenforceable for this reason.

4.8.3   Secrets and connection

Trade secrets do not include:

- the employee's skill and knowledge;

- information which is publicly available; or

- knowledge of general methods of running businesses.

The epitome of confidential information is a well guarded secret formula. For customer connection to be protected, there must be recurring and influential contact. So there is a relevant connection between estate agent, a doctor, and (the courts have held, though in the modern era it is doubtful that they are correct) a milkman with the client or customer, but probably not with a second hand car salesperson.

4.8.4   Reasonable between the parties

'Reasonable between the parties' means that the clause must not give the employer more protection than is necessary. If six months is sufficient to protect a hairdressing establishment, two years will be too broad, and the clause will fail. Similarly, if an area 250 yards round a salon would protect a hairdressers in a suburb, a covenant covering the whole town is too expansive. Facts alter cases: a covenant for an indefinite period may be reasonable.

4.8.5 Public interest

The clause must also be reasonable in the interests of the public. Covenants concerning employees are unlikely to be struck down on this basis at present. The exceptional cases are covenants attached to pension schemes, though they can perhaps be explained on the basis that they were unreasonable between the parties (see *Wyatt v Kreglinger & Fernau* (1933): in a pension agreement, there was a clause that the ex-employee would lose the pension if he took a job in the wool trade. The Court of Appeal held that the term was void for being contrary to the public interest).

4.8.6 Examples

There are many cases, of which the following are illustrative.

- *Commercial Plastics Ltd v Vincent* (1965)

  A covenant for one year after employment was held invalid where: (a) there was no limit on area; and (b) the clause covered the whole of the PVC field and not just the nearest area in which the employee was a research worker.

- *Fitch v Dewes* (1921)

  A restraint on a solicitor's clerk that he would never work as a solicitor's clerk within seven miles of Tamworth Town Hall was held to be valid because the restricted area was so small.

The rule is that the duration and area are inversely proportional to each other: the wider the area, the shorter the duration, and the smaller the area, the longer the duration. Where the clause protects confidential information, it need not be limited to the UK, for information is not restricted by national boundaries (*Scully UK Ltd v Lee* (1998)).

4.8.7 Practical help

Since each case in this area is judged on its own facts, guidance is hard to give. One hint is this: think of the area and time which would protect the business and then halve it. Even then, employers may lose. In relation to trade secrets there need be no limit on the area or duration of the covenant. Another matter of guidance is that a non-solicitation clause ('do not approach my client') is more likely to be upheld than one which forbids an employee from working in a certain territory (an area covenant). An example is *Office Angels Ltd v Rainer-Thomas* (1991). A clause forbidding an employee from opening an employment agency within a certain area, which included most of the City of London, was void because the coverage was too wide, even though the limitation was only for six months. But a covenant preventing the former employee's soliciting or dealing with clients would have succeeded, and it would have given the employers the protection they desired.

4.8.8 Construction and severance

Employers have two more bullets in their gun with regard to express restraint covenants: construction and severance.

*   The clause may be read in such a way that it is valid, provided that the parties meant it to be read in that fashion. A good illustration is *Home Counties Dairies Ltd v Skilton* (1970). A milkman covenanted that he would not 'serve or sell milk or dairy products'. One might have thought that the clause was invalid because it went beyond protecting the employee's business: it would have stopped the employee from serving in a grocer's shop. The court, however, construed the clause to restrain only employment as a milkman, since that was the intention of the parties. 'Dairy products' was therefore construed restrictively, and the covenant was valid. The courts have wavered substantially over the past 30 years in their attitude towards construction. The present position is that the power to construe widely should not be used to render enforceable an otherwise unreasonable covenant (*JA Mont (UK) Ltd v Mills* (1993)). Whether a covenant can be construed to be valid is judged at the date when the clause was entered into.

*   If a clause can be construed as two promises and grammatically one of those clauses can be struck out, the remainder, if supported by consideration, will be upheld if valid by itself. If the provision cannot be severed, the ex-employee is free to do what the clause forbade, even though the intention of both parties was to stop him performing acts which would harm the employers, such as dealing with clients. The excision must not offend the public policy which is at the heart of the restraint of trade doctrine (*Marshall v NM Financial Management Ltd* (1995)). This case restates the law of severance. So, if a salesperson promises not to compete for six months after termination 'in Leeds or elsewhere in the UK', the phrase 'or elsewhere in the UK' can be cancelled out, leaving a grammatically correct phrase of a covenant not to compete 'in Leeds'. If that clause passes the tests for restraint of trade, it is enforceable. An example is *Business Seating (Renovations) Ltd v Broad* (1989). An employee was forbidden to solicit customers of 'the company or any associated company'. The court excised the words 'or any associated company', thereby rendering the clause valid.

If, however, the clause contains only one promise, it cannot be severed. For example, in *Attwood v Lamont* (1920), the Court of Appeal held that a covenant that an employee would not serve as 'a tailor, dressmaker, general draper, milliner, hatter or haberdasher' could not be severed so as to restrain the employee from serving only as a tailor. There was only one promise. The deletion of the unenforceable stipulation would have changed the character of the covenant. The principle is the same nowadays. Clauses will not be excised if doing so would affect the main substance of the covenant. Severance cannot be used to carve out valid areas or durations from undifferentiated, longer durations or wider areas. For example, an invalid clause covering the whole of Devon cannot be whittled down to create a valid term applying only to Exeter. Severance in England is often called severance by the 'blue pencil' test, and will be more readily applied if there are separate clauses containing covenants rather than one 'catch-all' clause. Severance will not be used to strike out clauses which seek the continued existence of a covenant after a wrongful dismissal.

4.8.9 Breach

The clause must cover the breach. A clause preventing a person from carrying on a competing business does not stop him from being an employee of that business (*WAC Ltd v Whillock* (1990), a Scottish case).

4.8.10 Effect of wrongful dismissal

If an employer dismisses wrongfully, that is, without giving the correct length of notice and there is no justification for so doing, he cannot rely on a restraint covenant. So held the House of Lords in *General Billposting Co Ltd v Atkinson* (1909). English courts continue to affirm this rule, for example, *Rex Stewart Jeffries Parker Ginsberg Ltd v Parker* (1988). In that case, the covenant continued to apply because the contract expressly provided for termination to be with notice or for wages to be paid in lieu of notice. A summary dismissal (with wages in lieu) was therefore not a wrongful dismissal since the contract itself allowed the employers not to give notice provided that they paid wages in lieu. There is some debate whether that rule can be got round by inserting words into the clause to the effect that it will apply despite a wrongful dismissal, for example, a phrase such as the covenant applies after a termination 'however caused'. There is, however, no trace of such a rule in *Atkinson*. In *Owen and Briggs v Oates* (1990), Scott J thought that employers could not evade the rule in this way. The Court of Session in Scotland in *Living Design (Home Improvements) Ltd v Davidson* (1994) held that a covenant designed to take effect on termination, whether lawful or not, 'is manifestly wholly unreasonable'. The court struck down a clause which purported to give it the power to excise invalid stipulations and modify the rest to validate the covenant. English courts now reject this view (*Rock Refrigeration Ltd v Jones* (1996)). Moreover, since the policy of English law is against such promises, there is no necessity for striving to uphold them by means of such a device.

For there to be a wrongful dismissal, there has to be a dismissal. One form of dismissal is repudiation (which, particularly in the statutory claims of unfair dismissal and redundancy payments, is known as constructive dismissal). Whether there is a repudiation depends on whether or not the employers have broken a term going to the root of the contract. The answer to the question whether a repudiation exists is not always clear. One might have expected that non-payment or only part payment of salary would constitute a breach of a fundamental term. In *Cantor Fitzgerald International v Callaghan* (1999), it was said, *obiter*, that excuses such as an accountancy error, the breakdown of the payroll computer and illness meant that there was no breach of condition. What the employers intended was more important than the amount of difference between the due salary and the sum paid. Repeated part payment, however, indicates that there was a breach of a fundamental term.

4.8.11 Effect of repudiation

No doubt the principle in *Atkinson* applies where the employee is forced to leave because of the employer's repudiation of the contract, for example, by not paying salary (see *Dairy Crest Ltd v Wise* (1994) for an illustration of such a repudiatory breach rendering the covenant unenforceable no matter how reasonable it would otherwise have been). The breach of a fundamental term has obliged the employee to quit, a situation which is known as 'constructive dismissal' in the context of statutory employment claims.

4.8.12 Fall-back position

Where the covenant is unenforceable, the employers may still be able to rely on the implied duty of confidentiality, considered at 4.9.25, below.

4.8.13 Final remedies

If the covenant is enforceable, employers can claim at full trial both damages to compensate for past loss (for example, the solicitation of clients) and an injunction to stop future activities in contravention of the clause. The injunction will not last longer than the period stipulated in the contract. Where no time is stipulated in the contract, the covenant is construed as one of indefinite duration. Normally such a period is considered to be too long to be reasonable but it may not be excessive where the clause protects a formula, such as that for Coca-Cola. While courts will not force an employee to work for an employer, they generally will stop him working for someone else, provided that there is a clause in the covenant which is both enforceable and expressed in negative terms (this is known as the rule in *Lumley v Wagner* (1852)). Accordingly, an employer can stop the employee's violating the covenant, which is a clause expressed negatively: 'Thou shalt not disclose or use trade secrets.'

4.8.14 Interlocutory injunction

The principal remedy is, however, a so called 'interlocutory' injunction. That is one which is granted pre-trial to uphold the *status quo* before the alleged breach until trial. Since most cases do not proceed to trial, and since it is fairly easy to obtain such an injunction, employers normally have little to fear at this stage. Basically, courts dealing with interlocutory proceedings are instructed not to investigate the merits in order to avoid a 'mini-trial'. The law on this point was laid down by the House of Lords in *American Cyanamid Co v Ethicon Ltd* (1975). The application of *American Cyanamid* to restraint clauses was confirmed by the Court of Appeal in *Lawrence David Ltd v Ashton* (1989). There is the possibility of an order for speedy trial. Despite the application of *American Cyanamid* to covenants, the Court of Appeal said in *Lansing Linde Ltd v Kerr* (1991) that first instance courts could investigate the enforceability of the clause at the interlocutory stage. The reasoning is that unless judges do so, the covenant will often expire before trial. Accordingly, if the grant or refusal of an interlocutory injunction would in effect dispose of the claim, the court should look at the merits of the case; otherwise the merits will not be considered at all.

Both the interlocutory and final injunctions are subject to equitable principles. One effect is that an injunction will not be granted to enforce a covenant applying during employment when the issue of one would be tantamount to ordering the employee back to work for the employers. See, also, 7.2.24, below. The old employers can gain an interlocutory injunction to prevent the company which the former employee has set up from fulfiling contracts they have gained (*PSM International Plc v Whitehouse* (1992)). The Court of Appeal, by granting the remedy, injured a third party. Therefore, it is irrelevant that the defendant has already entered into contracts with third parties just as it is irrelevant that the effect of the restraint doctrine is to prevent the defendant making contracts in the future.

An injunction will not be granted to enforce a garden leave clause unless the employers have a contractual right to prevent the employee coming into work and can do so without providing work (*William Hill Organisation Ltd v Tucker* (1998)).

4.8.15 Damages not often helpful

In relation both to express and implied terms, it is wise to remember that employees are likely to be 'men of straw', unable financially to pay damages, and that legal claims by either party to the employment contract may well exacerbate industrial relations. For these reasons, actions by employers against employees are rare. For an exceptional case, see *NCB v Galley* (1958), discussed at 4.9.35, below.

4.9   Implied terms

If there is no express term, an implied one *may* take its place. If, for instance, there is no express mobility clause, the courts may imply one.

4.9.1   Illustration

An illustration is *Stevenson v Teesside Bridge and Engineering Ltd* (1971), a decision of the Divisional Court. The employee, a steel erector, refused to transfer to another site from one which was near his home. There was no express mobility clause. The court held that, since it was part of the nature of his job, and since the contract mentioned travelling and subsistence allowances, there was an implied term of mobility. In *Courtaulds Northern Spinning Ltd v Sibson* (1988), an employee was held to be under an implied duty to move to another site because he had worked there previously. His disobedience to an order to work there was a breach of this implied mobility clause and this was a breach of contract. Therefore, he was not constructively dismissed. The court said that on the facts some term as to mobility had to be incorporated. Slade LJ stated that the term was 'one which the parties would probably have agreed if they were being reasonable, not one which the parties, if asked, would have agreed to before entering the contract'. Emphasis is nowadays less on the presumed intention of the parties and more on the objective necessity for an implied term. The width of the term was determined by the parties' practice – reasonable commuting distance. The second depot was within that range. It is not always clear when the courts and tribunals will imply a mobility or flexibility clause. Moreover, the Court of Appeal held that the employee could be moved anywhere within reasonable commuting distance on the ground that the parties as reasonable people would have to agree, but no doubt if asked, the employee would have rejected such a stipulation.

A contrasting case is *O'Brien v Associated Fire Alarms Ltd* (1969). An electrician who had worked exclusively in Liverpool was asked to transfer to Barrow when orders in Liverpool dropped. There was no express agreement about mobility, and the court held that, though there was to be an implied one, that implied agreement stretched only so far as the area of daily travel. Since Barrow was beyond that limit, the employee won. How much easier it would have been for the employers to have an express term! In *Stevenson*, there would have been no dispute; in *O'Brien*, had any dispute arisen, the employers would have won it.

4.9.2   Practical guidance

The fact remains, however, that many employers do not think about the terms of employment, and accordingly the conditions under which an employee works are relegated to implied terms. The implied term which arises may not be one which the employer wanted. It is therefore worthwhile thinking seriously about either expressly agreeing on the terms orally or, better still, in writing. That way, both sides know the nature of the obligations. For example, if employers do not wish to pay sick pay, it is worthwhile expressly saying so; otherwise the courts may say that the employers implicitly promised to pay sick pay. Moreover, the more the terms are expressed in writing, the less room there is for the courts to imply terms.

4.9.3   How implied

There are several ways of incorporating terms, many of which apply to all contracts. For example, the House of Lords in the non-employment case of *Liverpool CC v Irwin* (1976) was willing to imply a term on the ground that the parties simply overlooked putting an express term into their contract. It is insufficient to imply a term on the grounds that it is reasonable, the principal authority being *Reigate v Union Manufacturing Co (Ramsbottom) Ltd* (1918). This is a case from general contract law but it applies to employment law. Reasonableness is, however, determinative of the width of the implied term once the court or tribunal has decided that there should be such a term in the contract. In *Sibson* (1988), Slade LJ said that where a contract had to have a term (for example, as to place of work), 'the implied term is one which the parties would probably have agreed if they were being reasonable'. Express terms override the sort of implied terms considered in this section but not terms which are implied (or better put imposed) by statute. An implied term cannot overturn an express one.

There is on-going debate as to whether an express term, such as a mobility clause, can be qualified by an implied term that the express term will not be exercised unreasonably. A classic statement is that of Roskill LJ in *Nelson v BBC* (1977): 'It is a basic principle of contract law that if a contract makes express provision in almost unrestricted language, it is impossible in the same breath to imply into that contract a restriction of the kind that the tribunal sought to do,' namely, to restrict an express term that the employee was to work where the employers required by an implied term that he was only to work on the Caribbean Service. In *Sibson*, there was a limit placed on an implied mobility term but none on the exercise of managerial discretion to move the worker between depots. No implied restriction, even on an *implied* term, was possible.

This decision is hard to reconcile with *Prestwick Circuits Ltd v McAndrew* (1990), noted below. *United Bank v Akhtar* (1989) supports the view that an express term can be qualified by an implied one. An express term that the employers could transfer the employee was held to be subject to an implied term that they would not do so unreasonably. An employee was not contractually obliged to uproot himself in the space of one weekend, despite the width of the express term. Other cases have held that a term that an employee should make up till shortages was subject to the implied term that the term did not apply where the deficit was due to a third party's dishonesty and that an express term permitting demotion for a disciplinary offence had impliedly to be exercised reasonably.

Similar arguments have been put in relation to 'flexibility' clauses; that is, terms which permit employers to transfer employees to different jobs. In *McClory v Post Office* (1992) a contractual power to suspend was held not to be exerciseable unreasonably. The use of an express flexibility clause to reduce hours of work and, therefore, pay when pay is based on hours, will be a breach of the duty of trust and confidence if it is exercised irresponsibly. However, only if the conduct of the employers made the position of the employee intolerable was there a breach of the implied term. In *Johnstone v Bloomsbury Health Authority* (1991), a case in which junior doctors sought to restrict their hours of duty, a majority of the Court of Appeal seemed to say that if employers asked for 168 hours per week they could do so under the contract, subject to a vaguely formulated duty not to break the health and safety legislation. Arguably, it is further subject to the implied duty of mutual trust and confidence noted at 4.9.19, below. *Johnstone* is not a clear authority.

United Bank is irreconcilable with cases such as *Rank Xerox Ltd v Churchill* (1988), where the EAT held that, where a term was unambiguous, the literal phrasing could not be modified by an implied term that the employers would not exercise their powers unreasonably. The effect is that employers could send an employee anywhere covered in the mobility clause, say from London to Carlisle, at any time and without a second's notice. There was no implied restriction that the employers would send the employee to places within daily travelling distance. The EAT case of *White v Reflecting Roadstuds Ltd* (1991), attempts to cut through this impasse by arguing that *United Bank* really decided that the employers could not enforce an express term in such a way that the employee could not perform her part of the contract. Other cases have adopted this theory. Where there do not exist reasonable grounds for moving the employee (or, in other words, the move was capricious), an attempt to transfer him is a breach of a fundamental term of the contract, that of trust and confidence, entitling the employee to resign and claim unfair dismissal. The judge said that 'there is an overriding implied term as to the relationship of trust and respect between employer and employee ...'. It is uncertain whether he meant that all express terms were subject to this overriding duty. (On the facts, a contractually permitted transfer to other work was not a breach of a contractually implied condition that the power was to be exercised only in a reasonable way; an express term was not subject to any such implied term. If the move was capricious, then there would be a breach of the implied term.) This argument seems to go contrary to the Court of Appeal's decision in *Western Excavating (ECC) Ltd v Sharp* (1978), where it held that reasonableness was irrelevant to the presence of a breach of contract. Again, the debate can be sidetracked by the insertion of an express term. The conflict between the authorities on the issue whether an express term may be subject to an implied restriction remains unresolved.

Courts and tribunals have taken the view that implied terms can be subject to implied restrictions. For example, an implied mobility clause may be restricted by a second implied term, that it will be exercised only on the giving of reasonable notice (*Prestwick Circuits Ltd v McAndrews* (1990)).

4.9.4   Business efficacy

Business efficacy is perhaps better put as 'business common sense'. The term is so basic that it is needed to make the contract function. A key term is missing and must be included. This is known as the rule in *The Moorcock* (1889). For instance, it may be necessary to imply a term like the place of work on this basis. It should be noted, however, that business efficacy may well work in the employers' favour. If one asks whether an employee really would have agreed to a term whereby his employers could transfer him anywhere at any time, one is likely to get a dusty answer. An example of a term implied through the business efficacy mode is *Star Newspapers Ltd v Jordan* (1994), where the EAT held that the company breached an implied term by not reconsidering the applicant's amount of commission when it reduced her area. Similarly, in *Hallstones v Staffordshire CC* (1997), the Court of Appeal held that there was an implied right to appeal against a sanction because that was a 'businesslike' effect of the employers' disciplinary procedure.

4.9.5   Officious bystander

If an officious bystander put it to the parties that a certain term ought to be in the contract and the parties said, 'Oh, of course!', then that clause is implied. In this way a gap can be filled. The case always cited for this proposition is *Shirlaw v Southern Foundries (1926) Ltd* (1939). MacKinnon LJ sought to use this test to supersede that in *The Moorcock*, which, as he noted, was *extempore* and expressed in general terms. It was not meant to be a principle of law. A more recent illustration is *Ali v Christian Salvesen Food Services Ltd* (1995). Employees agreed to work annualised hours. After those hours (1,824) they were to receive overtime pay. They were dismissed before they had completed the 1,824 hours. The EAT held that there was an implied term that in that situation they would be paid for hours over 40 they had worked each week. There was an obvious gap in the agreement which had to be filled. The Court of Appeal reversed that decision (in *Ali v Christian Salvesen Food Services Ltd* (1997)) on the ground that the omission to legislate for every eventuality in a collective agreement did not mean that the gap had to be filled by an implied term, but the issue was too complicated or controversial for changes to the main points of agreement to be made. Accordingly, no term was to be implied. The case illustrates that gaps cannot always be filled by implied terms. Clear and unambiguous terms cannot be overridden by a term implied on this ground (*Bradford v York Truck Equipment Ltd* (1988)).

4.9.6　Status

The relationship of the parties may necessitate the implication of a term. A certain term may be a necessary incident of an employment relationship. This method is not based on any presumed intention of the parties. As Lord Bridge said in *Scally v Southern Health and Social Services Board* (1993), the search for a term which the law implies as a necessary incident of a definable category of contract is 'based on wider considerations' than business efficiency. Where it is essential that some term has to be included in the contract, for example, whether there is sick pay, the Court of Appeal was once willing to invent a term of reasonable width (*Mears v Safecar Security Ltd* (1983)), but that court has now ruled that it is no longer open to employment tribunals to 'invent' terms as a last resort in pursuance of their duty to determine the content of the written statement (*Eagland v British Telecommunications plc* (1993)). An employment tribunal could rule as to what was the true formulation of the contract but it could not rule on what an employee's contractual term ought to have said, even though employees in the same category of post as herself had that term in their contracts. Teachers, for example, are under a professional obligation to do marking. In *Sim v Rotherham MBC* (1986), Scott J held that a teacher was under a duty to cover for absent colleagues. He said that a professional was subject to the expectation of the public. As Keith Ewing commented in *The Right to Strike*, 1991, it was 'a truly remarkable development' that 'the legal obligations of employees can be set by the social expectations of third parties'.

4.9.7　Custom

A custom in a certain trade can be implied into the contract, provided that it is certain, general (also called notorious) and reasonable. Some work practices fit this rule. An illustration is *Sagar v Ridehalgh* (1931). The court accepted that it was part of the custom and practice of the Lancashire cotton industry that employers could deduct money from weavers' pay for bad workmanship. Compare *Hardwick v Leeds AHA* (1975): it was an unreasonable custom to dismiss after expiry of sick pay. 'Unreasonable' here means 'unfair'. It is thought that an employee is subject to custom even though he does not know of it (never mind accept it), but the legal position remains unclear. For example, an employment tribunal in *Samways v Swan Hunter Shipbuilders Ltd* (1975) noted that employers knew of the practice of changing back from chargehands to labourers (with a consequent loss of pay) but their knowledge was insufficient to convert what had happened before into a custom. The mere fact that they acquiesced in the arrangement did not signify that they had agreed to it, for a better explanation of their behaviour was that if they did not acquiesce, they would be dismissed. The mere fact too that a practice is common in an industry does not make it into a contractual term. In *Duke v Reliance Systems Ltd* (1996), the EAT held that a custom could be contractual only if it had been drawn to the employee's attention and it had been applied for a lengthy period. Therefore, a unilateral change of management policy will not, of itself, change an employee's contract. Custom will rarely be a source of a term nowadays, for express agreements between employers and unions or employers and employees will largely have superseded it.

4.9.8 Works rules

Some rules in company handbooks may be held to have contractual force, but not all will. For example, the introduction of an equal opportunity policy by means of a circular to prison officers was held to be contractually binding in *Secretary of State for Scotland v Taylor* (1997), and this point was not disputed before the Court of Session (1999), whereas the introduction of a no smoking policy may not be in breach of contract because the change may only be in the non-binding company rules (*Dryden v Greater Glasgow Health Board* (1992)). Similarly, in *Grant v South-West Trains Ltd* (1998), the High Court held that an equal opportunities policy was not incorporated into the plaintiff's contract of employment. Therefore, she could not get a travel pass for her same-sex partner. There was no contractual intention. Moreover, the contract itself referred to partners of the opposite sex. A contractual flexibility clause will, for example, allow changes to the tasks an employee does, and depending on its terms, the time when he does them. In *Crédit Suisse Asset Management v Armstrong* (1996), a covenant in restraint of trade contained in a staff handbook was binding because the handbook was a contractual document, it was stated to be such and it was addressed to people whom the Court of Appeal called 'men of experience and sophistication'. A 'work-to-rule', that is, in accordance with the handbook, does not necessarily mean that the work-to-rule is valid, contractually speaking. The question is whether the parties wanted the rules to be contractually binding. For example, a notice on a noticeboard about sick pay was held in one case to be binding, but a string of highly detailed rules about how to carry on the business of running a railway was held not to be binding. For a case in this area, see *Secretary of State for Employment v ASLEF (No 2)* (1972), 4.9.31, below. It is thought that works rules are less of a source of law now than previously because of the growth of formal written contracts encouraged by the law on written particulars.

4.9.9 Implied in law/fact

Obligations implied in law are those which derive from the relationship or status being one of employment. Some terms are so fundamental that they are implied into every contract of employment. They are not dependent on the parties' intentions but are imposed on them, unless expressly excluded. They can be called 'default rules'; that is, if there is no express term, these implied terms apply. The term 'default rules' occurs in the speech of Lord Steyn in *Malik v BCCI Ltd* (1997). Terms imposed on employers can be seen as the courts' striving to restrain the freedom of managers to do as they please. Although the law is not settled, it is possible that some of these implied terms may override express terms. They are characteristic of a contract of employment, which the parties are deemed to accept. Duties of employers are dealt with at 4.9.10–4.9.20, below. Duties of employees are dealt with at 4.9.21–4.9.32, below.

The list of implied terms, whether of fact or of law, is not closed. There is substantial scope for flexibility and, as a corollary, uncertainty. For example, in *WA Goold (Pearmak) Ltd v McConnell* (1995), the EAT held that employers were under a duty to provide their employees with a grievance procedure (and that this duty was a fundamental one, breach of which constituted constructive dismissal), and, on appeal from Northern Ireland, the House of Lords in *Scally v Southern Health and Social Services Board* (1992) held that employers who failed to bring the right to purchase additional years of pension entitlements to the attention of doctors were in breach of an implied term to take reasonable steps to bring the terms to their notice. The decision is apparently limited to situations where the employees do not know of these rights. It is, however, not easy to convince the judges that an implied term not previously used exists. Moreover, *Scally* can be seen as a judicial attempt to protect people's entitlement to pensions, which, as a result of the Maxwell affair, were under attack at that time. Accordingly, perhaps it cannot be read widely. The courts still say that the relationship between employers and employees is not one to which natural justice applies and that there is no term to that effect implied by law (*McClory v Post Office* (1992)). Similarly, there is no implied term that an employee who does not qualify for a remedy for unfair dismissal will impliedly be treated under contract as if he were so qualified (*Focsa Services (UK) Ltd v Birkett* (1996) EAT). Therefore, he is restricted to damages for wrongful dismissal.

4.9.10 Pay

While there may be highly exceptional cases where the employer is under no duty to pay wages, normally he is. If the amount is not fixed by the parties, the courts imply a term that the employee is to receive a reasonable amount (*quantum meruit*). In *Way v Latilla* (1937), the defendant promised to look after the employee's interests if he secured for him a goldmining concession. The Lords held that he was entitled to £5,000 on the *quantum meruit* basis. Sometimes the contract may give the employee only the chance to earn wages. Where pay is fixed by contract, there exists a duty to continue to pay it. A non-contractual change in the method of assessing pay is a breach of contract. In *RF*

Hill Ltd v Mooney (1981), a change from a commission on all sales to the payment of commission only when the employee exceeded the target was a breach of contract. This term is subject to express terms. For example, a clause may permit the employer to suspend the employee without pay as a sanction for ill discipline, and, indeed, suspension without pay may be an implied term in some factories and trades.

4.9.11 Industrial action

While the point is not entirely free from doubt, it seems that an employee who is performing part but not the whole of the contract is entitled to payment for what is done, provided that the employers accept the work which is being done. In *Royle v Trafford BC* (1984) a teacher who was taking part in industrial action refused to have more than 31 pupils in his class, though he had been allocated 36. It was held that he was entitled to 31/36ths of his pay. If, however, the employers do not accept the reduced work, the employee is entitled to nothing (*Miles v Wakefield MDC* (1987)). Equitable set-off for non-performance of duties is a possibility (see *Sim v Rotherham MBC*, above).

4.9.12 Sick pay

There is apparently a slight presumption that wages are payable during sickness but the court must look at all the facts (for example, at practice) to determine whether there is a term (*Mears v Safear Security Ltd*, above). In that case, the employers had never awarded sick pay and the employee had never asked for it. Therefore, on the facts there was no sick pay. (Note, also, statutory sick pay under the Social Security and Housing Benefits Act 1982 as amended.) In fact, some 80% of employees are covered by a company scheme.

4.9.13 Short-time working

As with sick pay the express or implied terms govern wages during short-time or lay-off, for example, there may be a custom. Without such suspension withholding pay amounts to a repudiation of the contract. Basically speaking, pieceworkers have a right to earn remuneration, as do commission workers. Therefore, without the employee's consent an employer *cannot* close down his works because of a lack of orders where employees are paid by the piece (*Devonald v Rosser* (1906)). It is immaterial that the employers cannot make a profit. However, the position is different where the closure is outside the control of the employer (*Browning v Crumlin Valley Collieries Ltd* (1926) – closure of pit for repairs (though it must be said that the repairs were foreseeable) – or if in the industry there is a custom that lay-offs without pay are permissible). Employers would be well advised to include an express term. If an employee's contract contains an express clause that he will not be paid when there is no work, then he is not entitled to pay if he is laid off during industrial action by colleagues. The express term overrides the implied one. Note, also, guarantee payments under the ERA 1996.

4.9.14 Work

Employers must provide work for those who need publicity in their jobs, for example, actors, and for those paid on commission or by piece rates. Indeed, there may be an express term to such effect.

4.9.15 No duty to provide

It may be that highly skilled employees such as computer programmers must be given work. This exception may in time swallow the rule, and it has been said judicially that more employees than previously are owed a duty to provide work. This consideration has been treated as important in a case dealing with the lawfulness of 'garden leaves', that is, lengthy notice periods which the employers do not require employees to work out, the workers spending the time 'in the garden'. The preservation of a financial director's skill was a relevant factor in holding that he could move to a competing firm before the end of his garden leave (*Provident Financial Group plc v Hayward* (1989)). An injunction to enforce a garden leave will be restricted to the duration which a covenant in restraint of trade would have had (*William Hill Organisation Ltd v Tucker* (1998)). Otherwise, there is no duty to provide work. In the famous words of Asquith J in *Collier v Sunday Referee Publishing Co Ltd* (1940): 'Provided I pay my cook her wages regularly, she cannot complain if I choose to take any or all of my meals out.' Perhaps nowadays, however, chefs are such publicity seekers that we have to put them with other artistes such as actors. Failure to give work may amount to redundancy and may activate guarantee payments (both in the ERA 1996). In a series of cases, Lord Denning MR stated that there was a duty to provide work, but these rulings, such as *Langston v AUEW* (1974), seem to be part of his campaign against unions. They have not been followed since he retired.

4.9.16 Safety

In *Wilsons & Clyde Coal Co Ltd v English* (1938), the House of Lords laid down a threefold duty on employers. They must take reasonable care to provide safe equipment, a safe workplace, and safe fellow employees. So the employer can sack dangerous practical jokers. The duty to provide a safe system of work is non-delegable. If an employee is loaned out to a third party and is injured, the employers who loaned him out remain under a duty to exercise reasonable care; if they breach this duty, they are liable even though the employee is working for others at the time. There is, however, no implied term that employers will provide or give advice on insurance for workers they send abroad, even where the foreign country has no law permitting drivers to sue in negligence for road accidents and even when it is virtually impossible to find out the existence or non-existence of such a law. The Court of Appeal reached this conclusion in *Reid v Rush & Tompkins Group plc* (1989) by looking at the express terms. All kinds of terms, such as medical expenses, were in the contract, but there was no reference to insurance. Therefore, the alleged implied term did not exist. The case of *Johnstone* (see 4.9.3, above) has *dicta* from Stuart-Smith LJ that employers could not order employees to harm their health and safety, no matter what the express term said. If he is correct (and the majority did not agree), this implied duty overrides express contract clauses contrary to the classic concept of contract law. In *Walker v Northumberland CC* (1995), the High Court held that employers were under a duty not to cause psychiatric harm to an employee by overloading him with work. There is also a duty to warn cleaners of the dermatitis-causing effect of some cleaning agents.

4.9.17 Property

The employer is, however, under no duty to take care of the employee's goods (*Deyong v Shenburn* (1946)). Note, also, the Health and Safety at Work Act 1974 and the Employers' Liability (Defective Equipment) Act 1969.

4.9.18 Indemnity

An employer is under a duty to indemnify the employee for expenses necessarily incurred in the course of employment. This will cover, for example, defending legal proceedings for breaches committed by the employee.

4.9.19 Mutual trust

While the width of the duty of mutual trust and confidence (or respect) varies from job to job and some criticism by management must be expected in all jobs, since the 1970s there has developed a duty on employers to treat their employees with respect. They must protect employees against sexual harassment (*Bracebridge Engineering Ltd v Darby* (1990)). A series of events involving sexual innuendo amounts to a breach of the duty of trust and confidence (*Reed v Stedman* (1999)). Employers must not attempt unilaterally to reduce an employee's status or pay (*Arden v Bradley* (1994)). They must not criticise employees in front of their peers (the case best remembered by students is *Isle of Wight Tourist Board v Coombes* (1976), where the EAT held that a director's statement to an employee that his personal secretary was 'an intolerable bitch on a Monday morning' was conduct which breached the duty of trust and confidence, entitling her to resign) and they should not swear at a domestic gardener (*Wilson v Racher* (1974)).

The cases demonstrate the dynamic nature of implied terms. Thirty years ago there was no such term, and, for example, a failure to prevent what is now called sexual harassment would not have been in breach of any implied term. Lord Steyn, in *Malik v Bank of Credit and Commerce International* (1997), thought that the development of the term was 'sound'. The duty of trust and confidence can be seen as a hallmark of the employment relationship. The term was summarised by the EAT in *Woods v WM Car Services (Peterborough) Ltd* (1981): employers must 'not without reasonable and proper cause, conduct themselves in a manner calculated or likely to destroy or seriously damage the relationship of confidence or trust ... '. There is no need to show that the employers intended to get rid of the employee.

4.9.20 Death/injury

One point to bear in mind is that employers cannot contract out of or restrict liability to employees for death or serious injury (Unfair Contract Terms Act 1977).

4.9.21 Obedience

Employees are also subject to implied terms. An employee must obey lawful orders. The duty to obey a lawful and reasonable order has been said to be 'a condition essential to the contract of service' (*Laws v London Chronicle (Indicator Newspapers) Ltd* (1959)). What is lawful depends on the contract. Recall *O'Brien v Associated Fire Alarms Ltd*. The employer could not transfer the employee from Liverpool to Barrow. Therefore the order was not lawful and the employee need not have obeyed it. However, a disagreement over policy or the implementation of policy does not justify a refusal to obey an order.

4.9.22 Illegality

Moreover, the employer must not order something illegal, for example, falsify accounts (*Morrish v Henlys (Folkestone) Ltd* (1973)), and must not command an employee to go into immediate danger: in *Ottoman Bank v Chakarian* (1930), it was unlawful to order the employee to go to Turkey where he was under sentence of death. The Privy Council held that the danger by disease or violence must be 'immediately threatening'.

4.9.23 Duty to adapt

An example of a successful order is *Cresswell v Board of Inland Revenue* (1984): an order to work computers in PAYE administration was upheld because it was within the scope of the employee's duties that he would use new methods in doing his job. New methods of work fit under this head. The judge said that employers must provide training when the skills to be acquired were esoteric ones. It is interesting to see *Cresswell* in the context of classical contract law. At the time when the contracts of employment were made, computerisation could not be foreseen; nevertheless the employers were, by virtue of the implied term, provided with the power to order the employees to do the work in that unforeseen manner.

4.9.24 Care

Like employers, employees are under a duty to use reasonable care, for example, not to drive so carelessly that one knocks someone down. The principal authority is the well known House of Lords case of *Lister v Romford Ice and Cold Storage Co Ltd* (1957). An employee was held to be in breach of his implied contractual duty to take care of his fellow workers when he negligently ran down a colleague (who, as every tort student knows, was his father). And an employee is under an implied duty to be reasonably competent in the job.

4.9.25 Fidelity

The employee's duty of fidelity or faithful service takes several forms:

- not to take bribes;

- not to put his hand in the till;

- not to use his position to make a secret profit;

- not to keep secret the misconduct of colleagues even if by doing so the employee has to reveal his own wrongdoing;

- not to harm the employer's business by working in his spare time for a competing business;

- not to solicit customers before employment ends;

- not to tender for a contract which the employers were performing;

- not to use or disclose trade secrets, for example, formulae or blueprints. This duty terminates when the information enters the public domain, as occurred in *AG v Blake* (1996), provided the employee himself has not released the information.

An employee must not copy out a list of customers if the list is secret. There is no requirement that the employers stress to the employees that the relevant matter is confidential. The employee can, however, make preparations to enter into competition during employment to take effect after employment. What is acceptable and what is not is difficult to state in advance. Two examples of illegitimate preparation are *Marshall v Industrial Systems & Control Ltd* (1992), where the managing director had contacted clients and had taken fellow employees with him, and *Adamson v B & L Cleaning Services Ltd* (1995), where the applicant had put in a bid for a contract which his employers were performing while employed as their foreman. For a full analysis of the duty of faithful service, see Jefferson, M, *Restraint of Trade*, 1996.

While the vast majority of cases involve employees who have allegedly used or disclosed information, the term also applies to employers. For example, employers must not disclose the names and addresses of their employees to a local authority which is seeking to enforce a tax.

4.9.26 *Faccenda Chicken*

It is the duty concerning trade secrets which causes most difficulty. The law is now laid down in the wonderfully named case of *Faccenda Chicken Ltd v Fowler* (1987). This important case held that after employment ended the employer was entitled to protect only such legitimate interests as may be safeguarded by a covenant in restraint of trade: trade secrets (and highly confidential information) and customer connections. What is confidential varies from case to case. The employee's skill, and knowledge such as information concerning the amount of discount his former employers gave customers, was not covered: for protection against these there had to be an express covenant. The duty of confidentiality after employment does not extend to the recall (as opposed to the memorisation) of information.

4.9.27 Memory rule

The duty will apply not only where, for example, the employee has taken a written list of customers, but also where he has memorised a list. It may sometimes be difficult to prove that an employee memorised a list rather than just recalled it. This will be the case where there is only a small number of clients. It will be easier to prove that the employee memorised a document when, for example, it comprised coefficients.

4.9.28 Just cause or excuse

The duty, however, is subject to an exception, that of public interest or just cause or excuse. An interesting case is *Initial Services Ltd v Putterill* (1968). Employers had established a cartel to keep up prices. They blamed a new Government tax for keeping prices high. It was held that an employee was justified in revealing the companies' misdeeds to the press. The information must be disclosed to the appropriate body. In this case the press was appropriate. In other cases it may be appropriate to disclose it only to the police. There have been attempts in recent years in Private Members' Bills (which were in part based on the work of the Law Commission (see Report No 110, *Breach of Confidence*, 1981, Cmnd 8388)) to codify this defence but without success.

4.9.29 Remedy

If an employee has misappropriated a trade secret and disclosed it to a competitor, the employer has a whole battery of remedies available: damages against the employee and an injunction to stop further revelations; an injunction against the competitor; perhaps damages or perhaps account of profits; and delivery up for destruction of goods made with the confidential information. An example is *Camelot v Centaur Communications Ltd* (1998). The Court of Appeal ordered the defendants to return documents to the operators of the National Lottery so that the plaintiffs could discover which employee had disclosed them to the defendants. The disclosure was in breach of the duty of confidentiality.

4.9.30 Patent and copyright

For patents, see ss 39–40 of the Patents Act 1977. Copyright normally belongs to the employer. The Patents Act 1977 overrides any contrary agreement, whereas the provision on copyright may be overridden by agreement.

4.9.31 Co-operation

> I have no hesitation in implying a term into the contract of service that each employee will not, in obeying his lawful instructions, seek to obey them in a wholly unreasonable way which has the effect of disrupting the system, the efficient running of which he is employed to secure.

So said Roskill LJ (now Lord Roskill) in *Secretary of State for Employment v ASLEF (No 2)* (1972). On the facts, a work-to-rule was in breach of contract because it impeded the running of the employer's business. A more recent case is *Ticehurst v British Telecommunications plc* (1992), where a withdrawal of goodwill by a manager (who was also a union officer) was held to be in breach of her duty as manager to advance the interests of her employers. It did not matter that she was not acting wrongfully or negligently. It may be that *Ticehurst* represents a withdrawal by the judiciary. The court emphasised the position of the employee in the hierarchy, whereas in *ASLEF (No 2)* the Court of Appeal said that every contract of employment included a duty to co-operate. It must be said, however, that the court in *Ticehurst* phrased the duty as applying to employees who by the use of their discretion can disrupt the employers' business. It may be that, after *Ticehurst*, this implied duty is restricted to workers who have a good deal of discretion in what they do. The duty of co-operation gives free range to managerial discretion. Under the Health and Safety at Work Act 1974, there is a duty on employees to co-operate in the execution of duties under that statute (s 7).

4.9.32 Example

It is helpful to give an illustration of how the courts imply a term. In *Cole v Midland Display Ltd* (1973), Mr Cole was a manager hired on a 'staff' basis. He refused to do overtime without pay and was dismissed. It was held that:

- being a member of staff meant that he was paid whether there was work to do or not; and

- he was required to work reasonable overtime without pay.

My own employers seem to rely on reasonable overtime without pay a lot!

4.9.33 Reference

In *Lawton v BOC Transhield* (1987), it was held that there is no implied duty to supply a reference. Employers who supply references should be careful in so doing for otherwise they may now be liable in tort for negligent misstatement (*Spring v Guardian Assurance plc* (1995)). There is also the possibility of the tort of deceit. Lord Woolf in *Spring* said that, in appropriate circumstances, the courts would impose a duty on employers to look after their employees' 'economic well-being'. Reference was also made to *Scally* (see 4.9.9, above). In the light of this dictum, cases like *Reid v Rush & Tompkins Group plc* (4.9.16, above) and *Deyong v Shenburn* (4.9.17, above) require reappraisal.

4.9.34 Contractual effect

Express and implied terms may be conditions, warranties or innominate terms, depending on their importance. For example, in *Laws v London Chronicle (Indicator Newspapers) Ltd* (1959) (see 4.9.21, above), Lord Evershed MR said that the duty to obey was a fundamental aspect of the employment relationship.

4.9.35 Collective agreements

These are arrangements between managements and trade unions. Normally, they are not legally binding, that is, they are not contracts between those parties (but this presumption can be rebutted by an express term, as had occurred at times when foreign firms have established factories in the UK): the common law authority is *Ford Motor Co Ltd v AUEFW* (1969). Nevertheless they may be incorporated into the contract of employment and so be binding between employers and employees. Incorporation may be express or implied. The topic is dealt with after implied terms because only by knowing those methods can the reader understand the law. Even if the agreement says that it is binding in honour only it may still be contractually binding between employers and employees. Collective agreements are often made by laypersons. They are construed in the light of the matrix of the facts which gave rise to them and, as far as possible, a literal interpretation will not be used where to do so would lead to absurdity.

4.9.36 Ways of incorporation

There are several ways of incorporating terms. One is by express reference. A good illustration is *NCB v Galley* (1958). The defendant employee refused to work on Sundays. However, a term was incorporated from the collective agreement that he was to work 'as may reasonably be required', a phrase which covered working on Sundays. This contract referred to the collective agreement, which had become binding on him. The employee need not know of the collective agreement. Collective agreements may be incorporated by an express reference in the contract of employment to them 'as varied from time to time'. The parties to the contract will then be bound by the agreement in force at the time of the dispute.

4.9.37 Suitability

Not all terms are appropriate for incorporation into an individual's contract. There is no set test for determining which clauses are appropriate for incorporation and which are not, but in most cases the distinction is easy to draw. A case in point is *NCB v NUM* (1986): an agreement between these two parties to establish negotiation and conciliation procedures was not intended to take effect between the employer and the individual employees. In general, matters of policy will not be incorporated. In *Griffiths v Buckinghamshire CC* (1994), the High Court held that redundancy procedures including discussions with unions were not apt for incorporation. The agreement was not contractual in nature. As the court pointed out, if the clause alleged to be contractual is embedded among clauses which are mainly procedural, the likelihood is that it too is non-contractual. In *British Leyland UK Ltd v McQuilken* (1978), a collective agreement on retraining was not apt for incorporation. An example of a clause which was suitable for incorporation was one stating that the employers and the union would give each other notice of the termination of a bonus scheme (*Airlie v City of Edinburgh DC* (1996)). The distinction between those clauses apt for incorporation and others is not always clear-cut, but the principle is that purely collective matters such as recognition of the union are not suitable matters for incorporating into an individual's contract.

4.9.38 'No-strike' clauses

There is a special process for incorporating 'no-strike' agreements formerly found in s 18(4) of the Trade Union and Labour Relations Act 1974, now s 180 of the Trade Union and Labour Relations (Consolidation) Act 1992:

- it must state that there is a no-strike clause;

- it must be reasonably accessible to each employee during working hours at each workplace;

- the union must be independent;

- the contract must impliedly or expressly incorporate the no-strike clause.

In fact breach of a no-strike clause has little legal effect. Industrial action is, it seems, always a breach of contract anyway. The superadded breach of the clause does not increase damages for breach of contract. Moreover, statute forbids the courts to order strikers to return to work. The existence of a no-strike clause does not affect this prohibition.

4.9.39 As implied term

A collective agreement may also be impliedly binding on the grounds mentioned above, for example, under the officious bystander test: 'Are you employed on union rates?' 'Are you entitled to the wage increase the union has negotiated?' 'Oh, of course!' It may possibly be in small workplaces (as was the case when a union negotiated a redundancy package on behalf of a group of pilots) that the employee is bound by the doctrine of agency, but normally the device of agency will be inapplicable: staff turnover means that the principals are not identifiable at the time of the agency. Difficulties would also be encountered if a principal, a member, withdrew his or her authority for the union to act as agent. It was said in *Joel v Cammell Laird* (1969) that a member is bound only when he knows of the agreement and accepts it and there is evidence of incorporation.

4.9.40 National/local level

If a national collective agreement conflicts with a local one, it will be a question of fact as to which prevails and is incorporated. A case mentioned already, *Gascol Conversions v Mercer*, illustrates the proposition. The national agreement stated that the employee worked a 40 hour week; the local one said that he worked 54 hours. The employers gave him a written statement saying that he was bound by the national agreement and he signed it as being his new contract. As we have seen, the Court of Appeal held that he was bound by the national agreement because he had expressly agreed to it. No doubt normally, however, it will be the local agreement which will be binding because that agreement will be one which adds to the national one to adapt it to local conditions. It is worthwhile saying which agreement is the governing one. Because of the decline in national bargaining and the rise in negotiation at company or plant level, the difficulty occurs less in practice than might be thought.

4.9.41 Binding nature

If the clause in the collective agreement is incorporated, it will remain binding between the employer and the employee even though it has been terminated between employer and union. In *Robertson v British Gas Corp* (1983), the employers repudiated the agreement with the union. It continued, however, to be binding on them and their employees. Therefore, they were in breach of contract for failing to pay incentive bonuses. That term had become incorporated into the individual contracts of each employee. There is House of Lords' authority to similar effect (*Rigby v Ferodo Ltd* (1988)). A more recent case is *Edinburgh CC v Brown* (1999). Under an agreement made between the council and union representatives, successful applicants for regrading had their upgrading backdated to the date of application. This agreement was incorporated into contracts of employment. The council attempted unilaterally to vary this agreement by not making the pay increase retrospective. The EAT held that the attempted variation was unlawful and that, therefore, there was an unlawful deduction of wages. The outcome is the same if it is the union which withdraws from the agreement. The same applies the other way. Once bound by the contract as incorporated from the collective agreement, an employee cannot unilaterally withdraw and say that he is no longer bound. Of course, the contract of employment can be terminated by lawful notice. Employees may have to 'agree' to a change or face the sack.

4.9.42 Non-union members

The position with regard to non-unionists is not settled. If the contract refers expressly to the collective agreement, the non-union member is bound, but it seems that he is not bound where there is no express incorporation. So, if employers negotiate a change in the shift system with the union, that will not bind the non-member (*Singh v British Steel Corp* (1974)). The employers will have to reach a separate agreement with that person. The same principle applies where the employee is a member of a union but not of the union which negotiated the change in working practice (such as a reduction in the hours worked) (*Miller v Hamworthy Engineering Ltd* (1986)). The court may, however, say that among the terms incorporated into the individual contract is one whereby the parties agree to be bound to the collective agreement as varied from time to time. So the non-union member must also take the rough with the smooth. Similarly, employers who were part of a federation which negotiated an agreement remain bound until renegotiation, if they knew of the collective agreement.

4.9.43 Statute

Parliament's method of making women's pay equal to that of men is through the so called 'equality clause', if her work is so like that of the man that there are no practical differences, or her work has been rated as equivalent to that of the man, or the work of the woman and the man are of equal value to the employer. The women and men must be in the same employment.

4.9.44 Equality clause

The woman's contract is deemed to include an equality clause to the effect that any clause in her contract which is less favourable than a similar one in the man's agreement is treated as being no less favourable than the man's term, or if she does not have a term in her contract which the man has, her contract is deemed to include it. This law is stated in the EPA 1970, which is the subject of the next chapter.

4.9.45 'Imposed' terms

It might be better to call terms implied by statute 'terms imposed by law'. Even had the parties thought about the matter, they may not wish to have an equality clause; such a provision is not really an implied term. Moreover, even if the parties put expressly into the contract a clause which is contrary to the statutorily imposed one, that clause is overridden by the statute. This overriding is contrary to the usual rule that express terms prevail over implied ones. For instance, if the employer seeks to avoid the employee's rights under the ERA 1996, such a term is of no effect. In the jargon of employment lawyers, there is a 'floor of rights' for employees which the parties cannot contract out of. (As always with law there are exceptions, for example, an employee can contract out of a claim for unfair dismissal, provided that he does so in writing, the contract is for a fixed term of one year or more, and the contract is terminated by expiry of that fixed term.) Similarly, there can be no evasion of EC law by contract. An agreement, for example, to work beyond the times stipulated in the Working Time Directive is void.

4.9.46 Length of notice

Another way in which statute has intervened in the area of express/implied terms to protect an employee is in the length of notice he must give. The rules are, basically, if there is a period stated in the contract that will apply unless it is less than the statutory period. If there is no express notice period, there will be implied a period of reasonable length: what is reasonable depends on the facts of the case; if the reasonable length is less than the statute stipulates, the statutory period will take effect. The statutory period is one week for each year of service over two years up to a maximum of 12 years. It should be noted that the statutory minimum period for employees to give to employers is only one week, but this may be increased by agreement. An employee may waive the notice requirement and accept pay in lieu.

4.9.47 Dynamism

The subject of implied terms is sometimes presented in contract textbooks as being static. In fact, the topic is dynamic. A recent illustration is *Waltons and Morse v Dorrington* (1997): there is an implied term that employers will monitor workplaces in order to provide an environment reasonably conducive to employees' performing their contractual duties. This duty may entail preventing employees smoking. This case may lead to an implied term that the employers will not permit bullying or discrimination.

The mechanism of implying terms is one of the ways in which courts and tribunals can affect the content of the employment relationship. They may use it to favour employers. In *Secretary of State for Employment v ASLEF (No 2)*, the Court of Appeal held that employees were under a contractual duty not to disrupt their employers' business, even though what they were doing was fully in accord with the instructions of management. However, in a series of cases in the late 1970s and early 1980s, the EAT held that employers were under an obligation to treat their workers with respect. If they did not do so they were in breach of a fundamental implied term. That breach constituted a constructive dismissal; therefore, for the purposes of statutory employment rights, the employees had been dismissed. Therefore, they had a claim. With the growth of standard implied terms as an incident of the employment relationship and of terms statutorily imposed, the contract of employment is looking less like a contract and more like a status.

4.10 Variation

Employers are not permitted to alter contractual terms unilaterally, unless the clause allows such a change. A mobility clause, which was noted at 4.7.2, above, is an example of such a clause. This section discusses how employers can vary contracts where there is no flexibility under the contract at issue.

4.10.1 Contractual nature

The contractual nature of the service agreement is further illustrated by the need for a bilateral alteration of the terms for the parties to vary the contract. An important case is *Rigby v Ferodo Ltd* (1988). Employers sought to impose a wage cut unilaterally. The pay was contained in a collective agreement which was incorporated into the employee's contract. The House of Lords held that the employee was entitled to the difference between the pay he received after the cut and that to which he was due under his contract. Although the employers had repudiated the contract, the employees did not accept that repudiation and they continued working. Therefore, the contract was not terminated. The breach of contract continues until the employers retrieve the status quo. On the facts the amount of damages for wages lost by the pay cut continued to accumulate: the sum was not restricted to the period of notice the employers could have given.

Similarly, in one of the 'dinner lady' cases, *Burdett-Coutts v Hertfordshire CC* (1984), the employers reduced pay in a one-sided (as Mrs Thatcher would say) way. The Divisional Court held that the employees were entitled to the pay agreed by the parties. A proposal to vary unilaterally an employee's hours of work coupled with a proposal to give her notice that her contract would be terminated unless she consented was held to be an anticipatory breach in *Greenway Harrison Ltd v Wiles* (1994). In *Miller v Hamworthy Engineering Ltd* (1986), the Court of Appeal awarded an employee his full wages when he was unilaterally put on to short-time working by his employers. One way for employers to sidestep the rule as to acceptance is to insert a wide express term into the contract of employment, permitting them to do anything with regard to the employee's wages, place of work, job specification, and so on. It should be noted that even though the employers have broken the contract by varying the contract unilaterally, that does not mean that the employers will lose an unfair dismissal claim. They may have acted reasonably despite the breach. This point is of importance in the light of the dynamic nature of the contract of employment. For example, giving an employee extra responsibility may be a breach but dismissal for refusing to accept the burden may be fair because the employers have reasonably dismissed the employee for a substantial reason.

4.10.2 Protest

If an employee works under the unilaterally imposed conditions, after a time he will be deemed to have accepted them. Periodical protest is needed to preserve the pre-imposition terms. A case which at first sight is difficult to reconcile with this rule is *Jones v Associated Tunnelling Co Ltd* (1981). An employee was given a revised written statement. A clause purported to give his employers the power to move him from his place of work. He did not protest. They, four years later, tried to move him. He refused. The EAT held that he was entitled to refuse. His lack of protest was put down to the fact that the new clause did not affect him at the time when it was imposed. The position would have been different had the change had immediate effect, as a reduction in pay would have done. It has been held that a claim for unfair dismissal is not lost when the employee works under a new contract but objects to the change and says that he is working under the new contract without prejudice (*Hogg v Dover College* (1990)).

4.10.3 Dismiss

One contractual way for employers to obtain a variation is to dismiss employees lawfully (by applying the relevant notice period) and then re-employ them on new, revised contracts. There may be liability here for statutory unfair dismissal but none for contractual wrongful dismissal, for the contract has been lawfully terminated. It seems that the words of dismissal, whether verbal or in writing, must be unequivocal; otherwise what looks like a lawful termination with an offer to re-employ will be read as an unlawful unilateral variation.

4.11 Payment of wages

Normally, wages are agreed by the employers and employees, sometimes in a collective agreement. One area where the law intervenes is in relation to equal pay for men and women, which is discussed in the next chapter. This section deals with three issues in the law relating to wages: the legality of deductions, the former support for wages in various industries in the form of wages councils, and the national minimum wage.

4.11.1 Wages Act 1986

The Wages Act 1986, which replaced the Truck Acts and is now part of the ERA 1996, deals with, among other matters, unlawful deductions from wages. A deduction covers refusal to pay and simple non-payment as well as a deduction. A deduction not authorised by the Act is unlawful. An example is a reduction in wages made non-contractually and without the employee's assent. A cut of 10% from all wages is an unauthorised deduction. Therefore, the withdrawal of increased overtime rates to nightworkers is an unlawful deduction (*Bruce v Wiggins Teape (Stationery) Ltd* (1994) (EAT)). The same applies to non-contractual commission. All workers, including the self-employed who do the work personally, but not those in charge of their own business or members of a profession, are covered, except merchant seamen and those ordinarily working outside Great Britain. An agency nurse is a worker for this purpose. The Act applies to the Crown, but those serving in the armed forces are excluded. There are no longer restrictions on the ways in which wages may be paid. This rule is designed to facilitate cashless pay, such as by cheque or by transfer into a bank account.

'Wages' includes money paid by employers in respect of employment. Commission, holiday pay, bonuses, sums payable under an order for re-employment, statutory sick pay and statutory maternity pay are included. Discretionary bonuses and *ex gratia* payments are included within the definition of 'any sums payable ... in connection with ... employment', since the sums need not be paid under the contract. If they are normally paid (in other words, they would only not be paid in exceptional circumstances), they constitute wages. Excluded are payments in kind, such as accommodation; luncheon vouchers, however, are 'wages'.

4.11.2 Deductions

The exceptions are:

- deductions authorised by statute such as tax and national insurance;

- deductions notified in writing to the employee personally (a notice pinned to a wall is not enough), for example, trade union dues, repayment of a loan for a season ticket and payments to charity (though the fact that the employers have given a loan to the employee does not mean that he has agreed to any deduction from wages); and

- deductions authorised by contract, such as occupational pension contributions.

A deduction includes total non-payment and one which is the subject of a legal dispute. For instance, if an employee by contract is not to receive holiday pay if he is dismissed for gross misconduct, a refusal to pay the sum is a deduction where there is a dispute as to whether the employee's behaviour constituted gross misconduct. It is for the tribunal to determine this issue. If it decides that the conduct was not gross, there has been an improper deduction. Computing errors do not constitute deductions, but a decision not to make a payment because the employers believe wrongly that the contract permits them to do so is not an 'error of computation' which is disregarded. Here the dispute was as to whether a sum of money was properly payable.

With regard to the third exception, which largely covers deductions ('fines') for loss of stock and breakages, the Wages Act 1986 and the ERA 1996 lay down complex rules to protect those in retail employment, including shop assistants, insurance agents and bus drivers who collect fares. No deduction may exceed 10% of the gross wages on any one pay day in relation to retail workers. Employers must therefore wait to recover the whole loss. In respect of stock losses, deductions must be made within 12 months of the date when the loss was uncovered or ought reasonably to have been discovered. The employer must tell the worker in writing of his or her total debt and must make a demand in writing for payment on or before the date of the first deduction. If the worker leaves employment, the restriction to 10% is abrogated. It should be noted, however, that the Acts do not limit in any way the occasions on which pay may be deducted. For example, a deduction can still be made even though it was not the employee's conduct which led to the loss. The Acts govern only the *amount* of deduction.

4.11.3 Exceptions

Exceptions to the legislation are these: overpayment of wages or expenses (such as car allowances); deductions in respect of a strike or other industrial action; and payment of a court or tribunal order requiring an employee to pay something to his or her employers. In these instances deductions are lawful even if they would otherwise break the ERA 1996. (It may be, however, that the deductions are unlawful on other grounds.) If there is a dispute as to whether money was lawfully deducted in respect of a strike, this dispute must first be settled in the ordinary courts (*Sunderland Polytechnic v Evans* (1993)). The same rule applies to disputes about overpayments.

4.11.4 Enforcement and criticism

Enforcement lies in the hands of the wages inspectorate, but a worker may bring a claim before an employment tribunal for compensation or repayment. There is no limit on the amount claimed. Holiday leave accrued during garden leave is pay, even though the employee is not doing any work for the employers. Payment in lieu of wages (except when the employers lawfully terminate the contract but do not require the employee to work out the notice period) does not constitute 'wages'. Therefore, non-payment cannot be dealt with by the tribunal (*Delaney v Staples* (1992)). The proper forum is the county court or High Court. There is nowadays, however, a power in the tribunals to hear these cases under the Employment Tribunals (Extension of Jurisdiction) Order 1994 (SI 1994/1623), provided the contract has been terminated.

A point to bear in mind is that the ERA 1996 applies only to the amount of money to be deducted. It does not affect the grounds on which money is to be deducted. Employers may deduct money for reasons which to many are not fair. For instance, it is not unlawful to have a term in the contract of employment that an employee will make up losses at a petrol station even if such a deficit is not the fault of the employee, as when a customer has acted fraudulently by passing a dud cheque. The law on the deduction of wages is in truth procedural. It does not affect the substance. If the claim is non-payment of wages the civil courts have jurisdiction.

It should be noted that there is no financial limit to a claim for the unlawful deduction of wages, that the employers cannot counterclaim (compare the concurrent jurisdiction of employment tribunals over claims for up to £25,000 on termination of the contract), and that a claim can be brought while the employee is still working for the defendant employers (compare unfair dismissal).

4.11.5 Wages councils

From 1909 to August 1993 there existed wages councils which established minimum rates of pay in various low paid industries such as hairdressing. The then Government considered that they interfered with the free market and finally abolished them in the Trade Union Reform and Employment Rights Act 1993. At that time, the minimum ranged between £2.66 and £3.20 per hour. The Trades Union Congress has complained to the Social Affairs Directorate of the Commission that the Government had infringed Art 119 (now Art 141) of the EC Treaty, in that one of the 'effective means' of achieving equal pay had been abrogated. The Yorkshire Low Pay Unit reported in 1994 that pay in former wages councils' trades was being cut and there was no corresponding increase in jobs. The Agricultural Wages Board continues in existence. A study by the London School of Economics found that the effect of this Board was to increase, not destroy, jobs. It covers some 200,000 workers. The Government consulted to see whether it should be abolished but the interested parties opposed its destruction. The UK was, for a time, the sole EC State without provision for minimum wages.

An order of a wages council which took effect before abolition takes effect as a contractual term. Therefore, it cannot be varied except contractually. Employers wishing to force down wages will in law have to negotiate changes in the ways stated at 4.10, above.

4.11.6 National minimum wage

The National Minimum Wage Act 1998 came into effect on 1 April 1999. The Act applies to workers, not just employees. Wages include gross pay, bonuses and accommodation (up to £20 per week) but not tips distributed direct to staff, shift premia, overtime payments, and some benefits in kind, including company cars. The statute applies even where no work is available.

The minimum is £3.60 per hour for those aged 22 or over and £3.00 for those aged 18–21, inclusive (this figure will rise to £3.20 from June 2000). Those aged 16–17 are excluded. Pieceworkers are paid the national minimum wage over the pay reference period. No regard is taken of the worker's productivity.

The Act also deals with detriment and (automatic) unfair dismissal in respect of the minimum wage. Enforcement includes that performed by revenue officers and via criminal sanctions. The Act particularly improves the pay of women, ethnic minority workers, homeworkers and part-timers.

4.12   Working time

The Working Time Regulations 1998 (SI 1998/1833) implement the Working Time Directive (93/104) and the Young Workers Directive (94/33). The provisions are complex and only a summary is provided here.

The Regulations cover not just employees but also workers who personally perform any work or services. Working time is defined as any period when a worker is working or is at the employers' disposal and carrying out duties or activities, any period during which he is receiving training, and any other period which is treated as working time by a relevant agreement. That agreement could be a collective one or one agreed between the employers and their workers or a workforce agreement. The last is defined as an agreement in writing for a fixed period not exceeding five years which applies to all the workforce or, if the employers employ fewer than 20 workers, either by the workforce representatives or by a majority of the workers.

The 1998 Regulations impose a maximum working week of 48 hours averaged over 17 weeks. There are exceptions for those whose working time is not measured by time, such as executives. Individuals may agree not to be bound by the maximum but any agreement must be in writing and must be for a fixed duration or be of indefinite duration with the proviso that, if the latter, the worker can bring it to an end by giving notice for a period not exceeding three months. Employers must keep records, which are open to inspection by the Health and Safety Executive and those who have agreed not to be bound. The 48 hour week is a free-standing contractual right enforceable by workers: *Barber v RJB Mining (UK) Ltd* (1999). The High Court may award a declaration and an injunction.

Workers over 18 are entitled to a rest period of not less than 11 consecutive hours. Workers who change shifts or who work continental shifts are exempt, provided that they are given an equivalent rest period. Rest breaks must be provided every six hours for at least 20 minutes (unless there is a workforce or collective agreement to the contrary). Workers are also entitled to a weekly rest period of not less than 24 hours in each seven day period averaged over 14 weeks.

Night workers (defined as someone who works at least three hours between 9 pm and 7 am) are subject to particular protection. Their normal working hours should not exceed an average of eight in every 24 hours, averaged over 17 weeks. Free health assessments must be provided. If a night worker suffers health problems as a result of working nights, he must be transferred to daytime work if a suitable job is available.

From 1 October 1998, workers were entitled to three weeks' holiday per year. This rose to four weeks with effect from November 1999.

Enforcement of entitlements such as the 48 hour week is by the workers and there is protection against unfair dismissal and detriment not amounting to dismissal. The Health and Safety Executive enforce the record keeping duties imposed on employers. Limits are enforced by the Health and Safety Executive and local authorities.

The exclusions are large: doctors in training, police, the armed services; transport workers; and electricity, gas and waterworks workers. Those affected by foreseeable increases in work, for example, workers in the tourism sector, are also excluded. There is an exemption for unforeseen circumstances.

THE COMMON LAW OF CONTRACT

Common law contract

This chapter considered the content of common law contract of employment and the connected issue of statutory written particulars.

Offer and acceptance

There is no set form for offer and acceptance.

Infancy

A contract of employment is binding on a minor if, overall, it is to his advantage (*Leslie Frewin v Chaplin* (1966)).

Illegality

Contracts of employment which are illegal at inception are void, but ones illegal in performance are not. There is a growing jurisprudence on the courts and tribunals taking into account the seriousness of the illegality:

- *Newland v Simons & Willer (Hairdressers)* (1981);
- *Coral Leisure v Barnett* (1981);
- *Hewcastle Catering v Ahmed* (1991);
- *Leighton v Michael* (1996).

Form

Most contracts of employment need not be in writing.

Written statement

Parliament obliges employers to give written particulars to an employee within eight weeks of his commencing employment. This statement, which is not the contract, need not be supplied if there are in existence documents constituting the contract. Changes must be notified within four weeks. A tribunal cannot interpret the statement:

- *Mears v Safecar Security* (1983).

Express terms

Clauses expressly agreed take precedence over ones judicially implied:

- *Nelson v BBC* (1977).

Restraint of trade

Negative covenants are valid only if they protect a legitimate proprietary interest, are reasonable between the parties and are in the public interest. Covenants may be construed in order to validate them and can be severed. In the event of wrongful dismissal, the clause falls. The remedy most sought is an interlocutory injunction:

- *Herbert Morris v Saxelby* (1916);
- *Home Counties v Skilton* (1970);
- *General Billposting v Atkinson* (1909);
- *Lawrence David v Ashton* (1989);
- *Rock Refrigeration v Jones* (1996).

Implied terms

Terms may be implied by the judges:

- business efficacy: *The Moorcock* (1889);
- officious bystander: *Shirlaw v Southern Foundries* (1939);
- status: *Sim v Rotherham MBC* (1987);
- custom: *Sagar v Ridehalgh* (1931);
- works rules: *SSE v ASLEF (No 2)* (1972).

Terms may be implied as a result of the contract's being one of employment. The following duties are imposed on employers:

- pay: *Way v Latilla* (1939);
- (sometimes) work: *Devonald v Rosser* (1906);
- safety: *Wilsons & Clyde Coal v English* (1938);
- indemnity: employers must repay employees' expenses necessarily incurred in performing the contract, such as travel costs for sales representatives;
- mutual trust and confidence: *Wilson v Racher* (1974).

Employees are also subject to implied duties:

- obedience: *Cresswell v Inland Revenue* (1984);

- care: *Lister v Romford Ice* (1957);
- fidelity: *Faccenda Chicken v Fowler* (1987);
- co-operation: *SSE v ASLEF (No 2)* (1972).

Collective agreements can become part of an employee's contract either expressly or impliedly. Non-union members may be bound. Not all collective terms are appropriate for industrial enforcement. There is a special procedure for 'no-strike' clauses:

- *NCB v Galley* (1958);

- *NCB v NUM* (1986).

Terms may be implied by statute, an example being the 'equality clause' in the EPA 1970.

Variation

It is only possible to very terms bilaterally:

- *Burdett-Coutts v Herts CC* (1984).

Payment of wages

The Wages Act 1986, which is now part of the ERA 1996, deals with deductions from wages. Wages councils formerly provided minimum wages in some low paid industries.

National minimum wage

Since 1999, there is a national minimum wage in the UK, which is currently £3.60 for adults.

Working time

Subject to substantial exemptions, there is a maximum number of hours (48) in a working week. Nightworkers receive particular protection. The length of holidays has also been regulated for the first time.

CHAPTER 5

EQUAL PAY

5.1   Introduction

The Equal Pay Act (EPA) 1970 was intended to increase women's hourly earnings to the same level as those of men. It can also be seen as a measure aimed at preventing women's wages undercutting men's. Initially, the EPA 1970, which came into force in 1975, had some impact on female wages but the position has for some years been stabilised. Women continue to earn less than men overall. The equal value claim has also not had as significant an impact as commentators suggested it would have when it was introduced in 1983. The present figure is that women's hourly pay is about 80% of that of men. This continues an increase from 76% in 1989. It is thought that much of the difference is explained by women's traditional responsibility for child care. They often leave employment to have and look after children, and then return to work in a lower post than the one they left. Male earnings in manual jobs are often boosted by overtime pay, which means that gross pay difference is more substantial than the 80% figure would suggest. The weekly earnings of female manual workers are only 60% of that of men. If women have to look after children, they cannot do overtime. Some women may form part of the 'secondary labour force'; that is, unlike 'core' male workers, they are brought in to work only when the going is good for the firm; they are also the first to be sacked during a recession.

Many women work in 'occupationally segregated' jobs, that is, ones in which there are few or no male employees. These jobs, such as industrial cleaners, canteen assistants and typists, tend to be low paid, perhaps because there are so few men working in them. There is some suggestion that women face a 'glass ceiling'. They rise so far in corporate hierarchies but discrimination by men keeps them out of the top jobs. Women often work in jobs which are poorly unionised, and they suffer poorer wages as a result. Moreover, women often work in jobs which fit in with their child care responsibilities. Many part-timers do not have access to all the perks which full time employees have. As with the law on sexual and racial discrimination, the EPA 1970 is aimed at undermining stereotypical images; in this instance, women being worth less to employers than men. However, while women as a group may be affected by unequal pay, the basic rule is that only individual claims for equal pay are available. Yet payment systems apply generally.

The European Commission issued a Code of Practice on the Implementation of Equal Pay for Work of Equal Value for Women and Men in 1996 as a follow up to its Memorandum on Equal Pay for Work of Equal Value, 1994. It should be noted that, until the introduction of the national minimum wage, the only regulation of wages was via the EPA 1970. Both equal pay and the minimum wage are seen by those of the Right as interference with the free market. However, market forces, it is argued, are in turn partly the result of discrimination.

5.1.1 Application

The EPA 1970 applies only to terms of employment. It does not apply pre-employment, for example, at interviews. Where this statute does not apply, the Sex Discrimination Act (SDA) 1975 may apply. The courts have said that the two Acts fit together like a jigsaw puzzle to form one code. In general, the EPA 1970 applies to contractual benefits, the SDA 1975 to non-contractual ones such as promotion. 'Pay' is not restricted to money but extends to equivalents such as concessionary coal. The EPA 1970 is not restricted to employees but also applies to independent contractors who personally do the work (s 1(6)(a)). While the principal beneficiaries have been and were intended to be women, the EPA 1970 also applies to men who are not treated as favourably as women. There are exceptions to the Act: terms affected by protective legislation (s 6(1)(a)); terms connected with pregnancy or childbirth (s 6(1)(b)); and terms related to or connected with retirement and death (s 6(1A)(b) as amended). Where UK law is inconsistent with EC law, it is disapplied. EC law, which has profoundly affected UK law, is discussed below.

5.1.2 Equality clause

The main thrust of the EPA 1970 can be briefly stated. By s 1(1), a woman's contract is deemed to include an equality clause which states that:

- if any term of her contract is less favourable than a similar clause in a man's contract, her term is deemed to be no less favourable; and

- if her contract does not include a beneficial term which is in a man's contract, her contract is deemed to include that term.

If the applicant wins, she may be awarded damages (s 2(1)) or arrears of pay, but the claim for both used to be limited to the previous two years (s 2(5)). This issue was the subject of reference to the ECJ (*Levez v TH Jennings (Harlow Pools) Ltd* (1999)). The Court ruled that the two year limit does not apply when the employer had deliberately misrepresented to the employee the pay of persons of the opposite sex whom the applicant is using as a comparator. EC law, furthermore, precludes the application of a national rule which limits the amount of basic pay if, in comparison with similar domestic law, the rule disadvantages claimants. It is the national court which decides whether or not there is such a disadvantage. It is irrelevant that there is another cause of action (here, the tort of deceit). Section 2(5) was disapplied when the case returned to the EAT.

Claims are made to employment tribunals. There is no age limit, qualifying period or minimum hours of work. The burden of proof is on the applicant. According to *British Railways Board v Paul* (1988), there is no time limit for an applicant to bring an equal pay claim, but this case has been judicially criticised (and, it can be confidently asserted, is wrong: *Etherson v Strathclyde RC* (1992), a Scottish case). The limit in English law is six months from the termination of the contract. The House of Lords referred a question on the compatability of the six month time limit found in s 2(4) of the EPA 1970 to the ECJ in *Preston v Wolverhampton Healthcare NHS Trust* (1999). For time limits on pensions cases, see below.

It should be noted that a woman cannot obtain a proportional amount of a man's wage. If, for example, she presently earns 60% of a man's pay but should earn 75%, she cannot get the 75%, for that amount is not equal pay. If, however, she is presently earning less than the man but should be earning more, she can be awarded equal pay, at least when EC law applies (*Murphy v Bord Telecom Eireann* (1988)). The point is moot in English law (in *Waddington v Leicester Council for Voluntary Services* (1977), it was held that a female employee who worked more than a man but was paid less could not obtain equal pay!), but it is suggested that it is the same as EC law. Accordingly, if a woman earns 60% of the man's pay, but she should earn 115%, the tribunal inserts an equality clause to give her the man's pay (that is, she obtains 100%, but not 115%). A comparable situation occurred in *Evesham v North Hertfordshire HA* (1999). A female speech therapist claimed that her work was of equal value to that of a male clinical psychologist who earned more than she did. She was on point 6 of her pay scale; he was on point 1 of his. The EAT held that she was entitled to the same pay as he earned, but that she was not entitled to be put on point 6 of his pay scale.

5.1.3   Male comparator

For there to be an equality clause, the woman must be able to compare herself with a man in the same employment (the male comparator) and both must be employed on 'like work', 'work rated as equivalent' or 'work of equal value'. The woman can choose which man she wishes to have as her male comparator (*Ainsworth v Glass Tubes Ltd* (1977)). She may choose more than one comparator. The Conservatives suggested in 1994 that a woman should be able to compare herself against only one male comparator, but this proposal was not acted upon. The Court of Appeal in *British Coal Corp v Smith* (1994) held that the chosen man had to be a representative of the class of male employees from which he was selected. If he was not, the employees have a material factor defence (see below, 5.1.14). In that case, all the applicants had chosen more than one comparator and most had selected men from different establishments. The House of Lords (1996) did not refer to this matter, but where the male comparator is not representative, the employers may have a material factor defence (see 5.1.14, below).

An example of a situation where it may be easy for the tribunal to conclude that there were no reasonable grounds for a claim for equal pay is where the applicant claims equal pay with a man earning twice as much as she does. The ECJ in *Specialarbejderforbundet i Danmark v Dansk Industri* (1996) held that comparators must not be chosen arbitrarily. There is difficulty in finding male comparators in occupationally segregated industries. The applicant need not compare herself with a worker doing a similar task; for example, an administrative worker can compare herself with a male executive. It should be noted that separate claims must be brought by each woman, even though several or even thousands of women are using the same male comparator in their claims. While representative actions are possible, there is no 'class action' in the UK.

5.1.4 Same employment (s 1(6))

The restriction to 'same employment' means that a woman cannot compare her pay with that of men in other firms or industries. However, in the EPA 1970, being 'in the same employment' covers men working for companies associated with her employers (s 1(6)). In the important case of *Scullard v Knowles* (1996), the EAT held that EC terminology ('the same establishment or service') was wider than the statute, in that it embraced bodies which were not in the legal form of companies but which were under the control of a third organisation. Article 141 was not restricted to associated companies, but cross-industry comparisons were still not permitted. One had to enquire whether the applicant and comparator were in the same service, which in this case was that of regional education advisory councils. An answer could be sought by investigating whether common terms and conditions applied across the bodies. The law is now expressed in a looser form than it was before. Certainty has gone.

Scullard v Knowles cannot, however, be read as permitting comparisons between completely separate organisations. In *Lawrence v Regent Office Care Ltd* (1999), the EAT rejected a claim for equal pay by female school catering assistants whose jobs had been privatised following compulsory competitive tendering. They had been re-employed by the defendants on less favourable terms than those they had previously enjoyed when employed by a county council. It was held that they could not compare their wages against those of people still employed by the council. Morison J said that the applicant and the comparator must be, 'in a loose and non-technical sense, in the same establishment or service'. Cross-industry comparisons may not be made.

By s 1(6), 'same employment' is defined as the same establishment or different establishments where common terms and conditions of employment apply. A nursery nurse and a member of clerical staff each had common terms when a collective agreement applied to both (*Leverton v Clwyd CC* (1989)). In *British Coal Corp v Smith* (1996), the House of Lords held that female canteen workers and cleaners were in the same employment as male clerks and surface workers. The fact that they worked at different establishments and that there were incentive bonuses and concessionary coal for the surface workers did not undermine the conclusion that all worked under common terms and conditions, namely the national agreement.

The 'common terms and conditions' do not have to be the *same* terms and conditions. It is sufficient that the national agreement applied to women and men at the same establishment – in the above case, a pit. It did not matter that there were different provisions about concessionary coal and incentives. Therefore, 'common terms and conditions' includes those clauses which are broadly comparable. In *British Coal Corp v Smith* (1994), 1,286 women in seven types of job compared themselves with 150 men, a mammoth undertaking for the tribunal. Section 1(6) is being undermined by the move from collective bargaining to individual agreements: fewer workers will have common terms and conditions.

Though the EPA 1970 was not so worded, as a result of EC law, a woman can compare her pay with that of a male predecessor in her job (*Macarthys Ltd v Smith* (1980), a decision of the ECJ). It was held by the EAT in *Diocese of Hallam Trustees v Connaughton* (1996), in reliance on the ECJ's ruling, that a woman can compare her pay with that of a male successor to her job. It would be helpful if the EPA 1970 was amended to take account of these developments.

5.1.5   Like work (s 1(2)(a))

One of the three ways in which a woman can compare her wages with those of a man is if they are engaged in 'like work' for the same or associated employers. This term is defined in s 1(4) as being work 'of the same or broadly similar nature'. Any difference not 'of practical importance' is to be disregarded. The tribunal should take a broad brush approach in deciding whether the jobs are similar. In one case, the fact that the woman prepared 10 or 20 meals for directors at lunchtime, whereas the male comparators provided more meals at different times of the day, did not of itself signify that they were not doing broadly similar work (*Capper Pass Ltd v Lawton* (1977)).

Tribunals must investigate the work that the woman and the man actually do. The employment of a man to deter trouble makers at a betting shop does not justify a difference in pay if he has not been trained for the job or if there has never been any trouble (*Shields v E Coomes (Holdings) Ltd* (1978)). It is irrelevant that the man was contractually obliged to undertake additional work if he did not in practice do so. For example, in *Electrolux Ltd v Hutchinson* (1977), the EAT disregarded the fact that the men had to transfer to other jobs (if there was a demand) and work overtime (if there was a demand) because, in practice, they rarely performed these functions.

5.1.6 Practical difference

The time at which women and men work is irrelevant if the duties are in practice the same or broadly similar. Accordingly, the fact that women work on day shifts and men at night does not matter. There may, however, be a bonus for antisocial hours working, provided that the bonus is based on the antisocial nature of the time of work and not on difference of sex (*Dugdale v Kraft Foods Ltd* (1976)). The premium must not exceed the amount necessary to acknowledge the fact that the comparator works antisocial hours. Extra responsibility through working at night is the sort of factor which means that the two jobs are not broadly similar. Working alone at night was held to be a practical difference from working in a group during the day in *Thomas v NCB* (1987). A man's responsibility for items of greater value than those for which a woman was responsible defeated her claim in *Eaton Ltd v Nuttall* (1977). A mistake by him would be more serious than one made by her.

5.1.7 Work rated as equivalent (s 1(2)(b))

The second way in which a woman can obtain equal pay with a man working in the same employment is if their jobs have been equally ranked by a job evaluation scheme. As long as the grades are equally ranked, it does not matter that the points awarded to each job are not the same. In *Springboard Sunderland Trust v Robson* (1992), a woman's job was rated at 410 points. The job of the male comparator was rated at 428 points. The EAT held that, since both jobs fell within the same grade (410 to 449 points), her application for equal pay succeeded. The survey is binding even though the employers have not put it into effect (*O'Brien v Sim-Chem Ltd* (1980)). This has occurred where the evaluation has led to controversial outcomes. It must, however, have been accepted as valid by the parties (normally employers and the union) who agreed to carry it out (*Arnold v Beecham Group Ltd* (1982)). The employers cannot be forced to carry out job ranking.

5.1.8 Analytical nature

The Court of Appeal held in *Bromley v H & J Quick Ltd* (1988) that the evaluation had to be done analytically. That is, it is not sufficient that the study was performed subjectively. The survey must look at each element in both jobs and compare them; it is illegitimate to undertake what is called 'whole-job' comparison or to adopt the 'felt-fair' approach. The study must not itself be so sexually biased that the discrimination appears on the face of the record or is fundamental (*Eaton Ltd v Nuttall* (1977)). The criteria must be objectively justifiable. It should be said that *Bromley* has not been as effective in eradicating covert discrimination in job evaluation studies as it was thought that it would have been 10 years ago.

5.1.9   Equal value (s 1(2)(c))

When the EPA 1970 was originally passed, only the first two methods of acquiring equal pay were available. By acceding to the European Communities, the UK accepted the Treaty of Rome (now called the EC Treaty). Article 119 (now Art 141) inserted, as a result of French insistence, a statement that 'men and women should receive equal pay for equal work'. The UK Government contended that the two methods of claiming equal pay, 'like work' and 'work rated as equivalent', matched up to EC norms; that is, Art 141 was restricted to these methods. Indeed, this approach may have been the intention of the founding fathers of the EC. This view was successfully challenged by the European Commission. As a result of the ruling of the ECJ in *Commission v UK* (1982), the Government enacted a third mode of acquiring equal pay, that of 'work of equal value', by inserting a new paragraph into the EPA 1970 by means of the Equal Pay (Amendment) Regulations 1983 (SI 1983/1794). The ECJ held that the law before the amendment did not conform with Art 141 of the EC Treaty because workers could not ask a judicial body to carry out a job evaluation study. The Government reacted with bad grace and instituted a long-winded procedure for resolving equal value claims.

Recently, efforts have been made to speed up procedure both by giving tribunals the power not to commission experts and by not permitting employers to rely on the same defence at two different stages in the proceedings. Nevertheless, delays remain. Two well known cases, *British Coal Corp v Smith* and *Enderby v Frenchay HA*, took more than a decade to resolve. Lord Slynn in *British Coal* was particularly scathing about delay.

The cost of an equal value claim is also prohibitive. The EOC estimated in 1993 that the cost of such a claim is on average over £6,500 if the case does not go to appeal. If there is an appeal, costs may exceed £50,000.

5.1.10 Definition

The amended Act states that a woman is entitled to equal pay if her work:

> ... is, in terms of the demands made on her (for instance, under such headings as effort, skill and decision), of equal value to that of a man in the same employment.

For instance, in *Hayward v Cammell Laird Shipbuilders Ltd* (1988), a woman's claim that her work as a cook was of equal value to that of men working as painters, joiners and thermal insulation engineers was upheld. The House of Lords emphasised that the woman's application would be successful if one of her terms of employment fell short of one of the terms in the men's contract. It was immaterial that her 'job package', that is, the overall pay elements in her job, were equivalent to or better than the job package of the men. Some commentators have expressed concern that there could be a danger of 'leapfrogging' pay claims. If her pay was, for example, increased to the men's level, the effect might be that her supervisor's pay might be less than the woman's revised pay. The supervisor might, therefore, put in a claim for increased pay to preserve her differential. The effect might be to destroy (to 'dynamite' is the term used) long established pay structures. However, leapfrogging does not seem to have occurred in practice. Moreover, since the comparison is between individual terms in the contract, not between the female and the male job package, it could be that some terms in the men's contract are less favourable than terms in the woman's contract.

The effect of *Hayward* is to give workers the opportunity to claim that an equality clause should be inserted into their contracts in order to equalise upwards all their unfavourable terms and conditions. In fact, perhaps because of the lengthy procedure of equal value claims, leapfrogging does not seem to have occurred. The ECJ in *Barber v Guardian Royal Exchange* (1990) also said that each individual term has to be compared. The 'package' approach therefore cannot now be adopted by domestic courts or by Parliament. On this view, the House of Lords' decision in *Leverton v Clwyd CC* (1989), that the whole package of a female nursery nurse's and a male clerk's job should be compared when enquiring whether the employers had a genuine material difference defence, is incorrect. *Hayward* also illustrates how long-winded the process can be. The case took four years to conclude. Another criticism of equal value claims is that the requirements stated in s 1(2)(c), 'effort, skill and decision', are not necessarily gender-free. Merit pay, it appears, is more often given to men than to women. One might ask why 'merit' is not a gender-free term.

5.1.11 Procedure

The procedure for making an application is complex. The claimant commences the application in the tribunal. If there are no reasonable grounds for determining that the work is of equal value (including the material factor defence), the claim is dismissed. Since 1994, if a material factor defence was considered at this stage, it can only be considered at a later stage in exceptional circumstances: Employment Tribunals (Constitution and Rules of Procedure) (Amendment) Regulations 1994 (SI 1994/536). If there are reasonable grounds, either the tribunal decides the matter itself (this was introduced in 1996 as a way of reducing delays: see the Sex Discrimination and Equal Pay (Miscellaneous Amendments) Regulations 1996 (SI 1996/438)), or the case gets farmed out to an independent expert on industrial claims, that person being on a panel nominated by ACAS. There were 13 such experts in 1996. The expert drafts a report, taking into account representations made by the parties.

The experts seem to be inventing systems of evaluating jobs which are peculiarly their own. No one scheme is used. Parties are interviewed and usually, the applicant and her comparators are observed working by the expert.

The expert has, however, no right of access to the employers' premises. Under the legislation, he is expected to produce his report within 42 days. Since December 1993, experts have been under a duty to tell the employment tribunal within 14 days of the commission when they expect to submit the report and must inform the tribunal of any delay. In fact, the report can take over two years to complete.

The delay has been a source of constant criticism. If a report is commissioned, the tribunal cannot decide the issue until the report is received. If one party unreasonably delays the production of the report, she may lose the case or costs may be awarded against her. Similarly criticised is the fact that the expert has no power to order a person to give evidence. The report is not binding on the tribunal (*Tennants Textile Colours Ltd v Todd* (1989)). Throughout, the expert is striving to see whether the woman's and man's work are of equal value. The tribunal is under a duty to consider whether the result the expert has reached is one which could reasonably be reached. It seems that the experts do not attach weight to each factor they use, and the author suggests that this structure is challengeable, for any weighting or lack of weighting may be discriminatory. The expert must comply with the procedural requirements laid down by Parliament, and the report can be excluded if it is defective for some material reason or if its conclusion is perverse.

Challenges to the report must be made at this stage. If the report is not accepted, the tribunal instructs another expert. On acceptance, the tribunal holds a hearing. The expert can be cross-examined. The parties are allowed to call one of their own experts to challenge the tribunal's expert's conclusions. Usually, the tribunal will accept the expert's decision, at least when it is unchallenged, but the outcome must be reached after looking at all the evidence. If the report is rejected, the employment tribunal may commission a new report. There is debate as to how close to absolutely equal value the jobs must be. It has been held that, since a 'like work' claim expressly includes work of a broadly similar type, an equal value claim must be of exactly equal value, for there is no such breadth. However, it seems that most tribunals adopt what has come to be called the 'broad brush' approach and do not require absolute equivalence.

As stated above, tribunals can now investigate claims of equal value on their own. It is not known how many times they have not commissioned an expert report on this ground or how they proceed with their task. It is suggested that work measurement is a difficult job for which tribunal members will usually lack the expertise. In one employment tribunal case, a male maintenance worker was found to have significantly greater skills than a female cleaner, he had to take more decisions, and their efforts were equal. Therefore, the cleaner lost her equal value claim.

5.1.12 Defence

An equal value claim cannot be heard if there has been a job evaluation study which has ranked the comparison job unequally, provided that the study is not vitiated by sexual bias (s 2A(2)). Surprisingly, the claim is blocked if the survey is completed at any time before the final hearing (*Dibro Ltd v Hore* (1990)). The study will be vitiated if, for example, it ranks characteristics which have traditionally been recognised as feminine (for example, manual dexterity) lower than traditionally male traits (such as strength to lift heavy objects). The burden of proving that there has been an unbiased survey is on the employers.

5.1.13 No token male

The House of Lords held in *Pickstone v Freemans plc* (1988) that an equal value claim cannot be stopped, even if there are men other than the comparator who are doing 'like work' to the woman or whose jobs have been rated as equal by a job evaluation study. Accordingly, if a woman chooses a male who is not in these categories, her claim can proceed. This ruling was given in spite of the wording in s 1(2)(c), for the House of Lords considered that EC law gave women a right to claim that their jobs were of equal value to those held by men. The right is free-standing, that is, it is not dependent on whether the woman could rely on 'like work' or 'work rated as equivalent'. If, however, she chose as her male comparator a man working on 'like work' or 'work rated as equivalent', then, and only then, did she not have a right to make an equal value claim.

5.1.14 Genuine material difference: defences to equal pay claims (s 1(3))

By s 1(3), a woman loses her claim if her employers prove that the variation 'is genuinely due to a material factor which is not the difference of sex'. 'Genuinely' means that a defence such as market forces must not be a sham or subterfuge. 'Due to' connotes causation. The employers' intention is irrelevant just as it is in discrimination cases (*British Coal Corp v Smith* (1994) and *Ratcliffe v North Yorkshire CC* (1995)). In general, employers who rely on this defence in an equal value claim before an expert is assigned cannot rely on it again at a later stage in the proceedings (see 5.1.11, above). This defence is different from that of 'objective justification' in discrimination on grounds of sex. If there are genuine factors not tainted by discrimination which explain the difference, there is nothing which the employers have to justify. The employers have to prove that there is a factor which constitutes a genuine material difference between the woman's and the man's cases, but they do not have to show that there was an objective justification for the difference, that is, that they were adopting measures which corresponded to a real need and were appropriate and necessary to meet the need (*Tyldesley v TML Plastics Ltd* (1996), an EAT decision which seems to conflict with several House of Lords' cases, including *Rainey v Greater Glasgow Health Board* (1987), discussed below).

In *Strathclyde Regional Council v Wallace* (1998), the House of Lords held that a practice which was not concerned with sex did not have to be objectively justified. The employers had not awarded pay increases to persons who were doing the jobs of those above them. On the facts, a woman was claiming equal pay with those whose job she was doing, but the majority of the persons who were doing as she did were male. If, however, most of the unpromoted group had been female, the employers would have had to prove 'a material factor which is not the difference of sex'. Accordingly, only if the applicant can show that the employers' policy has a disparate impact on persons of her gender do the employers have to prove justification to succeed. *Tyldesley* was approved.

It used to be common to divide the defences of employers into two: 'material difference', which applies to 'like work' and 'work rated as equivalent'; and 'material factor', which applies to the equal value claim. In relation to 'like work' and 'work rated as equivalent', the defence is one of a material factor, which must be a difference between the man's and the woman's case. In relation to 'equal value', the material factor *may* be a difference between the woman's and the man's case. This division, however, has been largely rendered otiose by the House of Lords' decision in *Rainey v Greater Glasgow Health Board* (1987). Nevertheless, it remains convenient to retain the distinction.

The following have been held to be material differences:

- grading scheme (*National Vulcan Engineering Insurance Group v Wade* (1978));

- having acquired a training role and being involved in teaching others (*Baker v Rochdale HA* (1994));

- long service, superior qualifications, higher output, different location: *NAAFI v Varley* (1977): paying 'London weighting' to a male but not paying a supplement to a female employee of the same firm in Sheffield can be justified on this basis;

- demotion (this could be seen as an example of 'red-circling' (see below) (*Forex Neptune (Overseas) Ltd v Miller* (1987));

- economic necessity which leads to a later female employee being paid less than an earlier male one (*Albion Shipping Agency v Arnold* (1982));

- newcomer's wages protected when he joined an NHS department from private practice as a prosthetist (*Rainey* (above));

- 'administrative' convenience, plus the intention to cushion employees against the loss of their work, particularly older, long-serving employees (*Barry v Midland Bank plc* (1997) (EAT)), where a severance scheme based on the statutory redundancy payments scheme was justified on these grounds (*obiter*). *Barry* was confirmed by the House of Lords in 1999);

- full time employment when part-timers were not as economically productive as full-timers (*Jenkins v Kingsgate Ltd* (1981));

- a mistake by the employers in placing the comparator higher on the pay scale than the applicant (*Yorkshire Blood Transfusion Service v Plaskitt* (1994)). The error must be one that was genuine and the employers must try to correct the anomaly (*Young v University of Edinburgh* (1995)). Such decisions may be criticised on the grounds that, while the difference is a factor, it is not a material one, and they are inconsistent with EC law, which demands an objective justification (see 5.2.8);

- 'red-circling', that is, preserving wages of an employee's previous job when he works on a less well paid job, provided the red-circling is not the result of sex discrimination (*Snoxell v Vauxhall Motors Ltd* (1977)). The red circle must be phased out within a reasonable time (*Outlook Supplies Ltd v Parry* (1978)). If the reason for the difference disappears, so should the red circle (*Benveniste v University of Southampton* (1989)). Accordingly, a female lecturer appointed at a low point on the wage scale because of economic necessity should have her pay raised once that necessity has disappeared.

The EAT has said that there is no limit on the number of factors which can constitute a material factor (*Davies v MacCartneys* (1989)). In *North Yorkshire CC v Ratcliffe* (1995), the House of the Lords held that variation in pay caused by compulsory competitive tendering was not a material factor. Here, market forces were sexually discriminatory.

The Court of Appeal noted that the equal pay law was aimed at equality, not at establishing fair pay for the job, holding in *Calder v Rowntree Mackintosh Confectionery Ltd* (1993) that, where the employers relied on two or more genuine material differences, they do not have to prove which proportion each element contributes to the whole. A bonus for working on rotating day shifts was justified by the disturbance caused to men working on it, the men being paid a shift premium. (It may be that this rule is inconsistent with EC law: in *Enderby v Frenchay HA* (1993), the ECJ laid down the requirement that the whole of the difference must be justified, but the House of Lords approved *Calder* in *Strathclyde Regional Council v Wallace* (1998).) The same court held in *British Coal Corp v Smith* (1996) that there cannot be a material factor defence to an equal value claim where there is direct sex discrimination, for if there is, the employers have treated the applicant less favourably than a man 'on the grounds of her sex' (their Lordships did not deal with this issue). For example, if women's rates were depressed in order to win a tender, there would be discrimination (*North Yorkshire CC v Ratcliffe* (1995)). The law turns on whether the difference was due to a factor tainted by sex discrimination or otherwise. Financial constraint not based on sex is therefore a defence.

5.1.15 Separate pay systems

In *Reed Packaging Ltd v Boozer* (1988), the EAT held that lower female pay was justified when it resulted from two different collective bargaining systems. The use of two systems was administratively justified within *Rainey*. The Scottish EAT ruled in *Barber v NCR Manufacturing Ltd* (1993) that collective bargaining explained but did not justify differences in pay discrimination. The ECJ's decision in *Enderby v Frenchay HA* (1993), which requires the difference to be objectively justified (market forces can constitute such justification but whether they do or not is an issue for the national tribunal) and not due to sex, supports the Scottish EAT's approach.

Enderby was applied by the House of Lords in *British Coal Corp v Smith* (1996). Female cooks and male ancillary workers such as gardeners have separate bargaining systems. Collective agreements had assimilated the males to surface miners, but had not done so in respect of the women. The effect was that women were paid less than men. Again, the separate pay structures explained but did not justify the difference in pay. Since the employers could not justify that difference, the women were entitled to equal pay.

Employers cannot justify pay inequity by having separate collective bargaining agreements for groups largely consisting of men and women (see *British Road Services Ltd v Loughran* (1997), where it was held held that it did not matter that one of the pay systems did not apply to a group almost exclusively comprised of women) even if those arrangements are not discriminatory in themselves: separate pay bargaining is not by itself an objective justification, though, if it is not tainted by discrimination, it may be an element in determining whether there was such justification. Collective bargaining is not *per se* determinative but it provides some evidence that wages were non-discriminatory. This presumption contrasts with that which states that the more women there are in a group the easier it is to assume that there is discrimination. *Enderby* also demonstrates the effect of the lack of a 'class action'. A total of 1,395 female speech therapists brought a claim and the industrial tribunals had difficulty coping. Unfortunately, it also demonstrates how long winded equal pay claims can be. In *British Coal Corp v Smith*, there were 1,286 applicants, mainly canteen workers, working in 258 establishments.

5.1.16 Burden of proof

The burden of proof is on the employers. The standard of proof is on the balance of probabilities. It is not sufficient for the employers to show that they did not intend to discriminate on grounds of sex. What they have to show is that they have objectively justified grounds for the difference (*Rainey*, applying the ECJ authority of *Bilka-Kaufhaus GmbH v Weber von Hartz* (1986)). It is for the national court to determine whether there was justification. The ECJ held that differential pay could be justified only when the factors distinguishing the men's and women's remuneration:

> ... correspond to a real need on the part of the undertaking, are appropriate with a view to delivering the objectives pursued and are necessary to that end.

The ECJ clarified the issue of proof in *Enderby v Frenchay HA* by placing it on the employers once the employee has shown that statistics disclose a significant difference in pay between two jobs, one largely undertaken by men. The burden of proof, it was said in *British Coal Corp v Smith*, above, is not necessarily discharged by showing that there was no direct sex discrimination within the SDA 1975. Market forces can be taken into account.

5.1.17 Economic forces

The 'material factor' defence was intended by the Government to be wider than the material difference defence, in that it would also cover economic realities and market forces. In fact, *Rainey* has extended the 'material difference' defence to include these matters. Any distinction is now nebulous. The House of Lords in *Rainey* considered that administrative efficiency (which need not be based on economic forces) would provide the employers with a defence if their firm was not concerned with trade or business, but the main effect of *Rainey* is to give employers a defence to all three modes of claiming equal pay when economic factors dictate that the woman gets less pay than the man. This ruling is inconsistent with earlier cases which said that differences in pay were justified only where there was a difference in the 'personal equation' between the woman's and man's case, such as when he had undergone training courses but she had not. Nowadays, extrinsic factors such as market forces are relevant.

The principal criticism of this development is that the reasons why women are paid less than men include market forces. To allow free rein to the defence negates the whole point of the equal pay legislation. The Court of Appeal said in response to this point that the market forces must be ones which are untainted by sexual discrimination (*British Coal Corp v Smith*), and the House of Lords in *Ratcliffe v North Yorkshire CC* held that reducing women's wages to below those of male comparators was not permitted by the equal pay legislation. Both cases put a brake on the expansion of the market forces defence and mark something of a return to the original width of the exception of genuine material difference. The ECJ in *Hill v Revenue Comrs* (1998), an Irish case, held that increased cost arising from a jobshare was not a justification for any discrimination stemming from the jobshare.

One unresolved matter is whether, under s 1(3), each individual term has to be compared or whether the whole job package is the point of comparison. As we have seen, the House of Lords in *Hayward v Cammell Laird Ltd* held that, in relation to s 1(2)(c), the equal value claim, each term in the woman's contract must be compared against each term in the male contractor's contract. In *Hayward*, Lord Goff thought that the employers could have a s 1(3) defence if the female employee had better sick pay and pension but the men had higher pay; that is, if overall the jobs were such that there was no genuine material difference (see, also, *Leverton*, above). On the facts of *Hayward*, the woman's and the man's pay packages were determined through different pay structures. Lord Goff considered that the material difference defence failed, however, where sexual discrimination was part of the pay structures.

It may be that Lord Goff's approach has been undermined by the decision of the ECJ in *Barber v Guardian Royal Exchange* (1990), which is discussed below. *Barber* held that each part of the pay package has to be compared. Therefore, looking at the package in the round was not acceptable. *Barber* was, however, concerned with the situation where the males and females were governed by one pay structure, and is not necessarily applicable to cases such as *Hayward* where there are two structures, neither of which is discriminatory. The ECJ resolved this issue when it considered the claim of (female) speech therapists that they were doing work of equal value with (male) pharmacists in *Enderby* (above). The employers unsuccessfully argued that any unintentional indirect pay discrimination was the result of separate bargaining procedures, neither of which were in themselves discriminatory. *Reed Packaging Ltd v Boozer*, above, is overruled. The ECJ held that whether economic forces, such as a shortage of candidates, justify the difference is a matter for national courts, which should take into account the general principle of proportionality found in EC law.

The width of this exception undermines the thrust of the equal pay law. If market forces justify part of the difference but not the whole, discrimination may exist as to the remainder (*Enderby*). This is an important principle. Pleading and giving evidence of market forces does not automatically provide an objective justification.

5.1.18 Differences from SDA 1975

The differences of the EPA 1970 from the SDA 1975 should be noted.

- The EPA 1970 does not apply to unequal pay on the basis of marriage, whereas the SDA 1975 prohibits discrimination against married people.

- For the EPA 1970 to apply, there must be an actual male comparator; for the SDA 1975 to apply, it is sufficient to compare the woman with a hypothetical male. The EOC proposes to abolish this requirement in the EPA 1970 in order to improve the pay of women in occupationally segregated industries. The ECJ has not had the opportunity to rule on this point but it is interesting to note that in *Barber v Guardian Royal Exchange Assurance Group* there was no named female comparator, though in *Macarthys Ltd v Smith*, the ECJ held that there had to be a comparator of the opposite sex.

- The EPA 1970 does not expressly deal with indirect discrimination, whereas the SDA 1975 does. The House of Lords in *Ratcliffe v North Yorkshire CC* stated in the words of Lord Slynn that the English equal pay legislation 'must be interpreted ... without bringing in the distinction between so-called "direct" and "indirect" discrimination. The relevant question under the 1970 Act is whether equal treatment has been accorded for men and women ...'. However, the EAT held in *Jenkins v Kingsgate Ltd* (1981) that the EPA 1970 does apply to indirect discrimination. The basis for this decision was that the SDA 1975 prohibits indirect discrimination; the two Acts form part of one code; therefore, the EPA 1970 must also prohibit indirect discrimination which affects terms of employment. Lord Slynn said, to the contrary, that there was no provision expressly incorporating the concept. The ECJ in both *Jenkins* (1981) and *Enderby* (1993) did look at the concept of indirect discrimination in the context of an equal pay claim.

  Staffordshire CC v Black (1995) states that the English law on indirect discrimination applies to equal pay claims brought under Art 119 (now Art 141): there must be a requirement or condition with which considerably fewer women than men can comply, the requirement or condition must be detrimental to the applicant and the employers must not be able to justify the difference. It is suggested that this case is inconsistent with the ECJ decision in *Enderby*, above, which disapproved of applying the rules on indirect discrimination to equal pay claims. The EAT made no reference to *Enderby* and the decision looks *per incuriam*. It is also inconsistent with *Ratcliffe*.

  The Burden of Proof Directive (97/80), which is expected to come into force in 2001, will apply to equal pay as well as to equal treatment. Indirect discrimination, defined as 'provision, criterion or practice', will definitely form part of EC law.

- The defence of genuine material difference in the EPA 1970 is different from that of justification in respect of indirect sexual discrimination.

- The EPA 1970 does not require a 'requirement or condition' when dealing with indirect discrimination in 'pay', whereas the SDA 1975 in terms does. Once the Burden of Proof Directive (97/80) is transposed in UK law, the phrase 'requirement or condition' will have to be watered down to 'practice or procedure' or a similar phrase.

The EOC proposed in November 1998 that the EPA 1970 and the SDA 1975, as well as related material, should be amalgamated into one Sex Equality Act but, at present, the Goverment disagrees with this proposal.

5.2 Effect of EC law

As stated above, Art 141 (formerly Art 119) is, in some respects, more generous to women than English domestic law (see *Macarthys Ltd v Smith*, mentioned above). In such circumstances, applicants can rely on EC law and can do so in an industrial tribunal. There is some doubt, noted in Chapter 2, as to whether or not a tribunal has jurisdiction in such circumstances, but this point seems now to have been settled in favour of jurisdiction. The early EAT case of *Amies v ILEA* (1977), which denied jurisdiction, has not been followed (see, for example, *Albion Shipping Agency v Arnold* (1982) and *Griffin v London Pension Funds Authority* (1993)). The same point could have been at issue in the cases in English courts where domestic law fell short of EC norms, but the assumption has been that industrial tribunals have jurisdiction. There is jurisdiction to hear claims falling under the Treaty of Rome and EC directives. It has been held that, where English domestic law gives a remedy equivalent to that of EC law, the tribunal should not consider EC law (*Blaik v Post Office* (1994)). Only where English standards fall short of EC law should EC law be investigated.

The ECJ in *Defrenne v SABENA (No 2)* (1976) stated that Art 119 (now Art 141) has a dual aim: the prevention of price undercutting by countries which did not have equal pay rules; and the continued improvement of working conditions. Originally, it was economic policy which was to the fore; now, equal pay as part of anti-discrimination law is seen as a fundamental human right. The definition of 'pay' is read broadly in order to promote these policies.

5.2.1 Direct effect

Article 141 is directly effective insofar as the discrimination is direct. This was not an anticipated outcome. The ECJ at first restricted this point to discrimination which was 'direct and overt' (that is, obvious on its face) (*Defrenne v SABENA (No 2)* (1976)) but has since widened the right by dropping the need for overtness. However, where the discrimination is indirect, the ECJ held in *Jenkins v Kingsgate Ltd* (1981) that Art 141 was not directly effective. Accordingly, on this point, English law which prohibits indirect discrimination in pay is wider than EC law. The ECJ has now, however, moved to holding that indirect discrimination is covered by EC law. By Art 141, the 'equal pay for equal work' principle (to which was expressly added 'work of equal value' by the Treaty of Amsterdam), as clarified by the Equal Pay Directive (below), is not restricted by a narrow view of what constitutes pay. The legal nature of the pay is irrelevant, and pay is still 'pay' within Art 141 even though the employee is off work. It includes:

- pay under piece work schemes (*Specialarbejderforbundet i Danmark v Dansk Industri* (1996) (ECJ));

- concessionary fares for retired workers (*Garland v British Rail Engineering Ltd* (1982));

- sick pay (*Rinner-Kühn v FWW Spezial Gebäudereinigung GmbH* (1989) (ECJ));

- paid leave for taking part in training courses (*Arbeiterwohlfahrt der Stadt Berlin v Bötel* (1992) (ECJ) and *Kuratorium für Nierentransplantation eV v Lewark* (1996) (ECJ));

- pension scheme supplemental to the State provision (*Bilka-Kaufkaus* (above)). This is so even though the occupational pension simply substitutes for the State pension (see *Moroni v Firma Collo GmbH* (1994) (ECJ)); access to occupational pension schemes must be given to to married women (*Fisscher v Voorhuis Hengelo BV* (1994) (ECJ) and *Vroege v NCIV Institut voor Volkshuisvesting BV* (1994) (ECJ)) and to part-timers (*Vroege*)); pension schemes must not discriminate against men; the right to join these schemes is not affected by *Barber*;

- occupational pension schemes (which are contracted out from the State scheme) linked to the State retirement age, even when the difference is due to the State's pension age (*Barber v Guardian Royal Exchange Assurance Group* (1990)). Survivors' pensions are included (*Coloroll Pension Trustees Ltd v Russell* (1994) (ECJ)), however, pensions paid by statutory authority are excluded (*Griffin v London Pensions Fund Authority*, above, a case seemingly wrong after the ECJ decisions on pensions). *Barber* is limited to benefits in respect of periods of employment after the date when the case was decided: for example, *Neath v Hugh Steeper Ltd* (1994) (ECJ) (*Neath* and similar cases are in accord with the Maastricht Protocol mentioned at 5.2.2, below); *Neath* and *Coloroll* furthermore affirm that sex-based actuarial factors are permitted in determining the amount of pensions (in criticism it may be stated that class, job, race and general health are better predictors of life expectancy than sex and that other members of the EC do not use sex-based actuarial tables);

- compensation for unfair dismissal (*R v Secretary of State for Employment ex p Seymour-Smith* (1999)). It does not matter that this right derives from statute. However, reinstatement and re-engagement after unfair dismissal are governed by the Equal Treatment Directive 1976;

- *ex gratia* payments and contractual and statutory redundancy payments (see *Barber*). *Barber* held that the English method of comparing each term (the *Hayward* case) was correct;

- retirement ages: *Marshall v Southampton and South West Hants AHA* (1986), a decision which led to equalisation in s 2 of the SDA 1986 (amending s 6(4) of the SDA 1975), rendering illegal discrimination in relation to retirement, promotion, demotion, training, transfer and dismissal. The decision also led to the amendment of the then existing law in respect of the exclusion from unfair dismissal law of women above 60, whereas the age for men was 65, when there was no normal retirement age;

- fringe benefits fall within the EPA 1970 if they constitute pay, but fall under the SDA 1975 if they do not. An example is non-contractual discretionary bonuses, which fall under the 1970 and not the 1975 Act;

- a lump sum payment given exclusively to women on maternity leave is 'pay', and the fact that it is not given to men is irrelevant if it is designed to compensate for disadvantages (such as the introduction of new technology) which accrue during leave (*Abboulaye v Régie Nationale des Usines Renault SA* (1999)).

The ECJ held in *Gillespie v Northern Health and Social Services Board* (1996) that benefits paid by employers to women on maternity leave constituted pay. However, it ruled that women were not, under EC law, entitled to full pay during that period. The amount of pay was for the national authorities to determine, provided that the maternity pay was not so low that the purpose of the leave is jeopardised. This rule applies to both statutory and contractual maternity pay. Accordingly, the fact that a pregnant woman received maternity pay and not full pay during what would have been her holidays is irrelevant (*Edwards v Derry CC* (1998)). (The Pregnant Workers Directive 92/85 was not in force at the time when the facts of *Gillespie* arose. It provides for women on maternity leave to receive adequate allowances.) *Barber* may also qualify this principle.

The ECJ ruled in *Boyle v EOC* (1999) that contractual maternity pay which exceeded Statutory Maternity Pay was 'pay' within Art 141. Obliging a woman who did not return to work to repay the difference between the two amounts was not discriminatory. Women on maternity leave are not to be compared with sick men. Therefore, it was irrelevant that there was no contractual clause obliging men to repay sick pay if they did not return to work after illness.

5.2.2   Extent of *Barber* (1990)

As a result of *Barber*, some employers have been equalising retirement ages at 65. Pension rights must be equalised upwards after the date of *Barber*, but inequality is permissible before then in respect of pension benefits based on service before *Barber* (*Smith v Avdel Systems Ltd* (1994) (ECJ)). Trustees may raise the pension age to 65 to equalise benefits but, if they do so, men's benefits will have to be raised to the women's level from the date of *Barber* to the date of equalisation

(*Coloroll Pension Trustees Ltd v Russell* (1994) (ECJ)). The changes to pension rights made by the ECJ have been put into a statute. It should be noted that *Barber* does not apply to single sex pension schemes (*Coloroll*). There are vast financial implications in the outcome of these cases. The Maastricht Treaty has a Protocol under which *Barber* is restricted to prospective application. The Protocol applies to benefit from pension schemes. It does not affect the right to join schemes. This right applies from 1976, the date when the ECJ ruled that Art 119 (now Art 141) was directly effective. A worker can therefore join a pension scheme retrospectively but must pay the missing contributions.

The ECJ has ruled that *Barber* is prospective unless the claim was lodged before 17 May 1990 (the date of *Barber*) in *Ten Oever v Stichting Bedrijfspensioenfonds* (1993) ECJ (among others). This accords with the Maastricht Protocol. Its effect is to undermine the fundamental nature of the right to equality, a right which, indeed, the ECJ reaffirmed in its reasoning in some of the 1994 cases involving pensions; full equality will take 40 years. It should be noted that *Barber* does not apply to the right to join occupational pensions and, therefore, there is no temporal limit on access to pension schemes except for that in *Defrenne v SABENA (No 2)* (1976), when the ECJ first ruled that Art 119 (now Art 141) has direct effect. The Maastricht Protocol also does not apply to access to pension schemes (*Vroege* and *Fisscher*). However, as the ECJ ruled in *Fisscher*, the person excluded from the scheme has to pay contributions into it before being granted admission. Therefore, where access to certain benefits is given only to full-timers, there is a right to claim them back to 1976 (*Magorrian v Eastern Health and Social Services Board* (1998)). There is also no temporal limit on payment of benefits under occupational pension schemes, but – and this is a major condition – national time limits apply (*Dietz v Stichting Thuiszorg Rotterdam* (1997) (ECJ)). It must be admitted that the distinction between *Magorrian* and *Dietz* seems tenuous and, no doubt, a further reference to the ECJ is needed.

5.2.3 Article 141's limits

The ECJ has held that Art 141 does not cover deductions from gross pay which are paid into a company pension scheme, even though such deductions were not made from female workers' pay (*Newstead v Department of Transport* (1988)). The Court held that such deductions did not constitute a difference in pay, which Art 141 requires. The EAT held in *Manor Bakeries Ltd v Nazir* (1996) that payment for time off for trade union activities, such as attendance at annual conferences, was not pay within Art 141 because the employee was not at work during that time. It is suggested that this decision is incorrect. Money for attendance at a conference is paid because of the contract of employment. It is inconsistent with *Bötel* and *Lewark* (see 5.2.1, above), and Art 141 is not restricted to payment for working; it applies, for example, to holiday and sick pay. The Article states that 'pay' means any consideration which the worker receives from the employers in respect of employment. *Nazir* was not followed by the EAT in *Davies v Neath Port Talbot CBC* (1999) on these grounds. Moreover, social security schemes which are established by the State do not fall within the concept of 'pay' (*Defrenne v Belgium* (1971)). Payments to employees who retire early ('bridging pensions') to tide them over until the State pension age is not discriminatory (*Birds Eye Walls Ltd v Roberts* (1994) (ECJ)).

The House of Lords in *Barry v Midland Bank plc* (1999) held that, where severance pay was calculated according to an employee's rate of pay at the date of termination, the rule was not indrectly discriminatory against women. The claimant's argument was that there existed more women than men who had been in full time employment but who, at the termination of the contract, were in part time employment with their employers. The House of Lords stated that the scheme was not contrary to Art 141. The aim of the scheme was not to pay employees for what they had done in the past; therefore, the failure to take into account previous full time employment was immaterial. It should be noted that, since the scheme was not discriminatory, there was no need to try and justify it. In criticism, it may be said that the rule that previous employment was not considered did differentially affect men and women: if the rule is rephrased as 'full-timers get more severance pay than part-timers', this condition affected women more than men. It is therefore suggested that the criterion was indirectly discriminatory; if so, the burden would then switch to the employers to justify the requirement or condition. The payments on redundancy found in the ERA 1996 were held, however, to be 'pay' within Art 141 by the House of Lords in *R v Secretary of State for Employment ex p EOC* (1994). 'Pay' within Art 141 covers:

> ... any other consideration, whether in cash or in kind, which the worker receives, directly or indirectly, in respect of his employment, from his employers.

The fact that 'pay' does *not* arise out of the contract of employment is immaterial; it can arise out of the State 's action in legislating on the subject of 'pay'. The House of Lords referred the issue in *R v Secretary of State for Employment ex p Seymour-Smith* (1997). The ECJ ruled that compensation for unfair dismissal was pay within Art 141, but that the other remedies, reinstatement and re-engagement, were not. By comparison, there is no definition of pay in the EPA 1970.

5.2.4   Equal value covered

As originally drafted, Art 141 did not cover expressly equal pay for equal work. It was the Equal Pay Directive, noted in the next paragraph, which incorporated this type of claim. The Treaty of Amsterdam, however, rephrased Art 141 to include an express reference to equal value.

5.2.5 Equal Pay Directive

The EC enacted the Equal Pay Directive (75/117) in order to explain the width of the principle of equal pay for equal work in Art 141. It states that that principle:

> ... means, for the same work or for work to which equal value has been attributed, the elimination of all discrimination on grounds of sex with regard to aspects and conditions of remuneration.

As stated in Chapter 2, directives are enforceable only against emanations of the State (see *Marshall v Southampton and South West Hants AHA*, above). Accordingly, the Equal Pay Directive is effective only against State organs. Since, however, the Directive clarifies the extent of Art 141, rather than being a separate source of law, this restriction has not had much effect. Similarly, the wider the ambit of Art 141, the less need there is to rely on the Equal Treatment Directive 1976 (76/207), which, of course, is directly effective only against emanations of the State. Article 141, when it is directly effective, is so against both State and private employers. As the ECJ held in *Barber*, above, benefits paid by employers which are connected to an employee's compulsory redundancy fall within Art 141 as being 'pay'. Therefore, an employee can rely on the horizontally direct effect of Art 141, even though the benefits also fall within the Equal Treatment Directive which is, however, only vertically directly effective. The Equal Pay Directive and the Equal Treatment Directive are mutually exclusive. Pay falls within the former, not the latter. Therefore, for example, maternity pay is governed by the Equal Pay Directive because it constitutes 'pay' (*Gillespie v Northern Health and Social Services Board* (1996) (ECJ)). Accordingly, if the employers pay a woman less than her full pay because she is suffering from a pathological condition connected to pregnancy and therefore cannot attend work, that treatment is based on pregnancy and is discriminatory. The comparison to be made is with a worker who is paid in full if the illness is not connected with pregnancy.

5.2.6 *Danfoss* case

In *Handels-Og Kontorfunktionaerernes Forbund i Danmark v Dansk Arbejdsgiverforening* (1989) (the *Danfoss* case), the ECJ held that, under the Directive, pay differentials between men and women, such as those found in incremental pay schemes, had to be justified without reference to sex in order that they could still be lawful. Adaptability could be a lawful criterion if that criterion was important for the performance of the job. It could not be justified if it was not so related but simply had the effect of leading to the underpayment of women. The Court said that increments linked to seniority did not in general require justification, the argument being that experience is linked to performance. However, in criticism, it may be said that the connection is not a necessary one. In some jobs, such as assembling electrical components, experience does not lead to increased productivity.

It was also stated that the concept of transparency does not require employers to demonstrate exactly how they determined that the premium pay for a certain additional criterion was to be such and such an amount. The ECJ seems to have resiled from its position in *Danfoss* when it said in *Nimz v Freie und Hansestadt Hamburg* (1991) that increments based on length of service require justification where, overall, women are paid disproportionately less than men. What the ECJ is seeking is 'transparency'. That is, a woman must be able to work out why she has been placed at a certain pay point. If the reason why she has been placed where she has been is not transparent, the burden of proof is on the employers to demonstrate that their pay structure is not discriminatory. For example, merit pay must be justifiable.

5.2.7 Exclusions

Article 7(1)(a) of the Directive excludes provisions in relation to death and retirement 'and the possible consequences thereof for ... benefits'. Nowadays, this exemption is read narrowly (see *Marshall* and *Barber*).

5.2.8 Objective justification

The ECJ has allowed employers to have a defence to a claim of sexual discrimination in pay where the difference is objectively justified. The width of the defence of objective justification is the same as the English law defence of genuine material difference. The employers must have a real need for the difference in pay, the distinction must be appropriate 'with a view to achieving the objectives pursued', and it must be necessary. In *Rummler v Dato-Druck GmbH* (1987), the Court upheld a job evaluation study in a collective agreement by which points were awarded for muscular effort. The applicant argued that this criterion benefited men more than women. The Court did not accept her contention. It said that such a factor was permissible, provided that it was objectively justified. However, this criterion had to be balanced by factors which traditionally favoured women (presumably, matters such as manual dexterity). Once the factors had been set out, the evaluation of them, for example, by awarding a certain weighting to each factor, must not disadvantage employees of one sex; if it did, there was the possibility of indirect discrimination.

5.2.9 General

One way of viewing the effects of EC law on the EPA 1970 is that the former impliedly amends the latter. If, however, UK law is more favourable than Art 141, as restated in the Equal Pay Directive, UK claimants can rely on domestic law. If EC law is wider than UK law, UK claimants can use EC law as a 'free-standing' right enforceable by industrial tribunals. One difference between the two sets of laws arises from *Stadt Lengerich v Helmig* (1996) (ECJ). The Court held that a rule giving part-timers (who were largely female) overtime pay only when they had worked the same number of hours as full-timers before getting overtime payments was not discriminatory under Art 141 because part-timers and full-timers were treated alike. There was no different treatment and, therefore, no discrimination. Only if there was different treatment does a court have to enquire whether women were treated worse than men. In domestic law, there was a requirement or condition that part-timers must work full time hours before receiving extra pay. Could considerably more men than women comply with this? Was the rule justified? This case can be seen as one of several in which the ECJ has taken a less radical stance than it did in its earlier decisions. Cases such as *Barber*, with its 1990 cut-off date, and the cases on actuarial calculations, all reflect this trend.

Just as the law on trade unions and employees' rights has been consolidated, it would be helpful for students if the domestic and EC law of equal pay were put into one statute for reference purposes, though students should recall (see Chapter 2) that Articles of the EC Treaty may be directly applicable. Integration is necessary, for the law can be bewildering.

5.3   Critique

Some criticisms have already been mentioned, such as the 'volleying' of equal pay claim from UK law to EC law and back to UK law, the interrelationship between the Sex Discrimination and Equal Pay Acts, and the issue whether UK or EC law covers indirect discrimination. On the last, point the matter is crucial for UK women in relation to their employment law rights. Unlike the SDA 1975, there is no express reference to the concept of indirect discrimination in the EPA 1970. However, as we have seen, the English courts have sometimes read such a concept into the EPA 1970. The ECJ has also used the disparate impact argument in cases such as *Kowalska v Freie und Hansestadt Hamburg* (1990). In that case, the Court held that a redundancy scheme which excluded part time workers was discriminatory. The effect of the scheme was that substantially more women than men were excluded from the benefits. The court determined that part-timers should receive the money on a pro rata basis. This reasoning is important to UK women, for some 90% of part-timers in the UK are women, one of the highest proportions in the Community.

The EOC has strongly criticised the detailed workings of the equal value claim. In *Equal Pay for Men and Women – Strengthening the Acts*, 1990, it proposed among other matters that some experts should work full time, that experts should be trained and that they should be able to inspect the workplace. Time limits were also recommended in order to quicken the long-winded procedure. The report is worth studying by students in order to understand both the law and criticism of it. For instance, in relation to procedure, the Commission proposes that employers should be obliged to give equal pay to all women in the same employment who do 'like work' with a woman who has succeeded in her claim. This statutory duty would be a method of getting round the lack of a 'class action'. In November 1998, the EOC issued *Equality in the 21st Century: A New Equality Law for Britain*. Among the proposals were a duty on employers to monitor the pay of men and women, a power for employment tribunals to make awards applying to groups, and a power to be given to tribunals to vary collective agreements.

The Commission issued a Code of Practice on Equal Pay in 1996, which came into force in 1997. It recommends that employers should review their payment systems and, if need be, revise them to produce non-discriminatory wages, and that employers should adopt an equal pay policy.

EQUAL PAY

The Equal Pay Act 1970 is aimed at the upwards equalisation of women's pay with that of men. It operates by inserting a contractual 'equality clause', if the woman is engaged on 'like work', 'work rated as equivalent', or 'work of equal value'. Like work is defined as the same work or work which is so similar that there is no practical difference between the man's and the woman's job. Work rated as equivalent is where a job evaluation study has ranked the jobs equally. Work of equal value occurs where the jobs are of the same worth to the employers as determined by an independent expert. Employers have a defence of genuine material difference; examples are red-circling, London weighting and incremental payments for long service:

- *Shields v Coomes* (1978);

- *Bromley v Quick* (1988);

- *Hayward v Cammell Laird* (1988);

- *Rainey v Greater Glasgow Health Board* (1987);

- *Enderby v Frenchay HA* (1993);

- *North Yorkshire CC v Ratcliffe* (1995).

Effect of EC law

EC law, now based on Art 141 of the EC Treaty, has extended English law, but, at present, important issues await resolution by the ECJ:

- *Barber v Guardian Royal Exchange* (1990);

- *Smith v Avdel Systems Ltd* (1994).

Pay is widely defined under EC law and covers, for example, occupational pension schemes and payments on redundancy.

The width of Art 141 is clarified by the Equal Pay Directive 1975. The ECJ is seeking 'transparency' in payment systems and distinctions in pay are permitted only when they are necessary and appropriate. Separate collective agreements for men and women which in themselves are not discriminatory will not survive scrutiny by the ECJ where female and male earnings are unequal.

Criticisms

The law and procedure are complex, they are not found in one place, and, in places, they are uncertain:

- *R v SSE ex p EOC* (1993).

The equal value process has been severely criticised because of its long-windedness, the lack of expertise of the independent 'experts' and the time it takes to draft the report. To understand the law, knowledge of UK and EC law is needed, and several points remain unclear. A recent attempt, supported by the Equal Opportunities Commission, failed. The Conservative Government believed itself to be under a duty not to increase burdens on business.

CHAPTER 6

DISCRIMINATION ON THE GROUNDS OF SEX, RACE OR DISABILITY

6.1 Introduction: basic approach

The law on sexual bias in employment was laid down in the Sex Discrimination Act (SDA) 1975, and the law on racial discrimination in the Race Relations Act (RRA) 1976. The RRA 1976 had two precursors from the previous decade and some attempt had been made to open up the professions to women. Both Acts apply to areas which are not part of employment law, and those areas (such as schools) will be considered only insofar as they illustrate general principles. EC law on sex discrimination is restricted to the employment field. Only recently has power been given by the Treaty of Amsterdam to the Community institutions to 'combat discrimination based on ... racial or ethnic origin, religion or belief, disability, age or sexual orientation'.

The two statutes are similarly phrased. For example, both Acts prohibit indirect discrimination. To avoid duplication, this chapter will refer only to sex discrimination, except where racial discrimination law exhibits differences. Disability will be discussed separately. One difference is immediately evident: the SDA 1975 prohibits discrimination on the grounds of sex, whereas the RRA 1976 forbids discrimination on the grounds of race. (There are difficulties with persons who have been discriminated against on both grounds, for example, black women: they may be more than doubly disadvantaged.) Another difference is that claims that employers have sexually discriminated against an employee are brought under the Equal Pay Act 1970, whereas claims in relation to racial discrimination are brought under the RRA. The first such claim was *Wakeman v Quick Corp* (1999). The Court of Appeal rejected a discrimination claim by English employees that the defendant company was paying some of its Japanese workers more, because the latter were seconded from Japan.

One other difference needs noting: there are more exceptions to sexual discrimination than there are to racial discrimination. One may wish, on the grounds of decency, to prevent men from using women's lavatories, but there would be an outcry if black men were prohibited from entering white men's lavatories. This topic is dealt with under the exceptions to the SDA 1975 and RRA 1976, below. Both Acts were drafted in the English manner, that is, as rules followed by exceptions. EC law has reduced and modified the exceptions. The enforcement methods of the Equal Opportunities Commission and the Commission for Racial Equality are considered in Chapter 2. They have issued Codes of Practice on discrimination (SI 1985/387 and SI 1983/1081, respectively). As with equal pay, there is a directive on sexual discrimination (76/207). Being a directive, it is only vertically directly effective (see Chapter 2).

The House of Lords ruled in *R v Secretary of State for Employment* (1995) that the provisions (now repealed) which prevented part time employees from claiming a remedy for unfair dismissal contravened this Directive. The Government swiftly introduced legislation to give effect to this ruling in the Employment Protection (Part-Time Employees) Regulations 1995 (SI 1995/31), which now forms part of the Employment Rights Act (ERA) 1996. EC law has reached the stage where protection from sexual discrimination is seen as a fundamental human right. UK law is not so unequivocal.

The law concerned with disability on the ground of discrimination is based on the Disability Discrimination Act 1995. This statute differs in fundamental respects from the RRA and SDA and is, therefore, considered separately (see 6.10, below).

6.1.1 Aim of the discrimination legislation

The aim of the Acts is to provide equality of opportunity. There is little attempt to provide equality of outcome. The Acts can be seen as one part of the UK's human rights law. One problematic issue is that the remedy in English law is an individual one, whereas discrimination actually occurs against groups (blacks, women, etc). This problem is not as acute in disability discrimination law, where the focus is upon the individual. The case for non-discrimination from an economic perspective includes reduced turnover of staff, reduced costs of defending claims and a well motivated workforce. In this sense, anti-discrimination law provides an economic impetus: employers can select their employees from the widest possible range of talented people. What is sometimes called 'positive action', for example, the specific encouragement of Asian women to apply for places on training courses where they are underrepresented, is permitted, but in general, 'reverse discrimination' is not. For example, a firm cannot decide just to employ Afro-Caribbean men in the workforce because they are not represented at all at present, for that would be discrimination against white people.

The European Court of Justice (ECJ) ruled in *Kalanke v Freie Hansestadt Bremen* (1995) that a preference for a female candidate for promotion, all other things being equal (a rather weak form of positive discrimination), was unlawful when she was equally well qualified as a male employee. Shortly afterwards, however, the ECJ decided that positive discrimination was lawful where a female was promoted in preference to a male when they were both equally placed but women were under-represented, provided that the individual circumstances of the man could be taken into account (*Marschall v Land Nordrhein Westfalen* (1998)).

The Treaty of Amsterdam extended the small concession to positive discrimination found in the EC Treaty by permitting national measures to benefit the under-represented group. There is a Council Recommendation on Positive Action (84/635), and EC law was amended by the Treaty of

Amsterdam to include some forms of positive discrimination. Positive action is unaffected. It remains lawful to set up jobshares for women to return to work and to advertise in the ethnic press. While the Acts are directed at discrimination against women and ethnic minorities, they also apply to discrimination against men and white people. The Equal Opportunities Commission (EOC) reported in 1996 that it had received more complaints from men than women in 1995. It is moot how far the Acts have eradicated discrimination. The Conservative Government saw the Acts as burdens on business, but no attempt was made to repeal them. The EC regards non-discrimination on the grounds of sex as a fundamental human right. Exceptions are construed strictly; a directive passed under the Maastricht Treaty reverses the normal burden of proof as to defences; and the Fourth Action Plan 1996–2000 aims to achieve sexual equality. The Treaty of Amsterdam 1997 (which came into force in May 1999) provides that 'full equality in practice between men and women in working life' is the goal of EC law.

6.2 Coverage: effect and width

Until quite recently, the law was as stated *per* Lord Davey in *Allen v Flood* (1898):

> ... an employer may ... refuse to employ [a person] from the most mistaken, capricious, malicious or morally reprehensible motives that can be conceived, but the workman has no right of action against him.

In general, this statement remains true today. The law of contract governs, and that law is not constrained by any anti-discrimination principle. The rules of natural justice do not apply to prospective employees. Employers can turn down people whom they consider too old, too experienced, and so on. A trade union can refuse to employ a full time official because no money is available. The SDA 1975 changed the position in relation to sex. The SDA prohibits discrimination on the grounds of sex and marital status against women and men before, during and after employment. Accordingly, it applies even when no contract is in existence, such as at the interview stage pre-employment. The SDA 1975 also forbids discrimination on the grounds of married status (s 3) but not on the grounds that the applicant is single. The RRA 1976 also changed the law laid down by Lord Davey. Joining the EC in 1973 did not affect the statutes, either as a boost towards passing them or as a matter of drafting. Influence came from the USA. This may sound strange to modern employment lawyers, as nowadays influence comes from the EC.

The Acts extend beyond employees and apprentices to cover those working under a contract to do work personally Examples include a self-employed plumber who does the job himself and an articled clerk (*Oliver v JP Malnick & Co* (1983)). An insurance agent working on a commission only basis was held to be working under a contract to perform the work personally

(*Hill Samuel Investment Services Group Ltd v Nwauzu* (1994)). The definition excludes some jobs, for example, a subpostmaster, for he does not have to do the work personally, just supervise it (*Sheehan v Post Office Counters Ltd* (1999)). A doctor is also excluded because, in terms of the Acts, he does not act under a 'contract personally to execute any work or labour'. Foster carers are not employees of local authorities. Members of the armed forces used to be exempt from the requirements of the SDA 1975, but this is no longer the case, except where the discrimination is done to ensure effectiveness in combat: SDA 1975 (Application to Armed Forces, etc) Regulations 1994 (SI 1994/3276).

In relation to employment matters, the forum is the employment tribunal. There is no qualifying period or minimum number of hours. The claim must be made within three months of the prohibited act or omission, unless the employment tribunal considers it just and equitable to extend the limit: s 76 of the SDA 1975; s 68 of the RRA 1976. Cases on time limits in unfair dismissal claims are not binding in the context of discrimination. For example, it may be fair in discrimination cases to extend the limit when the claimant has received wrong legal advice or has gone through an internal appeals procedure. The Employment Appeal Tribunal (EAT) held in *Rastall v Midland Electricity plc* (1996) that it was just and equitable to extend the period where the ECJ had ruled that English law did not comply with EC law. Applicants had to put in claims within a reasonable time of the date on which they knew or ought to have known that they had a fair prospect of succeeding. A State should not be permitted to hide behind procedural limitations when it has not fully transposed a directive into national law. Leave to appeal was refused. The ECJ held that that SDA 1975 did not fully implement EC law (*Marshall v Southampton and West Hampshire AHA (No 2)* (1993)).

Time limits where English law falls short of EC norms do not run until the date of the full transposition of EC law into English law (not from the date of the ECJ judgment); otherwise, individual rights under EC law would not be protected. In that eventuality, the limit must not be less favourable than domestic limits; or, perhaps, it must be a reasonable one, that is, time runs from the date when it was reasonably clear to affected persons that a claim could now be brought (*Rankin v British Coal Corp* (1995)). Someone who has lost his case under English law but then discovers that EC law is wider can bring a claim in an employment tribunal in reliance on EC law, provided that he does so within a reasonable time of the clarification of EC law (*Methilhill Bowling Club v Hunter* (1995)).

6.2.1 Territorial ambit

The Acts apply only to employment at an establishment in Great Britain (s 10 of the SDA 1975; s 84 of the RRA 1976). Therefore, a cashier on a cross-channel ferry is not covered (*Haughton v Olau Lines (UK) Ltd* (1986)). However, s 84 is disapplied where the EC doctrine of free movement of workers applies. Accordingly, an Italian national is entitled to protection under the RRA on the grounds of nationality even though he works wholly or mainly outside Great Britain (*Bossa v Nordstress Ltd* (1998)).

6.2.2 Vicarious liability

Employers are responsible for the acts of their employees who discriminate unless they show that they took reasonably practicable steps to stop the discrimination (s 41 of the SDA 1975; s 32 of the RRA 1976). The employers' lack of knowledge and lack of approval are irrelevant. An equal opportunities policy or a policy of investigating every complaint of discrimination is evidence that the employers are taking such steps to prevent discrimination, but it has been held that an oral warning to perpetrators is sufficient. The Acts do require them to take 'such steps as [are] reasonably practicable to prevent the employee from doing that act', which can be read as '*all* such steps', for only then will discrimination be averted. The test of reasonable practicability is a higher one than reasonableness. An equal opportunity policy will not *per se* render the employers immune.

The extent of vicarious liability is controversial. In *Tower Boot Ltd v Jones* (1995), the EAT held that the test for vicarious liability was the tortious one. The employee's act must be one which falls within the scope of the fellow employee's employment, a phrase which covers doing an authorised act in an unauthorised way. If the colleague's behaviour cannot be called an unauthorised way of doing an authorised act by 'any stretch of the imagination', the employers are not liable. Therefore, if, as on the facts of the above case, an employee is racially abused and tortured by his so called workmates on racial grounds, the employers are not vicariously liable. Similarly, in *Waters v Metropolitan Police Comr* (1997), the Court of Appeal held that acts of discrimination, namely, victimisation on sexual grounds which took place off the employer's premises (a pub) and outside working time, did not make the respondent vicariously liable. Had the acts been done in the pub immediately after work or at a police social function, the employers would have been liable. *Tower Boot* and *Waters* have been trenchantly criticised. The tort test did not promote the anti-discrimination thrust of the statutes, and an employee who discriminates is in breach of the fundamental contractual duty to co-operate with colleagues. Therefore, harassment is done in the course of employment.

The Court of Appeal in *Tower Boot Ltd v Jones* (1997) overruled the EAT's decision. Waite LJ stated that employers should not be able to escape liability for discrimination through a tribunal's use of the common law principle of vicarious liability developed in one area of law (that is, tort) in another, wholly different one. 'To do so would seriously undermine that statutory scheme of the [Acts relating to discrimination] and flout the purposes which they were passed to achieve.' Whether something was done in the course of employment for the purposes of those statutes was to be decided by the tribunal, inquiring as a matter of ordinary language whether it was so done. Waite LJ rejected the tort concept (which remains unaffected by decisions on discrimination) on the basis that, by using it, 'the more heinous the act of discrimination, the less likely it will be that the employers would be liable'. Tribunals have to decide in a common sense way whether the act was done in the course of employment. Among relevant factors are whether the incident occurred in working hours, at the workplace or at employer-organised social events.

6.2.3   Instructing discrimination

It is unlawful for employers to give instructions to discriminate. Aiding or pressuring another to discriminate is illegal (s 42 of the SDA 1975; s 33 of the RRA 1976). It is in this way that an employee's colleague can be made liable for his own act of discrimination. A fellow worker can be liable under this provision even though the employers have a defence to vicarious liability by virtue of s 41(3) of the SDA, which provides that they are not liable if they took all such steps as were reasonably practicable to prevent the fellow worker from discriminating. Inducement to racial discrimination is also unlawful (s 31 of the RRA 1976).

6.3   Grounds of discrimination

Discrimination on the grounds of sex, marital status and race are discussed below.

6.3.1   Sex

The SDA 1975 applies to discrimination against both women and men (s 2(1)). It is thought that neither the SDA nor EC law applies to homosexuals (by analogy with *Grant v South-West Trains* (1998), an ECJ case on the Equal Pay Directive). However, discrimination against homosexuals is contrary to the European Convention. Within the SDA 1975, according to an employment tribunal in *White v British Sugar Corp* (1977), 'woman' means 'biological woman' (a proposition which has been under attack for 20 years and has not always been followed). A woman who dresses as a man and who has for many years been treated as a man remains a woman for the purposes of the SDA 1975.

However, the ECJ held in *P v S* (1996) that it was discriminatory to dismiss a transsexual who was undergoing gender reassignment, because of the general principle of EC law that there must be no discrimination on sexual grounds. *P v S* was applied to English law in *Chessington World of Adventures v*

Reed (1997), where the EAT held that the SDA could be construed in accordance with the Equal Treatment Directive. The SDA was amended by the Sex Discrimination (Gender Reassignment) Regulations 1999 (SI 1999/1162), but ministers of religion remain exempt from the law of sex discrimination. The court said that non-discrimination is a fundamental principle of EC law. However, it must be said that, from the viewpoint of English law, EC discrimination law seemed to be narrow because it did not include racial discrimination until the Treaty of Amsterdam came into force in 1999. Even now, the new Article merely permits EC legislation and is not directly effective.

For the present English position in relation to pregnancy, see below, 6.5.4. Since pregnancy is a condition which only women can have, it is automatically discriminatory to refuse to employ a woman or to dismiss her on the ground of pregnancy. In respect of homosexuals, sexual orientation can, like pregnancy, be defined only in terms of the complainant's sex. As pregnancy is a ground for sex discrimination, homosexuality should be treated in the same way.

6.3.2   Marital status

Section 3(1) of the SDA 1975 prohibits discrimination against married people. It does not, however, forbid discrimination against single people. This distinction looks inelegant, and appears to fall short of the Equal Treatment Directive (76/207) which prohibits discrimination 'in particular by reference to marital or family status'. Marital status assuredly includes the status of not being married. An early case exemplifies the effect of s 3(1) and the near-absurdity to which it can give rise. In *Bick v Royal West of England School for the Deaf* (1976), an employee was dismissed one day because she was going to get married on the next. She had no claim since, at the time of dismissal, she was not married. Cohabitees receive no protection. The Equal Treatment Directive's prohibition of discrimination on the grounds of sex does not extend to discrimination on the basis that the applicant has a child. There must, in all cases, be discrimination on the grounds of sex.

6.3.3   Race

The RRA 1976 is not restricted to 'race' in any narrow sense but extends to 'colour, race, nationality or ethnic or national origins' (s 3(1)). None of these terms is defined in the RRA 1976. In *Northern Joint Police Board v Power* (1997), the EAT held that the English and the Scottish had separate national origins. While the term 'nationality' relates to citizenship within a State, 'national origins' refers to history and geography, which point towards the fact that a nation existed at some time. Therefore, when a Scottish police force turned down an application for the post of chief constable because the applicant was

English, the rejection was on the grounds of national origins and, therefore, on the grounds of race.

An example of discrimination on the grounds of nationality is a refusal to employ an Irish person. In *McAuley v Auto Alloys* (1994), an Irish employee succeeded in a claim when he had been called a 'thick paddy' and was the butt of Irish jokes. The landmark authority on ethnic origin is *Mandla v Dowell Lee* (1983). Lord Fraser, relying on New Zealand authority, said that:

> ... a group is identifiable in terms of its ethnic origins if it is a segment of the population distinguished from others by a combination of shared customs, beliefs, traditions and characteristics derived from a common or presumed common past, even if not drawn from what in biological terms is a common racial stock.

On this approach, the English and Scots do not have different ethnic origins, for each group contains members of many ethnic backgrounds (*Power*). The last phrase in the above quote extends the coverage of the RRA 1976 to converts to religions included within the term 'ethnic origins'. Whether someone is within a certain ethnic group is a question of fact for the tribunal. A rule that no time off is to be given for attendance at mosques affects Asians more than whites, and Asians fall within the broad definition of 'race'. In *Mandla v Dowell Lee*, Sikhs were covered. In view of that decision and the policy behind the Act, Jews are covered, and the EAT did not doubt that this conclusion was correct in *Seide v Gillette Industries Ltd* (1980). However, adherents of other religions and sects, such as Catholics, Jehovah's Witnesses, Muslims and Rastafarians (*Crown Suppliers (PSA) v Dawkins* (1993)) are not included because they do not fall within Lord Fraser's definition – they are not identifiable in terms of their ethnic origins. (In fact, there are conflicting tribunal decisions on Muslims. In one tribunal case, *Hansard* was used to demonstrate that 'Asian Muslims' fell within a protected class. I thank my former student, Mohammed Dosanjh, for this information.)

In England, Wales and Scotland, there are no laws expressly forbidding religious discrimination. From the viewpoint of religion, present law appears absurd. For example, Jews are protected by the law of racial discrimination but Muslims are not. However, this outcome is consistent with Lord Fraser's definition of ethnic origins. After all, Parliament could easily have added 'religion' to s 3(1), but it did not do so. Discrimination on the grounds of language is not discrimination on the grounds of race. Therefore, a refusal to employ a person because he cannot speak Welsh is not discriminatory. Choosing a person at random is not discriminatory. However, discriminating against the Welsh people as a whole is unlawful because they constitute an ethnic group. An employment tribunal ruled that the Welsh:

- have a long shared history;
- have cultural traditions of their own;

- have a common geographical origin;

- have a language, albeit not spoken by all who claim to be Welsh;

- have a common literature and, probably even more distinctively, a common choral tradition peculiar to those of Welsh origin;

- have a predisposition to a particular religion, of those who are religious; and

- constitute a minority in terms of numbers compared, in the instant case, to the English.

In the 1991 Census, 5.5% of the population (just over three million people) classified themselves as non-white. Half of these came from the Indian subcontinent and 30% were black. There are some 285,000 Jews and 63,000 gypsies. The Welsh were not asked to identify themselves.

6.4 Definition

Sexual and racial discrimination are prohibited when they fall within the relevant statute. The several types of discrimination are discussed below.

6.4.1 Disparate treatment/impact

Both the SDA 1975 and RRA 1976 prohibit two forms of discrimination. These forms are generally called 'direct' and 'indirect'. The US terminology is 'disparate treatment' and 'disparate impact', those terms perhaps reflecting more closely what is prohibited than the English terms. Indirect discrimination was included by the then Home Secretary, Roy (now Lord) Jenkins, as a result of a visit to the USA. He was convinced that the law should root out practices which disfavoured women as well as straightforward discriminatory treatment (for example, advertisements stating that 'no women need apply'). Indirect discrimination is the tool for testing hidden or institutional discrimination.

6.4.2 Comparing

Both Acts require a comparison to be made between the man (or white person) and the woman (or ethnic person). Care must be taken to compare the two groups correctly. For example, in *Dhatt v McDonalds Hamburgers Ltd* (1991), the Court of Appeal held that there was no discrimination when the employers asked job applicants for their work permits when they were not EC nationals but did not ask for them when they were. The treatment of the applicant for the job, who was an Indian national, was to be compared with other non-EC applicants. Since all of them were asked to show their permits, there was no discrimination on the grounds of nationality. In criticism, it may be said that, if the court had applied the 'but for' test noted at 6.4.8, below, the result should have been different, for employers are entitled to ask EC nationals for their work permits.

If a union refuses representation at a disciplinary hearing to a male alleged to have sexually harassed a woman and it would have refused the same to a woman, there is no discrimination. The man and the woman would have been treated the same. The necessity for comparison has caused problems in relation to pregnancy. This issue is noted at 6.5.4, below. Difficulties also arise in respect of dress codes (see 6.5.4, below) and sexual harassment (see 6.4.10, below). The next sections deal with the modes of discrimination forbidden by the Acts.

6.4.3   Direct (s 1(1)(a))

This form of discrimination occurs where a man treats a woman less favourably than he treats or would treat a man. Unlike under the Equal Pay Act 1970, there is no need for an actual male comparison. A 'hypothetical male' is used – would these employers treat a (hypothetical) man more favourably than they treated this woman? An example occurred when the Army gave a smaller amount of non-statutory redundancy payments to members of the Women's Royal Army Corps than to similarly placed male soldiers. The Southampton employment tribunal held in 1995 that the women were entitled to compensation of £6,000–7,000 after the Ministry of Defence admitted liability. Since an aim of the law is to avoid employers' using stereotypes of women, discrimination is prohibited only if it was done on the grounds of sex. Accordingly, if the employers rejected a puny woman because the job required a strong person to do it, she has not been discriminated against because the unfavourable treatment, the rejection of her job application, is not on the grounds of her sex but because she cannot do the job. (See below for indirect discrimination.) If, however, all women were rejected because the employers considered that all women were weak, then the applicants would have been rejected on the grounds of their sex, not because they are weak.

Similarly, turning down a request for a jobshare from a woman returning to work after maternity leave is not discrimination so long as she is not treated less favourably than a man would have been treated in similar circumstances (*British Telecommunications plc v Roberts* (1996)). Pregnancy discrimination is direct discrimination (see 6.5.4, below). Less favourable treatment includes dismissing an employee or subjecting her to any other detriment. The latter phrase includes permitting someone within the employer's control to subject the employee to a detriment such as racial harassment (*Burton v De Vere Hotels* (1996), the Bernard Manning case). Here, the employers were directly (not vicariously) liable. Employers are, therefore, under a duty to protect their employees from discrimination by those under their control. On the facts of *Burton*, hotel supervisors could have reduced the effect of racial harassment by moving black waitresses out of the room in which the harassment was taking place.

Burton was applied to sex discrimination in *Chessington World of Adventures v Reed* (1997), where the employers knew about a campaign of harassment against a biological male who was changing his gender identity to female. They did not take adequate steps to prevent the campaign, even though they could have exercised control, and were accordingly directly liable. An employment tribunal, however, distinguished *Burton* when employers had done all they could (such as employing security staff) to prevent racial abuse.

It was held in *Burrett v West Birmingham HA* (1994) that it is not discrimination to apply a dress code to both sexes but to have different constituents in the code for each sex. This is a decision of the EAT; the Court of Appeal decision, which was to the same effect, is unreported. It is uncertain whether the case applies beyond dress codes. The fact that a female nurse thought it demeaning to wear a cap when men did not was not 'less favourable treatment'. It was a matter for the tribunal to decide on the issue. That is, the test is not whether the applicant considered there to be less favourable treatment but whether the employment tribunal decides that there is less favourable treatment. The cases on uniform are difficult to square with the Court of Appeal's ruling in *Gill v El Vino Co Ltd* (1983) that denying someone something, in this case the right to stand at a bar, was less favourable treatment. The ruling is also hard to reconcile with *James v Eastleigh BC* (1990), discussed below. Because the nurse was a woman, she had to wear a cap; male nurses did not. The uniform cases, however, hold otherwise. The difference in uniform was not less favourable treatment to the woman. The employers would penalise a male nurse who did not wear part of his uniform. See, also, 6.5.4, below.

6.4.4 Motive irrelevant

Contrary to early authority, the law is that the employers' motives are irrelevant. (See, also, 6.4.8, below.) If they think that it is not in the woman's best interests to promote her, there is discrimination. An important case is *Ministry of Defence v Jeremiah* (1979). The defendants refused to allow women to work in part of their plants. They did so because the job was dirty. However, there was more money in doing that job than in the work which the women actually did. The Court of Appeal rejected the idea that the employers' chivalry provided them with a defence. Their motive was irrelevant. (In fact, it was the men who were claiming: why should they alone do the dirty jobs?) Similarly, a refusal to employ a black person will be discriminatory even if opposition to his appointment among the workforce would lead to industrial strife.

6.4.5 Example

Hurley v Mustoe (1981) illustrates direct discrimination. A woman was sacked because the employer had a policy of not employing married women. He considered that, because of their childcare responsibilities, these women would be more likely to take time off to the detriment of his restaurant business than unmarried women without children. It was held that the rule was discriminatory against women and contravened the prohibition of discrimination on grounds of marital status. This case shows the law's attack on stereotypes.

6.4.6 *De minimis* **and unequal treatment**

There is a possibility that discrimination will not be unlawful if it is *de minimis*. Lord Denning MR was of this view in *Jeremiah*, above. The contrary view is that all sexual and racial discrimination should be expunged and, therefore, the *de minimis* exception should not apply. Eveleigh LJ expressed this view in the non-employment case of *Gill v El Vino Co Ltd* (1983), as did the EAT in *Greig v Community Industry* (1979). Another issue resolved in *Jeremiah* was that men were discriminated against by being given dirty jobs which were not given to the women, even though the employers compensated them for the dirt. Differently put, employers cannot buy the right to discriminate on sexual or racial grounds.

6.4.7 **Activating cause**

One limitation on direct discrimination should be noted. The discrimination must be the 'activating cause' of what the employers did (*Seide v Gillette Industries Ltd* (1980)). It is not sufficient that discrimination existed as a background factor. The fact that Mr Seide was Jewish was not the activating cause, just a factor explaining why the employers acted as they did in response to complaints about him. There is, therefore, no liability for racial or sexual discrimination if the treatment was made on non-racial or non-sexual grounds. On the other hand, provided that the discrimination was the cause of the employers' acting as they did, it does not matter that they had other motives. For example, a teacher at a Catholic school may be dismissed because she is pregnant. It does not, therefore, matter that her sexual partner was a priest and the school considered that she could no longer teach pupils about personal relationships and religious education. Had she not been pregnant, she would not have been dismissed.

6.4.8 **Objective cause**

There has been extensive discussion in the cases about whether or not the employers' intent or motive is relevant in discrimination cases. The principal authority is *James v Eastleigh BC* (1990). The council gave free admission to their swimming pool to women over 60 and men over 65. Those ages were the State pension ages. Men aged 60–64 had to pay, whereas women of the same age did not. The House of Lords held that the charging of fees to men aged 60–64 was discriminatory. Using the 'but for' test, men would have been treated as favourably as women but for their sex. The council's motive (to benefit the poor) or intention was irrelevant. Therefore, no matter how good the council's intent, the rule was discriminatory. The sole intent which is relevant is the intent to do the act/omission which is alleged to be discriminatory. The Lords' decision was only by a three to two majority (though it had earlier reached the same decision in a case involving the allocation of grammar school places) and has been criticised, but it seems to be correct both on the wording of the statutes and in terms of policy, the policy being the elimination of discrimination. *James* was approved by the House of Lords in *Nagarajan v London Regional Transport* (1999).

Take the following facts as an illustration of the 'but for' test. A woman is dismissed when it is discovered that she has married a man who works for a rival firm. Why has she been dismissed? Perhaps it is because she may divulge confidential information to her husband and, through him, to his employers. She has not been dismissed on the grounds of her sex. She would have been dismissed if she had been a male who cohabited with the rival employee. The tribunal, therefore, looks for the effective cause, which need not be the sole or even the main cause. A recent application of *James* was *Chief Constable of Greater Manchester Police v Hope* (1999). Questions about a white male sergeant's relationship with an Asian female civilian trainee would not have been asked but for his sex and race. The EAT again emphasised that the employers' intentions and motives were irrelevant to the issue of liability, though the lay members considered that they were relevant to compensation.

6.4.9 Stereotypes

Two cases have been selected to demonstrate how the law has been used to attack stereotyping by employers. In *Horsey v Dyfed CC* (1982), the council refused to send the applicant on a training course in the London area. Her husband was employed there. They assumed that she would stay in London on completion of the course and not return to her job with the council. The EAT said that the council would not have treated a married male employee in the same way if his wife lived near London. Accordingly, there was discrimination. In *Coleman v Skyrail Oceanic Ltd* (1981), a female booking clerk was dismissed when she married a man working for a rival firm. The Court of Appeal held that her dismissal was discriminatory: the employers had assumed that the husband would be the breadwinner. The breadth of such cases should be noted. If a female employee was dismissed for proposing to give up her job in order to join her husband in another town or for divulging confidential information to her partner, she would not have been dismissed on the grounds of her sex (though she might have been dismissed unfairly).

6.4.10 Sexual harassment

One aspect of disparate treatment is sexual harassment, whether verbal or physical. (Harassment may also be racial, as where a Japanese manager told a British national that he had a strange skin colour.) The term 'sexual harassment' does not appear in the SDA 1975 and there was some doubt as to whether this Act covered such conduct. In *Porcelli v Strathclyde Regional Council* (1985), the (Scottish) Court of Session held that sexual harassment, such as a male putting his hand up a woman's skirt, did constitute discrimination, for the man would not have acted in like manner towards another man. The applicant must have been subjected to a detriment on the grounds of sex. Calling out 'Hiya, big tits' to a woman is directly discriminatory. The remark is sex-related and would not have been made to a man (*Insitu Cleaning Co Ltd v Heads* (1995)). There is some authority that some forms of harassment are, by definition, based on sex. Therefore, no male comparator is needed (*British Telecommunications plc v Williams* (1997)). This argument already prevails in the context of pregnancy (see 6.5.4, below) and received the support of the President of the EAT in *Reed v Stedman* (1999):

> In a sexual harassment case, the answer [to the question whether the conduct was on the grounds of sex] will usually be quite clear without resort to a comparator, actual or hypothetical.

'Harassment' is an ill chosen word (and not one which appears in the statute), insofar as it connotes a sequence or series of acts. There is no doubt that one act is sufficient (*Bracebridge Engineering Ltd v Darby* (1990)). The EAT also held that the discrimination was done in the course of the harassers' employment because they were exercising their supervisory function when they performed the act of harassment. Accordingly, the employers were liable. One employment tribunal case involved a sales manager exposing his penis to a female sales representative; when she complained, the sales director exposed his penis to her. The tribunal held that both men's conduct was a detriment. The exposures would not have been made in front of male workers.

Not only will employers face compensation and legal expenses, but they will lose trained staff and productivity. In *Insitu*, the EAT said that whether one act was sufficient to found a complaint was a matter of fact and degree for the employment tribunal. Conduct of a sexual nature which may be welcome from one colleague may not be welcome when performed by another; in the latter event, there can be sexual harassment. It seems to be the law that there will not be discrimination if the affected employee was sensitive to the alleged harassment but a reasonable employee would not have been. However, it is suggested that, since the definition of harassment depends on the perceptions of the recipient, this type of thinking should not be used. Similarly, if the applicant finds the conduct unwelcome, it does not matter that the tribunal members would not have done so (*Reed v Stedman* (1999)).

There have been decisions which can be seen as anti-women. In *Wileman v Minilec Engineering Ltd* (1988), the EAT gave only a small amount of compensation because the applicant wore 'provocative' clothes and was in the habit of 'flaunting herself'. It is difficult to see how the way a woman chooses to dress can be relevant to the question of how she copes with alleged sexual harassment. In *Snowball v Gardner Merchant Ltd* (1987), the EAT permitted cross-examination concerning a woman's consensual sex life to see whether she had suffered a detriment in relation to unwanted advances, and seemed to say that any woman who called her bed her 'playpen' intended to 'play' with any man who made sexual overtures to her, while in *Stewart v Cleveland Guest (Engineering) Ltd* (1994), displaying nude pin-ups of women did not amount to treating the applicant less favourably than men, on the grounds that such photography may be as offensive to men as to women. The EAT held that the employment tribunal was the body best placed to determine the issue of whether the treatment of female employees was less favourable than the treatment of men, and added that employers should treat complaints of sexual harassment expeditiously and in a sensitive manner. This case is incompatible with the EC recommendation discussed below. There has been at least one employment tribunal case (*Salmon v David* (1998)) where prison officers openly looking at pornographic magazines was held to be sexual harassment of a female prison officer. It is also suggested that *Stewart* is inconsistent with *British Telecommunications plc v Williams* (1997), where it was held that there did not have to be a male comparator in a sexual harassment case.

6.4.11 EC on harassment

The EC has become increasingly interested in sexual harassment, which it sees as a widespread problem affecting the working lives of millions of women (though it is suggested that sexual harassment at work will not be stopped until society changes beyond the workplace). It commissioned a study (Rubenstein, M, *The Dignity of Women at Work*, 1987), issued a Code of Practice (1992) and has made a Commission Recommendation (1991) that Member States adopt the Code. The definition of sexual harassment in the Recommendation is:

> ... unwanted conduct of a sexual nature, or other conduct based on sex affecting the dignity of men and women at work, including conduct of superiors and colleagues.

The Code speaks of 'unwanted conduct', but that does not mean:

> ... that a single act can [n]ever amount to harassment because, until done and rejected, it cannot be said that conduct is 'unwanted'. We regard this argument as specious. If it were correct, it would mean that a man is always entitled to argue that every act of harassment was different from the first and that he was testing to see if it was unwanted: in other words, it would amount to a licence for harassment ... the word 'unwanted' is essentially the same as 'unwelcome' or 'uninvited'.

The word 'unwanted' also emphasises that sexual harassment is defined by reference to the way in which the recipient sees the behaviour of the alleged harasser. Harassment is not defined by reference to the intent of the perpetrator. The reference in the definition to 'superiors' is a recognition of the fact that sexual harassment is often an aspect of the power relationship at work.

Pressure is building up for a directive on sexual harassment as a matter both of improving health and safety at work and increasing competitiveness. The Treaty of Amsterdam amended the EC Treaty so as to give jurisdiction over 'equal opportunities and equal treatment'. This amendment provides a legal base for a directive on sexual harassment. The EAT in *Wadman v Carpenter Farrer Partnership* (1993) advised employment tribunals to have regard to the Recommendation. In *Insitu Cleaning Co Ltd v Heads* (1995), an employment tribunal held that a single act could not constitute harassment because a man could not know whether his conduct was 'unwanted' until it had been rejected; therefore, the first act would not be discriminatory. The EAT held that, if such an argument were adopted, men would have a licence to harass women. They could otherwise say that they were merely testing whether the behaviour was unwanted.

6.4.12 Indirect discrimination

Indirect discrimination (s 1(1)(b)), a concept which drives from US law, is defined as occurring where the employer applies to a woman a requirement or condition which he applies or would apply to a man but:

- which is such that the proportion of women who can comply with it is considerably smaller than the proportion of men who can comply with it;

- which he cannot show to be justifiable irrespective of the sex of the person to whom it is applied; and

- which is to her detriment because she cannot comply with it.

EC law on equal pay and sex discrimination does not provide a definition.

6.4.13 Examples of indirect discrimination

An example is *Price v Civil Service Commission* (1978). The Civil Service had age limits of 17–28 for the job for which the applicant wished to apply. She was 35. The EAT held that the rule's effect was to discriminate against women because, in practice, fewer women than men could apply for the job when they were aged between those age limits because they were away from the labour force, having and rearing children. Although women were not physically prevented from applying for the job, in practice, the condition of being aged between 17 and 28 affected women considerably more than men. It was to their detriment because a woman over 28 could not get the job and the employers could not demonstrate that the rule was justified.

In *Coker v Lord Chancellor* (1999), there was a requirement or condition that the person appointed as special advisor to the Lord Chancellor should be known to him. More men than women satisfied this requirement. In *Meade-Hill v The British Council* (1995), the Court of Appeal held that a mobility clause was indirectly discriminatory because, in practice, fewer married women than men could comply with the requirement that they transferred to any part of the UK as the defendant required – at that stage, it was for the employers to justify the inclusion of the clause. It did not matter that the employers had not attempted to enforce the clause. (The Sex Discrimination Act was amended in 1993 to cover this very point but the facts of the case arose before 1993.) It should be noted that Millett LJ stressed that it would be easy for employers to justify mobility clauses. A similar situation arose in *Clarke v Eley (IMI) Kynoch Ltd* (1982). The firm was faced with selecting workers for redundancy. Part-timers were chosen to be sacked first. The EAT held that the company's selection, the condition or requirement, amounted to indirect discrimination. The part-timers were women. They could not comply in practice with the requirement that they work full time in order to avoid redundancy. It was to their detriment, for they were dismissed. And the requirement could not be justified.

It was said in *Brook v London Borough of Haringey* (1992) that a policy of 'last in, first out' was justifiable because it was accepted industrial relations practice, even though women would be more likely to be dismissed than men because of their absence from the labour market through rearing children. This case seems to be wrong in the light of the EC standard on justification, discussed below, 6.4.20. Certainly, the EAT should have considered any attempted justification fully. In *Home Office v Holmes* (1984), the employers refused to allow a woman with children to do part time work. (Five times as many women than men work part time, and women comprise very nearly half the total workforce.) They did not attempt to justify the requirement of full time work. The requirement was discriminatory. However, full time work may be part of the nature of the job. In *Clymo v Wandsworth LBC* (1989), the EAT instanced the post of managing director. In other words, in that instance, the necessity to work full time would not be a 'requirement or condition' within the statute. However, an obligation on a cleaner to work full time would be a requirement or condition. Northern Ireland favours the approach of *Holmes* over *Clymo*. Full time working can become part of the nature of the job and, therefore, a requirement or condition (*Briggs v North Eastern Education and Library Board* (1990)). English tribunals may follow this lead. *Clymo* also seems inconsistent with EC law.

If a woman moves from full time to part time work, say, when coming back after giving birth, she cannot choose to work only those hours which suit her (*Greater Glasgow Health Board v Carey* (1987)). It must, however, be remembered that, if there is no discrimination, a refusal to allow a jobshare will not be sexual discrimination (*British Telecommunications plc v Roberts* (1996)). If there is no evidence that men's claims for a change to their contracts would not have been rejected, there is no discrimination against women who were refused a jobshare. The tribunal remitted the case to see whether there had been indirect discrimination.

6.4.14 Must

In *Perera v Civil Service Commission (No 2)* (1983), the Court of Appeal held, contrary to earlier authorities, that the phrase 'requirement or condition' was a 'must'. That is, absolute qualifications for a job, in this case that the applicant be a barrister or solicitor, constituted a requirement or condition, but factors influencing the decision to employ, such as whether the job applicant could communicate well in English, were not. With regard to three of the cases noted in the last section, in *Price*, there was a requirement or condition that the women be aged between 17 and 28. In *Clarke*, there was a requirement or condition that part-timers be dismissed first. In *Home Office v Holmes* (1984), there was a requirement or condition that employees worked full time. There is a 'requirement or condition' for the purposes of the test for indirect discrimination where there is a contractual clause, as in *Meade-Hill*, above. The 'requirement or condition' bar has been criticised on the basis that it may not match up to EC norms, which require only a discriminatory 'practice'. That term can cover criteria which are not absolute bars. Obviously, at present, employers can evade the law by making absolute bars into discretionary factors, though astute tribunals can check whether a preference is in fact a requirement, as occurred with age limits in *Jones v University of Manchester* (1993).

Perera was followed by the Court of Appeal in *Meer v LB of Tower Hamlets* (1988), but Balcombe LJ thought that the case may be inconsistent with the purposes of the legislation. Despite the authority of the Court of Appeal, the EAT sitting in Scotland concluded in *Falkirk Council v Whyte* (1997) that 'requirement' should be read broadly to include desirable qualities, such as the fact that the employee-to-be had to have supervisory experience. This wide construction was said to be demanded by EC law. *Falkirk* was not followed by the employment tribunal in *Coker v Lord Chancellor* (1999), which applied *Perera*.

Both the Commission for Racial Equality (CRE) and the EOC have called for the repeal of the necessity for an absolute bar and its replacement by the phrase 'practice or policy'. The ECJ ruled in the equal pay case of *Enderby v Frenchay HA* (1994) that no 'requirement or condition' rule applies in relation to discriminatory pay, but the EAT held in *Bhudi v IMI Refiners Ltd* (1994) that the rule continues to apply to sex discrimination law outside the field of pay. The phrase 'requirement or condition' occurs in the English legislation. It cannot be construed so as to comply with EC law without distorting its meaning. Therefore, the English rule continues to apply. The EAT thought that domestic legislation may have to be amended at some time. It is suggested that the problem lies with the drafters of the UK legislation and not with the judiciary.

Words such as 'practice' and 'factor' would be better suited to transferring EC norms into UK law. The Equal Treatment Directive is not restricted to 'musts'.

Once the Directive on the Burden of Proof in Cases of Discrimination based on Sex (97/80) is in force, *Perera* will be overruled. The Directive applies in situations where 'an apparently neutral provision, criterion or practice' exists.

6.4.15 Considerably smaller

Considering the words 'considerably smaller proportion', one might expect that, if no woman could comply, indirect discrimination would not apply, for 0% is not a considerably smaller proportion but no proportion at all. This argument was rejected, however, in *Greencroft Social Club and Institute v Mullen* (1985). In *Wetstein v Misprestige Management Services Ltd* (1993), the EAT held that the question whether one group was considerably smaller than another was a question of fact for the tribunal. Therefore, it could not interfere with an employment tribunal decision that the number of Jews who could comply with a requirement that they work on Friday evenings in winter (90–95%) was not considerably smaller than non-Jews who could comply (100%). 'Considerably' means 'much' or 'a good deal'. It does not mean 'worthy of consideration': *McCausland v Dungannon DC* (1993), a decision of the Northern Ireland Court of Appeal on the Province's fair employment legislation, which is worded similarly to the English sex and race statutes. The court said that whether one pool was considerably smaller than another was a matter for the employment tribunal members in their role as an industrial jury. The difficulty is that employers cannot say whether the pools are discriminatory without an employment tribunal decision. The word 'considerably' does not appear in the EC legislation, which speaks of 'no discrimination *whatsoever* on grounds of sex' (emphasis added). Once again, UK law may fall below EC norms.

6.4.16 Pool for comparison

The Court of Appeal in *Jones v University of Manchester* (1993) approved guidance in a social security case as to how the pool should be chosen:

> (1) Identify the criterion for selection. (2) Identify the relevant population, comprising all those who satisfy all other criteria for selection ... (3) Divide the relevant population into groups representing those who satisfy the criterion and those who do not. (4) Predict statistically what proportion of each group should consist of women. (5) Ascertain what are the actual male/female balances in the two groups. (6) Compare the actual with the predicted balances. (7) If women are found to be under-represented in the first group and over-represented in the second, it is proved that the criterion is discriminatory.

Accordingly, the two pools for comparison comprise, first, all those who satisfy the allegedly discriminatory requirement and, secondly, those who do not;

both pools must otherwise be the same. In the USA, the courts apply the 'four-fifths rule', that is, if women do not, for example, form 80% of the male workforce, there is a disparity which must be explained. There is no such rule in the UK – it was rejected in *McCausland* – and, surprisingly, the EAT held in *Greater Manchester Police Authority v Lea* (1990) that it was unable to interfere with the 'factual' holding of an employment tribunal that 95.3% was a considerably smaller proportion than over 99%. In *Staffordshire CC v Black* (1995), 89.5% was held not to be a considerably smaller proportion than 97%. In *London Underground Ltd v Edwards (No 2)* (1998), the Court of Appeal decided that the difference was considerable where 100% of the men could comply with a requirement but only 95% of women could do so. The court stressed that the tribunal should not look simply at percentages but also at the number of persons in each pool (here, 25 women but over 2,000 men). It did not matter that the sole person who could not comply with the requirement was the applicant. The court emphasised that whether there existed a 'considerably smaller' proportion of one sex was very much a question of fact for the tribunal.

The most criticised case in this area is *Kidd v DRG (UK) Ltd* (1985). An employment tribunal determined that it was not necessarily true that a greater proportion of married women looked after children than unmarried ones. The EAT held that it could not interfere, for the selection of the groups for comparison was a question of fact. The comparison pools must be appropriately selected. In *Pearse v Bradford Metropolitan Council* (1988), it was held that the pool consisted of those qualified to apply for a full time job as senior lecturer in the department of applied and community services and not just those men (47%) and women (22%) who worked full time: in other words, 'like' must be compared with 'like'. In *Boyle v EOC* (1999), the ECJ said that a criterion is discriminatory when, 'albeit formulated in neutral terms, it works to the disadvantage of far more women than men'.

6.4.17 Can comply

As *Price v Civil Service Commission* (6.4.3, above) demonstrates, 'can comply' does not mean 'can physically comply'. Women can comply with a requirement that they are aged between 17 and 28 when they are aged between 17 and 28. However, for various reasons, they might not in practice be able to comply with that requirement. The landmark authority is *Mandla v Dowell Lee*, above. A headmaster refused to let a Sikh boy who wore a turban into his Christian-ethic school. The boy could physically comply with a requirement that boys remove their headgear at school. However, in accordance with Sikh customs, he could not do so. The Lords held that 'can comply' means 'can consistently with the customs and cultural conditions of the racial group' comply. Since he was forbidden by the customs of his racial group from removing his turban, he could not comply with the school's requirement.

However, the fact that a person chooses not to comply with a rule that working must be full time does not show that he cannot comply with it.

6.4.18 Time of test

Two further points must be mentioned:

- the time of assessing whether an applicant can comply is the time of the non-satisfaction of the requirement or condition. In *CRE v Dutton* (1989), a pub banned travellers. Some gypsies were barred. The defendant unsuccessfully argued that gypsies could, in the past, have stopped being travellers; therefore, they could have complied with the 'no travellers' sign. It does not matter whether the applicant could comply with the rule in the past or at some time in the future;

- in *Enderby v Frenchay HA* (1992), the speech therapists' equal pay case considered in the previous chapter, the EAT held that the rule that the requirement or condition was indirectly discriminatory when a considerably smaller proportion of one sex could comply with it only applied where that requirement or condition caused the unfavourable treatment. It was not sufficient that there was a substantial difference in numbers. The Court of Appeal referred the case to the ECJ, which has not ruled on this matter. As a matter of English law, however, it must be said that the words of the statute do not support the EAT's judgment.

6.4.19 Detriment

Detriment means simply 'putting someone under a disadvantage': *Jeremiah*, (see 6.4.4, above). An example is the placing of women but not men onto reduced working weeks. There is no need for hostility towards women. Accordingly, the fact that the employers kept men on full time contracts because they considered that men were the breadwinners for families is immaterial.

The burden of proof is on the claimant. Whether something is a detriment depends on whether a reasonable worker would consider that she was disadvantaged in the job for the future (*De Souza v Automobile Association* (1986)). May LJ said: 'Racially to insult a coloured employee is not enough by itself, even if that insult caused him or her distress ...' Oral racial abuse is, therefore, not a detriment *per se*. The working environment must be affected. It should be added that *De Souza* is out of line with modern mores and has not always been followed by employment tribunals. Examples of 'detriment' include:

- transfer to a less interesting job (*Kirby v MSC* (1980)): this result follows even though pay and other conditions of work are unaffected;

- searching all black workers (*BL Cars Ltd v Brown* (1983));

- being deprived of the chance to apply for a job (*Coker v Lord Chancellor* (1999)); and

- a condition of continued employment that a woman worked full time (*Home Office v Holmes* (6.4.14, above)).

Surprisingly, a manager's saying 'Get the typing done by the wog' (*De Souza* (1986)) was held not to be a detriment, for the typist was not disadvantaged in the way in which she was to do the work. It had to be demonstrated that a reasonable worker would have considered himself to have been disadvantaged. It would have been a detriment had she been refused promotion because she was black. Compare *Bracebridge*, above, where the harassment was by a supervisor and so was done to her in relation to her employment. It was held by an employment tribunal not to be a detriment when employers withdrew a company car during maternity leave. During the leave, they were obliged only to provide statutory maternity pay.

6.4.20 Justified

There has been much debate over the breadth of the term 'justification'. In the USA, it approximates to 'business necessity'. UK law has fluctuated. From the viewpoint of women, the nadir was *Ojutiku v Manpower Services Commission* (1982). The Court of Appeal defined the term as 'acceptable to right-thinking people as sound and tolerable reasons'. Even in the period when this was the test, and even more so nowadays, it is not sufficient that the employers subjectively thought that their decision was justified. Since then, on the spectrum between 'convenient' and 'necessary', the law has shifted. The latest decisions hold that the requirement or condition must be objectively justified, a definition borrowed from EC law: see the equal pay case of *Rainey v Greater Glasgow Health Board* (1987) and the non-employment case of *Hampson v Department of Education and Science* (1989), a decision which was reversed by the House of Lords on another point. For EC law, see *Bilka-Kaufhaus GmbH v Weber von Hartz* (1986). The effect, said Lord Keith in *Rainey*, is to bring the law on discrimination into line with that on equal pay law's defence of material defence (s 1(3) of the Equal Pay Act 1970). *Bilka-Kaufhaus* requires:

- a real need on the part of the employers;

- that their practice must be appropriate in their determination to attain their objective; and

- that the practice must be necessary to attain it: if other means could be used, there is presumably no necessity and the practice is discriminatory.

Whether a practice is justified is a question for the national court. For example, in a preliminary reference ruling, the ECJ advised that it was for a Bavarian court to determine whether part-timers acquired skills more slowly than full-timers.

These rules are much more stringent than the *Ojutiku* test. It is common to deal with the three criteria as a whole rather than separately. The later ECJ authority, *Nolte v Landesversicherungsgewalt Hanover* (1996), reduces the final hurdle. No longer must the measure be necessary: it is sufficient that 'the national legislature was reasonably entitled to consider that the legislation was necessary'. There was no reference to *Bilka-Kaufhaus*. In *R v Secretary of State for Employment ex p Seymour-Smith* (1999), the ECJ held that generalisations that a certain law encourages recruitment are not sufficient justification. *Nolte*, which gave Member States a wide margin of discretion, was distinguished. Fundamental principles of EC law, such as equal pay, could not be frustrated by that discretion. The ECJ stated that the national tribunal:

> ... [had to ascertain,] in the light of all the relevant factors and taking into account the possibility of achieving the social policy aim in question by any other means, whether [increased recruitment] appears to be unrelated to any discrimination based on sex and whether the disputed rule, as a means to its achievement, is capable of advancing that aim.

It is not yet clear whether UK law in *Hampson* measures up to EC law. The Court of Appeal spoke of balancing the discrimination contained in the requirement or condition against the reasonable needs of the employers. The EAT spoke to similar effect in *Clymo*, above, which is an employment authority. Proportionality is the key concept, not that there is no way of achieving the object of the business. The House of Lords approved this test in *Webb v EMO Air Cargo (UK) Ltd* (1993). That test appears to be easier to satisfy than the *Bilka-Kaufhaus* ones of real need and appropriate and necessary measures. (A reasonable need is less of a need than a real need and a balancing test seems easier to satisfy than a proportionality test.)

The House of Lords in the equal access to employment rights case of *R v Secretary of State for Employment ex p EOC* (1994) accepted the *Bilka-Kaufhaus* test. Lord Keith said that the promotion of job opportunities for part-timers was a possible justification but the Government had, on the facts, failed to justify the exclusion of part-timers from the main employment rights. The European Commission has stated that employers' economic needs and administrative convenience can justify indirect discrimination. The Government did not specifically rely on these factors in *ex p EOC*, though Lord Keith did say that savings on indirect labour costs would not justify discrimination. It is difficult to see the difference between administrative convenience (justification) and savings on indirect labour costs (no justification).

The advice to employers is obvious: plead administrative convenience for every requirement or condition which is indirectly discriminatory. *Nolte*, however, gives support to the Government's losing arguments in *ex p EOC*, and the law on justification cannot be said to be clear at present. Balcombe LJ in the Divisional Court in *R v Secretary of State ex p Seymour-Smith* (1994) rephrased the test as: (1) Does the measure pursue a legitimate object of social policy? (2) Is it a suitable measure for attaining that aim? (3) Is it requisite for achieving that aim? If so, the Equal Treatment Directive is vertically directly effective and the UK statute, the SDA 1975, should be construed in conformity with it so far as possible: there is nothing in the statute to prevent such an interpretation. Be that as it may, the application of the *Hampson* test can be seen in *Greater Manchester Police Authority v Lea* (1990). The employers imposed a condition that they would not accept applications from those, *inter alia*, in receipt of an occupational pension. The EAT held that this requirement was not justifiable. The condition did not reflect a need by the authority. This good motive, the desire to help unemployed persons, was irrelevant.

In *R v Secretary of State for Employment ex p EOC*, above, the House of Lords held that attempts to justify the exclusion of part time workers from a remedy for unfair dismissal failed because there was no objective justification of the hours thresholds for making claims. The Government had argued that the abolition of the thresholds would add to the cost of employing workers and reduce job opportunities for part-timers, but Lord Keith commented that there was no 'factual evidence' in support. Certainly, employers cannot rely upon generalised propositions, such as 'part-timers are not part of the core workforce and therefore they should be paid less than full time employees'. In *London Underground Ltd v Edwards* (1995), the employers had not justified the introduction of flexible rostering which had an adverse impact on female drivers because 'it was feasible to cater for single parents or those with primary care of children ... without significant detriment to the objectives of the employer to achieve savings'. In *London Underground Ltd v Edwards (No 2)* (1997), the EAT held that the employers could justify not providing a crèche, but they could have accommodated a working mother by not making her work unsocial hours while her child was small. There was no appeal on this issue.

In *Board of Governors of St Matthias Church of England School v Crizzle* (1993), the EAT held that the requirement of a 'committed communicant Christian' was justifiable on the basis of the governors' legitimate and reasonable objective of preserving the school's Anglo-Catholic ethos. It was not out of proportion with its discriminatory effect on the complainant, who was of Asian origin. The EAT held that the employment tribunal was wrong to hold that the sole objective was efficient education: if it was, the applicant was the most suitable applicant. The EAT may have applied the *Hampson* test incorrectly. The needs of the school, for example, for serving mass, could be done by other members of staff.

German law which excluded employees of firms employing fewer than five employees from the coverage of its unfair dismissal law has been held to be justified by the need to protect small businesses from administrative, financial and legal constraints, even if it could be said that the exception was indirectly discriminatory (*Kirshammer-Hack v Sidal* (1993)). This case has been applied by the ECJ on other references from Germany and it has said that States have a margin of appreciation when it comes to social policy. The *Bilka-Kaufhaus* proportionality test would overturn some English decisions. In *Kidd v DRG (UK) Ltd*, above, the selection of all part-timers before any full time employees seems not to be justified by the slight advantage the firm gained: the gain was not proportional to the decision to dismiss part-timers first. In *Coker v Lord Chancellor* (1999), an employment tribunal rejected the defendant's attempted justification that he would appoint only a person personally known to him to the post of his special advisor, because that appointment would not be made on merit and the Lord Chancellor personally knew more men than women. It remains to be added that justification is a question of fact (*Clarke v Eley (IMI) Kynoch Ltd* (1982) and the House of Lords in *Mandla v Dowell Lee* (1983)). Moreover, the application of the test is one for the tribunals. It is possible for one tribunal to decide one way, another to decide differently, and the EAT is powerless to intervene, unless the outcome is perverse or a tribunal misdirected itself as to law.

An example of justification in the race discrimination area is the banning of beards in a chocolate factory on health grounds (*Singh v Rowntree Mackintosh Ltd* (1979)). Similarly, ordering Sikh women to remove their metal bracelet, which is a symbol of their faith, was justified when there was a risk of contamination on a food production line. It has been held justifiable on non-racial grounds that the employers have a requirement for all workers including Jews to work on the Jewish Sabbath. However, what is justifiable in one case in relation to certain employers may not be so with regard to all others. Payment of a bonus with the aim of making employees continue in employment until relocation was justifiable, even though women who were working part time as a result of a career break lost out because the bonus was directed at persuading employees to stay on, not at rewarding past service (*Barclays Bank plc v Young* (1994)).

A recent employment tribunal case, *Buckle v Abbey National plc* (1998), gives a flavour of what is happening at the tribunal level. The tribunal rejected the employers' attempted justification of excluding profit-related pay from casual workers because the company did not have to offer them work and they did not have to accept it. It held that the employee did work fixed hours on Saturdays; she was a committed and regular worker; and her hours were rostered a year in advance. Free shares were not given to casuals, the company arguing that the shares were distributed to reward those who had worked hard at the time of the takeover of another former building society. The tribunal held that the merger had affected everyone, including casuals. However, the tribunal accepted that it was justifiable not to provide private health insurance because the cost would have been about one-fifth of the applicant's salary.

There are indications in the judgment of the ECJ in *Webb v EMO Air Cargo (UK) Ltd* that direct discrimination may be justified, at least where the discrimination is based on pregnancy and the contract is for a short period. If so, and the jurisprudence has not been applied yet, potentially employers would be able to justify discrimination in both indirect and direct discrimination proceedings. This development would mark a change from English law. It should be noted, however, that what the ECJ said was *obiter* and the words need not be read to permit the justification of indirect discrimination. It is certainly hard to see why, in the light of anti-discrimination policy, employers should be allowed to justify direct discrimination based, for example, on market forces.

6.4.21 Third party

Third party discrimination, sometimes called 'transferred discrimination', has arisen through judicial interpretation. Under s 1(1)(a) of the RRA 1976, it is unlawful to discriminate 'on racial grounds'. If employers did dismiss an employee for serving a black customer, it can be said that she has been discriminated against on racial grounds. The principal decision is *Showboat Entertainment Centre Ltd v Owens* (1984). The employers instructed the applicant, the (white) manager of one of their slot-machine arcades, not to admit young blacks. He disobeyed the order and was dismissed. The tribunal held that he had been treated less favourably on racial grounds than a person who would have excluded blacks; that is, there was direct discrimination. It did not matter that the racial grounds related to customers, not to the person sacked. The EAT was strongly of the opinion that employees should not be placed in a position where they had to choose between obeying the law and disobeying an order (and so losing their job). The Court of Appeal approved the reasoning in *Showboat* in *Weathersfield Ltd v Sargent* (1999).

6.4.22 Problem in SDA 1975

It is uncertain whether the *ratio* of *Showboat* can apply to the SDA 1975. That statute prohibits unfavourable treatment of a woman 'on the ground of *her* sex' (emphasis added). If a woman is dismissed for serving a man when her employers have instructed her not to do so, it is difficult to say that she has been treated less favourably on account of her sex; rather, she has been treated less favourably on the ground of her potential customer's sex. Perhaps the drafter of the SDA 1975 did not anticipate this situation; presumably, there was no intent to distinguish between the SDA 1975 and the RRA 1976 on this point; there is, however, a demonstrable parliamentary intent to have the two statutes read together, and so the situation ought to be unlawful.

6.4.23 Victimisation

Both the SDA 1975 (s 4(1)) and the RRA 1976 (s 2(1)) prohibit the less favourable treatment of applicants who bring proceedings, give evidence or information, allege a breach of the SDA, the RRA or the Equal Pay Act 1970 or act under those Acts, or intend to do any of these. Giving a person a written warning for complaining about the selection of employees to be laid off on racial grounds is victimisation. Halting internal investigations into a complaint of racial discrimination when the employee has commenced a claim before an employment tribunal constitutes victimisation (*Northamptonshire CC v Dattani* (1994)). Similarly, failing to organise an internal appeal constitutes victimisation (*Allen v Cannon Hygiene Ltd* (1995)), as does the withdrawal of an offer of a transfer within the company. Another example is selecting for redundancy a worker who criticised her employers' equal opportunities record (*McGuigan v TG Baynes and Sons* (1998)). The treatment must be less favourable than the treatment accorded to one who does not perform these actions. A causal link must, therefore, be demonstrated. If the applicant was dismissed because he secretly taped discussions for use in a racial discrimination claim, it was held that, since a person who secretly taped matters for any other reason would have been expelled from the association, he was not victimised (*Aziz v Trinity Taxis Ltd* (1989)).

There are, however, other statements by the Court of Appeal which are inconsistent with modern law, as the House of Lords held in *Nagarajan v London Regional Transport* (1999): the motive of the alleged discriminator is now irrelevant in a direct discrimination case. Dismissal because trust and confidence between the employer and the applicant has broken down is not discriminatory. The victimisation must be the sole or dominating reason for the less favourable treatment (*TNT Express Worldwide (UK) Ltd v Brown* (1999)). The ECJ ruled in *Coote v Granada Hospitality Ltd* (1998) that the Equal Treatment Directive mandates Member States to provide a judicial remedy for those whose contract has been terminated and who claim to have been victimised. This decision overturned previous English authority. When the case returned to the EAT, it held that the SDA was capable of being construed to cover both women in employment and women who had been dismissed (*Coote v Granada Hospitality Ltd (No 2)* (1999)). The contrary English authorities were disapplied.

The ECJ in its reform proposals, *Equality in the 21st Century: A New Approach* (1998), recommended that interim relief should be available in respect of victimisation as it is for some unfair dismissals.

6.4.24 Segregation

In the RRA 1976 (s 1(2)), but not in the SDA 1975, there is provision that it is unlawful to provide separate facilities for persons of different races, even though the facilities are of equal quality. This stipulation prevents the development of apartheid as in South Africa and the 'separate but equal' doctrine which existed in US law until the 1950s. The main case is *Pel Ltd v Modgill* (1980). The employers had mainly white workers on one shift in their factory: Asian employees worked on another. There was, therefore, *de facto* segregation. It was held that the employers were under no duty to integrate the workforce by putting Asians into the mainly white shift. Therefore, s 1(2) prevents segregation where the employers have adopted a policy of segregation but does not oblige employers to destroy it once it has arisen, for example, by employee preference.

6.5 Scope

The scope for cases of discrimination in selection, job adverts, employment and dismissal are discussed below.

6.5.1 Discrimination in selection (s 6(1))

It is unlawful for employers to discriminate in the arrangements made for the selection of workers, in the terms on which they offer employment and in refusing or deliberately omitting to offer work to a woman (s 6(1)). A person seeking reinstatement on appeal is not being offered employment within this sub-section. However, s 6(1) does apply even though the claimant did not put in his application for employment, such as when a job is not advertised: *Coker v Lord Chancellor* (1999). It also applies when potential job applicants are told not to apply. The principal cases are *Saunders v Richmond LBC* (1978) and *Brennan v JH Dewhurst Ltd* (1984). In the former case, questions which were asked of a woman applicant wishing to be a golf professional but not of men were not discriminatory (but may be now). The fact the questions were asked by a woman may well have enabled the employers-to-be to win the case. She was indeed the chair of the selection board. In the latter case, the manager of a butcher's shop by his conduct implied that he did not want a female employee. The EAT held that his behaviour was unlawful, for the arrangements for selection were discriminatory, even though no one was in fact appointed to the job. Controversially, the EAT held that a discriminatory advertisement was not discrimination by the employers who inserted the advertisement because they did not discriminate in fact; they (only) intended to discriminate (*Cardiff Women's Aid v Hartup* (1994)). The remedy lay in the hands of the EOC or CRE, as noted below. As always, if there is discrimination, the reason for it is immaterial. If a man is turned down for a job because his female colleague-to-be refused to work with a male, there is discrimination. The employers-to-be have refused, or deliberately omitted to offer, employment.

6.5.2 Discrimination in job adverts

Section 38 of the SDA 1975 bans discriminatory job advertisements. Only the EOC can bring proceedings under s 38. The best illustration of s 38 is *EOC v Robertson* (1980). The employer advertised for 'a good bloke or blokess to satisfy the fool legislators'. The advertisement was held to be discriminatory. No one was fooled. It should be noted that, although only the EOC can bring an action under s 38, the same fact may constitute an arrangement for selection and fall within s 6(1). The equivalent provision of s 38 of the SDA 1975 in the RRA 1976 is s 29. Such actions are brought in the employment tribunals, but if the advertisement may be repeated, a county court can grant an injunction.

6.5.3 Discrimination in employment (s 6(2))

Employers are prohibited from discriminating against a woman in the way they afford or refuse to afford her an opportunity for promotion, transfer, training or any other benefit, facility or service, or if they subject her to any detriment. For instance, the award of postal rounds on the basis of seniority works against women who have not achieved the requisite number of years in service because of their absence from the job due to child rearing. A withdrawal of an offer of employment because the employee-to-be is pregnant is another illustration. A refusal to investigate allegations of discrimination constituted the refusal of access to 'benefits, facilities or services' (*Eke v Commissioners of Customs and Excise* (1981), a race discrimination case). The equivalent provision in the RRA covers discrimination 'in the terms of employment'; in this way, racially discriminatory pay is brought within the Act. For the meaning of detriment, see 6.4.19, below. Sexual harassment falls under the 'detriment' part of s 6(2).

6.5.4 Discrimination in dismissal (s 6(2))

There is no definition of 'dismissal' in discrimination law, but the same definition as in the rest of employment law is used (*Weathersfield Ltd v Sargent* (1998)). Employers who dismiss women or Asian employees and not men or white workers discriminate unlawfully. An example, though a controversial one, of a non-discriminatory dismissal is when employers dismiss a man for having long hair when they would not have dismissed a woman in similar circumstances (*Smith v Safeway plc* (1996)). The lay members of the EAT said that such conduct was discriminatory in the light of current social conditions, and they referred to the fact that the employers' 'short hair' rule affected non-working life. The employers had no rule banning long hair on women. The dissentient, Pill J, said that employers were entitled to have a dress code which applied to both sexes but which have different requirements for men and women depending on 'current perceptions' of convention.

The Court of Appeal, which declined to make a reference to the ECJ as to whether a dress code was permissible under the Equal Treatment Directive, agreed with Pill J. Discrimination on the grounds of sex was not permissible, but it was not necessarily discriminatory to distinguish between the sexes. Discrimination required the less favourable treatment of one sex or race: different treatment was permitted, provided that it was even-handed. Employers could have a rule requiring employees to be smart or conventional in appearance because that standard did not differentiate between the sexes. Dress was to be assessed as a whole, not item by item. Surely, however, this is the wrong approach. Less favourable treatment in respect of one item is not outweighed by better treatment on another.

Sacking a woman who is pregnant is the epitome of this type of discrimination in dismissal (*Hayes v Malleable WMC* (1985)). Coverage is not restricted to dismissal but applies to all 'scope' issues. For example, it is discriminatory to send a pregnant woman home on less than full pay on the grounds that she cannot do the work she was employed to do because she is pregnant, even though she is not unfit for work. The extent of this type of discrimination was explained in *Rees v Apollo Watch Repairs plc* (1996). A woman was dismissed after returning from maternity leave on the grounds that her replacement, another woman, was better at the job than she was. It was held that the 'effective cause' of the dismissal was the applicant's absence on maternity leave; such a dismissal was direct discrimination on the grounds of sex. The tribunal emphasised that what counted was the 'underlying reason' for the dismissal, not the 'immediate cause'. Leave to appeal was refused.

English law used to compare the situation of a woman who was dismissed for pregnancy against a man who was suffering from a long term illness. If she was dismissed but the man would not have been, there was discrimination. The previous law was that, since men cannot get pregnant, there was no even hypothetical male comparator; therefore, a woman sacked for pregnancy (etc) was not discriminated against on the grounds of her sex. The law was criticised for comparing pregnancy, which is not an illness, to illness (though some illnesses, such as prostate trouble, affect only men); and both English and EC law provide that special treatment for women in relation to childbirth is not discriminatory against men. The House of Lords in *Webb v EMO Air Cargo (UK) Ltd* (1993) referred the issue to the ECJ, which ruled that discrimination on the grounds of pregnancy was direct discrimination, at least where the contract was not a fixed term one and the absence lasted throughout it. There was no need to compare a pregnant woman with a male absent on health grounds.

One problem with this response in English domestic law is s 5(3) of the SDA 1975: 'A comparison of the cases of persons of different sex or marital status under s 1(1) or 3(1) must be such that the relevant circumstances in the one case are the same, or not materially different, in the other.' When the case returned to the House of Lords as *Webb v EMO Air Cargo (UK) Ltd (No 2)* (1995), it was held that, as a result of EC law, s 5(3) must be ignored when pregnancy is the cause of the discrimination. Their Lordships said *obiter* that, if the woman would be absent for the whole of her contract because of her pregnancy, it would not be discriminatory to dismiss her. On the facts, the applicant was on a permanent contract and her absence would have affected only part of her employment. Lord Keith raised the possibility of a non-discriminatory dismissal where the woman was totally absent, because it was unfair to the employers and it would bring the law into disrepute. In criticism, it should be said that this *dictum* raises the possibility of a defence of justification to a *direct* discrimination claim, which is impermissible as a matter of English law. In relation to Lord Keith's statement about the woman's absence for the *whole* of her contract, it may be that (if the exception is accepted) English law may be less beneficial to women than EC law, which may not require total absence for the contractual period.

Tribunals will have to be alert to employers seeking to use short-term contracts to evade the application of sex discrimination laws. In *Caruana v Manchester Airport* (1996), the EAT was mindful of this risk. The employers failed to renew a fixed term contract because an employee was pregnant. Since she would not be absent for the whole of the term, the EAT held that the non-renewal was direct sex discrimination. The ECJ has previously ruled that it is unlawful to refuse to employ a woman on the ground that she was pregnant, despite the fact that the employer would suffer serious financial hardship (*Dekker v Stichting Vormingscentrum voor Junge Volwassenen-Plus* (1991)). See, also, *Hertz v Aldi Marked K/S* (1991). Refusal to continue to allow a pregnant woman to work at nights where her contract was of indefinite duration is discriminatory (*Habermann-Beltermann v Arbeiterwohlfahrt* (1994)), again, at least where the contract is not for a fixed term. Where, however, a woman becomes ill after the end of her maternity leave through a pregnancy-related illness, the ECJ has ruled that then the tribunal must compare her with a sick male (*Hertz v Aldi Marked K/S* (1991) and *Webb*, relying on *Hertz*). The EAT applied *Webb* in *Iske v P & O European Ferries (Dover) Ltd* (1997). The employers refused to transfer the applicant, a stewardess on a cross-channel ferry, to shore leave. It was held that the refusal constituted discrimination on the grounds of sex.

The ECJ in *Brown v Rentokil* (1998) held that the Pregnant Workers Directive (92/85) prohibited dismissal from the onset of pregnancy to the end of the period of maternity leave. Therefore, the dismissal of a pregnant woman who had exhausted her entitlement to sick leave was on grounds of pregnancy, not sickness. Again, such a dismissal must be on the grounds of sex, because only women are affected by pregnancy. Therefore, absence during pregnancy and maternity leave are not to be considered as being due to sickness for the purposes of computing the amount of sick leave permitted by the contract of employment. However, after maternity leave, provided that the employers treat sick women and men equally, it is not discriminatory to count women's illness as part of sick leave, even though that illness derived from pregnancy or childbirth. *Brown v Rentokil* was applied in *Abbey National plc v Formoso* (1999). After rumours had been circulating that an employee had been having an affair with her manager, the employers called her to a disciplinary meeting. On the advice of her doctor, she refused to attend because she was emotionally unfit due to pregnancy. The hearing took place and she was dismissed. It was held by the EAT that she had been subjected to a detriment when the employers held the hearing in her absence, that absence being due to pregnancy. Dismissal of a woman during pregnancy for absence due to a pregnancy-related illness is direct sex discrimination.

The ECJ ruled in *Gillespie v Northern Health and Social Services Board* (1996) that it was not direct discrimination for women to receive maternity pay which is less than normal pay. The applicant contended that, since only women receive maternity pay, it was discriminatory to give less. The court held that women on maternity leave are not comparable to men and women in work; they are in a special class. Therefore, there was no discrimination. The amount of maternity pay was to be set by each Member State but the sum must not be so low that the protection of women before and after childbirth is undermined. The ECJ also ruled that women were entitled to receive the benefit of any increase in pay which they would have received had they not been in receipt of maternity pay. The main holding fits uneasily with *Webb*.

In *Caisse Nationale d'Assurance Vieillesse des Travailleurs Salariés v Thibault* (1998), the ECJ held that a rule that employees had to be at work for at least six months of the year in order to have the opportunity of qualifying for promotion was a breach of the Equal Treatment Directive, because women were discriminated against on account of absences occasioned by pregnancy and maternity leave.

6.5.5 Overlap with unfair dismissal

It should be noted that the same facts which give rise to an SDA or RRA claim can also give rise to an unfair dismissal claim. However, since 1999, there is generally a one year qualifying period for unfair dismissal remedies. There is no qualifying period under the SDA 1975 or RRA 1976. In relation to pregnancy and childbirth, it is automatically unfair to dismiss a woman for pregnancy (see s 99 of the ERA 1996). This provision means that the ECJ ruling in *Webb* is less important than it would otherwise have been. It should be noted that the amended s 99 still applies only to dismissal. Action short of dismissal continues to be dealt with solely under discrimination laws. There is also a financial limit on unfair dismissal claims. (This limit may be in breach of the Pregnant Workers Directive (92/85).) The questionnaire procedure is not available in applications for unfair dismissal (see 6.7.2, below).

The following differences between discrimination law and unfair dismissal should be noted:

• there is no qualifying period for discrimination law;

• discrimination law applies pre-employment;

• discrimination law applies to workers, not just to employees;

- there is no statutory cap on compensation for dismissal;

- the time limit in discrimination cases can be extended on the 'just and equitable' ground, whereas the exception is narrower in unfair dismissal claims: 'not reasonably practicable'.

6.5.6 Unions, etc

Sections 6 and 77 of the SDA 1986 render void discrimination in collective agreements and the rules of organisations, professions and occupations, even though they are not legally binding. Strange as it may seem, the Government did not give jurisdiction to any tribunal or court to rule non-contractual agreements and rules invalid until s 32 of the Trade Union Reform and Employment Rights Act 1993 inserted a new s 4(A–C) into the SDA 1986, allowing an employee or a potential one to complain to an employment tribunal about the rule's effect on her. The employment tribunal issues a declaration that the rule is void. It cannot rewrite the rule. Neither the EOC nor unions have *locus standi*. The change may still not measure up to EC norms.

6.6 Exceptions

If the employers fall within one of the exceptions, they may treat a member of one sex or race less favourably than they would treat a member of the other sex or another race. The exceptions constitute 'genuine occupational qualifications', which can be seen as justifications for discrimination even when the discrimination takes the form of direct discrimination.

6.6.1 Genuine occupational qualifications (s 7 of the SDA; s 5 of the RRA)

A worker may be excluded from a job or from a promotion or a transfer if the work or some of the tasks forming part of the job fall within one of the genuine occupational qualifications. If, however, the applicant is offered the job (or has obtained promotion or a transfer), the SDA and RRA apply with full vigour. Even if there is a genuine occupational qualification (often abbreviated to 'goq'), the employers must still consider whether or not it would be reasonable to use current employees in the relevant job (with the result that the potential worker can have a job to which the goq does not apply). This proviso applies to both sex and race goqs. In most instances, the existence of a goq is obvious and, in the 25 years that the legislation has existed, difficulties have been few.

6.6.2   In the SDA 1975

With regard to sex discrimination (including on the grounds of gender reassignment), the following constitute goqs:

(a) the nature of the job is such that one sex is needed because of physiology. The usual example is modelling, but a tribunal has held that working on a telephone sex line was a goq;

(b) the job is one in entertainment where authenticity is needed. An example might be that only male actors need apply for the role of King Lear. However, having radio shows presented by two persons, one of whom was required to be male and the other female, did not constitute a goq when a male was turned down, because it was not 'artistically preferable' to have both sexes;

(c) decency or privacy form the third goq. An example might be a female nurse whose job it is to change women's incontinence pads. A Northern Irish employment tribunal once held that the job of headmaster at a boys' boarding school fell within this exception. However, the job of practice nurse can be performed by either sex. This goq failed in the early case of *Wylie v Dee & Co (Menswear) Ltd* (1978). A refusal to employ a woman in a menswear shop was held to be discriminatory. Measurement of men's inside legs could be done by male shop assistants. On the other hand, it was held permissible in *Lasertop Ltd v Webster* (1998) to employ only a woman in a women-only health club as a seller of membership, because a man would have to relinquish his task at the door of the changing room. It is suggested that this ruling is inconsistent with EC law – one might ask why potential applicants to a health club need a tour of the changing room;

(d) the job involves a single sex establishment where the inmates require special supervision or care, for example, in prison or in a women-only hospital;

(e) the job involves personal services in the provision of welfare or education and can be done more effectively by members of one sex than another. An example might be the job of social worker with children who have been sexually abused by their fathers. Other examples are working for a rape crisis centre and at a women's refuge. It is moot whether this exception covers working as a receptionist at a birth control clinic. It has been held at an employment tribunal that services to female Asian muslims could more effectively be provided by a female interpreter than by a male one;

(f) the job consists of work abroad which, under that country's laws, can be done only by men. An example is that, in Saudi Arabia, women are not permitted to drive cars. Accordingly, a job agency can advertise for men only to act as chauffeurs;

(g) the job is one of two which can be held only by a married couple. The usual illustration is that of club stewards;

(h) it is impractical for the worker to live anywhere other than on the premises supplied by the employers; the only premises are available for men; and it is not reasonable for the employers to build separate premises for women. The usual example is a lighthouse. Here, it is cost which overrides the principle of equality. It is rare for this to happen;

(i) the post is likely to involve the worker's performing the job or living in a private house and must be held by a man because of the degree of social or physical contact with the person living in the home. An example is the provision of a male companion to an elderly man. The exemption also extends to knowledge of the intimate details of the private householder's affairs. It was added by s 1(2) of the SDA 1986 as a result of infringement proceedings brought by the EC Commission against the UK in the ECJ;

(j) the final exemption is detailed in s 4 of the Employment Act 1989. By this section, employers may offer employment only to men to comply with a statutory requirement existing before the enactment of the SDA 1975 which is for the protection of women in relation to pregnancy or maternity or other risks which are specially associated with women, to comply with the Health and Safety at Work Act 1974, or to comply with the laws mentioned in Sched 1 to the Employment Act 1989.

These exceptions apply even though not all of the duties associated with the job fall within the goq.

Article 2(4) of the Equal Treatment Directive provides an exception for positive discrimination particularly to remove 'existing inequalities which affect women's opportunities'. Like all exceptions to Community principles, this one is interpreted restrictively. It is arguable, however, that it should be read broadly, for it is actually a measure aimed at destroying inequality in the long run, though in the short term this derogation may exacerbate it. The Commission has extended this exception to permit discrimination in respect of access to employment and promotion if there is no quota system.

6.6.3   In the RRA 1976

The RRA 1976 provides a much shorter list of goqs than does the SDA 1975. Exceptions (a), (b) and (e) above, apply. There is also an exception for waiters in ethnic restaurants, for example, ethnic waiters in Chinese restaurants. 'Personal services' no doubt covers working as a receptionist at a treatment suite for victims of racial attacks. The personal services exception was utilised in *Tottenham Green Under Fives' Centre v Marshall* (1991). Looking after children in a nursery constituted a personal service. Some 84% of the children were of Afro-Caribbean origin. Someone was needed to talk and read to the children in

West Indian patois. Selecting someone of Afro-Caribbean or African origin for work in the nursery was a genuine occupational qualification. The fact that speaking patois did not constitute the whole of the job was irrelevant. Only if speaking patois was a sham was it relevant. In criticism, it may be said that it is wrong to assume that only an Afro-Caribbean person can speak the language.

The contrasting case is *Lambeth LBC v CRE* (1990). The personal services goq did not apply where the posts of group manager and assistant head of housing benefits did not have much contact with the public. Therefore, the post-holders did not need to have experience of the special problems faced by blacks and, accordingly, the employers were wrong to restrict job applicants to those of Asian or Afro-Caribbean origin.

Acts done to safeguard national security are permitted by s 52 of the SDA 1975 and s 42 of the RRA 1976, and discrimination on the ground of birth, nationality, descent or residence is allowed for jobs in the civil service and in various public bodies.

6.6.4   Other exemptions

- For the private household exemption in the SDA, see 6.6.2, above. The RRA retains the private household exception. It is not subject to the limits set out above in the amended SDA. Normally, the RRA is brought into line with the SDA when it is changed to bring it into line with EC law. It is suggested that the Government's respect for privacy among individuals should yield to the anti-discrimination principle. Though the RRA's exemption is not restricted to physical or social contact or intimate knowledge, it should be noted that the private household exemption does not apply where the discriminatory action alleged is victimisation.

- Charitable trusts: s 43 of the SDA; s 34 of the RRA. An illustrative case is *Hugh-Jones v St John's College* (1979). The college was a charitable trust. A woman was refused access to the senior common room. The EAT held that the college was not liable for sexual discrimination because it was a charitable trust.

- The SDA and RRA both permit reverse discrimination in a narrow set of circumstances, namely, in the provision of training for one gender or one (or more) racial groups if the number of persons from that group or groups or gender is nil or is comparatively small.

6.6.5 Other exemptions in the SDA

The SDA further exempts:

- sports and sporting facilities (s 17);

- police and police cadets in relation to height, uniform, equipment, pregnancy and pensions; prison officers in relation to height (s 18);

- ministers of religion, if the credo so provides (s 19) (compare the present position of the Church of England);

- special protection for women during pregnancy and childbirth;

- provisions in respect of death or retirement (s 6(4)).

To this exception, Parliament, in s 2(1) of the SDA 1986, engrafted exceptions, that is, where the SDA now applies. Section 6(4)(a) states that s 6(4) does not apply to the ways in which and terms on which promotion, transfer and training are made; nor does it apply to demotion, dismissal or any other detriment involving demotion or dismissal. Section 6(4)(b) as amended provides that benefits, facilities or services under an occupational pension scheme are not affected by the restriction found in s 6(4); s 6(4)(c) refers to dismissal. Changes were made in 1995 so that s 6(4) no longer applies to occupational pension schemes.

6.6.6 Death/retirement

The same exception in respect of death or retirement applies in the Equal Pay Act 1970. The ECJ ruled in *Barber v Guardian Royal Exchange Assurance Group Ltd* (1991) that payments under occupational pension schemes constitute 'pay' for the purposes of Art 119 (now Art 141). Since Art 141 is horizontally directly effective, s 6(4) was implicitly overruled by *Barber* where 'pay' in the EC sense was concerned. The law was amended in 1995 to comply with *Barber*.

6.6.7 Other exceptions in the RRA

The RRA further exempts:

- rules in relation to immigration;

- rules concerning qualifications for employment in the civil service (there are special rules in relation to the Ministry of Defence, the Diplomatic Service and the Cabinet Office);

- employment abroad on a ship (for example, British workers can be sacked in favour of cheaper Filipino or Lascar crew);

- qualifications (nationality, place of birth, duration of residence) for national and local sides (for example, the English football team);

- acts done under any statute or statutory instrument (s 41(1)).

6.6.8 Small employers

There used to be an exemption in favour of small employers, but the ECJ ruled that it contravened the Equal Treatment Directive (76/207) and the exception was repealed by the SDA 1986. It is possible that some of the exceptions which remain are inconsistent with the Directive.

6.7 Procedure

Some procedural matters require elucidation and are discussed below. Claims must be brought within three months of the last act of discrimination. An act which continues over a period is deemed to have been performed at the end of that period (*Barclays Bank plc v Kapur* (1994)), a race case which also applies to sex. A line is drawn between a continuing act and an act which has continuing consequences. The latter is not a continuing act. Accordingly, the appointment of a nurse at a certain grade was not a continuing act. The three months ran from the date of appointment (*Sougrin v Haringey HA* (1993)). An example of continuing discrimination is the refusal to grant a subsidised mortgage to a woman. In *Cast v Croydon College* (1998), the employers refused repeated requests to work part time. The Court of Appeal held that the refusals constituted a continuing act. Auld LJ stated:

> ... policy or no, a decision may be an act of discrimination whether or not it is made on the same facts as before, providing it results from a further consideration of the matter and is not merely a reference back to an earlier decision.

A series of discriminatory acts may demonstrate that the employers have been applying a policy of a continuing nature (*Osuwu v London Fire & Civil Defence Authority* (1995)). Mummery J(P) held that a series of acts can indicate a practice, which is a continuing act. Therefore, failures to upgrade could indicate continued discrimination. He said:

> A specific decision not to upgrade may be a specific act with continuing consequences. The continuing consequences do not make it a continuing act. On the other hand, an act does extend over a period of time if it takes the form of some policy, rule or practice ...

The employment tribunal may extend the limitation period if it considers it just and equitable to do so. For example, in *Aniagwu v London Borough of Hackney* (1999), it was just and equitable to extend the limitation period when the applicant had not brought the claim because he was appealing through the employers' appeals structure.

6.7.1 Burden of proof

There was a conflict as to where the onus of proof lies once the applicant has pointed to a *prima facie* case. The Court of Appeal in *Noone v North West Thames RHA* (1988) and *Baker v Cornwall CC* (1990) said that the legal burden switches to the employers once the applicant has established a *prima facie* case. Even after those cases, however, the EAT has continued to hold that the burden is on the applicant throughout (*British Gas plc v Sharma* (1991) and *King v Great Britain-China Centre* (1991)). The House of Lords approved *King* in *Zafar v Glasgow CC* (1998). The Court of Appeal in *King* held the law was that a tribunal may draw inferences from the facts, including discrimination (for example, a difference in treatment and a difference in gender is indicative of sex discrimination. But, if the employers treat all workers equally badly, it is difficult to draw the inference that they have acted towards one particular worker on a discriminatory ground); if so, it is then for the employer to provide an explanation.

In *Qureshi v London Borough of Newham* (1991), it was held that an inference of discrimination from the facts is a matter for the tribunal. The fact that the employers had acted incompetently towards a woman or a member of a racial group is not *per se* discriminatory. On the facts, failures to apply a policy against discrimination, to follow the employers' procedural rules and to supply the CRE with statistics in response to a questionnaire (see below) did not automatically mean that the employers had discriminated. In *Zafar*, the fact that the employers had acted in an unreasonable manner did not prove that they had treated the applicant less favourably than they would have treated another employee for the purposes of the law of racial discrimination. One has to compare treatment of two employees, not what reasonable employers would have done and what the defendant employers did do. Similarly, while there is no requirement that an appointments board should include at least one woman, her presence may be evidence that the employers did not discriminate, but, of course, such evidence is in itself not conclusive of the issue. In an unreported decision, the EAT held that failing to monitor an equal opportunities policy was strong evidence of discrimination. The burden of proof of 'justification' is on the employers.

The Labour Government accepted a Directive on the Burden of Proof in Sex Discrimination (97/80). Under this, the applicant has to prove less favourable treatment; then, the employers have to show that the less favourable treatment was not on the grounds of sex. The ECJ laid down the same law in *Specialarbejdforbundet i Danmark v Dansk Industri* (1996) (the *Royal Copenhagen* case) in relation to equal pay. Once the applicant establishes a *prima facie* case of discrimination, the burden of proof switches to the employers to justify the difference in pay. On the facts of the case, the burden switches when it is impossible to specify which factors determine the differences in pay based on piece work. It should be noted that the Directive applies only to sexual discrimination cases and that it will not come into force in the UK until January 2001. It also applies to equal pay, parental leave and the health and safety of pregnant workers.

Proving discrimination need not be difficult. In one employment tribunal case, an Asian male put in two applications for a job as a car fleet sales administrator, one in his own name, and one as a fictitious white female. The qualifications listed were similar. The dealership turned down his own application but offered an interview to the fictitious person. It was held that the firm had discriminated on the grounds of both sex and race.

6.7.2   Questionnaire

An employee may submit a questionnaire to her employers to gain information on discrimination. If they fail to reply, or do reply but do so evasively or equivocally, the employment tribunal may draw an inference of discrimination if it considers it 'just and equitable' to do so. See s 74 of the SDA 1975; s 65 of the RRA 1976.

6.7.3   Statistics

Statistical evidence may be of value in establishing discrimination. For example, the use of statistics may demonstrate a pattern of not employing black people. There is no duty on employers to undertake studies of patterns of employment in their firm, but, if there is such a study, the tribunal may draw adverse inferences from its non-disclosure (*Carrington v Helix Lighting Ltd* (1990)). While the tribunals have said that elaborate statistics are not required, use of these is increasing, and such evidence entitles the tribunal to draw an inference of discrimination when the employers do not adduce evidence to the contrary.

6.7.4   Discovery

The legal process of discovery is available in discrimination cases. For disclosure, the material in the hands of the employers must be relevant, necessary for the fair disposal of the case and not oppressive to them (for example, the documents can be obtained cheaply) (*West Midlands PTE v Singh* (1988)).

6.8   Remedies

The Acts empower tribunals to award several remedies. Two points should be emphasised: tribunals have no power to award exemplary damages; and the success rate (if the case should reach the tribunal at all) is not high.

6.8.1   Employment tribunal awards

The employment tribunal can do any or all of the following:

- make a declaration that the employee's rights have been infringed;

- order compensation (which was calculated up to a maximum of £11,000 until the ECJ's ruling in *Marshall (No 2)*, 6.8.4, below). Compensation is awarded if it is just and equitable to do so. Compensation covers both special damages, such as loss of salary, and general damages, such as for injury to feelings. It is thought that the tribunal can award compensation for personal injury (for instance, a mental breakdown) caused, for example, by sexual harassment. Tort law principles govern the assessment of compensation (*Ministry of Defence v Cannock* (1995)). The amount awarded is not restricted by justice or equity;

- make recommendations that the employers remove the discrimination.

Loss of earnings are assessed by referring to the chance that the employee would still have been in work had she not been dismissed for a discriminatory reason. The loss of that chance is expressed as a percentage. This mode of assessment is different from that adopted in respect of unfair dismissal claims, where the sum is assessed by refering to what reasonable employers would have done (*Abbey National plc v Formoso* (1999)). The tribunal can award damages for injured feelings (ss 66(4) and 57(4)), which they cannot do in unfair dismissal cases. The injury to feelings must be proved and the sum awarded is not to be used as a deterrent (*Cannock*). The courts and tribunals see injury to feelings as a fundamental part of compensation and, at times, it is the whole head under which compensation is awarded. Injured feelings includes the emotion felt at losing a congenial job, that is, loss of job satisfaction. While compensation for injured feelings is not automatically awarded, it is rare for it not to be granted (*Ministry of Defence v Sullivan* (1994)). In general, a sum of £500 is the minimum tribunals award on this ground (*Sharifi v Strathclyde Regional Council* (1992)). This figure is now, it seems, £750 in sex cases. As an example, the EAT increased an award of £50 to £750 in *Tullett v Page Group* (1998). The EAT rejected the contention made in *Orlando v Didcot Power Station Sports and Social Club* (1996) that this figure should be increased because the limit on compensation has been abolished. It stated that an apology from the employers could mitigate injury to feelings. The figure is higher in race discrimination claims: *Ministry of Defence v Hunt* (1996).

In cases where women had an abortion to comply with the rule that pregnant women could not serve in the armed forces, £5,000 was the going figure. Malice, deceit, humiliation of the complainant and dishonesty by the employers will increase the award. The median award in sex cases was £1,416 in 1992–93 (the median nearly doubled to £2,999 in 1993–94 and again to £5,700 in 1994–95), in race cases £3,333 in 1993–94 but £2,750 in 1994–95. Now that the financial limit has been removed, the median award is likely to increase. The Equal Opportunities Review found that the average was £4,556 in sex cases, £8,220 in race cases and £3,743 in disability cases in 1998.

Damages running into hundreds of thousands of pounds have been awarded by employment tribunals for dismissal from the armed forces for becoming pregnant. A Leeds employment tribunal awarded £10,000 in a sex case and a London employment tribunal awarded £20,000 in a race case for injury to feelings in a case involving a black prison officer who was ostracised. The EAT upheld the award (*Armitage v Johnson* (1997)). A Leicester employment tribunal awarded £3,500 to a black woman training to be a solicitor who was dismissed for failing her exams when two white trainees who had failed were retained. All these cases occurred in 1994–95. A 1999 employment tribunal case awarded £20,000 for injury to feelings when the employee suffered severe depression.

There should be no reduction on the ground that the sum looks excessive: to reduce on this ground would be to reintroduce the financial limit abolished by *Marshall (No 2)*: *Ministry of Defence v Hunt*, criticising *Cannock*, in which the judge had said that, once the sums were added together, the total should be looked at again to see whether it was a suitable amount. In *Noone v North West Thames RHA*, above, 6.7.1, the Court of Appeal awarded £3,000. This figure now seems on the low side, especially since the removal of the financial limit on awards (*Armitage v Johnson*). Awards must not be set so low that they diminish respect for the law, and comparisons can be drawn with personal injury claims (*Armitage*). The principles guiding the assessment of compensation for the dismissal of servicewomen who became pregnant were laid down in *Cannock*, but they apply generally to direct discrimination claims. (For example, if there was only a 25% chance of promotion, the sum would be reduced by 75%.) The tribunal has to estimate the chances of the woman returning to work, had she been allowed to take maternity leave; whether she would have been promoted; and whether she would have had more children. As tort law stipulates, she is to be put in the position she would have been in but for the employers' discriminatory conduct. Loss of a pension is compensatable.

Morison J criticised high awards (such as one for £300,000). Childcare costs are deducted from the sum. There is no separate head of compensation for loss of career prospects. The employee must mitigate her loss. Disability, race and sex discrimination are statutory torts and, therefore, the doctrine of mitigation applies. Reasonable steps to mitigate loss should be taken. There are conflicting

EAT decisions on the order of the deductions for mitigation and the possibility that the employee might have returned to work after childbirth. *Ministry of Defence v Hunt* put the former discount first; *Ministry of Defence v Bristow* (1996) applied the reverse order. Invalidity benefit is deducted from compensation for loss of earnings. No sum is deducted for contributory conduct. There should be no 'uplift' for compensation because the employers form part of the State.

The Court of Appeal ruled in *Sheriff v Klyne Tugs (Lowestoft) Ltd* (1999) that an employee's claim in respect of racial discrimination could include damages for personal injury, including psychiatric harm. Such were included within the statutory tort of racial discrimination. The same, of course, applies to sex discrimination and disability discrimination. It is uncertain whether Parliament intended this outcome. After all, when tribunals were, to a large degree, given concurrent jurisdiction with the ordinary courts over contractual disputes on termination of contracts of employment, personal injury actions were expressly excluded.

Compensation used not to be awarded for indirect discrimination if the employers did not intend to discriminate on the grounds of sex (s 66(3)). 'Intention' means that the employers want to bring about a state of affairs in which the employee is treated unfavourably on discriminatory grounds. It does not mean that the employers did wish to treat him or her less favourably on discriminatory grounds. Motives such as a desire to improve business efficiency are irrelevant. In *JH Walker Ltd v Hussain* (1996), the employers knew that Muslim employees wished to take off a day for a religious holiday and they knew that the holiday was important to Muslims. The EAT held that the refusal to permit leave was intentional. This lack of provision was criticised for failing to eradicate sexual discrimination. Employers would act strongly if they had to pay compensation for unintentional indirect discrimination. In 1994, a tribunal ruled that a female part time teacher was indirectly discriminated against when her employers decided that a job should be done by one full time teacher rather than two part time ones, and it awarded compensation for unintentional indirect discrimination in reliance on the Directive (*Tickle v Governors of Riverview CF School* (1994)). The Government reacted promptly and passed the Sex Discrimination and Equal Pay (Miscellaneous Amendments) Regulations 1996 (SI 1996/438).

Tribunals are empowered to grant compensation for unintentional indirect sex discrimination if it is considered just and equitable to do so and provided that the power to make a declaration and a recommendation is insufficient. The Regulations came into force on 25 March 1996. No change has been made to the law, which states that compensation cannot be awarded for unintentional indirect racial discrimination. There is a way round this failure to change the race discrimination law. If the tribunal issues a declaration that a requirement or condition was indirectly discriminatory, employers will find it difficult in later proceedings to argue that they were not acting intentionally. An example of the issue of competence to award compensation for indirect racial discrimination occurred when Asian aeroplane cleaners failed an English language test. One of them had worked for four years, showing that the test was unnecessary, but no compensation could be awarded.

6.8.2 Exemplary damages

The principal recent debate has been concerned with whether or not tribunals may award exemplary damages for discrimination. In a reserved judgment, the EAT in *Deane v London Borough of Ealing* (1993) ruled in reliance on a non-employment Court of Appeal authority that the Court of Appeal had been incorrect in *City of Bradford Metropolitan Council v Arora* (1991) to award exemplary damages under the RRA 1976. Such an award was available only in relation to torts which existed before the famous House of Lords decision in *Rookes v Barnard* (1964). Since neither the SDA 1975 nor the RRA 1976 existed in 1964, exemplary damages could not be granted for breach of those statutes.

Exemplary damages cannot be awarded in sex discrimination cases (*Ministry of Defence v Meredith* (1995)). It is irrelevant that the claim is based on the Equal Treatment Directive. It is suggested, however, that this case should be reconsidered: EC law demands that discrimination be deterred. Some of the sting in *Deane* may be reduced by tribunals awarding aggravated damages for injured feelings. No separate sum should be awarded: aggravated damages form part of damages for injury to feelings. This form of damage occurs when the applicant has been humiliated or has suffered distress, or where the employers have acted maliciously, insultingly or offensively. An example from the tribunal cases is where the employers accused the employee of making up allegations of racial discrimination. In another case, £8,000 was awarded where the employers took no interest in equal opportunities, they reacted with hostility when such issues were raised and they did not apologise. Aggravated damages are not awarded where the employers did not know of the unlawfulness of their conduct (*Ministry of Defence v Mutton* (1996)). The employee must also know (*Meredith*). The Law Commission in *Aggravated, Exemplary and Restitutionary Damages*, 1997, Report No 247, recommended exemplary damages in discrimination cases.

6.8.3 Recommendation

The recommendation is just that, a recommendation, not an order. For example, an employment tribunal cannot order the employers to provide showers (*Ministry of Defence v Jeremiah*, 6.4.4, above). Examples include a recommendation that the employer should counsel a woman when she next applied for a transfer within the company, a recommendation that the employee who sexually harassed the applicant be moved to a different job, and a recommendation that the employers apologise to the applicant. The EAT held that an employment tribunal was wrong to recommend that the applicant should be appointed to the next available job, because that was unlawful positive discrimination (*British Gas plc v Sharma*, 6.7.1, above). *Sharma* may be incorrect in the light of EC law, which requires effective remedies. This remedy is restricted to reducing or getting rid of the adverse effects of discrimination on the individual applicant. Therefore, general recommendations about the employers' employment practices cannot be made.

A recommendation is also limited to 'a specified period'. For this reason, a recommendation that the applicant should be promoted when a vacancy arose was held to be invalid in *Irvine v Prestgold Ltd* (1981). In that case, it was also held that it was not possible to include in a recommendation that, as an alternative to promotion, the applicant should receive the difference in pay between her present job and the post to which she was to be promoted. An example of a recommendation is found in *Dinar v Burger King Ltd* (1996):

> That within the next three months, the respondent company conduct an investigation into the systems in place for the allocation of menial tasks, the allocation of hours between employees, and promotion to service expert, to examine how they may be changed to ensure that each of the systems is operated fairly within the respondent company's equal opportunities policy and, within a further three months, to place a report including recommendations for improvements to the systems before the board of directors ...

Employment tribunals have done other things, such as ordering their decision to be displayed on noticeboards and instructing the employers to issue an apology. Monetary matters should fall within the award of compensation. If the employers do not carry out the recommendation, compensation may be awarded, or, if compensation has already been awarded, further compensation, if it is just and equitable (provided that the employers do not have a 'reasonable justification'), but only if it could have been awarded in the first instance. It is suggested that many employees do not want compensation but the prevention of discrimination in the future. The employment tribunal, however, has no such power, nor does it have jurisdiction specifically to enforce recommendations. The remedy for failure to comply with a recommendation is (increased) compensation. There is no power to order reinstatement or re-engagement, as can happen in unfair dismissal applications.

6.8.4 EC law

Interest on employment tribunals' compensation awards was not allowed (*Marshall v Southampton and South West Hants AHA (No 2)* (1990), a criticised authority). The court held that the word 'damages' in the English statute could not be construed as including interest on damages. The ECJ ruled in 1993 that national measures implementing EC law on sexual discrimination should be sufficiently powerful to achieve the objective of that law and be capable of effective enforcement in national courts. The objective was stated to be real equality of opportunity. Loss sustained by dismissal must be fully recompensed. An upper limit on the amount of compensation and the inability to award interest were inconsistent with achievement of the objective. Interest will now be awarded from the date of discrimination, not the date of the hearing. Compare unfair dismissal, where interest is payable only from 42 days after the award is promulgated.

It may be that English courts can construe 'damages' in EC law to include compensation for injury to feelings. If so, there would not be a difference between State and non-State employees (this is the *Marleasing* approach, discussed in Chapter 2). If such a construction is not possible, non-State employees will be able to rely on *Francovich* (also discussed in Chapter 2) to obtain damages against the failure properly to implement the Equal Treatment Directive. Accordingly, the English laws which limited the maximum amount to be awarded in an SDA claim and under which no provision was made for the award of interest in SDA claims were abrogated by the Sex Discrimination and Equal Pay (Remedies) Regulations 1993 (SI 1993/2798). The law on maximum compensation in racial discrimination cases was changed by the Race Relations (Remedies) Act 1994, which abolished the financial limit on compensation in race discrimination cases. The limit also was inconsistent with EC law because it did not provide a remedy which deterred employers from unlawful acts (*von Colson v Land Nordrhein-Westfalen* (1984)). The ECJ in *Marshall (No 2)* ruled that this limit was to be disregarded because otherwise, the principle of no discrimination on the grounds of sex would not be 'fully effective'. One effect of the ruling was to increase the amount for injury to feelings, that amount formerly being restricted by the overall limit on compensation. In the light of other ECJ decisions limiting the financial consequences of rulings, it is perhaps surprising that no limit was to be placed on the amount of compensation. It should be noted, however, that there is a financial limit on compensatory awards for unfair dismissal.

Article 6 of the Equal Treatment Directive 1976 obliges all Member States to adopt 'all the measures necessary to ensure that the Directive is fully effective'. In *Marshall (No 2)*, the Court of Appeal had held that Art 6 was not unconditional and precise enough to be directly effective, but it was wrong; however, it is only vertically directly effective. Certainly, the ECJ had no doubt that it did apply to emanations of the State. A claim for damages against the State by employees of private employers for improper implementation of the Directive is possible. Article 6 of the Directive is also to be read as imposing an obligation on Member States to introduce measures to deter employers from sexual discrimination. It cannot be said that English law acts as a deterrent, for its purpose is compensation. The 1979–97 Government rejected recommendations from the EOC for minimum awards, reversal of the burden of proof, class actions and wider EOC investigations. The Labour Government is also not prepared to alter the law, except in respect of the burden of proof.

The Treaty of Amsterdam gave the Community's institutions the power to make law on racial discrimination. Article 13 of the Treaty is not directly effective and unanimity is needed for its implementation. Another amendment was as to positive discrimination. Member States are permitted to introduce measures 'to ensure full equality in practice'. There is no doubt that, although UK discrimination law was, to a large degree, a transplant from the USA, its development has been the result of EC law.

6.9   Differences from equal pay and reform

- The Equal Pay Act 1970 applies only if there is a male comparator; under the SDA 1975, it is sufficient that there is a hypothetical male whom the employers would have treated better than the claimant.

- The SDA 1975 covers discrimination on the grounds of marital status, which the Equal Pay Act 1970 does not.

- A claim for equal pay used to be limited to two years' back pay, but the ECJ ruled that this limit adversely affected claimants, and so the EAT disapplied it. There is no such limit in sex discrimination law.

- The hurdle of 'requirement or condition' applies to the 1976 statute but not to equal pay claims where the applicant is claiming that the employers have indirectly discriminated against her. The EAT in *Bhudi v IMI Refiners Ltd* (1994) held that English law could not be construed in conformity with EC law on this point without distorting its meaning. It is suggested that the English statute could be construed to give effect to EC law by reading 'requirement or condition' as 'practice or policy'. Moreover, the same rules apply at the EC level to equal pay and equal treatment. The defence of material difference in the English equal pay law and the defence of justification in sex discrimination law should be read in the same way, despite the fact that they are drafted differently in the statutes. For both of these reasons, it is thought that *Bhudi* will not survive scrutiny in a higher court.

6.9.1   Pay

It should be remembered that the Equal Pay Act 1970 is not restricted to 'pay' but applies to all terms and conditions during employment. Once the worker has accepted the job, the Equal Pay Act 1970 applies, not the SDA 1975. This is not a problem with the RRA 1976, which covers contractual terms (such as pay) as well as conditions.

6.9.2 Effect of EC law

The effect of EC law must be understood. It is dealt with in general in Chapter 2 and, in the particular context of equal treatment, in the previous chapter. While the use of directives in the area of sex discrimination leaves the domestic government with a choice as to specific measures, 'the objective is to arrive at real equality of opportunity' and national 'measures must be such as to guarantee real and effective judicial protection and have a real deterrent effect on the employer', as the ECJ said in *Marshall (No 2)*. Had the policewoman in *Waters v Metropolitan Police Comr* (1997) (CA) relied on the Equal Treatment Directive (76/207) (discussed above), she may have been successful. There is ongoing debate on time limits of national claims based on EC law.

The European Commission's fourth Equal Opportunities Action Programme 1996–2000 proposes:

- an agreement between the social partners on the reconciliation between family and professional life;

- consultation with the social partners about reversing the burden of proof in sex discrimination cases and about atypical workers (many of whom are female);

- a Code of Practice on equal pay; and

- a report on the Recommendation on the Dignity of Men and Women at Work (that is, on sexual harassment).

One of the major proposals is on 'mainstreaming'; that is, all policy developments have to be checked to make sure they are not discriminatory. The EOC's *National Agenda for Action*, 1995, also proposes a similar approach: all existing and proposed legislation should be reviewed to make it non-discriminatory. 'Mainstreaming' is set to become a major buzzword and issue.

6.9.3 Reform

In 1999, the Government refused to contemplate drastic revision of race and sex discrimination law. For example, it decided not to amalgamate the Commissions. It nevertheless promised to revise the Commissions' powers to make investigations which had been stifled by *Re Prestige Group Ltd* (1984); to implement the Burden of Proof Directive (97/80); to change the definition of indirect sex discrimination to reflect that in the Directive; to consider amending race discrimination law to bring it into line with sex discrimination law in respect of the burden of proof and the definition of indirect discrimination; to revise the law so that courts and tribunals would be obliged to draw inferences when employers failed to complete questionnaires; and to abolish the rule that compensation cannot be awarded for indirect race discrimination. The CRE, in its *Reform of the Race Relations Act 1976: Proposals from the CRE* (1998), has proposed the reform of the definition of indirect discrimination and the abolition of the rule that compensation could not be awarded for unintentional indirect racial discrimination. It also recommended:

(a) providing protection for former employees, a recommendation which has, in part, been superseded by EC law;

(b) extending protection to office-holders and volunteers; and

(c) widening the definition of victimisation, except in relation to personal services, restricting genuine occupational qualifications to those jobs where the racial group of the workers is 'an essential defining feature'.

6.10 Disability discrimination

The Disability Discrimination Act 1995 came into force in December 1996. It prohibits discrimination (that is, less favourable treatment: but for the disability, would this employee have been treated as other workers were?) against disabled people (including those persons who have had a disability) in employment. Disability is defined as physical or mental impairment which has a substantial and long term adverse effect on a person's ability to perform some normal day to day activities. There can be an adverse effect even though the disabled person can perform some tasks. 'Substantial' means something that is not minor; 'long term' means something that has lasted or is likely to last for 12 months; day to day activities include mobility, speech, memory and dexterity. Among disabilities found in the cases are paranoid schizophrenia, a club foot, ME ('yuppie flu') and back injury. Medication and medical equipment are ignored in determining whether the impairment is substantial; so, for example, a person with an artificial limb is nevertheless substantially impaired under the Act. The mental illness which causes the mental impairment must be a clinically recognised one. Discrimination covers victimisation and both the direct and the indirect varieties (see the discussion above). The employers have a defence of justification to *both* types, unlike in respect of racial and sexual discrimination. There is no need to compare the disabled person against an able bodied person (cf, sex and race discrimination).

The Disability Discrimination Act 1995 applies to employees and applicants for employment and to apprentices and those independent contractors who personally perform the work, and recourse is available against employers and trade unions. It does not apply to those who employ fewer than 15 employees (reduced from 20 in 1998), and members of the armed services, police, fire and prison services are excluded. Also excluded are those who work on planes, ships and hovercraft. Complaints lie to the employment tribunals, and the questionnaire procedure is available as in race and sex discrimination. The tribunal may make a recommendation and award compensation. There is no limit to compensation. Compensation of over £103,000 was awarded in *Kirker v British Sugar plc* (1998). Interest may be awarded.

The Disability Rights Commission Act 1999 created the Disability Rights Commission (DRC). It replaces the previous enforcement body, the National Disability Council, and it has wider powers than its predecessor. It is expected to start functioning in Spring 2000. The powers of the DRC will be similar to those of the CRE and the EOC.

By s 5(2), employers discriminate against disabled persons if they fail to provide such reasonable adjustments to the workplace as are required by s 6 and such failure cannot be justified. Section 6(1) stipulates that, if a disabled person is at a substantial disadvantage in comparison with those who are not disabled, the employers must take such steps as are reasonable in the circumstances to eliminate the disadvantage. Section 6(3) provides a non-exhaustive list of reasonable adjustments, such as reallocating duties, altering hours of work and modifying equipment. Section 6(4) then provides a list of factors to be considered when determining whether or not the adjustment was reasonable. These include the cost and the employers' finances. The defence of justification also applies to this duty, and this is deemed as occurring when the reason for the failure to adjust is both material and substantial. There is no duty of reasonable adjustment in respect of racial or sexual discrimination. There is no duty on employers to provide carers to attend to an employee's personal needs (*Kenny v Hampshire Constabulary* (1998)).

6.11   Parental leave

The Employment Relations Act 1999 provides for several 'family friendly' laws. One of these is parental leave. The law is based on the Parental Leave Directive (96/34).

Parental leave is leave to look after a child or to make arrangements for the good of the child. Parents have a maximum of 13 weeks' unpaid leave per child; that is, looking after two children gives rise to 26 weeks' leave. The leave is given to parents of children under five born after 18 December 1999; to those who have adopted a child under 18 after that date (in which case, the leave period runs for five years or until the child reaches 18, whichever date comes first); and to those who acquired parental responsibility for a child born after 18 December 1999. The 'parent' must have one year's continuous employment, and part-timers have pro rata rights. The parent on leave remains employed, but is not bound by contractual terms except those relating to confidentiality; seniority and pension rights are preserved; and he or she has the right to return to the same job (or, if no longer available, to a similar or better one).

Collective agreements (or, where there is no union, workforce agreements) can build on the statutory scheme but, if there is no such agreement, a model scheme applies. Leave can be taken in blocks of one week or more; the employee must give at least four weeks' notice (if leave is for more than two weeks, he or she must give twice the amount of notice as the time to be taken off); and leave can be postponed by the employers if the needs of the business or the quality of service so demand. The maximum length of postponement is six months. An example of necessity occurs when the employers have to fulfil a large order. Employers can demand reasonable evidence to support a request for leave, for example, to see the birth certificate to check whether the child is under five.

6.12 Domestic emergencies

The Employment Relations Act 1999 provides for employees to have a reasonable amount of time off (which is unpaid) to deal with incidents involving dependants (that is, a spouse or partner, parent, child or someone who lives as part of the family). Leave is limited to births, deaths, injuries, illnesses, the failure of arrangements to look after dependants and emergencies affecting a child at school or on a school trip.

6.13 Non-discrimination against part-timers

Section 19 of the Employment Relations Act 1999 obliges the Secretary of State for Trade and Industry to make regulations with a view to ensuring that those in part time employment are treated no less favourably than those in full time jobs. Section 19 implements Directive 97/81 on part time work. By s 20, the Secretary of State is given power to issue a Code of Practice on part time work.

DISCRIMINATION ON THE GROUNDS OF SEX, RACE OR DISABILITY

Introduction

The Sex Discrimination Act 1975 and Race Relations Act 1976 prohibit discrimination on the grounds of sex and race respectively.

Coverage

The Acts cover employees and independent contractors doing work personally. Employers are vicariously liable.

Grounds

The Acts cover discrimination on the grounds of sex, married (but not single) status, and race, which includes ethnic origins:

- *Mandla v Dowell Lee* (1983).

Meaning

The Acts cover direct (unfavourable treatment) and indirect (requirement or condition, considerably smaller proportion, can comply, detriment, not justifiable) discrimination as well as third party discrimination, victimisation and, in the case of the RRA, segregation:

- direct: *Ministry of Defence v Jeremiah* (1979);
- motive irrelevant: *James v Eastleigh BC* (1990);
- harassment: *Porcelli v Strathclyde RC* (1985);
- indirect: *Price v CSC* (1978);
- requirement: *Perera v CSC* (1983); *Falkirk Council v Whyte* (1997);
- proportion: *Kidd v DRG (UK)* (1985);
- 'can comply': *Mandla v Dowell Lee* (1983);
- detriment: *Ministry of Defence v Jeremiah* (1979);
- justification: *Hampson v DES* (1989);
- third party: *Showboat Entertainment v Owens* (1984);

- victimisation: *Aziz v Trinity Taxis* (1988);
- segregation: *Pel v Modgill* (1980).

Scope

The Acts cover discrimination before, during, and after employment. Pregnancy dismissals constitute direct discrimination.

Exceptions

Exemptions called 'genuine occupational qualifications' and other exceptions are available:

- *Tottenham Green Under Fives' Centre v Marshall* (1991).

Procedure

To aid applicants, there are special rules on burden of proof, questionnaires, statistical evidence, and discovery:

- *King v Great Britain-China Centre* (1991).

Remedies

Employment tribunals can award a declaration, compensation and recommendation. Exemplary damages are no longer awardable:

- *Marshall (No 2)* (1993);
- *Deane v London Borough of Ealing* (1993).

Differences from equal pay

The Equal Pay Act 1970 applies to contractual terms.

Disability discrimination

The Disability Discrimination Act 1995 obliges employers not to discriminate against the disabled, either directly or indirectly. There is, however, a defence of justification which, unlike in racial or sexual discrimination, applies to both forms of discrimination. Employers are under a duty to make reasonable adjustments to accommodate their disabled staff.

Parental leave

The Employment Relations Act 1999 introduced leave for parents to look after children under five born after 18 December 1999. The leave is unpaid.

Domestic emergencies

The 1999 Act also provides for unpaid leave of a reasonable length to cope with emergencies involving dependants.

CHAPTER 7

TERMINATION OF THE CONTRACT OF EMPLOYMENT AT COMMON LAW

7.1 Termination without dismissal

When the contract of employment is terminated without the employee's being dismissed, he has no common law claim for wrongful dismissal and no statutory claim for a redundancy payment or unfair dismissal.

7.1.1 Death and winding up

The contract of employment is a personal relationship. If the employee dies, the contract cannot be enforced against him. If the employer is a natural person and he dies, the contract also terminates. If, however, the business is carried on by the employer's personal representatives, the contract is deemed to continue for the purposes of redundancy payments. If they do not carry on the business, the employee may claim a redundancy payment from them: ss 206–07 of the Employment Rights Act (ERA) 1996. If the employer is a company and the court winds it up, the employee is taken to be dismissed; if, however, the winding up is voluntary, the contract terminates only if the business is not carried on. Similarly, if the court appoints a receiver, the contract ends, but it usually continues if the debenture holders appoint the receiver. Dissolution of a partnership operates as termination of the contract of employment with the partners, but employment under a new partnership with some of the old partners constitutes a waiver of the right to sue in respect of the termination. For continuity of employment and the effect of the Transfer of Undertakings (Protection of Employment) Regulations (SI 1981/1794), see the relevant sections of this book.

7.1.2 Frustration

The contract of employment is automatically terminated if, without fault of either party, its performance becomes illegal, completion of the contract becomes impossible or performance of the contract would produce a situation radically different from that agreed. Subject to the possible exception of the imprisonment cases discussed below, the law is the same as that in general contract law. Accordingly, authorities such as the Coronation cases, *Davis Contractors Ltd v Fareham UDC* (1956) and *The Hannah Blumenthal* (1983) remain relevant. For example, in *Currie v Pinnacle Meat Processors Ltd* (1996), an employment tribunal held that the contract of employment of an ex-head boner was frustrated as a result of a statutory instrument which outlawed the de-boning of ox heads. Since 98% of the employers' business consisted of doing that, the contract was a 'radically different' one from that contemplated by the parties at the time when the contract was made.

7.1.3   Definition

An example is *Morgan v Manser* (1948), the case involving Charlie Chester, a Radio 2 disc jockey. He was called up for the army. His contract of employment was frustrated. The judgment of Streatfeild J (sic) sums up the law in one sentence:

> If there is an event or change of circumstances which is so fundamental as to be regarded by the law as striking at the root of the contract as a whole, and going beyond what was contemplated by the parties and such that to hold the parties to the contract would be to bind them to terms which they would not have made, had they contemplated that event or those circumstances, then the contract is frustrated by that event immediately and irrespective of the volition or the intention of the parties, or their knowledge as to that particular event, and this is even though they have continued for a time to treat the contract as still subsisting.

7.1.4   Effects

The effects of frustration are these:

- the contract is terminated by operation of law. Neither party need do anything;

- wages due up to the date of frustration may be recovered (Law Reform (Frustrated Contracts) Act 1943). Wages due after that date are not recoverable, unless it is just and equitable to award a sum representing the wages. Other contractual rights, such as pay in lieu of notice, also disappear;

- because the contract is determined by law, not by the act or will of either party, there is no dismissal. The principal employment claims, those of wrongful dismissal, redundancy payments and unfair dismissal, are all predicated on dismissal. If the employers have not dismissed the employee, no claim can arise. For example, without a dismissal an employee never reaches the stage of being able to argue that his dismissal was unfair because the employers acted in a procedurally unfair manner. To this rule there is an exception. By s 136(5) of the ERA 1996, if the frustrating event is the dissolution of corporate employers or the death of natural ones, the termination by frustration is deemed to be a dismissal for the purposes of redundancy payments. This rule applies even when Parliament has made the employment illegal. This area of law is sometimes known as 'deemed dismissal'.

7.1.5 Problems

Two particular frustrating events have caused problems to labour lawyers: sickness and imprisonment; though other events such as mobilisation, exclusion from premises by a customer of the employer and suspension on medical grounds also lead to frustration.

7.1.6 Sickness

A worker's contract may be frustrated by illness, as the classic case of *Poussard v Spiers* (1876) illustrates. An opera singer fell sick. She missed rehearsals and four performances. The contract was frustrated. Similarly, in *Condor v Barron Knights* (1966), a pop group's drummer fell ill and could not perform his agreement to drum seven nights a week. Again, the contract was frustrated. Both cases involved short term engagements. What of indefinite employment? Guidelines were laid down by Donaldson P in *Marshall v Harland & Wolff Ltd* (1972). A court or tribunal has to consider:

- the terms of the contract, including any term as to sick pay;

- how long the employment was likely to last in the absence of illness: a short term hiring was more likely to be frustrated than a long term one;

- the nature of the employment: for example, whether the employee was the holder of a key post;

- the nature of the illness and the prospect of recovery;

- the duration of past employment: the longer the length, the less the possibility of frustration.

The EAT in *Egg Stores (Stamford Hill) Ltd v Leibovici* (1977) added:

- the risk to the employers of being liable for a redundancy payment and unfair dismissal to an employee who is the replacement for the sick person;

- whether wages have continued;

- the acts and statements of the employers; and

- whether it was reasonable to expect the employers to wait any longer before dismissing.

An illustration is *Maxwell v Walter Howard Designs Ltd* (1975). An ill employee was off work for almost two years. However, there was no need for a permanent replacement. The contract was not frustrated.

7.1.7   *Notcutt v Universal Equipment*

The principal modern case is *Notcutt v Universal Equipment Co (London) Ltd*
(1986). The worker had been employed since 1957. He had a heart attack in
1983. His contract of employment stated that the employers could dismiss
him with one week's notice. There was no sick pay. After a while, it became
clear that he would never work again. The court held that the contract was
frustrated when the doctor told him that he would probably not work again,
and that the doctrine of frustration did apply to a contract which was
terminable by one week's notice. The fact that the employee would never
return constituted a fundamental change in the contract. The court
emphasised that the doctrine of frustration did apply to a contract
determinable with one week's notice and that attempts by employers to
plead frustration should be closely scrutinised to ensure that employees were
not deprived of their employment protection. The Court of Appeal stated that
a contract terminable by a short period of notice may, nevertheless, be the
subject of an expectation that it will continue indefinitely. Such an argument
in favour of the doctrine of frustration runs up against the counterargument
that, whenever frustration occurs, the employee is deprived of his right to a
statutory remedy dependent on the existence of a dismissal.

7.1.8   If no frustration

If the contract is not frustrated by sickness but the employers have dismissed
the employee for being ill, there exists a dismissal for common law and
statutory purposes. Where there is illness, that is a potentially fair reason for
dismissing someone. See Chapter 10.

7.1.9   Imprisonment

In contract law, the doctrine of frustration does not apply where the
frustrating event was self-induced. Nevertheless, the courts have held in
several cases that imprisonment can frustrate a contract of employment. In
Hare v Murphy Bros Ltd (1974), imprisonment for 12 months frustrated the
contract. Lord Denning MR said that the relevant event was the sentence of
the court, a matter outside the control of the parties. Therefore, imprisonment
was not self-induced. This argument looks thin.

7.1.10   *FC Shepherd v Jerrom*

The most important modern case is *FC Shepherd & Co Ltd v Jerrom* (1986). The
Court of Appeal said that a sentence of imprisonment was potentially a
frustrating event, but was not so if the parties had foreseen the eventuality (as
occurred on the facts), for neither party could rely on his own misconduct. In
the worker's contract of apprenticeship there was a clause that his employers

could dismiss him for misconduct. His misbehaviour was therefore a foreseen event, and no frustration occurred. Since it was the employers who were seeking to rely on the employee's misbehaviour, there was no frustration. There would have been frustration, had the employee been seeking to rely on his own misconduct.

This result is not necessarily in line with general contract law and is different from the view of Lord Denning MR mentioned in the previous paragraph. The Court of Appeal accepted that it would be contrary to common sense to hold that the employee had a claim for unfair dismissal if he had been at fault (for example, by doing the act which led to imprisonment) but no claim if there was frustration. Accordingly, the contract was frustrated by imprisonment. The time of frustration is when it was commercially necessary for the employer to decide whether to get a replacement or not (*Chakki v United Yeast Co Ltd* (1982)). On the facts of that case, the employee served only one day in prison when he was released pending his appeal. The EAT remitted the case for the tribunal to determine when a reasonable employer would have decided to replace the employee.

7.1.11 Expiry of a fixed term contract

Where the parties agree that a contract of employment shall last for a precise duration, when the agreement terminates there is at common law no dismissal. For example, a post which is accepted on the basis that it will terminate when external funding runs out ceases without dismissal on the occurrence of that event. There are, however, two important statutory consequences of the expiry of a fixed term contract:

- if such a contract is not renewed, non-renewal is deemed to be a dismissal for the purposes of redundancy payments and unfair dismissal: ss 136(1)(b) and 95(1)(b) of the ERA 1996 respectively;

- an employee under a fixed term contract can agree in writing to surrender his rights to redundancy pay if the contract is for two years or more: s 197 of the ERA 1996. Waiver comes into effect only on expiry; if the employers breach the contract during the fixed term, s 197 is not applicable. Until recently, an employee on a fixed term contract for one year or more could waive his right to unfair dismissal, but this rule was abolished by the Employment Relations Act 1999.

7.1.12 Definition

The definition of a 'fixed term' contract has caused some problems. It is one which expires on a particular date. It is not one which terminates on the completion of a certain job (such as completion of the Channel Tunnel) or the occurrence of a certain event (such as the non-renewal of funding). A contract which contains a clause concerning notice is still one for a fixed term if it otherwise fits the definition (*Dixon v BBC* (1979)). The waiver rule applies even though the fixed term has been extended, for example, because funding has been granted for an extra period (*Mulrine v University of Ulster* (1993), a decision of the Northern Ireland Court of Appeal). Where, however, there are in truth two or more separate contracts, one looks at the final contract to check whether it was one for a fixed term (*Open University v Triesman* (1978)). This definition applies in respect of both of the statutory consequences noted above. Therefore, employers may insert a break clause in a fixed term contract of two years or more and still be able to exclude a remedy for redundancy payments. If waiver is not fair to employees, this effect of the definition of fixed term contracts is doubly unfair.

7.1.13 Mutual consent

As with any other contract, a contract of employment is terminated by agreement. With regard to claims dependent on the existence of a dismissal, the employee will fail because a termination by mutual consent means that there has been no dismissal. On occasion, a finding of such termination works in favour of the accused. An interesting case is *SW Strange Ltd v Mann* (1965). The defendant was the manager of the plaintiffs' betting shop. In his contract, there was a clause stating that he would not compete with his employers after the termination of his contract. After arguments, he stopped being manager and took over the running of one department only. On his leaving, the plaintiffs sought to enforce the covenant in restraint of trade. The Court of Appeal held that the first contract had been terminated by mutual consent. When he started his job running the one department, his new contract did not contain the clause; therefore, it could not be enforced.

7.1.14 Cases

Termination by mutual consent worked in favour of the employee in this case. Normally, however, it will be the employee who suffers, for if there is termination of agreement there is no dismissal, and, therefore, no claim for wrongful or unfair dismissal or redundancy payments is possible. An important illustration is *Birch v University of Liverpool* (1985). Two members of the employers' staff opted for early retirement under a scheme agreed between the university and the union. The scheme gave the employees more money than the statute did and the agreement expressly included money in lieu of statutory redundancy payments. The court held that the contracts had terminated by agreement and, therefore, the employers had no statutory rights. Employees should be aware of the effect of such early retirement schemes. Termination by consent can even occur when the employee is under notice of redundancy. If an employee accepts the money, he will have no claim to a redundancy payment (though the scheme may well provide him with more money than the statutory payment, which is on the low side). For this reason, courts and tribunals have investigated whether there truly was consent or whether the facts really constituted dismissal. An offer to resign in an appeal hearing in disciplinary proceedings may in truth be a dismissal. The question which must be asked is: 'Who really terminated the contract of employment?'

In *McAlwane v Broughton Estate Ltd* (1973), the employee was given notice of dismissal. He was set to leave on 19 April. The employers agreed to his request to leave on 12 April. The employee contended that the employers should pay him a redundancy payment and compensate him for unfair dismissal. The employers argued that he had left by consent. The National Industrial Relations Court held that what occurred was merely an arrangement to alter the date of his departure, not an agreement that he should leave voluntarily. Therefore, he was dismissed and his claims could proceed. The Court of Appeal approved this decision by a majority in *Lees v Arthur Greaves (Lees) Ltd* (1974). Another case is *Caledonian Mining Co Ltd v Bassett* (1987). The employers intimated that they would have to make some employees redundant. The men found work with the National Coal Board. The employers contended that the employees had resigned, and so could not claim redundancy payments. The EAT held that the employers had by their actions (which included asking the men if they were interested in other employment) obliged the employees to resign. Therefore, the employees had been constructively dismissed and the contract had not been terminated by consent. In *Pearl Assurance plc v Manufacturing Science and Finance* (1997), insurance agents were put under pressure to resign. The EAT held that there was no termination by mutual agreement.

7.1.15 *Igbo v Johnson Matthey Chemicals*

The most important case is *Igbo v Johnson Matthey Chemicals Ltd* (1986). The employee requested extended leave to visit her husband and children in Nigeria. The employers granted it on condition that she signed a letter stating that: 'You have agreed to return to work on 28.9.86. If you fail to do this, your contract of employment will automatically terminate on that date.' She signed. She did not return on the due date because she was ill. The Court of Appeal held that the contract had not been terminated by agreement, but by dismissal. The letter the employee had signed was a means of avoiding giving her employment rights. Such a device was void under s 203 of the ERA 1996. The court thought that if the contract had been terminated by consent, all employers could insert similar clauses into the contracts, thereby depriving employees of their rights.

7.1.16 Further illustrations

Other instances of termination by mutual consent include: resignation to avoid disciplinary proceedings (*Martin v MBS Fastenings (Glynwed) Distribution Ltd* (1983)); resignation in order to obtain compensation after falling out with the company's owner (*Sheffield v Oxford Controls Co* (1979)); and a resignation to obtain a lump sum under a pension scheme, the alternative being a (lesser) redundancy payment (*Scott v Coalite Fuels and Chemicals Ltd* (1988)). On the other hand, in *Kwik Fit (GB) Ltd v Lineham* (1992), the EAT held that the employee had not resigned when he threw his keys onto the counter. The courts and tribunals look at whether the employee had a (fairly) free choice, but it must be said that they have only rarely taken into account s 203 of the ERA 1996. The Court of Appeal in *Martin* said that the question to be asked was: 'Who really terminated the contract of employment?'

7.1.17 Counter-notice

One point about mutual termination requires emphasis. If an employee is under notice and he give his employers notice that he wants to leave before the expiry of his employers' notice, he is deemed to have been dismissed for statutory purposes. Notice must be given in the period of notice provided by statute and not within such extra period stipulated in the contract. If these conditions are satisfied, he will retain his entitlement. The requirement of writing for one claim but not the other seems to act merely as a trap for the unwary and deserves to be abolished. The notice need not be in writing for unfair dismissal (s 95(2) of the ERA 1996), but must be in redundancy payments (s 136(3)). Employers may give a further notice which requires the employee to work until the termination of his contract. If he then leaves before termination, the tribunal may reduce the redundancy payment, and may do so even to nothing.

7.1.18 Performance

Like other contracts, a contract of employment is terminable by performance of all the obligations arising under it. In such circumstances, the employee is not 'dismissed' for the purposes of statutory rights (see, for example, *Ironmonger v Movefield Ltd* (1988)).

7.2   Termination by dismissal

This section considers situations where an employee is dismissed. The common law action of wrongful dismissal occurs where the employers dismiss the employee with short notice or with no notice at all and there is no justification. Claims founded on a dismissal obviously require there to have been a dismissal. In wrongful dismissal, which is a common law contractual action, there has to have been a repudiatory breach of contract. Examples include imposing new terms on employees without an agreement to vary and obliging an employee to undergo a medical examination when there was no contractual power to order the examination. Normally, it will be evident that there has been a dismissal but, on occasion, there may be a dispute as to whether the employers' act was sufficiently repudiatory. For example, a pay cut is a repudiation, but if the cut is small, the contractual effect may be only a breach of warranty and not a breach of condition. Repudiation may be of an express or implied term.

7.2.1   Notice

Contracts of employment usually have a term that they may be terminated by either party's giving notice. There may be a clause which restricts the reasons which may be given for dismissal. If there is no express term, the courts imply a term in the usual ways (for example, by using the officious bystander test). This term is of a reasonable length. All the circumstances, such as the type of job and the status of the employee, are taken into account. Custom and practice may be important. What is reasonable on one set of facts may not be so on another. In one case, it was held that an editor required 12 months' notice; in another, only six months was deemed to be necessary. The higher an employee is in the corporate hierarchy, the longer the length of notice is required. The duration of the period of reasonable notice may be longer than the statutory minimum period. Since the period of notice must be noted in the written statement, there is now less scope than previously for the implication of a term of reasonable notice. Since notice is a common law concept, the determination of implied terms and reasonable periods is for the ordinary courts.

7.2.2   Rules

Notice must be given to each employee individually. The dismissal notice must be such and not merely a warning of dismissal (*Morton Sundour Fabrics Ltd v Shaw* (1967); *Haseltine Lake & Co v Dowler* (1981)). Once notice is given, it cannot be withdrawn unilaterally. Both parties must agree to revocation (*Harris & Russell Ltd v Slingsby* (1977)). Dismissal takes effect when notice runs out.

7.2.3   Statutory period

The common law of notice could be used by employers to wreak injustice on employees. If the contract contained a clause that a worker could be dismissed with one hour's notice, then one hour was legally sufficient notice to terminate the contract lawfully. The employee had no remedy, despite perhaps working for the firm for 30 years. Parliament has intervened in favour of the employee. Statute overrides contractual provisions, unless the latter are longer than the statutory notice period. Under the ERA 1996, the length of the statutory period depends on how long the employee has worked for the employers. Section 86 stipulates the following:

- where the employee has worked continuously for the employers for under two years – one week;

- where he has worked for more than two years – one week for each year of service, to a maximum of 12 weeks.

Therefore, an employee with five years' continuous service is entitled to five weeks' notice; one with 30 years is entitled to 12 weeks. The right to a minimum of one week's notice does not apply if a casual worker is employed to do a particular task for under three months (s 86(5)), which was part of the Conservative Government's effort to reduce burdens on business. Merchant seamen, share fishermen and those working wholly or mainly outside Great Britain do not have this right. The law provides that an employee must give one week's notice if he has been employed for four or more weeks (s 86(2)). The difference between the lengths of notice to be given by employers and employees is justified on the basis that it is easier for employers to get new employees than it is for workers to find new jobs. In any case, their periods are minima, and employers can extend them by an express contractual provision. While the statute does not expressly provide any remedy for an employee's failure to give this minimum period of notice, presumably the employers would have an action for damages for breach of contract, though, in practice, most employees are not worth powder and shot. Any agreement purporting to reduce the statutory period of notice is void.

7.2.4 Application

Section 86 of the ERA 1996 provides, moreover, that the minimum statutory periods do not apply where either party is entitled to terminate the contract because of the other's conduct (see 7.2.5, below); either party may waive the right under s 86; and either party may accept payment in lieu of notice (s 86(3)). The right to pay in lieu of notice is lost if the employee waives notice (*Trotter v Forth Ports Authority* (1991), a decision of the Court of Session which was applied by the High Court in *Baldwin v British Coal Corp* (1995)). The waiver of notice means that there is no breach of contract. Since pay in lieu is damages for breach of contract, no pay is to be awarded where the employee has waived the breach. Where the employee does waive notice or accept pay in lieu, employment ends on that date, not when the notice would otherwise have run out.

This rule is important in relation to the amount of continuous employment the employee must have before claiming a statutory employment right. Employers can decide not to enforce the contractual requirement that an employee work out the period of notice. In this way, he cannot cause harm to the business, say, by poaching customers for his employers-to-be. Such an express term is known as a 'garden leave clause'. Where the contract gives the employers an election between terminating the contract with notice or making a payment in lieu, the employee is not under a duty to mitigate his loss because the term provides, in legal effect, that the payment is liquidated damages. In other words, the claim is one which lies in debt, and in that action there is no duty to mitigate, for example, by getting a new job. This law was confirmed by the Court of Appeal in *Abrahams v Performing Right Society* (1995). The effect is that the employee gets the money from the old job and the new one. Garden leave clauses are enforceable if they protect a legitimate interest of the employers and are reasonable in duration.

7.2.5 Cause

Employers may dismiss without giving notice if they have good reason to do so. This occurrence is known as 'summary dismissal'. For example, where the employee has repudiated the contract by breaking a condition of the agreement by going on strike, the employee breached a fundamental term of the contract, the duty to work (*Simmons v Hoover Ltd* (1977)). Other examples include where the employee has disobeyed a lawful order (even if that order has been given maliciously: *Macari v Celtic Football and Athletic Co Ltd* (1999)) or has misbehaved grossly, for instance, by stabbing a colleague. If the employee deals with money, theft of a small amount may be a good cause for dismissal (*Sinclair v Neighbour* (1967)). Often, the cause is gross misconduct. The Court of Appeal held in *Uzoamaka v Conflict and Change Ltd* (1999) that the ordinary concept of gross misconduct could be extended by the contract. On the facts, behaviour bringing the employers' project into disrepute was gross misconduct because there was an express term to that effect, even though, had there not been such a clause, the employee's conduct would not have constituted gross misconduct. The court also held that behaviour could constitute gross misconduct despite the employee's acting with the best of intentions.

7.2.6 Examples

Employers may be entitled to dismiss for one 'offence', depending on its seriousness (*Taylor v Alidair Ltd* (1978)). One bumpy landing by a pilot amounted to gross negligence. A series of incidents, for example, of drunkenness, will be evidence of gross misconduct (*Clouston v Corry* (1906)). Obtaining secret profits is gross misconduct (*Neary v Dean of Westminster*

(1999)). Two gardening cases illustrate the law. In *Pepper v Webb* (1969), a gardener refused to do some work and swore. The Court of Appeal held that his refusal and swearing were the last straw and the dismissal was lawful. In *Wilson v Racher* (1974), however, the gardener was ordered to use electric hedge cutters in the rain. He was sacked for refusing to do so. His dismissal was unlawful. One difference between those cases is that in the latter the event was isolated, whereas in the former it was part of a series of events. In *Wheatley v Control Techniques plc* (1999), the High Court held that an ultimatum to management that they should 'back me or sack me' was a breach of the fundamental term of trust and confidence entitling the employers to terminate the contract summarily. Employers should bear in mind that dismissal is a severe punishment and should only be done in response to a serious situation.

7.2.7   Various issues

Several points arise:

- the statutory period of notice in s 86 of the ERA 1996 does not apply where the employee is dismissed for cause (s 86(6));

- a dismissal for cause remains valid if the employers dismissed for one reason which turned out to be unjustified but, after dismissal, they discovered a valid reason (*Boston Deep Sea Fishing & Ice Co v Ansell* (1888)) (the position is different in unfair dismissal: employers must have a fair reason for dismissal at the time of dismissal – an after-discovered reason will not make fair a previously unfair reason: *W Devis & Sons Ltd v Atkins* (1977));

- employers need not give any reason for dismissal at law. However, by s 92 of the ERA 1996, as amended in 1999, they must provide written reasons to dismissed employees who have worked for them for one year continuously.

7.2.8   Wrongful dismissal

Where employers dismiss an employee without notice or with insufficient notice, they are said to have wrongfully dismissed him unless they have a good cause to dismiss with no or insufficient notice.

7.2.9   Definition

Wrongful dismissal covers situations both where the employers sack the employee expressly (for example, 'I sack you', 'get your cards', 'f... off and don't return') and where they act in such a manner that the employee is contractually entitled to leave and does so. The former situation has no title, although dismissal though the terms 'express dismissal', 'actual dismissal' and 'direct dismissal' are increasingly accepted. The second situation, breach of a fundamental term (such as non-payment of wages), is called 'repudiation'. In the event of an employee claiming a redundancy payment or unfair dismissal, the second situation is usually known as 'constructive dismissal'. Repudiation and constructive dismissal denote the same concepts, and the courts and tribunals use the terms more or less interchangeably.

7.2.10 No reason needed

It must be emphasised that, if the employers do comply with the notice requirement, there is no wrongful dismissal. There is no need for them to provide any reason at all why they dismissed the worker. If they do give a reason, there is no need for the reason to be a good or valid one. An employee at common law could not challenge being dismissed, for example, for having red hair, no matter how long he had worked for the firm.

7.2.11 Damages for notice period

The primary and usually the sole remedy is damages. As with other contractual actions, the plaintiff is entitled to be put into the position he would have been in had the contract been performed. The rule is that the employee can obtain damages only for the notice period, because at the end of that period the employers could have dismissed lawfully. The rule is that employers are deemed to have brought the contract to an end in the way most financially favourable to them (*Alexander v Standard Telephones and Cables Ltd (No 2)* (1991)). Statute provides that the minimum period of notice is to be taken into account when assessing damages for breach of contract. If the notice period, whether contractual or the minimum statutory one, is four weeks, that duration will be the basic quantum. The starting point is the net wage the employee would have earned in the relevant notice period. To be added are sums for the loss of contractual benefits such as bonuses and company car. The employee cannot, instead of suing for damages, sue in debt for his wages which should have been paid under the contract (*Marsh v Autistic Society* (1993)). The reasoning is that since the employee has not earned the money, there can be no claim for liquidated damages. Payment in lieu of wages is the equivalent to paying damages for the dismissal. There is no deduction for contributory fault, but if the employee was grossly at fault, he will lose his claim, for the dismissal will not have been wrongful.

7.2.12 Exceptions

To the rule that damages are only for the notice period, there are four exceptions, if they can be called exceptions at all:

- damages may be claimed for loss of employment rights which the employee would have acquired had he not been dismissed before the qualifying period (*Stapp v Shaftesbury Society* (1982) and *Raspin v United News Shops Ltd* (1999), but the Inner House of the Court of Session said in *Morran v Glasgow Council of Tenants' Associations* (1998) that this head of damages applied only when the employers do not have a right to make a payment in lieu of notice;

- if the contract is for something other than just wages, the employee may obtain damages for the further loss. For example, an apprentice who is sacked during the running of the apprenticeship can obtain damages for loss of training and of job prospects (*Dunk v George Waller & Son Ltd* (1970)). A public entertainer is partly rewarded through publicity: loss of publicity can increase damages;

- if the contract is for a fixed term and there is no provision for termination by notice (in the jargon, 'break clause'), damages are awardable for the period the employee would have worked under the contract, had the agreement been performed. For example, assume that the employee serves under a 10 year fixed term contract commencing in 1995; she is dismissed wrongfully in 1999. Her basic quantum is for salary for the remainder of the term, six years, which could be a substantial sum. The position would have been different if there had been a clause stating that her employers could dismiss by giving three months' notice. If they dismissed wrongfully, basic damages would only amount to the three months required contractually. Negotiation and drafting reveal their importance. Even in this situation, the employee must mitigate (see below);

- damages may be awarded for a period longer than the notice period when going through the contractual means for termination takes longer than the notice period (*Dietmann v London Borough of Brent* (1988)). In *Boyo v London Borough of Lambeth* (1995), the Court of Appeal held on the facts that five months was a reasonable period for going through a disciplinary procedure. The restraint on dismissal may be substantive, such as when employers may dismiss only for a reason stated in the contract, or procedural, as when the employee is contractually entitled to a hearing before dismissal. It is possible for there to be an implied term which restricts the ground for dismissal. In *Aspden v Webbs Poultry and Meat Group (Holdings) Ltd* (1996), it was held that notice of termination could not be given to an employee who was absent through illness when he had to be employed to benefit from a health insurance plan. The express term permitting dismissal with three months' notice was subject to an implied term that they would not do so if dismissal led to the loss of the insurance scheme.

Beyond these exceptional cases, the rule requires that in contract actions the aim is to put the aggrieved party in the position he would have been in had the contract been lawfully performed. A contract with a three month notice period can be terminated legally by giving notice of that length. Accordingly, damages are only for that period.

7.2.13 Uncompensatable losses

No damages are awarded for, first, loss of reputation or, secondly, the manner in which the employee was dismissed (*Addis v Gramophone Co* (1909)). This second rule can be evaded by arguing that the employees were dismissed in breach of the implied term of trust and confidence, in that the employers had been acting fraudulently and dishonestly with the effect that the employees had suffered such a stigma that they could not obtain jobs (*Malik v Bank of Credit and Commerce International SA* (1998) (HL)). Damages for such breach are assessed in the contractual manner. This is a narrow exception and does not extend to a situation where the employers have been incompetent. Furthermore, *Malik* is restricted to damages compensating for harm caused before the dismissal. There is still no compensation for the manner of dismissal, even when that results in psychological harm and an inability to work (*Johnson v Unisys Ltd* (1999)). Damages will not be awarded to compensate for an illness brought on by the dismissal (*Bliss v South East Thames RHA* (1987)). Similarly, stress and anxiety cannot be compensated. In *French v Barclays Bank* (1998), the employers altered the terms of a bridging loan. The court held that the change was both a breach of the loan contract and of the implied term of trust and confidence. Damages were awarded only in respect of financial loss. Furthermore, no compensation is awarded for the loss of job security (*Nicholson v Budget Insurance Ltd* (1998)).

7.2.14 Contractual benefits

Employees may obtain damages only to cover losses of benefits to which they were legally entitled. For example, in *Jancuik v Winerite Ltd* (1998), the EAT held that it was irrelevant that the employee might not have been dismissed if the employers had had a disciplinary procedure. There was no contractual right to such a procedure. If bonuses were at the discretion of employers, no compensation is payable for their loss. *Laverack v Woods of Colchester Ltd* (1967) demonstrates that no damages are granted to cover increases in remuneration during the period in which the contract should have continued where the employers have a discretion to award no increase. The High Court did, however, investigate what the employers would have paid the employee if they had exercised their discretion to increase pay in *Clark v BET plc* (1997). It held that, in the light of a contractual clause that the Board of Directors would review the employee's salary every year, he was entitled to an annual pay rise. If a pay increase *must* be awarded, as where the salary is inflation-proofed or the contract provides for an annual increase, that sum is brought into the calculations. Other examples of contractual benefits which will be compensated by the award of damages include membership of a private healthcare scheme and other perks, a contractual share option or profit-sharing scheme, and an occupational pension scheme. Compensation can be awarded for loss of an opportunity to obtain a redundancy payment. It is an open question whether damages can be awarded for loss of the chance to receive compensation for unfair dismissal.

7.2.15 Mitigation

As with other types of contract, employment law tells the aggrieved party to mitigate his loss. The mitigation doctrine applies also to sums due to the employee during the notice period. For example, the employee must, if possible, find a new job. An employee need not take any job that is offered: if the employers sack him and then offer him a job at a lower status than before, the employee need not take that offer into account (*Yetton v Eastwoods Froy Ltd* (1967)). Similarly, the employee need not take a job with the parent company of the firm which dismissed him. An employee is not expected to take a job in which his skills are not used or his status is reduced. Anything said by the Court of Appeal in *Abrahams v Performing Right Society*, above, to the effect that mitigation does not apply in a wrongful dismissal action is incorrect. As the court stated, the doctrine does not apply to claims in debt. Therefore, an action to recover wages due is not mitigable.

7.2.16 Tax

Damages of up to £30,000 are awarded net of tax under the rule in *British Transport Commission v Gourley* (1956), as amended by statute. Over £30,000 the amount is given gross, but it is taxed by the Inland Revenue.

7.2.17 Deductions

Both jobseeker's allowance and income support are deducted (*Parsons v BNM Laboratories Ltd* (1964)). Redundancy payments are not deducted (*Wilson v NCB* (1980)) neither are payments from a disability scheme. The compensatory award (but not the basic or additional award) for unfair dismissal is deducted, subject to the following limitation in *O'Laoire v Jackel International Ltd* (1991). If the employee's loss exceeds the amount awarded in the unfair dismissal claim, there is no deduction because the court cannot say that the amount falls within one or other of the heads of damages awarded in a wrongful dismissal action. The basic award is not deducted because it does not represent damages for dismissal. Payment for occupational pension schemes on termination of employment are not deducted because they comprise deferred pay to which the employee is entitled and are analogous to insurance (*Hopkins v Norcros plc*

(1994)). The aim throughout is to ensure that the employee does not make a profit out of being dismissed. It should be noted that there is no doctrine of contributory negligence in contract actions. Contributory conduct may, however, constitute gross misconduct, in which event the claim fails entirely.

7.2.18 Process

A wrongful dismissal action is one for breach of contract. It is, therefore, heard in the normal courts. Legal aid may be available. The limitation period is six years. Proceedings are the same as any other civil litigation. Claims for under £25,000 can be heard in employment tribunals. Legal aid is not available and the limitation period is three months.

7.2.19 Tabular representation of differences between wrongful and unfair dismissal

	Wrongful dismissal	*Unfair dismissal*
Basis	common law	statute (ERA)
Coverage	all employees	some exceptions
Qualifying period	none	one year (normally)
Dismissal	express and repudiation	express and constructive and non-renewal of fixed-term contract
Basis	no/ insufficient notice	dismissal and unfair
After-discovered reason	yes (*Boston*)	no (*Devis*)
Remedy	damages	reinstatement of re-engagement or compensation
Limit to damages	no	yes
Where	High Court/ County Court/ET	ET
Time limit	six years	three months
Legal aid	yes	ET – no; EAT – yes
Compensation for mode of dismissal	no	yes

7.2.20 Comparison with unfair dismissal

Wrongful dismissal looks to the form of the sacking. Employers may lawfully dismiss for any or no reasons, provided that they give the correct period of notice. Unfair dismissal concentrates both on procedure and substance. Both claims may be brought at the same time. Most contractual actions concerning dismissal can now be heard in employment tribunals. Where they are heard in different fora, the wrongful dismissal action will normally be stayed so that the unfair dismissal claim can be heard separately and quickly.

7.2.21 Survival of wrongful dismissal

Though unfair dismissal has largely displaced wrongful dismissal, it has not totally done so. An employee may be unable to claim a remedy for unfair dismissal, for example, because he does not satisfy the one year's continuous employment qualifying period. They are instances, mainly involving lengthy fixed term contracts without a notice clause, where an employee can obtain more in damages than he can in an unfair dismissal application. The latter has a statutory 'cap' to the amount of compensation. Legal aid is available for wrongful dismissal but not for unfair dismissal and, in 1996, the Conservative Government decided not to extend legal aid to tribunals in its White Paper, *Striking the Balance: The Future of Legal Aid in England and Wales* (Cm 3305). Sometimes, unfair dismissal may prove a better deal to employees. An illustration is that an employment tribunal may order the employers to reinstate the employee. Such a remedy is not possible in a wrongful dismissal action. Indeed, it was the existence of deficiencies in wrongful dismissal which was one of the motivating factors which led to the institution of a remedy for unfair dismissal in 1971. The drawbacks of unfair dismissal have in turn led to renewed interest in wrongful dismissal and a search for fresh remedies.

7.2.22 Summary of wrongful dismissal

To determine a case of wrongful dismissal, one should note the following:

(a) Has there been a dismissal? Dismissal may be either 'express' or repudiation of the contract by breach of a fundamental term.

(b) Was the dismissal wrongful, that is, with short or no notice?

(c) Can the employers justify their otherwise wrongful dismissal?

(d) If criteria (a) and (b) are fulfilled, and (c) is not demonstrated, how much can the worker obtain?

From an employee's viewpoint, the chief drawback of damages for wrongful dismissal is that they are calculated on the basis that the employers will dismiss him at the time most favourable to them. That sum is reduced by the doctrine of mitigation and is not added to, no matter how distressing the breach was. In the light of these rules, it may well be cheaper to dismiss an employee than to retain him.

7.2.23 Other remedies

The general rule is that neither employee nor employers can obtain specific performance of the contract or injunction restraining one party from doing something in breach of contract. A service agreement is a contract of personal service. Once the relationship is destroyed, the courts cannot force one party to work with another. By s 236 of the Trade Union and Labour Relations (Consolidation) Act 1992:

> ... no court shall, whether by way of:
>
> (a) an order for specific performance ... of a contract of employment; or
>
> (b) an injunction ... restraining a breach or threatened breach of such of a contract,
>
> compel an employee to do any work or attend at any place for the doing of any work.

Specific enforcement of a contract of employment is thought to be equivalent to forcing a husband and wife to live together after their marriage has irretrievably broken down. Courts will not grant orders which require supervision and damages are usually an adequate remedy in the view of the judiciary. If the automatic termination theory is accepted (see 7.2.28, below), there is no contract to be specifically enforced. One effect of the doctrine of no specific performance is that an employee at common law has no right to regain his old job. Even if an injunction is granted, the effect may be only to hold off dismissal. Provided the employers act properly, they may still dismiss. Nevertheless, one effect of the issue of an injunction is that there is now a method whereby management decisions can be challenged and reversed (if only for a short while). The remedy of damages cannot attain this end. There are exceptional situations listed below, 7.2.24–7.2.27, and these are of growing significance.

7.2.24 Negative covenants

Negative restraints in contracts (such as a covenant in restraint of trade) can be enforced by injunction, even though enforcement will indirectly persuade the employee to perform the contract. In *Lumley v Wagner* (1852), the court enforced an agreement not to perform for any other theatre owner during the contract. A negative clause will not be enforced if enforcement would lead to an employee either working for the employer or starving (*Rely-a-Bell Burglar & Fire Alarm Co v Eisler* (1926)). The courts also investigate whether the clause is a truly negative one rather than a positive one expressed in negative language, though the line between these is narrow, if it exists at all. The courts will not enforce a provision that the employee will not work for others after the contract has terminated but will enforce valid restrictive covenants (see 4.8, above). In such cases, damages will not normally be an adequate remedy.

7.2.25 Statute

Courts will grant an injunction to restrain dismissal where the contract of employment is derived from the royal prerogative or has 'statutory underpinnings' (see *R v East Berkshire HA ex p Walsh* (1985) *per* Donaldson MR: the Court of Appeal held that a senior nursing officer could not obtain an order for *certiorari* to quash his dismissal because proceedings for judicial review were available only for issues of public law, a concept which did not cover dismissal, even though the applicant was a public sector employee working under a contract regulated by the Secretary of State). Some public sector employees can be protected in this way. A teacher in a grant maintained school is in such employment, as is a prison governor. However, a police surgeon has to rely on private law. In *R v CPS ex p Hogg* (1995) the Court of Appeal held that a prosecutor's job with the CPS was not underpinned by statute but was an ordinary employment relationship. Therefore, his dismissal could not be challenged on public law grounds by judicial review. The Court thought that judicial review was perhaps available if he was dismissed for a reason which impugned his independence as a prosecutor.

Similarly a doctor's employment is a private law matter, but a refusal to accept a doctor on to a Family Practitioner Committee is a public law issue. This topic is normally dealt with in administrative law texts. The basic rule is that ordinary master and servant cases do not give rise to remedies other than damages (*Ridge v Baldwin* (1964) (*obiter*)), but public employment may do so. Public employment covers jobs where there is some kind of public office which is fortified by statute. Judicial review is available for public employment matters, such as a decision which affects a group of public employees, provided that the employee is not seeking to enforce private law rights. An employee who is not in public employment must rely on private law. For example, in *R v Secretary of State for Employment ex p EOC* (1994), the House of Lords held that an 'ordinary' employee could not challenge by means of judicial review the former qualification for unfair dismissal and redundancy payments that she had to have worked for five years at 16 or more hours per week. She could, however, rely on her private law right to bring her claim before an employment tribunal against her former employers.

Where the time limit for bringing an application for judicial review has elapsed, a public employee who is relying on a private law right is not debarred from using the civil courts. Declarations have been granted in relation to public employment and office holders and even employees affected by the *ultra vires* doctrine, for example, in relation to a trade union officer in *Stevenson v URTU* (1977). In such instances, *ultra vires* and natural justice comes into play, as does judicial review under Ord 53. From the viewpoint of the employee, the advantage of judicial review is that the employers' decision to dismiss may be quashed: no such remedy is available in a claim of wrongful dismissal. Judicial review also has the advantage to employees that a remedy is given to all relevant employees, not just the plaintiff or applicant.

It is uncertain how far the decision in *Stevenson* can be taken. Similarly the concept of 'office holder' is ill defined. Woolf J in *R v BBC ex p Lavelle* (1983) thought it arguable that all employees who qualified for a claim for unfair dismissal were office holders, but the point has not been debated in court since. The Court of Appeal went further in *Gunton v Richmond-upon-Thames LBC* (1980) when it granted a declaration that the plaintiff's contract of employment continued in existence until the period of notice which would have been due, had his employers followed the disciplinary procedure laid down in his contract. The effect was that the amount of damages he obtained was small.

It has been suggested that the applicant must show not solely a breach of natural justice but also that he has been materially prejudiced. Recent decisions seem to confirm the trend that more and more 'public' employment issues are being seen as private law ones. Civil servants are now said to work under contracts of employment, not under the royal prerogative, and the termination of the contract of a local authority worker is not a matter of public law.

7.2.26 Mutual trust

Where there remains mutual trust and confidence between the parties and damages are inadequate recompense, the employee may obtain an injunction to restrain dismissal where the dismissal is in breach of contract (*Irani v Southampton and South West Hants HA* (1985)). In *Irani*, damages were not adequate because, if the claimant lost his NHS appointment, he would not get another post in the NHS. This head of jurisdiction stems from *Hill v CA Parsons & Co* (1972). There are a growing number of authorities in this area. In *Anderson v Pringle of Scotland Ltd* (1998), the Outer House of the Court of Session granted an injunction to restrain the employers from selecting for redundancy on a basis other than 'last in, first out', which was incorporated into the contract of employment. There was still trust and confidence between the parties. There is a view that mutual trust is not required where the employee is not seeking to get his job back.

7.2.27 Workability

Where there is an elaborate system, for example, of appeals before dismissal, an injunction may be granted to restrain the employers' acting beyond their contractual powers by dismissing in breach of the terms (see, for example, *R v BBC ex p Lavelle* (1983), where Woolf J likened a modern day employee to an office holder, and *Robb v London Borough of Hammersmith and Fulham* (1991)). Where, as in *Robb*, the employee is seeking just to prevent a dismissal, there is no need for trust and confidence to remain between the parties. It is when the employee is trying to retain his job that trust and confidence must continue to exist. If it does not, no injunction will be granted. Employees are not restricted to the common law remedy of damages.

In *Jones v Gwent CC* (1992), Chadwick J granted both a declaration that a letter of dismissal was invalid because it did not comply with the contract and an injunction to restrain the defendants from treating him as being dismissed, despite the fact that there was no mutual trust and confidence. In Osman, C (ed), *Butterworths Employment Law*, 2nd edn, 1998, McMullen and Osman commented: '... the case is interesting, albeit adventurous, in that it completely ignores any requirement of trust and confidence *or* a "workable" relationship.' In this situation, it is sometimes said, the order sought must be 'workable' (see *Wadcock v London Borough of Brent* (1990)), though this condition has not always been required. Accordingly, the courts are nowadays much more ready to issue an injunction to restrain the employers from acting in breach of contractual provisions (such as not following disciplinary procedures). In *Peace v City of Edinburgh Council* (1999), Lord Penrose in the Outer House of the Court of Session said:

> ... where the parties are in agreement that the contract of employment subsists and should subsist ... there is no reason ... for declining to enforce provisions ... derived from the employment ...

7.2.28 Automatic termination

One (sometimes academic) point is the following. If dismissal led to the employment contract's being terminated automatically, that is, without any need for acceptance of the breach of a fundamental term by the employee, there would be nothing to perform specifically or to enjoin. General contract law is to the effect that the doctrine of what might be called 'elective termination' applies – the aggrieved party may elect whether to bring the contract to a close or to continue with it (and claim only a monetary remedy). The elective theory was summed up pithily in *Howard v Pickford Tool Co Ltd* (1951), 'an unaccepted repudiation is a thing writ in water and of no value to anybody'. Acceptance of the breach can be demonstrated by applying for a remedy for unfair dismissal. Employment law has shifted between the two theories. The present law is that the termination of the contract of employment must be accepted by the employee as a matter of law, but, in practice, the contract is terminated by the employers' repudiation (*Gunton v Richmond-upon-Thames LBC* (above) which is binding on the Court of Appeal and *Rigby v Ferodo Ltd* (1988)). In *Rigby v Ferodo*, the House of Lords accepted that the quote from *Howard* represented both contract law and employment law, though Lord Oliver did state that this was so except in 'the extreme case of outright dismissal or walk-out'.

The latest authority is *Boyo v Lambeth LBC* (1995), where the Court of Appeal reluctantly applied the elective theory, holding that they were bound by *Gunton*. Because elective termination is now adopted, there is the possibility of the issuance of an injunction to restrain the employers from acting in breach of contract. The question whether termination is automatic or elective is also important when deciding the date of termination: that decision may affect whether an employee has a statutory employment right. If the elective theory is adopted, the employee who does not accept the repudiation is entitled to sue in debt for wages and does not sue for damages for breach of contract (*Morgan v West Glamorgan CC* (1995)). The statement of law is controversial because, for many years, the rule has been that the employee cannot claim in debt under a contract of employment. This rule had been confirmed in the same year by the Court of Appeal in *Boyo*.

7.2.29 Effect of remedy

Before an injunction is granted, the courts act as they do in non-employment cases. An injunction is an equitable remedy awarded at the court's discretion following the maxims of equity such as inquiring whether the employee came with clean hands. No relief will be granted if damages constitute an adequate remedy.

TERMINATION OF THE CONTRACT OF EMPLOYMENT AT COMMON LAW

Termination other than by dismissal

Like other contracts, service agreements may be terminated by death, frustration, elapse of a fixed term, mutual consent and performance:

- *Notcutt v Universal Equipment* (1986);

- *Shepherd v Jerrom* (1986);

- *Birch v University of Liverpool* (1985);

- *Igbo v Johnson Matthey* (1986).

The principal issues which arise are the application of the contractual doctrine of frustration to short-term contracts of employment, the possibility of losing one's employment protection rights by leaving early, and the effect of the anti-evasion provision in s 203 of the Employment Rights Act (ERA) 1996.

Where the contract of employment ends by operation of law or agreement, there is generally no dismissal and, accordingly, no statutory or contractual claim.

Termination by dismissal

Contractual notice periods may be extended by statute. The notice period may be expressly stipulated in the contract; if there is none, it must arise impliedly and be of a duration reasonable in the circumstances. Statute (s 86 of the ERA 1996) builds on the contractual period. It is calculated by one of the following formulae:

- one week for up to two years; or

- one week for each year between two and 12 years; or

- 12 weeks for over 12 years.

The statutory minimum cannot be reduced by contract. An employee employed for whatever length of time must give his employers at least one week's notice.

Summary dismissal occurs when employers dismiss without giving the correct length of notice.

Employers may dismiss lawfully for cause (*Taylor v Alidair* (1978)).

Wrongful dismissal means summary dismissal without cause which is not justified. Justifications include disobedience, theft, swearing and clocking-in on behalf of a colleague, but each case depends on its own facts. Usually, one act of carelessness will not be sufficient to justify a dismissal.

The principal remedy is damages. Normal contract rules governing calculation and deductions, including mitigation, apply. In the normal run of cases, the amount of damages will be small because the sum is determined by the length of the notice period. At times, wrongful dismissal remains a better remedy for employees than unfair dismissal, such as when an employee is not qualified for the latter. Compensation for unfair dismissal is limited to a maximum amount. The limitation period for wrongful dismissal is six years in the courts, whereas the period is generally three months in typical unfair dismissal cases. Legal aid may be available for wrongful dismissal. It is not available for wrongful or unfair dismissal at the employment tribunal.

There is a growing jurisprudence on injunctions to restrain dismissals (*Irani v Southampton and SW Hants* (1985)). The law is not settled, but the cases have largely turned on the existence of statutory underpinning, the continued presence of mutual trust between the parties and the 'workability' of the remedy on the facts.

'Elective', not 'automatic', is the preferred theory of dismissal (*Gunton v Richmond LBC* (1981)). The elective theory is that, as with other contracts, a contract of employment is not terminated by the employers until the employee accepts the repudiation. He may wish to affirm the contract. The automatic thesis is that the contract is determined by the employers and the employee plays no part in the termination. In practical terms, the difference may be none. If the employers refuse to pay the employee, he cannot normally work for nothing and the doors may be closed on him.

CHAPTER 8

COMMON ISSUES IN REDUNDANCY PAYMENTS AND UNFAIR DISMISSAL

8.1 Statutory claims

Statutory redundancy payments and unfair dismissal claims share common features. This chapter deals with qualifications for the two claims, noting any differences. It begins with flowcharts (algorithms) detailing the stages in straightforward claims. Chapter 11 discusses unfair dismissal applications which do not fit within the general scheme.

8.1.1 Redundancy

Redundancy flowchart

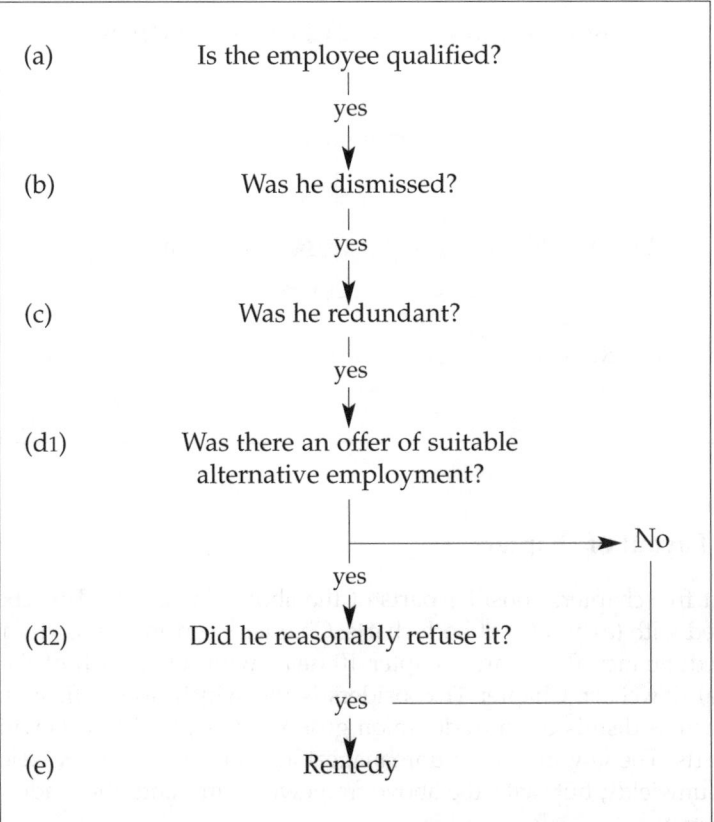

If the answer to (a), (b), (c) or (d2) is 'no', the worker has no remedy.

8.1.2 Unfair dismissal

Unfair dismissal flowchart

The sequence may be remembered as QDR3.

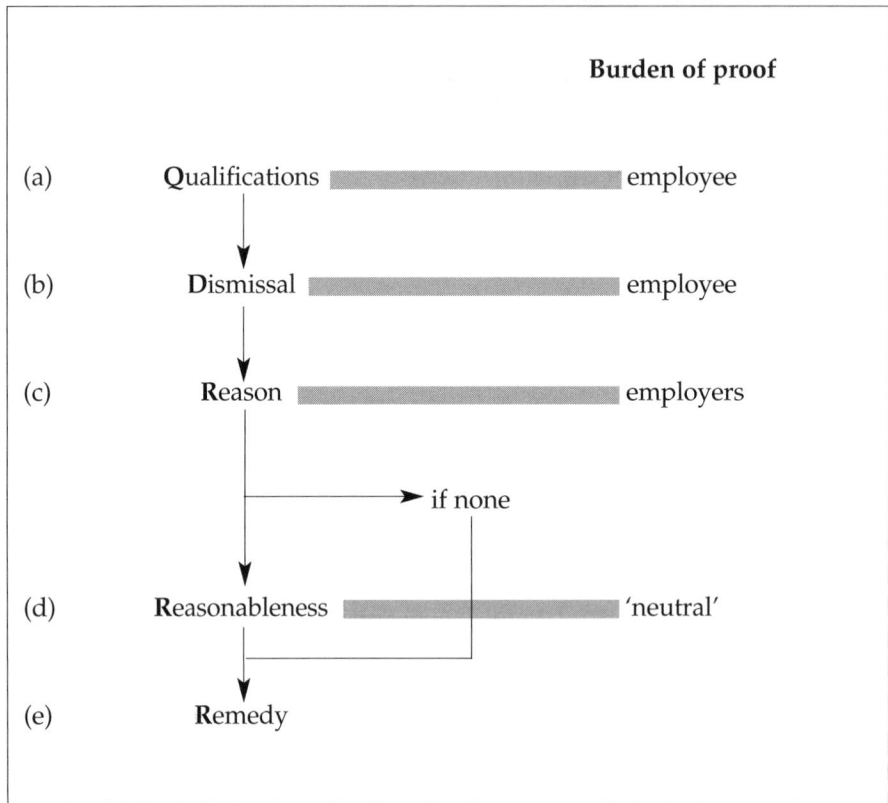

8.1.3 Layout of chapters

The next five chapters consider parts of the above flowcharts. This chapter is concerned with (a) and (b) of both charts. Chapter 9 considers (c), (d1) and (d2) of the redundancy flowchart. Chapter 10 deals with (c) and (d) of the unfair dismissal flowchart. Chapter 11 considers issues which do not fit within that chart, such as dismissal on trade union grounds. Chapter 12 deals with (e) of both charts. The law may look unmanageable, and certainly the caseload has become unwieldy, but, with the above frameworks in mind, the reader should not go astray.

8.1.4 Procedure

Both redundancy payment and unfair dismissal claims are made to employment tribunals (not the courts). Legal aid is not available for either at that stage: 'Green Form' advice is available. Both claims are made under the Employment Rights Act (ERA) 1996.

8.2 Policy

There has been much discussion of the policies underlying the law on redundancy payments and unfair dismissal. It has been argued that, although these policies favour employees, their effect has been to legitimise managerial prerogatives. In relation to redundancy, the aims are thought to be these:

- recompense to employees who are dismissed through no fault of their own, the remedy being compensation for long service;

- increase in the mobility of labour;

- money is given to employees to buy-off attempts to disrupt the restructuring of industry.

It has sometimes been argued that the law of redundancy payments recognised that employees had a right of property in their job. This argument is incorrect. After all, there is no such right until the employee is dismissed!

In the light of these industrial relations aims, one might expect that a wide interpretation would be given to the concept of redundancy, but, as will be seen, the judiciary has taken a narrow view.

The aims of the unfair dismissal legislation are thought to be the following:

(1) to promote the improvement of employers' treatment of employees;

(2) the improvement desired for companies' personnel records, linked with the improvement of treatment of employees;

(3) to prevent strikes concerned with dismissals. The law was drafted so as to provide more protection for employees than does the common law of wrongful dismissal (see Chapter 7);

(4) at the time of the enactment of the redundancy payment legislation, it was suggested that the aim of the law was to set 'minimum standards to ensure that the pace of voluntary action is both forced and underpinned': Lord Wedderburn (1966) 29 MLR 55. This rationale also underlies the unfair dismissal law.

Aim (2) has been achieved, though the true influence of the legislation is unknown. Aim (3) apparently has not been achieved. Aim (4) has to some degree. It should be noted that most claims are brought by applicants who are not members of unions, and that most claims are brought against small employers: perhaps unions keep employers up to the mark, and small employers continue to act like tsars. One effect of the legislation, but not an aim, has been that, overall, employers take more care in the selection of employees than they did in the 1960s.

8.3 Qualifications

The following qualifications apply to both redundancy payments and unfair dismissal. The burden of proving that he is qualified rests on the employee.

8.3.1 Employee

The applicant must be an employee or an apprentice (see s 230 of the ERA 1996). This matter is considered in Chapter 3. The self-employed have no claim. The more independent contractors there are, the less relevant unfair dismissal becomes.

8.3.2 Continuous employment

The employee must have two years' continuous employment for a claim for redundancy payments. The qualifying period for unfair dismissal was reduced from two years to one from 1 June 1999 by the Unfair Dismissal and Statement of Reasons (Variation of Qualifying Period) Order 1999. The previous exclusion of part time employees was repealed by the Employment Protection (Part-Time Employees) Regulations 1995 (SI 1995/31) as a result of *R v Secretary of State for Employment ex p EOC* (1994). The Government promised to keep the abolition of the hours requirement under review. The issue of continuity is dealt with separately in the next section. While there are varying definitions of part time work, there is no doubt that the proportion of part time to full time employment has increased over the last 20 years, just as the proportion of independent contractors has increased in relation to employees. The coverage of the law is decreasing. (There is no qualifying period for those dismissed for trade union membership or activities or for any other inadmissible reason.)

8.3.3 Excluded classes

The employee must not be a member of an excluded class such as share fishermen (that is, those paid by a share of the catch) (s 199). There are various other excluded classes of employees. For example, central government employees cannot claim a redundancy payment (they have better contractual arrangements), though civil servants can claim a remedy for unfair dismissal. Service personnel now have the right not to be unfairly dismissed unless they are dismissed for health and safety reasons. Section 193 allows a Minister of the Crown to exclude employees from their statutory rights on the grounds of national security. This power was famously used in relation to workers at the Government Communications Headquarters. Domestic servants are excluded if they are closely related to their employer.

8.3.4   Outside Great Britain

To get a remedy for unfair dismissal, the employee must not ordinarily work outside Great Britain (that is, England, Wales and Scotland) (s 196). There are slightly more complex rules dealing with redundancy payments. There is debate as to whether the 'contract' or the 'base' test applies. If it is not clear whether the employee works within Great Britain, the tribunal should investigate where the employee's base is (*Todd v British Midland Airways Ltd* (1978)). It must be stressed that it is the wording of the section which matters, and the tribunal should not become too wrapped up in deciding where the employee's base was.

There is also debate as to whether it is the base in the contract or the base in practice which counts. It does not matter that the employee spent more time away from base than at it; that is, one looks at the base in the contract, not at the base in practice (*Wilson v Maynard Shipbuilding Consultants AB* (1978)). Unfortunately, *Todd* says that one does investigate where the base was in practice, and Lord Denning MR said that contractual terms were often of little help in determining the base. A more recent authority, *Geest Line v Wright* (1995), stresses that the contract must first be construed to determine whether the employee worked ordinarily outside Great Britain; only if there was no clear answer should the tribunal investigate the base.The Court of Appeal in *Carver v Saudi Arabian Airlines* (1999) ruled that the contract test governed. *Wilson*, a Court of Appeal decision, was binding.

8.3.5   Normal retiring age

The employee must, for the purposes of unfair dismissal, not be over the normal retirement age for workers of his category in his firm. If there is no such age, the limit is 65 years for both sexes. The law is laid down by s 109 of the ERA 1996. It was held by an employment tribunal that the upper age limit for bringing a claim of unfair dismissal was indirectly discriminatory on the grounds of sex because it detrimentally affected more men than women (*Nash v Mash/Roe Group* (1998)). This was because more men than women stayed in work after the age of 65. For the purposes of redundancy payments, the maximum age is 65 or the normal retirement age if the employee is under 65: s 156 (that is, the test is different from unfair dismissal). In unfair dismissal claims, the House of Lords held in the leading authority of *Nothman v Barnet LBC* (1979) that, if there is a normal retirement age, only that age is considered. The age of 65 is only a fallback provision. Accordingly, if there is no normal retirement age, the maximum age one can claim at is 65. This rule was made clear by legislation in 1986, which also equalised the fallback age at 65 for both sexes.

The normal retirement age need not be the one stated in the contract but can be the date at which employees in the position of the applicant retire in practice (*Waite v GCHQ* (1983)). In other words, the contractual age is displaced when the reasonable expectations of the relevant class of employees point to a different age. However, there is a rebuttable presumption that the contractual age is the normal retiring age. In *Brooks v British Telecommunications plc* (1992), the contractual age was 60. Some employees in the same position as the applicant had been allowed to work beyond that age, but the reasonable expectation of employees in the same category as the applicant was that employees would retire at 60 and, accordingly, 60 was the normal age of retirement. The practice of permitting some employees to work beyond that age did not affect the reasonable expectation. The normal retiring age can be higher but not lower than the contractual age. The reasonable expectation can be altered by the employers informing the employees of a change (*Hughes v DHSS* (1985)). For a summary of the law, see *O'Brien v Barclays Bank plc* (1995).

The exemption concerning persons over the normal retiring age is not affected by the age at which the applicant is to get a pension. If the claimant is above the pension age but below the normal retiring age, he has a claim for unfair dismissal. An attempt to reduce the normal retiring age below that contractually agreed is void and does not take effect (*Bratko v Beliot Walmesley Ltd* (1996)). A consensual variation or a dismissal followed by a rehiring is needed. If an employer is in a unique position, there is no normal retiring age (*Age Concern Scotland v Hines* (1983)).

The age limit does not apply to unfair dismissal claims concerned with automatically unfair dismissals, such as sackings for being an employee representative for health and safety reasons or on a transfer or redundancy, asserting a statutory right or being pregnant or giving birth, membership of an independent trade union, taking part in its activities, or refusing to join or to remain a member of any union.

8.3.6 Exempted industry

The employee must not be employed in an industry which has been exempted from coverage of the legislation by the Secretary of State for Trade and Industry (s 110). The sole industry so treated is the electrical contracting industry. The Secretary of State may designate an agreement between employers and independent trade unions under s 110 only if the collective agreement provides better protection for employees than does the law of unfair dismissal. Section

110 was inserted to preserve collective bargaining over dismissals. The fact that it has been little used may be surprising to those imbued with the spirit of collective *laissez faire*. Section 110 was amended by the Employment Rights (Dispute Resolution) Act 1998, in an attempt to widen its appeal.

8.3.7 National security

With regard to dismissal for the purposes of safeguarding national security, the employee has no claim. There must be a ministerial certificate to this effect. This can be issued quickly.

8.3.8 Waiver

In respect of a claim for a redundancy payment, the employee must not have waived his right in writing. He must be employed on a fixed term contract lasting two years or more for redundancy payments purposes if he is to waive his rights. The definition of fixed term was given in Chapter 7. If a fixed term contract of the requisite length is extended and there is a waiver for the first period but not expressly in the contract extending that period, then, according to *BBC v Kelly-Phillips* (1998), the extension may be seen as a variation of the first contract only in respect of its length and the waiver will continue to apply. If the employee begins employment on an indefinite contract and then changes to a fixed term contract with a waiver, he loses her entitlement to claim, no matter how long he had served under the contract for an indefinite period. No consideration need be given for the waiver. The exemption applies only when the contract terminates at the end of the fixed term. It does not apply if the employers breach a fundamental term during the running of the contract. In that eventuality, the employee may make a claim. The law is laid down in s 197, as amended by the Employment Relations Act 1999. There is nothing to prevent employers from putting employees onto short term contracts and obliging them to waive their rights. It is uncertain whether short term contracts can be added together to arrive at the requisite two year period.

Section 197 was amended by s 18(1) of the Employment Relations Act 1999. There no longer exists the possibility of waiver of unfair dismissal rights.

8.3.9 Claim in time

In the case of unfair dismissal, the employee must apply within three months of the 'effective date of termination' (s 111(2)). The rule is to find the effective date, take the preceding day, and then add three months (*University of Cambridge v Murray* (1993)). In the case of redundancy payments, the limitation period is six months from the 'relevant date'. In both claims, where there is ambiguity, the date more favourable to the employee is taken. The limitation period does not start running until the employee knows that he has been dismissed. For example, in *McMaster v Manchester Airport plc* (1998), the employee was off work sick but he was on a day trip to France when the letter arrived dismissing him. Time did not run until he had read its contents.

The limitation period applies even when the claim is one brought by part-timers, who, before *R v Secretary of State for Employment ex p EOC* (1995), had no claim for redundancy payments: *McManus v Daylay Foods Ltd* (1995). The claim should have been brought within six months of the date of dismissal, even though before the House of Lords had spoken no one knew that a claim was possible. The House of Lords had, in reliance on EC law, abrogated the part-timers' exclusion retrospectively with the effect that part-timers had a claim from the time when the UK joined the EC. Surprisingly, the EAT said that the fact that the limitation period did not render it 'impossible in practice or excessively difficult to give effect to the directly effective ... rights conferred by Article 119 [now Art 141]', though this proposition is eminently contestable. Since the claim was one under what is now the ERA 1996, limitation periods in that statute applied.

In both claims, there is an exception. In redundancy payments, the limitation period can be extended by a further six months if the tribunal thinks it 'just and equitable' to do so (s 164). For unfair dismissal purposes, the claim may be heard if presented 'within such further period as the tribunal considers reasonable in a case where it is satisfied that it was not reasonably practicable for the complaint to be presented before the end of the period of three months'. 'Not reasonably practicable' does not apply to a mistake of law, but a mistake of fact may lead to the application of this extension. In relation to unfair dismissal proceedings concerned with sackings during a lock-out or industrial action when the employers have selectively re-engaged those directly interested in the lock-out or on strike (see s 238(2)–(3) of the Trade Union and Labour Relations (Consolidation) Act 1992), the limitation period is six months (s 239(2)). There is the usual extension to a period the tribunal deems reasonable if it was not reasonably practicable to present the claim within the six months. It should be noted that the law of discrimination is more favourable to ex-employees. The exception applies if it is 'just and equitable'.

8.3.10 Reasonably practicable

Ignorance of the right not to be unfairly dismissed is not sufficient to bring an employee within the 'reasonably practicable' exception. The fact that it was reasonable not to bring the action within the time limit is not to the point. A desire not to antagonise the employers is no excuse (*Birmingham Optical plc v Johnson* (1995)). Similarly, the fact that the employee has been going through the company's internal appeals procedure will not excuse him (*Palmer v Southend-on-Sea BC* (1984)). It is unfortunate that the Court of Appeal was unwilling to extend the deadline and thereby aid the voluntary settlement of disputes. Similarly, the fact that the employee was offered alternative work by the employers does not render it not reasonably practicable to comply with the three month deadline (*London Underground Ltd v Noel* (1999) (CA)).

Illness is one of the excuses for not complying with the time limit. In *Biggs v Somerset CC* (1996), the Court of Appeal held that the exception did not extend to a mistake of law. In *James W Cook & Co (Wivenhoe) Ltd v Tipper* (1990), the Court of Appeal decided that it was not reasonably practicable to present applications for redundancy payments when employees thought that the amount of work would shortly increase. Excuses given by the Court of Appeal in *Wall's Meat Co Ltd v Khan* (1979) were a physical impediment, a postal strike and an absence overseas. Discovering that the dismissal was given for a bogus reason more than three months after dismissal was treated as a valid excuse in *Churchill v A Yeates & Sons Ltd* (1983). If a solicitor does not present the claim in time, the remedy is an action in negligence against him for failing to meet the deadline.

8.4 Effective date of termination

The effective date of termination (often called EDoT or EDT) is the date from which the time limit for unfair dismissal claims runs. It is also the date up to which the one year qualification period runs. The same rules apply in redundancy payments law, except that the date is called the 'relevant date'. The law is laid down in ss 97 and 145 of the ERA 1996.

8.4.1 Rules

The rules are as follows:

- If either the employee or employers terminate the contract by giving notice, the EDoT is the date on which notice expires. This rule applies even if the notice was not of the requisite length. Where notice is given orally, the period begins on the next day. However, it has been held that the date cannot be earlier than that on which he himself knew that he was to be dismissed. Where the date given by the employers is stated ambiguously, the EDoT is the date to which the employee was paid, not the date when notice expires, for any vagueness should be interpreted in favour of the employee. The law on notice was considered in the previous chapter (see 7.2.1–7.2.4, above).

- If there is a lawful dismissal or resignation with no notice, the EDoT is when the termination takes effect. This rule applies even when the effect is to deprive the employee of the qualifying period for employment protection (*Stapp v Shaftesbury Society* (1982)). The rule applies even though the employee is dismissed summarily when already under notice of dismissal. The Court of Appeal in *Stapp* expressly held that the elective theory of termination did not apply in circumstances where the employers dismissed summarily.

- If the employee appeals against dismissal, the EDoT is when the original dismissal took place, not when the appeal was rejected (*J Sainsbury Ltd v Savage* (1981)). (The fact that the employee is appealing is not a good reason for not submitting an application for a statutory remedy within the relevant period, and employees should be advised to present their claim immediately on dismissal and not wait for the outcome of appeals.)

- If a fixed term contract expires, the EDoT is the date of expiry.

- If an employee under notice gives a counter-notice to end employment earlier, the EDoT is the date of expiry of the counter-notice (*Thompson v GEC Avionics Ltd* (1991)).

- If wages are given in lieu of notice, the EDoT is not when the employee accepts the breach as repudiating the contract but when the employee leaves, according to *Robert Cort & Son Ltd v Charman* (1981). This rule applies whether or not the dismissal was lawful. It should be noted that there is another line of cases which hold that, if dismissal is by notice but the employee is informed that he need not work out that period, the effective date is when the notice expires, not when he left.

- Neither s 97 nor s 145 deals with the EDoT where there is a constructive dismissal. The EAT held in *BMK Ltd v Logue* (1993) that the EDoT was the date when termination took effect. A constructive dismissal was treated as a dismissal without notice. Termination need not be on the date when the employee accepted the repudiation as terminating the contract. On the facts, removal of the applicant's directorship terminated the contract. The fact that he did not understand the true legal position was irrelevant. There is, however, another EAT authority, *GW Stephens & Sons v Fish* (1989), that the EDoT is the day when the employee terminates the contract.

8.4.2 Difference

While the effective date of termination is generally the same for both continuity of employment and limitation period purposes, there is one difference. For continuity purposes only, where the employers have dismissed with less notice than is provided by statute, that extra period (but not any contractual period) beyond the notice actually given is added on for the purposes of unfair dismissal (s 97(2)). The effect may be to push the employee over the two year qualifying period for statutory claims. Apparently, s 97(2) applies even though the dismissal is for gross misconduct (*Lanton Leisure Ltd v White* (1987)). The same rule applies to redundancy payments.

8.5 Continuity

Separate treatment is awarded to this topic because of its pivotal function. The effect of the Transfer of Undertakings (Protection of Employment) Regulations (TUPE) 1981 is considered in Chapter 13. References below are to the ERA 1996. The concept of continuity is a statutory one and the parties cannot contract out of it. The basic ideas behind the concept of continuity of employment are set out in this section.

8.5.1 Breach of continuity

If continuity is broken, the employee must start again to build up length of service for the purposes of both qualifying to claim and calculating the amount due. For example, if the employee has overall worked for the employers for five years and seven months ago he took an unauthorised holiday for a month but was then re-employed, subject to the rules below he has only six months' continuous employment. Therefore, if he is now dismissed, he does not have the requisite two years' qualifying period for a normal unfair dismissal claim. The requirement of one year's continuous employment works harshly against temporary employees such as seasonal workers and members of the peripheral labour force (see *O'Kelly v Trusthouse Forte plc* (1984), discussed in Chapter 3). Continuity is broken where an employee receives a redundancy payment and is then taken on again. Continuity is, however, preserved when an employee is reinstated or re-engaged after a successful unfair dismissal claim. The parties cannot contract out of the rules on continuity.

8.5.2 Counting

Sometimes, continuity is preserved but the week does not count. The principal provision is s 216, which applies both to strikes and lock-outs. For ease of reading, 'strike' in this paragraph includes 'lock-out'. If the employee has been on strike, the period of the strike does not count towards the qualifying period; however, the time before and after the strike does count. Therefore, the employee does not lose the years and months of work which he had accumulated before the strike. That period is added to the time after the strike. The whole of a week in which the employee was on strike does not count, even though the strike lasted for only a minute. It does not matter that a striker was dismissed and then taken back by the employers. Weeks between dismissal and reinstatement or re-engagement count. By s 215, weeks spent abroad do not count for the purposes of redundancy payments (but continuity is preserved).

8.5.3 Different jobs

It does not matter if the employee has had different jobs with the employers (or with the employers to whom the employee's contract has been transferred). Continuity runs from the commencement of employment, not from, for example, promotion or the change to a different department (*Wood v York City Council* (1978)). As that case demonstrates, it does not matter that the employee resigned from one council post to obtain another. The continuity provisions apply even though the previous employment with the relevant employers has come to an end through frustration (*Tipper v Roofdec Ltd* (1979)).

8.5.4 Presumption

There is a presumption of continuity (s 210(5)). (This presumption does not apply in relation to the transfer of a business: see 8.5.10, below.) If the employee shows that a week counts, the burden is on the employers to prove that other weeks do not count (*Nicoll v Nocorrode Ltd* (1981)).

8.5.5 Associated employments

Employment with an 'associated' employer counts. Section 231 states:

> Any two employers are to be treated as associated employers if one is a company of which the other (directly or indirectly) has control or if both are companies of which a third person (directly or indirectly) has control ...

This section applies only to companies. Therefore, the Commission for Racial Equality is not associated with Councils for Racial Equality because it is not a company.

Though the issue is not settled, the Court of Appeal held in *South West Launderettes Ltd v Laidler* (1986) that voting control was needed. Control in law is needed: the question 'who, in fact, controls the companies?' is irrelevant. A group of persons can be the controlling body (*Zarb v British & Brazilian Produce Co (Sales) Ltd* (1978)). This decision of the EAT was criticised in *Laidler* and the EAT refused to follow it in *Harford v Swiftrim Ltd* (1987), but it has not been overruled and was followed by the EAT in *Tice v Cartwright* (1999).

8.5.6 Re-employment

Where the employee is successful in an unfair dismissal claim and is reinstated or re-engaged by the employers, by their successors or by associated employers, continuity is preserved and the weeks between dismissal and re-employment count. The same applies to re-employment as a result of the intervention of a conciliation officer or a result of a voluntary agreement. See below, Chapter 12. Re-employment after redundancy breaks continuity.

8.5.7 Which weeks count?

Section 212(1) states:

> Any week during the whole or part of which the employee's relations with the employer are governed by a contract of employment counts in computing a period of employment.

The previous rules which excluded part time employees have been abolished as being sexually discriminatory. Part time employment no longer affects continuity. In *Colley v Corkindale* (1995), continuity continued even though the applicant worked only five and a half hours every other Friday. Provisions limiting part-timers' rights to claim for unfair dismissal were indirectly discriminatory and had not been justified. Their abolition in 1995 was not surprising.

8.5.8 Preserving continuity

The main difficulty surrounds s 212(3), which applies in four situations to preserve continuity where there is no contract of employment:

(a) if the employee is incapable of work through sickness or injury, s 212(3)(a) preserves continuity for 26 weeks. If a person is absent through illness and then remains absent for pension reasons, the latter absence breaks continuity (*Pearson v Kent CC* (1993)). Section 212(3)(a) applies if the applicant cannot do the work he is normally employed to do. Therefore, it does not matter if he can do other, lighter work for other employers;

(b) if he is absent because of a 'temporary cessation of work', continuity is preserved for the duration: s 212(3)(b). It is possible that continuity is preserved where the employee lost his first job and was later re-employed by the same employers on a different job (*Cannell v Council of the City of Newcastle-upon-Tyne* (1994), *obiter*). It is the employee's work which must have ceased. Whether the cessation was temporary is looked at with hindsight; that is, at the end of the cessation, can one say that it was temporary (*Fitzgerald v Hall, Russell & Co Ltd* (1970)? This provision will cover a phased return to work after industrial action. In *Ford v Warwickshire CC* (1983), the House of Lords held that a teacher with eight September–July contracts could include the weeks in between, for the time off between contracts was temporary. To break continuity the time between the contracts had to be assessed as longer than of short duration. Two years can be temporary (*Bentley Engineering Co Ltd v Crown* (1976)). However, the EAT held in *Berwick Salmon Fisheries Co Ltd v Rutherford* (1991) that a cessation was not temporary when the employee was laid off through lack of work for more time than he spent at work as a salmon-netter: the test in this case, whereby one looks at the whole period of employment, is inconsistent with the House of Lords' decision in *Ford* that one only looks at each interval and the following period of employment. The fact that the break was not permanent does not mean that it was not temporary;

(c) if the employee is absent by arrangement or custom (which means a practice in the establishment concerned), s 212(3)(c) operates to preserve continuity. An 'arrangement' means that, before the time away, there must have been some discussion or agreement. An expectation of returning is not sufficient (*Booth v USA* (1999)). This rule applies even though the employers intend by it to get round the legislation. The sub-paragraph covers a situation where the employee has been granted time off for personal reasons and where he is placed on a holding list pending return to work after a lengthy absence. Where no contract of employment was entered into because the applicant was to serve on a jury, continuity was not preserved because there was no custom to that effect (*Birkett v Workers Educational Association* (1999));

(d) if the employee is absent from work wholly or partly because of pregnancy or childbirth, s 212(3)(d) preserves continuity for 26 weeks. However, if the employee exercises her right to return in accordance with s 12(2) of the ERA 1996, all weeks count (that is, 11 weeks before childbirth and 29 weeks afterwards), but that provision applies only to women who, by already having two years' continuous employment, qualify for the right to return. The term 'childbirth' is defined in s 235(1) of the ERA 1996 as 'the birth of a living child or the birth of a child whether living or dead after 24 weeks of pregnancy'.

It should be noted that the purpose of s 212 is to preserve continuity. A person who is dismissed or made redundant is still dismissed or made redundant even though the sub-section applies.

8.5.9 Subsisting contract

Unlike its predecessor, s 212(3) applies whether or not there is a contract in existence during the contested period.

8.5.10 Transfer of employers

In the event of a change of employers, the basic principle is that continuity of employment is broken. There are, however, seven situations in which continuity is preserved by s 218:

(1) Where the trade, business or undertaking of the old employers is transferred (s 218(2)). While there is no express reference to the point in the statute, this proviso is read as covering transfer of part of an undertaking, provided that the part is not sold just as an asset (*Gibson v Motortune Ltd* (1990)). A person's continuous employment is preserved where he is retained by the old employers after sale of their business and then employed by the new ones, provided that the machinery of the transfer was taking place throughout that period. Moreover, a short gap in employment, even one for which the applicant claimed unemployment benefit, can be bridged by s 218(2). The test is whether there has been a transfer of the business as a going concern. Usually, there must be a transfer of goodwill. It is not enough that the employee has the same working environment or that only the lease of business premises has been transferred. The principal authority for these propositions remains *Woodhouse v Peter Brotherhood Ltd* (1972). Accordingly, s 218(2) will not apply if there has been merely a transfer of assets (*Melon v Hector Powe Ltd* (1981)). For example, in *Crompton v Truly Fair (International) Ltd* (1975), there was no transfer when the old employers made children's clothes, the new ones men's trousers. The provision does not apply where a franchise or maintenance contract is transferred. The burden of proving a transfer is on the employee (*Secretary of State for Employment v Cohen* (1987)) because the presumption that the employee did have continuity of employment does not apply to s 218(2).

(2) Where Parliament causes one company to replace another: s 218(3).

(3) Where an employer who is a natural person dies and the personal representatives take over: s 218(4).

(4) Where the employers are a partnership, personal representatives or trustees, and the composition of that body changes: s 218(5). A transfer from a partnership of four doctors to one is caught by s 218(2): *Jeetle v Elster* (1985).

(5) Where the employee is employed by an associated company: s 218(6). See 8.5.5, above, for the definition of associated employers.

(6) Where the employee is employed by the governors of a school maintained by a local education authority (LEA) or by the LEA itself, and he is transferred to governors of another school or to another LEA: s 218(7).

(7) Where the employee of one health service provider is transferred to another one: s 218(8).

8.5.11 Employee's role

It does not matter that the employee did not work for the transferees, as long as the business was transferred (*Lord Advocate v de Rosa* (1974)).

8.5.12 Moment of transfer

For s 218(2) to apply, the employee must be employed 'at the time of the transfer'. In *Teesside Times Ltd v Drury* (1980), the Court of Appeal (by a majority) controversially said that that phrase meant 'at the moment of transfer'. If he was not, continuity was not preserved. This decision is not in accord with the purpose of the legislation, which is to preserve continuity on a transfer (*Macer v Abafast Ltd* (1990)). However, the Court of Appeal in *Clark and Tokeley Ltd v Oakes* (1998) held that, in view of the complexity of transfers, the 'time of the transfer' covered the duration of the process of transfer. Therefore, an employee dismissed by the liquidator a week before the completion of the transfer was nevertheless employed at the time of the transfer.

8.5.13 Transfer regulations

Superimposed on s 218(2)–(8) is TUPE. TUPE 1981 partially but not totally replaces s 218(2), which is not repealed. Where TUPE applies, continuity is preserved. See Chapter 13 for TUPE. It should be noted that the enactment of TUPE does not affect the construction of s 218(2), which is read in the light of purely domestic authorities (*Green-Wheeler v Onyx (UK) Ltd* (1993)).

8.6   Dismissal

For both redundancy payments and unfair dismissal purposes there are three types of dismissal (ss 95(1) and 136(1)). The burden of proof is on the employee.

8.6.1   Express

'Express', 'actual' or 'direct' dismissal occurs where the employers terminate the contract with or without notice. Such a dismissal occurs where the employers say, for example, 'You're fired' or 'Get your cards'. There have been cases where tribunals have had to consider whether the words used did constitute dismissal, for example, 'Fuck off' may not amount to dismissal (*Futty v D & D Brekkes* (1974)). The tribunals have also held that words of dismissal spoken in anger can be withdrawn and that words indicating a dismissal were not to be taken as such when they occurred in the heat of the moment (*Tanner v Kean* (1978)). Giving the employee a choice between resigning or being dismissed and deceiving the employee into resigning constitute dismissal.

8.6.2   Non-renewal of fixed term contract

The expiry of a fixed term contract without renewal was deemed by Parliament to be a dismissal in order to prevent employers' putting workers on to such contracts to avoid the employment protection legislation. The ending of a contract of apprenticeship is the expiry of a fixed term contract and, by definition, it cannot be extended. It should be noted that, in any case, there is an anti-avoidance provision in s 203 of the ERA 1996 (see *Igbo v Johnson Matthey Chemicals Ltd* (1986) in Chapter 7).

8.6.3 Constructive

There has been debate about the meaning of the handy phrase 'constructive dismissal'. The Court of Appeal in *Western Excavating (ECC) Ltd v Sharp* (1978) held that constructive dismissal is the same as the common law concept of repudiatory breach. The employee must be contractually entitled to leave because of the employers' breach of a fundamental term or because they have evinced an intention no longer to be bound by the contract (that is, anticipatory breach). Whether there had been a breach of a fundamental term is determined objectively without regard to the employers' intention.

An example of anticipatory breach is *Greenaway Harrison Ltd v Wiles* (1994). The employers proposed to vary the applicant's hours of work unilaterally unless she agreed, and they said that they would dismiss her in accordance with her contract otherwise. It did not matter that the threat to terminate the contract was lawful. The EAT said that if they were not correct, employers could avoid constructive dismissal simply by threatening to give notice of dismissal. (It may be enquired which condition in the contract the employers were proposing to breach, for, after all, *Western Excavating* requires such a breach.) The reasonableness of the employers' conduct is irrelevant. For example, in *Courtaulds Northern Spinning Ltd v Sibson* (1988), the Court of Appeal held that an order to move to a nearby site was permitted impliedly by the contract.

Whether the order was unreasonable was immaterial. However, the development of implied terms in the past 20 years has sidestepped this issue. What is unreasonable is likely to be a breach of the duty of mutual trust and confidence. There must be no waiver of the breach. Express and constructive dismissal were dealt with in the previous chapter. Both can give rise to a common law action for wrongful dismissal. Except for the non-renewal of a fixed term contract, what does not amount to a dismissal at common law does not amount to a dismissal under the ERA 1996. For example, an employee has no claim for unfair dismissal if his contract of service is terminated by frustration.

In all three instances of dismissal, the touchstone is the termination of the employment contract. It is immaterial that because the employee waives the breach and works under protest, the employment relationship continues, as it does if an employee is sacked and is then taken back on. In this situation, there is a dismissal because the employers have sacked the employee (*Hogg v Dover College* (1990)). The employee does not, therefore, have to resign in order to claim a remedy for unfair dismissal. The outcome is that, where the employers unilaterally impose a radical variation of the contract, the employee is to be treated as being 'expressly' or 'directly' dismissed and not as constructively dismissed. In one case, the imposition of a new type of shift system constituted dismissal. The existing contract was terminated and the implementation of the shifts was an offer of a new contract. It is for the tribunal to decide whether the change was so substantial as to amount to a dismissal or whether it amounted only to a repudiatory variation. Where there is the former, the employee who remains at work does so under a new contract and he has a claim for unfair dismissal in respect of the old one.

The tribunal investigates whether the constructive dismissal was the effective cause of the employee's resignation. It need not be the sole cause. In *Jones v F Sirl and Son (Furnishers) Ltd* (1997), there occurred a series of incidents which amounted to constructive dismissal. The final incident took place on 25 October 1993. The employee received an offer of employment with a rival firm on 17 November and left work on 24 November. The EAT held that she resigned in response to the breaches of fundamental terms in her contract. The fact that there was a concurrent cause, the offer of a new job, did not matter.

8.6.4 Examples

The following cases are a few of the multitude dealing with constructive dismissal:

- giving an employee an unjustified warning: *Walker v Josiah Wedgwood & Sons Ltd* (1978);

- using extremely foul language: *Palmanor Ltd v Cedron* (1978);

- failing to provide a safe system of work: *British Aircraft Corp v Austin* (1978);

- deliberately failing to pay wages, no matter how small the unpaid sum is: *RF Hill Ltd v Mooney* (1981). However, though failure to pay is a breach, it is not always a breach of a fundamental term. If the failure is due to 'a temporary fault in the employer's technology, an accounting error or simple mistake, of illness, of accident, or unexpected events', the tribunal can easily conclude that there was no breach going to the root of the contract (*Cantor Fitzgerald International v Callaghan* (1994), *obiter*);

- imposing a penalty disproportionate to the offence: *BBC v Beckett* (1983);

- being unfairly critical on several occasions: *Lewis v Motorworld Garages Ltd* (1985). This case is an illustration of a 'last straw' dismissal. It does not matter that the last breach was not repudiatory, as long as the breaches cumulatively destroyed the trust underlying the contract;

- giving an unlawful order: *Weathersfield Ltd v Sargent* (1999), where an employee was told not to hire out vehicles to 'coloureds or Asians';

- dressing down an employee in front of colleagues: *Hilton International (UK) Ltd v Protopapa* (1990);

- appointing another person to do the employee's job, even though the employers believed on reasonable grounds that he would not be returning: *Brown v JBD Engineering Ltd* (1993). The fact that there has been a mistake is relevant to whether there has been a repudiation, but does not *per se* decide it.

A case where there was no constructive dismissal is *Dryden v Greater Glasgow Health Board* (1992). The employers introduced a no smoking policy but without breaking contract. Since there was no breach of contract, there could be no constructive dismissal. Many instances of constructive dismissal stem nowadays from breach of the implied term of trust and confidence, which includes the duty not to treat employees arbitrarily or capriciously. Another recent illustration is *Woodhall v Greggs plc* (1999), where the EAT held that the failure to have regard to a contractual term stipulating that there had to be consultation before the shift pattern was changed was not a breach going to the root of the contract.

8.6.5   Problems

Whether the conduct of the employers is sufficiently serious to entitle the employee to leave immediately is a question of fact for the tribunal (*Woods v WM Car Services (Peterborough) Ltd* (1982)). Accordingly, a tribunal may find that conduct is repudiatory in one case but not in the next, and the EAT cannot intervene in the interests of consistency. Moreover, should a tribunal wish to give itself jurisdiction to hear the merits of the case, it will hold that there has been a constructive dismissal, for without a dismissal the claim cannot proceed. Since constructive dismissal is largely dependent on there being a breach of a fundamental term and that term may be an implied one, tribunals may invent or discover novel implied terms, such as the duty to treat employees with respect (see Chapter 4), thereby giving themselves jurisdiction. It is interesting to note the number of reported cases from the late 1970s in which tribunals sought to get round the need to find breach of such a term, after the court had ruled in *Western Excavating* that constructive dismissal required breach of a fundamental contractual term.

8.6.6   Who terminates?

One sophisticated point is this: where the employers break the contract and the employee leaves as a result, is this a dismissal by the employers or a constructive dismissal? The answer would seem to be both. Which it is matters when discovering the EDoT (see 8.4, above).

COMMON ISSUES IN REDUNDANCY PAYMENTS AND UNFAIR DISMISSAL

Statutory claims

Redundancy payments and unfair dismissal are employment protection laws created by Parliament.

Policy

Parliament's aims include recompensing employees for loss of their jobs and improving personnel management.

Qualifications

Employees must be qualified to apply for these remedies. Basically, they must have one year's continuous employment for unfair dismissal or two years for redundancy payments, must not be members of excluded classes, must not ordinarily work outside Great Britain, must not be over the retirement age, must not have waived their right, and must claim in time:

- *Nothman v Barnet LBC* (1979);

- *Palmer v Southend-on-Sea BC* (1984).

Effective date

The effective date of termination is the date to which continuous employment runs and from which the limitation period runs. Where the employers dismiss with notice, the effective date is when the notice expires.

Continuity

Employment must be continuous for statutory claims, and weeks count towards the qualifying period (and the quantum of compensation). The rules are complex. Continuity is preserved in the absence of contract by s 212 and on transfer by s 218 of the ERA 1996:

- *Fitzgerald v Hall, Russell* (1970);

- *Ford v Warwickshire CC* (1983);

- *Woodhouse v Peter Brotherhood* (1972).

During a strike, continuity is not broken but the weeks on strike do not count. There is a presumption of continuity: the burden of disproof lies on the employers. The effects of the Transfer of Undertakings (Protection of Employment) Regulations 1981 are considered in Chapter 13.

Dismissal

For statutory purposes, 'dismissal' covers dismissal by employers, non-renewal of fixed term contracts and constructive dismissal. The last is defined in contractual terms and covers, for example, 'last straw' cases:

- *Western Excavating v Sharp* (1978);

- *Lewis v Motorworld* (1985).

There are hundreds of cases on what amounts to constructive dismissal, that is, to conduct entitling the employee to leave without notice. Since constructive dismissal is defined in contractual terms, employment tribunals have to consider whether or not a fundamental term, whether express or implied, has been breached. Tribunals may 'invent' an implied term in order to give themselves jurisdiction to hear the merits of the case, which they cannot do if they conclude that there has been no dismissal.

CHAPTER 9

REDUNDANCY PAYMENTS

9.1 Introduction

The statutory scheme for redundancy payments is found in Pt XI of the Employment Rights Act (ERA) 1996. Private schemes may be more advantageous to employees than the State scheme, which provides only a minimum (a 'floor of rights') supplementable by contractual or *ex gratia* payments. The maximum state payment is £6,600, but private schemes, for example, in coalmining and shipbuilding, provide substantially more. When redundancy payments were first introduced in 1965, they were intended to ease demanning in traditional heavy industries. Their purpose now would seem to be to facilitate dismissals without friction.

9.1.1 Coverage of chapter

A flowchart on redundancy was provided at the beginning of Chapter 8, which also deals with the first two stages of the claim: was the employee qualified and was he dismissed? This chapter considers the next two stages: was the employee redundant and did the employers make a suitable offer of alternative employment, and, if so, did the employee reasonably refuse it? Also considered is the procedure for handling redundancies now found in ss 188–98 of the Trade Union and Labour Relations (Consolidation) Act (TULR(C)A) 1992 and amended by the Collective Redundancies and Transfer of Undertakings (Protection of Employment) (Amendment) Regulations 1995 (SI 1995/2587). The amount of compensation is detailed in Chapter 12.

9.2 Misconduct

The misconduct exclusion is such that an employee will not be awarded a redundancy payment if dismissed for misconduct (s 140(1) of the ERA 1996).

9.2.1 Effect

The contract of employment must be terminated without notice or with insufficient notice. If full notice is given, the employers may give notice in writing that they are contractually entitled to dismiss summarily ('special notice'). In *Simmons v Hoover Ltd* (1977), the EAT held that a strike was misconduct. Section 140(1) applies where the employers could have dismissed for gross misconduct as defined at common law (see Chapter 7) but, in fact, dismissed for redundancy. This ruling explains why s 140(1) exists, for a person who is dismissed for misconduct is not dismissed 'by reason of redundancy'. In other words, s 140(1) seems to state the obvious unless this interpretation is used.

9.2.2 Deduction

If dismissal for misconduct occurs during the period of notice of redundancy, an employment tribunal is empowered to pay all or part of the redundancy payment, depending on the justice and equity of the case (s 140(3)). If the dismissal is for a strike during the statutory notice period, the employee retains the right to the payment (s 140(2)). The aim of s 140(2) is to preserve the right when industrial action is undertaken as a reaction to management's decision to declare redundancies. Since both s 140(1) and s 140(3) refer to misconduct, it might seem uncertain what the relationship between the two subsections is. Under s 140(1), the right is lost totally; under s 140(3), the right survives but the quantum is reduced. The law seemingly provides inconsistent norms. The difference lies in s 140(3)'s applying only during the redundancy notice period.

9.2.3 Extension notice

If s 140(2) applies, employers may serve a 'notice of extension' on the employees. This notice obliges the workers to make up the days lost through their action. If the employees do not do so, they lose their right to redundancy payments.

9.3 Definition of redundancy

Parliament has defined 'redundancy' in a special way. If the definition is not satisfied, there can be no claim for a redundancy payment, no matter how 'redundant' the employee might be said to be in ordinary language.

9.3.1 By reason of redundancy

For a claim to succeed, the dismissal must be 'by reason of redundancy'. If the dismissal was for another reason, it will not be 'by reason of redundancy'. In *Sanders v Ernest A Neale Ltd* (1974), a strike caused the closure of a factory. The National Industrial Relations Court held that the employees were not dismissed 'by reason of redundancy'.

9.3.2 Presumption

If an employee is dismissed, there is a statutory presumption in favour of redundancy (s 163(2)). Therefore, the burden of disproof is on the employers. It should be noted that this presumption does not apply to unfair dismissal where one of the potentially fair reasons is that the employee was redundant. What sometimes surprises readers is that employers often argue in favour of redundancy. They do so because the definition of redundancy is the same for the purposes of unfair dismissal and redundancy payments; compensation for the former is at a higher rate than for the latter; therefore, the employers try to prove redundancy as a potentially fair reason to dismiss.

Redundancy payments were instituted in 1965, and payments for unfair dismissal in 1971. The efforts by employers to prove redundancy were not foreseen by Parliament in 1965. It may be that the employee is seeking to demonstrate that he is not redundant, with the effect that the employers have to show that the reason why they did dismiss was a *prima facie* fair reason for dismissal within the unfair dismissal legislation, unfair dismissal leading to greater compensation than redundancy payments. In other words, it is to the employee's benefit not to be redundant. Previously, employers used to get a rebate from the State for part of the costs of redundancy payments. This rebate has been abolished. Employers ought to be more ready to contest redundancy claims than was the case before.

9.3.3 Section 139(1) of the ERA 1996

Redundancy is defined in s 139(1) of the ERA 1996. The dismissal must be wholly or mainly attributable to:

- the employers' ceasing to carry on the business for the purposes of which the employee was employed or intending to do so; or the employers' ceasing to carry on the business in the place where the employee was employed or intending to do so; or

- '... the requirements of that business for employees to carry out work of a particular kind or for employees to carry out work of a particular kind in the place where he was employed, have ceased or diminished, or are expected to cease or diminish.'

In the discussion below, 'work of a particular kind' is abbreviated as WOPK. WOPK has been defined as 'work which is distinguished from other work of the same general kind by requiring special aptitudes, special skills or knowledge' (*Amos v Max-Arc Ltd* (1973)). The cessation of a business may be permanent or temporary. If a business is closed down and a different one is re-opened by the employers on the same premises, there is a cessation of business; however, the closure of a hotel restaurant and the re-opening of it as a brasserie is not.

9.3.4 Statute prevails

Only the statutory definition is used in determining whether or not an employee is redundant. The fact that an employee is 'redundant' in ordinary language is immaterial. The case of *Vaux Breweries Ltd v Ward* (1968) strongly emphasises this point. The applicant was dismissed as not satisfying the requirements of her employers. They thought her too old to fit the image they were trying to present. Your parents might say that she was redundant, but, as we shall see, because the requirements of the business for WOPK had not ceased, she was not *statutorily* redundant. Similarly, local authorities' contracting out of services does not seem to lead to statutory redundancy, for the WOPK, for example, collecting dustbins, remains to be done.

9.3.5 Reason for redundancy

If the definition applies, it does not matter what the reason for the redundancy was. Perhaps management bungled, or, as in *Moon v Homeworthy Furniture (Northern) Ltd* (1977), the employer dismissed the employees because their factory had a bad industrial relations record. No investigation is undertaken by the tribunal of the true ground behind the redundancy when s 139(1) applies. Kilner Brown J stated that legislation 'has taken away all powers of the courts to investigate the rights and wrongs of industrial disputes ...'. A façade of political neutrality is preserved.

9.3.6 Applying the law

For many years, it was unclear which test was to be applied to WOPK. On one view, it was the contractual approach which governed. This test was that there was a redundancy if there was a diminution in the type of work for which the employee had been engaged under his contract of employment. For example, in *Nelson v BBC (No 2)* (1980), the employee was not redundant because, under his contract, he could be assigned to any task within the BBC and, of course, the BBC had not closed down. The second test, the 'function' test, was: did the employers need fewer employees to do the sort of work the employee was doing?

The House of Lords, on appeal from Northern Ireland in *Murray v Foyle Meats Ltd* (1999), ruled that both of these tests were incorrect. Both of them missed the point. The tribunal should look at the pure and simple words of the statute: have the requirements of the business for employees to carry out WOPK ceased or diminished? If so, was the dismissal wholly or mainly attributable to that state of affairs? On the facts, the employers, who ran a slaughterhouse, did not need as many employees because of a decline in business. Therefore, the applicant was redundant. The contract and the function tests are, therefore, both incorrect.

9.3.7 Work of a particular kind

WOPK is a difficult concept. Five Court of Appeal cases in which work had not ceased or diminished are listed below in chronological order.

- *Vaux Breweries Ltd v Ward* (1968)

  A barmaid was sacked when the employers decided to modernise a pub to attract a younger, more free-spending clientele than previously. She was replaced by 'bunny girls'. Her WOPK had not ceased or diminished. There was still work to be done serving customers.

- *Hindle v Percival Boats Ltd* (1969)

  A boatbuilder was used to working with wood. He was dismissed for being 'too good and too slow' when the yard changed from wood to fibreglass. He was not redundant. The particular kind of work had not changed.

- *Chapman v Goonvean and Rostowrack China Clay Co Ltd* (1973)

  The employers withdrew the bus service they had provided to take seven employees to work. The service had become uneconomic, and the employers wished to save money. There was no redundancy. Indeed, the seven men were replaced.

- *Johnson v Nottinghamshire Combined Police Authority* (1974)

  Women workers' five day week was reorganised into a six day shift system. Because the amount of work remained the same, they were not redundant. The court did say, however, that the tribunal can investigate whenever the reorganisation was a smokescreen hiding redundancy.

- *Lesney Products & Co v Nolan* (1977)

  The employers changed from day and night shifts to double day shifts, one result being that the employees lost overtime pay. There were no redundancies: the work remained the same.

Therefore, a change in contractual terms may mean that there has been a constructive dismissal, but does not *per se* mean that a redundancy payment is due. The law of redundancy payments does not act as much of a restraint on managerial prerogative. As these cases demonstrate, replacing employees by cheaper workers does not mean that the employees are redundant. It is suggested that the authorities run contrary to the law's aim, which is to compensate (to some degree) employees who have lost their jobs through technological advances.

9.3.8   Efficiency reorganisations

As can be seen from these five Court of Appeal cases, if the employers reorganise the work in the interests of efficiency (for example, to stop losses or to increase profits) and they dismiss employers actually or constructively, the workers have not been dismissed by reason of redundancy. Therefore, they did not succeed in their claims for redundancy payments – despite their jobs being reorganised away. They got nothing; yet the employers saved or gained money through dismissing them. Lord Denning MR was a strong upholder of employers' rights to reorganise their business 'in the interests of efficiency', as he put it in *Chapman*, above, with consequential changes to contractual terms but without redundancy. If a remedy for unfair dismissal is claimed, a reorganisation in the interests of efficiency is treated as 'some other substantial reason', which is one of the five potentially fair reasons. Provided the employers have acted reasonably, the employees will have no remedy. The concomitant effect of the narrowness of the definition of redundancy is that it is difficult for employers to demonstrate that a dismissal was for redundancy in an unfair dismissal case.

9.3.9   Narrowness of definition

As a result of these cases, one can say that WOPK ceases when the employee's job function has been superseded, for example, when his job is done by someone else (*Sutton v Revlon Overseas Corp* (1973)). In *European Chefs (Catering) Ltd v Currell* (1971), the employee's job as one type of chef disappeared. His WOPK had ceased, despite there being a demand from his employers for another type of chef. This case amply illustrates the precision with which WOPK is defined. In another case, an employment tribunal held that the job of an unsupervised night mechanic was different from that of an ordinary daytime mechanic. Since whether the work is WOPK is a question of fact, one tribunal's decision may be inconsistent with another's and the EAT cannot intervene. For example, if the WOPK was serving mild and bitter to old fogies in *Vaux Breweries Ltd v Ward*, the employee's WOPK would have ceased when the business requirements were for serving Pernod to young trendies. There may be a redundancy even though the employee knew that the job was only temporary (*Nottingham CC v Lee* (1980)). It should be noted that, consistently with the period in which the redundancy payments scheme was established, the era of the 'white heat of the technological revolution', the definition of WOPK is phrased so as to cover the situation where the requirements of the business for an employee to do WOPK have ceased or diminished. It does not matter that the work done by the employers has in fact increased. Accordingly, an employer who is replaced by a machine is redundant, and is so even though the employers automated production in order to step up output because demand had increased. *A fortiori*, the employee is redundant when the work is the same but the number of employees to do it is reduced (*McCrea v Cullen & Davison Ltd* (1988), a decision of the Northern Ireland Court of Appeal). The test is whether the reorganisation:

> ... results in the employee's work being encompassed in other posts and whether the employer's business is such that it no longer has a requirement for a separate and additional employee to carry out the work [*Sutton v Revlon*, above].

Therefore, the dismissal of staff taken on in the expectation of a large order which did not materialise is by reason of redundancy because the words of the statute are fulfilled (*O'Hare v Rotaprint Ltd* (1980)). The main point remains the difficulty in determining what is WOPK. If a plumber who dealt with the heating is dismissed when the employers replace him with a heating technician, have the employers' requirement for employees to do WOPK ceased or diminished? The Court of Appeal thought so in *Murphy v Epsom College* (1985), but the answer is not obvious.

9.3.10 Bumping

One particular kind of redundancy dismissal should be noted. If, as a result of a downturn in demand in one department there is a need for redundancy, and the employers transfer a person from that department into a second department and sack an employee in the second department, that employee is dismissed for redundancy (see, for example, *W Gimber & Sons Ltd v Spurrett* (1967)). The industrial relations term for this situation is 'bumping'. In the mid-1990s, it was doubted whether a person who was sacked as a result of 'bumping' could be redundant within the terms of the statute, but the House of Lords held in *Murray v Foyle Meats Ltd* (1999) that she could be. Her dismissal was attributable to reduced demand for employees. The issue was simply one of causation.

9.4 Suitable employment unreasonably refused

If the employers, successors or associated employers (or the new employers on a transfer of the business) offer the employee a renewal of the contract or offer suitable alternative work before the end of the contract, there is no redundancy if the employee unreasonably refuses the offer (ss 138 and 141). The offer must contain details of the job. The renewal or re-engagement must take effect immediately on termination of the previous contract or within four weeks thereof. Continuity is preserved.

9.4.1 Suitability

What is suitable depends on an objective test. The best known case is *Taylor v Kent CC* (1969). A former headmaster was offered a place in a 'floating pool' of teachers, that is, he was to do supply work as and when required. The Divisional Court held that, because of the loss in status, the offer was not of suitable employment (even though his pay remained the same). It was as if a company director had been offered the job of navvy. Similarly, in *Sheppard v NCB* (1966), the loss of fringe benefits made the job offer unsuitable. Tribunals should not investigate the financial situation of the employers to determine whether an offer of a job with substantially reduced terms was suitable for the employee (*Sennitt v Fysons Conveyors Ltd* (1994)). In *Carron Co v Robertson* (1967), Lord Parker CJ said:

> ... in deciding as to the suitability of employment in relation to an employee, one must consider not only the nature of the work, hours and pay, the employee's strength, training, experience and ability, but such matters as status.

The burden of proof is on the employers to demonstrate suitability. In *Anglia Regional Co-operative Society v O'Donnell* (1994), the employers failed to show that a transfer fell within the terms of a mobility clause and that the employee had accepted new terms and conditions which would have permitted them to move her, but they did demonstrate that the offer to move her was suitable alternative employment which she had unreasonably refused.

9.4.2 Reasonableness

Even if the offer is suitable, the employee will retain the right to a redundancy payment if refusal of it is reasonable. What is reasonable is judged subjectively: was it reasonable for this employee to refuse the offer of alternative employment? Reasonable reasons include family commitments, lack of good schools for the employee's children, loss of friends and travel problems. In an important decision, *Thomas Wragg & Sons v Wood* (1976), it was held that fear of future redundancy in the new job coupled with the employee's being near retirement age made the refusal reasonable. It has, however, been said that a personal fad is not a good reason. *Fuller v Stephanie Bowman Ltd* (1977) illustrates this proposition. A female employee was asked to move from Mayfair, a salubrious part of London, to an office above a sex shop in Soho. The court, surprisingly, held that she unreasonably refused the offer. The job was the same; therefore, it was suitable. The offer was refused unreasonably as a consequence of a 'personal fad'. The fact that work will not last for long does not *per se* mean that refusal was reasonable.

9.4.3 Separate stages

Though the tribunals and courts have treated the (un)reasonable refusal of suitable alternative employment as separate, factors relevant to one may also be relevant to the other (*Spencer v Gloucestershire CC* (1985)).

9.5 Trial periods

If the employee wishes to try out the job, there is a trial period of four calendar weeks (s 138(2) and (3)). If he does not like the new job, he retains the right to a redundancy payment. The four week trial period may be extended by the parties for a period which must be expressly stated, provided they do so in writing and do so for the purposes of retraining (s 138(3)). The EAT held in *Kentish Bus and Coach Co Ltd v Quarry* (1994) that the trial period was preceded by a common law 'thinking time' of a reasonable duration, during which the employee could consider whether to accept the new terms. For the purpose of redundancy payments, the employee is treated as not having been dismissed; however, he may still have been dismissed for the purposes of the law of unfair dismissal (*Jones v Governing Body of Burdett Coutts School* (1997)).

9.5.1 Effect of repudiation

Where the employee is constructively dismissed on the grounds of redundancy, it has been held several times that the employee is entitled to a common law trial period (of reasonable duration), followed by the s 138(2) trial period. For example, in *Air Canada v Lee* (1978), the employers moved the employee to another office. They were not permitted to do so under her contract. She agreed to the change on a trial basis. She left after two months. There was no doubt that she had been constructively dismissed, but she had left after the statutory four week period. The EAT held that she had left within the common law trial period. The statutory period had not even begun to run. What is a reasonable length depends on the facts. Twelve months were held to be of a reasonable duration in *McKindley v William Hill (Scotland) Ltd* (1985). What is reasonable is dependent on the common law concerned with acceptance of a breach of a fundamental term or affirmation of the contract.

9.5.2 Deemed redundancy

If the employers dismiss the employee during the trial period for whatever reason (for example, incompetence), the employee is treated as having been dismissed for redundancy; that is, his claim springs up again. If he resigns during the period because he has sampled the job and does not like it, he is deemed to have been dismissed, but whether the job was suitable and whether the ground for leaving was reasonable are matters for the tribunal. If, however, the employee remains in the job, there is deemed to have been no dismissal; therefore, there can be no claim for unfair dismissal based on redundancy.

9.6 Time off

An employee who is given notice of dismissal by reason of redundancy is entitled to a reasonable amount of time off work to seek employment or retraining (s 52 of the ERA 1996). Only employees who have worked for two years continuously may claim. The application is made to an employment tribunal if the employers unreasonably refuse time off. The maximum award the tribunal may give is two-fifths of a week's pay, but the award may be less, for it is otherwise based on the pay which the employee would have received had he been allowed time off. If the employee does obtain a new job during the time off, the liability of the employers to make a redundancy payment is unaffected. (Indeed, the same applies generally: a payment is still due even if an employee steps into a new job the moment after dismissal.)

9.7 Redundancy procedure

The Employment Protection Act 1975 introduced a special procedure for handling redundancies. The then Government considered that that law fulfilled, and was indeed broader than, EC law. The Conservative Government, however, found that the English provisions fell short of EC norms and drastically amended the law in 1993 and 1996 to embody the relevant EC directive.

9.7.1 Consultation

When contemplating redundancies, employers have a duty under s 188 of TULR(C)A 1992 to consult with 'authorised representatives' of recognised independent trade unions or elected representatives of the employees on redundancy. Redundancy is defined in s 195, as inserted by the Trade Union Reform and Employment Rights Act 1993, as dismissal not being for a reason – such as misconduct – connected with the individual employee; that is, 'redundancy' is wider in ss 188–98 than it is in the previous sections of this book and in the next three chapters: the pre-1993 definition was held by the ECJ in *Commission v UK* (1994) to fall short of EC standards. Consultation must take place 'in good time'. In the event of non-compliance, an employment tribunal may award a 'protective award' unless there are 'special circumstances' excusing non-compliance. Consultation may reduce the number of employees to be dismissed or other work may be found. In practice, redundancies are rarely avoided. There is a presumption of redundancy in s 195.

9.7.2　Recognition and non-recognition

Recognition is discussed in Chapter 14. Since recognition is not obtained through law, employers can refuse recognition or derecognise without legal sanction. The non-implementation of EC law in these circumstances was strongly condemned in *Commission v UK* (1994). The Government changed the law so that there is now a duty to consult with employee representatives even though no recognised union exists. Where both representatives of a recognised independent trade union and representatives of the employees exist (whether elected for the purpose of the consultation exercise or elected for any other purpose and it is appropriate to consult them), the employers consult with the union's representatives: Collective Redundancies and Transfer of Undertakings (Protection of Employment) (Amendment) Regulations 1999. Where consultation is with trade union representatives, it does not matter that no employee to be dismissed is a member of that union, provided that he falls within a category of employees in respect of whom the trade union is recognised. Where consultation is with non-trade union representatives, it is difficult to see how the representatives can gain advice from the persons whom they represent in the time allowed. This law should be contrasted with the detailed regulation of union elections.

9.7.3　Authorised representatives of unions

Section 196 of TULR(C)A 1992 defines authorised representatives as elected representatives or officials or other persons authorised to carry on collective bargaining with the relevant employers. An example is a shop steward (*GMWU v Wailes Dove Bitumastic Ltd* (1977)). On the facts of that case, there was no duty on the employers to consult with a full time union officer because he had never taken part in collective bargaining with the employers. Bargaining had been with the shop steward.

9.7.4　Consultation defined

The term 'consultation' is not fully defined in the statute. Certainly, full-blooded negotiation is not required. Consultation need not lead to agreement. In a case on a statute dealing with the same terms, *R v British Coal Corp ex p Price* (1994), Glidewell LJ defined the term 'fair consultation' as:

> (a) consultation when the proposals are still at a formative stage; (b) adequate information on which to respond; (c) adequate time in which to respond; (d) conscientious consideration by an authority of the response to consultation.

The Court of Appeal held that there was consultation despite the employers' paying non-statutory redundancy payments before the end of the consultation period was reached. The employers must disclose in writing the number of jobs to go; the reason for the redundancies; the total number of employees; the method of selection for redundancy; the length of notice and the amount, if any, they will give above the statutory redundancy payment; and the method of calculating the sum payable on redundancy. The names of those to be dismissed need not be given. Providing the union with the number of those to be made redundant analysed into manual, clerical and technical/management grades is insufficient to comply with the duty to disclose 'the numbers and descriptions of employees whom it is proposed to dismiss as redundant'. Therefore, merely telling the representatives that there will be redundancies is not enough (*Electrical & Engineering Association v Ashwell-Scott Ltd* (1976)).

Consultation must be concerned with ways of avoiding dismissals, reducing the number of employees to be dismissed, and mitigating the effects of the dismissals (s 188(6), as revised). While consultation does not mean negotiation and certainly does not mean that an agreement must be reached, it goes beyond simply telling the representatives that dismissals will occur shortly. In *TGWU v Ledbury Preserves (1928) Ltd* (1985), the employers informed the union of the dismissal half an hour before giving the workforce their notice of dismissal. This was not consultation, but a sham. The consultation must be with a view to reaching agreement. This change reinforces the view in this case that the consultation must be meaningful. The amendment makes consultation more like negotiation than previously.

9.7.5 Special circumstances

Parliament has given a defence to the employers if they are afflicted with special circumstances (s 188(7)). (There is no such defence in the Directive relevant to the area: see below, 9.7.16.) If the defence applies, sub-s (7) nevertheless imposes a duty on them to:

> ... take all steps towards compliance ... as are reasonably practicable in those circumstances.

'Reasonably practicable' steps could mean that the duty may be satisfied by the employers' doing nothing.

The burden of proving special circumstances and reasonably practicable compliance is on the employers (s 189(6)). The sort of situation envisaged by the special circumstances defence occurred in *USDAW v Leancut Bacon Ltd* (1981). The employers were heading for insolvency. Their directors undertook talks with a third party to buy shares, but the talks broke down. Employees were dismissed for redundancy. The company's bank withdrew credit and a receiver was appointed. It was held that special circumstances existed. The employers thought that there would be a rescue operation but, virtually at the last moment, their hopes evaporated. The EAT considered in *Association of Patternmakers & Allied Craftsmen v Kirvin Ltd* (1978) that a line was to be drawn between a reasonable hope that the company would be saved (as in *Leancut Bacon*) and a foreseeable insolvency, the latter not amounting to a special circumstance. This distinction represents current law. (The hope, in the former instance, must not be one based on no evidence: the employers have no defence if they are wilfully blind, that is, if they shut their eyes to the obvious.) This law leaves something to be desired. In *Leancut Bacon*, it could hardly be said that the withdrawal of credit was unforeseeable.

A well known instance of a foreseeable redundancy was *Clarks of Hove Ltd v Bakers' Union* (1978). The employers found that they had insufficient money to carry on. They realised what was happening but did not tell their workforce until two hours before they closed down. On the facts, the employers should have consulted with the union well before the closure, for they knew that the shutdown was inevitable. The court said that, in order for employers to have this defence, the circumstances must be uncommon or out of the ordinary, such as those which occur when the factory burns down, the main suppliers suddenly stop delivery or, as in *Hamish Armour v ASTMS* (1979), the failure to obtain a loan from the Government leads to dismissals for redundancy. An administration order does not make it impracticable to comply. Employers do not have a special circumstances defence where failure to consult is due to a controlling person's not giving them the information: s 188(7). The effect is that an English company has no defence if its parent company based abroad does not provide it with the requisite information. If the defence applies, no protective award (see 9.7.9, below) is awarded. Surprisingly, the defence of special circumstances was not discussed in *Commission of the European Communities v UK* (1994).

9.7.6 In good time

Section 188(1A) provides that, where employers are proposing to make redundant 100 or more employees within a 90 day period, consultation must take place 'in good time and in any event ... at least 90 days ... before the first of the dismissals take effect'. The minimum period for 20–99 employees within a 90 day period is 30 days.

Since 1995, there has been no duty to consult when the number of workers to be made redundant was 19 or fewer. The Government said that the amendment would free 96% of UK businesses from the duty to consult. It was expected by the Conservative Government that the savings to firms from this reduction in coverage would more than outweigh the increased cost of the new duty to consult where there was no union. There has been no empirical research on this issue.

It must be stressed that the need to consult in good time occurs before the specified number of days in s 188(1A), the latter being only a fallback position if consultation cannot take place before then. Where the employee representatives are elected for the purpose of consulting on redundancy, TULR(C)A 1992, as amended in 1995, provides that 'in good time' means that consultation must start as soon as practicable after the election. The consultation period can begin before the information for consultation is provided. 'Proposing' to dismiss covers situations where there is a settled intention to do so but not where the employers think that there is only a remote possibility of dismissal for redundancy (*NUPE v General Cleaning Contractors* (1976)). Similarly, thinking about a problem, the solution to which may be dismissal, is not proposing to dismiss (*Hough v Leyland DAF Ltd* (1991)). The duty on the employers to consult exists even though consultation would have made no difference (*Sovereign Distribution Services Ltd v TGWU* (1989)).

The relevant EC Directive applies at an earlier stage, when employers were contemplating redundancies: see *R v British Coal Corp ex p Vardy* (1993), the case on the Government's proposal to close most collieries. Indirect effect would be given by interpreting 'proposing' to mean 'contemplating'. The court granted an injunction to restrain the defendants from closing the pits in breach of a statutory procedure. 'Contemplating' is subjective. The employers need not act as reasonable employers would have acted. The numbers who count within s 188(2) need not be union members, nor, indeed, do they have to be employees who are qualified to bring redundancy payments claims (for example, they need not have worked continuously for two years), but the numbers exclude employees on fixed term contracts for 12 weeks or less or on task contracts where the task is not expected to last more than 12 weeks.

Under the 1995 Regulations, it seems that employers will be able to avoid the duty to consult if they invite the employees to elect representatives but they do not do so. In this respect, the Regulations may not comply with the Directive.

9.7.7 Establishment

Section 188 requires the employees to be at one establishment. The ECJ held in *Rockfon A/S v Specialarbejderforbundet i Danmark* (1996) that the term meant the unit to which the employees to be made redundant were assigned. The unit may not have its own management structure. Employers cannot evade the application of the law by splitting their activities into separate divisions. The principal English authority is *Barratt Developments Ltd v UCATT* (1978). Employers proposed to dismiss 24 construction workers across eight sites (out of their 14 sites). The EAT confirmed an industrial tribunal's decision that, since all sites were administered from one location, they formed one establishment. Therefore, the number of workers could be aggregated to bring what is now s 188(1A) into play. Presumably, one looks at the autonomy of the individual locations.

9.7.8 Employer/employee

One technical matter is that associated employers do not constitute one employer for the purposes of the protective award. Therefore, one cannot aggregate employees of different but associated employers to trigger a larger protective award than would otherwise be given (*E Green & Son (Castings) Ltd v ASTMS* (1984)). This was so even though the three companies on the facts of this case shared accounting and personnel services and they were subsidiaries of a holding company (and so were associated employers for other purposes).

9.7.9 Protective award

The remedy for non-compliance with the duty to consult is the award by an employment tribunal of a protective award to individual employees on the application of the recognised independent trade union. There is no statutory procedure for obliging the union to act. The award, which is discretionary, orders the employers to pay remuneration based on the employees' normal working hours (that is, excluding voluntary overtime) for the 'protected period' (s 189(3)). By s 189(4), as amended in 1995 and 1999:

... [t]he protected period –

(a) begins with the date on which the first of the dismissals to which the complaint relates takes effect, or the date of the award, whichever is the earlier; and

(b) is of such length as the tribunal determines to be just and equitable in all the circumstances having regard to the seriousness of the employer's default in complying with any requirement of s 188; but shall not exceed 90 days.

The 'protected period' continues despite the company's being wound up by court order.

Unions cannot obtain an injunction to oblige employers to consult (*Griffin v South West Water Services Ltd* (1995)). The sole remedy is the protective award.

9.7.10 Compensation

The protective award is intended to be compensatory, not penal (*Talke Fashions Ltd v Amalgamated Society of Textile Workers & Kindred Trades* (1977)). The gravity of the employers' misconduct and the loss occasioned to the employees must be considered. The seriousness of the default is measured by the increased loss to the employees. In *Barratt Developments Ltd v UCATT* (1978), the award was said to be based on the amount payable as wages or in lieu of notice which the employee would have obtained had consultation procedures been followed. Loss is, therefore, not calculated by reference to the financial loss suffered by the employee during the protected period. Accordingly, money may still be payable despite the fact that the employees immediately obtained other jobs.

Because the amount awarded is based on the 'just and equitable' criterion, no compensation award may be given. In *Amalgamated Society of Boilermakers v George Wimpey & Co Ltd* (1977), the EAT did not make an award where the employees were kept informed but the employers had not complied with the obligation to provide information in writing. Similarly, no award was made in *ASTMS v Hawker Siddeley Aviation Ltd* (1977) where the employers and union had agreed on the payment of wages in lieu of notice. The rule enforcing set off between the protective award and wages due or damages for breach of contract was abolished in 1993. Previously, the sanction of the protective award was rendered nugatory where the award was wiped out by the payment of wages in lieu. Even after the change, the compensation is not of such a level as to make the right effective to satisfy EC law. If the relevant directive were directly effective, employees would be able to rely on it to gain compensation beyond the present limits. Those limits and the previous set off were condemned by the ECJ in *Commission of the European Communities v UK*, above. The sanctions were not adequate to deter employers.

9.7.11 Exclusions

A protective award is not granted where the employee is not ready and willing to work; joins industrial action; is dismissed (fairly) for a reason other than redundancy; unreasonably terminates his contract; is offered suitable alternative employment; or his contract is renewed and the renewal takes effect before or during the protected period (see s 191 of TULR(C)A 1992).

9.7.12 Limitation period

The time limit is laid down in s 189(5):

> An employment tribunal shall not consider a complaint under this section unless it is presented to the tribunal –
>
> (a) before the date on which the last of the dismissals to which the complaint relates takes effect; or
>
> (b) during the period of three months beginning with that date; or
>
> (c) where the tribunal is satisfied that it was not reasonably practicable for the complaint to be presented during the period of three months, within such further period as it considers reasonable.

9.7.13 Non-compliance

The remedy for non-compliance with the award is an individual complaint to an employment tribunal (s 192).

9.7.14 Comment

The protective award is a strange remedy in several respects. It is one enforceable by a trade union but paid to individual employees. What if one or more of those employees are not union members? Can they oblige the union for their workplace to undertake proceedings for their benefit? The answer is unknown. Moreover, while the right is one to consultation, the remedy is not one to enforce consultation, neither does it seem effective enough to comply with EC law

Representatives have the right not to be subjected to a detriment by the employers for performing or proposing to perform 'any functions or activities as such an employee representative or candidate'. Dismissal on this ground is automatically unfair.

9.7.15 Notification

Employers have a duty to notify the Secretary of State in writing that they are proposing to dismiss for redundancy: s 193. The revised s 195 definition of redundancy applies to s 193 (see 9.7.1, above). As with consultation with recognised independent trade unions or other representatives, there is a 'special circumstances' defence in situations where it was not reasonably practicable for the employers to comply with the law on notification; if the excuse applies, the employers must 'take all such steps towards compliance with that requirement as are reasonably practicable in the circumstances': (s 193(7)). It is an offence punishable by a fine (currently up to £5,000) to fail to give notice (s 194(1)). It is thought that the object of s 193 is to enable the Government to have in place retraining schemes and job placement opportunities. It would be interesting to know whether s 193 does actually have this effect. The definitions of, for example, 'establishment' and 'special circumstances' are as in the previous paragraphs. It should be noted that notifying the Secretary of State is a duty separate from that of consultation. Both obligations must be fulfilled.

9.7.16 Critique

Comments on consultation and notification:

(a) Provided employers do consult and notify, there is nothing to prevent employers from dismissing for redundancy many employees ('mass redundancy'). The laws on consultation and notification are, moreover, procedural, not substantive, in effect. Non-compliance does not stop sackings.

(b) Linked with consultation on redundancy is the obligation to consult under the TUPE 1981 (SI 1981/1794), as amended. For this obligation, see Chapter 13.

(c) There is debate as to whether present law complies with EC norms, which is found in the Directive on the Approximation of Laws of the Member States relating to Collective Redundancies (75/129, as amended by 92/56). The aims of the 1975 Directive are 'to ensure comparable protection for workers' rights in different Member States and to harmonise the costs which such protective rules entail for Community undertakings' (*Commission of the European Communities v UK* (1994)). The changes in the 1993 Act were necessitated by the two Directives. They came into force on 30 August 1993. In one respect, until 1995, UK legislation was more favourable to employees than EC law. The Directive applies only if 20 or more are to be dismissed whereas UK law was not so limited. The Government, however, amended UK law by increasing the threshold to 20. The change from 'earliest opportunity' to 'in good time' reflected a change from pro-employee law which was not in the Directive. In brief the following matters arise:

- the Directive obliges the national Department of Employment to try to solve problems arising from mass redundancies. This obligation has not been transposed into English law;

- the Directive applies when redundancies are contemplated, the UK legislation when they are proposed. English cases are divided on whether contemplating and proposing are the same concept or whether contemplating occurs before proposing. As a matter of language, the latter construction is correct. The ECJ ruled in *Commission of the European Communities v UK* (1994) that English law fell short of EC standards in this respect. English law is brought into line by reading 'proposing' as 'contemplates'. When it enacted the consultation procedures in 1975, the then Government thought that they were complying with EC law. Interestingly, the Directive expressly does not apply to public administrative bodies. In *Griffin v South West Water Services Ltd* (1995), Blackburne J held that a privatised utility was not a 'public administrative body' within the Directive (although it was an emanation of the State for the purposes of the doctrine of direct effect). He suggested that OFWAT, the water services regulator, was such a body;

- where consultation is to be with representatives of a recognised independent trade union, there is nothing to prevent employers from derecognising the union and thereby ending this route to consultation, as occurred in *Griffin*. Employers are then free to consult with a body elected for the purpose of consultation, members of which may come from a non-independent staff association.

- Blackburne J stated *obiter* in *Griffin* that the protective award was 'adequate' within the definition that bears in discussions of remedies for EC purposes. It is, however, suggested that the remedy is inadequate. The compensation is capped; the worker cannot obtain re-employment; and the union receives no compensation for the employers' failure to consult. The award does not, therefore, act as a deterrent to employers who fail to consult.

It is uncertain whether the Collective Redundancies Directive is directly effective. Some Articles seem to be unconditional and sufficiently precise. It is also uncertain whether an action against the State for non-implementation would be properly brought by an individual or by a union. The issue of who are the workers' representatives within Arts 2 and 6 was said not to be unconditional and sufficiently precise in *Griffin*. This proposition has been criticised above, 2.4.1. This issue will no doubt be referred to the ECJ soon.

(d) The Divisional Court ruled in *R v Secretary of State for Trade and Industry ex p UNISON* (1996) that the 1995 Regulations did comply with the EC law: EC law permitted a threshold of 20 employees before the provisions on consultation were triggered and it did not specify that elections for employee representatives had to take place in any particular manner. The court also rejected the argument that the remedy was inadequate. It held that the withdrawal of consultation rights where fewer than 20 were to be made redundant was not indirectly discriminatory on the grounds of sex, since the rule did not disproportionately affect women. Certainly, women were disproportionately employed in small enterprises, but that did not mean that they were necessarily at risk when firms made fewer than 20 employees redundant. For damning criticism, see P Skidmore (1996) 25 ILJ 225.

(e) Just as occurs with regard to redundancy payments, tribunals cannot investigate the reason for the redundancy (*Association of University Teachers v University of Newcastle-upon-Tyne* (1987)). No judicial body can prevent redundancies by checking the managerial prerogative to dismiss. As will be seen in the chapter dealing with the calculation of redundancy payments, the remedy for breach of the legislation is not re-employment in the same or similar job but pecuniary compensation. The remedy, therefore, does not prevent dismissals but puts a monetary tariff on them. Since most employers pay up without a tribunal hearing, there is not even the satisfaction that some employees might get through having their complaint heard by a public body.

(f) The widened definition of 'redundancy' noted above, 9.7.1, may lead to unforeseen problems. Consultation and notification requirements apply if dismissal is for a reason unconnected with the individual employee. Assume that the employers wish to cut the pay of their workers. They give each employee the requisite length of notice lawfully to terminate the contracts, and in the same letter offer re-engagement but with less pay. Within s 195, as amended, there is dismissal not related to an individual employee. Therefore, consultation is a legal necessity. Certainly, redundancies in the interests of efficiency fall within s 195. It would seem, however, that 'dismissal' within the Directive, as amended, does not include constructive dismissals such as may occur when employers suspend payment of their debts and the employees leave.

(g) 'It may be argued that requiring employers to consult in the face of impending financial collapse will hasten the failure of the business. At a sensitive time, employers may be understandably reluctant to publicise the economic instability of the business. The direct clash between workers' rights and business needs does, nonetheless, highlight the very shaky foundations of the provisions of this Directive.' (Burrows and Mair, *European Social Law*, 1996, p 214.)

REDUNDANCY PAYMENTS

Introduction

Qualified employees dismissed by reason of redundancy have the right to claim in an employment tribunal that they should be awarded a redundancy payment.

Misconduct

Employees dismissed for misconduct lose this right. Misconduct includes industrial action:

- *Simmons v Hoover* (1977).

Definition

There is a presumption of redundancy. Accordingly, the burden of disproof is on the employers. The definition includes the closure of the business at the place the employee works and the diminution in the requirements of the business for the employee to do work of a particular kind:

- *Vaux Breweries v Ward* (1968);
- *Hindle v Percival Boats* (1969);
- *Johnson v Notts CPA* (1974);
- *Murphy v Epsom College* (1985);
- *Murray v Foyle Meats Ltd* (1999).

Suitable employment unreasonably refused

Employees lose their entitlement if they unreasonably reject an offer of suitable alternative employment. Suitability is judged objectively, reasonableness subjectively:

- *Taylor v Kent CC* (1969);
- *Thomas Wragg v Wood* (1976).

Trial periods

There is a statutory four week trial period in the new job; however, if the employee is constructively dismissed, there is a common law trial period of reasonable length in addition:

* *Air Canada v Lee* (1979).

Time off

Employees under notice of redundancy have a right to reasonable time off work to seek employment or retraining.

Redundancy procedure

In the event of redundancies, employers must consult with authorised representatives of recognised independent trade unions or, if there are none, with other representatives, in good time. The remedy is a protective award. There is a defence of special circumstances:

* *TGWU v Ledbury Preserves* (1985);

* *Clarks of Hove v Bakers' Union* (1978).

There is a duty on employers to notify the Secretary of State of mass redundancies.

The definition of redundancy in the context of the procedure for handling redundancies is wider than that in the earlier parts of this chapter. It covers dismissal for any reason not connected with the individual employee.

CHAPTER 10

UNFAIR DISMISSAL: GENERAL APPROACH

10.1 Introduction

In an unfair dismissal claim, once the employee has shown that he is qualified and has been dismissed (see Chapter 8), the burden switches to the employers to demonstrate a potentially fair (also called *prima facie* valid) reason for the dismissal. If they cannot do so, the employee wins. If they can do so, the question for the employment tribunal is whether the dismissal was fair or not, having regard to the size and administrative resources of the firm and equity and the substantial merits of the case. The issue of the remedy is considered in Chapter 12. The next chapter deals with particular instances of fair or unfair dismissal which do not fall within the general run of unfair dismissal (for example, dismissal for a trade union related reason). Accordingly, in this chapter, two stages are considered, the third and fourth, in a straightforward unfair dismissal application, the reason and the reasonableness – see the diagram at the start of Chapter 8. This chapter also contains a discussion of the effect of an employee's request for written reasons for dismissal within s 92 of the Employment Rights Act (ERA) 1996.

10.1.1 Unfair

The description of this claim as 'unfair dismissal' must not mislead the reader. What the term really means is 'dismissal contrary to statute', just as wrongful dismissal is concerned with dismissal at common law. One must apply the law set forth in the statute, not simply say: 'Gosh! Didn't those employers dismiss unfairly!'

10.1.2 Right to be accompanied

Section 10 of the Employment Relations Act 1999 introduces a right to be accompanied at disciplinary and grievance hearings when the worker makes a reasonable request to that effect. Only one person may accompany the worker. He must be a trade union official or a colleague of the worker. He is permitted to address the hearing but not to answer questions on behalf of the worker. He must be given time off to attend.

Non-compliance with these rules is remedied via a complaint to an employment tribunal (s 22). Compensation must not exceed two weeks' pay (up to the statutory maximum). No award is available if a supplementary award (given as a result of the Employment Rights (Dispute Resolution) Act 1998) for a failure to permit the worker to appeal internally is granted. A dismissal for exercising this right is automatically unfair, and the usual rules that there is no qualifying period or upper age limit apply. Detriment (previously action short of dismissal) is also prohibited.

10.2 Written reasons

An employee who is dismissed is entitled to receive in writing the reason for the dismissal, provided that he has been continuously employed for one year.

10.2.1 Right

There was no right at common law to be informed of the reason for one's dismissal. By virtue of s 92 of the ERA 1996, an employee who is dismissed by his employers with or without notice or whose fixed term contract is not renewed may request from them a statement in writing concerning the reason for dismissal. It should be noted that an employee who is constructively dismissed is not entitled to written reasons. There was a qualifying period of two years (s 92(3)) but this was reduced to one year by the Unfair Dismissal and Statement of Reasons for Dismissal (Variation of Qualifying Period) Order 1999. The employers must reply within 14 days, if that is reasonably possible, stating the reason(s) for dismissal. There is no need for more than a brief statement. The employers need not add any reference as to why they believed the reason to be an acceptable one to use (*Harvard Securities plc v Younghusband* (1990)). The statement may refer to documents, such as letters already sent to the employee, and it may be sent to a representative of the dismissed employee, not to each employee individually (*Kent CC v Gilham* (1985), a dinner ladies' case).

10.2.2 Unreasonable failure to provide reasons

If the employers unreasonably fail to provide reasons or the reasons given are incomplete or false, the employee may complain to an employment tribunal (s 93). The application must be made within the notice period or within three months of the effective date of termination. The employment tribunal has a discretion to extend the time limit if it was not reasonably practicable to present the claim within those three months. If the claim is successful, the tribunal will award two weeks' pay. There is no statutory maximum. This remedy has been held to be a penal one and, therefore, under English canons of construction, it is subject to strict interpretation. In *Lowson v Percy Main & District Social Club Institute Ltd* (1979), it was held that the employers did not unreasonably refuse the request where they did not communicate with their solicitors but the company gave reasons when the solicitors realised that the request of the employee had not been satisfied. However, in *Brown v Stuart Scott & Co Ltd* (1981), it was reasonable not to provide reasons when the employers believed that they had not sacked the employee. If the written reasons are incomplete or false, the employment tribunal may investigate the true reasons.

10.2.3 Effect

The written statement is admissible as evidence in an employment tribunal (s 92(5)). In an unfair dismissal claim, an employment tribunal will not look favourably on employers who give one reason for the purposes of s 92 and another to defend the claim.

10.2.4 Critique

Controversy over s 92 centred on the increase of the qualifying period to two years (reduced in 1999 to one year). The Conservative Government's view was that the increase from six months brought the law on written reasons in line with that of unfair dismissal. There is, however, no necessary link between s 92 and s 94 (which states that every employee has a right not to be unfairly dismissed), for every employee surely ought to know the reason for dismissal, and that argument indeed applies even to workers employed for fewer than six months. Furthermore, even if he does not qualify for unfair dismissal, surely the employee ought to be provided with a reason for the purposes of other claims.

10.3 Reason for dismissal

Once the employee has proved that he is qualified and has been dismissed, the burden switches to the employers to show that they had a reason to dismiss.

10.3.1 Definition and effect

To defend an unfair dismissal claim, the employers must have a 'reason' for dismissal. The reason is 'the set of facts known to the employer or beliefs held by him which cause him to dismiss the employee' (*Abernethy v Mott, Hay and Anderson* (1974)). The knowledge of the employee is irrelevant. It is sufficient that the employers believe that they dismissed on a certain ground; they need not demonstrate that that ground was fully supported by all the evidence. The employers' motive is relevant in determining what their true reason for dismissing was. Sham reasons are disregarded. The reason given has to be the real reason, not necessarily the one provided by the employers. For example, if a housing association sack an employee on the grounds that his job has been taken over by independent contractors, that reason may be a 'smokescreen' to hide the true reason, which might be that the employee pilfered property or spied on inhabitants of the block of flats. Where there are two or more reasons, the employment tribunal must define which was the ground that motivated the employers to sack (*Carlin v St Cuthbert's Co-operative Association Ltd* (1974)). In *Smith v City of Glasgow DC* (1987), the House of Lords held that, where the employers put forward several reasons and one of them is not accepted, they must prove that that reason was not the principal reason. Accordingly, if they cannot show that the surviving reasons constituted the principal reason, they lose at this stage.

10.3.2 Reliance on reason

The law on reasons provided by employers is a little confusing. Basically, employers cannot argue before the employment tribunal a reason which they did not write in the Notice of Appearance. However, if the different reasons are in reality simply different labels covering the same facts, the employment tribunal may determine that the real reason was pleaded. The usual example is that, until the case is heard, it may not be clear whether the facts give rise to redundancy or to a reorganisation falling within 'some other substantial reason'. *Hotson v Wisbech Conservative Club* (1984) illustrates the law. The employers' Notice of Appearance said that the employee was dismissed for 'inefficiency'. This reason is one of incapacity; in fact, he was sacked for dishonesty, that is, for misconduct. The EAT held that the employers were not entitled to change their reason before the tribunal because the employee was not given a sufficient opportunity to meet the real allegation. It has been suggested that, if the employee knows the real reason why he has been sacked, it does not matter which reason the employers gave. The problem with this suggestion is that the employee may not know which reason to argue against.

10.4 After-discovered reasons

If employers wrongfully dismiss a worker but, between the sacking and trial, discover a reason which would have justified them dismissing summarily had they known of it, they have a defence to the action (*Boston Deep Sea Fishing & Ice Co v Ansell* (1888)). The law is of opposite effect in unfair dismissal. Employers cannot use an after-discovered reason to make fair an unfair dismissal: *W Devis & Sons Ltd v Atkins* (1977), one of the leading cases in UK employment law. The employee was dismissed for refusing to obey a lawful order. After dismissal, the employers uncovered evidence that he had been dishonest. The House of Lords held that the employers could not rely on the subsequently discovered evidence to convert an unfair dismissal into a fair one.

An example of the effect of *Devis v Atkins* is a prosecution of the employee for a crime committed during employment. If the employers reasonably believe that the employee committed the offence (for example, a theft), they may dismiss and, provided that an adequate investigation was carried out, the likelihood is that the dismissal will be fair. The fairness is not affected by a jury's post-dismissal finding that the employee was not guilty. The law that after-discovered reasons cannot be used applies to reasons discovered after dismissal. Reasons discovered between the date when notice of dismissal was given and the date at which the dismissal took effect can be taken into account, according to the Court of Appeal in *Alboni v Ind Coope Retail Ltd* (1998), where *Parkinson v March Consulting Ltd* (1997) was applied. The following points should, however, be noted.

10.4.1 Exceptions

- While a dismissal is not fair, the compensation may be reduced – even to nil – by the presence of a reason subsequently discovered. In *Devis v Atkins* itself, the compensation was reduced to nothing because the employee had suffered no loss.

- Where the employee is dismissed and is then refused the right to appeal through the company's complaints procedure, that refusal is taken into account in assessing the reasonableness of the dismissal, according to the House of Lords in *West Midlands Co-operative Society Ltd v Tipton* (1986). The House of Lords reconciled their decision with that in *Devis v Atkins* by saying that that authority related to after-discovered reasons justifying dismissal of the employee, whereas the refusal of the employers to permit the employee to start the grievance procedure related to the employers' conduct and was, therefore, a reason which had to be taken into account by the tribunal when determining the equity and substantial merits of the case. Their Lordships considered that the appeal process was part of the dismissal; in other words, dismissal did not, for this purpose, take place until the appeals procedure was exhausted. Evidence relating to the dismissal can be used if discovered in the appeal, but such evidence cannot be led if it relates to a different ground for dismissal. Yet the House held that the date of dismissal was the date when the employers fired the employee, not the date when they refused to start the appeal process (or the date when that process would have ended, had it started). It does not matter whether the appeal was a matter of contractual entitlement or not.

- Evidence relating to the particular reason for dismissal (for example, conduct) may be taken into account, even though it is uncovered after dismissal (*Tipton*). However, as we have seen, after-discovered evidence in relation to what would have been a potentially fair reason for dismissal is not admissible.

- Medical evidence which appears during an appeal against dismissal can be used (*National Heart and Chest Hospitals v Nambiar* (1981)). The law may be wider than this proposition.

- It may cover situations where the employee is kept on until the end of internal appeals and fresh information is discovered during the process. Evidence confirming the initial decision to dismiss may be led, but evidence which uncovers a different potentially fair reason to dismiss may not be used (*Monie v Coral Racing Ltd* (1981)).

- Matters occurring between the date of giving notice of dismissal and the date of its expiry can be looked at. Moreover, the fact that an appeal did not take place until after the effective date of termination does not matter for the purposes of determining reasonableness (*Rank Xerox (UK) Ltd v Goodchild* (1979)).

- Evidence may be given of matters which the employers did not know but ought to have known at the time of dismissal 'if it was a proper case to carry out a further investigation and if they had carried out that investigation' (*W Weddel & Co Ltd v Tepper* (1980), interpreting *dicta* of Viscount Dilhorne in *Devis v Atkins*).

10.4.2 Later dismissal

Though the after-discovered reason cannot be used to render fair an unfair dismissal, there is nothing to prevent the employers from using that ground as a potentially fair reason on dismissal for that reason; that is, the employers lose the first claim but win on any second claim by the employee, which could occur if he is reinstated by the employment tribunal.

10.5 Potentially fair reasons: burden of proof

To defend a claim, the employers must prove that they have a substantial reason justifying dismissal. If they cannot, the dismissal is unfair. If they can, the employment tribunal moves to the next stage, consideration of the reasonableness of the dismissal. Accordingly, though s 94 of the ERA 1996 proclaims that every employee has a right not to be unfairly dismissed, that right is defeasible.

10.5.1 Five reasons

The ERA 1996 lays down five reasons which can justify dismissal:

- conduct, for example, theft, fighting at work and absenteeism;

- capability or qualifications of the employee for performing the work he was employed to do, for example, incompetence. Illness by statute falls within this *prima facie* fair reason;

- redundancy;

- contravention of statute, for example, a delivery driver cannot do his job because he has lost his licence;

- some other substantial reason justifying dismissal of the employee from the post he held.

Since the fifth reason is *some other* substantial reason, the first four reasons must also be substantial ones.

10.5.2 Reason and reasonableness

There is a tendency to run together the issues of whether the employers had a *prima facie* valid reason to dismiss and whether they acted reasonably. However, by statute, the issues are separate and there is a different burden of proof: in relation to the former, the onus is on the employers, but there is no formal burden in relation to the latter, the employment tribunal deciding by reference to all the circumstances.

10.5.3 Conduct (s 98(2)(b))

Conduct cases are very much based on their own facts, but common instances include failure to obey lawful orders (such as refusing to sign a letter apologising to a customer); theft from the employers; doing 'foreigners' (that is, using the company's materials on work other than the company's); setting up a rival company; violence at work; gross negligence; and (gross) swearing. A refusal to work non-contractual overtime has been treated as misconduct, in that the order was a reasonable one. In one case, the employee's leaving money in the till while he went to the lavatory was misconduct.

Cases cannot be used as precedents. The same swear words may be acceptable on a building site between a tiler and a foreman but not between the master of ceremonies and the principal speaker at the Chancellor of the Exchequer's speech at the Guildhall in London. Similarly, wearing a badge saying 'Lesbians ignite!' might be acceptable among university lecturers but not among audit clerks (*Boychuk v HJ Symons Holdings Ltd* (1977)).

10.5.4 Capability or qualifications (s 98(2)(a))

By s 98(3), capability includes 'skills, aptitude, health or any other physical or mental quality', while qualifications are defined as 'any degree, diploma or other academic, technical or professional qualification relevant to the position which the employee held'. A finding of incompetence may spring from one incident or from several. In *Taylor v Alidair Ltd* (1978) (while the case was in the EAT), Bristow J gave the following illustration of jobs where a single bad incident could make a dismissal fair:

... the scientist operating the nuclear reactor; the chemist in charge of research into the possible effects of, for example, thalidomide; the driver of the Manchester to London express; and the driver of an articulated lorry full of sulphuric acid.

The Court of Appeal endorsed those illustrations. The requirements, for example, of a driving licence, need not be laid down in a written contract. Note that, in respect of health, employers are under a duty to make reasonable adjustments under the Disability Discrimination Act 1995.

10.5.5 Redundancy (s 98(2)(c))

The term 'redundancy' is defined as per s 139 of the ERA 1996. Refer to Chapter 9.

10.5.6 Contravention of statute (s 98(2)(d))

This reason covers the situation when 'the employee could not continue to work in the position which he held without contravention (either on his part or that of his employer) of a duty or restriction imposed by or under any enactment' (s 98(2)(d)). An illustration is *Sandhu v Department of Education and Science* (1978). The Secretary of State dismissed the employee, a teacher, for being unsuitable. The dismissal was under his statutory powers. The claimant could not continue to work lawfully: he would have done so in contravention of statute. Therefore, the employers' reason fell within s 98(2)(d). In the discussion below of procedural fairness, there is no special section dealing with contravention of a statute. The same principles as apply elsewhere govern procedural fairness in relation to this reason; for example, could the employers who dismissed a driver for not having a licence have put him on to different work?

10.5.7 Some other substantial reason (s 98(1)(b))

By statute and statutory instrument, two forms of dismissal are deemed to be for a substantial reason. By s 106, a temporary employee who is engaged to fill the place of a permanent worker who is pregnant or has been suspended on medical grounds will have been dismissed for a substantial reason if he is warned that his post is only temporary and is then dismissed. By virtue of the Transfer of Undertakings (Protection of Employment) Regulations (TUPE) 1981, the employee is deemed to have been dismissed for a substantial reason where it is done for 'economic, technical or organisational reasons entailing a change in the workforce' when the undertaking is transferred. The TUPE is considered in Chapter 13.

10.5.8 Common examples

Outside s 106 and TUPE, certain situations have been seen as falling within the category of 'some other substantial reason' (SOSR). These situations are noted below, but the categories of SOSR are not closed and, in *RS Components Ltd v Irwin* (1973), the court rejected the argument that this fifth category of potentially fair reasons should be construed *ejusdem generis* with the previous four reasons.

Pressure from customers

In *Dobie v Burns International Security Services (UK) Ltd* (1985), the employers provided security at Speke airport, Liverpool. The employee was a security officer. The airport authority refused to let him continue in employment after various incidents for which he was allegedly to blame. Employers should provide evidence of this reason. It should be noted that threatened or actual industrial action cannot be used by the employee as a potentially fair reason. See chapter for further discussion on this point.

Reorganisations in the interest of efficiency

Redundancy dismissals fall within s 98(2)(c), discussed above. If the statutory definition of redundancy is not satisfied, there may nevertheless be a *prima facie* valid reason within s 98(1)(b). It should be noted that a dismissal in this area, as in others, can be fair, despite the fact that it was the employers who were in breach of contract. The test whether the reason is a substantial one has varied over the years. The reasonableness of the new terms is not the sole criterion, for the tribunal has to look at the decision to dismiss and see whether dismissal was reasonable. In that context, the new terms may be of importance, but they are not conclusive on the issue of reasonableness. In *Robinson v British Island Airways Ltd* (1978), the EAT demanded a 'pressing business reason', but, in *Bowaters Containers Ltd v McCormack* (1980), the change had to be merely 'beneficial', that is, beneficial to the employers. The most authoritative case, *Hollister v National Farmers' Union* (1979), demanded a good, sound business reason. More recently, the EAT has suggested that the true test is a balancing one: were the employers reasonable in their belief that the advantage to them as reorganised outweighs the detriment to the employee (*Chubb Fire Security Ltd v Harper* (1983))? There is no need for the employers to demonstrate that the business reasons for the change were so pressing that, unless the employee accepted the revised terms, the enterprise would collapse (*Catamaran Cruisers Ltd v Williams* (1994)).

Academic comment is that this line of cases gives employers a large amount of power when it comes to the issue of changing contracts without an unfair dismissal claim. Employers cannot simply say that the reorganisation was needful. They must act on reasonable information. For example, in *Orr v Vaughan* (1981), the employers accepted the recommendation of a bookkeeper that a certain beauty salon in which the employee worked should be closed down. The employers did not provide further evidence that it was that salon which was losing money. The EAT held that there had been no reasonable investigation of the needs of the business. The tribunal said that the information had to be reasonably acquired. Presumably, that phrasing indicates that the data need not be specially commissioned or too expensive to track down on a cost/benefit analysis.

One important point about SOSR is demonstrated by the cases. The employers may have a potentially fair reason to dismiss, even though their actions are in breach of contract. Moreover, an employee may be fairly dismissed despite his seeking to rely on the contractual position. In other words, he is bound his contract but the employers do not necessarily dismiss unfairly when they seek to change his contractual terms to his detriment! Rights under contract are subordinated to the employers' right to manage efficiently.

Unilateral changes to contractual terms

A refusal to accept new contract terms may amount to SOSR. In *RS Components Ltd v Irwin* (1973), the employees refused to accept a covenant in restraint of trade. The court held that they were dismissed for SOSR. The firm's profits had been bitten into when some workers left to establish a competing company. The dismissals of the employees who refused were for a substantial reason.

Temporary workers

In situations falling outside s 106, dismissal of those on temporary contracts may be for SOSR. In *North Yorkshire CC v Fay* (1985), the expiry of a fixed term contract of a teacher was a dismissal for SOSR when the employee knew that the job was temporary.

10.5.9 Categories not closed

SOSR covers many other situations. An example is the dismissal of a wife where her husband is dismissed, their being engaged on a 'joint contract', for example, where they are club stewards. In *Saunders v Scottish National Camps Ltd* (1980), the Court of Session, the Scottish equivalent of the Court of Appeal, held that dismissal was for SOSR where the employers dismissed a homosexual employee in the belief that persons of such sexuality were more likely to interfere with children than heterosexuals. In one of the first important unfair dismissal cases, a refusal by colleagues to work with an employee because she insisted on boasting about her sexual dalliance with a 'toyboy' was held to be SOSR (*Treganowan v Robert Knee & Co Ltd* (1975)). The dismissal of an apprentice when the contract of apprenticeship has expired is SOSR. The term also covers the following situations: dismissal for an unacceptable attendance record, even though the absence was caused by sickness; a refusal to live within a certain distance of the workplace contrary to an express term in the contract of employment; failing to reveal a criminal conviction or chronic mental illness;

and driving so badly that the employers lose confidence in the employee. The Court of Appeal in *Dobie* (above) said that a reason is not substantial if it is 'a whimsical or capricious reason which no person of ordinary sense would entertain', a phrase which gives a wide, pro-employer meaning to 'substantial'.

10.5.10 Commentary

The following criticisms of SOSR may be made.

The meaning of 'substantial'

Courts and tribunals have accepted that SOSR is satisfied by something less than a real need of the business. Only if the reason is 'trivial or unworthy', as the Court of Appeal put it in *Kent CC v Gilham* (above, 10.2.1), is it not substantial. This test is an easily satisfied one, arguably not in line with the ordinary meaning of 'substantial' and surely not in line with the intention of Parliament. Most reasons advanced for doing something as serious as sacking an employee are assuredly not trivial or unworthy. Moreover, what is trivial? What is unworthy?

Management description of a reason for dismissal has rarely been questioned. If the employers consider the reason to be important, it is 'substantial' (*Banerjee v City and East London AHA* (1979)). The reason is challengeable only on the basis of no evidence.

Managerial prerogative

In a well known article, Bowers and Clarke (1981) 10 ILJ 34 argued that the elasticity of SOSR meant that tribunals could preserve rule by management by holding the reason for dismissal to be SOSR. Yet one object of the unfair dismissal was to rein in managerial prerogative at the point of dismissal. It might have been helpful if Parliament had provided a definitive list of substantial reasons.

Exploitation

The principal types of SOSR mentioned above are readily exploited by employers. If employers repudiate the contract and the employee accepts, there is a wrongful dismissal. However, there may not be an unfair dismissal. The employers may contend that the change was SOSR; therefore, the issue then turns on the fairness of the dismissal. One might have expected unfair dismissal to be more favourable to employees than wrongful dismissal, but that expectation may be disappointed.

10.6 Reasonableness

If the employers demonstrate a potentially fair reason, the employment tribunal must determine whether the dismissal was fair or unfair, having regard to that reason and taking into account whether, in the circumstances, including the size and administrative resources of their undertaking and equity and the substantial merits of the case (s 98(4)), the employers acted reasonably. The tribunal must address the issue of reasonableness in terms of s 98(4): *Haddon v Van den Bergh Foods Ltd* (1999) (EAT).

This section looks at various matters which an employment tribunal may consider when dealing with the fairness of the dismissal. It opens with a discussion of general matters, then looks at specific matters connected with particular potentially fair reasons. It must be noted throughout that matters relevant to one reason may well be relevant to another: to some extent, the law on procedural fairness is applied to all the reasons. However, for the purposes of exposition, it is convenient to divide up the various aspects of fairness, and some issues, such as warnings, are closely linked to some reasons (for example, a warning not to repeat conduct or a warning to improve standards) but not to others (for example, if employers come under customer pressure to dismiss, a warning to the employee that they are under such pressure is hardly feasible).

It should be noted that the fact that the employers repudiated the contract does not mean that they acted unreasonably. There can be a fair constructive dismissal. The reason for the dismissal and the reasonableness of it are separate issues. There are three points of interpretation in s 98(4). First, 'equity' means not the rules and maxims of equity but 'common fairness', as Donaldson LJ put it in *Union of Construction, Allied Trades and Technicians v Brain* (1981). The second point is that s 98(4) directs the employment tribunal to concentrate on the behaviour of the employers, not on any injustice to the employee. The House of Lords emphasised this interpretation in *Devis v Atkins*, above. Finally, s 98(4) does not give tribunals much guidance on how to determine whether a dismissal was a reasonable one. A large amount of discretion is left in their hands, and the exercise of that discretion is reviewable only if the tribunal has misdirected itself in law or if its decision is perverse. There is a serious possibility of inconsistent determinations. The Court of Appeal noted this point in *Kent CC v Gilham*, above, but held that decisions of tribunals were not binding on other tribunals.

An example of the final point is *Lovie Ltd v Anderson* (1999). Police informed the employers that they were going to charge the employee with indecent assault. Because of the charges, as well as previous complaints by members of the public and his inadequate explanation of what he had done, the employers dismissed him with immediate effect. The EAT said that the situation was sometimes so blatant that the employers had a reasonable belief as to guilt. Sometimes, as, for example, where the first the employers hear of misconduct is when the police inform them of criminal charges, it is reasonable to undertake some kind of investigation. Between the two situations is a spectrum of circumstances. On the facts, the employers should have afforded the employee a further opportunity to give his side of the story.

10.6.1 Reasonable grounds

In relation to the reason for the dismissal, the employers need not know, for example, that the employee was incapable: it suffices that they believed on reasonable grounds that he was so. The employers do not have to prove that they had reasonable grounds because, since 1980, the burden of proof at this juncture has been neutral between the parties. This law is sometimes known as the rule in *British Home Stores Ltd v Burchell* (1980). There is a three stage test:

(a) Did the employers believe the reason?

(b) Did they have 'in mind reasonable grounds upon which to sustain that belief'?

(c) Did they carry out 'as much investigation into the matter as was reasonable in all the circumstances of the case'?

This test, which runs together the reason for and reasonableness of the dismissal, raises the issue of procedural fairness, which is discussed below. Accordingly, merely believing that the employee was incompetent is insufficient. There must be some objective grounds for that belief and the employers must reach the decision to dismiss in a fair manner, for example, after warnings about raising standards. The *Burchell* test originated in a case involving theft but has been widely applied and received the imprimatur of the Court of Appeal in *W Weddel & Co Ltd v Tepper* (above). Stephenson LJ added that the employers should not 'form their belief hastily without making the appropriate enquiries'. Nevertheless, *Burchell* remains a principle rather than a law. It is not *per se* an error of law for an employment tribunal not to go through the test. The statutory words govern: *Haddon v Van den Bergh* (1999). It should also be noted that *Burchell* is irrelevant where the facts are clear, for example, where it is clear that the employee had stolen the item or the misconduct is obviously gross, as when a male employee is found 'entertaining' a young lady in his office late at night. If a jury has convicted the employee of an offence, it is reasonable for the employers to believe that he did commit the crime (*P v Nottinghamshire CC* (1992)). This last case is illustrative of the proposition that the trust and confidence in the employment relationship can be broken by what the employee did out of work hours.

10.6.2 *Iceland Frozen Foods v Jones*

Browne-Wilkinson J (as he then was) stated in *Iceland Frozen Foods v Jones* (1983):

> ... the correct approach for the ... tribunal to adopt in answering the question posed by [s 98(4) of the ERA 1996] is as follows: (1) the starting point should always be the words of [s 98(4)] themselves; (2) in applying the section, an [employment] tribunal must consider the reasonableness of the employer's conduct, not simply whether they [the members of the ... tribunal] consider the dismissal to be fair; (3) in judging the reasonableness of the employer's conduct, an [employment] tribunal must not substitute its decision as to what was the right course to adopt for that of the employer; (4) in many, though not all, cases, there is a band of reasonable responses to the employee's conduct within which one employer might reasonably take one view and another quite reasonably take another; (5) the function of the ... tribunal, as an industrial jury, is to determine whether in the particular circumstances of each case the decision to dismiss the employee fell within the band of reasonable responses which a reasonable employer might have adopted.

The 'reasonable responses test' has become standard. If these employers did dismiss and reasonable employers might have dismissed, the dismissal is fair. If the employers acted within the band of reasonable responses, their conduct was fair. For example, a dismissal for a second, though minor, job-related fraud is within the range of reasonable responses. It is immaterial that, had the members of the employment tribunal been the employers, they would have done more before dismissing. There are many cases to this effect. For instance, dismissing a teacher for gross indecency outside work may not always lead to fair dismissal but it is within the reasonable range of responses which employers may make. Therefore, sacking a teacher on this ground is reasonable. Similarly, a dismissal for phoning up a pornographic line is within the range of reasonable responses. The inquiry into whether the employers have acted unreasonably does not accord with the words of the statute, which instructs the tribunal to consider whether they have acted reasonably. Steven Anderman's comment in *Labour Law*, 3rd edn, 1998, p 158, is incisive:

> In effect, the judiciary has read into the act a self-denying ordinance which attempts to ensure that rather than imposing upon employers an objective notion of fairness in the interpretation of the statutory standard, it is to be limited to reflecting the lowest common denominator of acceptable managerial practice.

10.6.3 Size

Size does matter. Section 98(4) directs the employment tribunal to consider the size and administrative resources of the employers. It may, for instance, be reasonable for one enterprise to dismiss, but, on the same facts, it might be unreasonable for another undertaking to do so. A large firm may be able to wait for an employee to return from illness, whereas a small firm may not be in such a position. It would not be reasonable for the owner of a corner shop to provide several layers of appeals, whereas it might be reasonable for a chain of high street stores to provide an appeal structure. Similarly, firms with fewer than 20 employees need not provide details of disciplinary procedures in the written statement. However, the Advisory, Conciliation and Arbitration Service (ACAS) Code of Practice, considered below, is expressed to apply to all businesses regardless of size and, under s 98(4), small firms must follow a procedure which is fair in the circumstances.

10.6.4 Guidelines

The Court of Appeal has instructed employment tribunals not to act legalistically but to use common sense (for example, *Kent CC v Gilham (No 2)* (1985)). In *Duffy v Yeomans & Partners Ltd* (1994), the Court of Appeal said that:

> ... there is a grave danger that this area of law is becoming ever-sophisticated, and that there is an attempt to lay down matters which are no more than factors which an [employment] tribunal should take into account in reaching its decision whether the employer acted reasonably in the circumstances of the particular case.

As the quote above from *Iceland Frozen Foods* demonstrates, employment tribunals are to act as industrial juries (and, therefore, not as industrial courts). One effect is that the Employment Appeal Tribunal cannot correct employment tribunal decisions which are different on the same facts. Indeed, the Court of Appeal has several times trenchantly rebuked the EAT for laying down guidelines for employment tribunals to follow. In the Court of Appeal in *Bailey v BP Oil (Kent Refinery) Ltd* (1980), Lawton LJ stated: '... it is unwise for this court or the Employment Appeal Tribunal to set out guidelines and wrong to make rules and establish presumptions for [employment] tribunals to follow or take into account.' Only if the EAT or the Court of Appeal can say that there was an error of law or say something to the effect of 'My goodness, that must be wrong' may they intervene (*Neale v Hereford and Worcester CC* (1986), *per* May LJ). The tribunal 'has to look at the question in the round and without regard to a lawyer's technicalities. It has to look at it in an employment and industrial relations context': *UCATT v Brain* (above). (It may surprise members of the Court of Appeal that their brethren have not always refrained from endorsing guidelines.)

Since employment tribunals must not substitute their own ideas for the employers' assessment of reasonableness, the term 'industrial jury' is something of a misnomer. Despite the Court of Appeal's criticism of guidelines and legalism, it is suggested that guidelines promote consistency of decision making and that legalism is unavoidable when tribunals are seeking to apply the law to control managements' freedom to do as they will.

10.6.5 Importance of procedure

Procedural fairness is a major concern of tribunals when considering whether a dismissal was fair. The question being asked is whether employers reached the decision to sack in a fair way. Did they, for example, issue a warning that they would dismiss the employee for the next 'offence'? Did they consult with the employee when considering whether to dismiss on medical grounds? There are hundreds of cases in the law reports and excerpted in journals such as *IDS Brief* and *Employment Trends*, as well as thousands of unpublished transcripts from employment tribunals and the EAT. There follows an outline of the topic, with emphasis on only the more significant cases and on the relevant ACAS Code of Practice and its accompanying handbook. Indeed, this style of approach has received the blessing of the EAT. In *Hillman v London General Transport Services Ltd* (1999), it said that employers should take into account only the most obvious propositions of employment law and any other relevant law brought to their attention by the employee. In the words of Lord Donaldson MR in *Piggott Bros & Co Ltd v Jackson* (1992):

> [In deciding whether the employer acted reasonably or unreasonably in treating the employee's conduct, an employment tribunal] will have to consider what alternative courses of action were open to the employer – should he, for example, not have dismissed at all or should he have taken further steps to persuade the employee to desist from such conduct and only have dismissed if that proved ineffective?

10.6.6 Renewed emphasis

A series of decisions downgraded the importance of procedural fairness. Where a fair procedure had not been followed, tribunals were encouraged to ask whether it would have made any difference to the question of dismissal. Employers could establish that a dismissal was fair, despite an unfair procedure, by showing that they would probably still have dismissed if a fair procedure had been followed. This approach was, in effect, overturned by the House of Lords in *Polkey v AE Dayton Services Ltd* (1988). It is now irrelevant whether or not the defect in procedure made a difference. The test is: was it reasonable for the employers, in the light of their knowledge at the time of dismissal, to adopt the procedure they did? (But see *Duffy*, below, 10.6.7.) The result is that tribunals once again place great emphasis on whether a fair procedure was followed before dismissal. So, for example, these procedural matters could make a dismissal unfair:

- conduct – a dismissal for misconduct without giving the employee an opportunity to answer the allegations or without revealing the identity of the person who made them;

- capability – a dismissal for poor performance without sufficient warnings and an opportunity to improve;

- redundancy – a dismissal for redundancy without warning or consultation or without consideration of alternative jobs.

The defect in procedure must be quite a serious one. For example, it has been held that there is no such defect where the employers do not give the employee the gist of the 'charges' against him when it is obvious to him what they were (*Fuller v Lloyds Bank plc* (1991)).

10.6.7 Exception

The House of Lords qualified the general rule by stating that, if it was clear to the employers at the time of dismissal that following the proper procedure would have been 'utterly useless', failure to follow that procedure may be justified. (*Polkey* itself might have been such a case.) The Court of Appeal held in *Duffy v Yeomans & Partners Ltd* (1994) that employers need not actually make a decision not to consult. It is sufficient that a reasonable employer might not have consulted. This case looks like a return to the pre-*Polkey* law. *Polkey* reasserted the need for the employers actually to know the circumstances which led to the dismissal. *Duffy* is a case where consultation would have made no difference to the outcome; consultation would have served no purpose. It is also inconsistent with the decision of the Scottish EAT in *Robertson v Magnet Ltd (Retail Division)* (1993). Despite this qualification, the better view is that an employer should always follow a fair procedure in *every* case of dismissal. One illustrative case is *Charles Robertson (Developments) Ltd v White* (1995), where the employers' argument was that it would have been utterly useless to adopt a fair procedure because the employee had been caught stealing by a video camera. Holland J said:

> ... each applicant was a well established employee and each theft, while inexcusable as such, was not of the most heinous nature ... in either case, a disciplinary interview, so far from being useless, had a potential value as an aid to a balanced decision as to dismissal, and one that could be seen to be fair.

10.6.8 Effect on remedy

The 'any difference' test will still be relevant to the question of remedies. Take, for example, a misconduct case. If it is shown that, though the employer had not investigated the matter adequately, the employee was nevertheless 'guilty', compensation may be reduced.

10.6.9 Code and handbook

The ACAS Code No 1 on Disciplinary Practice and Procedures (issued first in 1977 and revised in 1998) is supplemented by an ACAS advisory handbook, *Discipline at Work* (1987). The advisory handbook complements the ACAS Code No 1 by giving more practical advice. It does not impose any binding legal obligations. It is an attempt to show what is good industrial relations practice. It is not a Code of Practice and the guidelines must not be applied rigidly. The handbook was to have been an ACAS Code, but the then Secretary of State for Employment rejected it as being too legalistic and too difficult for small employers to use.

ACAS Code No 1 operates in a different fashion. An employment tribunal (but not a court) is empowered to take the Code's provisions into account when determining the fairness of a dismissal. Section 207(2) of the Trade Union and Labour Relations (Consolidation) Act 1992 stated that the Code 'shall be taken into account', not that it may be taken into account. However, non-compliance with the provisions of the Code will not automatically render a dismissal unfair. Compliance or non-compliance is one of the factors for consideration. The aim of a set of procedures is not primarily to impose sanctions but rather to ensure that employees are treated fairly and consistently. The importance of following proper procedures can become crucial in relation to a dismissal, since the way in which the dismissal has been handled can be challenged before an employment tribunal. Fairness in handling a dismissal will be judged by reference to whether the employer acted reasonably in all the circumstances. Failure to follow a proper procedure can make what is otherwise a dismissal for good cause an unfair dismissal. A checklist for handling a disciplinary matter is set out in the advisory handbook.

10.6.10 Rules

Rules are necessary to advise employees of the kind of acts and behaviour which constitutes a breach of discipline. In the words of the advisory handbook:

> They set standards of conduct at work and make clear to employees what is expected of them.

In the words of the ACAS Code, para 7:

> Rules should be readily available and management should make every effort to ensure that employees know and understand them.

This paragraph reflects *Meyer Dunmore International Ltd v Rogers* (1978). One way of ensuring that employees know of the rules is to have an induction course.

Each organisation will have varied requirements. Neither the advisory handbook nor the ACAS Code contains a universal set of rules. It is doubtful whether a complete set of rules appropriate to all situations could be devised. Moreover, some rules are so obvious that they do not need stating. For example, a rule to say that fraudulently claiming expenses constitutes misconduct is hardly necessary. An example from the cases is *Ulsterbus Ltd v Henderson* (1989): a bus conductor did not have to be instructed by a rule that not issuing tickets was a sackable offence. However, some factors will be common to all organisations.

10.6.11 Contents

The advisory handbook gives the following examples which might be appropriate in a small company.

Timekeeping

Are employees required to 'clock in'? Clocking-in offences have led to fair dismissals where the rule was clear (for example, *Dalton v Burton's Gold Medal Biscuits Ltd* (1974)). What rules apply to lateness?

Absence

Who authorises absence? Who approves holidays? Whom should employees notify when they are absent from work? When should notification of absence take place? When is a medical self-certificate sufficient? When will a doctor's certificate be necessary?

Health and safety

Are there special requirements regarding personal appearance or cleanliness, for example, length of hair, jewellery or protective clothing? Are there special hazards? Are there non-smoking areas? Is alcohol prohibited?

Use of company facilities

Are private telephone calls permitted? Are employees allowed to be on company premises outside working hours? Is company equipment generally available for personal use?

Discrimination

Is it clear that racial and sexual abuse or harassment will be treated as disciplinary offences? Is there a rule about clothing or uniform which is disproportionately disadvantageous to a racial group and which cannot be justified on non-racial grounds? Is there a rule requiring higher language standards than are needed for safe and effective performance of the job? Is there a requirement about mobility of employment which cannot be justified on operational grounds and is disadvantageous to one sex?

Gross misconduct

Are the kind of offences that are regarded as gross misconduct and which could lead to dismissal without notice clearly specified? In *Lock v Cardiff Railway Co Ltd* (1998), the EAT stated that 'it seems to us essential that employees should be given due warning of which types of misconduct will, on a first breach, lead to dismissal'.

The advisory handbook gives these examples of gross misconduct: theft; fraud; deliberate falsification of records; fighting; assault on another person; deliberate damage to company property; serious incapability through alcohol or being under the influence of illegal drugs; serious negligence which causes unacceptable loss, damage or injury; and serious acts of insubordination.

Rules should be clearly stated and the penalties for breach should be expressed in the rules.

10.6.12 Application

Employment tribunals may question the application of the rules to particular facts. For example, the EAT was satisfied in *Roberts v British Railways Board* (1997) that the employers did not have a blanket policy of sacking employees who had tested positive for alcohol or drugs but had investigated the employee's claim that he had passively inhaled cannabis which was being smoked by his brother. On the other hand, in *Ladbroke Racing Ltd v Arnott* (1983), the employers implemented a rule that employees were not permitted to place bets, on pain of dismissal. Bets had certainly been placed but the breaches of the rule were minor and the employees did not gain any monetary advantages from their breaches. The Court of Session held that the employers had acted unreasonably. This latter case demonstrates that not even clear rules prevent the employment tribunal from investigating the fairness of the dismissal. Similarly, in *Dairy Product Packers Ltd v Beverstock* (1981), the EAT held that, if employers wished to treat the drinking of alcohol off the premises during working hours as more serious than doing so on the premises, the rule to that effect must be pellucid.

10.6.13 Inconsistency

Furthermore, inconsistency of treatment may give rise to an unfair dismissal. If there is a rule that both employees will be dismissed if one clocks the other in, but the rule has not been enforced in the past, dismissal is probably unfair should the firm decide on one occasion to apply the rule. Warnings that the rule is going to be enforced for the future should be used. Similarly, dismissing employees for 'lewd behaviour' at a Christmas party is unfair if, previously, other employees performing similar acts had not been dismissed. Different outcomes may, however, be justified by the circumstances: see, for example, *Securicor Ltd v Smith* (1989), which was applied in *London Borough of Harrow v Cunningham* (1996) to distinguish a person who was on a final warning and one who was not. For instance, where two employees are seen fighting at work, it may be reasonable to dismiss one but retain the other if the former has a worse disciplinary record than the latter. In *Paul v East Surrey HA* (1995), Beldam LJ said:

An employer is entitled to take into account not only the nature of the contract and the surrounding facts but also any mitigating circumstances affecting the employee concerned.

It is fair to dismiss all employees who might have stolen an item, provided that the employers cannot identify the true perpetrator and have undertaken an investigation (see *Monie v Coral Racing Ltd* (1981) and *Parr v Whitbread & Co plc* (1990)). If, however, the employers believe that one among the potential thieves did not take the property, they may keep him while sacking the others (*Frames Snooker Centre v Boyce* (1992)). In this case, a father did not sack his daughter, but he did dismiss two other employees. The EAT held that, if employers have 'solid and sensible grounds' for differentiating among the employees, they can do so without the others succeeding in their claim for unfair dismissal.

10.6.14 Interpretation

Disciplinary rules can act as warnings. Therefore, in relation to fair procedure (discussed below), rules can replace warnings. The rule, however, must still cover what occurred and must be applied. 'Liable to instant dismissal' does not mean 'will be dismissed' (*Meridian Ltd v Gomersall* (1977)).

10.6.15 Procedures

The ACAS Code of Practice's guidance on the form of disciplinary procedures is well established. Procedures should:

* be in writing;

* specify to whom they apply;

* provide for matters to be dealt with quickly;

* indicate the disciplinary actions which may be taken;

* specify the levels of management which have the authority to take the various forms of disciplinary actions and ensure that immediate supervisors do not normally have the power to dismiss without reference to senior management;

* provide for individuals to be informed of specific complaints against them and to be given an opportunity to state their case directly to those considering disciplinary action before decisions are reached;

* give individuals the right to be accompanied, either by a trade union official where a trade union is recognised or by a fellow employee of their choice;

* ensure that any investigatory period of suspension is with pay (unless the contract of employment clearly provides otherwise) and specify how pay is to be calculated during such a period;

- ensure that, except for gross misconduct, no employees are dismissed for a first breach of discipline;

- ensure that disciplinary action is not taken until the case has been carefully investigated (any decision has to be taken on a basis of adequate facts, which in turn demands adequate investigation);

- ensure that individuals are given a written explanation for any penalty imposed;

- provide a right of appeal and specify the procedure to be followed and the action that may be taken by those hearing the appeal.

A case illustrating these points is *Charles Robertson (Developments) Ltd v White* (1995). Two employees were dismissed for theft of a small quantity of sweets from a stockroom. The store manager dismissed them without hearing their case and without advising them of their 'rights' under the ACAS Code, including the right to be accompanied by a representative of their choice. In many circumstances, consultation before dismissal is important. It gives the employee the opportunity to suggest alternative work or retraining, to say that he will work for less money, and so on. It also gives employers the chance to put forward and respond to ideas. Consultation is also a matter both of good etiquette and good industrial relations practice.

10.6.16 Enforcement

In respect of implementing disciplinary action, the advisory handbook suggests:

> Before deciding whether a disciplinary penalty is appropriate, consider the employee's disciplinary and general record, whether the disciplinary procedure points to the likely penalty, action taken in previous cases, any explanations and circumstances to be considered and whether the penalty is reasonable.

The advisory handbook suggests that the following procedure be adopted (and provides specimen disciplinary procedures suitable for adoption either by any organisation or by small firms in Appendix 3):

- 'In the case of minor offences, the individual should be given a formal oral warning and told that a note that it was given will be kept for reference purposes.'

- 'In the case of more serious offences or where there is an accumulation of minor offences, the individual should be given a formal written warning.'

- 'If the employee has received a previous warning, further misconduct may warrant a final written warning or consideration of a disciplinary penalty short of dismissal' (including disciplinary transfer, disciplinary suspension without pay, demotion, loss of seniority, or loss of increment, provided these penalties are allowed for by an express or implied term of the contract of employment).'

• There may be occasions when misconduct is considered not to be so serious as to justify dismissal but serious enough to warrant only one written warning which will be both the first and final.

• A final written warning should contain a statement that any further misconduct will lead to dismissal. If all previous stages have been observed, the final step will be dismissal.

10.6.17 Stages

It will be seen that a three stage procedure is recommended before dismissal, namely: formal oral warning; first written warning; and final written warning. This does not, however, mean that three warnings must always be given before any dismissal is considered. There may be occasions when, depending on the seriousness of the misconduct involved, it will be appropriate to enter the procedure at stage two (written warning) or stage three (final written warning). There may also be occasions when dismissal without notice is applicable. Moreover, the fact that an employee is on a final warning does not mean that an employer is justified in dismissing him immediately. The circumstances must still be considered. It is unlikely that dismissal for one act of misconduct will be fair. For example, in *Lock v Cardiff Railway Co Ltd* (1998), a train guard put off a teenager who did not have a valid ticket and could not pay the excess fare. The EAT held that the employment tribunal should have taken into account the Code of Practice (the ACAS Code), para 10(h), which states that, 'except for gross misconduct, no employees are [to be] dismissed for a first breach of discipline'.

10.6.18 Misconduct defined

In order to follow such a procedure, it is necessary for a company to indicate which types of misconduct will attract the various penalties. The types of misconduct can be grouped in order to indicate the likely disciplinary sanctions that will be imposed. Examples are set out below. (There is no guidance on this in the advisory handbook.)

Written warning

• lateness or bad timekeeping;
• unauthorised absence from place of work;
• less serious cases of negligence;
• minor incidents of insubordination or disorderly conduct;
• poor performance of job duties;
• time wasting;

- minor breaches of safety regulations;
- refusal or failure to carry out the legitimate instructions of a manager.

Final written warning

- repetition of an offence or the commission of a different offence after a first written warning has been given;
- disciplinary offences of the type detailed above and of a sufficiently serious nature to warrant a more serious sanction than a first written warning.

Dismissal

- prolonged unauthorised absence after the issue of a final warning;
- repetition of offences of a less serious nature when taken individually after a final warning and/or suspension.

Dismissal without notice for gross misconduct

- theft of property from the company or other employees while on company premises;
- falsification of company documents, whether or not for personal gain;
- making a false statement in regard to matters affecting employment;
- assault or battery on site against any person;
- unauthorised use of company vehicles;
- habitual or gross intoxication on company premises;
- flagrant violation of safety rules;
- deliberate damage to company property or the property of other employees;
- serious negligence.

Dismissal for gross misconduct should only take place after the normal investigation to establish all the facts. The employee should be told of the complaint and be given an opportunity to state his case and be represented. Witness statements need not be given to the employee if it is fair and reasonable not to do so: *Hussain v Elonex plc* (1999) (CA).

10.6.19 Counting warnings

One problem which has arisen is whether employers are entitled to move from oral to written warning, etc, where the warnings relate to different matters. There may be a warning for arriving slightly drunk and another for theft of paper clips. While the law is uncertain, it is thought that employers are entitled to add together such warnings; otherwise, they do not get a rounded view of the employee's behaviour and competence. The EAT held in *Auguste Noel Ltd v*

Curtis (1990) that employers could add together warnings on different subjects. A number of different incidents of bad behaviour may add up to serious misconduct. Another issue is that, as a matter of both good industrial relations practice and (probably) law, a warning should be wiped off the record after, say, six or 12 months.

10.6.20 Appeals

With effect from 1 January 1999, the Employment Rights (Dispute Resolution) Act 1998 inserted s 127A into the ERA 1996. By this section, an employment tribunal may reduce the compensatory award by up to two weeks' pay if the employee fails to go through an internal appeals procedure.

The ACAS Code makes it clear that provision should always be made in a disciplinary procedure for an appeal (ACAS Code, para 10(k)). Employers should:

- provide for appeals to be dealt with speedily;

- wherever possible, use a procedure which is separate from the general grievance procedure;

- wherever possible, provide for the appeal to be heard by an authority higher than that taking the disciplinary action;

- pay particular attention to any new evidence introduced at the hearing and allow the employee to comment on it;

- examine all the issues fully and not be afraid to overturn a wrong decision;

- realise that the provision of an appeal is an indispensable part of any disciplinary procedure. It is as important as the need to have a full investigation of the facts and to give the employee a chance to put his side of the case forward.

The Court of Appeal in *Sartor v P & O European Ferries (Felixstowe) Ltd* (1992), approving earlier EAT cases, stated that an appeal can retrospectively cure a bad first hearing, provided that it took the form of a full rehearing and that, if possible (as it will be in a medium or large firm), representatives of the management should not be the same at hearing and on appeal. On the facts, although there were defects in the procedure, these did not render the dismissal unfair. This doctrine applies to redundancy dismissals (*Lloyd v Taylor Woodrow Construction* (1999)). The employers' failure to comply with the contractual appeals procedure does not make the process void and is not such a fundamental defect that the dismissal by that body is unfair (*Westminster CC v Cabaj* (1996): the court held that the issue was whether the defect at the appeal stage rendered it impossible for the employee to obtain a fair hearing). Rather surprisingly, the EAT held in *Post Office v Marney* (1990) that, if the initial hearing was fairly held, it did not matter that the appeal was unfair. It is suggested that this decision is wrong. Procedural fairness in general demands the provision and use of an internal appeals structure. A misuse of that system should be considered unfair.

10.6.21 Notification

In respect of notifying employees of disciplinary rules and procedures, employers are required to give employees a written statement of the main terms of employment together with a note of the disciplinary rules and procedure. See Chapter 4. On the issue of a written statement and disciplinary rules, an employee should be required to give a receipt.

10.6.22 Absence

In its advisory handbook, ACAS gives guidance on the procedure for handling absences. A distinction is made between absences on grounds of ill health (see below) and absence for reasons which may call for disciplinary actions. The following points are made by ACAS:

- Accurate record keeping is vital. The records should show:
  - lateness and any reasons therefore;
  - the duration of any absence and any reasons therefore.

  In this way, management can pick up and deal with any problems at an early stage.

- Absences should be investigated promptly and the employee asked to give an explanation. In the absence of a good reason for absence, the matter should be dealt with under the disciplinary procedure.

- The employee should be told what improvement in attendance is expected and warned of the likely consequences if this does not happen.

- If there is no improvement, the employee's age, length of service, performance, the likelihood of a change in attendance, the availability of suitable alternative work and the effect of past and future absences on the business should all be taken into account in deciding appropriate action.

The advisory handbook gives separate guidance covering employees who fail to return from extended leave on the agreed date.

10.6.23 Incompetence

Dismissals on the basis of inadequate performance or lack of skill or competence should be handled differently from cases of misconduct. Part of the fault may be the employers', for example, lack of adequate training or adequate supervision or lack of care in the recruitment and selection process.

Normally, one act of shoddy performance will not be sufficient to justify dismissal, but may be so on the facts (*Alidair Ltd v Taylor* (1978): the bumpy landing of an aeroplane led to the employers losing confidence in the pilot).

The advisory handbook makes the following points.

- The standard of work required should be explained and employees left in no doubt about what is expected of them. Accurate job descriptions obviate disputes. (However, dismissal may be fair when a person high in the employers' hierarchy is sacked when he ought to have known of the standard.)

- The consequences of any failure to meet the required standards should be explained.

- Proper training and supervision are essential to the achievement of satisfactory performance. Appraisal systems may be useful as evidence.

- An employee should not normally be dismissed because of poor performance unless warnings and a chance to improve have been given. Consideration should be given to finding suitable alternative work (for example, *Vokes Ltd v Bear* (1974)), but there is no requirement to create an alternative job (*MANWEB v Taylor* (1975), a case of general application). A warning in a case involving substandard work serves a different purpose from one given for misconduct. It can be used to show the employee how to improve on his performance.

10.6.24 Illness

How would you deal with the following? An employee was absent over two years with dizzy spells, anxiety, nerves, bronchitis, virus infection, cystitis, althruigia of the left knee, dyspepsia and flatulence. In the four quarters of one year, she was absent for 20%, 27%, 22%, and 37% of her time. Most, if not all, of the illnesses were covered by a doctor's note. She had received three warnings, and a final warning. Employers had followed their own procedure correctly. The GP whom the company employed thought that none of the sicknesses could be verified at the present time and that the employee did not seem to be suffering from any long term illness, but, of course, he could not query the employee's own doctor's certificates.

The case is *International Sports Co Ltd v Thomson* (1980). An employment tribunal held the dismissal to be unfair, but the EAT allowed the employers' appeal. They said that the employee had been fairly dismissed for absenteeism, a 'conduct' reason. Employers do not need to determine the *bona fides* of doctors' notes: no reasonable employer would have done that. There is no need for a formal medical examination where employee's complaints are intermittent and unconnected:

> What is required ... is, firstly, that there should be a fair review by the employer of the attendance record and the reasons for it; and, secondly, appropriate warnings, after the employee has been given an opportunity to make representations.

A fully detailed medical investigation is not needed.

10.6.25 Relevance

In unfair dismissal cases, the issue of sickness arises in two situations:

- because of sickness, the contract of employment cannot be performed. In law, this failure is called 'frustration'. Where there is frustration, employment has not been terminated by dismissal. Since there is no dismissal, there can be no unfair dismissal (see Chapter 7);

- sickness may be a potentially fair reason for dismissal, in the same way that redundancy and misconduct are. There has been a dismissal, and the employers are arguing that the dismissal was for sickness. If they show that reason, it is for the employment tribunal to decide whether, in all the circumstances of the case, the employers acted fairly in dismissing the employee.

10.6.26 Consultation

The basic rule is to carry out such investigation as is reasonable. If the employers cannot be expected to wait any longer before dismissing, the dismissal will normally be fair (*Spencer v Paragon Wallpapers Ltd* (1977)). To decide this question, employers should look at:

- the nature of the illness;

- the potential length of absence;

- the employee's personal circumstances;

- the urgency of filling the employee's post;

- the size and nature of the employers' firm.

Consultation will normally be a prerequisite (*East Lindsey DC v Daubney* (1977)). There is a need for 'sensitive consultation and discussion' with the employee. Consultation may well bring new facts to light. Consultation should be undertaken sensitively. When the employee believes, contrary to the true position, that he is getting better, *Eclipse Blinds Ltd v Wright* (1992) states that employers are entitled not to consult. Employers should keep in touch with the employee so that they know the true position before dismissal. There is no duty on the employee to inform the employers of any progress (*Mitchell v Arkwood Plastics (Engineering) Ltd* (1993)). The employers need not discover the true diagnosis of the employee's illness. It is sufficient that they know the medical position of persons in general with that ailment. Relying on the company doctor's report will usually not be sufficient, and the employers have no implied right to order an employee to submit to a medical examination by the company's doctor or by an independent practitioner. A doctor's note is not conclusive.

In *Hutchinson v Enfield Rolling Mills Ltd* (1981), the employee was certified sick for one day but he was seen in Brighton at a union demonstration. It was held that he had been fairly dismissed. It is not by itself fair to sack where sick pay has run out, and it may be fair to dismiss even though sick pay has not run out (*Hardwick v Leeds AHA* (1975)). Requests for reports from the employee's doctor are regulated by the Access to Medical Reports Act 1988. This statute does not apply to reports from the company's own doctor. The Act permits employees to gain access to their own records and to comment on them. If, because of illness, an employee's behaviour is dangerous to others, employers may dismiss fairly even though no one has (yet) been injured.

10.6.27 Other procedures

Polkey emphasises the need for correct procedures, for example, to check the precise details of the illness and prognosis; to give the employee the chance to state his case; to keep in touch with the employee; and to ask the employee's GP when the employee may return to work. If there is any doubt about the reason for the employee's absence, the employers should ask the employee to see the company doctor (if the employee refuses, the firm should warn him of the possibility of dismissal) and allow him to be accompanied by a trade union representative, if there is one, or by a friend. However, a failure to follow a contractual disciplinary procedure does not automatically mean that the dismissal was unfair. It should be noted that it is immaterial that the employers caused the employee's illness. The tribunal must look at the fairness of the dismissal, not at the responsibility for the illness which led to the dismissal. In *London Fire & Civil Defence Authority v Betty* (1994), the employers accused the employee of racial discrimination and harassment of his colleagues. There were no grounds for these allegations. He fell ill and had a nervous breakdown. The EAT told the employment tribunal to consider procedural fairness and not investigate responsibility for the breakdown.

10.6.28 Futility

Consultation is not always necessary, for example, there may be a risk to health of fellow employees; good eyesight in some jobs may be a necessity; there may be a need to cope with the Christmas rush or for the employee constantly to attend machines; or the employee may be medically unfit for, for example, work on North Sea rigs. The test of futility is objective.

10.6.29 Redeployment

A reasonable employer may, instead of dismissing, put an employee on to lighter work or put him into a 'holding group'.

10.6.30 Considerations

The ACAS advisory handbook states that:

> If there is no improvement, the employee's age, length of service, performance, the likelihood of a change in attendance, the availability of suitable alternative work and the effect of past and future absences on the business should all be taken into account in deciding appropriate action.

On self-certification, the handbook suggests that:

> Where there is no medical advice to support frequent self-certified absences, the employee should be asked to consult a doctor to establish whether medical treatment is necessary and whether the underlying reason for absence is work-related.

10.6.31 Redundancy

Polkey (1988) is itself a case where the employers selected the employee on the grounds of redundancy. The employee was employed by employers as one of four van drivers. The employers were losing money. They decided to reduce overheads by replacing the drivers with van salesmen and they had to act quickly. They sacked three of the drivers, including the employee, because they did not think they would be suitable salespeople. The employee was told he was being made redundant, handed a letter to that effect, and sent home. He complained that he had been unfairly dismissed. He supported his argument by saying that he ought to have been consulted or warned. There had also been no consultation with his union. The tribunals and the Court of Appeal ruled that, since the employers would have sacked him even if there had been consultation, the employee was fairly dismissed. However, the employee successfully appealed to the House of Lords. There, it was held that the rule which the courts had been following was incorrect. That rule was called the 'no difference' rule or the *British Labour Pump* rule. It was called the 'no difference' rule because it was said that a failure to follow the correct procedure did not make a dismissal unfair if it would have made no difference had the right procedure been adopted. It was called the *British Labour Pump* rule because the main case in which the 'no difference' rule was stated was *British Labour Pump Ltd v Byrne* (1979). In *Polkey* (1988), the House of Lords overruled the *British Labour Pump* rule.

10.6.32 *Polkey*

In *Polkey* (1988), the House of Lords restated the law. The task facing the employment tribunal is to decide whether employers acted reasonably in dismissing, not whether justice was done. *Per* Lord Mackay:

> The subject matter for the tribunal's consideration is the employer's action in treating the reason as a sufficient reason for dismissing the employee. It is that action and that action only that the tribunal is required to characterise as reasonable or unreasonable. That leaves no scope for the tribunal considering whether, if the employer had acted differently, he might have dismissed the employee.

Therefore, one has to look at the conduct of employers, not at whether employee has suffered any injustice. The following should be taken into account in deciding whether the employers acted reasonably:

- Was the correct procedure followed?

- The fact that employers would have dismissed anyway is irrelevant. One must look at what employers did, not what they might have done.

- What happens if employers would have dismissed had they gone through the correct procedure? As we have seen, they will normally lose the issue of liability for unfair dismissal. Nevertheless, compensation may be reduced if following the correct procedure would have made no difference. (It should be emphasised that compensation for a dismissal which is unfair because of substantive (and not procedural) defects is not affected by this rule.) The selection of criteria for making individuals redundant is an example of a substantive defect. Of the three remedies for unfair dismissal, reinstatement, re-engagement and compensation, the most likely award for an unfair redundancy is compensation. This is divided into two parts. The compensatory award may be reduced on the grounds that there has been no loss or that it is 'just and equitable' to award a lesser sum. The second part is the basic award, which is calculated according to the employee's age, weekly earnings and the time he has worked for his employers. It cannot be reduced except for contributory fault, for example, misconduct, or for the sum which the employers have expended as a redundancy payment. Even if the tribunal awards no compensatory award, employers should be aware that they will face paying the basic award. One cannot predict what percentage reduction a tribunal might make. For example, it could be 20% or it could be 100%.

- 'In judging whether what the employer did was reasonable, it is right to consider what a reasonable employer would have had in mind at the time he decided to dismiss as the consequence of not consulting or not warning' (*per* Lord Mackay). For instance, one must judge the dismissal against what a reasonable employer would have done. If a reasonable employer would have consulted and this employer did not, the outcome will normally be unfair dismissal.

'Normally' is used because there are exceptional situations where employers do act reasonably in dismissing without consultation. Various phrases have been used: 'complete waste of time'; no possible 'explanation or mitigation'; where the offence is 'heinous'. Lord Mackay in *Polkey* said:

> It is quite a different matter if the tribunal is able to conclude that the employer himself, at the time of dismissal, acted reasonably in taking the view that, in the exceptional circumstances of the particular case, the procedural steps normally appropriate would have been futile, could not have altered the decision to dismiss and therefore could be dispensed with.

The illustration often given of a futile procedure is an investigation after the employer saw the employee stab a fellow worker. Besides futile procedures being rare – and it might not be futile to investigate in the stabbing example: there may be provocation – futile procedures must be especially rare in redundancy cases because, as the Court of Appeal said in *Polkey*:

> ... the system adopted for the selection of the individual for redundancy may be at the very centre of the inquiry when the tribunal comes to determine whether the employee has acted reasonably or unreasonably in treating redundancy as a sufficient reason for dismissing the employee concerned.

Therefore, to defend an unfair dismissal claim successfully, employers must go through the correct procedures. Only exceptionally will they win if they do not do so, and this principle applies even though consultation would have made no difference to the result. With the *Polkey* approach, employers lose more unfair dismissal cases than before unless they put their house in order. It is obviously worthwhile putting one's house in order to avoid, for example, bad publicity and the stigma of being branded a bad employer.

10.6.33 Summary

To sum up, a dismissal on the grounds of redundancy may well be unfair if the rules of procedure have been broken. *Polkey* emphasises the need for a fair procedure. While it is true to say that a failure to adopt fair procedures will not *per se* lead to a finding of unfair dismissal, the chances are that it will. And the fact that employers win on one occasion because of special circumstances does not mean that they will win on the next occasion. Certainly, a tribunal will be loath to hold a dismissal unfair if the substantial merits are with the employers and it will not require a perfect procedure, but it is no use trying to guess how a tribunal might react to an unfair procedure. It is worthwhile, for legal purposes, getting things right in the first place. Surely, it is also worthwhile getting things right for the sake of industrial relations, good employee-management relations and reduced incidence of strikes.

10.6.34 Other options

As Lord Mackay said in *Polkey*:

> ... in the case of redundancy, the employer will normally not act reasonably unless he warns and consults any employees affected or their representatives, adopts a fair basis on which to select for redundancy and takes such steps as may be reasonable to avoid or minimise redundancy by redeployment within his own organisation.

Possible options include:

- a call for volunteers;

- the transfer of the employee to another job, even if the new post represents a demotion (give employee a trial period in it);

- short-time working (could still be redundancy);

- a call for early retirement;

- possibly look for a job in the rest of the group.

10.6.35 Procedure

In unfair redundancy cases, the stress upon fair procedure takes two forms:

- reliance on the ACAS Code; and

- stricter application of the steps laid down in *Williams v Compair Maxam Ltd* (1982) to see whether a fair procedure has been used.

10.6.36 Code of Practice

The Code of Practice is like the Highway Code. It is not by itself law but may be taken into account by the employment tribunal. Failure to comply with the Code does not necessarily mean that the dismissal was unfair, but it is strong evidence that it was so. A failure to follow the Code may lead to the conclusion that a dismissal was unfair and which, had the Code been followed, would have been fair. The Code does not have much to say specifically about redundancy, but the following principles may be drawn from it:

- the rules should be written down. This ensures that employees know what they must do, and it reduces the chances of misunderstanding;

- the rules should be simple;

- the rules should not discriminate on the grounds of race, sex or marital status;

- the rules should be generally available, for example, in the company handbook, on the noticeboard or given to employees as part of the written statement when they join the firm;

- special care should be devoted to those whose mother tongue is not English;

- if a rule is no longer applied or has not been consistently applied, any change in practice should be told to the employees.

There is Northern Irish authority for the proposition that no system of appeals need be provided in redundancy cases because there is no mention of appeals in this context in the ACAS Code. It is suggested that this ruling misrepresents the nature of the Code, which is not the maximum the employers are obliged to do. If an aspect of procedural fairness is not stated, that does not mean that it is never a consideration for the tribunal.

If the Code is followed, employers will usually win the case, but must still have a sufficient reason to dismiss and their decision to dismiss must be within the band of reasonable responses to the situation.

10.6.37 *Williams v Compair Maxam*

The much criticised case of *Williams v Compair Maxam Ltd* (1982) lays down the sort of procedure that firms ought to follow if they are to defend successfully a claim of unfair dismissal on the ground of redundancy:

- there should be no unfair selection procedure; for example, retention of those who would, in the opinion of management, keep the company viable is a subjective criterion and therefore unfair. Criteria for selection should be reasonably objective and precise, for example, length of service, skill, attendance record and loyalty. Details of why particular marks had been given to individuals when assessing whom to select need not be disclosed. The relevant critieria differ from job to job. For example, in deciding which teacher to dismiss, a governing body might take into account such criteria as exam results, ability to teach several subjects or one subject at several levels, academic qualifications and so on;

- employers should make reasonable efforts to find an alternative job and consider alternatives to redundancy, for example, cutting costs in other ways. There is, however, no duty to offer the employee a job which came up after he had been dismissed (*Octavius Atkinson & Sons Ltd v Morris* (1989)). A fair process is the main requirement, and not every selection process requires individual consultation They should consult with employees and warn of impending redundancy. This is said to be one of the fundamentals of a fair procedure, though there is no duty to consult an individual employee where his union prohibits individual consultation. Employers must give individual employees the opportunity to contest their marks if they have used a points system for redundancy selection (*John Brown Engineering Ltd v Brown* (1997)). They should consult with the trade union.

Both types of consultation are usually needed, whether the dismissal is for redundancy or another potentially fair reason (*Huddersfield Parcels Ltd v Sykes* (1981), for example). But, in *Mugford v Midland Bank plc* (1997), consultation with the union only was sufficient on the facts, the EAT stating that a failure to consult with the employee individually did not necessarily make the redundancy unfair. Usually, both must take place before the final decision to make someone redundant; for example, presenting the union with a list of those to be made redundant is not consultation. The Court of Session in *King v Eaton Ltd* (1995) approved the law stated by Glidewell LJ in *R v British Coal Corp ex p Price* (1993):

> Fair consultation means:
>
> (a) consultation when the proposals are still at the formative stage;
>
> (b) adequate information on which to respond;
>
> (c) adequate time in which to respond;
>
> (d) conscientious consideration by an authority of a response to consultation.

The Scottish EAT also adopted this definition in *John Brown Engineering*. See Chapter 9 for consultation with recognised unions pre-redundancy dismissals. There is no need for consultation in an emergency, for example, sudden loss of orders or the urgent need to find a purchaser for a business which is in dire financial straits (*Warner v Adnet Ltd* (1998)). Other possible reasons for not consulting include sabotage and demoralising the workforce. The latter reason, however, does not seem to be a good one: does not every redundancy lead to some demoralisation? It is suggested that employers should not rely on this reason for not consulting. An example of failure to consult occurred in a case where it was company policy not to consult with employees, who were managers, about dismissals. It was held that the dismissal was unfair. The EAT held in *University of Glasgow v Donaldson* (1995) that the duty to consult applies even when the employee is on a fixed term contract. The lengths to which employers should go to consult differ, depending on whether the contract is permanent or for a fixed term, but for both types there is an obligation to consult. This duty applies even though the post was externally funded.

10.6.38 Guidelines

Compair Maxam lays down guidelines, not rules. The guidelines do not always apply. The chances are that not all the guidelines have to be followed by small firms which are non-unionised (though even so a small business may as well get procedure right). The employment tribunal must look at how a reasonable employer would have treated this employee. The guidelines are helpful pointers in deciding that question. If the procedure for redundancy has been agreed with the trade union, there is less necessity to follow the guidelines. Despite the above, the EAT has said:

... it is not necessarily enough for an employer to say 'I adopted reasonable criteria' if after consulting as a reasonable employer would have done, different criteria leading to a different result might have been adopted.

When the Court of Appeal has not specifically endorsed *Compair Maxam*, there are signs in the speeches in *Polkey* that the House of Lords is in favour of the approach, no matter how much the Scottish EAT disagrees with the guidelines.

10.6.39 Further considerations

- Instead of compensation, a tribunal in an unfair redundancy case might award re-engagement 'in employment comparable to that from which he was dismissed or other suitable employment'. The tribunal will take into account the wishes of the employee, practicability of re-engagement and justice if the employee caused or contributed to the dismissal. As Lord Bridge said in *Polkey*:

  > In a case where an [employment] tribunal held that dismissal on the ground of redundancy would have been inevitable at the time when it took place, even if the appropriate procedural steps had been taken, I do not ... think this would necessarily preclude a discretionary order for re-engagement on suitable terms ...

- An employee may be unfairly dismissed even though by the time of the dismissal the employers have offered to dismiss another person instead.

- *Brown v Stockton-on-Tees BC* (1988) is important. Where a female employee is selected for redundancy because she needs maternity leave, the dismissal is for a 'reason connected with her pregnancy' and is automatically unfair. There is no need to see whether a reasonable employer would have done as this employer did. Therefore, employers must disregard the inconvenience of the fact that one of the potential persons to be made redundant is pregnant and will have to be off work.

- As stated above, the criteria for selection for redundancy must be free from bias on the grounds of race, sex and marital status. For example, if redundancies are based on the criteria of 'part-timers first', that may be discrimination if men form the full time work force and women are the part time employees.

10.6.40 Case law effects

Cases illustrating the effects of *Polkey* include:

- *Brown v Gavin Scott* (1988)

  The employers reorganised management structure to cut costs. They sacked the employee, the general manager of three shoe shops, without consultation. It was held that the dismissal was unfair. Consultation would not have been useless because a different solution might have emerged.

- *Mining Supplies (Longwall) Ltd v Baker* (1988)

  The employers decided to make redundant 29 manual workers. Negotiations were held with the union and volunteers were sought. There were insufficient volunteers and the union said that 'last in, first out' was the sole criterion which they were prepared to accept. The employers disagreed. They decided to discuss the matter with individual employees. The final choice came down between one with 19 years' service and one with 20. The company chose the former on the basis of 'what most fits the company's needs'. He was not told the reason why he was selected for redundancy. The EAT followed *Polkey*, holding the dismissal to be unfair because the employers had not adopted a fair procedure. They said that, on the basis of the facts of this case, proper consultation would have required two weeks, and they gave a compensatory award for those weeks.

- *GEC Energy Systems Ltd v Grufferty* (1988)

  The employers carried out work for X at a power station. X did not renew the contract. The employers served redundancy notices on their staff. They then entered into negotiations with the CEGB for work at another power station. The CEGB made it clear that fewer workers were needed. They identified the staff they wished to keep. The employee was not one of them. The employers did not say why they were not keeping the employee on. The redundancy was held to be unfair because:

  (a)   no real attempt had been made to find the employee another job; and

  (b)   too little account had been taken of the employee's length of service, good record and the difficulty he would find in obtaining employment elsewhere.

  In this case, a full and skilled consultation process was required. Therefore, the dismissal was unfair. *Polkey* was applied. The case was sent back to the employment tribunal to assess compensation.

10.6.41 Some other substantial reason

In order for a dismissal in a business re-organisation to be fair, there must normally be discussion and consultation with the employees affected, to avoid misunderstanding and any possible injustice to an employee. However, the ultimate question is whether the employer has acted reasonably, not whether it is reasonable for the employee to accept new terms. An employee may be acting reasonably in refusing to accept, for example, because the new terms are disadvantageous to him, yet the employer may be acting perfectly reasonably, for example, because pressing business needs demand that overtime has to be worked.

10.6.42 Temporary workers

Where a temporary employee is dismissed, the dismissal is not automatically fair So, if, for example, there is suitable alternative employment available, a failure to offer it may render the dismissal unfair.

10.6.43 Customer pressure

Dismissal at the behest of customers may be fair if the complaint is valid, for example, misconduct or incompetence on the employee's part subject to the usual safeguards of investigation and a fair hearing, etc. If the commercial situation is such that the employer is forced to bow to the customer's wishes, the employer must first try to resolve the situation in an alternative way, for example, by changing the employee's workload to prevent contact or dissuading the customer.

UNFAIR DISMISSAL: GENERAL APPROACH

Employees have a right to be accompanied at a disciplinary or grievance hearing.

Written reasons

By statute, employees employed for one year or more are entitled to written reasons explaining their dismissal.

Reason

Employers must prove the reason which activated the dismissal:

* *Smith v City of Glasgow DC* (1987).

After-discovered reasons

Subject to exceptions, fair reasons to dismiss discovered after dismissal are not acceptable though compensation may be reduced:

* *Devis v Atkins* (1977);

* *West Midlands Co-op v Tipton* (1986).

Potentially fair reasons

There are five potentially fair reasons: capability (including illness), conduct, redundancy, illegality and 'some other substantial reason' (SOSR):

* *Taylor v Alidair* (1978);

* *Hollister v NFU* (1979).

Conduct covers, for example, violence at work, theft from employers and gross negligence.

Capability covers lack of skill and lack of an academic degree or professional qualification.

Illegality includes a delivery driver's loss of licence.

SOSR is not defined in the statute. It includes a business re-organisation not amounting to redundancy and dismissal at the behest of customers.

Reasonableness

Employment tribunals decide fairness, having regard to the size and administrative resources of the firm and equity and the substantial merits of the case. Of importance is procedural fairness, for example, warnings and investigation:

- *BHS v Burchell* (1980);

- *Iceland Frozen Foods v Jones* (1983);

- *Bailey v BP Oil* (1980);

- *Polkey v Dayton Services* (1988);

- *Spencer v Paragon Wallpapers* (1977);

- *Williams v Compair Maxam* (1982);

- *Mugford v Midland Bank plc* (1997);

- *Lock v Cardiff Railway Co* (1998).

The tribunal may take into account ACAS Disciplinary Practice and Procedure (a Code of Practice), as expanded by its advisory handbook, *Discipline at Work*, which gives employers practical advice on avoiding unfair dismissal claims. It should be emphasised that even small workplaces are subject to the principles of procedural fairness, though such principles may be attenuated for the smallest of employers. The Code recommends the use of a series of warnings, but that procedure can be short-circuited depending on the nature of the incident. It should be recalled that tribunals are not subject to EAT rules and may reach inconsistent outcomes.

CHAPTER 11

UNFAIR DISMISSAL: PARTICULAR PROBLEMS

11.1   Introduction

This chapter examines the various situations where dismissal is either 'automatically unfair' or 'automatically fair'. The term 'automatically unfair' means that the employment tribunal does not investigate the reasonableness of the dismissal, as it does with regard to the five potentially fair reasons, such as conduct, discussed in the previous chapter. 'Automatically fair' is the term given to reasons where the dismissal is fair without reference to the reasonableness of the dismissal. The topic of 'industrial pressure' in the context of unfair dismissal is also noted.

11.2   Automatically unfair

By s 152(1) of the Trade Union and Labour Relations (Consolidation) Act (TULR(C)A) 1992, it is unfair to dismiss an employee if the reason or principal reason for the dismissal was that he:

(1) was or proposed to become a member of an independent trade union (s 152(1)(a)); it need not be shown that he intended to join any particular union;

(2) had taken part or proposed to take part in the activities of an independent trade union at an appropriate time (s 152(1)(b)); or

(3) was not a member of any or a particular trade union or of one of a number of particular trade unions, or had refused or proposed to refuse to become or remain a member (s 152(1)(c)).

'Membership' includes making use of the union's services, such as joining a trade union in order to have its support against the employers: *Speciality Care plc v Pachela* (1996), applying *Discount Tobacco & Confectionery Ltd v Armitage* (1990) and not following *dicta* of the House of Lords in *Associated British Ports v Palmer* (1995) and *Associated Newspapers Ltd v Wilson* (1995). See 11.2.7, below.

The employment tribunal looks at the employers' state of mind, not just at 'but for' causation (*CGB Publishing v Killey* (1995)). This decision is out of line with the law on racial and sexual discrimination. If the employers wrongly believe that the employee has been taking part in union activities, s 152(1) applies. The reason for dismissal can fall within this provision even though the employers do not act out of a desire to get rid of a union activist who is a thorn in the flesh (*Dundon v GPT Ltd* (1995)). Therefore, if the reason for selection for redundancy is that the employee was spending too much time on union duties, that falls within the section. It does not matter that the consent to the performance of those duties had been given impliedly and reluctantly.

Section 146, which deals with detriment (previously called 'action short of dismissal'), is dealt with below, but the two claims are similarly phrased (for example, 'appropriate time'). Cases on one are used in the other. There are also laws aimed at preventing dismissal or detriment for refusing to make payments to charity (in lieu of union dues).

Protection is given only to employees, whereas the International Labour Organisation's Convention No 98, the Right to Organise and Collective Bargaining, applies to all workers. There are the usual exceptions, such as share fishermen.

11.2.1 (In)dependence

The difference in wording between point (1) on the one hand and points (2) and (3) on the other should be noted (see above, 11.2). Point 3 applies to any trade union, independent or not. Points (1) and (2) require the union to be independent. The definition of 'independent' is discussed in Chapter 14, below. Section 152(1)(a) and (b) form part of the protection given to employees who wish to associate together; they are part of the laws guaranteeing freedom of association. Section 152(1)(c), however, was part of the previous Government's attack on the closed shop, the means whereby some unions in some workplaces could restrict the supply of labour. However, it is not restricted to closed shop situations but covers non-members in all situations, whether a closed shop exists or not.

11.2.2 Activities

Dismissal for taking part in the activities of an independent trade union (a phrase which is not defined in the statute) includes the dismissal of an activist by his present employers for the disruption he caused in his previous job (*Fitzpatrick v British Railways Board* (1992)). Other activities include attendance at union meetings (for example, *British Airways Engine Overhaul Ltd v Francis* (1981)), acting as a shop steward (*Driver v Cleveland Structural Engineering Ltd* (1994)), speaking at a company's training event (*Bass Taverns Ltd v Burgess* (1996)) and attempting to recruit new members (for example, *Lyon v St James Press Ltd* (1976)). Leading a strike is taking part in the activities of a trade union (*Britool Ltd v Roberts* (1993)). However, actually taking part in industrial action is not an activity of an independent trade union and, even if it were, it would not satisfy the requirement that it take place at an appropriate time; instead, the employment tribunal may not hear and determine the case, subject to exceptions (see 11.3, below). A possible example of industrial action which does fall within 'activities' is taking part in a ban on voluntary overtime. Such a ban would also occur at an appropriate time. It was suggested in *Lyon* that acts which were wholly unreasonable, extraneous or malicious would not be protected, but these *dicta* have not as yet been applied.

11.2.3 Criticised cases

Two cases have been subject to criticism. In *Carrington v Therm-A-Stor Ltd* (1983), employees were dismissed when the union sought recognition from the employers. The court held that they had been dismissed, not for their own union activities, but, as it were, for the union's union activities. For the right to apply, employees have to be dismissed for what they do, not for what the union does. Therefore, since s 152 was not fulfilled, they were unprotected. In *Chant v Aquaboats Ltd* (1978), an employee was dismissed for organising a petition complaining about safety at work. He was a member of a union. The EAT held that his complaint did not fall within s 152. What he did was not taking part in union activities, for the trade union had not invited him to organise the petition; and he was not a trade union official. The union was not involved. Therefore, the activities were not those of a trade union but were undertaken on his own account. This outcome was not affected by the fact that a union official had approved the petition. It should be noted that an employee has a right not to be dismissed or victimised if he has alleged that the employers have violated health and safety rules.

11.2.4 Appropriate time

The phrase 'appropriate time' in s 152(1)(b) means, by sub-s (2), time outside the working hours or time within working hours during which, 'in accordance with arrangements agreed with or consent' given by his employers, the employee may take part in the activities of a trade union. There is, accordingly, no general right to engage in union activities at any time. Consent may be implicit (*Marley Tile Co Ltd v Shaw* (1980)). The court, however, held that the implication was not to be made when the employers simply kept silent when they were informed that a union meeting was to be held in working hours.

In *Zucker v Astrid Jewels Ltd* (1978), the EAT held that, by talking about the advantages of union membership while working, an employee was taking part in a union's activities at an appropriate time because the employers had not prohibited talk during work. As that case also shows, lunchtimes and tea breaks are appropriate times, even though the employee is paid for them. In *Burgess v Bass Taverns Ltd* (1996), the Court of Appeal held that a shop steward talking at an induction course for trainee managers was taking part in union activities at an appropriate time.

11.2.5 Procedure

There is no qualifying period or age limit (s 154 of TULR(C)A 1992, as rewritten by Sched 7, para 1 of TURERA 1993). There are special rules on compensation, and these are discussed in the next chapter. Three matters require mention here:

- In assessing compensation where the unfair dismissal falls within s 152, the employment tribunal takes into account the contributory conduct of the employee, but not if the conduct constitutes a breach or proposed breach of a requirement:

    (a) to be or become a member of any trade union or of a particular trade union or one of a number of particular trade unions;

    (b) to cease to be, or refrain from becoming, a member of any trade union or of a particular trade union or one of a number of particular trade unions; or

    (c) not to take part in the activities of any trade union or of any particular trade union or of one of a number of particular unions [s 55(2)].

    An example of conduct contributing to the applicant's dismissal is *Dundon v GPT Ltd* (1995), where the EAT assessed the deduction at one-third of the award. It considered that there could well be a difference between the percentage in an ordinary unfair dismissal case and one in an automatically unfair claim. One criticism of *Dundon* is that it is difficult to see that the applicant did anything blameworthy, as demanded by the EAT, which contributed to his dismissal; the fact that his union activities were protected by statute did not contribute to his dismissal.

- Awards may be made against third parties for the reason specified below (see 11.2.9).

- Under s 152, an applicant may apply to an employment tribunal for interim relief within seven days of the effective date of termination (s 161). Where the dismissal is for a reason falling within s 152(1)(a) or (b), the employment tribunal cannot proceed unless there is a document in writing, signed by an authorised official of the independent trade union of the employee who is or was proposing to become a member, stating that, at the date of dismissal, the employee was or proposed to become a member of that union and there seem to be reasonable grounds for supposing that the reason for dismissal was the one alleged. If it is likely that s 152 has been breached, the tribunal asks the employers to reinstate the employee in the same job or re-engage him in a similar job. If the employers do not attend the hearing or are unwilling to reinstate or re-engage the complainant, the tribunal must make an order for the continuation of his contract of employment, by which his employment rights (for example, pay, seniority and pension) are retained until settlement or resolution of the dispute. (If the employee loses the unfair dismissal claim, he nevertheless keeps the money.) If the employers do not comply with the reinstatement or re-engagement, the tribunal must make an order for the continuation of the employee's contract and order compensation on the usual 'just and equitable' basis, having regard to:

(i)   the infringement of the employee's right to be reinstated or re-engaged in pursuance of the order; and

(ii)   any loss suffered by the employee in consequence of the non-compliance [s 166(1)].

If the employers do not comply with the order to continue the employment contract, the employment tribunal determines the amount of pay owing, if non-payment is the breach; if the non-compliance is in respect of something other than non-payment, the tribunal orders the employers to pay compensation on the 'just and equitable' basis, having regard to the employee's loss occasioned by the non-compliance.

Interim relief is also available in respect of a protected disclosure under the Public Interest Disclosure Act 1998.

11.2.6 Burden of proof

If the employee does not have the one year's continuous service for an ordinary unfair dismissal claim, he must prove that he was dismissed for a reason falling within s 152 (*Smith v Hayle Town Council* (1978)). If he satisfies the qualifying period, the burden is on the employers. Similarly, the burden of proof switches to the employers if he can show the s 152 reason (see *Maund v Penwith DC* (1984)).

11.2.7 Detriment

As well as protection from dismissal on trade union grounds, employees (with the usual exceptions, such as share fishermen) have a right not to be subjected to detriment as individuals (s 146(1) of TULR(C)A 1992, as amended by the Employment Relations Act 1999). Accordingly, it is unlawful to: apply a detriment to an employee for the purpose of preventing or deterring him from seeking to become or being a member of an independent trade union, or for penalising him for so doing; prevent or deter him from taking part in the activities of an independent trade union at an appropriate time; or compel him to become or be a member of any trade union, independent or not. The words 'as an individual' in s 146(1) are meant to preclude the argument that adverse action against a union is, by itself, detriment to a union member.

An example of the application of s 146(1) is *FW Farnsworth Ltd v McCoid* (1999), where an employee's post as shop steward was derecognised. It was held that this was action taken against him as an individual. The detriment is one based on the same grounds as s 152 (with amendments to the wording). The detriment must be taken 'for the purpose of' the grounds listed. One looks at the employers' purpose, not the effect on the employee (*Gallacher v Department of Transport* (1994)). Refusing to promote a union official because he did not possess proven managerial experience, and, in order to get that experience, he would have had to give up his full time union job, did not fall within s 146(1). The employers' purpose was to ensure that only those with appropriate experience were promoted. Neill LJ said that 'purpose' connoted 'an object which the employer desires or seeks to achieve'. Purpose, therefore, means intent. Similarly, derecognising a shop steward because he is unfit for the job does not violate s 146(1).

The effect of the employers' action is irrelevant. The House of Lords held in *Associated British Ports v Palmer* (1995) that the employers' aim was to achieve flexibility when they replaced union negotiated terms with personal contracts, and it held in *Associated Newspapers v Wilson* (1995) that a refusal to negotiate with the union, with the objective on getting the employees on to personal contracts, had as its purpose the abrogation of collective bargaining. In neither case was the employers' purpose to deter the employees from continuing to be union members, nor was it to penalise members for remaining members, even though those who signed personal contracts received pay increases which those who remained on union-negotiated contracts did not obtain. The House of Lords did not accept that making use of the union's services such as collective bargaining was the same as being a member of a union, a highly controversial ruling. Protection was given only for membership. Also controversial was the House of Lords' use of statutory material in its construction of the relevant provision.

The line between act and omission was, before 1999, not clear cut: for example, was a refusal to pay a contractually agreed pay rise an action or a failure to act? The interpretation was a serious inroad on freedom of association. Bob Simpson tellingly wrote:

> Since a trade union is by definition an organisation of workers whose principal purposes include the regulation of relations between workers and employers …, it is remarkable that the House of Lords should conclude that this part of the Social Contract labour legislation was enacted to protect only workers' rights to benefits from union membership which have nothing to do with regulating relations with employers [(1995) 24 ILJ 235, p 243].

Fortunately, the Employment Relations Act 1999 defines 'detriment' to cover both act and omission. 'Detriment' means treating the employee less favourably than another employee would be treated on the relevant ground, such as when an employee who takes part in a union meeting is denied promotion but one who did not is granted it. It does not matter that the worker's terms and conditions of employment are not affected, as when an employee lost recognition as a shop steward in *Farnsworth*, above. Section 146 also covers penalising employees for being or seeking to become a member of a trade union and for taking part in trade union activities at appropriate times. 'Penalising' means putting the employee at a disadvantage, and covers the refusal of a car park space (*Carlson v Post Office* (1981)). Non-renewal of a fixed term contract is not detriment: it is a dismissal; this is because of the definition of 'dismissal' found in TULR(C)A 1992 and its precursors (*Johnstone v BBC Enterprises Ltd* (1994)). Since the applicant had waived his right to unfair dismissal (which at that time was lawful), he had no remedy.

11.2.8 Pressure and purpose

By s 148(2), the employment tribunal is instructed to disregard pressure exercised by calling, organising, procuring or financing industrial action such as a strike. If there is evidence of that and evidence of a purpose which falls within s 146, then, by s 148(3) (as inserted by s 13 of TURERA 1993), the tribunal is directed to consider only evidence that the employers' purpose was to further a change in the relationship with all or any class of their employees . In other words, s 146 has been severely restricted. If the purpose was to improve efficiency, that purpose is irrelevant even if, as a side effect, union membership is required.

The aim of s 13 was to reverse two Court of Appeal cases, *Associated British Ports v Palmer* (1993) and *Associated Newspapers Ltd v Wilson* (1993), which had held that it was action short of dismissal (the forerunner of detriment) when employees were given 'sweeteners' to make them sign personal contracts (that is, ones which had no place for the union) when those who refused to sign did not get the extra money. In fact, the decisions were reversed by the House of Lords in 1995, thereby rendering the amendment otiose. Lord Bridge held that 'action' short of dismissal did not include an omission to give a benefit to union members. Accordingly, if employers paid more to employees who were not members of a union than to those who were, they were not liable.

Although Lord Bridge investigated the legislative history of the provision, he failed to refer to the political history behind the law. It was introduced at the time of the Social Contract between the Labour Government and the unions. The failure to provide expressly for an omission was not deliberate. The drafter may have felt it evident that 'action' covered 'omission'; or it may be that he failed to notice the issue. The case has gone to the European Court of Human Rights. The new s 148(3) provides that, if the employers' action was one which no reasonable employer would take, the employment tribunal may then investigate whether there was detriment within s 146.

11.2.9 Procedure and remedy

There is the usual time limit of three months from the date of the last detriment, or, if it was not reasonably practicable for the complaint to be made within that time, within a reasonable further period (s 147). The burden of proving the purpose for which detriment was given lies on the employers (s 148(1)). If the employment tribunal upholds the complaint, it makes a declaration and may award compensation (which is not financially limited by statute):

> ... such as the tribunal considers just and equitable in all the circumstances, having regard to the infringement complained of and to any loss sustained by the complainant which is attributable to the action which infringed his rights [s 149(2)].

'Loss' covers, for example, frustration felt on failing to join a union. Injury to feelings may be included in the award of compensation. The employers must not be punished.

Mitigation must take place, industrial pressure is disregarded, and contributory fault may reduce the compensation (s 149(4)–(6)). A third party who puts pressure on the employers to make the employee join a trade union may be joined (by either the complainant or the employers) as party to the proceedings and ordered to pay compensation (s 160). It should be noted that tribunals do not have the power to order the unfair treatment to stop. See 11.4, below, for analogous provisions on industrial pressure and joinder in the context of unfair dismissal.

11.2.10 Selection for redundancy on union grounds

By s 153 of TULR(C)A 1992, where an employee is redundant but is selected for redundancy on a ground specified in s 152(1) (see above), for example, trade union activities, the dismissal is deemed to be unfair. Redundancy is defined as in Chapter 9. Comparison must be made with the positions of comparable employees who were not dismissed. The employment tribunal, when making the comparison, must not take into account anything the dismissed employee did as a trade union official (*O'Dea v ISC Chemicals Ltd* (1996)). Even so, if there was no comparable employee, the claim fails. It is difficult to see the reason for this decision. If the selection for redundancy was made on trade union grounds, why should it matter that there was no comparable employee? There has been no qualifying period for this right since 1993.

11.2.11 National minimum wage

To dismiss a worker because he receives the minimum wage or because he is seeking to obtain it amounts to automatic unfair dismissal.

11.2.12 Pregnancy/childbirth

Section 99 of the ERA 1996 derives from s 24(1) of TURERA 1993. By it, dismissal is automatically unfair if the reason or principal reason for it was any of the following:

- pregnancy or any reason connected with pregnancy, such as an abortion, according to an employment tribunal case ('any reason connected with pregnancy' would presumably also cover dismissing a woman because she was pregnant on the grounds that the institution did not employ unmarried parents for religious reasons);

- childbirth (a phrase which includes the birth of a dead child after 24 weeks of pregnancy) or any reason connected therewith;

- the use of maternity provisions;

- incapability of working following childbirth if the employee has a medical certificate stating that, 'by reason of disease or bodily or mental disablement', she is incapable of working after maternity leave, dismissal taking place within four weeks of the end of her leave;

- in consequence of a statutory requirement contained in a Code of Practice on health and safety or recommendation in relation to the right to return after maternity;

- redundancy within the maternity leave period and s 77 of the ERA 1996 has not been complied with (offering her a suitable alternative vacancy). It should be noted that, in a normal redundancy situation, there is no law which compels the employers to offer a suitable vacancy.

Caledonia Bureau Investment and Property v Caffrey (1998) is an example of the first of the reasons. Because of post-natal depression, an employee could not return to work at the end of her maternity leave. She was dismissed. The EAT held that her dismissal was due to a pregnancy-related illness. Section 99 applied and the applicant was held to have been unfairly dismissed. It did not matter that the dismissal occurred after the maternity leave period, provided that the contract continued. The decision has been criticised on the grounds that the first reason is restricted to pregnancy and does not extend to maternity.

If the employers do not know of the pregnancy, s 99 does not apply. The reason for dismissal is not pregnancy. Section 99 is a result of the Pregnant Workers Directive (92/85). This measure is based on the Framework Directive (89/391) on health and safety. Voting on health and safety matters is by qualified majority voting, and opposition by the UK can thereby be overridden. In fact, the Government abstained on the vote.

11.2.13 No qualifying period

Section 99 deems the reason for dismissal to be unfair: the reason does not have to be proved unreasonable. There is no qualifying period. The claim of the applicant in *Webb v EMO Air Cargo (UK) Ltd* (1993) could now be brought under s 99. However, a refusal to employ on the grounds that the candidate was pregnant cannot be brought because s 99 applies to dismissal, not refusal to employ.

11.2.14 Written statement

As a supplementary to s 99 of the ERA 1996, s 92(4) gives a woman a right to a written statement of the ground of dismissal if she is dismissed while she is pregnant or while she is on maternity leave after childbirth. There is no need for her to make a request and there is no minimum length of continuous service.

11.2.15 Dismissal for assertion of statutory right

Since 1993, there has existed the right not to be dismissed for asserting a statutory right. This right is now contained in s 104 of the ERA 1996:

(1) The dismissal of an employee by an employer shall be regarded for the purposes of this Part as having been unfair if the reason for it (or, if more than one, the principal reason) was that the employee –

    (a) brought proceedings against the employer to enforce a right of his which is a relevant statutory right; or

    (b) alleged that the employer had infringed a right of his which is a relevant statutory right.

(2) It is immaterial for the purposes of sub-section (1) whether the employee has the right or not and whether it has been infringed or not, but, for that sub-section to apply, the claim to the right and that it has been infringed must be made in good faith.

(3) It shall be sufficient for sub-section (1) to apply that the employee, without specifying the right, made it reasonably clear to the employer what the right claimed to have infringed was.

(4) The following statutory rights are relevant for the purposes of this section, namely –

    (a) any right conferred by this Act for which the remedy for its infringement is by way of a complaint or reference to an industrial tribunal;

    (b) the right conferred by section 86 of this Act; and

(c)   the rights conferred by the following provisions of the Trade Union and Labour Relations (Consolidation) Act 1992, namely, sections 68, 86, 146, 168, 169 and 170 (deductions from pay, union activities and time off).

It is interesting to note that, despite the fact that the right to a minimum period of notice cannot be enforced in an employment tribunal, the s 104 right nevertheless applies. Section 146 of TULR(C)A 1992 is dealt with above, 11.2.7. 'This Act' is the ERA 1996. Therefore, assertions of unfair dismissal and redundancy are covered. There is a time limit of three months. The burden of proof is on the employee.

11.2.16 No qualifying period

A dismissal under s 104 is deemed to be an inadmissible reason and there is no qualifying period or minimum hours of work. Selection for redundancy because the applicant has asserted a statutory claim is automatically unfair.

11.2.17 Victimisation

Section 104 reflects a growing concern with the penalisation of persons who brought, for example, claims that action short of dismissal had been taken against them and had complained to an employment tribunal, in consequence of which they had been actually or constructively dismissed. This concern found expression in the Offshore Safety (Protection against Victimisation) Act 1992 (which is repealed by TURERA 1993 but widened beyond the narrow situation covered by that Act). If, however, dismissal was for threatening behaviour and not for asserting a statutory right, this right is inapplicable.

11.2.18 Health and safety

Section 100 of the ERA 1996 gives employees (including whistleblowers) protection against dismissal in health and safety matters. (The section protects against dismissal: it does not advantage safety representatives over other employees. Therefore, additional points in redundancy selection procedure should not be given to a health and safety representative for performing his duties.) The Employment Relations Act 1999 removes the statutory limit on the compensatory award for this head of liability.

(1)   The dismissal of an employee by an employer shall be regarded for the purposes of this Part as having been unfair if the reason for it (or, if more than one, the principal reason) was that the employee –

    (a)   having been designated by the employer to carry out activities in connection with preventing or reducing risks to health and safety at work, carried out, or proposed to carry out, any such activities;

(b)   being a representative of workers on matters of health and safety at work, or a member of a safety committee –

   (i)   in accordance with arrangements established under or by virtue of any enactment, or

   (ii)   by reason of being acknowledged as such by the employer, performed, or proposed to perform, any functions as such a representative or a member of such a committee;

(c)   being an employee at a place where –

   (i)   there was no such representative or safety committee, or

   (ii)   there was such a representative or safety committee but it was not reasonably practicable for the employee to raise the matter by those means, brought to his employer's attention, by reasonable means, circumstances connected with his work which he reasonably believed were harmful or potentially harmful to health or safety;

(d)   in circumstances of danger which he reasonably believed to be serious and imminent and which he could not reasonably have been expected to avert, left, or proposed to leave, or (while the danger persisted) refused to return to, his place of work or any dangerous part of his place of work; or

(e)   in circumstances of danger which he reasonably believed to be serious and imminent, took, or proposed to take, appropriate steps to protect himself or other persons from the danger.

There is a defence to this head of liability that the employee had taken or intended to take steps which were so negligent that a reasonable employer would have dismissed; if that is the case, the dismissal is fair. If the employee's belief in harm is not reasonable, there is no claim (*Kerr v Nathan's Wastesavers Ltd* (1995)). As long as the employee is carrying out health and safety matters, it is irrelevant that he is doing so in a confrontational or inflexible manner (*Goodwin v Cabletel UK Ltd* (1998)).

These provisions derive from the so called 'framework' Directive (89/391) on health and safety. There are similar provisions covering detriment short of dismissal on the grounds in s 44 of the ERA 1996. If the employee was subjected to a detriment for performing the functions of a safety representative, 'it is no defence that he intended to embarrass the company in front of external safety authorities, or that he performed those functions in an unreasonable way, unacceptable to the employer': *Shillito v van Leer (UK) Ltd* (1997).What is 'serious and imminent' is left to case law.

11.2.19 Other automatically unfair dismissals

It is automatically unfair to dismiss protected shop workers and betting workers if they refuse to work on Sundays (s 101 of the ERA 1996), to dismiss employee-nominated trustees of pension funds for exercising their functions (s 102 of the ERA 1996), and to dismiss representatives in pursuing their tasks of consultation under the Collective Redundancies and Transfer of Undertakings (Protection of Employment) (Amendments) Regulations 1995 (SI 1995/2587), reg 14. Detriment is also unlawful.

11.2.20 No qualifying period

Dismissal for this reason is deemed to be an automatically unfair reason. There is no qualifying period. A selection for redundancy on this ground is deemed to be automatically unfair and interim relief is available, as it is for pension trustees and employee representatives. Action short of dismissal on health and safety grounds is also compensated on the 'just and equitable' basis with the usual deductions, but there is no maximum limit on compensation.

11.2.21 The Public Interest Disclosure Act 1998

This Act gives protection to whistleblowers. It inserts new sections into the ERA 1996. The statute is a complex one and its principal provisions are summarised below. Employees are protected only if they make a qualifying disclosure. This consists of the disclosure of information which, in the reasonable belief of the worker, tends to show that:

- a crime has been, is being or is likely to be committed;

- a person has failed, is failing or is likely to fail to comply with a duty imposed by law;

- a miscarriage of justice has occurred or is likely to occur;

- the health and safety of an individual has been or is likely to be imperilled;

- the environment has been or is likely to be damaged; or

- information revealing any of these has been or is likely to be intentionally concealed.

Disclosure must be only to certain persons or bodies, principally the employers or their officers. Legal advisers and Ministers of the Crown are such persons. There is a lengthy list of organisations to which disclosure may lawfully be made. There are two further instances where the worker is protected. The first is where:

(a) the worker discloses the information in good faith;

(b) he believes in the truth of the allegation;

(c) he does not act with a view to make a personal gain;

(d) it is reasonable in all the circumstances to make the disclosure (the Act gives various factors to be used to determine reasonableness, such as whether the worker was acting in breach of confidentiality); and

(e) the worker believes on reasonable grounds that he will be subjected to a detriment if the material is disclosed to the employers or other prescribed persons; or, where there are no prescribed persons, the worker believes on reasonable grounds that the information will be destroyed or concealed; or the worker has previously disclosed the information to the employers or a prescribed person.

The second is that, if the information is of exceptional gravity, the disclosure need not be to certain persons only but can be made generally, provided that:

(a) the information is of sufficient gravity;

(b) the worker believed on reasonable grounds that it was true;

(c) he did not reveal the information to make a personal gain; and

(d) it is in all the circumstances reasonable to make the disclosure. In determining that question, the tribunal is to take into account the identity of the person or organisation to whom it was revealed.

By s 103A, the dismissal of an employee in breach of these rules is automatically unfair. There is no maximum compensatory award. There is no minimum qualifying period or normal retiring age. Interim relief is available. Protection is similarly granted from selection for redundancy on these grounds and from detriment short of dismissal. Provisions in contracts purporting to exclude these rights are void (s 43J).

11.2.22 Right to be accompanied

The Employment Relations Act 1999 makes it automatically unfair to dismiss a person for seeking to exercise the right to be accompanied (or to accompany a worker) at a disciplinary hearing. As usual, there is no upper age limit or qualifying period. The Act also provides similar protection in respect of detriment.

11.3 Automatically fair

Where Parliament has stated that the reason for the dismissal is an automatically fair one, the tribunal cannot deal with the case, even though the employee is qualified and has been dismissed.

11.3.1   Industrial action/lock-out

Dismissal during industrial action/lock-out was originally designed to keep employment tribunals out of collective disputes. It has, however, been successively altered, with the result that its original purpose has been seriously undermined. Where this law applies, the employers can dismiss the workforce and take on new employees without having to compensate those dismissed. Calls have been made to the effect that dismissals during industrial action should be heard and, if employment tribunals get involved in the merits of strikes, so be it. In fact, tribunals cannot avoid getting involved in the matter of disputes, as when employers selectively re-engage official strikers (see 11.3.2, below). If this exception does not apply, the employment tribunal has jurisdiction to hear and determine the cause in the ordinary way, as detailed in Chapter 10 (see *TNT Express (UK) Ltd v Downes* (1993)). If s 238 is inapplicable, *Downes* holds that the employment tribunal may investigate any justification for the industrial action.

11.3.2   Effects

By s 238(1) of TULR(C)A 1992, an employment tribunal may not investigate the issue of fairness if, at the time of dismissal, the employee was taking part in official industrial action, such as a strike, or the employers were conducting a lock-out, provided that all employees involved were dismissed and none was re-engaged within three months of dismissal. To s 238(1) there are two exceptions. First, a claim for unfair dismissal may be heard if not all 'relevant employees' have been dismissed or only some have been re-engaged within the three months (s 238(2)). The tribunal must now consider the claim: the effect of s 238(2) is not to make the dismissal automatically unfair. It may be reasonable to dismiss some strikers but keep others. In other words, normal unfair dismissal law governs.

The second exception was created by the Employment Relations Act 1999. This exception can easily be seen by the words which have to be put on pre-strike ballot papers:

> If you are dismissed for taking part in strike or other industrial action which is called officially and is otherwise lawful, the dismissal will be unfair if it takes place fewer than eight weeks after you started taking part in the action and, depending on the circumstances, may be unfair if it takes place later.

The industrial action must be lawful. There is no qualifying period or age limit. Protection is also given to those sacked after the eight week period, if the employers have not taken reasonable steps to resolve the dispute.

Normal unfair dismissal law includes the deduction for contributory fault. If the industrial action is not endorsed or authorised by a trade union (under s 20(2) of TULR(C)A 1992), that is, if it is unofficial, no employee may apply for a remedy for unfair dismissal (s 237). Industrial action is not unofficial if none of the employees is a member of a trade union. If the action was official but the union has repudiated it, it does not become unofficial until the end of one working day after repudiation (s 237(4)), that is, the workers have a day's grace before s 237(1) applies. If s 238 does apply so that the employment tribunal has jurisdiction, the limitation period is six months from the date of dismissal, or, if it was not reasonably practicable to bring a claim within that period, within such time as the employment tribunal considers reasonable (s 239(2)). A person is not taking part in a strike if he has communicated the intention to return. Section 137 does not apply to workers dismissed for being whistleblowers within the Public Interest Disclosure Act 1998.

11.3.3 Definitions

For the purposes of ss 237–38, strike, industrial action and lock-out are undefined. There is a definition of strike found in s 246 of TULR(C)A 1992 which, it appears, applies to ss 237–38. A strike is 'any concerted stoppage of work'. In s 216 of the ERA 1996, which defines it for the purposes of continuity of employment, a lock-out is the closure of the workplace, suspension of work or the employers' refusal to continue to employ some employees. It seems that a breach of contract is not necessary. Industrial action covers work-to-rule, go-slows, and even withdrawal of voluntary overtime (that is, there is no need for a breach of contract) (*Faust v Power Packing Casemakers Ltd* (1983)). Therefore, even though the employees are not in breach of contract, they lose the protection of employment law. Even if the strike was provoked by the employers, the employees have no remedy. In *Wilkins v Cantrell and Cochrane Ltd* (1978), the employees refused to drive overloaded lorries. The employers dismissed them. The employees had no remedy, despite the employees being provoked into the strike.

The contrast between *Faust* and *Wilkins* is amazing. Employees who do not commit a breach of contract can be dismissed. If the employers do break the contract and the employees go on strike as a result, they can be lawfully dismissed. In *Rasool v Hepworth Pipe Co Ltd* (1980), however, taking part in an unauthorised mass meeting during working hours, the meeting being held to consider employees' views on forthcoming wage negotiations, did not constitute industrial action (rather, it was taking part in trade union activities but at an inappropriate time: see above). No pressure was being put on the employers.

According to the much criticised EAT decision of *Lewis v E Mason and Sons* (1994), an individual protest is a strike. A refusal to drive a lorry from Wales to Edinburgh in winter because it did not have an overnight heater was held to be industrial action. His refusal to obey a lawful order constituted such action. The EAT said that the issue of whether industrial action was occurring was an issue of fact for the employment tribunal, and the present finding of the tribunal was not perverse. At the time of that decision, the TULR(C)A definition did not apply. Nevertheless, it cannot be said that there was *concerted* action. It is suggested that, in this context, 'taking part in' means 'participating with others in'. Industrial action is a collective, not individual matter. (It is also suggested that the order was unlawful.)

According to *Manifold Industries Ltd v Sims* (1991) – there are contrary cases – the test for deciding whether an employee was taking part in the action is objective. It is irrelevant whether the employers knew that he was participating. A belief that the employee was on strike where in reality he was not does not excuse the employers (*Thompson v Woodland Designs Ltd* (1980)).

11.3.4 Taking part

'Taking part' in action is also determined objectively. It does not matter what the employee's motive was. A person is taking part in a strike even where he is taking part in the action merely because he is acting as bosses' spy . In *Coates v Modern Methods and Materials Ltd* (1982), the employee was held to be taking part in a strike, even though her reason for joining in was that she was afraid of abuse from her colleagues if she did not. A person on sick leave is not taking part in a strike (*Hindle Gears Ltd v McGinty* (1985)). General expression of support for a strike by a sick employee does not mean that he is taking part in the action. However, an employee who is on strike but becomes ill remains on strike for the purposes of ss 237–38 (*Williams v Western Mail and Echo Ltd* (1980)).

The employees must be actually participating in action; it is insufficient that a strike has been threatened (*Midland Plastics Ltd v Till* (1983)). The taking part in the action relates to the time of the dismissal. *Lewis*, above, can also be criticised on this point. A threat of industrial action, that no employee would come to work on the following day, was held to be industrial action at the time when the employee was dismissed, but surely a threat of action is not the same as action, as, indeed, *Midland Plastics* had held. A surprising case is *McCormick v Horsepower Ltd* (1981). An employee was dismissed for redundancy. He had earlier refused to join a picket line. Since he had been dismissed, the employment tribunal had no jurisdiction.

11.3.5 Action or activity?

If the employees' conduct does not amount to a strike or other industrial action, it may constitute a union activity, in which case the protection afforded between s 152(1) of TULR(C)A 1992 comes into play. If so, the employees have greater protection than in a normal unfair dismissal claim. A mass meeting is instanced as not being industrial action (even though production is stopped) but as being a union activity. The line is fine.

11.3.6 Relevant employees

'Relevant employees' in relation to industrial action are, by s 238(3):

> ... those employees at the establishment of the employer at or from which the complainant works who at the date of his dismissal were taking part in the action.

The definition excludes employees who have died, retired or resigned. Therefore, if a co-worker has to return to work before the claimant was dismissed, he does not count as a relevant employee for the purposes of s 238(2). The effect is that employers can wait and see who comes back, then sack all those still out, the latter no doubt being the ones whom they consider to be troublemakers. It seems, furthermore, that the dismissals of those taking part in action can take place at any time up to the end of the employment tribunal hearing. If all those taking part are dismissed before then, they are 'relevant employees' (*P & O European Ferries (Dover) Ltd v Byrne* (1989)). This Court of Appeal decision may not accord with the legislative intent.

In relation to lock-outs, 'relevant employees' are defined, again in s 238(3), as those 'directly interested in the dispute', a term which includes those who have returned to work (*Campey & Sons v Bellwood* (1987)). Therefore, this definition is wider than that in respect of industrial action. Another difference is that in relation to a lock-out, there is no restriction as to establishment, whereas in respect of industrial action the relevant employees must work at the same establishment as the employee. 'Establishment' is undefined. The effect of 'establishment' may be demonstrated thus. Assume that during a recession a firm is faced with the need to cut the workforce. As a reaction to proposed cuts, employees at two factories, one in London and the other in Norwich, go on strike. The employers can now close one of the plants, say London, without fear of unfair dismissal claims despite the fact that the employees at the other establishment are still on strike. For a discussion of 'establishment' in the context of handling redundancies, see Chapter 9.

11.3.7 Offer of re-engagement

By s 238(4), an offer of re-engagement under s 238(2) is defined as an offer by the employers, their successors or associated employers to re-engage the employee:

> ... either in the job which he held immediately before the date of dismissal or in a different job which would be reasonably suitable in his case.

A job offer remains suitable even though it is treated as the second stage in disciplinary procedures. In *Williams v National Theatre Board Ltd* (1982)), since the employees turned down that offer, they had no claim. The Court of Appeal also held that there is an offer within the sub-section when the offers vary in the terms and conditions. The court opined that job offers with seriously reduced terms would not be within s 238(4). There can be an offer of re-engagement within s 238(2) even though the employers did not know that they had previously dismissed an employee for taking part in industrial action (*Bigham v GKN Kwikform Ltd* (1992)). (This situation can occur in large firms.) An advertisement to the world does not constitute an offer.

11.3.8 Exceptions

Sections 237(1) and 238(2) do not apply if the reason or principal reason for dismissal was the health and safety ground found in s 100 of the ERA 1996 or the maternity ground found in s 99 of the same Act: Sched 8, paras 76–77 of TURERA 1993. Section 99 was substituted for the old law by the same statute. These sections are discussed above.

11.3.9 Critique: comments on ss 237–38

The law makes:

> ... the process of dismissal of a striking workforce into something like a game of hazard on which the winner takes all, in which defeat or victory turns on the fall of a single card [*Hindle Gears Ltd v McGinty* (1985), *per* Waite J].

It has become so encrusted with exceptions that everything depends on interpretation. Is what is happening a strike or other industrial action? If so, s 237 applies; if not, the dismissal may be for trade union reasons, with the result that the dismissal is automatically unfair and the employers have to pay an increased level of compensation. The problem is exacerbated by the facts that 'strike' is left undefined and the issue of whether there is 'industrial action' is a question of fact for the tribunal; and the EAT cannot intervene to determine which of two tribunals holding diametrically different views is correct where the issue is deemed to be one of fact. The latter rule has been said judicially not to be in accord with the development of orderly industrial relations.

The protection from claims which ss 237–38 provide applies even though the employers have provoked the strike. TURERA 1993 gives employees some protection where the industrial action was a response to health and safety matters, but, outside of that area, employees have no claim. For employees, the position is made even worse by the provision on lock-outs. The employer can lock the employees out for whatever reason and thereby avoid any unfair dismissal liability. If, for example, the employers cut wages, the employees refuse to accept the cuts and, in return, the employers lock them out and then dismiss them, the employment tribunal has no jurisdiction. When Rupert Murdoch sacked 5,500 workers for refusing to move from Fleet Street to Wapping, the dismissals could not be challenged.

Sections 237–38 apply, no matter the reason the employers had for dismissing. There is no reason to show that the industrial action was the activating cause. It is sufficient that industrial action or a lock-out was taking place at the date of dismissal. This point reinforces the second point above, about employers' provoking a strike, then dismissing the employees without fear of legal sanction.

One anomaly can be demonstrated by reference to *Faust v Power Packing Casemakers Ltd* (1983). Employers sacked employees for refusing to work voluntary overtime. The refusal was linked to a pay claim. Since the workers were taking part in industrial action at the time of dismissal, the employment tribunal had no power to hear their claim for unfair dismissal. If, however, the employers had dismissed just one employee for the refusal, only he being in dispute over pay, he would, no doubt, have won a claim for unfair dismissal. One person cannot act in concert or in combination, as appears to be necessary before ss 237–38 apply. Yet the sole difference is that, on the actual facts of *Faust*, three were dismissed; on the hypothetical facts, only one was. Why should numbers make a difference? When s 238 was first drafted, the answer was: to keep employment tribunals away from questioning the merits of collective disputes. With the changes to s 238 (and the enactment of s 237), that argument is no longer fully sustainable.

The Committee of Experts of the International Labour Organisation in 1989 condemned the precursor of s 238 on the grounds that it deprived employees of their right to challenge the fairness of their dismissal before a judicial body in breach of the Convention No 87, 1948, on Freedom of Association and Protection of the Right to Organise.

11.3.10 National security

Dismissal on grounds of national security is automatically fair.

11.4 Industrial pressure

With regard to any unfair dismissal claim, in considering whether employers acted fairly in dismissing, employment tribunals cannot take into account the fact that the sacking was brought about by industrial pressure such as a strike or the threat of one (s 107 of the ERA 1996). An example is *Colwyn Borough Council v Dutton* (1980). Trade union members refused to act as crew to the claimant when he drove a dustbin lorry. They considered that he drove dangerously. The employment tribunal could not take into consideration his colleagues' action.

11.4.1 Joinder

Section 160 of TULR(C)A 1992, noted above, permits the claimant or employers to join unions as parties to proceedings where the employers were induced to dismiss the employee as a result of actual or threatened strike or other industrial action, where the pressure was exercised because the employee was not a member of any or any particular trade union or of a number of particular unions. The employment tribunal can order compensation to be paid by the union.

UNFAIR DISMISSAL: PARTICULAR PROBLEMS

Automatically unfair

It is automatically unfair to dismiss an employee on the following grounds: union membership/non-membership; union activities at appropriate times; for reasons of pregnancy or childbirth; because the employee deals with health and safety matters, is a pension funds trustee, an employee representative for consultation on redundancy or transfer of an undertaking; or is a protected shop worker or a betting worker who refuses to work on Sunday:

- *Fitzpatrick v BRB* (1991);

- *Carrington v Therm-A-Stor* (1983);

- *NCB v Ridgway* (1987).

The rights to become a member and to take part in activities apply only in relation to independent unions, whereas the right not to be dismissed for not being or refusing to become a member applies to both independent and sweetheart unions. 'Appropriate times' include after work. 'Last in, first out' may be a customary arrangement. An agreed procedure may be a system to which the parties have impliedly given their consent.

Employers must not subject their employees to a detriment on these grounds.

Automatically fair

It is automatically fair to dismiss employees during a strike, other industrial action or a lock-out, except when the action is official and either not all relevant employees have been dismissed or there has been selective re-employment within three months of the dismissal:

- *Faust v Power Packing* (1983);

- *Coates v Modern Methods* (1982).

The Employment Relations Act 1999 adds that dismissal of those undertaking industrial action is automatically unfair if dismissal occurs within eight weeks of the commencement of participation in the action.

Management prerogatives were progressively widened on this point throughout the 1980s and early 1990s. It should be noted that there is no longer any protection for unofficial strikes, even when colleagues have been selectively re-engaged:

- *Hindle Gears v McGinty* (1985).

Dismissal is automatically fair even though the employers have provoked the action.

The aim behind the law was to prevent tribunals' being concerned with the merits of industrial disputes, but the amendments to the law have undermined this purpose.

National security is an automatically fair reason.

Industrial pressure

Tribunals must not, in unfair dismissal claims, take into consideration industrial pressure such as a strike. However, employees and employers may join the party organising the pressure, and that party may be ordered to pay the compensation:

- *Colwyn BC v Dutton* (1980).

CHAPTER 12

REDUNDANCY PAYMENTS
AND UNFAIR DISMISSAL REMEDIES

12.1 Coverage

This chapter deals with the remedy where employees are made statutorily redundant or are unfairly dismissed. The law is found in the Employment Rights Act (ERA) 1996. An employee cannot get both a redundancy payment and a basic award for unfair dismissal unless the dismissal was unfair because it was for an inadmissible reason.

12.2 Redundancy payments

These are calculated according to a set formula which is dependent on the employee's normal working hours and remuneration. The Employment Relations Act 1999 links the maximum week's pay to the retail prices index.

12.2.1 Calculation

Redundancy payments are calculated according to a statutory formula (s 162 of the ERA 1996): the week's pay up to £220 x the number of years of continuous employment to a maximum of 20 x a multiplier based on the age of the employee, that multiplier being 1.5 for each full year the employee is over 41, 1 for each year between 22 and 40 and 6.5 for each year between 18 and 21, and only the best 20 years are counted. Examples:

- Assume the employee is 63, earns £275 per week and has worked continuously for the employers for 37 years. Only 20 years are counted. Work backwards 20 years from 63. Therefore, the years between the ages of 43 and 63 count. For years over 41, the multiplier is 1.5. Only £220 out of the £275 count. The calculation is £220 x 20 x 1.5 = £6,600. As can be seen, £220, 1.5 and 20 are the maximum amounts under statute; accordingly, £6,600 is the maximum redundancy payment. There is no deduction for contributory fault.

- Assume the employee is aged 45 and is earning £185 per week. She has been working continuously for the employers for 10 years. She has worked four full years over the age of 41; assume she has worked six full ones below 41. Therefore, the sum is £185 x 4 x 1.5 plus £185 x 6 x 1. Note that the fact that she is over 41 does *not* mean that her pay up to the maximum is multiplied by 1.5. It is the years over 41 which count.

It should be noted that, unlike when calculating the basic award for unfair dismissal, years of employment under 18 do not count for redundancy payments. If the employee is aged 64, one 12th is deducted from the payment for each month the employee is over 64. (No claim is possible if the employee is over the normal retiring age if it is lower than 65; if there is no such age, the limit is 65.) If the employers give the employee a redundancy payment without an employment tribunal being involved, they must give him a written statement demonstrating how they calculated the amount. If no statement is given, the employee may request one in writing, specifying a date, at least one week from the date of the letter, by which the employers must reply.

The maximum week's pay and the maximum total seem small in modern conditions, especially in the light of the fact that only employees with 20 or more years' continuous employment who are over the age of 41 and earning £220 can obtain the maximum. The Law Society estimated in 1995 that the figure should be £500 per week if it was to be increased in line with inflation. Dismissal for reason of redundancy remains quite a cheap option for employers.

12.2.2 Week's pay

The calculation of the week's pay is stated in the ERA 1996. Where the express or implied terms of the contract of employment (and not practice unless there has been a contractual variation) determine the number or minimum number of hours, the employee is said to have normal working hours. The amount of week's pay is dependent in this instance on the normal working hours. If an employee works 37 hours per week, the week's pay is that remuneration for those hours. Overtime causes problems. What happens if the employee receives basic pay for 37 hours but extra pay for overtime? The principal authority is *Tarmac Roadstone Holdings Ltd v Peacock* (1973). The court held that only if overtime was compulsory on *both* sides was it to be counted towards the week's pay. An employee was paid a basic wage for 40 hours, but he regularly worked an extra 17 hours overtime per week. He had to do the overtime if offered, but the employers did not contractually have to offer it. Therefore, overtime was not compulsory on both sides and was not counted when calculating the week's pay. That pay was based on the 40 hours he was contractually obliged to do. By the ERA 1996, his 'week's pay' was less than he received as pay per week; that is, a statutory definition, not a common sense definition, applies. The effect is to reduce the redundancy payment to which an employee would otherwise be entitled.

12.2.3 Non-time workers

With regard to piece workers, 'week's pay' is calculated by reference to the normal hours of work multiplied by the average hourly rate of pay (excluding overtime payments) in the 12 weeks preceding the last complete week before the calculation date. A similar calculation is made for shift workers (whose hours may also need to be averaged) and those who have no normal working hours, such as double glazing salespeople and lecturers. One point of interest with regard to the categories of employees mentioned in this paragraph is that the 12 week period must consist of weeks in which the employee earned money. The effect can be dramatic. If a firm is going to make workers redundant, it may well reduce pay towards the date of dismissal, for example, a piece worker may find that there are fewer pieces to be made. Yet the week's pay is calculated according to the average of the last 12 weeks of work. If no work is performed, with the result that no remuneration is earned, that week is not counted and the week immediately preceding the 12 is substituted. If the employee has worked for fewer than 12 weeks with the present employers, then, if continuity of employment is preserved with his previous employers, weeks worked for the latter count.

12.2.4 Remuneration

'Remuneration' in s 224 includes contractual bonuses and commission, including incentive bonuses (see *British Coal Corp v Cheesbrough* (1990)). If bonuses are annual payments, a proportionate amount is included in the week's pay. *Ex gratia* bonuses such as Christmas bonuses are excluded (*Skillen v Eastwoods Froy Ltd* (1967)). Expenses are included if the sum paid towards them by the employers exceeds the amount spent by the employee (*S & U Stores Ltd v Wilkes* (1974)), but note that this situation may be a fraud on the Inland Revenue, rendering the contract illegal and void. Compulsory service charges which are divided up among staff constitute pay (*Tsoukka v Potomac Restaurants Ltd* (1968)) but tips paid by the customer direct to the employee are not, because they are not payments from the employers (*Palmanor Ltd v Cedron* (1978)). The value of payments in kind, for example, a company car and free lodgings, are not included (*S & U Stores* (above)). Holiday pay is excluded because its payment relates to remuneration during employment, not to payment during normal *working* hours. State benefits are excluded.

12.2.5 Week ending

Pay means gross pay. The 'week' ends on a Saturday unless pay is calculated weekly, in which case the week ends on the day when the employee is paid.

12.2.6 Calculation date

Which week's pay is the relevant one is determined by looking at the 'calculation date' as defined in s 225. If the employers dismissed with insufficient contractual notice, it is the date on which the statutory minimum period of notice would have expired (that is, s 86 of the ERA 1996 applies: see

Chapter 7). This provision ensures that pay rises which take effect after dismissal but before the statutory period of notice has elapsed are taken into account.

12.3 Unfair dismissal

Unlike redundancy payments, unfair dismissal need not be redressed by money. There is the possibility that the ex-employee may get his job back.

12.3.1 Possible remedies

In a straightforward unfair dismissal claim, there are three possible remedies: reinstatement, re-engagement and compensation. The employment tribunal must consider the remedies in that order, that is, reinstatement is meant to be the primary remedy. The remedies are not cumulative. The successful claimant receives only one remedy, not a medley of them. By s 112(2) of the ERA 1996, the tribunal has the duty of explaining what reinstatement and re-engagement are and, even if the applicant is legally represented, it must ask whether the applicant wishes the tribunal to order one of these remedies. Reinstatement and re-engagement are together sometimes called re-employment. Here, that term will be used to cover both orders.

If re-employment is ordered, continuity is preserved and the weeks between dismissal and order count. The law is laid down in the Employment Protection (Continuity of Employment) Regulations 1993 (SI 1993/2165), which apply where the employment tribunal has ordered re-employment and where an ACAS conciliation officer has blessed a settlement between the parties.

Conciliation settlements under the Trade Union Reform and Employment Rights Act (TURERA) 1993 also preserve continuity. If there is no order or ACAS intervention, continuity is, it seems, preserved by s 212 of the ERA 1996 (*Ingram v Foxon* (1984)) (see 8.5.7 and 8.5.15, above). Contributory fault does not necessarily preclude an order to re-employ.

12.3.2 Reinstatement

A tribunal may order the employers to reinstate the employee. Reinstatement means that the employee is restored to his pre-dismissal job. All the benefits of that job are retained (for example, pension, holiday entitlement, length of service and pay including increments and sick pay). He is treated as not having been dismissed (s 114(1)). Accordingly, benefits, such as pay increases, which would have been received had there been no dismissal, are given to the employee. There is no statutory maximum. Another consequence is that, since the employee is treated as not having been dismissed, he has to relinquish any money he did receive from his employers, such as an *ex gratia* payment. Any money he received from new employers during the period between dismissal and reinstatement is deducted.

12.3.3 Unreasonable refusal

If the employers are ready to reinstate but the employee refuses the offer unreasonably, the basic award may be reduced (s 122(1)). An offer must be made: inviting the ex-employee to discuss the situation is insufficient.

12.3.4 Re-engagement

An order for re-engagement is one by which the employee is placed into 'employment comparable to that from which he was dismissed or other suitable employment', the terms so far as reasonably practicable being as favourable to him as if he had been reinstated (s 115(1)). Re-engagement may be with a successive or associated employer. As with reinstatement, rights are preserved. The employment tribunal must specify the name of the employers; the nature of employment; the rate of pay; any arrears of pay (there is no maximum limit); any right which must be restored to the employee, including any pension and seniority rights; and the date by which the employers must comply with the order. Without these specifications, the order is invalid.

Contributory fault can be taken into account in the terms of the order. There is no power to order re-engagement on better terms and conditions than the employee would have had, had he been reinstated. In *Rank Xerox (UK) Ltd v Stryczek* (1995), the EAT held that an employment tribunal had been wrong to order re-engagement in a job with a company car and better pay than the one the employee had been dismissed from. If there is only one vacant job, the order can direct the employers to engage the employee in this job. Since the order puts the employee into the position he would have been in had he not been dismissed, he is awarded pay (including improvements in terms) he lost out on between dismissal and re-engagement (*City and Hackney HA v Crisp* (1990)). There is no duty to mitigate.

12.3.5 Re-employment: procedure (s 116 of the ERA 1996)

The employment tribunal first inquires whether the claimant wishes to be re-employed. If so, it determines whether to order reinstatement; if it decides that it will not, it determines whether to order re-engagement. In considering either order, the employment tribunal must consider (the first of these would be better phrased as a prerequisite, because no tribunal will order re-employment contrary to the applicant's wishes):

- the wishes of the claimant (for example, he may not want to be re-employed because of a personality clash), including whether reinstatement or re-engagement is desired;

- the practicability of re-employment; and

- whether he caused or contributed to the dismissal: if he did, the employment tribunal must inquire whether it is 'just' to order re-employment. Contributory fault is the same concept as that used in awards of compensation for unfair dismissal (see below). Therefore, the fact that the employee contributed to a large degree can preclude reinstatement, but the employment tribunal may instead order re-engagement without full back-pay.

The tribunal is not restricted to considering these factors. A failure by an employment tribunal to follow this process does not render the order null and void, but the EAT can set aside the decision if there is a possibility of injustice (*Cowley v Manson Timber Ltd* (1995)). The court said in that case that any other ruling would be inconvenient.

12.3.6 Practicable

Discussion in the cases centres around whether it is practicable for the employers to reinstate. For example, it is not practicable in the normal run of cases to re-engage when trust between the parties has broken down (*Wood Group Heavy Industrial Turbines Ltd v Crossan* (1998)). 'Practicable' is quite a strong word. It does not mean 'expedient' (*Qualcast (Wolverhampton) Ltd v Ross* (1979)). Impracticability is not impossibility. In *Port of London Authority v Payne* (1994), the Court of Appeal held, in accordance with this proposition, that employers did not have to call for members of the workforce to take voluntary severance. The burden of proof is on the employers. In *Payne*, the court said that employment tribunals should take into account the commercial judgment of the management and that employers should not have to investigate 'every possible avenue which ingenuity might suggest'. It stressed that tribunals could not instruct employers how to run their business. The reference to 'commercial judgment' paves the way for the employers to win every case on the issue of practicability. Nevertheless, tribunals must use their experience and rely on common sense. The following factors have been held to make it impracticable to re-employ:

- opposition to re-employment from the workforce (*Coleman v Magnet Joinery Ltd* (1975)) (for example, re-employment would lead to a strike (*Langston v AUEW (No 2)* (1974));

- breakdown of a personal relationship, such as where the firm has few employees (*Enessy Co SA v Minoprio* (1978)). Lord McDonald in the Scottish EAT said that an employment tribunal should not force re-employment on small employers who were reluctant to take back the employee unless there was powerful evidence that the order would succeed;

- taking back the employee would mean the dismissal of another (*Freemans plc v Flynn* (1984)). There is no duty to create a vacancy.

It has been held to be impracticable to reinstate a caretaker who was known to be a member of the British National Party when he worked with ethnic minorities. It may also be impracticable if the employee would have been made redundant in the period between dismissal and re-employment had he still been employed. Unfitness is another reason, as is the fact that there would be insufficient work for the employee to do because he could no longer do part of his job because he had lost his driving licence. The lack of a vacancy does not make it impracticable to re-employ.

12.3.7 Permanent replacement

If the employers have taken on a permanent replacement, the employment tribunal may not take that situation into account when determining the practicability of the re-employment unless the employers can show that:

- it was not practicable to arrange for the dismissed employee's work to be done except by a permanent replacement (s 116(5)) (for example, a typist may easily be replaced but a computer programmer may be hard to replace); or
- the replacement was engaged after the lapse of a reasonable time, without the dismissed employee having contacted them to say that he wished to be re-employed, and it was no longer practicable to arrange for his work to be done except by the replacement (s 116(6)).

The effect is that it is easier for a small employer to rely on s 116(5) than a large one.

If the employers could defeat a claim for re-employment merely by engaging a permanent replacement, they could easily avoid having to take the dismissed employee back.

12.3.8 Practicability as defence

The issue of practicability in s 116(1) may be raised both when the employment tribunal is considering which remedy to award and when dealing with total non-compliance (see 12.3.9, below).

12.3.9 Additional award: sanction for non-compliance (s 117 of the ERA 1996)

If employers refuse to have the employee back, the employment tribunal must make an award of compensation in the normal way (considered in the next section) and may make an award of additional compensation, usually called an 'additional award' (s 117(3)). This award is between 26 and 52 weeks' pay and, since the Employment Relations Act 1999, applies in all cases. 'Week's pay' was defined above (see 12.2.2, above). The maximum week's pay is the same as that in respect of the basic award (at present, £220). Now that the special award is abolished, the additional award is 26–52 weeks' pay in all instances. The additional award is not tied to the loss suffered by the employee. It is a penal, deterrent remedy (*George v Beecham Group* (1977)). However, a failure to mitigate can be taken into account in determining the amount. The additional award will not be granted if the employers can prove that it was not practicable to comply with the order (s 117(4)). However, s 117(4) is disapplied where the dismissal was for an automatically unfair reason. This reference to practicability has been criticised for giving employers two bites of the cherry. They can raise it both pre- and post-order. It might be said that the second occasion gives the employers opportunity to raise matters which have arisen since the order, but it is not so restricted.

A possible way of reconciling the contentions of 'two bites' and 'only post-order', and one which has come to be accepted in the cases, is this: when considering whether to order re-employment, statute tells the employment tribunal to have regard to practicability, whereas, at the present stage, impracticability is a full defence. That is, at the first stage, the employment tribunal can potentially hold that the re-employment may be impracticable but still order it, whereas, under s 117, impracticability provides the employers with an excuse or justification for non-compliance with the order (*Timex Corp v Thomson* (1981)). An example of impracticability is where the employers would have to dismiss another employee to take the complainant back. The fact that the employers have lodged an appeal does not make it impracticable to comply.

12.3.10 Unreasonable prevention

The award of compensation which the tribunal must make is subject to a deduction if the employee has unreasonably prevented the order being complied with. The unreasonable prevention is treated as failure to mitigate (s 117(8)).

12.3.11 Partial compliance

If the employers comply only partly with the order, the tribunal must order such compensation as it thinks fit, having regard to the employee's loss. (Reinstatement on less favourable terms is treated as a total failure to comply and, in that event, the tribunal makes the additional award.) The statutory maximum may be exceeded 'to the extent necessary to enable the award fully to reflect the amount specified as payable under s 114(2)(a) or 115(2)(d) ...' (s 124(3), as inserted by s 30(2) of TURERA 1993). Sections 114(2)(a) and 115(2)(d) relate to payments which the complainant might reasonably have expected to have, but for dismissal between the date of termination and re-employment. An example is non-contractual overtime which the applicant might reasonably have been expected to have earned. Accordingly, pay arrears and the loss of other benefits can be recompensed even if the normal statutory maximum is exceeded. The aim is to put the employee into the position he would have been in had he not been dismissed.

12.3.12 No specific performance

It should be noted that employment tribunals have no jurisdiction to put the employee physically back into his workplace. The sanction for non-compliance is monetary. Specific enforcement is not an option. Moreover, the 'additional award' is just that – it is awarded on top of the basic and compensatory awards.

12.3.13 Critique

Reinstatement is sometimes called 'the lost remedy' (see Dickens *et al* (1981) 10 ILJ 160). Since the inception of unfair dismissal, it has been seen as the primary remedy: the employment tribunal is instructed to consider it first. Since 1975, the tribunal has been empowered to order the employers to reinstate (before then, re-employment could only be recommended). Nevertheless, the proportion of employees who actually get their job or a similar one back through the tribunal system is low, at present about 1% of cases heard. This figure is substantially below that obtained outside the tribunal system through arbitration and mediation, which often involve trade unions, and is below that of the USA.

12.3.14 Primary remedy's failure

The following reasons have been suggested for the low rate of re-employment:

- tribunals have not insisted on re-employment being impracticable (see Lewis (1982) 45 MLR 384);

- legalism in tribunals has led to the importation of concepts from the common law. The common law set its face against the specific enforcement of contracts of personal service. Since the chair is a lawyer and the parties are often represented by lawyers, employment tribunal proceedings may be imbued with common law principles. The employment tribunal is searching, it is said, for an agreement to reinstate;

- employees may not wish to be re-employed. They may fear victimisation. In addition, there was, until 1993, no remedy for dismissal on grounds of assertion of statutory rights (see s 104 of the ERA 1996); the employee had to make another (normal) unfair dismissal claim. One reason for not wanting re-employment might be that the employee has a new job.

These reasons do explain a good part of the failure of re-instatement to fulfil expectations that it would be the primary remedy. Nevertheless, it is suggested that there should be little problem in re-employing workers in large firms and employers would not find their authority undermined substantially by taking employees back when they have been unfairly dismissed. It might also be said that the remedy will be more correlative with the right than is presently the case.

12.3.15 Compensation

If neither reinstatement nor re-engagement is ordered, the employment tribunal considers the award of compensation. The Employment Relations Act 1999 links the maxima to the retail prices index. In a normal unfair dismissal case, both a basic and a compensatory award are granted (s 118(1)). The basic award may still be awarded even though nothing is given as the compensatory award. The median award for these in 1992–93 was £2,616. In 1993–94, it was £2,773, £3,289 in 1994–95 and £2,499 in 1995–96. Part of the reason for this low figure is that many of those unfairly dismissed lose their jobs early in their career and, in any case, they are on low pay. There may be an extra 'additional award', which was considered above.

12.3.16 Basic award: calculation (s 119)

This award is calculated in the same way as a redundancy payment, except that full years of continuous employment under the age of 18 count (from the age of 16). As with redundancy payments, there is a one 12th deduction for each month the employee is over 64. The basic award is at least a minimum figure (currently £2,900) if dismissal was for an inadmissible reason. For the minimum in trade union cases, see 12.3.18, below. A basic award is payable even though the employee has not lost money through being dismissed. It remains payable even though there is no compensatory award granted by the tribunal.

12.3.17 Deductions

By s 122(2) of the ERA 1996, misconduct which was uncovered after dismissal may be used to reduce the basic award (though it cannot be used to make an unfair dismissal fair: *W Devis & Sons Ltd v Atkins* (1977)). The employment tribunal may make a 100% deduction in respect of an after-discovered reason.

The basis on which the statute directs the employment tribunal to make a percentage deduction is the 'just and equitable' one; that is, the award is reduced only if it is just and equitable so to do. The effect is that there is no need to show that the misconduct caused or contributed to the dismissal (cf compensatory awards, 12.3.20, below). Neither this deduction nor the following one applies if the dismissal was for redundancy (s 122(3)), unless the dismissal was unfair on grounds of selection for redundancy for trade union reasons or because the employee was a safety representative, a representative for the purpose of consultation or a trustee of an occupational pension scheme.

Where the employers dismiss two employees, not knowing which stole money from them, no deduction is made for contributory fault, for it has not been proved that the individual employee contributed to his dismissal.

If the employee unreasonably refuses an offer of reinstatement, this award may be reduced by a just and equitable amount (s 122(1)). It will not be reduced where the employee thought that he would be victimised if he went back to his old job. The award is not reduced by failure to accept an offer of re-engagement.

Redundancy pay is deducted (s 122(4)), whether the payment was under the State scheme detailed in Chapter 9 or under a private one (see *Boorman v Allmakes Ltd* (1995)), unless the dismissal was for an inadmissible reason. If the basic award is totally extinguished by this deduction, the excess is deducted from the compensatory award.

If the employers make an *ex gratia* payment to compensate the employee for losing his right, that sum may (but need not) be set off against the basic and compensatory awards. The presumption is in favour of a set off.

It should be noted that there is no power to reduce the basic award where the applicant has not mitigated his loss (*Lock v Connell Estate Agents* (1994)). The EAT held in *Chamberlain Products Ltd v Patel* (1996) that the basic award is not to be reduced because the employers could have dismissed anyway, had they followed a fair procedure. Therefore, the deduction for contributory fault must not be lumped together with this deduction to form one global percentage reduction.

12.3.18 Particular provisions

Where the dismissal is unfair because the employee was dismissed on trade union grounds (s 152) or was selected for redundancy on trade union grounds (s 153), the basic award is one of not less than £2,770, subject to a deduction for contributory fault in relation to the s 153 reason (s 156(1) and (2) of the Trade Union and Labour Relations (Consolidation) Act (TULR(C)A) 1992. There is no deduction for any 'fault' in relation to being or not being a union member. What are trade union grounds is discussed in Chapter 11.

There is a minimum sum which applies to dismissal on health and safety grounds, with the normal deduction for contributory fault.

The maximum basic award is two weeks' pay where the employee has been made redundant and unreasonably refuses an offer to renew the contract or one of suitable alternative employment or unreasonably terminates the contract during the trial period (s 121). 'Week's pay' is defined above, 12.2.2.

12.3.19 Comment

It is sometimes said that the basic award represents compensation for the loss of an employee's proprietary rights in his job. Certainly, the sum is not based on actual economic loss, but it is a small amount to pay to buy out proprietary rights and, since 1980, there has been no irreducible minimum below which the award may not go.

12.3.20 Compensatory award

Unlike the basic award, the compensatory award is determined by reference to what the employee lost. That sum is based on net pay and is not limited by a maximum amount of weekly pay. It is subject to a statutory maximum, which is currently £50,000. The additional award is extra to this financial limit. The scheme for calculating the compensatory award is a statutory one and additions and deductions must not be made unless permitted by the statute. The employee has to demonstrate loss (*Adda International Ltd v Curcio* (1976)). However, the EAT has said that the employment tribunal should not hide behind the burden of proof when determining loss (*Barley v Amey Roadstone Corp Ltd (No 2)* (1978)). The amount need not be as scrupulously proved as it is in a High Court action for personal injuries. If the loss is nothing, a nil compensatory award is given. If, for example, a dismissal is unfair because of lack of consultation but the employee would have been dismissed anyway had there been consultation, the remedy is just for the length of time consultation would have taken.

The Employment Rights (Dispute Resolution) Act 1998 provides: (1) if an employee is prevented from using an appeals procedure, a supplementary award of up to two weeks' pay is awarded; and (2) if the employee refuses to go through this procedure, a deduction of a similar sum may be made.

12.3.21 Just and equitable

The fundamental rule of compensatory awards (including the amount of loss) is laid down in s 123(1):

> ... the amount of the compensatory award shall be such amount as the tribunal considers just and equitable in all the circumstances, having regard to the loss

> sustained by the complainant in consequence of the dismissal in so far as that loss is attributable to action taken by the employer.

A recent Court of Appeal authority on s 123(1) is *Jones v Lingfield Leisure plc* (1999). A duty manager at a fitness centre was dismissed. She had been permitted to act as a self-employed personal trainer. Losing her managerial job meant that she also lost her job as trainer. The court held that, on the facts, no compensation could be awarded for the loss of her earnings as a self-employed person.

Tribunals are instructed to 'have regard' to the loss. They are not instructed to award the employee compensation for loss. Accordingly, they have discretion in calculating compensation (*Cox v Camden LBC* (1996)). Furthermore, s 123(1) is a statutory code for calculating compensation. Tribunals are not bound by common law authorities on quantum. This is different from racial and sexual discrimination, which are deemed to be statutory torts. Therefore, tort concepts such as remoteness are irrelevant (*Leonard v Strathclyde Buses Ltd* (1998)). It is 'just and equitable' to deduct half the invalidity benefit the employee receives from the compensatory award (*Rubenstein v McGloughlin* (1996)). There is, however, another authority requiring the whole of this benefit to be deducted, and yet other cases have decided that none should be deducted! We await a Court of Appeal ruling.

Behaviour subsequent to dismissal is not taken into account when determining what is just and equitable. Therefore, breach of the implied duty of confidentiality after termination of employment is irrelevant (*Soros v Davison* (1994)).

The employee who suffers no loss receives no compensation: it is not unjust to award a nil payment. The assessment is:

> ... often a difficult question, but one which the industrial tribunal in their capacity as an industrial jury are well suited to answer, and in respect of which they will not go wrong if they remember that what they are trying to do is to assess the loss suffered by the claimant, and not to punish the employer for his failure in industrial relations [*British United Shoe Machinery Co Ltd v Clarke* (1978)].

On the facts, no compensation was given because, even if there had been consultation, the employee would have been made redundant. The EAT held that, where a dismissal for redundancy was unfair because of a failure to consult and it was uncertain whether he would or would not have been retained if consultation had taken place, the employment tribunal should assess the probability of his being retained as a percentage and then use that percentage to determine the loss attributable to the employers within s 123(1) (*Dunlop Ltd v Farrell* (1993)). Where, however, unfairness resides not in procedural unfairness but in substance (in this case, the employers had artificially narrowed the pool from which to select for redundancy), the employment tribunal should not reduce the award in such a way (*Steel Stockholders (Birmingham) Ltd v Kirkwood* (1993) (Scottish EAT)). In other words, one does not now inquire whether the employee would have been selected in any event.

It must be said that the line between procedure and substance is not pellucid. The Court of Appeal repudiated the distinction in *O'Dea v ISC Chemicals Ltd* (1996), though the Court of Session has not done so. It has also been held that no deduction should be made from the compensatory award when the employers' unfairness results from their misconduct as opposed to nonfeasance (*Boulton & Paul Ltd v Arnold* (1994)). As criminal lawyers know, the line between commission and omission is not clear.

12.3.22 Statutory maximum

The maximum is applied only after deductions (considered below, 12.3.30) have been made (*Walter Braund (London) Ltd v Murray* (1991)).

12.3.23 *Norton Tool*

When assessing compensation, employment tribunals must not simply award a global sum but must refer to heads of compensation. In *Norton Tool Co Ltd v Tewson* (1973), the court laid down several heads. The sum must recompense the employee, not penalise the employers. It is for the employee to prove the loss. Deductions made under the principle in *Polkey v AE Dayton Services Ltd* (1988) that the employee would have been dismissed anyway, despite her being unfairly dismissed, are made at the first stage of calculating compensation, the 'just and equitable' stage, and deductions for contributory fault and redundancy payments above the statutory minimum are made when the *Polkey* deduction has been made (*Cox v Camden LBC* (1996)). The *Polkey* deduction is made from the loss after calculating what the loss was. In other words, this part of the calculation goes to 'just and equitable', not to 'loss'. It is for the employers to adduce evidence to demonstrate that their failure to take the correct procedural steps was reasonable so that the *Polkey* deduction should be made. A deduction of 100% can be made when applying *Polkey*. An investigation or hearing may be futile.

12.3.24 Loss to hearing date

The employment tribunal looks at the complainant's loss of earnings, including profit-related pay and increases in pay, net of tax and national insurance up to the time of the hearing. This sum is based on the actual loss, not on 'week's pay' as defined above. Accordingly, overtime pay and tips are included. Money expended on training and setting up a business can be recompensed under this head. If there is a dispute as to the correct remuneration, the issue is decided by the tribunal even though the dispute is a contractual one. Having determined the loss, the tribunal deducts money earned elsewhere, that is, mitigation applies. (It has been said that, if the employee obtains employment before the hearing but then loses it, compensation should cover only the period between the dismissal and the fresh job (*Courtaulds Northern Spinning Ltd v Moosa* (1984)), provided that the new employment is better paid than the old (*Fentiman v Fluid Engineering Products Ltd* (1991)). Jobs known to be temporary do not count for this purpose but pay from them is deducted.) If the pay is the same or less, the loss under this head runs to the date of the hearing, with deduction for pay from the new employers (*Ging v Ellward (Lancs) Ltd* (1978)). However, if the employee earns money from a source other than his employers during the notice period, that sum will not be deducted (*TBA Industrial Products Ltd v Locke* (1984)). This rule was said to be in accord with good industrial relations practice.

In a wrongful dismissal action, both mitigation and a failure to mitigate reduce the award; in unfair dismissal, a failure to mitigate results in a deduction but not mitigation itself. This rule is inconsistent with the statute, which obliges the tribunal to apply to unfair dismissal compensation the same rule on mitigation as applies to common law actions. (If, however, the employee substantially exceeds his pay from the employers, that sum is deducted, for that mitigation is said to be good industrial practice.) Contrariwise, if the employers dismiss with pay in lieu of notice, that sum is deducted (*Addison v Babcock FATA Ltd* (1987)). *Ex gratia* payments on unfair dismissal are deducted (*Horizon Holidays Ltd v Grassi* (1987)), unless the payment would have been given to the employee had the dismissal been fair (*Roadchef Ltd v Hastings* (1988)). The law on payments during the notice period and *ex gratia* payments cannot be said to be settled (see, also, 12.3.33, below).

12.3.25 Expenses and perks

Expenses and perks are covered as losses reasonably incurred as a result of dismissal, for example, removal expenses and, in the case of a dismissed university lecturer, the cost of buying the *Times Higher Education Supplement* (s 123(2)). Losses of contractual benefits such as membership of a private health insurance scheme, a low interest mortgage, subsidised meals, a company car if private use was allowed and travel allowances are included. Unfortunately for employees, legal expenses are not covered by this head.

12.3.26 Future loss

The employment tribunal chooses a multiplier based on the amount of time after the date of hearing that the particular employee's losses may continue. There is no maximum length of time. For example, the fact that the dismissal leads to depression and anxiety can be taken into account by the tribunal in determining how long the employee would take to get back into work (*Devine v Designer Flowers Wholesale Florist Sundries Ltd* (1993)). The cut off point is when the illness is no longer attributable to the employers' action, for, after that date, it is no longer just and equitable to award compensation. Similarly, the tribunal can take into account the fact that the employee is unlikely to get another job because he is near retirement age or is a single parent with small children. If the employment tribunal finds that the employee would have stayed in the job after the normal retiring age, compensation can extend to that extra period. This multiplier (refer to tort law, where the same principle applies) is affected by any relevant factors such as turnover of staff and whether the employee might have left the labour market, whether there were suitable job opportunities in the vicinity and whether work is seasonal in nature (as in a seaside resort). It is possible, having regard to such factors, for an employment tribunal to find that the former employee will never work again.

The multiplier is, as in the previous head, affected by perks and overtime pay during the estimated period of future loss (see above). If the employee who was unfairly dismissed would have been dismissed anyway because, for example, redundancies took place shortly after dismissal, the sum awarded will be low. The tribunal is under an obligation to explain how it reached the multiplier (*Qualcast (Wolverhampton) Ltd v Ross* (1979)). Except for the statutory maximum, there is no limit on the sum which can be awarded under this head. For example, in *Morganite Electrical Carbon Ltd v Donne* (1988), the EAT held that future loss covering 82 weeks was not wrong or perverse. The EAT rejected an argument that, at the very most, six to 12 months' loss should be compensated.

If the employee would find it more difficult than an average employee to obtain work, the sum will be increased. An example which has occurred is where the employee had defective vision. When calculating both losses, no account is taken of insurance moneys paid on termination. Similarly, if the unemployment rate is high, the tribunal is entitled to take into account the fact that the employee may never work again.

12.3.27 Accelerated receipt

As with wrongful dismissal, there may be a deduction for accelerated receipt in respect of this head of compensation.

12.3.28 Accrued rights

Accrued rights covers such matters as the loss of the period of continuous employment. The employee has to start building up the length of service necessary to qualify for rights such as unfair dismissal. Similarly, the employee will have to build up notice periods. Normally, half the statutory entitlement is given. It is normal practice to award a nominal sum of £100–200 under this head for loss of the chance to claim a remedy for unfair dismissal (*SH Muffett Ltd v Head* (1987)). However, there is no rule stating that tribunals must always award this sum (*Harvey v Institute of the Motor Industry (No 2)* (1995)). Nothing will be awarded if the loss was too remote. Loss of pension rights are also recompensed, often by reference to a report prepared by the Government Actuary's Department which sets out various ways of assessing loss.

12.3.29 Manner of dismissal

Compensation may be awarded for the way in which the employee was dismissed if he lost (some of) his employability as a result (*Vaughan v Weighpack Ltd* (1974)). No award is, however, made for distress or demotivation. The law was summed up in *Norton Tool*: 'Loss does not include injury to pride or feelings.' No sum is added if the employers have behaved in a particularly blameworthy manner.

12.3.30 Deductions

Even if the loss has been substantial, little or no compensation may be awarded if it would be unjust or inequitable to award a figure which truly compensates the employee. An example of a deduction is a contractual or *ex gratia* redundancy payment which is higher than the statutory one. According to the Court of Appeal in *Digital Equipment Co Ltd v Clements (No 2)* (1998), that sum should be deducted in full from the compensatory award before making the deduction in respect of the chance that the employee would be dismissed anyway, had the dismissal not been procedurally unfair (the '*Polkey*' deduction). The law on the order of deductions is complex and ever changing. Some sums, such as housing benefit, are not deducted (*Savage v Saxena* (1998)). It should be noted that the deduction under *Polkey* applies to the compensatory award but not to the basic award.

12.3.31 Contributory fault

Once the employment tribunal has determined the amount of compensation available by adding together moneys due under the *Norton Tool v Tewson* heads of compensation, it may deduct part or the whole, that is, 100%, of that sum for any action of the employee which caused or contributed to his dismissal. Tribunals should take a common sense view in deciding whether the employee did cause or contribute to the dismissal. The standard of proof is on the balance of probabilities. Tribunals have been deducting a percentage reduction based on the employee's fault. It may be, however, that s 123(6) should be read as being restricted to factual causation: but for the employee's behaviour, would he still be employed? Did his conduct contribute to his dismissal?

The proportion is determined on the 'just and equitable' basis: 100% can be deducted if the employee was entirely to blame for the dismissal. If there is a deduction under the general principle in s 123(1) (for example, because the applicant's employment would have ceased anyway shortly after the date on which he was unfairly dismissed), the amount of that deduction should be taken into account when calculating contributory fault compensation under s 123(6) (*Rao v Civil Aviation Authority* (1994)). The Court of Appeal held in that case that the s 123(6) deduction should be made before the s 123(1) one because a deduction for fault may affect what it is just and equitable under s 123(1). Accordingly, a deduction for contributory fault is made before any deduction under the 'just and equitable' ground. There have been conflicting decisions, but it seems that, if there is contributory fault, the basic and compensatory awards need not be reduced by the same percentage, though the EAT thought in *RSPCA v Cruden* (1986) that a difference would be justifiable only in exceptional circumstances.

The most recent authority is *Charles Robertson (Developments) Ltd v White* (1995). With regard to the basic award, s 122(2) permits a just and equitable reduction on account of the applicant's conduct. That conduct need not have caused or contributed to the dismissal. In respect of the compensatory award, however, s 123(6) is restricted to conduct which caused or contributed to the dismissal. The EAT upheld an employment tribunal's decision to reduce the compensatory award by 100% on the ground that the employees, by stealing a small amount of sweets, had caused their dismissal, but reduced the basic award by only 50% because of the employers' failure to adopt a fair procedure on dismissal. The Court of Appeal said that the effect of the law in *Rao*, above, may be that different percentages may occur, for 'the deduction which is just and equitable under s 122(2) is not the same as that which is just and equitable under s 123(6)'.

The employment tribunal looks at the proportion with a broad brush approach, considering all the circumstances. There are, on this approach, four categories: (1) the employee is solely to blame; (2) he is largely to blame; (3) both parties were equally at fault; (4) the employee was at fault but to a lesser degree than the employers. Examples from the cases include coming back drunk after a Christmas lunch; failing to inform the employers why the employee had been absent; putting a body into the wrong coffin; and walking out of a meeting called to discuss contractual issues.

One point of interpretation should be noted. 'Fault' is necessary. Therefore, if the employee was not at fault, there is no contributory fault. *Morrish v Henlys (Folkestone) Ltd* (1973) was mentioned in Chapter 4. The employee was told to falsify accounts. This order was unlawful. Accordingly, he did not cause or contribute to his dismissal when he refused to 'cook the books'. Another example is that, when an employee is dismissed during an official strike, then, in cases where the employment tribunal has jurisdiction to hear the application (see Chapter 11), participation in the action is not contributory fault. If it were, so holding would defeat the purpose of the provision (*Courtaulds Northern Spinning Ltd v Moosa* (1984), approved by the House of Lords in *Tracey v Crosville Wales Ltd (No 2)* (1997)). However, 'individual blameworthy conduct additional to or separate from the mere act of participation in industrial action' constitutes contributory fault. 'Fault' also covers incapability to do the job where the employee could have put it right (*Sutton and Gates (Luton) Ltd v Boxall* (1979)), situations where the employee is not in breach of contract (*Nelson v BBC (No 2)* (1979)) and inciting industrial action.

In *Nelson*, the Court of Appeal said that employee's conduct was to be considered if it was foolish, bloody-minded or perverse, but it was not to be taken into account where the employee was merely sticking to his legal rights. Brandon LJ looked for blameworthy conduct. Employment tribunals must consider only the fault which led to the dismissal and not any other faults of the employee (*Hutchinson v Enfield Rolling Mills Ltd* (1981)). There can be contributory fault even though the dismissal was a constructive one (*Polentarutti v Autokraft Ltd* (1991)), though it is sometimes said that only exceptionally can a deduction be made in this situation. Other examples of blameworthy conduct taken from the cases are going on holiday without permission, establishing a competing business and having a bad attendance record.

12.3.32 After-discovered reason

In an after-discovered reason case (the *Devis v Atkins* scenario), the contributory fault provision does not apply because the employee's behaviour did not cause or contribute to the dismissal. Instead, the compensatory award is reduced on the grounds that the sum is given on the 'just and equitable' basis under s 123(1) (quoted above, 12.3.21). It has been argued that the House of Lords was incorrect to award nil compensation on the grounds that s 123(1) says that the employment tribunal shall award compensation, but that argument does not take into account the following words of the sub-section. It may be just and equitable to award nothing.

12.3.33 *Ex gratia* payment

If the employers make an *ex gratia* payment, this amount should be deducted from the compensatory award before the fault deduction.

12.3.34 Illness

It has been said that only rarely will ill health justify a deduction (*Slaughter v C Brewer & Sons Ltd* (1990)). An exception may be when the employee has persistently refused a medical examination or to obtain medical reports. Section 123(6) speaks of 'action of the complainant'. Is ill health 'action'? If, however, the sickness renders the employee incapable of working, there may be a deduction in accord with the general 'just and equitable' ground noted above, 12.3.21.

12.3.35 Mitigation (s 123(4))

The compensatory award may be reduced by the employee's failure to mitigate. Mitigation means the same as at common law (see 7.2.16, above, but see 12.3.24). The employee must take reasonable steps to find a new job. This will include going to a job centre, reading the trade press and joining an agency. The ex-employee may have to accept a job at a lower rate of pay. The onus of proof lies on the employers to disprove that the particular employee took reasonable steps (*Bessenden Properties Ltd v Corness* (1974)). A refusal to accept worse terms and conditions offered by the employers before dismissal is not a failure to mitigate. Where the offer is made post-dismissal, the terms of the offer are investigated in order to determine whether they were reasonable: since it was the employers who were at fault, the standard of reasonableness is not a high one.

It may be reasonable to refuse to return to the same job when the employee was sacked in a humiliating fashion. It has been held that to refuse an offer of reinstatement by one's employers is a failure to mitigate, because the duty to mitigate applies only after the termination of the contract. However, it was decided in *Seligman and Latz Ltd v McHugh* (1979) that non-use of a grievance procedure did not constitute a failure to mitigate. In *Lock v Connell Estate Agents* (1994), the EAT held that non-use of the internal appeals procedure did not constitute a failure to mitigate, for the applicant is not under a duty to make the defendants change their minds, though there are several contrary *dicta*. Not applying for another job before dismissal is irrelevant because, again, the duty arises only after dismissal. The sum involved in the mitigation calculation is determined by considering how long the employee would have been out of work if he had mitigated; it is not done by reducing the compensatory award by a percentage (*Smith, Kline and French Laboratories Ltd v Coates* (1977)). A 100% deduction for failure to mitigate is rare (*Savage v Saxena* (1998)). Expenses such as moving house to get a new job in an attempt to mitigate are part of the employee's loss, for which he is compensated. Mitigation does not apply to the basic award except when the employee unreasonably refused re-employment (see above, 12.3.3).

12.3.36 Recoupment

By the Employment Protection (Recoupment of Jobseeker's Allowance and Income Support) Regulations (SI 1996/2349), the employment tribunal does not deduct from the sum payable for loss to the date of the hearing the amount paid in income support or unemployment benefit. The employment tribunal orders the employers not to pay over compensation to the employee for loss to the date of the hearing. The Department of Employment then serves on the employers what is called a 'recoupment notice', instructing them to pay the Department the sum of jobseeker's allowance/income support which the employee has received. The employers then pay over the remainder to the employee. The effect is that he gets only what has been lost financially. If the employee did not receive any such State benefit, the Regulations do not apply.

12.3.37 Disqualification

In relation to that part of the compensatory award which covers loss of future earnings, the employee is disqualified from jobseeker's allowance and income support over whatever period the employment tribunal decides to make the award.

12.3.38 Comment

Compensation in unfair dismissal cases tends to be on the low side. The median award is the equivalent of a few months' wages: it is not enough to deter dismissals.

12.3.39 Abolition of the special award

The special award was a sum paid in addition to the basic and compensatory award where the dismissal was for a trade union reason. It was abolished by the Employment Relations Act 1999.

12.3.40 Joinder

The union may be joined as defendant to the claim by either the employee or the employers. Compensation may be awarded against it (s 160). Similar provisions apply if dismissal is for an automatically unfair reason.

12.3.41 Detriment

Detriment (see Chapter 11) is recompensed under the terms of s 149 of TULR(C)A 1992 by the employment tribunal's having regard to the 'just and equitable' basis. There is no maximum. Compensation may be awarded for injured feelings (*Cleveland Ambulance NHS Trust v Blane* (1997)).

REDUNDANCY PAYMENTS
AND UNFAIR DISMISSAL REMEDIES

Redundancy payments

These are calculated according to a statutory formula dependent on length of continuous employment, age and week's pay. Pay is capped at £220 per week. 'Pay' excludes non-compulsory overtime:

* *Tarmac Roadstone v Peacock* (1973).9

Unfair dismissal

A tribunal may award reinstatement (same job), re-engagement (comparable job) or compensation. Compensation comprises the basic and compensatory award, the latter consisting of money for loss to the date of hearing, future loss, loss of accrued rights and compensation for the manner of dismissal. It is subject to deductions for contributory fault and failure to mitigate. An additional award is granted for failure to comply with a re-employment order:

practicability: *Coleman v Magnet Joinery* (1975);

compensatory award: *Norton Tool v Tewson* (1973);

future loss: *Morganite v Donne* (1988);

accrued rights: *Muffett v Head* (1987);

manner of dismissal: *Vaughan v Weighpack* (1974);

fault: *Sutton & Gates v Boxall* (1979);

mitigation: *Seligman v McHugh* (1979).

CHAPTER 13

TRANSFER OF UNDERTAKINGS

13.1 Introduction

The topic of transfer of undertakings has been reserved for separate consideration because of its complexity. It is a textbook case of the influence of the EC on domestic law, and because EC law in this area is ever changing, so, too, is English law. There was, furthermore, a conflict between the 1979–97 Government's aim of a flexible labour force and the EC's social policy, dating from the mid-1970s, of preserving employees' rights on the transfer of an undertaking.

13.1.1 'Layers' of law

To understand the topic, one must grasp that there are several overlapping 'layers' of law. If one layer is for some reason inapplicable, one should look at the next layer. This chapter deals with the common law, English statutory law pre-EC (which still exists) and EC law, both as part of English law as a result of the Transfer of Undertakings (Protection of Employment) Regulations (TUPE) 1981 (SI 1981/1794) and as a result of decisions of the European Court of Justice (ECJ). Unfortunately, the ECJ has not been consistent in its interpretation of EC law.

13.1.2 Flowchart

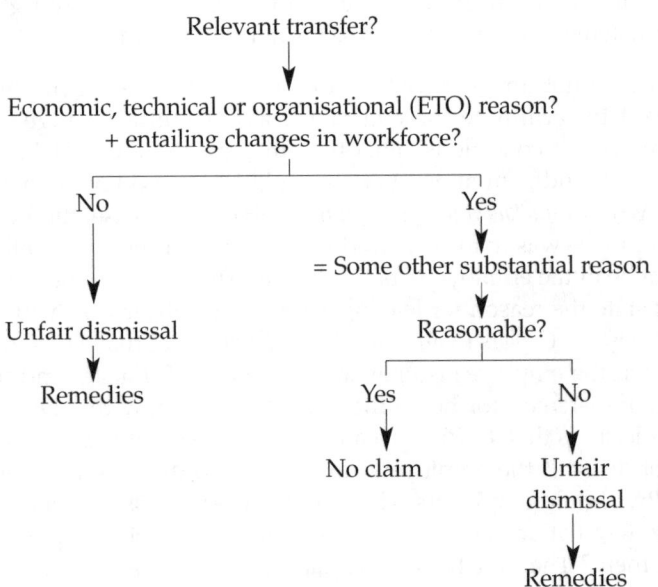

13.1.3 Changes to TUPE 1981

The reader should also be aware of the significant changes in this aspect of law made by the Trade Union Reform and Employment Rights Act (TURERA) 1993 and the Employment Relations Act 1999:

- TUPE was previously restricted to undertakings in the nature of a commercial venture. Section 33(2) abolishes that restriction. Non-profit making bodies and charities are now covered. Before these changes came into effect, teachers who were dismissed from two schools which were closed and then re-opened because one did not fall within TUPE had to rely on the Directive. Prior UK law was held to be in breach of the Acquired Rights Directive (77/187) in this respect in *Commission v UK* (1994). Claims can be made against the State for failure to implement directives fully when transposing them into national law.

- By s 33(4), new paras (4A) and (4B) are inserted into reg 5 of TUPE, with the effect that the rights and obligations are not transferred if the employee objects to being employed by the transferee employers (in other words, if he objects to the fact of transfer); instead, the contract is terminated, but the employee is not to be treated as being dismissed by the transferors. He has no right to claim unfair dismissal and redundancy payments. Employers have no duty to inform their workforce of this law. The surprising effect of this is that the employee is given a right to object, but if he exercises that right, he is dismissable and, if dismissed, he has no remedy. Regulation 5(4B) deems the employee not to have been dismissed. Therefore, the employee has no claim where his action is based on his having been dismissed, nor does he have any right against the transferees, because the contract is not transferred.

  One cannot imagine well advised employees exercising this option. The right to terminate the contract if a substantial change is made to an employee's conditions, other than that arising under TUPE, is unaffected. This amendment attempts to bring UK law into line with EC law as laid down in *Katsikas v Konstantinidis* (1993). In this case, the ECJ held that an employee was not transferred without his consent. After all, transfer may not be in the employee's best interests. The employee need not give notice or state the reason for leaving. Controversially, it was held by the EAT in *Photostatic Copiers (Southern) Ltd v Okuda* (1995) that TUPE does not apply when the employee is unaware of the fact of transfer and the identify of the transferees, for how otherwise does he know that he can object? The criticism is that TUPE normally acts for the employee's benefit, but it will not do so if the employers do not inform the employee of the transfer. Why should employers who play their cards close to their chest not have the Regulations applied to them when more open employers are subject to them? The EAT held in *Secretary of State for Industry v Cook* (1997) that

Photostatic Copiers should not be followed because it did not promote employment protection. Since the Regulations are to be read purposively (that is, to protect employees), this case (*Okuda*) is incorrect, a conclusion which is fortified by an understanding of one of the aims of the Regulations, the *automatic* transfer of obligations from the old to the new employers. The decision is also out of line with *Charlton v Charlton Thermosystems (Romsey) Ltd* (1995), where employees were transferred from a company to its owners when the company was dissolved without their knowing of the dissolution. Transfer takes place without the consent of the parties provided that the worker does not object, a principle irreconcilable with *Okuda*.

- There were other minor changes affecting the scope of TUPE: the non-transfer of occupational pension schemes and the duty to consult with unions (there are also changes to the procedure for handling redundancy found in the Trade Union and Labour Relations (Consolidation) Act (TULR(C)A) 1992, provisions which are in some respects parallel to consultation of a transfer).

- Section 38 of the Employment Relations Act 1999 permits the Secretary of State for Trade and Industry to make regulations which extend the application of the Acquired Rights Directive to situations where there is no transfer within the Directive. It is expected that this power will be used to make it clear that contracting out and transfer of employees of public bodies fall within the ambit of TUPE.

13.2 Laws

At law, an employee could not be compelled to serve a new master, and the new master was not compelled to continue to employ the employee (*Nokes v Doncaster Amalgamated Collieries Ltd* (1940)). The employee had no rights against the transferees, only against the transferors, who might in any case be insolvent. The implementation of EC law in the UK substantially ameliorated this position for employees.

13.2.1 Common law

Common law survives where statute, statutory instrument and EC law relating to transfers do not apply. Where those laws do not apply, the employee may well have a claim for a redundancy payment. A purchase of shares does not change the identity of the employer. The company remains the company.

13.2.2 Section 218

From 1963, Parliament intervened to protect employees in the event of the transfer of a business. The most important provision is s 218 of the ERA 1996. This law was discussed in Chapter 8.

13.2.3 The influence of EC law

Directive 77/187 (as amended by Directive 98/50) on the approximation of the laws of the Member States relating to the safeguarding of employees' rights in the event of transfer of undertakings, business or parts of businesses, was grudgingly enacted by the Government in TUPE. The aim of the Directive, as stated in its preamble, is the safeguarding of employees on a transfer. The Directive originated as a measure designed to give the EC a 'human face'. The restructuring of industry and commerce during the formation of the common market would hit workers unless they received protection. Social and political resistance to economic change was to be bought off by employment protection laws. The legal base was what was then Art 100 (now Art 94) of the EC Treaty. If TUPE falls short of EC standards in the Directive, an applicant can rely on the Directive where it is unconditional and sufficiently precise in an action against an emanation of the State (that is, the Directive is only vertically directly effective). An employee cannot rely on the Directive against a non-State employer. TUPE must also be construed in conformity with the Directive. For a general discussion of the effect of EC law, see Chapter 2.

The Directive is often known as the Acquired Rights Directive (ARD). Another name is the Business Transfers Directive. The Directive applies to 'employees'. TUPE defines an employee as 'any individual who works for another person, whether under a contract of service or apprenticeship or otherwise'. The definition is wider than that adopted generally in employment law, that is, a person working under a contract of service. The concept of 'employee' is for the Member State to determine; there is no Community-wide definition. The rationale for the non-uniform definition of employee is that the Directive effects only a partial harmonisation of EC law. If UK law does not match up to EC law, there are the usual claims by State employees and for the Government's failure to implement EC law fully. Section 38 of the Employment Relations Act 1999 gives the Secretary of State for Trade and Industry power to extend TUPE to situations where the ARD does not apply.

Article 137 of the EC Treaty (as inserted by the Treaty of Amsterdam) states that social policy directives should not impede the creation and development of small and medium enterprises. It may be difficult to reconcile this provision with the ARD's purpose of preserving employment rights on the transfer of an undertaking.

13.2.4 TUPE 1981

The basic thrust of TUPE can be summarised thus. In the event of a relevant transfer, the contract of employment is automatically transferred from the old to the new employers at the time of the transfer (therefore, if there was no contract of service but a contract for services, or if the employee is not part of the transferors' 'human stock', then the applicant was not employed by the transferors and neither the Directive nor the Regulations apply (*Gale v Northern General Hospital NHS Trust* (1994))); similarly, collective agreements are transferred. The intentions of the transferors and the transferees are irrelevant. The law is mandatory. A dismissal connected with a transfer is automatically unfair unless the employers have an economic, technical or organisational reason for dismissing. Controversially, it has been held that, where there has been no dismissal, the employees cannot even agree to a variation in their contractual terms where the variation is connected with a transfer that is taking place (*Wilson v St Helens BC* (1998) (HL)). Therefore, the old terms remain in effect. The condition would seem to block all contracting out, including compulsory competitive tendering, which seeks to cut costs by reducing wages. For trenchant criticism, see M Rubenstein [1996] IRLR 317 and 534.

Perhaps the principal criticism of TUPE is that it does not operate on a transfer by share purchase, which is the main method by which businesses are transferred in the UK. TUPE does not apply because the employers remain the same in formal terms, though the effect on employees may be the same as when the Regulations do apply: both the workers in the enterprise as it existed before the change of ownership and the workers in the purchasing firm may be adversely affected by the takeover. The old and the new owners may take completely different approaches to the treatment of their employees. The Regulations do not apply to employees who ordinarily work outside the UK (reg 13). An agreement to contract out of the Regulations is void (reg 12). The remedies given by the Regulations are exclusive. The High Court has no power to award an injunction (*Betts v Brintel Helicopters Ltd* (1996)).

13.2.5 Relevant transfer

TUPE applies only to transfers of an undertaking, or part of one, which take place by sale, other disposition or operation of law. Where only part of an undertaking is transferred and the employee used to work both in that part and in a part retained, the question of whether he was attached to one part or the other depends on whether he was assigned to the transferred part. Though the issue is disputed, he is assigned to the part where he forms part of the staffing structure (*Duncan Web Offset (Maidstone) Ltd v Cooper* (1995)). The issue is one of fact for the tribunal. The EAT emphasised that the tribunal should not be misled by the technicalities of the situation, but should take care not to deprive an employee of the protection of the Regulations.

The contrasting approach is to ask where the employee performed most of his activities. In the light of the EAT's reference to policy, these theories ought not to lead to different results. Accordingly, the fact that the employee worked in two parts of a building, one of which is shut down, does not preclude him from being transferred to a company which took over the part kept open. 'Other disposition' includes the contracting out of a service, such as the cleaning of a hospital, as well as the situation where a company is dissolved and the employees continue working for the former directors and sole shareholders. No property need be transferred. Several ECJ cases have made this point. One such authority is *Merckx v Ford Motor Co Belgium SA* (1996). One car dealership closed and another took its place. The first recommended that its customers use the second. No assets were transferred. Nevertheless, there was a transfer within the Directive. It does not matter that the first dealership had gone into liquidation, for the Directive exists to protect employees and they would not be protected if liquidation prevented the transfer of their rights.

Regulation 2(1) provides that 'undertaking' includes trade or business. It is possible that the use of the term 'undertaking' means that the contracting out of one piece of work on one occasion will not result in a transfer within TUPE. The ECJ has said that the Directive applies when the undertaking is transferred and retains its identity (*Spijkers v Gebr Benedik Abattoir CV* (1986)). If there is a transfer, it is irrelevant that there was a contractual mobility clause under which the transferors could have moved the employee to a part of their business which was not transferred (*Securicor Guarding Ltd v Fraser Services Ltd* (1996)). It is sufficient that the activities performed immediately before and immediately afterwards are the same. It applies even though only one employee was transferred (*Schmidt v Spar- und Leihkasse der früheren Ämter Bordesholm, Kiel und Cronshagen* (1995)). It did not matter that the part transferred was merely ancillary to the main business or that no tangible assets were transferred. See, however, the discussion of *Süzen*, below.

The Regulations are construed to give effect to the Directive (*Kelman v Care Contract Services Ltd* (1995), a decision of the EAT which summarises present law). Mummery J emphasised that the Regulations form part of the law aimed at protecting employees. Therefore, property, company or insolvency law perspectives should not be used. It does not matter whether tangible assets are transferred. The usual point must be made: the words of English law must not be distorted. The Regulations used to be restricted to transfers in the nature of a commercial venture but, as a result of *Dr Sophie Redmond Stichting v Bartol* (1992), the law was widened in 1993 to cover such an undertaking. See below, 13.2.7, for further discussion.

The type of factors which are important in s 218 of the Employment Rights Act (ERA) 1996, such as goodwill, may be also important under the Regulations, but the important issue remains:

... whether, having regard to all the circumstances, the economic entity identified prior to the transfer can be found after the transfer ... not, has the same business continued in existence nor has the goodwill been transferred? [*Council of the Isles of Scilly v Brintel Helicopters Ltd* (1995), *per* Morison J].

However, even though the basic activity remains the same, there is no transfer if the transferees do not take over any assets or employees and the place of business moved (*Betts v Brintel Helicopters Ltd* (1997) (CA)). A transfer of only fixtures and fittings was held not to be a transfer of an undertaking in *Robert Seligman Corp v Baker* (1983). However, in the light of the *Schmidt* case, this ruling seems incorrect, for the fact that there is no transfer of goodwill does not rule out a transfer within the Regulations. The ECJ's decision in *Rygaard v Stro Molle Akustik A/S* (1996) that there is no transfer where only one contract is transferred is restricted to that situation (*BSG Property Services v Tuck* (1996)). It is sufficient that a stable entity is transferred. Again, it was said that no assets need be transferred.

Whether there has been a transfer is one of fact. The EAT will not interfere with a tribunal's determination, even though another tribunal might have decided differently. If the applicant was employed in a part of a group of companies which was not transferred when other parts were, he is not protected by the Regulations (*Michael Peters Ltd v Farnfield* (1995)). In company law terms, the corporate veil is not lifted. The competition law concept of a group of companies forming one economic unit was rejected, but the EAT was open to the suggestion that, on other facts, subsidiary companies may be part of the holding company for the purposes of the Regulations. The Regulations do, however, apply to a person who was employed in a transferred part but who continued to work for the receivers of the transferors for some time after the transfer (*Sunley Turriff Holdings Ltd v Thomson* (1995)). In the latter case, the Scottish EAT held that it was immaterial that the transferees and receivers were mistaken about the effects of the contractual position. *Duncan Web Offset* (above, 13.2.5) may be helpful to employees in this area. The EAT's view that the Regulations should be applied broadly and in favour of the protection of employment may override the contractual niceties when determining in which part of the business the applicant was employed. Morison J said that employment tribunals should 'be astute to ensure that the provisions of the Regulations are not evaded by devices such as service companies or by complicated group structures which conceal the true position'.

Rygaard has been seen as marking a retreat from the broad definition of 'undertaking' found in *Spijkers* and applied in cases such as *Schmidt* and *Sophie Redmond*. Whether this is so is not yet clear. *Schmidt* was roundly criticised in Germany for increasing business costs and prioritising the policy of protecting employees on a transfer over the policy of saving money by contracting out. Both cases were mentioned with approval by the ECJ in *Merckx*. *Rygaard* will certainly not normally affect the law that contracting out is covered by the Regulations (see below, 13.2.7). It is suggested that the requirement laid down by the ECJ of a stable economic entity may be limited to the facts of the case, which concerned the completion of building works. The Directive also does not apply to the reorganisation of administrative functions of local authorities, since it is concerned with business, not with the exercise of a public authority power to reorganise itself. *Sophie Redmond* seems to be inconsistent.

In the landmark case of *Süzen v Zehnacker Gebäudereinigung Krankenhausservice* (1997), the ECJ held that there was no relevant transfer when only an activity such as cleaning was transferred. This decision, which may be seen as contrary to previous authorities, means that transferees can avoid the application of the ARD and TUPE by not re-engaging the transferors' employees. This outcome is contrary to the ARD's aim of safeguarding rights on transfer. Surprisingly, the ECJ held that they were applying the test in *Spijkers* and did not say that *Schmidt* was wrong.

Also surprising was the fact that the Court of Appeal in *ECM (Vehicle Delivery Service) Ltd v Cox* (1999) ruled that *Süzen* had not altered the previous law. The transferees argued that there was no relevant transfer when a contract to deliver cars was lost and they were awarded the contract; all that had been transferred was the service, that is, the delivery of cars. Mummery LJ held that tribunals had to apply *Spijkers*: a large range of factors had to be considered. On the facts, the customers were the same, the work was the same and the service's economic identity was unchanged. He said that:

> ... although the *Süzen* decision has been described as involving a shift of emphasis or a clarification of the law, nothing was said ... which casts doubt on the correctness of the interpretation of the Directive in ... earlier decisions.

He added that *Spijkers* and *Schmidt* had not been overruled. *Süzen* was also distinguished as a case involving the loss of a contract with only one customer; *ECM* was also different from *Betts*, where there was a loss of a contract for one location only. In criticism of *ECM*, it may be said that there is no scope for a subjective approach to be taken in the definition of a 'relevant transfer'; the reason behind the employees not being taken on should be irrelevant. Furthermore, *ECM's* facts look very much like *Süzen*, as in both there was a loss of a contract and little was transferred.

13.2.6 Leases: franchises

Regulation 3(1) states that the transfer must be from one person to another. There is normally no difficulty in demonstrating that this has occurred. Difficulty has arisen at the ECJ level about the termination or forfeiture of a lease where the owners retake possession and then grant a lease to new lessees. There has been held to be a transfer both where the employees were dismissed on the expiry of the lease by the old lessees (*Daddy's Dance Hall A/S v Foreningen af Arbejdsledere i Danmark* (1989)) and where they were dismissed after expiry of the lease (*P Bork International A/S v Foreningen af Arbejdsledere i Danmark* (1989)). Franchise arrangements have caused difficulty in the ECJ and English courts, but, depending on the facts, the Directive and Regulations can apply (*Landsorganisationen i Danmark v Ny Molle Krø* (1989)). The last case emphasises that the Directive applies where there has been a change of employers; it does not matter that there has been no change of owners.

Regulation 3 was amended in 1993 to ensure that leases and franchises are covered. There need be no transfer of property and the transfer can take place on a series of transactions. For example, in *Bork*, all the employees were dismissed when the lease on a factory expired. The purchasers of the freehold of the factory then engaged more than half of them. The ECJ held that the Directive applied despite there being negotiations between the old and new employers.

13.2.7 Privatisation

Much has been written on the application of TUPE to privatisation. Contracting out is cheaper than keeping services in-house if costs, particularly wages and pensions, can be reduced. The abolition of the rule that the part transferred had to be in the nature of a commercial venture partly resolves the issue. Collecting dustbins or maintaining property may well not be in the nature of a commercial venture, but that fact is now irrelevant. Contracting out, privatisation and market testing were thought, pre-*Süzen*, almost always to lead to a transfer taking place. The ECJ case of *Rask v ISS Kantineservice A/S* (1993) held that there is a transfer where an identifiable economic entity is transferred: the legal form of the transaction is irrelevant. The Court said:

> ... the decisive criterion for establishing whether there has been a transfer within the meaning of the Directive is whether the business retains its identity, as would be indicated, in particular, by the fact that its operation was actually continued or resumed.

It did not matter that the part transferred was ancillary to the main business, such as a canteen in an electrical factory, but certainly there was no need for a transfer of goodwill or even of assets. Therefore, for example, contracting out cleaning and security services was caught by TUPE and the Directive. It did not even matter that the service was to be performed for a fixed fee. This case seemed to block Government efforts to contract out, for the employees' transfer is caught by the Directive and it cannot save money by contracting out. The policy of compulsory competitive tendering was doomed. The case has proved controversial in Germany.

The Conservative Government misled businesses into believing that TUPE did not apply to contracting out; since it does, many firms (transferees) have had to shoulder costs they did not expect. A transfer of further education colleges from the control of local authorities to corporations was, it was conceded, a relevant transfer. The High Court in *Kenny v South Manchester College* (1993) held that there was a transfer within the Acquired Rights Directive when, as a result of competitive tendering, prison education was transferred from a county council to the defendants, even though there was no transfer of assets, no employee was to be transferred and there was no direct transfer from the council to the new providers. Applying *Sophie Redmond*, the EAT held in *Wren v Eastbourne BC* (1993) that a transfer of services as a result of compulsory competitive tendering fell within TUPE. The change was simply one of contractors. A transfer of a privatised cleaning contract from one contractor to another is within the Regulations even though no equipment, material or goodwill is transferred (*Dines v Initial Health Care Services Ltd* (1995)). The Court of Appeal held that an economic unit had been transferred.

Though the Court of Appeal in *Betts v Brintel Helicopters* (1997) stated that *Dines* was correct on its facts, *Dines* would appear to be incorrect if *Süzen* (ECJ) and *Betts* are applied. In *Dines*, it did not matter that the cleaning service was handed back to the hospital and was on the next day given to the second contractors for, as EC cases demonstrate, a transfer may take place in two stages. Moreover, it was immaterial that there was no contract between the two employers.

Indeed, it is possible that the two employers do not know each others' identity: in a tendering process the names of the bidders are kept secret. Similarly, a transfer of school cleaning services from a local authority's direct service organisation to governors when a school obtained grant-maintained status was a transfer within the Directive (and, after the removal of the non-commercial venture exception, is within the Regulations) (*Governors of Highams Park School v Odger* (1994)). The employee, a cleaner and supervisor, was assigned to that part of the transferors' 'organisational framework' which was transferred.

Similarly, a transfer of paediatric and neonatal services from two district health authorities to an NHS trust was a transfer within the Regulations (*Porter v Queen's Medical Centre* (1993)). The fact that the services were carried out in a different way did not prevent there being a transfer; nor did it matter that, under the relevant English statute providing for the transfer, there were no contractual rights and liabilities. The transfer was, nevertheless, one by law and was therefore 'legal' within the Directive.

The Regulations apply to the contracting out of council services, even though the council put detailed rules into the contract (*Birch v Nuneaton and Bedworth BC* (1995)). Indeed, the EAT thought that the council's continuing control supported the ruling that the undertaking, the provision of leisure facilities, retained its identity. It must, however, be remembered that continuing control is not necessary for there to be a transfer. TUPE also applies to the 'contracting in' of services, as occurs when a council contracts out a function to a company, the company goes into liquidation and the council resumes the service (*Council of the Isles of Scilly v Brintel Helicopters Ltd* (1995)). However, the ECJ's ruling in *Rygaard* may affect this law in a 'one-off' switch of provider (see 13.2.5, above). The court held that the Directive applies only where a 'stable economic entity' is transferred. It does not apply where 'the transferor undertaking merely makes available to the new contractor certain workers and material for carrying out the works …'.

13.2.8 Hiving down

The application of the Regulations to the practice of 'hiving down' is one area where, in respect of employees' rights, English law is in advance of EC laws, though it has been argued that English law may not give effect to the purpose of the Directive, that purpose being the protection of employees on the transfer of a business. Hiving down occurs when the receiver or liquidator sells (or tries to sell) a unit of a business which is insolvent. The employees remain in the service of the bankrupt firm. Their services are provided to the buyers through a wholly-owned subsidiary of the bankrupt firm. The buyers now can select which employees they wish to engage.

Before the Regulations, the employees' rights lay against the insolvent firm and, through them, against a State-run fund where redundancy payments were claimed (in other respects they were unsecured creditors). TUPE 1987 (SI 1987/442) operates to safeguard the rights of the employees now working for the wholly owned subsidiary. By reg 4, the transfer to the subsidiary is deemed not to take effect until immediately before either the transferee company ceases to be a wholly-owned subsidiary of the transferors (this provision does not apply in the event of a winding up) or the business is transferred by the transferee company to another person. The effect is that, where the hiving down is successful, the employees remain in the employment of the company which is parent to the wholly-owned subsidiary until the business is transferred to the buyer. They are then automatically transferred to the subsidiary and thence to the buyers.

13.2.9 Transfer of contract

Where there is a relevant transfer, the contract of employment of an employee employed by the transferors immediately before the transfer is not terminated by the transfer; instead, the contract is treated as if it were made with the transferee employers (reg 5(1)). No transferee need be identified at the time of the transfer for the Regulations to apply (*Harrison Bowden Ltd v Bowden* (1994)). One looks with hindsight to see what happened. Rights and duties, powers and liabilities in connection with that contract are transferred and the transferees become liable for anything except criminal liability done or incurred by the transferors. For example, a claim of sex discrimination against the former employers is transferred (*DJM International Ltd v Nicholas* (1996)). Not only is the contract transferred but things done to the employee are also transferred. Mummery J said that the Directive's scope covered expressly 'an employment relationship existing at the date of the transfer'. It was immaterial that the applicant had been dismissed from her full time job on reaching 60 and was taken on again 10 days later as a part-timer – the discrimination claim related to the former contract.

Liability is not joint between the transferors and transferees. In *Stirling DC v Allan* (1995), the Court of Session held that the Regulations were clear on this point. The Directive provided for the transfer of obligations. Member States were given the option to provide for joint liability but the UK did not take up that option. The court called for a change in the law to provide for joint liability, which would be a change which promoted the purpose of the Regulations, the protection of employees. Among matters transferred are continuity of employment and an accrued right not to be unfairly dismissed by the transferors (*Green-Wheeler v Onyx (UK) Ltd* (1993)). However, the employee may make a claim for unfair dismissal against the transferees (see below) but the employers may have a defence. If it is uncertain against whom the claim should be brought, the claimant may complain against both. The employment tribunal will decide against whom the claim should be brought.

Where the transferees engage the employees and then seek to negotiate a change in the terms, any change is ineffective and the terms agreed with the transferors remain in force (*Wilson v St Helen's BC* (1998) (HL)).

13.2.10 Immediately before

Where the employee was dismissed before the date of the transfer for a reason unconnected with the transfer, the dismissal may or may not be unfair, depending on normal principles (see Chapter 10). It is not automatically unfair. For a case where there was held to be no connection, see *Longden v Ferrari Ltd* (1994), where the EAT upheld an employment tribunal decision that the receivers dismissed the employees because of pressure from the bank and not at the behest of the purchasers, despite the fact that the transferees had told the receivers which workers they wished to retain. M Rubenstein [1994] IRLR 151 commented that: 'It must be strongly arguable that selection for retention and non-selection are two sides of the same coin, and that the EAT's holding ... opens the door to abuse.' The rights and duties under the contract are not transferred because the employee was not employed at the moment of transfer (*Secretary of State for Employment v Spence* (1987)). In that case, a three hour gap prevented transfer even though the three hours were on the same date. The receivers had relinquished any hope of saving the business at the time of the dismissals. This decision was approved *obiter* by the House of Lords in *Litster v Forth Dry Dock and Engineering Co Ltd* (1990). In *Litster* there was collusion, but the case applies generally (*Harrison Bowden Ltd v Bowden* (1994) and *Ibex Trading Co Ltd v Walton* (1994)).

Turning to the facts of *Spence:* at 11 am, there was no work. The employees were dismissed. The purchasers of the business took over at 2 pm, apparently not knowing of the sackings. They re-employed the whole workforce. Since there had been no transfer, the employees' rights were against the old employers (only), but they were insolvent and, accordingly, the employees' redundancy payments had to be made by the State. The decision worked in favour of these employees who wanted redundancy payments, not the continuance of work. The new employers were not liable to make these payments. They would have been liable had there been a transfer. The House of Lords in *Litster* approved the ruling in *Spence* on the grounds that the old employers and the new did not collude with the aim of selling off the business at an advantageous price without the employees. The employees truly were dismissed for redundancy and not on account of the transfer.

Spence has been heavily criticised. One point is that the Regulation speaks of 'date': why should 'date' be read as 'moment'? The employees did end and restart employment on the same date. Furthermore, the factual basis of the ruling in *Spence* may be questioned. The old employment folded at 11 am because the contractors with whom the old employers had done 80% of its business had withdrawn, but, by 2 pm, the new employers had signed an agreement with the contractors. There may not have been actual collusion between the old and the new employers, but something underhand may have occurred.

13.2.11 Date of transfer

For the purposes of reg 3(1), the date of the transfer is when the transferees take over, not the time when the legal process of a sale (or other transfer) is completed. The transfer occurs:

> ... as soon as there is a change ... of the natural or legal person responsible for operating the undertaking who, consequently, enters into obligations as an employer towards employees working in the undertaking, and it is of no importance to know whether the ownership of the undertaking has been transferred [*Daddy's Dance Hall A/S v Foreningen af Arbejdsledere i Danmark* (1988)].

13.2.12 *Litster v Forth Dry Dock*

If the contract of employment has been terminated for a reason connected with the transfer before the date of transfer, the dismissal is automatically unfair. In *Litster*, the employees were dismissed an hour before the transfer. The transferors were in receivership. A new company was established to take over the business but it did not wish to take on the transferors' employees. It wished to use workers from elsewhere who would work for lower wages than the employees. Those employees claimed for unfair dismissal. Were they employed 'immediately before' the transfer? Since the employees were dismissed one hour before the transfer, one might be permitted to think that, applying *Spence*, TUPE did not apply. The House of Lords held, however, that the dismissals were for a reason connected with the transfer. Regulation 8(1) applied. Rights under the employment contracts were transferred to the transferees. The House of Lords said that the Regulations had to be read in conformity with the EC Directive, as interpreted by the ECJ in *Bork International*.

Regulation 5 now applies not just to those who were employed at the date of the transfer but also to those who would have been so employed if they had not been unfairly dismissed within the circumstances prescribed in reg 8 (see below). The House of Lords stated that the Regulations were intended to protect employees who would not be protected if employers could dismiss without incurring liability. The effect is to stop evasion of the Regulations. In *Spence*, however, there was no attempt at evasion.

13.2.13 Transfer of what?

Where there has been a relevant transfer, all rights, powers, duties and liabilities of the transferors arising under or in connection with the contract of employment are transferred to the transferees (reg 5(2)(a)). An example is a share option scheme (see, also, 13.2.9, above). On the facts of *Litster*, the claims for unfair dismissal were against the new company, not the old one. Regulation 5(2) transfers not just contractual but statutory and tortious duties too. The transfer of tort duties, including personal injury claims, was mentioned in *Spence* (possibly, vicarious liability is not transferred). The High Court held in *Bernadone v Pall Mall Services Group* (1999) that liability for the tort of negligence is transferred. A sexual discrimination claim was held in *DJM International Ltd v Nicholas* (1996) to be transferred.

If the wording of the English Regulations ('in connection with') is too narrow to include statutory obligations, Art 3(1) of the Directive will operate and reg 5(2)(a) must be interpreted in conformity with it. The effect is that claims for breach of contract (for example, arrears of pay) and personal injury are transferred and the transfer takes place without the consent of the employee. For the position where he objects, see 13.1.3, above. However, criminal liabilities such as breaches of the Health and Safety at Work Act 1974 are not transferred (reg 5(4)). The effect of reg 5 is often described as a statutory novation of the contract. It is as if the employment contract had from the start been made with the transferees.

It has been held that the protective award is not transferred (*Angus Jowett & Co Ltd v NUTGW* (1985)). This ruling may be incorrect: if a sex discrimination claim is transferred, so should a protective award. Continuity is preserved and weeks continue to be counted as if there had been no transfer. It should be noted that the Directive protects only rights upon a transfer; afterwards, any protection depends on national law.

13.2.14 Dismissal or ineffective?

If there is a dismissal in connection with the transfer, two interpretations are possible. First, the dismissals are void. Therefore, the contract is not terminated by the dismissal and the employee remains in employment with the transferees. There is support for this approach in *Bork International* and in Lord Oliver's speech in *Litster*. The second view is that the dismissal does terminate the contract: all the Regulations do is to say which employers are liable. The second approach is more in line with English thinking and the House of Lords held that dismissals in connection with a transfer were effective and not a nullity in *Meade v British Fuels Ltd* (1998). It is suggested that the normal reasons militating against reinstatement do not apply in the context of the transfer of an undertaking. Payment of additional compensation on a failure to re-employ may not be an effective remedy in EC terms. *Litster*, however, preserves continuity and the transfer of the contract in any event.

13.2.15 Substantial change

Regulation 5(5) of TUPE states that an employee has the right to terminate his contract without notice if a substantial change is made to the conditions of work and that change is to his detriment. The majority view is that 'substantial change' is a wider concept than the English doctrine of constructive dismissal. Browne-Wilkinson LJ in *Berriman v Delabole Slate Ltd* (1985) said that 'any detrimental change in … working conditions' sufficed. A change in only the identity of the employers does not give the employee this right unless the change was, in all the circumstances, a significant one to his detriment. The effect of the opening part of reg 5(5) is to preserve the employee's right to resign when there has been a substantial change in his employment (that is, constructive dismissal). So, if an employee's pay is reduced after and because of the transfer, there is a constructive dismissal. Regulation 8(1) (see 13.2.18, below) applies and the dismissal is automatically unfair. The defence in reg 8(2) does not apply because, even if there is an economic, technical or organisational reason, there is no change in the workforce. By reg 5, the transferees will be liable.

13.2.16 Non-contractual benefits

Regulation 5(5) seems to apply even though the change is not one to the contract of employment; for example, there may be a change to promotion prospects or to prospects for continued employment.

13.2.17 Occupational pensions

Regulation 5 does not operate to transfer occupational pension schemes (reg 7(1), as it now is). However, that restriction has been narrowed to old age, invalidity and survivors' benefits (s 33(5) of TURERA 1993, inserting a new reg 7(2) into TUPE). Accrued rights under the transferors' pension schemes are protected. There is no duty on the transferees to provide pension rights equivalent to those guaranteed by the transferors (*Walden Engineering Co Ltd v Warrener* (1993)). This interpretation is not inconsistent with Art 3(3) of the ARD, which prevents a transfer of these pensions only where it is impractical to transfer them (*Adams v Lancashire CC* (1996)). Other matters, such as contractual benefits on redundancy, are now transferred.

13.2.18 Regulation 8

A dismissal is automatically unfair if the reason or principal reason for it was the transfer or a reason connected with it (reg 8(1)). There will be no transfer within this provision when the employees are dismissed at a time when no purchaser of the business could be identified or there was no certainty that any sale of the business would occur (*Ibex Trading Co Ltd v Walton* (1994), where the possibility of a transfer was said to be 'a mere twinkle in the eye'). This interpretation is a narrow one, inconsistent with the aim of protecting employees' rights on a transfer which takes place. Insolvency practitioners will no doubt exploit this loophole by dismissing employees.

The employers may demonstrate that the reason or principal reason was:

> ... an economic, technical or organisational reason entailing changes in the workforce of either the transferor or the transferee before or after a relevant transfer [reg 8(2)].

If this defence applies, the employers' reason is treated as one of the potentially fair reasons, that is, some other substantial reason, and the employment tribunal has to consider s 98(4) of the ERA 1996: was the dismissal fair taking all the circumstances including procedural fairness (such as consultation) and the size and administrative resources of the employers into account? (See Chapter 10.) Deeming the dismissal to be 'some other substantial reason' does not affect claims for redundancy payments (*Gorictree Ltd v Jenkinson* (1984)). This ruling is consistent with the aim of the Directive and Regulations, which is to preserve employees' rights. Those rights would be diminished if employees could not claim redundancy payments. The thinking behind this is that reg 8(2) deems an economic, technical or organisational reason to be 'some other substantial reason', but it may also be another potentially fair reason, such as redundancy. For the remedy for unfair dismissal, see Chapter 12. It is likely that compensation will be ordered. This remedy may not be adequate and effective in EC terms. Accordingly, an employee may be able to rely on the Acquired Rights Directive to get his job back without loss of rights.

13.2.19 Connection with transfer

There is no restriction upon the time beyond which a reason cannot be connected with the transfer. As long as there is a link, a dismissal years later suffices. If the dismissal is not in connection with the transfer, the normal law of unfair dismissal applies. Where the transferors give notice of dismissal and that notice expires after the transfer, the 'reason' within reg 8(2) is that of the transferors, even though liability is transferred to the transferees (*BSG Property Services v Tuck* (1996)).

13.2.20 ETO

The phrase 'economic, technical or organisational reasons entailing changes in the workforce' is taken straight from the ARD. There is no ECJ judgment detailing its meaning and no attempt has been made to fit it into UK domestic law.

A dismissal for an economic, technical or organisational reason (often called an 'ETO') may nevertheless be a redundancy (*Gorictree Ltd v Jenkinson* (1984)). Pressure put by the purchasers on the transferors to dismiss the workforce before the transfer is not an ETO on the grounds that TUPE is meant to protect employees, and 'economic' must be read *ejusdem generis* with technical or organisational, that is, it must relate to the conduct of the business and not to its attractiveness to purchasers (*Wheeler v Patel* (1987)). A dismissal of employees at the request of the transferees is not an economic reason. However, the term is not restricted to situations in which those dismissed would have been dismissed anyway, had there been no transfer (*Trafford v Sharpe & Fisher (Building Supplies) Ltd* (1994)). There is no definition of these terms in the Regulations or elsewhere in employment law.

An example of transferee employers successfully claiming an ETO reason is *Porter v Queen's Medical Centre* (1993). A reorganisation at a hospital which led to new specialisms being demanded of consultants was an ETO reason entailing changes in the workforce. The plaintiffs' contracts of employment terminated when notice given by their (transferor) employers elapsed. In *Warner v Adnet Ltd* (1998), the Court of Appeal held that a dismissal by administrative receivers before the transfer was for an economic reason; the employee was redundant. It was held by the EAT in *BSG Property Services v Tuck* (1996) that transferees cannot rely on the ETO defence when the employees are dismissed by the transferors because the latter does not have the ETO defence in mind when they dismiss.

13.2.21 Entailing changes

It used to be thought that 'entailing changes in the workforce' meant that the number of employees or their functions had to change. In a significant decision, the Court of Appeal in *Berriman v Delabole Slate Ltd* (1985) held that reg 8(2) does not apply where there was a change in an employee's contract to his disadvantage. The number of workers did not change. The employers' aim was to standardise the contracts of their workers after a transfer, an aim which might be laudable. However, the reduction in the employee's terms and conditions (a cut in his pay) was a constructive dismissal which he did not accept. It was automatically unfair. The court said that 'entailing changes in the workplace' encompassed both a change in the overall numbers and a change in the functions of the employees. A change of pay was, therefore, not a change in the workforce. A change in numbers meant a change in the number of staff, not a change where one employee is replaced by another. The court looked to the purpose of the Directive, which was to preserve employees' rights, including 'their existing terms of service', on a transfer. If the transferees seek instead to get the transferors to dismiss the employees, *Litster* applies. An example of a change in functions is *Crawford v Swinton Insurance Brokers Ltd* (1990). A clerk was asked to become an insurance salesperson. The EAT held that reg 8(2) applied. There was a change in the workforce because the employers needed one clerk less and one salesperson more.

13.2.22 Qualifications

It appears that the claim for unfair dismissal must be made by an employee who is qualified to bring the complaint. Therefore, rules such as the qualifying period of one year's continuous employment apply (see Chapter 8 for the qualifications). The EAT once said that the then two year qualifying period for unfair dismissal did not apply where the Regulations did, but the Collective Redundancies and Transfer of Undertakings (Protection of Employment) (Amendment) Regulations 1995 (SI 1995/2587) reinstated the qualifying period. The Divisional Court held that this rule was not indirect sex discrimination in *R v Secretary of State for Trade and Industry ex p UNISON* (1996).

13.3   Trade unions and other consultative organs

In the event of a transfer, reg 10 of TUPE, as amended by the Collective Redundancies and Transfer of Undertakings (Protection of Employment) (Amendment) Regulations 1995, imposes on employers (whether transferors, transferees or both) a duty to inform and consult with authorised representatives of affected employees, whether elected for this purpose or otherwise, or with representatives of an independent trade union which they recognise. Where there are both sets of representatives, the employers must choose the union's representatives: Collective Redundancies and Transfer of Undertakings (Protection of Employment) (Amendment) Regulations 1999 (SI 1999/1925). An 'employee' in this context is defined as an employee, apprentice or other worker but does not include those who work under a contract for services.

The procedure for handling redundancies (discussed in Chapter 9) applies only to the employers who dismiss. Another difference is that the duty to consult in reg 10 applies even though no one is to be made redundant. As a result of the decision in *Commission v UK* (1994), the then Government changed English law in an attempt to attain European standards. The ECJ said that EC-wide law on this matter had to be comparable among Member States and had to impose similar costs on employees across the Community. While the then Government set its face against the compulsory recognition of unions and the establishment of works councils, it did amend the law to oblige employers to consult but provided them with an option: they could consult with union representatives (if there were any) *or* with other representatives of employees, whether there was a union or not, and these other representatives of employees may be ones who came together solely for the purpose of being consulted on the transfer. The employees' representatives must be elected by the employees and the union must be an independent one (see Chapter 4). The representatives must have reasonable time off work to perform their duties and it is automatically unfair to dismiss a representative or a candidate for this office.

Employers are also under a duty not to subject a representative or candidate to any detriment. One interesting point about the 1995 Regulations was that there was no system for electing the representatives stipulated, but a detailed scheme for elections is now provided by the 1999 Regulations. If there is no election, employers must give the information to individual employees. Where consultation is with trade union representatives, the union must be independent. No such condition applies to non-trade union representatives. Non-union representatives may find it difficult to act freely in a takeover situation.

13.3.1 Information

Information must be provided to the representatives about the fact of transfer, when it will take place and the reasons for it; about the 'legal, economic and social implications' for those employees who will be affected; and about the measures which will be taken in relation to those 'affected employees'. That term includes not just those who will be transferred but anyone who may be affected by the transfer or measures taken in connection with it (reg 10(1)). A representative (of a union) is an official or other person authorised to carry out collective bargaining (reg 2(3)). If it is the transferors who are under the duty to consult, the transferees must give them the relevant information (reg 10(3)). The law on handling redundancies is narrower than TUPE for only in the latter must there be information about the legal, economic and social complications of the transfer. What are legal, economic and social implications is unclear. Moreover, information needs be provided only about the fact of transfer. The law on handling redundancies extends to proposals for redundancy.

13.3.2 When?

The information must be given 'long enough before a relevant transfer to enable consultations to take place'. There are no minimum time limits, as there are in the procedure for handling redundancies (see Chapter 9). Certainly, information need not be given at the stage when there are only proposals for transfer: it would appear that it need be given only when the parties are agreed on the transfer. The Directive speaks of the fact of transfer, not of proposals for transfer. The position is otherwise in the law on handling redundancies. In this respect, the law is more pro-employees in redundancy dismissals than is the right discussed here.

13.3.3 Consultation

Where the employers, whether transferors or transferees, will be taking measures with regard to the affected employees, they must consult with representatives 'with a view to seeking that agreement to measures to be taken'. The words in inverted commas were added to reg 10(5) by s 33(6) of TURERA 1993. The duty arises when the employers have decided on the transfer. The employers must consider the objections and reply to them, giving reasons for rejections. The economic, legal and social implications of the transfer must be addressed.

One effect of the House of Lords' decision in *Wilson v St Helens BC* (13.2.4, above) should be noted. It was held that employees could not agree to a variation in their terms and conditions when the attempted consensual variation stemmed from a transfer because the Directive was mandatory in its effect. If this ruling is correct, it renders almost otiose the provisions of consultation with the representatives of employees, for what use is it to consult when no changes may be made?

13.3.4 Special circumstances

Regulation 10(7) gives employers a 'special circumstances' defence of apparently the same width as on the law on handling redundancies (see Chapter 9). If there are circumstances making it not reasonably practicable for the employers to inform or consult, they must take all reasonably practicable steps to comply with their duties. The burden of proof of special circumstances and all reasonably practicable steps is on the employers.

13.3.5 Sanction

Enforcement is by the bringing of a claim to an employment tribunal: reg 11(1). A claim may be brought by the employee representatives or by the recognised independent trade union (reg 11, as amended by the 1995 Regulations). The claim must be made within three months of the completion of the transfer (reg 11(8)). A claim may be made before the date of transfer (*South Durham Health Authority v UNISON* (1996)). The remedy is a just and equitable sum to a maximum of 13 weeks' pay (reg 11(11), as amended by s 33(7)(a) of TURERA 1993 and the 1999 Regulations). The tribunal is instructed to have 'regard to the seriousness of the failure of the employer to comply with his duty'. There is no longer any set off for the protective award for failure to consult on redundancy (reg 11(7), as amended by s 33(7)(b)). The repeal of this set of provisions may encourage unions and others to use TUPE more, though the sanction remains derisory. The protective award discussed in Chapter 9 is of more significance than this exceptionally weak remedy. The small size is a breach of the Directive, which, like all legally enforceable directives, must be accompanied by an adequate remedy. In *Commission v UK* (1994), the previous set off and the present financial limit were condemned.

The dismissal of an employee representative is automatically unfair if the employers' principal reason was that he 'performed, or proposed to perform, any functions or activities as such an employee representative candidate' in order to become one. There is a corresponding right not to be subjected to a detriment on the same grounds.

13.3.6 Collective agreements

By reg 6, 'any collective bargain agreed by the transferor shall have effect as if made by the transferee'.

13.3.7 Recognition

If an undertaking or part of an undertaking is transferred and it retains an identity distinct from the remainder of the transferees' business, any recognition of a union by the transferors is transferred to the transferees (reg 9). However, the transferees may resile from recognition in the usual way whenever they wish. Moreover, there is no enforcement mechanism provided in reg 9. Unions must rely on industrial muscle to retain recognition. And if the identity is not preserved, reg 9 is inapplicable. The effect is that, if the transferred part of the undertaking is merged with the transferees' business, there is no transfer of recognition.

13.4 Reform

The ARD was amended in 1998. Member States have until 17 July 2001 to change domestic law. The main amendments are as follows:

- a relevant transfer is one involving an economic entity which retains its identity;

- public undertakings are expressly covered but there is an exception for the re-organisation of public administrative bodies;

- Member States may put transferees under a duty to inform transferors of all the rights and obligations consequent on a transfer;

- Member States *may* include occupational pension rights among the rights which are transferred;

- it is no defence to a claim that the employers did not provide information that the parent company did not supply it; and

- information must be provided to individual employees if (through no fault of the employees) there are no representatives to be informed and consulted.

TRANSFER OF UNDERTAKINGS

Laws

At common law, contracts of employment could not be transferred, but the Transfer of Undertakings (Protection of Employment) Regulations (TUPE) 1981 operate on a relevant transfer to preserve continuity of those employed immediately before the transfer, and rights and duties under the contract are automatically transferred. A dismissal in connection with the transfer is automatically unfair unless the employers have an economic, technical or organisational reason entailing changes in the workforce, in which case, the dismissal is potentially fair. The transfer need not be in the nature of a commercial venture but the entity transferred must be stable:

- *Dr Sophie Redmond Stichtung v Bartol* (1992);
- *Rygaard v Stro Molle Akustik* (1996);
- *Süzen v Zehnacker Gebäudereinigung GmbH Krankenhausservice* (1997).

Leases and franchises may be transferred:

- *Daddy's Dance Hall* (1989);
- *Ny Molle Krø* (1989).

Privatisation continues to cause problems to English courts and tribunals:

- *Wren v Eastbourne BC* (1993);
- *Porter v Queen's Medical Centre* (1993);
- *Dines v Initial Health Care Services Ltd* (1995).

Criminal liability and some aspects of occupational pensions are not transferred.

An 'ETO' includes a redundancy:

- *Litster v Forth Dry Dock* (1990);
- *Berriman v Delabole Slate* (1985).

Trade unions

There is a duty to inform union representatives about the transfer and a duty to consult 'with a view to seeking agreement to measures to be taken'. If there is no union, consultation with *ad hoc* bodies suffices. Collective agreements are transferred, as is recognition where the identity of the part transferred is preserved. Since there is no duty under English law to continue recognition of unions, this provision can be easily circumvented. The ECJ ruled in *Commission v UK* (1994) that the Government had failed to satisfy the standards of the EC in several respects, including restricting consultation to situations in which there was a recognised union.

CHAPTER 14

TRADE UNIONS

14.1 Coverage

This chapter considers the definition of trade unions and their legal status, history and independence; recognition by employers; the right to information for collective bargaining purposes; various rights to time off; and the political fund. The next chapter deals with the internal affairs of unions (that is, the relationship with their members). The final chapter deals with some aspects of collective bargaining and industrial action. Some of this material may be differently ordered on your course.

14.2 Definition

This section looks at trade unions, special register bodies and employers' associations.

14.2.1 By statute

Section 1 of the Trade Union and Labour Relations (Consolidation) Act (TULR(C)A) 1992 defines a trade union for the purposes of the Act as:

... an organisation (whether temporary or permanent) –

(a) which consists wholly or mainly of workers of one or more descriptions and whose principal purposes include the regulation of relations between workers of that description or those descriptions and employers or employers' associations; or

(b) which consists wholly or mainly of –

(i) constituent or affiliated organisations which fulfil the conditions in paragraph (a) (or themselves consist wholly or mainly of constituent or affiliated organisations which fulfil those conditions); or

(ii) representatives of such constituent or affiliated organisations, and whose principal purposes include the regulation of relations between workers and employers or between workers and employers' associations, or the regulation of relations between its constituent or affiliated organisations.

The definition is important because trade unions have various benefits and are subject to various burdens, as this and the following chapters show. There are some 300 unions, down from around 450 in 1979.

The principal authority is *Midland Cold Storage Ltd v Steer* (1972). Though the definition covers temporary bodies, it does not include an *ad hoc* committee of shop stewards. The court held that the body's function was not the regulation of employment relations but the organisation of industrial action. It was formed for the purpose of blacking a company and, even though it was an organisation of workers (it consisted of shop stewards of various unions and had a convener and a secretary), it did not constitute a union because its purpose was not that stated in s 1(a).

As long as the principal purpose is the regulation of employment relations, it does not matter that the union does not perform all possible purposes of a union, that the (express) objects of the organisation do not include the regulation of such relations or that it does not have the industrial muscle to carry out collective bargaining fully (*BAALPE v NUT* (1986)). There is no minimum number of members.

14.2.2 Federations

The definition of 'union' covers a federation of unions, the best known union being the International Transport Workers Federation (see, for example, *NWL Ltd v Woods* (1989), a case involving an affilation of unions). For this reason, the Trades Union Congress is thought to be a union.

14.2.3 Workers

The definition in s 1 refers to 'workers'. This term is wider than that of 'employees', but it does not cover all persons who, in ordinary language, perform 'work'. By s 296 of TULR(C)A 1992, 'workers' include employees and all those who agree to perform personally a service for another person, but not those whose relationship with the person who engaged their service is that of professional and client. Because of the definition, authors are not workers because they do not come under a duty to perform services (*Writers' Guild of Great Britain v BBC* (1974)), and The Law Society is not a union because the relationship of solicitor and client is one of professional and client (*Carter v The Law Society* (1973)).

14.2.4 Special register bodies

Certain bodies do seek to regulate employment relations but their principal purpose is the maintenance of professional standards of practice, not regulation. The two main organisations are the British Medical Association and the Royal College of Nursing. There are 13 other bodies. These are called 'special register' bodies. The main advantage of being on the register is that, like trade unions, the bodies' rules and purposes are not affected by the restraint of trade doctrine (see 14.4, below), provided that their actions deal with industrial relations. No more organisations may be added to the register.

14.2.5 Employers' associations

By s 122(1) of TULR(C)A 1992, an employers' association is:

> ... an organisation (whether temporary or permanent) ... which consists wholly or mainly of employers or individual owners of undertakings of one or more descriptions and whose principal purposes include the regulation of relations between employers of that description or those descriptions and workers or trade unions ...

Like the definition of 'trade union', this definition also covers constituent and affiliated organisations. The Certification Officer (CO) keeps a list of employers' organisations. There were 117 bodies on the list in 1995 and 107 in 1997. Unlike trade unions, these associations may (but need not) be companies. If the association is unincorporated, it is treated as a quasi-corporate body, just as a union is. The restraint of trade doctrine does not apply to employers' associations.

14.3 Legal status of unions

Section 10(1) of TULR(C)A states:

> A trade union is not a body corporate but –
>
> (a)   it is capable of making contracts;
>
> (b)   it is capable of suing and being sued in its own name, whether in proceedings relating to property or founded on contract or tort or any other cause of action; and
>
> (c)   proceedings for an offence alleged to have been committed by it or on its behalf may be brought against it in its own name.

Therefore, a union is not a company and, indeed, by s 10(3), it cannot be registered as a company, friendly society or industrial and provident society. The side-note to s 10 reads: 'Quasi-corporate status of trade unions'; that is, unions are not companies but have some of the rights and obligations of companies.

14.3.1 Trusts

Section 12(1) vests union property (including its records) in trustees on trust for the union. In this respect, trade unions differ from unincorporated associations, such as clubs, where the property is held on trust for the members. If the trustees act unlawfully, a union member may apply to the High Court for various orders, including the removal of the trustees and the appointment of receivers. Such orders took place in the miners' strike 1984–85, though at that time, the court's power was not found in statute as it is now.

14.3.2 Libel

Despite s 10(1), a trade union does not have sufficient legal personality to suffer injury to its reputation. Accordingly, it cannot sue for libel (*Electrical Electronic Telecommunications and Plumbing Union v Times Newspapers Ltd* (1980)). O'Connor J said that not merely was a union not a company, it was not to be treated as a company. Therefore, it did not have the requisite personality. However, it had earlier been held that unions could sue for defamation.

14.4   Restraint of trade

By s 11(2) of TULR(C)A 1992, 'no rule of a trade union is unlawful or unenforcable by reason only that it is in restraint of trade'. This sub-section is self-explanatory. However, one aspect of the restraint of trade doctrine needs discussion at this point. Section 11(2) assumes that trade union purposes are in restraint of trade, but is that so? Trade union objectives may well now be considered as not unreasonable between the parties, not contrary to the public interest and protective of a legitimate interest.

14.4.1 Purposes

By s 11(1) of the same statute:

> ... the purposes of a trade union are not, by reason only that they are in restraint of trade, unlawful so as – (a) to make any member of the trade union liable to criminal proceedings for conspiracy or otherwise, or (b) to make any agreement or trust void or voidable.

There is a possibility that even this wide provision might be outflanked by the common law. In *Edwards v SOGAT* (1971), Lord Denning MR postulated that individuals had a right to work exercisable against trade unions (though not against employers or the State). If so, union purposes which conflicted with this right to work could be struck down as being in restraint of trade. What interferes with an individual's right to work also is contrary to the doctrine of restraint of trade. Little has been heard of this notion since Lord Denning retired.

14.5 Listing

The CO keeps a list of trade unions: s 2(1) of TULR(C)A 1992. Membership of this list is voluntary. The list comprises those unions which were on a list kept in 1974, together with any union which the CO has since put on the list. Unions may apply to the CO to be added to the list. The CO must put a union's name on the list if he is satisfied that the organisation is a trade union, that the form containing the body's rules, officers, address and name has been duly completed, and that the organisation's name is not the same as another union or so similar to another that it is likely to deceive the public (s 3). There is also a charge. There are, as of 1994, 267 unions, down from 287 in 1993. Listing is not a condition for an organisation's being classed as a trade union.

14.5.1 Advantages

The advantages of listing are these:

(a) membership of the list is evidence that the body is a trade union (s 2(4));

(b) listing is a prerequisite of a certificate of independence (s 6(1));

(c) tax relief is available on income and gains applied for provident benefits.

For present purposes, (b) is the most important. Listing is a step towards the certificate, and only if a union is independent does it and its members enjoy certain rights.

14.5.2 Removal

The CO may remove the name of a body from the list if it is no longer a union and must remove it if so requested or if he is satisfied that the organisation no longer exists (s 4). There is an appeal to the EAT against refusal to list and removal from the list (s 9(1)). Surprisingly, the appeal may be on a question of fact, not just of law (s 4(4)). The same applies to the certificate of independence.

14.6 Independence

Certain rights and privileges are given only to trade unions which are independent. Organisations of workers which are not independent of employers are sometimes called 'sweetheart (or house) unions' or staff associations, though a staff association can take on so much of the mantle of a trade union that it becomes independent.

14.6.1 Definition

By s 5 of TULR(C)A 1992, an independent trade union is a trade union which:

(a) is not under the domination or control of an employer or group of employers or of one or more employers' associations; and

(b) is not liable to interference by an employer or any such group or association (arising out of the provision of financial or material support or by any other means whatsoever) tending towards such control.

14.6.2 Liable to interference

In s 5(b), 'liable to interference' means 'vulnerable to, or at the risk of, interference' (*Squibb UK Staff Association v CO* (1979)). The test is not whether the trade union is likely to suffer interference in practice but whether intervention may occur. On the facts of *Squibb*, the union was not independent. It had a small membership base and its attempts at collective bargaining with management were largely unsuccessful. Although the employers did not at that time interfere in the running of the union, there was the possibility that it might do so later. Indeed, the union could not continue without the employers' involvement.

14.6.3 Criteria

The CO determines whether the trade union is independent. Various criteria have been set out, and these were accepted in *Blue Circle Staff Association v CO* (1977). These factors do not appear in the statute but are his own.

History

If the union was set up by management or with management's help, it is unlikely to be classified as independent for some time. Nevertheless, it can, after a while, grow apart from the employers so that it is no longer vulnerable to influence. On the facts of *Blue Circle*, the staff association was not independent. It originated as a management tool ('a sophisticated instrument of personnel control') and was not free from 'paternal control'.

Membership

If a union is formed which recruits only among employees of one company, it is not likely to be independent. As with all these guidelines, this one is not a condition of independence. For example, the National Union of Mineworkers (NUM) is independent despite the fact that it recruits largely among employees of one company.

Financial aspects

If a union receives a subsidy from the employers, it is unlikely to be independent.

Facilities

If the employer provides amenities, such as free phones, the union may not be independent. In *Squibb*, the employers provided free offices, free internal mail and time off with pay. The court held that the union was not independent. It is fascinating to note that, once a union has been declared independent, it is expected that such facilities will be provided by the employers!

Collective bargaining

The lack of 'robustness' in negotiation on industrial matters is a mark of non-independence.

Internal affairs

In *Blue Circle*, the employers nominated the chair of the Joint Central Committee. This ability demonstrated that the union was liable to interference. In *Government Communications Staff Federation v CO* (1993), the EAT held the federation to be liable to interference because the Director of GCHQ could withdraw his approval for its existence. This veto has since been withdrawn.

The Union of Democratic Mineworkers satisfied these factors and was granted a certificate of independence after the miners' strike. It is not always easy for breakaway factions to be credited with independent status.

14.6.4 Procedure

A trade union desirous of independence applies to the CO for a certificate (s 6(1)). Applications are fairly rare. There were three in 1994, a figure fairly constant throughout the 1990s. The union must be a listed one (see above, 14.5). The CO makes 'such enquiries as he thinks fit' and takes into account 'any relevant information submitted ... by any person', including rival unions. The CO then uses the criteria stated above to determine whether the union is truly independent. An appeal against refusal of a certificate is made to the EAT and may be as to fact or law (s 9). The EAT hears the case *de novo* and may take into account information which the CO did not know. Only a union aggrieved by the refusal of a certificate may appeal. A trade union which dislikes the grant of a certificate to another union may not appeal. The CO may revoke the certificate 'if he is of the opinion that the union is no longer independent' (s 7). Again, there is an appeal on fact or law to the EAT. There is nothing to stop a union which has been refused a certificate from applying again. In his reasons for refusing to grant the certificate, the CO may give the union advice as to how it can gain the certificate in the future.

14.6.5 Effect

Once issued, the certificate:

> ... is conclusive evidence for all purposes that a trade union is independent; and a refusal, withdrawal or cancellation of a certificate of independence ... is conclusive evidence for all purposes that a trade union is not independent [s 8(1)].

Where an issue relating to independence arises in a court, an employment tribunal, the EAT, ACAS or the Central Arbitration Committee, the matter is stayed until the issue is resolved by the CO (s 8(4)).

14.6.6 Advantages

Independence is important on a number of grounds. Only independent trade unions have the rights to:

- obtain information for collective bargaining purposes;
- appoint health and safety representatives; and
- be consulted on redundancy and on the transfer of undertakings.

Only members of independent trade unions have the right to engage in trade union activities and to time off work for union duties and activities. They must not have detriment applied against them on trade union grounds.

14.7 Recognition

Recognition may be defined as the situation where employers undertake to negotiate with trade unions on collective bargaining issues 'to any extent' (s 180(3) of TULR(C)A). A union may be recognised for one, some or all purposes. Being recognised for one purpose does not mean that the union is automatically recognised for all purposes. The acquisition, retention and widening of recognition is a matter of custom and practice, the arrangements often reached after years of contention and, sometimes, industrial action. There may be a trade dispute over recognition. If so, ACAS may employ its officers to aid in reaching a settlement. Recognition may be the outcome of an express agreement or implied arrangement (such as occurred when a firm consulted with the union about the allocation of work, job security, and discipline), but merely allowing the union to represent members, for example, at disciplinary hearings, is insufficient (*USDAW v Sketchley Ltd* (1981)).

Since recognition is voluntary, so too is derecognition, of which there were a number of well publicised incidents in the 1980s. It is thought that the number of employees whose employers recognised unions for collective bargaining over basic pay fell from two-thirds to a little over a half between 1980 and 1990. Sometimes, derecognition is partial, in that unions are deprived of only part of their role. The general decline in union density in the 1980s has increased the number of derecognitions, as has the move from collective agreements to individual contracts. There is evidence that, since 1993, there have been more recognition agreements than derecognitions.

14.7.1 Voluntary nature

There used to be a way in which unions could extend recognition to new workplaces by law, but that procedure was abolished in 1980 as being incompatible with the British tradition of voluntarism and the then Government's desire to rein unions in. Because there is no legal enforcement of recognition, employers can withdraw from agreements recognising unions at will. The National Coal Board could break an agreement to give exclusive recognition to the National Union of Mineworkers without incurring legal liability (*NCB v NUM* (1986)). Both collective agreements in general and recognition agreements in particular cannot be visited by legal sanctions if broken. It is present Government policy to enforce recognition when a majority of the workforce desire it (see 14.7.2, below).

The most important case remains *NUGSAT v Albury Bros Ltd* (1979). Recognition by an employers' association of which the firm was a member did not mean that the firm recognised the union. Recruitment of a small number of employees, a letter to the firm about pay and one meeting did not constitute recognition. Negotiations which may lead to recognition do not constitute recognition. There had to be bargaining.

14.7.2 Recognition under statute

When the provisions of the Employment Relations Act 1999 come into force, a new Sched A1 will be incorporated into the Trade Union and Labour Relations (Consolidation) Act 1992. This provides for a statutory recognition procedure where employers and unions cannot agree voluntarily. Recognition will normally be automatic if either the majority of the workers in the bargaining unit are union members or 40% of the workers in the bargaining unit vote in favour *and* a majority of that 40% are voting in favour. Disputes will be handled by the revamped Central Arbitration Committee (CAC). The procedure exempts employers who employ 20 or fewer workers. It will be unlawful to dismiss a worker or subject him to a detriment in respect of recognition. It will also be unlawful to select for redundancy on this ground. Derecognition under statute will be treated in a manner similar to recognition.

14.7.3 Transfer Regulations

There is a reference to recognition in the Transfer of Undertakings (Protection of Employment) Regulations (TUPE) 1981 (SI 1981/1794), whereby the transferee employers must continue to recognise unions recognised by the transferors where the transferred undertaking or part of an undertaking is transferred as a unit and is not merged with the transferees' trade or business. There is no legal method, however, of preventing derecognition after the transfer.

14.7.4 Advantages

Only independent recognised unions have rights, for example, to be consulted on redundancies and transfers of undertakings, to obtain information for collective bargaining purposes and to appoint safety representatives. Only members of recognised independent trade unions have various rights to time off work. Information for collective bargaining and time off are discussed below. Information and consultation and redundancies and transfers have been discussed above (Chapters 9 and 13 respectively).

14.8 Collective bargaining information: duty to provide

By s 181(1) of TULR(C)A, which derives from the Industrial Relations Act 1971:

> ... an employer who recognises an independent trade union shall, for the purposes of all stages of collective bargaining about matters, and in relation to descriptions of workers in respect of which the union is recognised by him, disclose to representatives of the union, on request, the information required by this section.

The union must, therefore, be independent and recognised. Recognition means recognition at the date of the request. Subsequent derecognition is irrelevant. The right extends only to those issues on which the employers recognise the union (*R v CAC ex p BTP Tioxide Ltd* (1981)); that is, this right cannot be used to broaden the matter in respect of which the union is recognised. For example, if unions are not recognised for the purpose of closing workplaces, they cannot receive disclosed information (such as losses) relating to the closure. Recognition can come about through custom and practice. 'Representatives' means trade union officials and others authorised by the trade union to carry on collective bargaining, such as shop stewards. The aim behind the legislation is to smooth the way towards collective agreements. Information must be provided even though the employers have decided not to negotiate on a certain matter.

14.8.1 Included matters

By s 181(2):

> ... the information to be disclosed is all information relating to the employer's undertaking which is in his possession, or that of an associated employer, and is information –
>
> (a)   without which the trade union representatives would be to a material extent impeded in carrying on collective bargaining with him; and
>
> (b)   which it would in accordance with good industrial relations practice that he should disclose to them for the purposes of collective bargaining.

It is difficult to understand how a trade union could be materially impeded in bargaining in one year if it had never had the information in previous years, for, in those years, it was presumably not materially impeded! A union is materially impeded where the information is relevant and significant.

14.8.2 Code of Practice

In determining what is to be disclosed, reference may be made to the ACAS Code of Practice No 2, 'Good Industrial Relations and Disclosure of Information to Trade Unions for Collective Bargaining Purposes' (1997). The Code invites negotiators to take into account the subject matter of the bargaining, the issues, the level of negotiations (for example, are they at factory or company level?), the firm's size and its type of business. Among matters which might be raised are pay and benefits, conditions of service (for example, redundancy, criteria for promotion and appraisal), manpower (for example, turnover and planned changes to equipment), performance (such as productivity) and financial matters including assets and liabilities. Research by Gospel and Lockwood ('Disclosure of information for collective bargaining: the CAC approach' (1999) 28 ILJ 233) shows that the occasions on which trade unions obtained information about non-labour costs, redundancy proposals, corporate strategy and profits were rare. The Code has the same legal status as other ACAS Codes. It is not law but tribunals may consider it.

14.8.3 Collective bargaining

Collective bargaining is defined in s 178(1) as negotiations relating to or connected with a collective agreement which is:

> ... any agreement or arrangement made by or on behalf of one or more trade unions and one or more employers or employers' associations and relating to one or more of the matters specified in s 178(2).

Section 178(2) states:

the matters referred to above are –

(a) terms and conditions of employment, or the physical conditions in which any workers are required to work;

(b) engagement or non-engagement, or termination or suspension of employment or the duties of employment, of one or more workers;

(c) allocation of work or the duties of employment between workers or groups of workers;

(d) matters of discipline;

(e) a worker's membership or non-membership of a trade union;

(f) facilities for officials of trade unions; and

(g) machinery for negotiation or consultation, and other procedures, relating to any of the above matters, including the recognition by employers or employers' associations of the right of a trade union to represent workers in such negotiation or consultation or in the carrying out of such procedures.

(The same list appears in relation to the definition of trade dispute as a defence to claims in tort in respect of industrial action (s 244(1)). See Chapter 16.) Recent claims have involved matters such as performance-related pay and contracting out. The list, while lengthy, does not cover everything in relation to which a union might be recognised, for example, investment plans for the next decade. The duty to disclose applies notwithstanding the employers' declaration that they will negotiate on a particular issue.

14.8.4 Exemptions

Disclosure is not permitted where it would breach national security or a statute where; there would be a breach of confidentiality; it relates to an individual (unless that individual consents to disclosure); disclosure would cause 'substantial injury' to the undertaking 'for reasons other than its effect on collective bargaining'; or the information was created in connection with legal proceedings (s 182(1)). These exceptions are wide. By s 182(2)(b), employers are not required to compile information if doing so 'would involve an amount of work or expenditure out of reasonable proportion to the value of the information in the conduct of collective bargaining'. Employers need not provide the original documents. The obligation is fulfilled by providing copies.

An example of confidentiality is *Civil Service Union v Central Arbitration Committee* (1980). A firm put in a tender when the Government was contracting out cleaning. The cost of contracting out was on a form marked 'In confidence'. It was held that the information, including the number of cleaners at the Ministry of Defence, could not be disclosed. The Code of Practice suggests:

... substantial injury may occur if, for example, certain customers would be lost to competitors, or suppliers would refuse to supply necessary materials, or the ability to raise funds to finance the company would be seriously impaired as a result of disclosing certain information.

The Code states that the burden of proof is on the employers. It might be said that this embargoed information is the sort of data which would be most useful to a trade union wishing to promote the interests of its member vis à vis their employers.

14.8.5 Redress

The remedy is long-winded. The union complains to the CAC. The CAC refers it to ACAS if there is a reasonable likelihood that the matter can be resolved by conciliation, which is often successful. If there is no such likelihood or conciliation fails, the CAC, comprising both the Chair (or a deputy) and the industrial members, hears and determines the complaint, giving reasons. If the complaint is well founded, the CAC so states and specifies a period longer than a week by the end of which the employers must disclose the relevant information. If, by the end of that time, the data has not been divulged, the trade union may present a further complaint to the CAC. Again, the CAC considers and determines the complaint, giving reasons for its rulings. If the further complaint is well founded, the CAC so states. Unions have won over half these claims.

At the same time or after presenting the further complaint, the trade union may claim before the CAC that the members specified in the claim should receive the terms and conditions in their contracts requested in the claim. If the employers comply with the request for information, the whole claim falls. If, however, they do not, the CAC, after hearing both parties' arguments, may order the employers to observe the terms and conditions specified in the claim or such other terms and conditions as it considers appropriate.

The new terms and conditions, like the equality clause in the law of equal pay, become part of the employees' contract, provided that they are suitable for incorporation (and are enforced in the normal way) until superseded or varied by a collective agreement, a later award of the same type or an agreement between the employers and employees covered. In the event of the latter, the change must be favourable to the employees. There is no punitive element. The right and the remedy are out of kilter. There is no remedy that the union is to be provided with the information, and the CAC cannot prescribe what the employers must disclose in future negotiations. Complaints can be heard only if they relate to past failures. One interesting matter is that there is no appeal from the award of new terms and conditions.

The long-winded nature of the procedure is shown by the fact that CAC awards are made many months after the annual negotiations about which the trade union has complained have been settled. The complaints procedure is not much used, perhaps because some firms voluntarily disclose information.

There are about 20 references a year to the CAC. The highest figure in recent years was 37 in 1993. This right to information, which was established in its current form in 1975, was not limited by the Conservative Government, perhaps because the remedy is tortuous and the uptake small, though there was a proposal in the White Paper, *Industrial Action and Trade Unions*, Cm 3470, 1996, that the right should be abolished. An alternative view is that the information makes unions moderate their demands.

14.8.6 Other statutes

Besides information which must be supplied for collective bargaining, there are also duties on employers to provide information to safety representatives and employees covered by occupational pension schemes. Information about redundancies and transfers of undertakings have already been considered (see Chapters 9 and 13 respectively). The Employment Act 1982 states that companies employing more than 250 workers must include in their annual report a statement about action taken to inform and consult with their employees. It seems that this provision is more honoured in the breach than in the observance. One might have thought that the reports on corporate governance (Cadbury (1992) and Hampel (1998)) would have devoted space to a consideration of disclosing information to employees, but they do not.

14.9 Time off

Parliament has provided several rights to time off – for trade union duties and activities, health and safety representatives, public duties and antenatal care.

14.9.1 Time off for trade union duties and training (paid)

By s 168(1) of TULR(C)A 1992:

> ... an employer shall permit an employee who is an official of an independent trade union recognised by the employer to take time off during his working hours for the purpose of carrying out any duties of his, as such an official, concerned with –

> (a) negotiations with the employer related to or connected with matters falling within s 178(2) (collective bargaining) in relation to which the trade union is recognised by the employer; or

> (b) the performance on behalf of the employees of the employer of functions related to or connected with matters falling within that provision which the employer has agreed may be so performed by the trade union.

Section 178(2) is set out above. The duties the official is performing must, under s 168(1)(a), be ones which are concerned with negotiations with his own employers. In 1999, the legislation was extended to receipt of information from employers in connection with the transfer of undertakings and collective redundancies. There is no right to time off nowadays for general industrial relations duties. The right extends to attending a conference on matters which are not currently issues for collective bargaining, but which will be so in the future.

In *London Ambulance Service v Charlton* (1992), the EAT held that officials had a right to time off to attend a meeting of the District Co-ordinating Committee because its activities were 'related to or connected with' collective bargaining. Since the right to paid time off during working hours, the employee has no right to pay for performing union duties at other times or, indeed, to payment in lieu. This rule causes difficulty for those who work shifts or part time, for such workers seem not to be entitled to paid time off. Take, for instance, a night shift worker who attends a meeting in the daytime. To be awake at the meeting, she misses one of her shifts. She apparently cannot receive pay for missing the night shift because attendance at work was not contemporaneous with attendance at the meeting.

Employers must also permit the official to undergo industrial relations training which is relevant to the performance of his collective bargaining duties mentioned in s 168(1) and which is approved by his trade union or the Trade Union Congress (s 168(2)). Employers do not break their duty to give time off if they do not know of the official's request for it. By s 168(3):

> ... the amount of time off ... and the purposes for which, the occasions on which and any conditions subject to which time off may be so taken are those that are reasonable in all the circumstances having regard to any relevant provisions of a Code of Practice issued by ACAS.

The relevant Code of Practice is No 3, 'Time off for Trade Union Duties and Activities' (1991) (SI 1991/968), which was revised in 1997. The Code notes that, if the trade union representative's constituents are undertaking industrial action but the employee is not, it may be reasonable to give time off and, as a matter of good industrial relations, management should consider giving facilities such as premises to hold meetings in order that trade union officials can more easily perform their duties.

In *Adlington v British Bakeries (Northern) Ltd* (1989), the Court of Appeal held that a preparatory meeting fell within the business for which time off was available. The test of reasonableness is the same as that found in unfair dismissal, the 'range of reasonable responses' test (*Ministry of Defence v Crook* (1982)). This decision has been criticised for incorporating into 'time off' law a requirement derived from the entirely disparate law of unfair dismissal. The amount of time off is a reasonable amount according to the statute, not an amount which falls within employers' reasonable responses. The Court of Appeal held in *Thomas Scott & Sons (Bakers) Ltd v Allen* (1983) that it was unreasonable for all 11 shop stewards to have time off at the same time, while the EAT said in *Wignall v British Gas Corp* (1984) that it was reasonable to refuse time off when the worker had already had 12 weeks off. The needs of the school and the objections of parents made it unreasonable for a teacher to take time off in *Borders Regional Council v Maule* (1993).

14.9.2 With pay

The right is to time off with pay (cf the right to time off for trade union activities, 14.9.4, below) (s 169(1)). In the case of piece workers and others whose pay varies with the amount of work done, the amount is calculated by reference to 'the average hourly earnings' of the employee:

> ... or, if no fair estimate can be made of these earnings, the average hourly earnings for work of that description of persons in comparable employment with the same employer or, if there are no such persons, a figure of average hourly earnings which is reasonable in the circumstances [s 169(3)].

Earnings can include voluntary overtime (cf the definition of 'week's pay' in the Employment Rights Act (ERA) 1996; see Chapter 12). Of course, an official is not entitled to pay if the meeting takes place at a time when he is not expected to work.

14.9.3 Remedy

The remedy for not allowing time off or not paying for it is a complaint to an employment tribunal within three months of the failure or, if the tribunal was satisfied that it was not reasonably practicable for the complaint to be presented within that period, within such further period as the tribunal considers reasonable. If the complaint is upheld, the tribunal makes a declaration if the breach is one of failure to allow time off and may award compensation on the 'just and equitable' basis, 'having regard to the employer's default in failing to permit time off ... and to any loss sustained by the employee ...' (s 172(2)). If the complaint is of non-payment, the tribunal must order the employers to pay the sum due. The tribunal can order the employers to provide time off in the future. There is no power to order that the employers must act in a certain way in the future.

14.9.4 Time off for trade union activities (unpaid)

Section 170(1) of TULR(C)A states:

> ... an employer shall permit an employee of his who is a member of an independent trade union recognised by the employer in respect of that description of employee to take time off during his working hours for the purpose of taking part in –
>
> (a) any activities of the union; and
>
> (b) any activities in relation to which the employee is acting as a representative of the union.

The employers must know that time off has been requested. The amount, purposes, occasions and conditions of time off must be reasonable, having regard to the ACAS Code of Practice (s 170(3)). Time off does not cover activities consisting of industrial action (s 170(2)). The remedy is a complaint to an employment tribunal within three months or a reasonably practicable period. The employment tribunal must make a declaration if the complaint is well founded. It may make an award of compensation on the 'just and equitable' basis, having regard to the employers' default and the employee's loss. Again, the employers cannot be ordered to give a certain amount of paid time off for activities to take place after the declaration is granted.

It should be noted that s 170, unlike s 168, is not restricted to time off for collective bargaining purposes. In *Menzies v Smith & McLaurin Ltd* (1988), the employee applied for paid time off for training. The EAT held that the subjects of the training were not connected with collective bargaining: they involved issues relating to import controls and North Sea oil. The matters did, however, fall within s 170 as being union activities. The Code of Practice instances attendance of union conferences and of emergency meetings. Though time off under s 170 is without pay, there is nothing to prevent the parties reaching a contract to provide for pay. If a trade union official cannot get paid time off within s 168, unpaid time off within s 170 may nevertheless be available. One interesting case is *Luce v Bexley LBC* (1990). The EAT held that lobbying against the Education Reform Act 1988 was a political, not a trade union, activity. Therefore, union officials could not get time off, despite the lobbying being about a matter which concerned all teachers and despite its being organised by the Trade Union Congress. This decision has been criticised for going against the intention of Parliament, which wanted 'activities of the union' to be read broadly.

14.9.5 Time off for health and safety representatives (paid)

Health and safety representatives of recognised trade unions have a right to reasonable time off, with pay, to perform their functions. The right extends to training to do their jobs. The law is laid down in the Safety Representatives and Safety Committee Regulations 1977 (SI 1977/1500). If the employers already provide a course, a representative may be lawfully denied time off to attend a course sponsored by the Trade Union Congress on the same subject. The remedy for refusing time off is compensation, awarded by an employment tribunal and assessed on the 'just and equitable' basis. The remedy for failing to pay for the time off is the amount which should have been paid. In neither case is there a statutory limit. The restriction to trade unions has been heavily criticised for some years; and it should be remembered that recognition can be withdrawn at any time without legal sanction.

14.9.6 Other leave requirements

The aim behind the time off provisions is to improve industrial relations and, in respect of time off for health and safety representatives, to improve workplace safety. There are also rights to:

- time off with pay for study and training (for 16–18 year olds);

- time off without pay (though the work must be proportionally reduced) for public duties, for example, for Justices of the Peace and members of police authorities (s 50 of the ERA 1996: the amount of time off must be reasonable);

- time off with pay for antenatal care (s 55 of the ERA 1996: this provision dates from 1980). The aim of this provision is to reduce perinatal mortality (it is uncertain whether s 55 covers time off for seeing to pregnancy-related illness);

- time off with pay for occupational pension scheme trustees (s 58);

- time off for employee representatives or candidates for election, including (since 1999) training (s 61, as amended); and

- time off with a maximum of two-fifths of a week's pay, as defined in Pt XIV, Chapter II of the ERA 1996, when an employee is under notice of dismissal for redundancy and is refused time off (s 52 of the ERA 1996). If the employee is given time off but is not paid for it, the amount which should have been paid is awarded, subject to the maximum of two-fifths of a week's pay.

The employee need not disclose details of interviews to be undertaken. In the case of ante-natal care, the remedy for unreasonably refusing time off is the amount which would have been paid; if the employers fail to pay for the time off, the remedy is the amount which should have been paid. Since the right is to reasonable time off, employers may not be liable where a part-timer refuses to take up an appointment in his non-working time. There are no statutory limits on either award. As for public duties, the award is of compensation assessed on the 'just and equitable' basis, with no limit. There is no qualifying period for any of the rights to time off. There is also no minimum size of the undertaking at which the employee works. In no case can the employers order the employee to do extra work to compensate for the time off. The right is to time off work with or without pay. Tribunals have no power to recommend the amount of leave in the future. However, there is nothing to stop employers from encouraging employees to attend at union and other activities out of working time.

One criticism of all these provisions for time off is that any claim brought will not be heard until after the meeting for which the worker seeks leave. It should also be noted that employers are permitted to add together time off for several different reasons to assess whether time off on the relevant occasion is reasonable.

14.10 Political fund

In the famous case of *Amalgamated Society of Railway Servants v Osborne* (1910), the House of Lords decided that trade union funds could not be used for political objects, for example, to pay salaries to Labour MPs. The Trade Union Act 1913 reversed this ruling. It stated that union moneys could be used for any purpose mentioned in the trade union's constitution but that such moneys had to be donated from a separate fund, the political fund. In 1984, the Conservative Government introduced the law that trade union members must be balloted every 10 years to see whether or not they desired to maintain a fund. The law is now found in TULR(C)A 1992, Chapter VI, as amended by the Trade Union Reform and Employment Rights Act (TURERA) 1993. Over five million members subscribe, and there were 38 unions with such funds at the end of 1998.

14.10.1 Basic law

A special fund must be established to hold money to be expended on political matters (s 71(1); s 82(1)). Before one can be established, there must have been a 'political resolution' approving political objects as objects of the union (s 71(1)(a)). Union rules must provide for exemption from payment of any member objecting to contributing (s 71(1)(b)). Contribution to the fund must not be a condition of membership (s 82(1)(d)). A union cannot finance political objects out of its general fund, nor can it transfer money from its general to its political fund. It may be that political fund money can be spent on general objects, at least if the rules so permit.

14.10.2 Political objects

Political objects are defined in s 72(1) as expending money:

(a)   as any contribution to the funds of, or on the payment of expenses incurred directly or indirectly by, a political party;

(b)   on the provision of any service or property for use by or on behalf of any political party;

(c)   in connection with the registration of electors, the candidature of any person, the selection of any candidate or the holding of any ballot by the union in connection with any election to a political office;

(d)   on the maintenance of any holder of a political office;

(e)   on the holding of any conference or meeting by or on behalf of a political party or of any other meeting the main purpose of which is the transaction of business in connection with a political party;

(f)   on the production, publication or distribution of any literature, documents, film, sound recording or advertisement the main purpose of which is to persuade people to vote for a political party or candidate or to persuade them not to vote for a political party or candidate.

By s 72(4), 'political office' connotes the office of MP, MEP, member of a local authority or any position within a political party. 'Service' in (b) would seem to cover the loan of staff. Sub-section (e) covers the annual Labour Party Conference. Money spent on the Labour Party's Headquarters was for a political purpose (*Richards v NUM* (1981)) (s 72(1)(b) expressly covers such expenditure: before 1984, it was for the CO to determine if such expenditure was for a political purpose). 'Maintenance' includes finance for research facilities (*ASTMS v Parkin* (1984)). Campaigning at general election time against cutbacks in public services was political (*Paul v NALGO* (1987)). Paying subsistence expenses to union members assisting MPs at a general election must be paid out of the political fund.

If employers do not deduct the money to be paid into the political fund, the employee may apply to an employment tribunal.

14.10.3 Protected property

Where there is a political fund, the money in it cannot be used to satisfy a judgment against the union, but it can be sequestered to pay a fine for contempt of court. In the jargon, the fund is 'protected property'.

14.10.4 Voting

By s 73(1), a political resolution must be approved in a vote on a ballot of the members. Voting must be carried out by marking a paper in a fully postal ballot, not by show of hands. All union members (except members overseas) are entitled to vote on the continuance of a fund; overseas members are entitled to vote where a resolution has expired. A simple majority is needed. A new resolution is needed every 10 years (s 73(3)). The ballot must be held in accord with rules approved by the CO (s 76(1)). The TULR(C)A 1992, as amended by TURERA 1993, lays down detailed rules about the appointment of an independent scrutineer, the entitlement to vote, voting, counting by an independent person (who may be the scrutineer) and the scrutineer's report on the ballot. Perhaps the main provisions are s 77(3) and (4). By s 77(3):

Every person who is entitled to vote in the ballot must –

(a)   be allowed to vote without interference from, or constraint imposed by, the union or any of its members, officials or employees, and

(b)   so far as is reasonably practicable, be enabled to do so without incurring any direct cost to himself.

By s 77(4):

> ... so far as reasonably practicable, every person who is entitled to vote in the ballot must –
>
> (a) have a voting paper sent to him by post at his home address, and
>
> (b) be given a convenient opportunity to vote by post.

Since 1988, a workplace ballot has not been possible. The vote must be fully postal. Those who may vote must not be exclusively those who currently contribute. Only overseas members can be excluded from the vote.

14.10.5 Remedy

A member of a trade union may apply to the CO or the High Court (which deals with breaches of statute) when the union has not acted in accord with the rules for a political ballot approved by the CO. The time limit is one year from the day of the announcement of the result of the ballot (ss 79–81 of TULR(C)A 1992). If the application is made to the court, the court may issue an 'enforcement order', instructing the union to hold the ballot properly to remedy the defect or to desist from doing a specified act. The CO had no such power until he was given it by the Employment Relations Act 1999. There is an appeal from the CO to the EAT. Formal complaints to the CO are rare. Only three were made in 1998.

14.10.6 Non-contributors

A person who does not wish to contribute to the political fund is exempted (s 82(1)(b)). If the employers deduct money in breach of this exemption, the employee may apply to an employment tribunal. The union must tell the members that they have a right to be exempted (s 84(2)). A person cannot be refused admission to the union on the ground that he is unwilling to contribute to the political fund. By s 82(1)(c):

> ... a member shall not by reason of being so exempt –
>
> (i) be excluded from any benefits of the union, or
>
> (ii) be placed under a disability or a disadvantage as compared with other members of the union (except in relation to the control or management of the political fund) ...

The main case is *Birch v NUR* (1950). An exempted member complained that the union's national executive committee had stripped him of his office of branch chair because he did not pay the political levy. The judge held that his removal was unlawful.

The CO ruled unlawful a provision that a non-contributing member paid five-thirteenths of one penny each week which was refunded in a lump sum every quarter (*McCarthy v APEX* (1979)). It is also unlawful for unions to charge higher subscriptions to members who do not pay the political fund than those who do. If the employers operate a check-off system for union dues, they cannot refuse to operate a check-off for those union members who do not pay the levy (s 86). Non-payment of the political fund is often called 'contracting out'. The previous Government at times suggested that the law should be changed so that members have to 'contract in' to the fund but, as yet, this proposal has not been enacted. It might be argued, however, that the present law on balloting is unfair to those who wish to pay. Why should they be denied the opportunity of contributing to the levy by fellow members who do not wish to contribute? After all, non-contributors are protected against discrimination.

14.10.7 Lapse

Where the political resolution lapses because a ballot has not been held within 10 years or has been defeated, the trade union must stop collecting money for the fund. In 1997, the CPSA's political fund lapsed and, later that year, its members voted against re-establishing it. Any money collected after the lapse must be refunded. No money can be added to the fund (except interest on the sum). The union may transfer the whole or part of the political fund to another fund, or it can freeze the fund in the hope that a later vote may revive it.

14.10.8 Comment

In 1984, the Government introduced the provision relating to ballots' having to be held every 10 years. It believed that the re-ballots would lead to fewer political funds than before, the effect being that trade unions' financial support for the Labour Party would haemorrhage. Some £4 million per year is given to the Labour Party by unions, but the proportion of the Party's income derived from unions is declining. In fact, unions which had political funds successfully retained them in the mid-1980s and a few unions which did not have them ran successful ballots to establish them, the argument being that unions should be able to speak on political matters affecting their membership, especially because the definition of 'political' was a wide one covering, for example, campaigns against government cutbacks. Some unions have political funds but are not affiliated to the Labour Party. One contention was that trade unionists who vote for the Conservatives – and about one-third of them do – should not stifle the expression of views by their colleagues, and the link with the Labour Party was played down, though there is nothing to prevent unions supporting the Conservatives or Liberal Democrats. Similar results to those obtained in

1985–86 were obtained in the first decennial ballots in 1994–96. The average percentage in favour was 80%. The restrictions on political funds do not apply to companies. Companies donated over £2 million to the Conservative Party in 1994, but donations by them to other political parties are small in comparison.

There are no restrictions on companies giving money for political purposes, the sole law being that they must disclose donations of above £200, and companies tend to stop donations for reasons other than shareholders criticising these gifts. Cost-cutting, globalisation of commerce and anger at Government policies are some of the stated reasons. Shareholders have no right to contract out of political donations. It has seemed unfortunate to the present writer that he could not contract out of subsidising one political party when buying food, beer and new houses!

TRADE UNIONS

Definition

Trade unions are organisations of workers, the principal purpose of which is the regulation of employment relations:

- *Midland Cold Storage v Steer* (1972).

The association need not be permanent and need not have industrial muscle.

Legal status

Unions are quasi-corporate bodies able to make contracts, to sue and be sued and be prosecuted. They cannot, however, sue for libel:

- *EEPTU v Times Newspapers* (1980).

Restraint of trade

Unions' rules and purposes are not in restraint of trade. It has been postulated that unions' rules may be struck down on the basis that they interfere with an individual's right to work.

Listing

Unions may be placed on the Certification Officer's list.

Independence

Unions free of employers' control and not liable to interference have various rights:

- *Squibb v CO* (1979);
- *Blue Circle v CO* (1977).

The Certification Officer investigates the union's history, membership, finance, facilities, role in collective bargaining and internal affairs.

The rights include being consulted on collective redundancies and on the transfer of undertakings and to receive information for collective bargaining purposes.

Recognition

Employers' recognition of unions is not supported by statute:

- *NUGSAT v Albury Bros* (1979).

Collective bargaining information

Recognised independent unions must be given information for collective bargaining purposes. Some matters are exempted:

- *R v CAC ex p BTP Tioxide* (1981).

Time off

Union officials must be given reasonable time off with pay for aspects of collective bargaining for which the union is recognised. Members have a right to time off without pay for union activities:

- *Adlington v British Bakeries* (1989);
- *Luce v Bexley LBC* (1990).

Political fund

Unions wishing to expend money on political objects must establish a separate fund in a fully postal ballot. Non-contributors must not be discriminated against.

- *Paul v NALGO* (1987);
- *Birch v NUR* (1950).

Political objects include the maintenance of MPs and campaigns against cuts in public services.

Voting must be fully postal and must be held every 10 years. There are detailed rules on balloting and counting.

CHAPTER 15

TRADE UNION GOVERNANCE

15.1 Introduction

This chapter considers freedom of association, the legal status of the rule book, various rights of an applicant for membership and rights of a member against his trade union, whether arising under contract, public law or statute. It concludes with discussion of elections for certain union positions and the linked members' rights such as to be a candidate. Current law is highly restrictive of union autonomy. In relation to freedom of association, the reader is also directed to detriment and dismissal on trade union grounds, discussed in Chapter 11.

15.2 Association and dissociation

Various international treaties state that individuals have a right to form organisations such as trade unions. Examples are Art 20 of the Universal Declaration of Human Rights 1948 and Art 11 of the European Convention on Human Rights. The International Labour Organisation (ILO), an arm of the United Nations, has conventions on this topic which States may ratify. Both the European Social Charter 1961 and the EC Social Charter 1989 upheld freedom of association. These treaties are not, however, binding on the UK until ratified and, once ratified, they can be denounced. The repeal of the Fair Wages Resolution and the Truck Acts involved the denunciation of two conventions of the ILO. The Treaty of Amsterdam 1997 (in force 1999) states that the EC has no competence in matters concerning freedom of association.

15.2.1 International standards

The ILO has, on several occasions, found the UK to be in breach of its international obligations. Examples include the abolition of collective bargaining for teachers and the banning of unions at GCHQ. A majority of the European Court of Human Rights (ECHR) held in *Young, James and Webster v UK* (1981) that Art 11 of the Convention was broken when the employers dismissed employees in a closed shop situation despite Art 11 stating only that employees had a freedom to associate and freedom not to leave unions and despite the *travaux préparatoires*. The ECHR has since ruled that Art 11 is breached by a failure to provide a right not to join a trade union. It is arguable that the law on unjustifiable discipline is contrary to Art 11. Choice of moving workplace or rejoining a union is not (*Sibson v UK* (1993)).

15.2.2 Membership and non-membership

The UK does not ban the formation of unions, but members of the police force and GCHQ cannot join unions and would be in breach of their contracts if they did so. Members of the armed forces may join but they must not participate in union activities which conflict with their service duties. Section 137 of the Trade Union and Labour Relations (Consolidation) Act (TULR(C)A) 1992 prohibits employers' refusing to employ persons on the grounds of trade union membership or non-membership. It was held by the EAT in *Harrison v Kent CC* (1995) that a refusal to re-employ an applicant who had previously been a shop steward and had displayed anti-management attitudes breached s 137. It was a question for the employment tribunal whether a refusal to employ because of his union activities was a refusal to employ because he was a trade union member. Mummery J said that:

> ... a divorce of the *fact* of membership and the incidents of membership is illusory ... membership of a union means more than the bare fact that a person ... holds a union membership card. Participation in the activities of a union is one of the ways in which membership of a union is manifested ...

The Government equated rights to membership and non-membership. These had previously been seen as being totally different. Membership supported collective bargaining, which was considered a good thing. Non-membership undermined it; therefore, it was a bad thing. Employers can still refuse to employ union members who are classified as troublemakers. The right in s 137 extends to cover a requirement that a person should donate money to a charity if he did not wish to subscribe to a union. Such donations were one way in which unions sought to get round the 'free rider' problem – persons who took advantage of benefits obtained by unions, such as increased pay, but who did not pay union dues. The remedy is a complaint to an employment tribunal within three months of the employers' refusal or, if it was not reasonably practicable for the complaint to be presented within that period, within a reasonable time of the end thereof. The burden of proof is on the applicant. If the complaint is well founded, the employment tribunal makes a declaration and may make an award of compensation calculated as for the tort of breach of statutory duty, the maximum being the same as that of the compensatory award for unfair dismissal. Compensation for injured feelings may be awarded. The employment tribunal may make:

> ... a recommendation that the respondent take within a specified period action appearing to the tribunal to be practicable for the purpose of obviating or reducing the adverse effect on the complainant of any conduct to which the complaint relates [s 140(1)(b)].

15.2.3 Joinder

If the individual or employers claim that the latter were induced to act by pressure which a trade union exercised on them 'by calling, organising, procuring or financing a strike or other industrial action, or by threatening to do so' (s 142(1)), the employment tribunal must include the union in the action if requested before the hearing of the complaint and may include it if the request is made after the start of the hearing but before its conclusion. The employment tribunal may order compensation to be paid wholly or partly by the union (s 142(2)).

15.2.4 Goods and services

Complementary to s 137 are ss 144–45 of TULR(C)A 1992. By s 144:

> ... a term or condition of a contract for the supply of goods or services is void in so far as it purports to require that the whole, or some part, of the work done for the purposes of the contract is done only by persons who are, or are not, members of trade unions or of a particular trade union.

By s 145(1):

> ... a person shall not refuse to deal with a supplier or prospective supplier of goods or services on union membership grounds.

'Union membership grounds' means grounds where there is a requirement that persons working under the contract are or are not members of any trade union or any particular trade union. Section 145 gives rise to a right in persons with whom there is a refusal to deal and those who may be 'adversely affected' by breach of s 145 (s 145(5)). Violation is actionable as a breach of statutory duty and the defences to that tort are available to this action.

15.2.5 Pre-entry closed shop

Section 137 marks the culmination of the then Government's attacks on one form of union security, the closed shop. The right applies to pre-entry closed shops (that is, ones in which individuals must be a member of a certain trade union or trade unions before the employers can consider them suitable for the job). There is now no legal support for pre- or post-entry shops, even if the employers do not wish to upset existing arrangements in order to support good industrial relations.

Two points of interpretation of s 137 should be noted. It applies only to refusal on grounds of membership of a trade union. If the member is turned down because he is an activist, he has no right. Membership without activity is not totally meaningful. In *Discount Tobacco and Confectionery Ltd v Armitage* (1990), a member's recourse to a trade union official to ask him to help determine her terms and conditions was a function of membership, not an activity. This case would seem to be restricted to its own facts as a result of *Associated Newspapers Ltd v Wilson* (1993) and *Associated British Ports v Palmer* (1995), where the House of Lords drew a line between the membership of a union and using its services: deterring members from using the union's services was not the same as deterring members from continuing membership, a decision which has attracted great criticism on the grounds that being a member and using the union's power are the same.

Despite this criticism of *Discount Tobacco* by the House of Lords, the EAT said in *Speciality Care plc v Pachela* (1996) that employment tribunals could find that a sacking for seeking help from the union in a dispute over a variation in hours was a dismissal for membership of the union. Similarly, it would seem that s 137 would not apply to refusals of employment on the grounds that the applicants had participated in industrial action. Another point to note is that s 137 has a tendency to upset settled industrial relations practices. If the employers wish to bargain collectively with only one or a small number of unions, their wish is undermined by persons joining other unions. It is uncertain whether the decisions of the House of Lords in the *Associated* cases will affect *Harrison v Kent CC* (15.2.2, above). The decision of the Lords is in line with Conservative Party thinking, which sees a place for unions as purveyors of services such as insurance and legal help.

15.3   Union rules

The union rule book is both a constitution for the union and a contract between the trade union and the member. Unions have a statutory duty to provide a copy of the rules to any person on request. A reasonable fee may be charged. The sanction for breach of this duty is a fine. The maximum fine is £5,000. Traditionally, Parliament has not intervened, but there are now several members' rights against unions which supersede contrary rules. Statutory remedies are becoming more important than contractual rights, which, unlike in many other areas of employment law, retain their importance. In one instance, there is an implied term:

> In every contract of membership of a trade union ... a term conferring a right on the member, on giving reasonable notice and complying with any reasonable conditions, to terminate his membership of the union shall be implied [s 69 of TULR(C)A 1992].

What is reasonable is not defined. The union may postpone the resignation's taking effect until the member has been disciplined and paid any arrears of duties.

15.3.1 Judicial intervention

Accordingly, it is for the judges to determine how long reasonable notice is and which conditions are reasonable. Besides statutory changes, judges have a powerful role to play in the control of union rule books through the construction of the rules and the application of natural justice. It has been argued that the judiciary lean too far in favour of maverick individuals at the expense of union collectivism. Judicial intervention was justified by Lord Denning MR in *Breen v Amalgamated Engineering Union* (1971) on the ground that:

> ... the rules are in reality more than a contract. They are a legislative code ... This code should be subject to control by the courts just as much as a code laid down by Parliament itself.

After a consideration of the interpretation of rule books, the remainder of this section looks at common law and statutory intervention. Common law terms remain important, for statute may not cover the issue. Freedom of association, the right which underpins the autonomy of trade unions in the UK, has been severely restricted by recent statutes.

15.3.2 Construction

It is the dual legal role of the union rule book which underlies the judges' approach to it. As a contract, it must be construed as such. If there is, for example, no power to expel expressly stated, contractual rules on implied terms govern. As a code, the rules are subject to administrative law, such as the doctrines of *ultra vires* and natural justice. Cutting across the contractual and administrative law approaches is the knowledge that rule books are often drafted without legal help. Taking a strict, contractual approach to interpretation may not be in tune with what the drafters believed they were writing.

A cynic might say that the courts adopt whichever mode gives an anti-trade union result. The most authoritative case, *Heatons Transport (St Helens) Ltd v Transport and General Workers Union* (1972), went beyond a strict construction to see whether, at common law, the union was vicariously liable for the actions of its shop stewards. To decide that question, the House of Lords investigated custom and practice when the contract, that is, the rule book, was silent. It is arguable that the courts take a broad approach to the rules when they are investigating constitutional matters (for example, is the union vicariously liable?) and a narrow one where the matter involves individual members (for example, has the union the power to suspend a member?).

15.3.3 Contract

Since membership of a trade union gives rise to a contract, a member deprived of his rights under the contract may claim in the ordinary courts that the contract has been broken by the trade union. Legal aid may be available. The normal remedies – damages, injunction or both – are available. A declaration may be awarded. One might have expected that, where collective and individual interests conflicted, the former would prevail, but this has rarely been the case. The courts have said that, absent a rule, there is no common law power in a trade union to expel. Therefore, if a union wishes to expel a member, there must be a rule and the union must apply that rule, including any procedure under it (*Hiles v Amalgamated Society of Woodworkers* (1968)). Similarly, the courts have refused to imply a term that a member would obey all reasonable instructions of the trade union and that a union can set aside the result of a ballot for the general president (unless perhaps he or she was not qualified to stand). There are many cases dealing with whether unions had power under their rules to perform various functions. Going through all the cases would be piling Pelion on Ossa. A small sample of what may be called classic cases follows:

- *Hopkins v NUS* (1985)

  A levy on members to support the National Union of Mineworkers was not allowed by the rules and an injunction was granted. However, the expenditure of this levy was lawful because the union's objects clause permitted it to spend money on the improvement of conditions and the protection of all members of the union. Since coal was transportable in ships crewed by the National Union of Seamen, it was arguable that financial support to the NUM was lawful.

- *Lee v Showmen's Guild of Great Britain* (1952)

  A member was fined by a union committee for engaging in unfair competition. The court held that what he had done did not constitute such competition. That is, the court held that it could intervene where there was no evidence to support the finding of unfair competition.

- *McVitae v UNISON* (1996)

  The court held that a term that a union could discipline its members for misbehaviour could be implied into a contract between them. The High Court said that, on the facts, a rule was implied as to discipline in respect of conduct before amalgamation permitting the new union to take disciplinary action when both of the old unions had such rules during their existence. This case marks something of a departure from orthodox analysis of contracts of membership. Terms have rarely been implied in the past. It remains to be seen whether this case marks the start of a trend.

- *Esterman v NALGO* (1974)

  Templeman J ruled that a committee was wrong to hold that refusing to participate in a strike was 'conduct which, in the opinion of the branch committee, renders her unfit for membership'. He held that the courts could prevent unlawful discipline and not just intervene when the action had been taken. It should be noted that the court intervened despite the subjective phrasing ('in the opinion of ... ') of the clause. The basis of Templeman J's ruling was that no reasonable tribunal could have come to the conclusion that it did: to discipline members for not taking part in industrial action when only 41% had voted in favour. In criticism, it may be said that the courts are intervening in unions' internal affairs at the time when unions need their collective power most, namely, when they are involved in industrial action.

These cases demonstrate the courts' power to control discipline and expulsion through interpretation of the rule book. Not even subjectively phrased rules, such as that in the last case, escape review. Besides control in these ways, the courts' power to rule on implied terms give judges power to give effect to their policies. For example, in *MacLelland v NUJ* (1975), it was held that members had to be given reasonable notice of important meetings.

15.3.4 Further examples

The courts have tended to intervene if the union has, in their view, misinterpreted the relevant rule. In *Kelly v NATSOPA* (1915), the court held that a union was wrong to hold that taking a part time job was 'conduct prejudicial to the union's interests'. In *MacLelland v NUJ* (1975), the court held that a member had been improperly disciplined for failing to attend a union meeting. He had turned up and signed in but had not stayed for the duration. It was held that what he had done was enough to constitute attendance. Accordingly, the union did not by contract have the power to discipline him.

The courts have, on the one hand, strongly upheld the principle that their jurisdiction must not be ousted by the rules of domestic tribunals, yet, on the other, they have given leeway to rules which are couched in wide language, such as a rule whereby a member may be expelled for engaging in conduct which, in the view of the national executive committee, is prejudicial to the interests of the union.

15.3.5 Remedies

Courts are restricted to damages and remedies which prohibit action in reliance on the rule, but they cannot enforce the rules by ordering specific performance (*Taylor v NUM (Yorkshire Area)* (1984)). The court could not order the holding of a ballot required by the rules. There is no statutory limit on damages in contractual actions against unions.

15.3.6 Exhaustion of internal remedies

One particular instance of judicial control is whether a member must follow a union rule that internal remedies must be exhausted before he can go to the courts. In *White v Kuzych* (1951), the Privy Council held that internal remedies (such as an appeals process) had to be gone through first, but judges in later cases have stated that such a rule cannot oust the jurisdiction of the court, though a good reason must be given for non-exhaustion (for example, *Leigh v NUR* (1970) and *Radford v NATSOPA* (1972)). This non-ouster is supported by s 63 of TULR(C)A 1992. Any union or judge made rule calling for the exhaustion of internal remedies is void if a member or ex-member has applied to the trade union for a determination of the matter and no determination has been made within six months of the submission. Section 63 overrides contrary union rules, but it is arguable that it does not overrule the law in cases such as *Leigh v NUR*, that is, that the non-ouster principle still applies before the six months have elapsed. If the rule were phrased not merely that internal remedies must be exhausted but there was no appeal from union decisions, a *fortiori* it would be void as contrary to public policy (*Lee v Showmen's Guild of Great Britain* (1952) and s 63 of TULR(C)A 1992).

15.3.7 Intervention pre-decision

It is not yet clear whether a court can intervene to prohibit proceedings before a decision has been reached. Among cases upholding such jurisdiction are ones from the 1984–85 miners' strike. In *Taylor v NUM (Derbyshire Area)* (1984), the court prevented the application of disciplinary rules on the grounds that, since the strike was not official because it had been called in breach of the rules, disciplining for not taking part was illegal. In *Clarke v Chadburn* (1985), disciplining was unlawful because the rule had not been validly adopted. More recently, however, the Court of Appeal stated in *Longley v NUJ* (1987) that, in advance of a determination, the courts will be loath to intervene. This decision heralded a period during which the courts did not often intervene using common law techniques, but it is unclear whether the period is genuinely one of judicial abstentionism or whether it simply reflects the fact that there are now other, statutory, modes of intervention.

15.3.8 *Foss v Harbottle*

There has been debate, especially in recent years, about whether the company law rule in *Foss v Harbottle* (1843) applies to unions. By that rule, a member of a company cannot, subject to exceptions, bring an action for redress of harm done to the company, partly because the company alone is the 'proper plaintiff' to remedy harm to itself and partly because the court will not restrain something which the company might ratify. One exception is that a company cannot ratify an *ultra vires* act. Since that act is unlawful, it cannot be made lawful by ratification. A recent discussion appears in *Taylor v NUM (Derbyshire Area) (No 3)* (1985). The judge, Vinelott J, said in relation to a claim that the area officers should refund the £1.7 million they had spent on the miners' strike on the grounds that they had acted in breach of their fiduciary duties to the union in supporting an unlawful strike:

> *Foss v Harbottle* applies to a union but does not bar the right of an individual to an action joining the union and its officers as defendants and claiming that a particular application by the union and its officers was *ultra vires* ... and requiring the officers to make good the loss to the union. Being *ultra vires*, the misapplication cannot be ratified by any majority of the members.

Chadwick J said the same in *Wise v Union of Shop, Distributive and Allied Workers* (1996). The astute reader may be asking the question why a company law concept is applied in labour law. After all, Parliament has stated not just that a trade union is not a company but that it is not even to be treated as one (see s 10(1) and (2) of TULR(C)A 1992). The position remains uncertain as to whether *Foss v Harbottle* applies and, if so, whether the exceptions apply. On the facts, the judge held that the courts will not grant an injunction if it will not serve a useful purpose. Certainly, *Foss v Harbottle* does not apply where the wrong is done not to the union/company but to the member in his capacity as a member. The wrong is so done when the union fines or expels him.

15.3.9 Natural justice

Besides contract, the courts intervene on the grounds of natural justice. These rules, *nemo judex in sua causa* ('no one shall be claimant and judge') and *audi alteram partem* ('hear the other side'), are the same as those found in public law. For example, the member must have notice of the rule he allegedly broke. Natural justice is distinct from contract. Contract cannot be used to exclude natural justice (*Radford v NATSOPA* (1972)). Such a rule is contrary to public policy. Though the issue has not clearly been resolved, it seems that a fair appeal cannot cure a bad first hearing. It should be recalled that natural justice is concerned with procedure, not with substance. The fact that the decision was unjust is irrelevant if the way in which it was reached was just.

15.3.10 Bias

The most famous case on bias is *Roebuck v NUM (Yorkshire Area) (No 2)* (1978). Mr Scargill, President of the union, sued a newspaper for libel on its behalf. The plaintiffs, who were union members, gave evidence for the paper. Mr Scargill claimed that one plaintiff had contradicted in court what he had told the union's solicitors out of court and the editor had divulged union correspondence to the paper's lawyers. The behaviour was, in his opinion, detrimental to the interests of the union. The area council, which was chaired by Mr Scargill, said that the conduct was detrimental. It referred the issue to the area executive council, which was also chaired by Mr Scargill. It recommended suspension of the members. The area council, again chaired by Mr Scargill, confirmed the decision. The court said that Mr Scargill had acted as 'the complainant, the pleader, the prosecutor, the advocate and the chairman'. The proceedings were tainted with the appearance of bias and so were contrary to natural justice.

It should be noted that, as perhaps occurred in the above case, there need not be actual bias. It is sufficient if there is a semblance of bias – a real possibility of prejudice. It is obviously difficult to provide totally bias-free persons where a union official is accusing a member of breach of a rule and another official forms the tribunal, but the courts have taken a broad approach and have not struck down decisions easily. There is authority for the proposition that it is not always the law that a person cannot sit at first instance and on an appeal in the same matter, at least where the union rules so permit.

15.3.11 Notice and hearing

A union member is entitled to receive notice of the misconduct alleged and to be given enough time to defend himself (for example, *Stevenson v United Road Transport Union* (1977)). No notice need be given if everyone involved knows the nature of the charge. The member is still entitled to answer the allegations.

15.3.12 Width

The courts have said that the right to be heard does not extend to the right to be legally represented (*Enderby FC v Football Association* (1971) (not a trade union case)). In the view of Lord Denning MR, as stated in that case, a clause in the union's rule book purporting to exclude legal representation is contrary to public policy, because all tribunals have the inherent discretion to permit such representation. It may be that an appeals system is not a requirement of natural justice, and there are conflicting cases as to whether a defect at first instance may be cured on appeal. The width of natural justice varies from case to case.

15.3.13 Right to work

The contractual method of controlling unions' decisions can work only where there is a contract. If an applicant for membership is turned down, there is no contract in existence. There are statutory rules relating to turning individuals away on sexual and racial grounds and, as we shall see, on the right to membership of a union. At common law, Lord Denning MR said on interlocutory motion in *Nagle v Feilden* (1966) (again, a non-trade union case) that individuals had a right to work. He applied his doctrine (in *obiter dicta*) to unions in *Edwards v SOGAT* (1971) on the grounds that the closed shop interfered with the worker's right to work when the union refused to re-admit him, and there may be life in his doctrine. If so, the courts would have power to strike down union rules, concocted out of spite or whimsy, which interfered with this right. It may be that, if it exists, it is restricted to situations where the union holds a monopoly position. However, as stated in Chapter 14, the doctrine seems to have quietly died since Lord Denning's retirement, at least in relation to unions. *Nagle v Feilden* is now considered to be an illustration of public law, to be dealt with in judicial review proceedings. Unions can be seen as having a public law function, particularly when a closed shop exists. The contrary argument is that a public interest does not convert a private matter into a public law matter.

15.3.14 Illegality

Courts have said that they have jurisdiction to strike down rules which are illegal at common law. In *Drake v Morgan* (1978), it was said *obiter* that a rule providing for the repayment of fines of members convicted of illegal picketing was unlawful. Doing so is nowadays statutorily illegal (s 15 of TULR(C)A 1992).

15.3.15 Comment

It is unlikely nowadays that expulsion from a trade union will lead to the loss of a job, whereas a dismissal, by definition, means that an employee no longer has a job. Yet union rules are more strictly controlled by judges than are sackings. The principles of natural justice do not apply to ordinary master and servant cases. A radical might say that the difference represents the judges' class bias. They favour capitalists, that is, employers, at the expense of labour unions. When Lord Denning spoke in favour of the individual against the big battalions, he was not speaking of an employee against the employers but of a member against the trade union.

15.4 'Bridlington': the principles

Trade unions, meeting at the Trades Union Congress in Bridlington, Yorkshire, agreed a set of principles regulating recruitment at the workplace. The principles are non-contractual. The principles were amended in 1993 to take account of changes in the law. Principle 5, which was renumbered Principle 3 in 1993, states that:

> ... no union shall commence organising activities at any establishment or undertaking in respect of any grade of workers in which another union has a majority of the workers employed and negotiate terms and conditions, unless by arrangement with that union.

Principle 2 prohibits unions from accepting applicants who are or recently have been members of a union affiliated to the Trades Union Congress without making enquiries of that union. The notes to the principles are of equal standing to the principles. Principle 1, note (e), which is now part of the new Principle 3, states that no union shall enter into a sole negotiating agreement or any arrangement whereby other unions would lose their rights of recognition, and no union may negotiate unless those unions concur. In the event of a dispute, the Trades Union Congress's Disputes Committee has jurisdiction and Trades Union Congress unions must obey its rulings. It can order a union to compensate the union from which it has taken members, and it has the power to censure the poaching union. The Disputes Committee cannot nowadays require a trade union to expel a member who has been admitted in breach of the 'Bridlington principles'.

15.4.1 Right to membership

Section 14 of TURERA 1993 substitutes new ss 174–77 into TULR(C)A 1992. The heading is 'right to membership of trade union'. The old ss 174–77 provided members with a right not to be unreasonably excluded or expelled from a trade union, a right granted originally in ss 4–5 of the Employment Act 1980. The new sections widen that right, which applied only when there was a closed shop. The old ss 174–17 are repealed. So the right to membership of a trade union replaces the right not to be unreasonably excluded or expelled from a trade union. The right does not replace the common law right to sue for breach of contract.

One might have thought that the 1993 Act was needed less now because of the swift decline of the closed shop in the 1980s. The statutory rights discussed here and below, 15.5, have been seen as grave intrusions on the principle of freedom to organise. The principle of union autonomy, which some say is necessary in a democratic society, has been undermined.

15.4.2 Definition

By s 174(1), an applicant or member must not be excluded or expelled from a trade union except as detailed below. Exclusion includes the situation where:

> ... an individual's application for membership of a trade union is neither granted nor rejected before the end of the period within which it might reasonably have been expected to be granted [s 177(2)(a)].

Expulsion includes the situation where:

> ... an individual ... under the rules of a trade union ceases to be a member of the union on the happening of an event specified in the rules [s 177(2)(b)].

The latter provision will take effect if there is a rule that membership lapses if fees have not been paid for a certain time. Should this occur, there is a right against the trade union unless one of the defences (or perhaps, better put, exceptions) apply. However, expulsion does not cover the situation where the member resigns as a protest against policy or where there is a breach of a fundamental term in the contract of membership. In other words, there is no doctrine of constructive expulsion. 'Exclusion' means exclusion from the union. It does not include exclusion from the benefits of a trade union while remaining a member (*NACODS v Gluchowski* (1996)). Therefore, suspension is not included in the definition. A suspended member may, however, have other remedies. It is noteworthy that the tribunal drew support from anti-union cases, which distinguished between membership and the benefits of membership, to reach a pro-union decision.

15.4.3 Exceptions

The exceptions are found in s 174(2):

> The exclusion or expulsion of an individual from a trade union is permitted by this section if (and only if) –
>
> (a) he does not satisfy, or no longer satisfies, an enforceable membership requirement contained in the rules of the union;
>
> (b) he does not qualify, or no longer qualifies, for membership of the union by reason of the union operating only in a particular part or particular parts of Great Britain;
>
> (c) in the case of a union whose purpose is the regulation of relations between its members and one particular employer or a number of particular employers who are associated, he is not, or is no longer, employed by that employer or one of those employers; or
>
> (d) the exclusion or expulsion is entirely attributable to his conduct.

Paragraph (b) covers the National Union of Mineworkers' areas, each of which is a separate union. Paragraph (c) permits single employer unions. Since the sus-section is not restricted to independent trade unions, 'house' unions can exclude or expel those protesting against the 'sweetheart' relationship without infringing this right. If the applicant falls within one of the exceptions, the question of whether or not the exclusion or expulsion was reasonable is irrelevant.

15.4.4 'Enforceable' requirement

By s 174(3), a requirement is 'enforceable' if it 'restricts membership solely by reference to one or more of the following criteria:

(a) employment in a specified trade, industry or profession;

(b) occupational description (including grade, level or category of appointment); and

(c) possession of specified trade, industrial or professional qualifications or work experience.

There is not much room for the application of the Bridlington principles. Accordingly, the statute gives an impetus to predatory unions. Inter-union disputes may increase with a concomitant threat to industrial relations. Section 174(3) does, however, safeguard craft unions.

15.4.5 Conduct

Conduct is negatively part-defined in s 174(4) to exclude:

> ... his being or ceasing to be, or having been or ceased to be –
>
> (i)   a member of another trade union;
>
> (ii)   employed by a particular employer or at a particular place; or
>
> (iii) a member of a political party.

It further excludes conduct covered by the right not to be unjustifiably disciplined by a trade union (s 65 of TULR(C)A 1992), on which, see below, 15.5. Nevertheless, this sub-section does permit a union to refuse to admit membership to a person who is in arrears of subscription with another union.

15.4.6 Remedy

The remedy is a little complex. The complainant makes a claim to an employment tribunal within six months of the exclusion or expulsion or, if it was not reasonably practicable to bring the complaint within that period, within a reasonable further time. Time runs from the receipt of the decision, not from the date of the decision (*Smith v UNISON* (1998)). If the complaint is well founded, the employment tribunal makes a declaration. The complainant may now apply for compensation, either to the tribunal if the complainant has been admitted or re-admitted to the trade union, or to the EAT under all other circumstances. That is, in this instance, the EAT has original jurisdiction. This claim is made not before four weeks and not after six months from the date of the declaration. Compensation is awarded on the 'just and equitable' basis, with reduction for contributory fault. ('Fault' has included applying for a job with employers whom the applicant knew had a closed shop agreement: 15% was deducted.) The maximum compensation is 30 times the current limit on a week's pay for the purpose of calculating the basic award in unfair dismissal (£210) plus the maximum compensatory award. Where the claim is determined in the EAT, there is a minimum award of £5,000. This minimum is not reduced by any contributory fault. Appeals lie on points of law from the employment tribunal to the EAT. It is uncertain whether the sum must be reduced through the doctrine of mitigation. There is no express power in the statute, but there was such a power in the repealed law.

15.4.7 Comment

Depending on one's viewpoint, the new right may be seen either as an extension of the policy of statutory regulation on unions in an effort to destroy them through undermining their autonomy or as safeguarding individuals when they are oppressed by collective bodies. Unions argue that, as voluntary bodies, they should be able to control who can become members. The new law is wider than common law, under which a union could exclude a person for any reason and could specify any qualifications for membership, provided that the rule was not arbitrary (on the last point, see *Nagle v Feilden*, 15.3.13, above). Section 14 is akin to the widening of the law against unjustifiable discipline created in s 3 of the Employment Act 1988, now found in s 65 of TULR(C)A 1992 and expanded by s 16 of TURERA 1993.

The effect of the new ss 174–77 would appear to be the destabilisation of management-union agreements. Employers will have to deal with more unions, and some unions may be subject to undermining; perhaps breakaway unions will be encouraged. One side effect may be that firms which have entered into single union deals may find their agreements upset. A few years ago, one might have commented that the destruction of single union deals was not in accord with Conservative Government policy which sought, during Labour administrations, to diminish inter-union disputes and, during the early Conservative era, to reduce complexity in industrial relations by encouraging single union deals in the hope that Japanese and US companies would come to greenfield sites. But Conservative policy was to destroy collective bargaining and this right was another brick in the wall. It was ironic that government policy backfired (as it did with regard to the political fund) and that unions became less complacent about recruiting members than they had previously been. The Rules were amended in November 1993 to comply with the legislation. The model rule, mentioned above, 15.4, is no longer efficacious. The sole reasons for exclusion or expulsion are those stated in s 174, which is quoted above, 15.4.3.

15.4.8 Overlap

Encouraging or advising a union not to accept an applicant may amount to unjustifiable discipline, which is discussed next.

15.5 Unjustifiable discipline

Section 3 of the Employment Act 1988 created a right not to be unjustifiably disciplined. This right is now found in ss 64–65 of TULR(C)A 1992, as expanded by s 16 of TURERA 1993. This right is in addition to any contractual action. Its aim is to deter the penalisation of strikebreakers. The two main provisions in the extended s 65(2), which exhaustively defines the types of conduct in relation to which an employee is unjustifiably disciplined, are sub-ss (a) and (g):

(a)   ... failing to participate in or support a strike or other industrial action (whether by members of the union or by others), or indicating opposition to or a lack of support for such action; ...

(g)   ... resigning or proposing to resign from the union or from another union, becoming or proposing to become a member of another union, refusing to become a member of another union, or being a member of another union.

Paragraph (a) applies even though the majority of members have voted in favour of the action. Unions have strongly criticised this provision as being an attempt to undermine the power of collective action. Union solidarity has been undermined. 'Other industrial action' does not cover all instances of pressure exerted by unions on employers.

In *Knowles v Fire Brigades Union* (1996), the trade union expelled members who had, contrary to the union's policy, become standby firemen when they were already full time officers. The EAT held that there had to be 'some action directed against the employer with the object of obtaining some advantage for the employees'. Accordingly, the expulsions were not unjustifiable within the definition. The Court of Appeal upheld the decision that no industrial action had been taken.

Paragraph (g) can be seen as another step towards the undermining of the closed shop whereby employees had to be members of the union before performing a job. The definition of unjustifiability in s 65(2) is wide, but it is exhaustive and does not cover all kinds of conduct a union might adopt in relation to a member, such as suspending him for secretly taping a meeting of the branch executive.

The Committee of Experts of the ILO felt that the precursor of s 64 contravened Convention No 87 on Freedom of Association and Protection of the Right to Organise (1949). However, the Government in 1993 widened the scope of s 65 and did not respond to criticism from the Committee.

15.5.1 Disciplined

By s 64(2), being 'disciplined' by a trade union means that a determination has been made or purportedly made, either under the union's rules or by an official of the union or a number of persons including an official, that:

(a)   he should be expelled from the union or a branch or section of the union;

(b)   he should pay a sum to the union, to a branch or section of the union or to any other person;

(c)   sums tendered by him in respect of an obligation to pay subscriptions or other sums to the union, or to a branch or section of the union, should be treated as unpaid or paid for a different purpose;

(d)   he should be deprived to any extent of, or access to any benefits, services or facilities which would otherwise be provided or made available to him by virtue of his membership of the union, or a branch or section of the union;

(e)   another trade union, or a branch or section of it, should be encouraged or advised not to accept him as a member; or

(f)   he should be subjected to some other detriment ...

An example of (d) is suspension from the union.

'Detriment' is undefined. Whether something is a detriment is a matter for the tribunal. It might be interpreted as 'putting under a disadvantage,' as it is in the discrimination field. A recommendation that a member be disciplined is not a determination (*TGWU v Webber* (1991)). Specifying that a person was on a strike-breaker in a circular is a detriment, at least when the union intends to cause embarrassment.

15.5.2 Defences

Two defences are given in s 65. If the individual asserts that the union, an official or a trustee of it is breaking or proposes to break a requirement imposed by the rules or any other agreement or statute and the assertion is false and is known by the individual to be false, discipline is not unjustified (s 65(6)). The second exception occurs when the union would have penalised the member irrespective of his conduct, which falls within s 65(2), such as where the conduct is in breach of a professional code or where the union acted solely on the reason falling outside s 65(2).

15.5.3 Remedy

The remedy for breach of the right not to be unjustifiably disciplined is an application to an employment tribunal (s 66(1)). The claim must be presented within three months of the determination, unless the tribunal finds that it was not reasonably practicable for the claim to be brought within that period or that the delay was attributable to an appeal against the determination, in which cases the individual has such further period as the tribunal considers reasonable (s 66(2)). Whether the applicant was appealing depends on the substance of the facts, not on the form. If the claim is well founded, the tribunal so declares (s 66(3)). If a claim is successful, the member cannot also succeed in a claim under the revised s 174 of TULR(C)A 1992, the right to be or not to be a union member (discussed in the previous section) (s 66(4) of that Act as substituted by para 50, Sched 8 of TURERA 1993); however, common law remedies are unaffected. One point of procedure should be noted: while the limitation period for this right is three months, that under s 174 is six months.

15.5.4 Compensation

If the employment tribunal declares that the complaint was well founded, the applicant may ask for compensation (s 67(1)). Any fine is repayable. Application is made to the EAT if:

(a) the determination infringing the applicant's right not to be unjustifiably disciplined has not been revoked; or

(b) the union has failed to take all the steps necessary for securing the reversal of anything done for the purpose of giving effect to the determination ... [s 67(2)].

Otherwise, the claim is to the employment tribunal. The claim is made between four weeks and six months after the declaration (s 67(3)). The four week period gives the trade union a chance to change its decision. Compensation is awarded on the 'just and equitable' basis (s 67(5)). The union must put the member back into the position he was in before disciplining, even though he himself could have restored the position (*NALGO v Courtney-Dunn* (1991)). The applicant must mitigate his loss (s 67(6)). The sum must be reduced if the member caused or contributed to his being disciplined (s 67(7)).

Nowadays, after the calculation has been made, s 67(8) operates to fix a minimum and a maximum. The minimum in a case originally heard by the EAT under s 67 is the same as that found in the revised s 176 of TULR(C)A 1992, now £5,000. There is no minimum in an employment tribunal case. Before the massive increase to £50,000 in 1999, the maximum was the aggregate of 30 times the maximum 'week's pay' (£220) and the maximum compensatory award (£12,000), that is, £18,600.

In *Bradley v NALGO* (1991), the EAT awarded the then minimum. The remedy was compensatory, not punitive. The complainants, who had been expelled for not participating in a strike, did not have their job prospects diminished because of their expulsion. They claimed to be entitled to compensation for their injured feelings. The EAT held that it was not their expulsion which had caused any injury to their feelings but the reaction of their workmates to it. Accordingly, no recompense under this head was ordered.

It is, however, suggested that there is no power to award compensation for injured feelings in respect of unjustifiable feelings. Employment tribunals are creatures of statute; Parliament sometimes grants them jurisdiction to award compensation for injured feelings, but it has not done so for breach of this right; therefore, employment tribunals lack this power in this jurisdiction. The protection for non-strikers against their union should be compared with the lack of protection for strikers against their employers.

15.5.5 Sex and race

Unions may not exclude discipline or expel members on sexual or racial grounds (s 12 of the Sex Discrimination Act 1975; s 11 of the Race Relations Act 1976). Unions may, however, reserve seats for women when to do so would preserve an irreducible minimum of women serving on the union's executive.

15.6 Ballots

Parliament has imposed the requirement that votes be held for the posts of various union officials, including members of the national executive, except those who merely provide factual or legal information.

15.6.1 Executive

By s 46 of TULR(C)A 1992, elections committees must be held for various union posts, namely, the president, general secretary, member of the (principal) executive (committee) and any post by virtue of which a person is a member of the executive. It does not matter whether the executive committee member had a vote and, since the early 1990s, ballots must be fully postal. It is interesting to note that the worst instance of corruption, that by the Electrical Trades Union in the late 1950s and early 1960s, involved postal voting.

By s 46(3):

> Member of the executive means a person who may attend and speak at some or all of the meetings of the executive, otherwise than for the purpose of providing the committee with factual information or with technical or professional advice
>
> ...

An example might be a solicitor. Elections need not be held for the posts of president or general secretary if the applicants for those posts are not voting members of the executive or an employee of the trade union holds the position under the rules for under 13 months *and* has not within the 12 months preceding the engagement held either position. There also need be no election where a member is elected to one post and retains a post after his term of office expires if the second post is dependent on the first; an example is where the president keeps his seat on the executive as the immediate past president. Re-elections must take place within five years. The Act overrides contrary union rules. There are exceptions for newly formed unions (s 57) and those who are within five years of retirement (s 58).

The principal executive committee, which TULR(C)A 1992 renamed the 'executive', is the body which runs the trade union on a day to day basis (s 119). Accordingly, a committee which deals with conditions of employment is not such a body (*Paul v NALGO* (1987), a decision of the Certification Officer (CO)).

Generally speaking, unions accept the legitimacy of elections for the national executive. Elections are conducted by an independent person, who also normally acts as the scrutineer.

15.6.2 Candidature

By s 47(1), 'no member of the trade union shall be unreasonably excluded from standing as a candidate'. Exclusion is not unreasonable if the union excludes all persons of a class to which the individual belongs (s 47(3)), the usual example being Communists. The CO upheld a rule that candidates could not stand for office when they could not complete the term of office before retirement. 'No candidate shall be required, directly or indirectly, to be a member of a political party' (s 47(2)). The union must not discriminate on the grounds of sex or race, but it may reserve posts on elected committees for members of one gender (s 49 of the Sex Discrimination Act 1975).

15.6.3 Election addresses and scrutineers

There are various stringent requirements in relation to addresses (s 48) and the independent scrutineer of the election (s 49, as extended by TURERA 1993). For example, the scrutineer's name must be notified to the voters. One task of the scrutineer is to inspect the register of members. He must comment on its accuracy in his report on the election. There must be a scrutineer even where the election is not contested.

15.6.4 Constituencies

Section 50 governs the entitlement to vote. Unions may exclude (all) members who are out of work, (all) in arrears of dues or (all) apprentices, trainees, students or new members (s 50(2)). Entitlement to vote may be restricted by reference to:

(a) a class determined by reference to a trade or occupation;

(b) a class determined by reference to a geographical area; or

(c) a class which is by virtue of the rules of the union treated as a separate section ... [s 50(3)].

Overseas members may be excluded.

15.6.5 Voting and counting

Voting is carried out by marking a ballot paper (s 51(1)). Therefore, other forms of voting, such as show of hands, are unlawful. Indirect voting, for example, at a delegate conference, is outlawed. The paper is sent and returned by post 'so far as is reasonably practicable' (s 51(4)). In the jargon, voting is 'fully postal' –

the paper is sent out and returned by post. This law was enacted in 1988: previously, a workplace ballot was lawful. By s 51(3):

> ... every person who is entitled to vote at an election must –
>
> (a) be allowed to vote without interference from ... the union or any of its members, officials or employees; and
>
> (b) so far as is reasonably practicable, be enabled to do so without incurring any direct cost to himself.

The union may state that candidates are on an official 'slate' (*Paul v NALGO* (1987)). Counting must be done fairly and accurately, though an inaccuracy is disregarded 'if it is accidental and on a scale which could not affect the result of the election' (s 51(5)). (Unions are under a duty to keep accurate lists of members: now s 24 of TULR(C)A 1992.) The outcome of the election may be determined by a 'first past the post' system or by the single transferable vote method. There are detailed provisions in relation to the scrutineer's report (s 52 as broadened by ss 1–2 of TURERA 1993). For example, details of his report must be made available to individual members. Counting must be done by independent persons (s 51A, as inserted by s 2 of TURERA 1993).

15.6.6 Remedy

A member or a candidate, but not the union, may apply to the CO or the High Court for a declaration that his rights have been infringed. By s 56(4):

> ... where the court makes a declaration it shall also, unless it considers that to do so would be inappropriate, make an enforcement order; that is, an order imposing on the union one or more of the following requirements –
>
> (a) to secure the holding of an election in accordance with the order;
>
> (b) to take such other steps to remedy the declared failure as may be specified in the order;
>
> (c) to abstain from such acts as may be so specified.

Breach of an enforcement order is contempt of court, punishable by an unlimited fine or imprisonment or both. If the application is to the CO, he is limited to making a declaration. If the complaint fails before the CO, the member may still apply to the court, but if the union fails, it has no such right. Judicial review is a possibility. Even if the CO has not determined the complaint, the aggrieved individual may bring proceedings in court (*Lenehan v UCATT* (1991) (Hoffmann J)). Complaints to the CO have been rare. There were no decisions made by him in 1992, but there were two in 1995 and 12 in 1998. It should be noted that, even if the challenge to the election is successful, the result remains valid.

15.6.7 Additional to common law

The statutory rules on ballots are additional to union rules. If the union rule book is not followed, there is a breach of the contract of membership; for example, in *Taylor v NUM (Yorkshire Area)* (1984), the question was whether or not the failure to ballot members in respect of the 1984–85 strike was a breach of the rules.

15.6.8 Funds and premises

There used to be provisions, dating from 1980, permitting the Secretary of State for Employment to provide funds for trade union ballots (s 115 of TULR(C)A 1992) and giving independent trade unions the right to use employers' premises for secret ballots (s 116), but these were abolished by s 7 of TURERA 1993. No funds were available after 31 March 1996. Section 116 was repealed as otiose. As mentioned earlier in this chapter, statutory ballots must now be fully postal. There is nothing to prevent unions and employers reaching arrangements with regard to facilities for non-statutory ballots, such as those for elections to the post of shop steward.

The Trades Union Congress was originally very much against the provision of State funds for balloting in union elections before industrial action and before continuing political funds, seeing it as an encroachment on union autonomy, a 'sweetener' for the bitter pill of government regulation. The position changed; since unions had to hold elections, money for them had to come from somewhere. The squeeze on union finances caused by a reduction in membership in the 1980s led to a shift towards acceptance of State funds. The withdrawal of funds for stationery, printing and postage has hit some unions hard. State funding was seen by the Conservative Government as part of the policy of 'giving unions back to their members', that is, getting rid of unrepresentative officials. The statutory stipulation that ballots must be held but funding will not be provided does not look evenhanded.

TRADE UNION GOVERNANCE

Association and dissociation

Refusal to employ on the grounds of trade union membership or non-membership is unlawful. Trade unions may be joined and may have to pay compensation:

- *Young, James and Webster v UK* (1981).

Union rules

Union decisions and rules are controlled through contract law and principles of natural justice. There is debate as to whether the rules may be unenforceable when conflicting with 'the right to work', whether they may be struck down for illegality, and whether *Foss v Harbottle* applies:

- *Hopkins v NUS* (1985);

- *Lee v Showmen's Guild* (1952);

- *Leigh v NUR* (1970);

- *Taylor v NUM (Derbyshire Area) (No 3)* (1985);

- *Roebuck v NUM (Yorkshire Area)* (1978);

- *Stevenson v URTU* (1977);

- *Edwards v SOGAT* (1971).

Bridlington principles

Trade Union Congress-affiliated unions strive to avoid poaching; however, there is a right to membership of trade unions which undermines the Bridlington principles. Statute prohibits the exclusion and expulsion from unions, subject to exceptions. The exceptions include an enforceable membership requirement, such as that the union recruits only in one industry, which is of relevance where the worker does not work in it.

Unjustifiable discipline

There is a statutory right not to be unjustifiably disciplined by a trade union. This includes a fine for not participating in strikes despite a majority in favour.

- *TGWU v Webber* (1991);

- *Bradley v NALGO* (1991).

Ballots

Fully postal ballots must be held for elections to the union's principal executive committee. Members have a right to stand as candidates. There are technical rules relating to the holding of ballots. State funding for ballots has been phased out, and independent unions are no longer entitled to use employers' premises for ballots. The repeal of the latter legislation is consistent with the move towards fully postal voting.

CHAPTER 16

INDUSTRIAL ACTION

16.1 Coverage

This chapter considers the law on collective agreements between unions and management; the effect of industrial action, such as strikes, on individual contracts of employment; unions' liability in respect of tort (including remedies against them and their representatives); and picketing. Use of the law has increased over the last decade and the Conservative Government of 1979–97 increased the range of possible plaintiffs. As early as 1982, Donaldson MR said in *Merkur Island Shipping Corp v Laughton* (1983) that parties to industrial disputes 'should know what is and what is not offside. And they must be able to find out for themselves by reading plain and simple words of guidance'. Since then, the law has become even more complex and has, on several occasions, been condemned on that account by the Committee of Experts on the Application of Conventions and Recommendations of the International Labour Organisation. The number of days lost to strikes in England continues to decline, as it does in other democracies. The average for the 1970s was 12.9 million, but there were only 278,000 days lost in 1994. (These figures do not include action short of strikes.)

16.2 Collective agreements

The law relating to collective agreements has changed substantially over the past 30 years. There is no set form: an exchange of letters is sufficient. Originally, they were not contracts, for the reason that they were not intended to be legally binding. The Industrial Relations Act 1971 created a presumption that they were legally binding but that presumption was rebutted by a clause to the effect that the agreement was not contractual, a TINA LEA clause ('this is not a legally enforceable agreement'). It is thought that, between 1971–74, there was only one agreement that was legally enforceable. After 1974, collective bargains reverted to their common law status (now s 179 of the Trade Union and Labour Relations (Consolidation) Act (TULR(C)A) 1992).

Few collective agreements are legally binding; exceptions include the collective agreement at GCHQ (1997). A clause stating that an agreement is 'binding' is read as one that it is binding in honour only (*NCB v NUM* (1986)). There have been calls over the past decade for collective agreements to be legally enforceable (for example, the Green Paper, *Industrial Relations in the 1990s*, Cm 1602, 1991, which noted that most other EC States had legally enforceable agreements) but no change has been made. It is thought that the reluctance to proceed with this measure stemmed from the then Government's desire to exclude unions from bargaining on behalf of workers. Legislation would certainly lead to inflexibility, a undesirable vice in industrial relations. Unions continue to bear an antipathy towards law and lawyers, and that antipathy would be worsened by employers' suing them for breach of contract. Nowadays, unions may wish to see legal enforceability, which would provide a brake on the movement towards derecognition and individual contracts. Collective bargaining demonstrates that the parties wish to continue their relationship.

16.2.1 Auxiliary support

For a large part of the period 1909–79, there were various 'props' or auxiliary mechanisms supporting collective bargaining. For example, wages councils provided minimum wages in various industries and there was a procedure whereby agreements could be 'extended' across industries. From 1979, the Government withdrew these props, the final one, wages councils, being abolished in 1993. There remains support for ending industrial action, for example, ACAS may be involved (see Chapter 2). Conservative Government policy was 'to move pay determination away from centralised collective bargaining and make it more responsive to local needs' (White Paper, *People, Jobs and Opportunities*, Cm 1810, 1992, para 4.4). Fewer than half the workforce is now covered by collective agreements, a decline from the figure of three-quarters in 1980. The International Labour Organisation's World Labour Report 1997–98 thought that coverage may be as low as 25%.

16.2.2 Individual contract

Despite the fact that agreements between unions and management are not legally enforceable, provided that the terms are appropriate, they may be incorporated into individual contracts of employment. As stated in Chapter 4, there is a special method of embodying 'no-strike' clauses.

16.2.3 Breach

Disputes over changes to collective agreements may lead to industrial action, which can thus be seen as a normal part of industrial relations. Since collective agreements are not legally enforceable, judicial remedies are not available for breach. Leaving aside the coal industry, there has been a general decline in the number of strikes over the last 20 years. Despite the large increase in the legal provisions governing industrial action, few employers use that law, for industrial relations must continue after the dispute has been settled.

16.3 Effect on employment contract

Industrial action will almost certainly breach individual contracts of employment, despite both parties not contemplating or desiring that outcome. The UK has ratified the Council of Europe's Social Charter 1961 and the United Nation's International Covenant on Economic, Social and Cultural Rights 1966, both of which guarantee the right to strike. However, current UK law is inconsistent with these international obligations.

16.3.1 Breach

A contract of employment has been described as a wage-work bargain. The employee agrees to work in return for a wage. In contractual terms, there is an implied term that the employee will be ready and willing to work. This term is a condition, breach of which provides the employers with the choice either to terminate the contract (that is, dismiss) or to treat it as continuing; whichever option they choose, the employers may claim damages in the ordinary courts. In practice, employers rarely sue employees who are likely to be 'men of straw' and legal action is likely to exacerbate industrial relations. An exceptional case is *NCB v Galley* (1959), discussed in Chapter 4.

Dismissal may not be an option if the employee is skilled. It cannot be said that law and practice are consistent. The problem lies in the law's deeming the contract to have terminated when the strike was merely a 'blip' in a long term relationship. This lack of fit is made worse by the law that any type of industrial action, for instance, a strike, a go-slow, or work-to-rule, is almost certainly a breach of contract. This law renders nugatory the view sometimes advanced that there is a right to strike in UK law. Even when employees kept strictly to the works rules, the Court of Appeal has held that they had broken the implied duty to co-operate with their employers in the running of the business (*Secretary of State for Employment v ASLEF (No 2)* (1972)).

Not every worker realises that he has no legal redress if dismissed while on strike. This rule applies even though the industrial action was provoked by the employers. The courts have said that there is no breach of contract where the employees give notice that they are terminating employment, but the ending of the relationship is not what they want: they want improved terms, not no job. Lord Denning MR suggested in *Morgan v Fry* (1968) that giving notice merely suspended the contract for the duration of the action, but this idea was rejected in *Simmons v Hoover Ltd* (1977) as being inconsistent with employment protection law, which is predicated on there being a repudiation of the contract. Therefore, action remains a breach of contract.

However, it is suggested that any technical objections to suspending the contract during industrial action can be resolved by legislation. Canada and Ireland have such a law. All industrial action can be seen as a breach of the implied duty of co-operation. This duty is a fundamental one. Therefore, action is repudiatory of the contract of employment. A strike notice is thus notice of a breach of contract and not, as Davies LJ suggested in *Morgan v Fry*, a notice of termination and an offer to work on different terms and conditions.

It is hard to agree with the claim that there is a right to strike in the UK. And the contractual rules apply even if it is the employers who provoked the dispute. If, however, employees resigned lawfully to put pressure on employers, there is no breach of contract (*Boxfoldia Ltd v NGA 1982* (1988)). Giving notice of industrial action, on the other hand, does not prevent a breach from occurring. The law that all industrial action was necessarily a breach of contract was criticised by Lord Denning MR in *Morgan v Fry*: '... if that argument were correct, it would do away with the right to strike in this country.'

16.3.2 Other effects

Three effects of industrial action on the contract should be noted. First, a dismissal for taking part in a strike is for misconduct and, accordingly, the employee cannot claim a redundancy payment (see *Simmons v Hoover Ltd*, discussed in Chapter 9). A protest against redundancy leads to the loss of redundancy payments! Secondly, unless there is selective re-engagement in an official strike, dismissal is fair for unfair dismissal purposes (see Chapter 11). Even if those who participate in industrial action are immune from liability (see below), they will still be liable for breach of contract. Employees can, therefore, be lawfully dismissed for taking part in a lawful strike. Thirdly, as was seen in 4.9.11, above, employers can deduct or stop pay for industrial action.

16.3.3 No specific performance

No order for specific performance of a contract of employment may be made and no injunction restraining a breach of or threatened breach of such a contract may be granted where the effect in either case would be to oblige the employee to do work or attend at any place for the purpose of doing work (s 236 of TULR(C)A 1992).

16.4 Restricted strikes

There are various restrictions on strikes. Most apply only to specific categories of workers, for example, the police force. There is a statutory tort of inducing a prison officer to withdraw services or commit a breach of discipline, found in s 127 of the Criminal Justice and Public Order Act 1994. Two restrictions apply more broadly. By the Emergency Powers Act 1920, as amended in 1964, the Government may proclaim a state of emergency lasting for a month when:

... events of such a nature and on so extensive a scale as to be calculated, by interfering with the supply and distribution of food, water, fuel or light, or with the means of locomotion, to deprive the community or any substantial proportion of the community of the essentials of life [have occurred or are immediately threatened] ...

The Government may make regulations under the Act, as it most famously did in the three day week of the early 1970s. The regulations must not make it a crime to take part in a strike or to persuade others peacefully to join in.

Section 240(1) of TULR(C)A 1992 states:

A person commits an offence who wilfully and maliciously breaks a contract of service or hiring, knowing or having reasonable cause to believe that the probable consequences of his so doing, either alone or in combination with others, will be –

(a)   to endanger human life or cause serious bodily injury; or

(b)   to expose valuable property, whether real or personal, to destruction or serious injury.

Malice is irrelevant. The offence is triable only summarily, with a maximum imprisonment of three months or a fine up to level 2 on the standard scale (presently £100) or both. No doubt it could cover strikes by doctors and nurses. The most obvious candidates for inclusion are firefighters.

One outcome of the Industrial Relations Act 1971 was a decision not to imprison individual trade union members or organisers. In prison, they could be presented as martyrs and gain public support. For this very reason, the Conservative Government sought throughout not to imprison trade unionists. Using s 240 would have destroyed its policy. As far as is known, no prosecution has ever been brought under this section, even though it has existed since 1875.

16.4.1 Post Office Act 1953

An example of the criminalisation of a strike in a specific industry is s 58 of the Post Office Act 1953, which makes it an offence wilfully to delay or procure the delay of a postal packet. Individuals do not have *locus standi* to ask for an injunction to restrain industrial action which gives rise to such a crime. The Attorney General may, in his discretion, bring a relator action. In *Gouriet v UPOW* (1978), the Attorney General refused to grant an injunction to stop the defendants inducing their members to boycott post to South Africa. The House of Lords held that no injunction could be sought to stop breaches of the criminal law by a member of the public in the absence of special damage or infringement of his private rights.

16.4.2 Sit-ins

It should also be noted that offences may be committed during sit-ins. Besides criminal damage and other 'normal' crimes, criminal law penalises several forms of trespass (see Pt II of the Criminal Law Act 1977). Conspiracies to commit these crimes are contrary to s 1 of the the Criminal Law Act 1977.

16.5 Liability for action

Students often find difficulty in tackling problems involving industrial action. The law looks unmanageable. Certainly, it is complex (partly because it developed in a piecemeal fashion and partly because it is drafted obscurely) and it depends on the interrelationship between common law and statute. The way to deal with the law is to do what the courts do and adopt a sequential view:

- Do the employers have a common law cause of action?
- If so, does statute give immunity from tort?
- If so, is that immunity removed by statute?

These are also rules on pre-strike ballots. Remedies must be considered after establishing liability. Trade unions are nowadays liable to the same extent as individuals, subject to a maximum limit on damages. The fact remains that 'the present law relating to industrial action is ludicrously unbalanced and ridiculously complex' (Pitt, G, 'The right to strike: a shift in focus', in McColgan, A (ed), *The Future of Labour Law*, 1996, p 109).

16.5.1 Inducing breach

This economic tort is the principal one committed in industrial disputes. Trade unions will usually induce employees to break their employment contracts; these breaches will, in turn, induce employers to break their commercial contracts. The classic definition is that of Jenkins LJ in *DC Thomson & Co Ltd v Deakin* (1952).The employers must show:

> ... first, that the person charged with actionable interference knew of the existence of the contract and intended to procure its breach; secondly, that the person so charged did definitely and unequivocally persuade, induce or procure the employees to breach their contracts of employment with the intent mentioned; thirdly, that the employees so persuaded, induced or procured did in fact break their contracts of employment; and fourthly, that the breach of the contract forming the alleged subject of interference ensued as a necessary consequence of the breach of the employees concerned of their contracts of employment.

The House of Lords approved this statement in *Merkur Island Shipping Corp v Laughton* (1983).

16.5.2 Direct form

The simplest form of this tort may be represented as in the folowing diagram.

(E = employee, Rs = employers, TU = trade union or organiser or other person.) Between E and Rs there is a contract of employment.

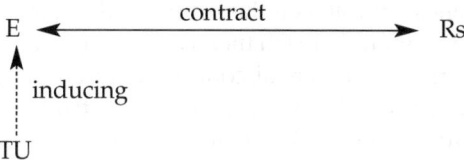

The trade union induces the employee to break his contract with the employers. This form of the tort is sometimes known as 'direct inducement'.

16.5.3 Indirect form

A second form, indirect inducement, arises where the trade union puts pressure on suppliers to or distributors of the Rs with whom the trade union is in dispute. The trade union is seeking to boycott or 'black' Rs. This activity is sometimes known as 'secondary action'. Primary action occurs when employees put pressure on their own employers.

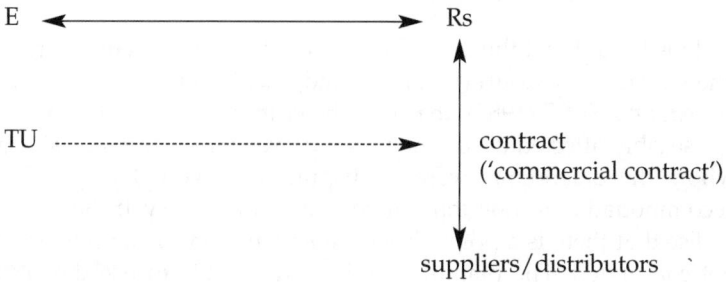

The trade union is inducing a breach of contract between Rs and suppliers/distributors in order to put pressure on Rs to improve E's terms and conditions. All the suppliers and distributors may bring actions. The procuring of the breach of contract constitutes the unlawful means necessary for the indirect form of the tort.

16.5.4 Example

In the second form of the tort, there must be unlawful means. An illustration of indirect inducement is *Torquay Hotel Co Ltd v Cousins* (1969). The trade union brought pressure on suppliers (of oil) to stop deliveries to the employers, with whom the trade union was in dispute. The pressure was that the trade union would call out its members at suppliers if the suppliers did not stop deliveries, that is, members at suppliers would breach their contracts of employment if the suppliers did not breach their commercial contract with the employers. (The tanker drivers were already on strike, so the case was, in truth, one of indirect interference, though Lord Denning MR treated the facts as ones of direct interference.) This demand constituted unlawful means for the purposes of this tort. The majority were of the opinion that there was a breach induced by the defendant. A *force majeure* clause in the contract between the suppliers and the employers simply excused the suppliers from liability for breach of contract; it did not mean that there was no breach.

In the indirect form, it is accepted that interference is sufficient. It should be noted that, in the tort of interference with contract of business, unlawful means must be proved for both the direct and the indirect forms. This is so despite the fact that the tort seems to have developed in response to the narrowness of the present tort, for which breach has to be demonstrated. Unlawful means include the commission of torts such as trespass, nuisance and inducing breach of statutory duty.

16.5.5 Constituents: intent

Jenkins LJ said that the defendants must intend to procure a breach. A judge at Sheffield County Court (that is, the judgment is not binding) held, however, in *Falconer v ASLEF* (1986), that it sufficed that the plaintiff was a member of a foreseeably affected class – he was a passenger on British Rail transport, with whom the defendants were in dispute. (He won damages for two nights' accommodation in London.) Intent was unnecessary. If the defendants do not realise that there is a possibility of their action inducing the breach, this tort is not committed. The plaintiff would now be able to use the citizen's right of action (see 16.10.1, below).

16.5.6 Knowledge

Jenkins LJ said in *Thomson v Deakin* that defendants would be liable only if they knew of the contract's terms. This requirement has been watered down. It suffices that they know of the contract – they no longer need to know of the terms. Wilful blindness as to terms suffices. There is nothing to stop well advised employers sending details of contracts to trade union and officials. In *Merkur Island Shipping Corp v Laughton* (1983), a case on indirect interference by unlawful means, the defendants knew the terms of the contract, a time charter, because they had a copy of it. The House of Lords, however, agreed with the Court of Appeal that the defendants must be deemed to have been aware of the contract. The effect is that the trade union need not know that a particular contracts exists. The case involved interference with business (see 16.5.19, below) but the torts are the same on this point. However, if the union does not know of the contract, breach of which it is alleged to have induced, there is no liability (*Timeplan Education Group Ltd v NUT* (1997)).

16.5.7 Breach

The dispute must lead to a breach of contract in the direct form of this tort. If there is no breach induced, there is no tort. This requirement was widened in *Prudential Assurance Co v Lorenz* (1971) to cover breach of an equitable duty. A trade union induced members not to pass insurance premiums they had received to Rs. Not doing so was breach of their (equitable) duty to account. The court held that the trade union was to be forbidden from inducing breaches of this duty. However, the Court of Appeal, in a non-labour case, thought that this tort did not exist, or at least that there was no tort of inducing a breach of trust.

There is no tort of inducing an unfair dismissal (*Wilson v Housing Corp* (1997)), nor is there a tort if the contractual term is void for illegality. There is no tort of inducing a person not to enter into a contract – a contract must exist before a person may be induced to break it.

16.5.8 Inducement

The courts distinguish inducement from advice. A statement of fact is not inducement (*Thomson v Deakin*; in *Camellia Tanker SA v ITF* (1976), inducement was stated to cover 'pressure, persuasion, or procuration'). Telling members of the progress of negotiations did not constitute inducing them to break their contracts. Whether providing information constitutes inducement on the facts of a particular case is a matter for the court. It is, however, an inducement where the third parties are ready and willing to act in breach of their contract with the employers. The presence of pickets may constitute an inducement.

16.5.9 Cause

It must be proved that the trade union's acts did cause the suppliers/distributors to not perform their contract with the employers (*Thomson v Deakin*). On the facts of the case, the plaintiff could not prove that another firm's decision not to supply them with newsprint was occasioned by the union's inducing its members at the firm to join in industrial action.

16.5.10 Unlawful means

Unlawful means are required for the 'indirect' variant of this tort. They may be a breach of contract, a tort or some other form of civil liability. Trespass in order to change tyres at a motor show has been held to be unlawful means. Presumably, a crime is sufficient, though the cases are in conflict. It is uncertain how far 'unlawful means' extend beyond actionability in tort. In the words of Lord Denning MR in *Torquay Hotel Co Ltd v Cousins* (1969):

> ... a trade union official is only in the wrong when he procures a contracting party directly to break his contract or when he does it indirectly by unlawful means.

A breach of statutory duty is unlawful means (*Meade v Haringey LBC* (1979)). Whether such a breach occurs is a matter of construction of the statute (*Lonrho Ltd v Shell Petroleum Ltd (No 2)* (1982); *Associated British Ports plc v TGWU* (1989)). It should be noted that the statutory protection covers inducing breach of contract, not inducing breach of statutory duty.

The requirement of unlawful means distinguishes this tort from the situation in *Allen v Flood* (1898), where the House of Lords held that it was not a tort to oblige a third party to act in such a way as to affect the plaintiff detrimentally, even when the defendant intended to injure the plaintiff.

16.5.11 Illustration

An example of a breach of contract being of unlawful means is *Emerald Construction Co Ltd v Lowthian* (1966). A trade union called out its members at the employers. The employers worked for a firm which had subcontracted work to them. The employers fell behind and they were in breach of contract with the firm, that is, the trade union had induced the employers to break the contract with the firm by inducing the employers' workers to breach their contracts. The workers' breach was the unlawful means for this form of inducing breach of contract. An interesting point is that the workers were, in fact, independent contractors for, and not employees of, the employers.

16.5.12 Justification

Potentially, justification is a defence to inducing breach of contract (and presumably to inducing breaches of equitable and statutory obligations) but it has succeeded in only one case, *Brimelow v Casson* (1924). The court held the tort to be justified when chorus girls were induced to go on strike for more pay, the alternative being to become prostitutes. Protecting their morals was a justification. It has been suggested that the defence is available only when the defendants are acting in pursuance of a legal, and not a moral, duty. In an early case, the House of Lords held that defendants were liable despite the fact that they were acting simply in furtherance of their aspirations and were not activated by malice (*South Wales Miners' Federation v Glamorgan Coal Co Ltd* (1905)). A protest against a wage cut did not fall within the defence of justification. Perhaps nowadays this defence could be read more broadly than it was in the early part of the last century. More recent is *Greig v Insole* (1978), the world series cricket case, where it was held that the motives of the International Cricket Council did not justify the procuring of breaches of contracts between individual cricketers and the Packer group.

16.5.13 Intimidation

In *Rookes v Barnard* (1964), the House of Lords held that there was a tort of intimidation. It covered not just a threat of violence but also a threat to break a contract or to commit some other unlawful act. A union said that its members would withdraw labour if a non-unionist was not dismissed by his employers. They did dismiss him. The dismissal was lawful because it was made with the correct length of notice. Accordingly, the tort of inducing breach of contract did not apply, for no contract was broken. The House of Lords held, though, that the union had acted tortiously. It threatened to act in breach of contract, namely, in breach of a no-strike clause in a collective agreement. (Counsel had, surprisingly to modern readers, conceded that the clause was legally binding.) Exemplary damages were awarded.

16.5.14 Criticism

Leaving aside the exemplary damages point, *Rookes v Barnard* has been severely criticised. Controversy has centred on the invention of this tort. The last similar case dates from 1793 and the facts related to threats of violence. One might have thought that the tort had died out or that it was narrowly drawn, but the House of Lords really created a novel tort. The effect was that since, at that time, the tort was not one covered by a statutory immunity, trade union organisers were liable; yet trade union members would not have been liable had they gone on strike, because the immunity attached to breaches of contract (that is, breaches of contract attracted immunity but the threats to break contracts did not).

16.5.15 Meaning of intimidation

The boundaries of the tort are hard to see. Cases are rare. Certainly, a line is drawn between intimidation and advice, and it seems that the threat must be one which is powerful enough 'to induce the other to submit' (*per* Lord Denning MR in *Morgan v Fry* (1968)). A threat to take lawful action is not intimidation. Justification is possibly a defence.

16.5.16 Interference with contract, business or trade

Interference with contract has been accepted fairly recently as a tort, and there have been intimations that there exists a tort of 'interference with the trade or business of another person by doing unlawful acts', as Lord Diplock put it in *Merkur Island Shipping Corp v Laughton* (1983). This possible tort would be a 'super tort' or the genus of which inducing breach of contract is a species. Similarly, intimidation would be a species of this tort. Lord Reid in *T Stratford & Son Ltd v Lindley* (1965) considered that the tort of inducing breach of contract was not restricted to breaches of contract. Lord Denning MR in *Torquay Hotel Co Ltd v Cousins* (1969) said, *obiter*, that the tort of interfering with contract existed, and the House of Lords recognised its existence in *Merkur Island* and *Hadmor Productions Ltd v Hamilton* (1983). The tort is aimed at protecting the commercial expectations of the parties.

16.5.17 Width

The parameters of the tort of interference with contract were laid down by Lord Denning MR in *Torquay Hotel*:

> First, there must be interference in the execution of a contract. The interference is not confined to the procurement of a breach of contract ... Secondly, the interference must be deliberate. The person must know of the contract, or, at any rate, turn a blind eye to it and intend to interfere with it ... Thirdly, the interference must be direct.

Whether the interference is direct or indirect, the interference must be by unlawful means. On the facts of *Torquay Hotel*, Lord Denning MR held that the suppliers would not be liable for failure to supply if failure was caused by an industrial dispute. Since there was no breach of contract there could be no tort of inducing breach of contract, but the present tort fitted the facts.

16.5.18 Interference with business

It is thought that the tort of interference with trade or business, where it is established, would extend beyond interference with contracts, for no contract need exist. The predominant purpose to injure is necessary. In *Barretts and Baird (Wholesale) Ltd v IPCS* (1987)), the mere fact of interference was insufficient. This decision, however, was only at first instance. Further clarification is needed. This case is also inconsistent with *Falconer v ASLEF* (see 16.5.5, above), which did not require an intent to injure. *Falconer*, in turn, is inconsistent with *Deakin*.

There must also be unlawful means. The nature of those means has been substantially debated by the House of Lords in non-employment cases. It seems that, in this tort, both the direct and indirect interference forms must have unlawful means. In *Barretts*, the judge thought that breaches of their own contracts of employment by the workers constituted unlawful means, but this proposition has been doubted. A breach of statutory duty has been said to be unlawful means for this tort. Violence is enough, as are threats amounting to intimidation.

In *Middlebrook Mushrooms Ltd v TGWU* (1993), the employers dismissed workers who protested against their wages being cut. The ex-employees 'picketed' local supermarkets, trying to discourage shoppers from buying the company's produce. The Court of Appeal held that the leaflets handed out by the pickets were not aimed at inducing breaches of contract between the shopkeepers and the company. There was no direct interference with contracts. The pickets were seeking to persuade shoppers not to buy. The shoppers had no contract with the company. No doubt the effect hoped for was that the supermarket owners would not place orders with the company. The possible tort was one of indirectly inducing the shopowners not to enter into contracts in the future. Being of the indirect form, unlawful means were necessary. Since none were used, there was no tort. Neill LJ opined that, when employers sought injunctions against unions and their members, the court should take into account Art 10 of the European Convention on Human Rights, which sets out the right to freedom of speech.

16.5.19 Cases

The width of the tort is uncertain and is best viewed through the cases.

Brekkes Ltd v Cattel (1972)

The tort is committed when there is interference with an expectation that a contract will be made.

Hadmor Productions Ltd v Hamilton (1983)

A television station had a licence to broadcast but was not contractually obliged to do so. The union threatened to ask its members at the station not to broadcast programmes made by the plaintiffs. The House of Lords held that there was an expectation that the plaintiffs' programmes would be broadcast, and this expectation was not fulfilled. On the facts, the tort of intimidation had also occurred.

Merkur Island Shipping Corp v Laughton (1983)

The International Transport Workers Federation has for a long time tried to increase pay for seafarers by attempting to bring pressure on shipowners to pay union rates. The plaintiffs' ship was 'blacked'. Tugmen and lock keepers refused to aid the boat's leaving port. There was an exemption clause in the charterparty that there would be no liability 'in the event of loss of time due to boycott of the vessel in any port ... by shore labour or others'. Therefore, there was no breach of the term that voyages would be made with utmost despatch. Nevertheless, there was an interference with contract. The unlawful means were procuring the tugmen and lock keepers to break their contracts of employment.

The existence of this tort of interference with trade or business by unlawful means is significant because it is not one of the torts rendered lawful in trade disputes, as discussed below, 16.6. It has the potential to swallow up the other economic torts. If breach of contract constitutes unlawful means for the purposes of this tort, businesses affected by industrial action will be able to sue those on strike for loss and there will be no statutory immunity.

16.5.20 Conspiracy

Civil conspiracy is 'the agreement of two or more to do an unlawful act or to do a lawful act by unlawful means' (*Mulcahy v R* (1868), *per* Willes J). A conspiracy to injure is different. It does not require an independent wrong and it occurs where the predominant purpose is to injure the plaintiffs, not to advance the defendants' legitimate interests. Pecuniary loss must be caused. An unlawful means conspiracy will also amount to interference with trade or business by unlawful means. It was said that the first type also required the defendants to intend to injure the plaintiffs (*Lonrho Ltd v Shell Petroleum Ltd (No 2)* (1982)). However, the House of Lords decided that a person was liable even without having the predominant purpose of injury to the plaintiff in a conspiracy to use unlawful means (*Lonrho plc v Fayed* (1992)). In that case, Lord Bridge said:

> Where conspirators act with the predominant purpose of injuring the plaintiff and in fact inflict damage on him, but do nothing which could have been actionable if done by an individual acting alone, it is the fact of their concerted action for that illegitimate purpose that the law, however anomalous it may now seem, finds a sufficient ground to condemn their action as illegal and tortious. But when conspirators intentionally injure the plaintiff and use unlawful means to do so, it is no defence for them to show that their primary purpose was to further their own interests.

Unlawful acts include crimes (which amount to torts: *Lonrho v Shell Petroleum*, above) and torts. It is debatable whether breach of contract is unlawful for this purpose. Unlawful means include an agreement to cause loss with the intention to injure the plaintiffs (*Huntley v Thornton* (1957)). Members of a district committee were liable when they expelled a trade union member out of spite. Any strike involves an agreement with the purpose of injuring the employers (the plaintiffs).

There is debate as to whether a breach of contract constitutes unlawful means in this tort. Potentially, all strikers are liable for the tort of conspiracy. However, this variant of the tort is not committed where the predominant purpose of the defendants is to promote a legitimate interest (*Mogul SS Co v McGregor, Gow & Co* (1892)). If causing injury, not promoting the union's interests, is the predominant purpose, there is a conspiracy to injure (*Quinn v Leathem* (1901)).

Since that case, union objectives have been held to be legitimate. The most famous case is *Crofter Hand Woven Harris Tweed Co v Veitch* (1942), where it was decided that a closed shop was a legitimate purpose. Lord Wright said:

> ... the rights of the employer are conditioned by the rights of the men to give or withhold their services. The right of workmen to strike is an essential element in the principle of collective bargaining.

Also legitimate is pressure to oblige employers to start employing union members (*DC Thomson & Co Ltd v Deakin* (1952)) and to get rid of a colour bar (*Scala Ballroom (Wolverhampton) Ltd v Ratcliffe* (1958)).

Criticism is often made of the fact that what is not tortious if done by one person can be the tort of conspiracy if done by several people. This criticism was most deftly put by Lord Diplock in *Lonrho Ltd v Shell Petroleum Co Ltd (No 2)* (1982):

> To suggest that acts done by one street-corner grocer in concert with a second are more effective and dangerous to a competitor than the same acts done by a string of supermarkets under a single ownership, or that a multinational conglomerate ... does not exercise greater economic power than any combination of small businesses is to shut one's eyes to what has been happening in the business and industrial world ...

16.5.21 Economic duress

The House of Lords suggested in *Universe Tankships Inc of Monrovia v ITWF* (1983) that economic duress made a contract void, with the effect that money paid under coercion was recoverable. The House of Lords said that, though the statutory immunity (discussed below) does not directly apply to economic duress, industrial action which amounted to duress would be immune on the same basis. That is, economic duress would be treated as though it constituted an economic tort, and would thus be rendered immune by s 219 of TULR(C)A 1992. Certainly, if there was no protection from the economic torts, few, if any, instances of industrial action would be lawful. There are some statements in this case which appear to say that economic duress is a tort, but it is suggested that these are wrong: see *Allen v Flood*, below.

16.5.22 *Allen v Flood*

The existence of this tort is seemingly inconsistent with one of the classic cases of the common law, *Allen v Flood* (1898), where it was held that action done with the purpose of injuring another was not tortious *per se*.

16.6   Immunity

English law has for many years granted the organisers of industrial action an immunity from liability in tort. It is unfortunate for unions that their exemption from liability has been called 'immunity'. This terminology suggests that the protection for unions is a privilege, to be withdrawn whenever a government feels like doing so. What the immunities represent are social and political rights which should not be withdrawn at will. Continental members of the European Union generally have a right to strike, and this right is enshrined in some States' constitutions, a matter which demonstrates the true significance of such a right.

16.6.1 Definition

Section 219(1) and (2) of TULR(C)A 1992 reads:

(1) An act done by a person in contemplation or furtherance of a trade dispute is not actionable in tort on the ground only –

   (a)   that it induces another person to break a contract or interferes or induces another person to interfere with its performance; or

   (b)   that it consists in his threatening that a contract (whether one to which he is a party or not) will be broken or its performance interfered with, or that he will induce another person to break a contract or interfere with its performance.

(2) An agreement or combination by two or more persons to do or procure the doing of an act in contemplation or furtherance of a trade dispute is not actionable in tort if the act is one which if done without any such agreement or combination would not be actionable in tort.

The side note to s 219 reads: 'Protection from certain tort liabilities.' Perhaps terminology should change from 'immunity' to 'protection'.

Nowadays, a union has the same immunity as an individual. It is no longer totally immune. Note that s 219(1)(a) and (b) cover any contract, not just contracts of employment as was once the case. The aim was to protect secondary action, but that aim has been frustrated by the withdrawal of the immunity from such action.

16.6.2 Effect

Section 219(1) and (2) protects persons who would otherwise be tortfeasors from liability in tort. It does not protect from other forms of liability, notably criminal law and breach of contract. Furthermore, protection is limited to the torts specified. There is no protection from other torts such as breach of statutory duty, trespass and harassment. There has been controversy over the meaning of 'not actionable'. What it means is that, in relation to the torts mentioned, no one is allowed to sue. Otherwise put, the activity is rendered lawful. What is made lawful is not unlawful means for another tort such as interference with trade by unlawful means. Therefore, although there is no direct protection against this tort, there is indirect protection from liability.

16.6.3 Conspiracy

The immunity from conspiracy in s 219(2) requires brief discussion. It does not make lawful conspiracies to commit unlawful acts, for those acts are actionable if done by only one person. It only renders immune conspirators who use unlawful means. If, however, the unlawful means are rendered immune, there is no tort of conspiracy to use unlawful means.

16.6.4 Workers and their employers

Section 244(1), which defines 'trade dispute', is restricted to 'workers and their employer'. By s 244(5), 'worker' means:

(a) a worker employed by [his] employer; or

(b) a person who has ceased to be so employed if his employment was terminated in connection with the dispute or if the termination of his employment was one of the circumstances giving rise to the dispute.

The employers against whom the workers are taking industrial action must, in law, be their employer. The corporate veil will not be pierced (*Dimbleby & Sons Ltd v NUJ* (1984)). Employers can establish a company between themselves and their suppliers/distributors. A strike against the wrong firm will lose the immunity it would have had, had it been against the right firm. It is not always easy to find who the employers are. The shift from national to company bargaining weakens this part of the immunity. A dispute between a union and the employers where the workers are not involved no longer attracts the immunity.

The International Transport Workers' Federation's lengthy campaign against ships flying flags of convenience is not protected because there is no dispute between the crew and the shipowners. In *University College London NHS Trust v UNISON* (1999), the Court of Appeal ruled that s 244 did not apply where a strike was held in order to obtain protection from an unknown future employer. The dispute must be between the workers and their *current* employers.

16.6.5 Worker and worker

The restriction to 'workers and their employer' means that disputes between two sets of workers are not protected. Therefore, demarcation disputes no longer attract immunity unless there is also a dispute with the employers. Employers may find it difficult to avoid involvement. A *dictum* of Lord Diplock in *Dimbleby* (1984), that demarcation disputes between employees employed by the same employer are immune when disputes between employees alone are not, should presumably be read in this light.

16.6.6 Dispute

There must be a dispute. It need not be a full-blown one. A dispute 'exists wherever a difference exists, and a difference can exist long before the parties become locked in combat' (*per* Lord Denning in *Beetham v Trinidad Cement Ltd* (1960)). The term is widened by s 244(4):

> ... an act, threat or demand done or made by one person or organisation against another which, if resisted, would have led to a trade dispute with another, shall be treated as being done or made in contemplation or furtherance of a trade dispute with that other, notwithstanding that because that other submits to the act or threat or accedes to the demand no dispute arises.

Accordingly, if the employers cave in to the claim on presentation thereof, there is nevertheless a dispute. This in fact occurred in *Hadmor Productions* (see 16.5.19, above). There will, however, be no dispute attracting the immunity where it has been settled. Similarly, there is no dispute where employees were happy to be paid less than other workers.

16.6.7 Golden formula

The phrase 'in contemplation or furtherance of a trade dispute' is often known as the 'golden formula'. A trade dispute is defined in s 244(1) as a:

> ... dispute between workers and their employers which relates wholly or mainly to one or more of the following –
>
> (a)   terms and conditions of employment, or the physical conditions in which any workers are required to work;
>
> (b)   engagement or non-engagement, or termination or suspension of employment or the duties of employment, of one or more workers;
>
> (c)   allocation of work or the duties of employment between workers or groups of workers;
>
> (d)   matters of discipline;
>
> (e)   a worker's membership or non-membership of a trade union;
>
> (f)   facilities for officials of trade unions; and
>
> (g)   machinery for negotiation or consultation, and other procedures relating to any of the above matters, including recognition by employers or employers' associations of the right to a trade union to represent workers in such negotiation or consultation or in the carrying out of such procedures.

Only the matters listed attract immunity.

16.6.8 Wholly or mainly

The term 'relates wholly or mainly' should be noted. It is a closer link than that formerly required, which was that the dispute be connected with one of the listed matters. In *Mercury Communications Ltd v Scott-Garner* (1984), a dispute was held to be relating wholly or mainly to upholding British Telecom's monopoly, not relating wholly or mainly to the threat to jobs at British Telecom. The action was not immune. It would have been immune before the change. However, in *Wandsworth LBC v National Association of Schoolmasters* (1993), the Court of Appeal held that a boycott of standard assessment tests was one brought about by an increased workload for teachers. Accordingly, it was concerned with their terms and conditions of employment. It was not wholly or mainly one relating to a protest against educational policy. The task of deciding which motivation is predominant places a substantial power in the hands of the courts.

16.6.9 Trade

The restriction to the matters listed is meant to limit lawful strikes to those which are non-political. An example of industrial action which fell on the 'political' side is *BBC v Hearn* (1977). Television technical staff threatened not to transmit the FA Cup Final to South Africa as a protest against apartheid. The trade union argued that there was a term in its members' contracts that they should not be contractually obliged to transmit broadcasts to South Africa as long as apartheid continued. The court held that, at the time of the action, this issue had not arisen, that is, the workers were not striking to enforce this term in their contracts. Accordingly, none of the matters in s 244(1) were the subject of dispute and there was no immunity. If there had been a dispute as to contractual terms, there would have been a dispute. Indeed, the court was willing to go further to include disputes about practices which were not contractually binding. But the *ratio* of the case demonstrates that the mere fact that there is threatened action does not bring the immunity into play. There must be a difference over a listed matter. The House of Lords has said that industrial action is not simply converted into a trade dispute by the union's arguing that the way to resolve the matter is to include it as a term in the employees' contracts (*Universe Tankships Inc of Monrovia v International Transport Workers' Federation* (1983), *obiter*). No protection is afforded to the following situations: where unions act out of 'ruffled dignity' (*Huntley v Thornton* (1957); inter-union rivalry leading to annoyance with the plaintiffs (*Stratford v Lindley* (1965); and an *ad hominem* attack on a person who criticised the trade union (*Torquay Hotel v Cousins* (1969)).

16.6.10 Contemplation or furtherance

According to Lord Loreburn in *Conway v Wade* (1909), 'contemplation' is when 'a dispute is imminent and the act is done in expectation of and with a view to it', and 'furtherance' is when 'the dispute is already existing and the act is done in support of one side to it'. An act done when a dispute is only a possibility is not done in contemplation of it. Similarly, boycotting a contractor who drove through a picket line is not action taken in furtherance of a trade dispute, for the dispute was at an end. The boycott came too late to attract the immunity.

Preparation by the union is not, by itself, in contemplation of a dispute. Where a union official sought to find out about employers' wage bills and weekly sales, no immunity to inducing breach of contracts of employment was available because no dispute was imminent. Where, however, a union told its members not to co-operate with a private contractor, it was held that the act was in contemplation of a dispute. The line is fine. If the defendants honestly believe that what they are doing is in furtherance of the dispute, that is sufficient. The courts have no power to withdraw immunity on the ground that the acts were too remote from the dispute or that it is commercially impossible to comply with the demand (*NWL Ltd v Woods* (1979); *Express Newspapers Ltd v McShane* (1980); and *Duport Steels Ltd v Sirs* (1980), a famous trilogy of cases, which have been superseded by legislation). Strikes cannot be in contemplation or furtherance of a trade dispute if the dispute has been settled.

16.6.11 Political strikes

This paragraph considers strikes against the Government. As stated above, a line is drawn between trade and political disputes. A strike against the Government may appear to be political. However, in industrial relations, the Government may have a role not just as the formulator and enforcer of policy but also as an employer. What about action against a pay freeze? There is no difference on this point between Government and other employers. The immunity applies. For example, in *Sherard v AUEW* (1973), the union threatened to strike against a pay standstill. Since other employers could also impose a pay freeze, the Government was treated in the same way as ordinary employers.

The courts have gone further. If denationalisation threatens jobs, a protest strike against it is immune (*General Aviation Services (UK) Ltd v TGWU* (1974)). However, protests against more general government policies, such as the passing of the Industrial Relations Bill, are not immune (*Associated Newspapers Group Ltd v Flynn* (1970)). A 'day of action' against economic policy was not immune (*Beaverbrook Newspapers Ltd v Keys* (1980)). Both strikes were adjudged to be political despite the subject matter affecting workers.

The Court of Appeal held in *London Borough of Wandsworth v NUS/UWT* (1993) that a boycott of school assessment tests was related wholly or mainly to workload or working hours and was therefore a trade dispute. Since 1982, action is not protected unless it is 'wholly or mainly' related to one of the listed matters. This phrase means, then, that more disputes are political after 1982 than before because, though the matter might have been connected with a listed subject, it is not wholly or mainly relating to it. Part of the Conservative Government's strategy was to restrict the width of the immunity.

16.7 Impermissible purpose

Lawful strikes can be rendered unlawful by impermissible purpose. By ss 222–25 of TULR(C)A 1992, industrial action for several reasons is not protected by the immunity. Action against employers to enforce union membership is not protected (s 222). This provision is part of the attack on the closed shop. It is not, however, restricted to situations where a closed shop exists. The strike is impermissible where even one of the reasons behind it was to press for the dismissal of non-members. By s 223:

> ... an act is not protected if the reason, or one of the reasons, for doing it is the fact or belief that an employer has dismissed one or more employees in circumstances such that by virtue of s 237 (dismissal in connection with unofficial action) they have no right to complain of unfair dismissal.

This provision reinforces the position of employers who have dismissed unofficial strikers. Interlocutory injunctions restraining the industrial action are available. See Chapter 11 for dismissals for unofficial strikes.

Section 224 deals with secondary action, discussed below. Action is not protected if it involves pressure on employers to impose a term in a contract that their suppliers or distributors should recognise unions (s 225). Action is not immune if only one of the reasons for the dispute relates to s 222 or s 225.

The introduction of s 223 did not lead to a change in the definition of 'trade dispute' in s 244(i). Accordingly, industrial action over the dismissal of unofficial strikers is a trade dispute and is at the same time impermissible.

16.8 Secondary action

Secondary action is defined in s 224(2) as being:

> ... when ... a person –
>
> (a) induces another to break a contract of employment or interferes or induces another to interfere with its performance; or
>
> (b) threatens that a contract of employment under which he or another is employed will be broken or its performance interfered with, or that he will induce another to break a contract of employment or to interfere with its performance, and the employer under the contract of employment is not the employer party to the dispute.

The effect of this is to outlaw industrial action in solidarity with other workers. Some people view the curtailment of such strikes as a body blow to unions' perceptions of their role. To get round the prohibition of sympathy strikes, union officials have to try and convert the industrial action into primary action; that is, they must try to involve other employers in the dispute and then call out the employees. There is no similar ban on secondary or sympathetic action by employers.

16.8.1 Former immunity

Before 1980, trade unions had immunity where they undertook industrial action against one employer in order to bring pressure on another. The Employment Act 1980 reduced the width of the immunity. The law was complex and was criticised for so being. Instead of reformulating it, the then Government abolished the immunity for secondary action in 1990. There is an exception, which is more nominal than real, for peaceful picketing, considered below.

16.9 Strike ballot

For acts done by unions to be immune, a ballot is necessary. (There is no obligation on employers to ballot their shareholders before going to the aid of companies who are engaged in industrial action, and this sympathy action is not unlawful.) The Government's stated aim was to oblige unions to adopt 'proper democratic procedures' (*Industrial Relations in the 1990s*, Cm 1602, 1991).

This section of the book does not apply to industrial action which is unofficial, that is, not union-backed. Such industrial action remains protected. Trade unions which take part in industrial action, even trade unions which are not recognised, are not immune without a ballot (s 226(1)). This provision was introduced in 1984. Most ballots have been in favour of striking. For instance, in 1992, 90% of votes were in favour. A sample voting paper must be sent to the employers not later than three days before the ballot and notice of the ballot must be given to them not less than seven days before the vote (s 226A, inserted by s 18 of TURERA 1993). This provision gives the employers more time to react to the call for industrial action. Pre-strike ballots are now an accepted part of the industrial scene, and ballots to end action are becoming common. There is a Code of Practice on Industrial Action Ballots and Notice to Employees, 1995, which courts and tribunals may take into account. Some parts of the Code do not have a statutory footing: for example, it suggests that internal disputes settlement procedures should be exhausted before a ballot is arranged.

16.9.1 Loss of immunity

If this process does not take place, immunity is lost from those employers but not otherwise. A union has to appoint an independent scrutineer in order to retain any immunity (s 226A, inserted by s 20 of TURERA 1993). Trade unions must inform the relevant employers of the outcome as soon as is reasonably practicable (s 231A, inserted by s 19 of TURERA 1993). (There need be no scrutineer where there are fewer than 50 members entitled to vote.) To secure immunity, ss 227–32 must be complied with. There must be a majority in favour (s 232 relates to ballots of overseas members).

16.9.2 Entitlement to vote

Those entitled to vote are those who:

> ... it is reasonable at the time of the ballot for the union to believe will be induced to take part ... in the industrial action in question, and no others [s 227(1)].

If a significant number of those entitled to vote are denied the opportunity, the ballot is invalid (*RJB Mining (UK) Ltd v NUM* (1997)). A simple mistake, however, does not invalidate the ballot. Independent contractors who personally do work or perform services must be allowed to vote. If persons who were not members at the time when the vote was held are called out as a result of that ballot, the union retains its immunity (*London Underground v RMT* (1995)). As Millett LJ put it: 'It is the industrial action which must have the support of a ballot, not the participation of those who have been induced to take part in it.'

The basic rule as to voting constituencies is that separate ballots must be held for each workplace (s 228(1), as amended by the Employment Relations Act 1999). The aim is to prevent gerrymandering to produce a militant constituency out of several workplaces where moderates are in the majority. The place of work, until the amendment in 1999, was defined as:

> ... the premises occupied by [the employee's] employer at or from which that person works or, where he does not work at or from any such premises or from more than one set of premises, the premises occupied by his employer with which his employment has the closest connection.

'Occupied' is read in a broad, industrial relations sense. Train operating companies occupy railway stations even though it is a different company which legally owns the platforms, concourse, rails and so on (*InterCity West Coast Ltd v National Union of Rail, Maritime and Transport Workers* (1996)). The two employers' staff had a licence to walk on Manchester Piccadilly Station for business purposes and, accordingly, the employers occupied it. It did not matter that the employees of each employer reported to separate offices.

The 1999 Act redefined workplace as:

(a) if the person works at or from a single set of premises, those premises; and

(b) in any other case, the premises with which the person's employment has the closest connection.

There is a complicated exception in s 228(3), the thrust of which is that there can be just one ballot for employees of one occupational description who work in different places. If there is a breach of s 228(3), it does not matter that, if the ballot had been held properly, it would have made no difference to the result (*RJB Mining (UK) Ltd v NUM*). A ballot may be held covering employees of different employers if it is reasonable for the unions to believe that there is a common factor (*University of Central England v NALGO* (1993)). Surprisingly, there must even be a ballot where the union consists only of other unions and has no individual members (*Shipping Co Uniform Inc v ITF* (1985)).

16.9.3 Voting

Voting is by marking a paper (s 229(1)). Papers, so far as is reasonably practicable, must be sent out and returned by post (with the exception of merchant seamen) (s 230(2) of TULR(C)A 1992, as inserted by s 17 of TURERA 1993). The effect is that workplace and semi-postal ballots no longer attract any statutory immunity (and this is so despite the fact that some unions achieve a higher turnout of voters in workplace ballots than in fully postal ones). The Code of Practice on Trade Union Ballots on Industrial Action (revised version, 1991) suggests that the union gives members a fortnight to vote when second class post is used. This recommendation undercuts the necessity that unions act very promptly or members' interest will wane rapidly. Postal ballots will hold back fervour. The Code also suggests that internal procedures for resolving disputes should be exhausted before a ballot is called, a provision which is not in the legislation. The paper must specify who may call the industrial action (s 229(3)). It must contain either or both of the following:

> ... a question (however framed) which requires the person answering it to say, by answering 'Yes' or 'No', whether he is prepared to take part or, as the case may be, to continue to take part in a strike; or
>
> ... a question (however framed) which requires the person answering it to say, by answering 'Yes' or 'No', whether he is prepared to take part or, as the case may be, to continue to take part in industrial action [s 229(2)].

Both questions must be put if both forms of action are proposed (*Post Office v Union of Communication Workers* (1990)). If both questions are put, a majority in either suffices for that type of action; the fact that, altogether, the votes against action outweigh those in favour is irrelevant (*West Midlands Travel Ltd v TGWU* (1994)).

A 'strike' is defined in s 246 as 'any concerted stoppage of work'. Since bans on overtime and rest day working are concerted stoppages of work, they are strikes for the purpose of ballots before industrial action (*Connex South Eastern Ltd v National Union of Rail, Maritime and Transport Workers* (1999)). A strike, therefore, need not be a cessation of all work. This decision left little to be included as industrial action short of a strike. Presumably, go-slows and works-to-rule are covered. The problem for unions with this decision is that they may win non-strike ballots but will lose strike ballots. *Connex* was overturned by the Employment Relations Act 1999, which stated that an overtime ban was action short of a strike in s 229.

The paper must also contain the following words: 'If you take part in a strike or other industrial action, you may be in breach of your contract of employment' (s 229(4)). This phrase has come to be known as the 'health warning'. No explanation must be added to this written declaration (even if the action will not amount to a breach!). However, the union may provide a separate leaflet detailing its stance and commenting on s 229(4). The aim behind this sub-section is to dampen enthusiasm for industrial action. However, the Employment Relations Act 1999 provided protection for those taking industrial action if they are dismissed within eight weeks of the start of the action. By s 229(1)(A), inserted by TURERA 1993, the name of the scrutineer must be on the ballot paper except for constituencies of fewer than 50 members (s 226C, inserted by TURERA 1993). Ballot papers must also be consecutively numbered.

16.9.4 No interference

There must be no interference by the union with its members or officials in the vote (s 230(1)). The voting must be in secret and the votes must be fairly counted, though inaccuracies are disregarded if they do not affect the outcome (s 230(4)). Secret voting by post was the Government's response to traditional methods of voting in trade unions – by show of hands, at mass meetings, at the workplace and at branch meetings.

16.9.5 Information

All persons entitled to vote must be told of the result, including 'yes' and 'no' votes and spoilt ballot papers (s 231). Employers must be told as soon as reasonably practicable (s 231A, inserted by TURERA 1993). If not the defendants lose immunity totally.

16.9.6 Non-provision

Immunity is, in relation to the relevant employers, (only) forfeited if the employers are not informed of the industrial action (s 234A, inserted by s 21 of TURERA 1993 and amended by the Employment Relations Act 1999). The notice must specify those employees ('containing such information in the union's possession as would help the employer to make plans'), state whether the action will be continuous or not (such as a series of one day strikes), and state that the notice is given for the purposes of s 234A. The effect of s 234A is to permit employers to know which employees are covered by the notice of industrial action. The obligation was held to include a duty to inform employers of the names of individuals when there is no other means of disclosing who is affected (*NATFHE v Blackpool and the Fylde College* (1994). This Court of Appeal decision came in for strong criticism, partly because it did not reflect the intention of Parliament). It was overruled by the Employment Relations Act 1999. If the action is discontinuous, the union must inform the employers of the dates of the action; the effect is that random dates to maximise disruption cannot be chosen. Notice must be given within the period from the ballot to seven days before the action. This provision is perhaps the most controversial one in TURERA 1993, for employees may be susceptible to nobbling and may be victimised. Forewarned is forearmed.

16.9.7 Call to action

The calling of industrial action must be by a 'specified person' (s 233), that is, the one mentioned in s 229(3) (see 16.9.3, above). There must have been no call for industrial action before the ballot. The ballot is not effective after four weeks, or for up to eight weeks if the union and employers agree (s 234, as amended by the Employment Relations Act 1999). Time runs from the day of the ballot (that is, this day is counted), not from the day after the ballot. Midnight is counted as the previous day. It will, however, be valid for 12 weeks if a court order prohibiting the action is set aside. In *Post Office v Union of Communication Workers* (1990), the Court of Appeal held that a ballot in September 1988 did not render lawful a strike in September 1989, even though there had been industrial conflict in the interim. The effect of s 234 and s 234A is to give unions little time for the outcome of the ballot to be utilised. If the action is not called by the correct person, immunity is lost.

16.10 Citizen's and member's right

'The citizen's right of action' and the member's right are discussed in this section.

16.10.1 Citizen's right

By s 235A, inserted by TURERA 1993, any individual (a term which normally excludes a company) may make a claim for an order to the High Court if a trade union or another person has done an unlawful act to induce a person to take part in industrial action and the effect of the action does or is likely to prevent, delay or reduce the quality of goods or services to him. There is no right to damages. 'Unlawful' includes actionability in tort. But the tort need not be actionable at the suit of the plaintiff, and it includes the situation where the member's right (discussed below) is infringed. It does not matter that the person was not entitled to receive the goods or services. The action need not be intended to affect the individual who brings the action. No loss need be caused. The sort of person who could bring this action is the plaintiff in *Falconer v ASLEF* (see 16.5.5, above), and there would be no need for him to have a right of action in tort. The right gets round the restrictions on economic torts discussed earlier.

The order requires the trade union to desist from inducing persons to participate in industrial action. Inducement is done by the trade union if it is 'authorised or endorsed' by the union within s 20(2)–(4) of TULR(C)A 1992. There used to be a Commissioner for Protection against Unlawful Industrial Action whose function was to assist individuals in bringing the 'citizen's right of action', but the post was abolished by the Employment Relations Act 1999.

Employers may not wish to resort to law for fear of inflaming the situation. This right undercuts that desire. It is thought that an injunction will not help resolve industrial disputes.

16.10.2 Member's right

Section 235A refers to 'unlawful' acts. Besides tortious acts, which are not immune, 'unlawful' means a breach of s 62 of TULR(C)A 1992 (as amended by Sched 8, para 47 of TURERA 1993). By s 62(1), a trade union member:

> ... who claims that members of the union, including himself, are likely to be or have been induced by the union to take part or continue to take part in industrial action which does not have the support of a ballot may apply to the court for an order.

The order requires the trade union to ensure that there is no inducement to members to participate in action. Acts are those of the trade union if authorised or endorsed under s 20(2)–(4). Persons working for the Crown are deemed to be employees for the purpose of defining industrial action ('a strike or other industrial action by persons employed under contracts of employment' (s 62(7))).

16.10.3 Comment

The new action does not apply to lock-outs. It does not apply when firms cut back services or reduce standards: one cannot sue Virgin Cross-Country for withdrawing trains. Unions and management will not be able to deal with disputes themselves. The law discussed in 16.9 and 16.10, above, were part of the Conservative Government's plan to decrease strikes and union power by increasing the number of requirements for a lawful industrial action. The member's action is in addition to any contractual right he may have under the union's rule book (see, for example, *Taylor v NUM (Yorkshire Area)* (1984), where the plaintiffs succeeded in the action to restrain the union from imposing discipline in breach of its rules, in other words, in breach of contract).

16.11 Vicarious liability

A union may be responsible in law for the actions of its officials, including shop stewards. Vicarious liability for the economic torts, the ones normally involved in industrial action, is laid down in statute. Otherwise, the common law applies.

16.11.1 Statute

By s 20(1) of TULR(C)A 1992:

> ... where proceedings in tort are brought against a trade union:
>
> (a) on the ground that an act –
>
>   (i)   induces another person to break a contract or interferes or induces another person to interference with its performance; or
>
>   (ii) consists in threatening that a contract (whether one to which the union is a party or not) will be broken or its performance interfered with, or that the union will induce another person to break a contract or interfere with its performance; or
>
> (b) in respect of an agreement or combination by two or more persons to do or to procure the doing of an act which, if it were done without any such agreement or combination, would be actionable in tort on such ground,
>
> then, for the purpose of determining in those proceedings whether the union is liable in respect of the act in question, that act shall be taken to have been done by the union if, but only if, it is to be taken to have been authorised or endorsed by the trade union in accordance with the following provisions.

16.11.2 Authorised or endorsed

By s 20(2):

> ... an act shall be taken to have been authorised or endorsed by a trade union if it was done, or was authorised or endorsed –
>
> (a) by any person empowered by the rules to do, authorise or endorse acts of the kind in question; or
>
> (b) by the principal executive committee or the president or general secretary; or
>
> (c) by any other committee of the union or any other official of the union (whether employed by it or not).

In (c), 'other official' includes a shop steward, even though union rules do not allow him to call a strike, and a 'committee' may be one established for the purpose of conducting the industrial action at issue ((c) was added in 1990). The next sub-section makes the union liable for the acts of a group of persons and individuals within that group where a union official was a member of the group and the purposes of the body included the organising of industrial action. This rule was also added in 1990.

An illustration of s 20(2) occurred in the unreported High Court case of *British Railways Board v National Union of Rail, Maritime and Transport Workers* (1992). Members of a staff committee set up by a collective agreement between the plaintiffs and defendants were not union officials. Therefore, industrial action led by these people was unofficial. The outcome was that a strike in their favour after they has been dismissed was unofficial and was, therefore, impermissible under s 223 (see 16.7, above).

16.11.3 Repudiation

If the act was authorised or endorsed under s 20(2)(c), it can be repudiated by the executive, president or general secretary, provided they repudiate as soon as they know of the facts (s 21(1)). The repudiation must be in writing and the trade union:

> ... must do its best to give individual written notice of the fact and date of repudiation, without delay –
>
> (i)   to every member of the union who the union has reason to believe is taking part, or might otherwise take part, in industrial action as a result of the act; and
>
> (ii)   to the employer of every such member ... [s 21(2)].

This statement must be included:

> Your union has repudiated the call (or calls) for industrial action to which this notice relates and will give no support to unofficial industrial action taken in response to it (or them). If you are dismissed while taking unofficial industrial action, you will have no right to complain of unfair dismissal [s 21(3)].

Section 21(2) and (3) became part of the law in 1990. Repudiation ceases to be effective if the executive, president or general secretary acts inconsistently with it (for example, by nodding and smiling at shop stewards who are carrying on the action). If, within three months (Sched 7, para 17 of TURERA 1993) of the purported repudiation, a person who is party to a commercial contract and who has not previously been given written confirmation seeks confirmation of it, the repudiation is ineffective if repudiation is not 'forthwith confirmed in writing' (s 21(6)). Commercial contracts are defined to exclude contracts of service and contracts to perform work or services personally. The whole thrust of this law is to make unions centralise their decision-making process and to split the union hierarchy from the members. Centralisation remains inconsistent with the structure of many unions.

16.11.4 Nods and winks

Section 21 was the Conservative Government's response to what it saw as unions' encouragement of unofficial strikes. Unions may not wish to show their hand but, by nods and winks, they may encourage members to take unofficial action. Section 21 ensures that unions take control, the sanction being damages in tort up to the maximum stated below, 16.12. Section 21 is otiose, for, as the Court of Appeal held in *Express and Star Ltd v NGA (1982)* (1986), a union is liable for contempt when it encourages members to strike unofficially, even though that contempt is based on disobedience to an order based on a tort covered by s 20.

16.11.5 Common law

Section 20 applies to only the economic torts and to contempt proceedings based on breach of an injunction in respect of these torts. With regard to other torts, the common law in *Heatons Transport (St Helens) Ltd v TGWU (1972)* (HL) applies.

16.12 Damages

There is a limit on the amount of damages which may be awarded against a trade union in tort. If there are fewer than 5,000 members, the maximum is £10,000; for 5,000–25,000 members: £50,000; for 25,000–100,000 members: £125,000; and more than 100,000 members: £250,000 (s 22). The statute does not state the date on which numbers are to be calculated. These limits have remained static since they were introduced in 1982. This maximum applies to each action, not each dispute. If a dispute gives rise to 10 suits by employers, each employer can sue up to the maximum.

These maxima do not apply to tort actions concerning personal injury through negligence, nuisance or breach of duty, property and product liability under the Consumer Protection Act 1987. The maximum can be exceeded by adding interest to the damages. By s 23, certain trade union funds are 'protected property' which cannot be used to pay damages. These include the provident and political funds. Property which is 'protected' cannot be used for paying damages, whether the claim is brought in tort or otherwise.

16.12.1 Effect of changes

For many years before 1982, unions were not liable in tort. When the law was changed, the Government thought that, if there was no limit, trade unions would quickly be made bankrupt. The narrowing of the immunities and the technicalities of the ballot may lead to increased losses to union funds.

16.12.2 Width of law

Section 22 is limited to tort. Unlimited fines remain available for contempt of court. For example, the National Graphical Association was fined £675,000 for contempt in 1984. There is no limit on the amount payable by individuals. Inerlocutory injunctions may break strikes.

16.13 Injunctions

'Holding the ring' is the jargon phrase for this area of law. The courts are meant to act as umpires in boxing matches act. Their decisions may, however, affect the outcome of industrial action.

16.13.1 Effect

Most cases against trade unions never reach trial. Therefore, courts rarely have to consider damages against unions. Trade union officials are likely to be 'men of straw'. What employers and other affected individuals want is an interlocutory injunction to stop the industrial action. This type of prohibitory order is granted by the High Court pre-trial and may be granted without notice, the aim being to preserve the status quo pre-trial. Since, however, few trade dispute cases reach trial (fewer than one in 15 cases, according to McKay (*The Law on Industrial Action under the Conservatives*, 1996, Institute of Employment Rights)), it is the grant of this order which in practice is important. The union, if injuncted, will find it hard to re-motivate its members when the interlocutory injunction is lifted.

Most unions obey injunctions. The employers will argue that they will suffer financial loss if the remedy is not awarded. The changes in the law provided employers and trade union member with more rights against unions. Over 200 claims for injunctions were made between 1983 and early 1996. Many concerned the new legal provisions such as balloting and secondary action, but some concerned the common law. Injunctions against pickets are rare now.

The decline in industrial action over the past decade has been matched by a reduction in the application for injunctions. One major problem for unions is that they are not always represented at the grant of these orders. Affidavit evidence is not available, and proceedings need not take place in open court in the daytime. The remedy can be granted over the telephone. The choice for the unions is one between obeying the order or defying it and suffering the consequences of being in contempt of court.

16.13.2 Financial loss

Generally, judges grant interlocutory injunctions if plaintiffs have an arguable case (*American Cyanamid Co v Ethicon Ltd* (1975)). The courts have strongly adhered to the principle that, at this stage of the proceedings, there must be no 'mini-trial' on the merits. Merits are for the full trial. Because employers can point to pecuniary loss as a result of industrial action and trade unions cannot point to such damage if the injunction is granted, employers usually gain this relief despite the fact that support for action may disappear over time, a matter which has not yet been considered properly by the courts. If the remedy is granted, plaintiffs have to give an undertaking to pay damages at full trial if they then lose, but this promise is nugatory because full trials are rare and trade unions cannot calculate their losses in economic terms. In the words of Lord Diplock in *NWL Ltd v Woods* (1979), the 'practical realities' are that the grant of an interlocutory relief 'is tantamount to giving final judgment against the defendants'. One factor for consideration by the court has been said to be the public interest (*Associated British Ports v TGWU* (1989)), a point not dealt with by the House of Lords. So far, no account has been taken of the public interest behind the freedom to strike.

16.13.3 *Ex parte*

Parliament sought in s 221 to defuse trade union anger at the grant of prohibitory orders. By s 221(1):

> ... where –
>
> (a)   an application for an injunction ... is made to a court in the absence of the party against whom it is sought or any representative of his; and
>
> (b)   he claims, or in the opinion of the court would be likely to claim, that he acted in contemplation or furtherance of a trade dispute, the court shall not grant the injunction ... unless satisfied that all steps which in the circumstances were reasonable,
>
> have been taken with a view to securing that notice of application and an opportunity of being heard with respect to the application have been given to him.

This sub-section thereby restricts *ex parte* orders. The effect is to put the likelihood of the defence's success into the balance.

16.13.4 Consideration

Section 221(2) reads:

> ... where –
> (a) an application for an interlocutory injunction is made to a court pending the trial of an action; and
> (b) the party against whom it is sought claims that he acted in contemplation or furtherance of a trade dispute, the court shall, in exercising its discretion whether or not to grant the injunction, have regard to the likelihood of that party's succeeding at the trial of the action in establishing any matter which would afford a defence to the action under section 219 (protection from certain tort liabilities) or section 220 (peaceful picketing).

Section 221(2) is a consciousness-raising provision.

If it is probable that the defendants have a s 219 or s 220 defence, the remedy is refused (*NWL Ltd v Woods* (1979)), though this law has not always been applied by the High Court. Section 221(2) does not apply if there are immediate threats to health and safety (*Beaverbrook Newspapers Ltd v Keys* (1980)) or fundamental rights, for example, freedom of the press (*Express Newspapers Ltd v McShane* (1980)) or, perhaps, if the national economy will be harmed (*Associated British Ports Ltd v TGWU* (1989)). It will also not apply when the strike action has ceased.

16.13.5 Application

Since s 221(2) applies only in relation to those economic torts mentioned in s 219, in relation to the other torts the *American Cyanamid* test applies. In a restraint of trade case, *Lansing Linde Ltd v Kerr* (1991), however, the Court of Appeal said that *American Cyanamid* did not apply with full force where trial was unlikely. Since trial is unlikely in industrial matters, this statement may require reconsideration; otherwise, the courts have been acting in error for many years. Contrariwise, Lord Diplock in *NWL Ltd v Woods* said that the courts retained a residual discretion to grant an interlocutory injunction, even when the immunities apply, if the action would be 'disastrous' to employers and the community. There are similar suggestions in other cases, but no judge has as yet relied on them.

16.13.6 Contempt

Breach of injunction is penalised by punishment for contempt of court and sequestration of the defendant's assets. Contempt, at least if it is wilful, is punishable by a fine or imprisonment (up to two years) or both, at the court's discretion. There is no maximum limit on the fine. No union property is exempt. An example is *Austin Rover Group Ltd v AUEW* (1985). The judge held that the general secretary of the trade union should have done something to help implement an order that the trade union should not issue any instruction to take industrial action. No fine was ordered because the breach was not serious. Arthur Scargill was fined £1,000 in 1984.

Substantial fines have been ordered in other cases against trade unions. A defiance of the court order will lead to a heavy fine. In *Richard Read (Transport) Ltd v NUM (South Wales Area)* (1985), the defendants were fined £50,000. Similarly, if a union takes a long time to withdraw instructions to strike, a large fine may be imposed. The contempt may be purged by the contemnor accepting the jurisdiction of the court, though often an apology is needed.

16.13.7 Sequestration

If sequestration is ordered, commissioners seize the defendant's assets. Obstruction of them is a contempt. Money can then be used to pay fines. The union must pay for the costs of the sequestration. The trade union's accountants must co-operate. Trustees can be removed if they attempt to save union assets from sequestration (*Clarke v Heathfield (No 2)* (1985)).

16.14 Picketing

Picketing is a form of protest during disputes, whether industrial or not, whereby demonstrators seek one or more of several objectives: to communicate the fact that they are in dispute, to seek support for their action, and to stop replacement labour and supplies. What is sometimes known as 'secondary picketing' occurs when others join in to bring pressure on the employers who are parties to the primary dispute or where employees picket other than at their place of work. The restriction to one's place of work was intended to deter flying pickets. Picketing can give rise to offences and to civil liability.

16.14.1 Crime

Besides offences such as criminal damage, assault, battery and offences contrary to the Public Order Act 1986 (such as s 3, affray), certain offences classically may occur. Note, also, ss 11–16 of the 1986 Act, which deal with public demonstrations and processions. The Criminal Justice and Public Order Act 1994 inserted s 4A into the Public Order Act 1986 to create the offence of intentional harassment, causing alarm or distress. A person will be liable if he shouts insulting words at a non-striker with intent and causes another person harassment, alarm or distress. Criminal liability was also established for displaying writings, signs or other visible representations which are threatening, abusive or insulting. Perhaps a sign saying 'scab' is sufficient.

16.14.2 Breach of the peace

Breach of the peace occurs when a person behaves in such a way as to be likely to cause, or in fact causes, a breach of the peace. That person can be a picket, the persons picketed or anyone else. In *Piddington v Bates* (1960), Lord Parker CJ held that a constable was acting lawfully when he limited the number of pickets to two at the entrance to a factory when he contemplated that a breach of the peace was a real possibility. As that case demonstrates, the accused is guilty even though he did not use or threaten violence. In *Kavanagh v Hiscock* (1974), a policeman had reason to believe that a breach of the peace might occur if he did not clear all pickets from the entrance to a hospital. The court held that he was justified in doing as he did.

Pickets have no right to stop vehicles, even ones which contain replacement labour. The police have a right to stop vehicles carrying pickets miles away from the site if they apprehend a breach of the peace (*Moss v McLachlan* (1985)). Again, the police could use this power to prevent any pickets reaching the site. Going through a police cordon constitutes a breach of the peace.

16.14.3 Obstruction

The offence of obstruction of the highway is now found in s 137 of the Highways Act 1980. The wilful obstruction of the free passage without lawful authority or excuse is a crime. Whether the offence occurs is dependent on the duration and place of the obstruction, its purpose, and whether there was an actual rather than a potential obstruction (*Nagy v Weston* (1965)). There is no right to stop vehicles (*Broome v DPP* (1974)).

16.14.4 Nuisance

Public nuisance is a common law crime and is committed when free passage is blocked by pickets, but it is thought that picketing *per se* does not amount to public nuisance. Forty pickets walking in a circle at an entrance to a workplace was a public nuisance (*Tynan v Balmer* (1967)). Picketing a person's home is also a nuisance (*Thomas v NUM (South Wales Area)* (1985), *per* Scott J).

16.14.5 Obstructing a constable

Section 86(3) of the Police Act 1996 creates the offence of obstructing a police constable in the execution of his duty. 'Duty' includes preventing trouble at a picket line. If the protesters object to what the constable is doing when he tells them to go home, this offence may have been committed. Obstructing a constable is not an arrestable offence but a police officer may arrest without warrant when he reasonably apprehends a breach of the peace; a police officer may well apprehend a breach of the peace when obstructed.

16.14.6 Watching or besetting

By s 241(1) of TULR(C)A 1992:

> ... a person commits an offence who, with a view to compelling another person to abstain from doing or to do any act which that person has a legal right to do or abstain from doing, wrongfully and without legal authority –
>
> (a)   uses violence to or intimidates that person or his wife or children or injures his property;
>
> (b)   persistently follows that person about from place to place;
>
> (c)   hides any books, clothes or other property owned by or used by that person, or deprives him of or hinders him in the use thereof;
>
> (d)   watches or besets the house or other place where that person resides, works, carries on business or happens to be, or the approach to any such house or place; or
>
> (e)   follows that person with two or more other persons in a disorderly manner in or through any street or road.

The crime is punishable by a fine not exceeding £2,000 or six months' imprisonment or both. This crime was created in 1875 but was very rarely used until the 1984–85 miners' strike. The fine was substantially increased in 1986 as a result of the strike and the crime was made an arrestable offence in that year. 'Compelling' does not cover efforts to persuade people not to do something.

16.14.7 Wrongfully

'Wrongfully' means that the act must be tortious independently of the crime (*Ward, Lock & Co v OPAS* (1906) and *Thomas v NUM (South Wales Area)* (1985)). Therefore, if the picketing is lawful, there is no crime under this section. The contrary decision in *J Lyons & Sons v Wilkins* (1899) is nowadays regarded as incorrect. 'Intimidates' covers 'putting persons in fear by the exhibition of force ... or the threat of violence' (*R v Jones* (1974)). There is no need for violence against the person. Violence against property suffices. James LJ suggested in *Jones* that 'harsh words' would also constitute 'intimidates', but he may be wrong. Scott J held in *Thomas*, above, that mass picketing amounted to intimidation for the purposes of this offence. 'Watches or besets' covers sit-ins. The offence is not restricted to the industrial context but has been used against an anti-roads protester. As criminal law students will remember, agreements to commit torts are generally not criminal (ss 1, 5 of the Criminal Law Act 1977) but agreements to commit crimes are conspiracies. For example, an agreement to attack a non-striker is an offence and remains so even if done in contemplation or furtherance of a trade dispute.

16.14.8 Effect of civil immunity

Even if the picketing is rendered civilly lawful by s 219 of TULR(C)A 1992, it can still be a crime contrary to s 241 (*Galt v Philp* (1974), a Scottish case). The High Court of Justiciary held that a work-in amounted to watching or besetting. In other words, watching or besetting can be committed not only by persons outside the premises but inside too. The crime is not restricted to the industrial context but can apply to anti-roads protesters and stalkers.

16.14.9 Effect on tort

The fact that this crime has been committed does not *per se* mean that the defendants are tortiously liable (*Thomas v NUM (South Wales Area)* (1985)).

16.14.10 Bail conditions

As a condition for bail, magistrates may impose a condition that the defendant shall not picket or demonstrate to support the dispute in connection with which he was arrested (*Mansfield Justices ex p Sharkey* (1984)). The magistrates' condition did allow the defendant to picket his usual workplace. A person may receive a more severe sentence for breach of bail conditions than for the offence for which he was arrested.

16.14.11 Police role

Various discretions, such as that of arrest, are left in the hands of the police. These discretions have been criticised by civil libertarians as leaving too much power in the hands of the police. The arrest of pickets may worsen an industrial dispute.

16.14.12 Civil law

Other torts may occur, such as interference with business by unlawful means (*Thomas*, above) and trespass to land, as occurred when a defendant, a union official, addressed a meeting on the employers' premises without permission. However, the following are the more important ones. The economic torts, such as inducing breach of contract, have already been discussed (see 16.5, above).

16.14.13 Private nuisance

The tort of private nuisance is committed when the defendant unlawfully interferes with the plaintiff's use or enjoyment of his land. Scott J in *Thomas*, above, held that interference with an individual's right to use the highway was a private nuisance. Mass picketing was held to constitute this tort.

Working miners were unlawfully harassed by striking colleagues, who were prohibited from blocking vehicles and preventing people from entering premises. The correctness of this decision awaits a judgment by the Court of Appeal, and the proposition has been condemned as judicial legislation. Even if picketing is peaceful, it can amount to the tort of private nuisance where the defendants have not restricted their activities to the communication of information (*Mersey Dock and Harbour Co v Verrinder* (1982)).

16.14.14 Harassment

Scott J in *Thomas* thought that there was a tort of harassment actionable at the suit of those being picketed, but his decision was doubted by Stuart-Smith J in *News Group Newspapers Ltd v SOGAT 1982* (1987). In a non-employment case, the Court of Appeal said that there is a tort of harassment. Public nuisance (see 16.14.4, above) is also tortious.

16.14.15 Trespass to highway

Except for passing and repassing, use of the highway is trespass (*Hickman v Maisey* (1900)). An assembly of 21 people on the highway has been said to be sufficient. Special damage is required. Only owners of the highway may sue in respect of this tort.

16.14.16 Immunity

Section 220 of TULR(C)A 1992 gives immunity from civil and criminal liability to pickets in several situations. By s 220(1):

> ... it is lawful for a person in contemplation or furtherance of a trade dispute to attend –
>
> (a) at or near his own place of work; or
>
> (b) if he is an official of a trade union, at or near the place of work of a member of the union whom he is accompanying and whom he represents, for the purpose only of peacefully obtaining or communicating information, or peacefully persuading any person to work or abstain from working.

This sub-section is to the effect that flying pickets and persons who join the picket line but are not employed by the employers in dispute have no immunity. The narrow width of the protection afforded by this sub-section was demonstrated in the Wapping dispute (*News Group Newspapers Ltd v SOGAT 1982* (1987)). Closure of newspaper offices near Fleet Street and their transfer to Wapping resulted in illegal picketing at Wapping: the employees had never worked there; therefore, they were not 'at or near' their place of work. Picketing their former workplace would have no effect because the employers no longer were there.

The rest of s 220 reads:

(2) If a person works or normally works –

    (a) otherwise than at any one place; or

    (b) at a place the location of which is such that attendance there for a purpose mentioned in sub-section (1) is impracticable;

    his place of work for the purposes of that sub-section shall be any premises of his employer from which he works or from which his work is administered.

(3) in the case of a worker not in employment where –

    (a) his last employment was terminated in connection with a trade dispute; or

    (b) the termination of his employment was one of the circumstances giving rise to a trade dispute in relation to that dispute his former place of work shall be treated for the purposes of sub-section (1) as being his place of work.

(4) A person who is an official of a trade union by virtue only of having been elected or appointed to be a representative of some of the members of the union shall be regarded for the purposes of sub-section (1) as representing only those members; but otherwise an official of a union shall be regarded for those purposes as representing all its members.

Section 220(4) permits national officials to picket with others. The expectation is that he will restrain the other pickets.

16.14.17 Secondary picketing

Secondary picketing is lawful if the pickets are at their own place of work. By s 24(1), secondary action which is lawful picketing is protected. Section 224(3) defines lawful picketing as:

... acts done in the course of such attendance as is declared lawful by section 220 (peaceful picketing) –

(a) by a worker employed (or, in the case of a worker not in employment, last employed) by the employer party to the dispute; or

(b) by a trade union official whose attendance is lawful by virtue of sub-section (1)(b) of that section.

It should be remembered that, by s 244, 'trade dispute' is defined as a dispute between workers and their employers. Picketing against other employers is unlawful. This type is sometimes called 'sympathy picketing'. Unfortunately, this action sometimes also goes by the name of 'secondary picketing'. The question to ask is: where was the defendant picketing?

An example of s 224 is this. Persons picket a factory. Lorry drivers bringing supplies from a firm to the employers turn back. The effect of s 224 is that the pickets will not be liable, provided they do not go beyond what is permitted by s 220. Picketing the place where the lorries are based is unlawful.

16.14.18 Width of immunity

Picketing is permissible within s 220(1) only in industrial disputes, only for the purposes mentioned and only in respect of torts concerning attendance; torts beyond attendance are not rendered immune; and pickets cannot prevent persons entering premises (*Tynan v Balmer* (1967)) or stop vehicles (*Broome v DPP* (1974), 16.14.3, above). 'At or near' covers picketing at the entrance to a private industrial estate on which the employers' factory was sited (*Rayware Ltd v TGWU* (1989)). If the pickets had been closer, they would have been trespassing.

The 1991 version suggests that, if there is a choice as to places to picket, picketing should take place only at the closest spot, otherwise, the picketing will not be regarded as being 'at or near' the place of work. If their place of work has closed down, pickets cannot picket at the new workplace (*News Group*, 16.14.14, above, the 'Wapping case') – effectively, they cannot lawfully picket anywhere.

16.14.19 Numbers

Immunity in the statute is not limited to a maximum number of pickets. In other words, mass picketing is not *per se* unlawful. However, the Department of Employment's Code of Practice on Picketing 1980, revised in 1991 (SI 1991/476), states that mass picketing may be tortious and recommends not more than six pickets at each entrance, adding: '... frequently, a small number will be appropriate.' Scott J in *Thomas* thought that mass picketing constitutes intimidation and that six was the correct maximum. He stated that large numbers were unnecessary for peaceful persuasion.

The Code has therefore had an effect on the law, though its legal status is solely that it is admissible in evidence and may be taken into account by a court, an employment tribunal or the CAC (s 207(3) of TULR(C)A 1992). It should be noted that the Code does not affect the police's right (mentioned above, 16.14.2) to limit the number of pickets. Certainly, mass picketing may tend to show that the protesters' purpose is not that of attendance for peaceful communication, but this remains a matter of evidence, not substantive law (*per* Lord Reid in *Broome v DPP* (1974)).

16.14.20 Code on essential services

The Code also states that picketing should not stop 'the operation of essential services, such as police, fire, ambulance, medical and nursing services', nor should it interfere with public health, for example, water purification operations. The law, however, states that peaceful picketing is lawful. Perhaps surprisingly, it advises that trade union members should not be disciplined or expelled for crossing picket lines. In this respect, breach of the Code may help to demonstrate that the union member has been unjustifiably disciplined (see Chapter 15).

16.14.21 Critique

The narrowness of lawful picketing is striking. It is difficult to say that there is a right to picket in English law because the legality of picketing is hedged around with restrictions. For example, as the Code of Practice puts it, a picket may not 'attend lawfully at an entrance or exit from any place of work which is not his own, even if those who work there are employed by the same employer or covered by the same collective bargaining arrangements'.

The inability of pickets to stop vehicles and then communicate peacefully with the drivers is a major drawback of the legislation for pickets. The basic structure of the law was laid down in 1875 when there were no cars or lorries. In a traditional phrase, the legislation was drafted for the horse and cart era. Individuals walking to work can be communicated with; drivers cannot. The inability perhaps exacerbates any existing tendency to violence at the picket line. It is hard to credit the fact that even as good a judge as Lord Reid thought (in *Broome v DPP*) that pickets' rights were the same as those of hitchhikers. It is arguable that official pickets in an official dispute who are clearly so marked should be allowed peacefully to communicate their message. In practice, sometimes, the police do hold up traffic to allow pickets to pass on their message. It is only when this discretion is exercised that there is a 'right' to picket.

The Code of Practice has influenced the development of the law despite its not being a statute. Such 'soft law' or 'legislation by the backdoor' is disliked by democrats. Criticism is especially strong on the limit of six per entrance and the attempt to prohibit picketing of so called essential services: there is no ban on strikes in the essential services. If the Government wishes to prohibit them, it should do so by statute. (One interesting point in conclusion is that the 'citizen's right of action' mentioned above was originally intended to have covered only essential services. It was widened between the Green Paper, *Industrial Relations in the 1990s*, Cm 1602, 1991, and the Act.)

Picketing has declined in efficacy and number since the mid-1980s. The numbers of strikes in 1994 was, at 205, amounting to the loss of 0.28 million working days, the lowest since records began in 1891. Since strikes and picketing are not a problem, it is surprising that so much law has been introduced to combat industrial action over the last 20 years.

INDUSTRIAL ACTION

Collective agreements

Agreements between managements and unions are not normally legally binding but may affect the individual's contract.

Effect on employment contract

Industrial action is normally a breach of contract:

- *Simmons v Hoover* (1977).

The courts have been astute to find that even working to rule is a breach of contract – the implied term to co-operate in the smooth running of the employers' business.

Restricted strikes

Various statutes criminalise effects of action. The Emergency Powers Act 1920, as amended, is the principal statute.

Liability for action

Unions and others may be liable for various torts, including inducing breach of contract, intimidation, interference with contract and conspiracy. There is also a tort of breach of statutory duty and, possibly, torts of inducing breach of an equitable obligation and interference with trade or business. (The last three are not immune from liability.) The possibility of economic duress arising is noted:

- *Thomson v Deakin* (1952);
- *Torquay Hotel v Cousins* (1969);
- *Rookes v Barnard* (1964);
- *Hadmor Productions v Hamilton* (1983);
- *Merkur Island v Laughton* (1983);
- *Crofter Hand Woven Tweed v Veitch* (1942);
- *Universe Tankships v ITWF* (1983).

Immunity

Section 219 of TULR(C)A provides immunity from most of the usual economic torts where action is taken in contemplation or furtherance of a trade dispute (the 'golden formula'):

- *Mercury v Scott-Garner* (1984);

- *BBC v Hearn* (1977).

Impermissible purpose

Some strikes that are otherwise immune no longer attract immunity for certain activities, for example, enforcing union membership.

Pressure on employers to recognise a union by imposing a term in the contract to that effect is not allowed.

Secondary action

The former rules on secondary action have been abolished, except in relation to the effects of picketing. Picketing at one's workplace remains lawful even though its effect is detrimental to suppliers and distributors.

Strike ballot

A fully postal strike ballot is needed to keep the immunity for official action. The rules, which are technical, require, for example, the appointment of an independent scrutineer.

Citizen's and member's rights

An individual has a right of action to restrain tortious strikes.

Vicarious liability

By statute, a union is liable for actions authorised or endorsed by the relevant officers or not repudiated by them.

Damages

Generally, unions are liable only up to a specified sum; for example, a union with more than 100,000 members is liable to a maximum of £250,000 in relation to each employer. There is no limit on fines for contempt of court.

Injunctions

Employers gain interlocutory injunctions subject to statutory restrictions. Breach is a contempt of court and may lead to sequestration:

- *NWL v Woods* (1979).

Picketing

Criminal offences and torts abound in relation to picketing. Peaceful picketing at one's place of work for the purpose only of communicating information is rendered lawful by statute. Bail conditions may be imposed:

- *Piddington v Bates* (1960);

- *Thomas v NUM* (1985);

- *Mansfield Justices ex p Sharkey* (1984).

FURTHER READING LIST

Official publications

Report of the Royal Commission on Trade Unions and Employers' Associations, Cmnd 3623, 1968 HMSO (the Donovan Report)

Trade Union Immunities, Cmnd 8128, 1981, HMSO

Democracy in Trade Unions, Cmnd 8778, 1983, HMSO

Trade Unions and their Members, Cm 95, 1987, HMSO

Removing Barriers to Employment, Cm 655, 1989, HMSO

Unofficial Action and the Law, Cm 821, 1989, HMSO

Industrial Relations in the 1990s, Cm 1602, 1991, HMSO

Resolving Employment Rights Disputes – Options for Reform, Cm 2707, 1994, HMSO

Industrial Actions and Trade Unions, Cm 3470, 1996, The Stationery Office

Fairness at Work, Cm 3968, 1998, The Stationery Office

Promoting Disabled People's Rights – Creating a Disability Rights Commission for the 21st Century, Cm 3968, 1998, The Stationery Office

Modern labour law

Arthurs, HW, 'Labour law without the State?' (1996) 46 UTLJ 1

Auerbach, S, *Derecognition and Personal Contracts: Fighting Tactics and the Law,* 1993, Institute of Employment Rights

Blanchflower, D and Freeman, R, *Did the Thatcher Reforms Change British Labour Market Performance?*, 1993, Centre for Economic Performance

Cully, M *et al, The 1998 Workplace Employee Relations Survey: First Findings,* 1998, DTI

Davies, P and Freedland, M, *Labour, Legislation and Public Policy,* 1993, Clarendon

Deakin, S and Wilkinson, F, 'Rights vs efficiency? The economic case for transnational labour standards' (1994) 23 ILJ 289

Deakin, S and Wilkinson, F, *The Economics of Employment Rights*, 1991, Institute of Employment Rights

Deakin, S, 'Equality under a Market Order' (1990) 19 ILJ 1

Dickins, L, *Whose Flexibility?* 1991, Institute of Employment Rights

Ewing, K 'Economics and labour law in Britain: Thatcher's radical experiment' (1990) 28 Alta LR 632

Ewing, K (ed), *Working Life: A New Perspective on Labour Law*, 1996, Lawrence & Wishart

Ewing, K, 'Swimming with the tide' (1993) 22 ILJ 165

Ewing, KD, Gearty, CA and Hepple, BA (ed), *Human Rights and Labour Law* 1994, Mansell

Fairhurst, J, 'The Working Time Directive' (1999) Web Journal of Current Legal Issues

Ferner, A and Hyman, R (eds), *Industrial Relations in the New Europe*, 1992, Blackwell

Fosh, P *et al*, 'Politics, pragmatism and ideology' (1993) 22 ILJ 14

Fredman, S, 'The new rights' (1992) 12 OJLS 24

Hanson, CG, *Taming the Trade Unions*, 1991, Macmillan

Hendy, J, *A Law unto Themselves: Conservative Employment Laws*, 3rd edn, 1993, Institute of Employment Rights

Hepple, R, 'The future of labour law' (1995) 24 ILJ 303

Hoath, DC (ed), *75 Years of Law at Sheffield*, 1985, University of Sheffield Printing Unit (article by Sir John Wood)

Institute of Employment Rights, *Just the Job?*, 1995, Institute of Employment Rights

Lewis, R and Clark, J, *Employment Rights, Industrial Tribunals and Arbitration* 1993, Institute of Employment Rights

MacMillan, J, 'Employment tribunals: philosophies and practicalities' (1999) 28 ILJ 33

McCarthy (Lord) (ed), *Legal Intervention in Industrial Relations*, 1991, Blackwell

McColgan, A (ed), *The Future of Labour Law*, 1996, Pinter

Moher, J, *Trade Unions and the Law – The Politics of Change*, 1995, Institute of Employment Rights

Mückenberger, U and Deakin, S, 'From deregulation to a European floor of rights' (1989) 3 Zeitschrift für Ausländisches und Internationales Arbeits- und Sozialrecht 153

Rideout, R, 'Industrial relations – the Empire Strikes Back' [1997] CLP 361

Ryan, B, 'Unfinished business? The failure of deregulation in employment law' (1996) 23 JLS 506

Tremlett, N and Banerji, N, *The 1992 Survey of Industrial Tribunal Applicants*, 1994, Employment Department

Wedderburn (Lord) (ed), *Labour Law in the Post-Industrial Era*, 1994, Dartmouth

Wedderburn (Lord), 'Freedom of association and philosophies of labour law' (1989) 18 ILJ 1

Wedderburn (Lord), *Labour Law and Freedom*, 1995, Lawrence & Wishart

EC law

Barnard, C and Deakin, S, 'European Community social law and policy' (1997) 1 IRJ European Annual Report 131

Barnard, C, 'A Social Policy for Europe' (1992) 8 International Journal of Comparative Labour Law and Industrial Relations 15

Barnard, C, Clark, J and Lewis, R, *The Exercise of Individual Employment Rights in the Member States of the European Community*, 1995, Employment Department

Barnard, C, *EC Employment Law*, revised edn, 1996, Chancery Wiley

Bercusson, B, 'The dynamic of European labour law after Maastricht' (1994) 23 IRJ 1

Bercusson, B, 'The European Community's Charter of Fundamental Social Rights for Workers' (1990) 53 MLR 624

Bercusson, B, *European Labour Law*, 1996, Butterworths

Betten, L, 'The democratic deficit of participatory democracy in Community social policy' (1998) 23 EL Rev 20

European Commission, *European Social Policy – a Way Forward for the Union*, 1994, COM (94) 333

Fitzpatrick, B, 'Community social law after Maastricht' (1992) 21 ILJ 199

Hepple, R, 'Social values and European law' [1995] CLP 39

Hepple, R, 'The implementation of the Community Charter ...' (1990) 53 MLR 643

Hervey, T and Rostant, P, 'After *Francovich*' (1996) 25 ILJ 259

Hervey, T, 'The rise and rise of conservatism in Equal Pay' (1996) 18 Journal of Social Welfare and Family Law 107

Hoskyns, C, *Integrating Gender*, 1996, Verso

McGlynn, C, 'An exercise in futilities: the practical effects of the social policy opt-out' (1998) 49 NILQ 60

Nielsen, R and Szyszczak, E, *The Social Dimension of the European Community*, 3rd edn, 1997, Handelshojskolens Forlag

Sciarra, S, 'Social values and the multiple sources of European public law' (1995) 1 ELJ 60

Shaw, J and More, G (eds), *New Legal Dynamics of European Union*, 1995, Clarendon

Shaw, J, 'European Community judicial method' (1990) 19 ILJ 228

Steiner, J, 'The limits of State liability for breach of European Community law' (1998) 4 EPL 69

Discrimination

Banton, M, *Discrimination*, 1994, Open UP

Barnard, C, 'The principle of equality in the Community context' (1998) 57 CLJ 352

Clayton, G and Pitt, G, 'Dress codes and freedom of expression' [1997] EHRLR 54

Dex, S and McCulloch, A, *Flexible Employment in Britain – A Statistical Analysis* 1995, EOC

Docksey, C, 'The principle of equality ... under Community law' (1991) 20 ILJ 258

Ellis, E, 'Recent developments in EC sex equality law' (1998) 35 CMLR 379

Ellis, E, *European Community Sex Equality Law*, 2nd edn, 1998, Clarendon

Equal Opportunities Commission, *Flexibility in Practice*, 1995, EOC

Feminist Legal Research Unit, *Making Ourselves Heard*, 1995, FLRU, University of Liverpool

Fenwick, H and Hervey, T, 'Sex equality in the Single Market' (1995) 32 CMLR 443

Fitzpatrick, B, 'Equality in occupational pensions' (1991) 54 MLR 271

Fredman, S, *Women and the Law*, 1997, OUP

Fredman, S,'The poverty of equality: pensions and the ECJ' (1996) 25 ILJ 91

Hepple, R and Szyszczak, E (eds), *Discrimination: the Limits of Law*, 1992, Mansell

Hepple, R *et al*, *Improving Equality Law: The Options*, 1997, Runnymede Trust

Hervey, T and O'Keeffe, D, *Sex Equality Law in the European Union*, 1996, Chichester: Wiley

Honeyball, S, *Sex, Employment and the Law*, 1991, Oxford; Blackwell

Houghton-James, H, *Sexual Harassment*, 1995, Cavendish Publishing

Lester, A and Rose, D, 'Equal value claims and sex bias in collective bargaining' (1991) 20 ILJ 163

McColgan, A, *Just Wages for Women*, 1997, Clarendon

McColgan, A, *Pay Equity*, 1994, Institute of Employment Rights

McCrudden, C, 'Equal treatment and occupational pensions' (1995) 46 NILQ 376

McCrudden, C, 'The effectiveness of European equality law' (1993) 13 OJLS 320

Millward, N, *Targeting Potential Discrimination*, 1995, EOC

Moore, S, 'Justice doesn't mean a free lunch' (1995) 20 EL Rev 159

More, G, '"Equal treatment" of the sexes in European Community law' (1993) 1 Fem LS 45

Peters, A, 'The many meanings of equality and positive action in favour of women under European Community law' (1996) 2 ELJ 177

Prechal, S, 'Combatting indirect discrimination in the Community law context' [1993] Legal Issues of European Integration 81

Rubenstein, M, 'Sexual harassment' (1992) 21 ILJ 70

Rubenstein, M, *Preventing and Remedying Sexual Harassment at Work*, 1992, Industrial Relations Services

Rubery, J, *The Economics of Equal Value*, 1992, EOC

Sinclair, A, 'Harassment: discrimination and interpretation' (1998) Web Journal of Current Legal Issues

Skidmore, P, 'Sex, gender and comparators in employment discrimination' (1997) 26 ILJ 51

Townshend-Smith, R, *Discrimination Law*, 1999, Cavendish Publishing

Townshend-Smith, R, 'Justifying indirect discrimination in English and American law' (1995) 1 International Journal of Discrimination and the Law 103

Welsh, C, Knox, J and Brett, M, *Acting Positively: Positive Action under the Race Relations Act 1976*, 1994, Employment Department

Whiteford, E, 'Lost in the mists of time: the ECJ and occupational pensions' (1995) 32 CMLR 801

Wintemute, R, 'Recognising new kinds of direct discrimination: transsexualism, sex orientation and dress code' (1997) 60 MLR 343

Terms

Bercusson, B, *Working Time in Britain: Towards a European Model*, 1994, Institute of Employment Rights (Pts I and II)

Bielenski, H, *New Forms of Work and Activity*, 1994, European Foundation for the Improvement of Living and Working Conditions

Collins, H, 'Market power, bureaucratic power, and the contract of employment' (1986) 15 ILJ 1

Freedland, M, *The Contract of Employment*, 1976, Clarendon

Gurry, F, *Breach of Confidence*, 1984, Clarendon

Hepple, R, 'A right to work?' (1981) 10 ILJ 65

Hepple, R, 'Restructuring employment rights' (1986) 15 ILJ 69

Honeyball, S, 'Employment law and the primacy of contract' (1989) 18 ILJ 97

Jefferson, M, *Restraint of Trade*, 1996, Chichester: Wiley

Kidner, R, 'Vicarious liability: for whom should the "employer" be liable?' (1995) 15 LS 47

Mogridge, C, 'Illegal employment contracts' (1981) 10 ILJ 23

Napier, B, 'Aspects of the wage-work bargain' (1984) 43 CLJ 337

Rideout, R, 'Confidentiality or protection of trade secrets?' (1986) 15 ILJ 183

Rideout, R, 'The contract of employment' [1966] CLP 111

Vickers, L, *Protecting Whistleblowers at Work*, 1995, Institute of Employment Rights

Warburton, J, 'The employment of home workers' (1984) 13 ILJ 251

Termination

Bowers, J and Clarke, A, 'Unfair dismissal and managerial prerogative' (1981) 10 ILJ 34

Carty, H, 'Dismissed employees: the search for a more effective range of remedies' (1989) 52 MLR 449

Collins, H, 'The meaning of job security' (1991) 20 ILJ 227

Collins, H, *Justice in Dismissal*, 1992, Clarendon

Dickens, L, 'Comparative systems of unjust dismissal' (1994) 536 Annals of the American Academy 4

Dickins, L et al, *Dismissed*, 1985, Blackwell

Elias, P, 'Fairness in unfair dismissal' (1981) 10 ILJ 201

Enonchong, N, 'Contract damages for injury to reputation' (1996) 59 MLJ 592

Ewing, K and Grubb, A, 'The emergence of a new labour injunction?' (1987) 16 ILJ 145

Ewing, K, 'Remedies for breach of the contract of employment' [1993] CLJ 405

Forrest, H, 'Political values in individual employment law' (1980) 43 MLJ 361

Fredman, S and Lee, S, 'Natural justice for employees' (1986) 15 ILJ 15

Freer, A, 'The range of reasonable responses test – from guidelines to statute' (1998) 27 ILJ 335

Goulding, P, 'Injunctions and contracts of employment' (1990) 19 ILJ 98

Grunfeld, C, *The Law of Redundancy*, 3rd edn, 1989, Sweet & Maxwell

Hardy, S and Adnett, N, 'Entrepreneurial freedom versus employee rights' (1999) 9 Journal of European Social Policy 127

Korn, A, *Compensation for Dismissal*, 2nd edn, 1997, Blackstone

Lewis, R and Clark, J, *Employment Rights, Industrial Tribunals and Arbitration: The Case for Alternative Dispute Resolution*, 1993, Institute of Employment Rights

Lofaso, AM, 'Pre-termination job rights of British workers affected by collective redundancies' (1996) 16 Yearbook of European Law 277

Macdonald, E, 'Contractual damages for mental distress' (1994) 7 Journal of Contract Law 134

McMullen, J, 'Atypical transfers, atypical workers and atypical employment structures – a case for greater transparency in transfer of employment issues' (1996) 25 ILJ 286

McMullen, J, 'Frustration of the contract of employment and statutory labour law' (1986) 49 MLJ 785

McMullen, J, 'Takeovers, transfers and business re-organisations' (1992) 21 ILJ 15

McMullen, J, 'The resurgence of proceduralism in unfair dismissal law' (1988) 51 MLJ 651

McMullen, J, *Business Transfers and Employee Rights*, 2nd edn, 1992, Butterworths

Trade unions

Dunn, S and Metcalf, D, *Trade Union Law Since 1979: Ideology, Intent, Impact*, 1994, Centre for Economic Performance

Dunn, S and Wright, M, *Managing Without the Closed Shop*, 1993, Centre for Economic Performance

Dunn, S *et al*, 'Workplace industrial relations in transition' (1993) 31 British Journal of Industrial Relations (special edition) 169

Elias, P and Ewing, K, *Trade Union Democracy, Members' Rights and the Law*, 1987, Mansell

Ewing, K, 'Trade union recognition' (1990) 19 ILJ 209

Leader, S, 'The European Convention on Human Rights, the Employment Act of 1988 and the right to refuse to strike' (1991) 20 ILJ 39

Leader, S, *Freedom of Association*, 1992, Yale UP

Leopold, JW, 'Trade unions, political funds ballots and the Labour Party' (1997) 35 British Journal of Industrial Relations 23

Miller, K, 'some legal consequences of union derecognition' [1996] Juridical Review 13

Morris, G and Archer, TJ, *Trade Unions, Employers and the Law*, 2nd edn, 1993, Butterworths

von Prondzynski, F, *Freedom of Association and Industrial Relations*, 1987, Mansell

Smith, P *et al*, 'Ballots and union government in the 1980s' (1993) 31 British Journal of Industrial Relations 365

Syrett, K, '"Immunity", "privilege" and "right": British trade unions and the language of labour law reform' (1998) 25 JLS 388

Townshend-Smith, R, 'Refusal of employment on grounds of trade union membership or non-membership' (1991) 20 ILJ 102

Undy, R *et al*, *Managing the Unions: The Impact of Legislation on Trade Unions' Behaviour*, 1996, Clarendon

Industrial action

Auerbach, S, 'Legal restraint of picketing' (1987) 16 ILJ 227

Auerbach, S, *Legislation for Conflict*, 1990, Clarendon

Bentil, JK, 'Improper interference with another's business or trade interest as a tort' [1993] Journal of Business Law 519

Carty, H, 'Intentional violation of economic interests' (1988) 104 LQR 250

Elgar, J and Simpson, R, *The Impact of the Law on Industrial Disputes in the 1980s*, 1992, Centre for Economic Performance

Elgar, J and Simpson, R, *Union Negotiators, Industrial Action and the Law*, 1993, Centre for Economic Performance

Elias, P and Ewing, K, 'Economic torts and labour law' [1982] CLJ 321

Ewing, K, 'The right to strike' (1986) 15 ILJ 142

Ewing, K, *The Right to Strike*, 1991, Clarendon

Gall, G and McKay, S, 'Research note: injunctions as a legal weapon in industrial disputes' (1996) 34 British Journal of Industrial Relations 567

Miller, K, 'The legal regulation of industrial action since 1979' [1998] Juridical Review 150

Morris, G, 'Industrial action in essential services: the new law' (1992) 21 ILJ 89

Morris, G, 'Industrial action: public and private interests' (1993) 22 ILJ 194

Pitt, G, *The Limits of Industrial Action*, 1995, Institute of Employment Rights

Wallington, P, 'Injunctions and the right to demonstrate' [1986] CLJ 86

Wallington, P, 'Some implications for the policing of industrial disputes' [1987] CLR 180

Welch, R, *The Right to Strike: a Trade Union View*, 1991, Institute of Employment Rights

INDEX